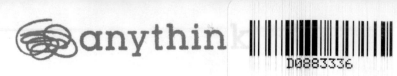

FOR MY PARENTS

CONTENTS

[**ACKNOWLEDGMENTS**]

This book could not have been written without the generous assistance of many people and institutions. It is a pleasure to be able to thank them here. The research for this book was supported by major grants from the German Academic Exchange Service (DAAD), the Mabelle McLeod Lewis Memorial Fund, and the Harry Frank Guggenheim Foundation. In addition, I was fortunate to spend a year as Geballe Dissertation Fellow at the Stanford Humanities Center and a later year as a James Bryant Conant Post-Doctoral Fellow at the Center for European Studies at Harvard University. The University of Maryland General Research Board and the National Endowment for the Humanities provided summer stipends at key points in the project.

The librarians of the Staatsbibliothek Preussischer Kulturbesitz in Berlin, Green Library at Stanford University, Widener Library at Harvard, the International Legal Studies Reading Room of the Harvard Law School Library, the National Library of Medicine in Bethesda, and McKeldin Library at the University of Maryland facilitated access to many of the sources on which this study is based. I am particularly indebted to the Interlibrary Loan offices at Stanford, Harvard, and the University of Maryland, who worked hard to locate rare materials. The archivists of the Bundesarchiv, Abteilung Potsdam, the Bayerisches Hauptstaatsarchiv in Munich, and the National Archives in College Park, Maryland, allowed me to consult crucial archival materials.

I have benefited greatly from the advice and encouragement of many friends and colleagues. Peter Becker, David Blackbourn, Arthur Eckstein, Richard Evans, Gabriel Finder, Thomas Green, Larry Joseph, Robert Kunath, Andrew Lees, Paul Lerner, Oliver Liang, Laura Mayhall, Jerry Muller, Suzanne Marchand, Jeannie Rutenburg, James Sheehan, Jon Sumida, and Nikolaus Wachsmann were kind enough to read all or parts of the manuscript and offered valuable suggestions. I am deeply grateful to all of them.

I am also greatly indebted to Lewis Bateman for showing interest in my work and agreeing to publish this book; to Thomas Green, my principal series editor, who read the manuscript with great care and made many valuable suggestions; and to Hendrik Hartog for accepting this book in the Studies in Legal History series, which he coedits with Thomas Green. Ron Maner was an excellent project editor, and Trudie Calvert did an exceptional job copyediting the manuscript.

I owe a special debt of gratitude to James Sheehan, who taught me how to think about history. I want to thank Larry Joseph, without whose support this book could never have been completed. And, finally, I want to thank my parents for their love and encouragement throughout the years. This book is dedicated to them.

ABBREVIATIONS

AfK	*Archiv für Kriminologie*
AKK	*Archiv für Kriminalanthropologie und Kriminalistik*
ARGB	*Archiv für Rassen- und Gesellschaftsbiologie*
ASS	*Archiv für Strafrecht und Strafprozeß*
AZP	*Allgemeine Zeitschrift für Psychiatrie*
BA	Bundesarchiv
BDC	Berlin Document Center
BfG	*Blätter für Gefängniskunde*
BHStA	Bayerisches Hauptstaatsarchiv, Munich
BVP	Bayerische Volkspartei
DDP	Deutsche Demokratische Partei
DJZ	*Deutsche Juristen-Zeitung*
DNVP	Deutschnationale Volkspartei
DR	*Deutsches Recht*
DVP	Deutsche Volkspartei
DZGGM	*Deutsche Zeitschrift für die gesamte gerichtliche Medizin*
EOG	Erbgesundheitsobergericht
FNPG	*Fortschritte der Neurologie, Psychiatrie und ihrer Grenzgebiete*

GRR   *Gesetz zur Verhütung erbkranken Nachwuchses,* bearbeitet und erläutert von Arthur Gütt, Ernst Rüdin und Falk Ruttke (Munich: Lehmann, 1934)

IKV   Internationale Kriminalistische Vereinigung

JW   *Juristische Wochenschrift*

KPD   Kommunistische Partei Deutschlands

MDRG   *Monatsblätter des Deutschen Reichsverbandes* [from vol. 3: *Reichszusammenschlusses*] *für Gerichtshilfe, Gefangenen- und Entlassenenfürsorge*

MIKV   *Mitteilungen der IKV*

MKBG   *Mitteilungen der Kriminalbiologischen Gesellschaft*

MKS   *Monatsschrift für Kriminalpsychologie und Strafrechtsreform*

N.F.   Neue Folge

NSDAP   Nationalsozialistische Deutsche Arbeiterpartei

RJM   Reichs-Justizministerium

RMI   Reichsministerium des Innern

SPD   Sozialdemokratische Partei Deutschlands

StGB   Strafgesetzbuch

ZGNP   *Zeitschrift für die gesamte Neurologie und Psychiatrie*

ZStW   *Zeitschrift für die gesamte Strafrechtswissenschaft*

ZStA   Zentrales Staatsarchiv, Potsdam

INVENTING THE CRIMINAL

INTRODUCTION

European historians have become increasingly interested in the history of crime and criminal justice since the 1970s. Much of the work in this area has approached the subject of crime from the perspective of social history, in the form either of quantitative studies aimed at reconstructing the historical development of crime rates[1] or of local studies or microhistories of particular criminals or crimes, especially those associated with social conflict.[2] Other historical studies have focused on the legal, institutional, and political history of criminal justice and penal reform. Most of the work in this field was explicitly conceived as a critique of earlier studies that had presented the development of criminal justice since the late eighteenth century as a story of progress driven by the humanitarianism of penal reformers. The revisionists, by contrast, emphasized the social control function of criminal justice.

While many of the revisionists were Marxists offering class analyses of criminal justice,[3] Michel Foucault advanced a different version of the social control approach. Without paying much attention to class relations, Foucault's book on the birth of the prison stressed the development and diffusion of more effective "technologies of power" in the criminal justice system and throughout

1. See, for instance, Howard Zehr, *Crime and Development in Modern Society: Patterns of Criminality in Nineteenth-Century Germany and France* (London: Croom Helm, 1976); Eric Johnson, *Urbanization and Crime: Germany, 1871–1914* (New York: Cambridge University Press, 1995).

2. Pioneering: Douglas Hay et al., eds., *Albion's Fatal Tree: Crime and Society in Eighteenth-Century England* (New York: Pantheon, 1975); E. P. Thompson, *Whigs and Hunters: The Origin of the Black Act* (New York: Pantheon, 1975).

3. See, for instance, Douglas Hay, "Property, Authority and the Criminal Law," in *Albion's Fatal Tree*, ed. Hay et al., 17–63; Michael Ignatieff, *A Just Measure of Pain: The Penitentiary in the Industrial Revolution, 1750–1850* (New York: Pantheon, 1978).

society.[4] Foucault called attention to the connection between power and knowledge and, more particularly, to the important role that criminological knowledge played in the development of criminal justice. But Foucault's *Discipline and Punish* dealt primarily with the early nineteenth-century birth of the prison, rather than the birth of criminology. It examined the development of new "disciplinary" practices in a variety of institutions and offered a highly abstract, functionalist analysis of the role of the prison in society. Foucault used the writings of prison reformers to draw an ideal-type picture of the institutional practices of prisons. He did not, however, examine the writings of criminologists, and he did not pursue his story into the late nineteenth century, when scientific criminology first became an important force.

The present book takes its cue from Foucault in the sense that it follows up on his suggestion that criminological knowledge played an important role in the development of criminal justice. Yet it differs from Foucault's work because it avoids the functionalist approach characteristic of Foucault and others in the social control school. Instead of reducing criminology to an auxiliary role in the mechanism of social control, I seek to reveal the tensions inherent in the development of criminology and the complexity of the relationship between criminological knowledge and penal policy. Besides these Foucauldian origins, this book grew out of my ongoing research on late nineteenth- and twentieth-century German penal reform, from which I learned that the ambition to provide criminal justice with a "scientific foundation" was one of the major forces behind modern penal reform. This book differs from most of the existing literature by approaching the history of crime and criminal justice from the perspective of intellectual history and the history of science, rather than social, legal-institutional, or political history.

The book's main story begins in the 1880s because it was in the last two decades of the nineteenth century that the emergence of a new penal reform movement and Cesare Lombroso's work on the "born criminal" gradually gave birth to "criminology" as a recognized field of scientific inquiry. Throughout the period studied, criminological research was conducted by people working in

4. Michel Foucault, *Surveiller et punir: Naissance de la prison* (Paris: Gallimard, 1975), translated as *Discipline and Punish: The Birth of the Prison* (New York: Pantheon, 1978). For an early critique of the social control approach, see Michael Ignatieff, "State, Civil Society and Total Institutions: A Critique of Recent Social Histories of Punishment," in *Social Control and the State*, ed. Stanley Cohen and Andrew Scull (Oxford: Robertson, 1983), 75–105. For other work critical of the social control approach, see Robert Nye, *Crime, Madness and Politics in Modern France* (Princeton: Princeton University Press, 1984); Martin Wiener, *Reconstructing the Criminal: Culture, Law, and Policy in England, 1830–1914* (Cambridge: Cambridge University Press, 1990).

other disciplines, primarily psychiatrists and criminal jurists. But although criminology did not attain the status of an academic discipline, several developments, such as the founding of criminological journals and academic associations, indicated that criminology was becoming a recognized interdisciplinary field of inquiry engaged in a shared discourse. After placing the origins of criminology in contemporary context, the book traces the development of German criminology from the late nineteenth-century reception of Lombroso through the Nazi regime. The end date of 1945 was chosen because it marked a definite hiatus in the development of German criminology, but it should not be interpreted in a teleological sense.

The history of criminology speaks to a number of larger issues. First, the development of German criminology reflects the psychiatric profession's efforts to extend its expertise to criminal behavior and to offer medical solutions to the crime problem. The history of criminology therefore provides an excellent opportunity to examine the interaction between the social and natural sciences and between law and medicine. Because criminological research was truly interdisciplinary, jurists who studied crime had to grapple with the research of psychiatrists and vice versa. As a result, criminological research began to transform the relationship between psychiatry and criminal justice from an adversarial into a symbiotic one. Second, following the development of German criminology through three different political regimes, from Imperial Germany through the Weimar Republic to the Nazi period, affords us the opportunity to gauge the impact of politics on scientific research and its applications. Finally, the recent resurgence of biological and genetic research on crime gives a history of criminal-biological research from Lombroso to the Nazis striking contemporary relevance.

While the histories of British and French criminology have been the subject of several works published in the last fifteen years, the history of German criminology still remains largely uncharted territory.[5] A short legal disserta-

5. On French criminology, see Laurent Mucchielli, ed., *Histoire de la criminologie française* (Paris: L'Harmattan, 1994), and Nye, *Crime, Madness and Politics*. On British criminology, see David Garland, *Punishment and Welfare: A History of Penal Strategies* (Aldershot: Gower, 1985); Garland, "British Criminology before 1935," *British Journal of Criminology* 28 (1988): 131–47; Terence Morris, "British Criminology, 1935–1948," ibid., 150–64. On England and France, see Marie-Christine Leps, *Apprehending the Criminal: The Production of Deviance in Nineteenth-Century Discourse* (Durham: Duke University Press, 1992). Note the absence of chapters on Germany in the following collections: Piers Beirne, *Inventing Criminology: Essays on the Rise of "Homo Criminalis"* (Albany: State University of New York Press, 1993); Beirne, ed., *The Origins and Growth of Criminology: Essays on Intellectual History, 1760–1945* (Aldershot: Dartmouth, 1994); Paul Rock, ed., *History of Criminology* (Aldershot: Dartmouth, 1994).

tion from 1972 made an initial attempt to survey the development of criminology under the Nazi regime; then, starting in the 1980s, a younger generation of criminologists published a handful of articles on the history of their discipline during the Third Reich.[6] But apart from a recent German dissertation on the reception of Lombroso, there are no studies of the history of German criminology by historians.[7] Hence this book represents the first attempt to chart the history of German criminology from its inception through the Nazi regime. It is therefore almost entirely based on primary sources.

The historiography on German crime and criminal justice is more developed, although here, too, the literature on Germany lags far behind the literature on France and England.[8] Our knowledge of the social history of crime in nineteenth- and twentieth-century Germany is still extremely limited, but a handful of works have begun to shed light on some aspects of the subject.[9] The last

6. Reinhard Schütz, "Kriminologie im Dritten Reich: Erscheinungsformen des Faschismus in der Wissenschaft vom Verbrechen" (J.D. diss., University of Mainz, 1972); Marlis Dürkop, "Zur Funktion der Kriminologie im Nationalsozialismus," in *Strafjustiz und Polizei im Dritten Reich*, ed. Udo Reifner and Bernd Sonnen (Frankfurt: Campus, 1984), 97–120; Klaus Rehbein, "Zur Funktion von Strafrecht und Kriminologie im nationalsozialistischen Rechtssystem: Eine Wissenschaft begründet die Barbarei," *MKS* 70 (1987): 193–210; Dieter Dölling, "Kriminologie im 'Dritten Reich,'" in *Recht und Justiz im "Dritten Reich,"* ed. Ralf Dreier and Wolfgang Sellert (Frankfurt: Suhrkamp, 1989), 194–225; Franz Streng, "Der Beitrag der Kriminologie zu Entstehung und Rechtfertigung staatlichen Unrechts im Dritten Reich," *MKS* 76 (1993): 141–68. Karl-Heinz Hering, *Der Weg der Kriminologie zur selbständigen Wissenschaft* (Hamburg: Kriminalistik Verlag, 1966), focuses on the Italian criminal anthropologists and the French criminal sociologists; German developments are addressed only in brief sections on Liszt and Aschaffenburg; developments after 1914 are sketched in a brief epilogue. Achim Mechler, *Studien zur Geschichte der Kriminalsoziologie* (Göttingen: Otto Schwartz, 1970), focuses on French and British developments in the first half of the nineteenth century, with only a few pages on German prison reformers of that period. A useful collection of essays titled *Kriminalbiologie*, edited by Justizministerium des Landes Nordrhein-Westfalen (Düsseldorf, 1997), which examines different aspects of criminal biology under the Nazi regime, appeared (only in 1998) after this manuscript was virtually finished.

7. Earlier versions of Chapters 2 and 3 of this book appeared in Richard Wetzell, "Criminal Law Reform in Imperial Germany" (Ph.D. diss., Stanford University, 1991). See also Mariacarla Gadebusch Bondio, *Die Rezeption der kriminalanthropologischen Theorien von Cesare Lombroso in Deutschland von 1880–1914* (Husum: Matthiesen, 1995).

8. For recent surveys of the British, French, and German literature, see Clive Emsley, "Albion's Felonious Attractions: Reflections upon the History of Crime in England," in *Crime History and Histories of Crime: Studies in the Historiography of Crime and Criminal Justice in Modern History*, ed. Clive Emsley and Louis Knafla (Westport: Greenwood, 1996), 67–86; René Lévy, "Crime, the Judicial System and Punishment in Modern France," ibid., 87–108; Alf Lüdtke and Herbert Reinke, "Crime, Police and the 'Good Order': Germany," ibid., 109–37.

9. Recent studies are Richard Evans, *Tales from the German Underworld: Crime and Punishment in the Nineteenth Century* (New Haven: Yale University Press, 1998); Johnson, *Urbaniza-*

decade has also seen the appearance of some work on the representation of crime in literature, art, and popular media.[10] While the social history of crime is usually written by historians, most German legal history is written by German legal scholars, and most of it deals with civil rather than criminal law. To this day, the standard survey of the history of German criminal justice dates from 1947.[11] When German *historians* have turned their attention to legal history, they have focused mainly on the Nazi period and, to a somewhat lesser extent, the Weimar Republic.[12] As a result, the history of German criminal justice in the nineteenth century and in Imperial Germany largely remains to be written, a situation that is only just beginning to change.[13] The only aspect of criminal

tion and Crime; Richard Evans, ed., *The German Underworld: Deviants and Outcasts in German History* (London: Routledge, 1988); Regina Schulte, *Das Dorf im Verhör: Brandstifter, Kindsmörderinnen und Wilderer vor den Schranken des bürgerlichen Gerichts* (Hamburg: Rowohlt, 1989), translated as *The Village in Court: Arson, Infanticide, and Poaching in the Court Records of Upper Bavaria, 1848–1910* (Cambridge: Cambridge University Press, 1994). Pioneering: Dirk Blasius, *Bürgerliche Gesellschaft und Kriminalität: Zur Sozialgeschichte Preussens im Vormärz* (Göttingen: Vandenhoeck, 1976); Blasius, *Kriminalität und Alltag: Zur Konfliktgeschichte des Alltagslebens im 19. Jahrhundert* (Göttingen: Vandenhoeck, 1978).

10. Jörg Schönert, ed., *Literatur und Kriminalität: Die gesellschaftliche Erfahrung von Verbrechen und Strafverfolgung als Gegenstand des Erzählens. Deutschland, England und Frankreich, 1850–1880* (Tübingen: Niemeyer, 1983); Schönert, ed., *Erzählte Kriminalität: Zur Typologie und Funktion von narrativen Darstellungen in Strafrechtspflege, Publizistik und Literatur zwischen 1770 und 1920* (Tübingen: Niemeyer, 1991); Maria Tatar, *Lustmord: Sexual Murder in Weimar Germany* (Princeton: Princeton University Press, 1995).

11. Eberhard Schmidt, *Einführung in die Geschichte der deutschen Strafrechtspflege* (Göttingen: Vandenhoeck, 1947; 3d ed., 1964).

12. Heinrich Hannover and Elisabeth Hannover-Druck, *Politische Justiz, 1918–1933* (Frankfurt: Fischer, 1966); *NS-Recht in historischer Perspektive* (Munich: Oldenbourg, 1981); Robert Kuhn, *Die Vertrauenskrise der Justiz (1926–1928): Der Kampf um die Republikanisierung der Rechtspflege in der Weimarer Republik* (Cologne: Bundesanzeiger, 1983); Ingo Müller, *Furchtbare Juristen: Die unbewältigte Vergangenheit unserer Justiz* (Munich: Kindler, 1987); Lothar Gruchmann, *Justiz im Dritten Reich, 1933–1940: Anpassung und Unterwerfung in der Ära Gürtner* (Munich: Oldenbourg, 1988); Dreier and Sellert, eds., *Recht und Justiz; Im Namen des deutschen Volkes: Justiz und Nationalsozialismus* (Cologne: Verlag Wissenschaft und Politik, 1989); Gerhard Werle, *Justiz-Strafrecht und polizeiliche Verbrechensbekämpfung im Dritten Reich* (Berlin: de Gruyter, 1989); Ralph Angermund, *Deutsche Richterschaft, 1919–1945* (Frankfurt: Fischer, 1991).

13. Richard Evans, *Rituals of Retribution: Capital Punishment in Germany, 1600–1987* (Oxford: Oxford University Press, 1996); Johnson, *Urbanization and Crime*; Wetzell, "Criminal Law Reform." Pioneering: Blasius, *Bürgerliche Gesellschaft*; Blasius, *Kriminalität und Alltag*. The lack of historical studies of the criminal justice system in Imperial Germany is reflected in the fact that the chapter on law in the most recent historiographical survey of Imperial Germany makes no mention of criminal law: Michael John, "Constitution, Administration and the Law," in *Imperial Germany: A Historiographical Companion*, ed. Roger Chickering (Westport: Greenwood, 1996), 185–213.

justice on which there is a well-developed historical literature is the history of juvenile justice, which is frequently studied in the context of youth welfare policy.[14] There is a growing historical literature on the police[15] but still almost no work on the history of German prisons, prison reform, or prison societies, which is especially striking in comparison with the rich literature on prisons in Britain and France.[16]

This history of German criminology is an attempt to contribute to the further development of German criminal justice history. The book's expansion of chronological focus to include Imperial Germany is designed not only to provide information about a neglected period of criminal justice history but also to permit a better assessment of which features were and which were not unique to the Weimar and Nazi periods. This study also shifts focus from the well-researched topic of the criminal justice system's treatment of political enemies and racial minorities to one aspect of its treatment of "ordinary" criminals. Finally, because the development of criminology affected most aspects of criminal justice, from the prisons to penal policy to judicial practice in the courts, this

---

14. Christa Hasenclever, *Jugendhilfe und Jugendgesetzgebung seit 1900* (Göttingen: Vandenhoeck, 1978); Heinz Cornel, *Geschichte des Jugendstrafvollzugs* (Weinheim: Beltz, 1984); Detlev Peukert, *Grenzen der Sozialdisziplinierung: Aufstieg und Krise der deutschen Jugendfürsorge von 1878 bis 1932* (Cologne: Bund-Verlag, 1986); Michael Voss, *Jugend ohne Rechte: Entwicklung des Jugendstrafrechts* (Frankfurt: Campus, 1986); Jörg Wolff, *Jugendliche vor Gericht im Dritten Reich* (Munich: Beck, 1992); Elizabeth Harvey, *Youth and the Welfare State in Weimar Germany* (Oxford: Clarendon Press, 1993); Edward Ross Dickinson, *The Politics of German Child Welfare from the Empire to the Federal Republic* (Cambridge, Mass.: Harvard University Press, 1996); Gabriel Finder, "Education, Not Punishment: Juvenile Justice in Germany, 1890–1930" (Ph.D. diss., University of Chicago, 1997).

15. For a review of the literature, see Lüdtke and Reinke, "Crime, Police and the 'Good Order.'" Recent studies include Ralph Jessen, *Polizei im Industrierevier: Modernisierung und Herrschaftspraxis im westfälischen Ruhrgebiet, 1848–1914* (Göttingen: Vandenhoeck, 1991); Alf Lüdtke, ed., *"Sicherheit" und "Wohlfahrt": Polizei, Gesellschaft und Herrschaft im 19. und 20. Jahrhundert* (Frankfurt: Suhrkamp, 1992); Elaine Glovka Spencer, *Police and the Social Order in German Cities: The Düsseldorf District, 1848–1914* (DeKalb: Northern Illinois University Press, 1992); Herbert Reinke, ed., *". . . nur für die Sicherheit da . . . ?" Zur Geschichte der Polizei im 19. und 20. Jahrhundert* (Frankfurt: Campus, 1993); Patrick Wagner, *Volksgemeinschaft ohne Verbrecher: Konzeptionen und Praxis der Kriminalpolizei in der Zeit der Weimarer Republik und des Nationalsozialismus* (Hamburg: Christians, 1996).

16. Thomas Berger, *Die konstante Repression: Zur Geschichte des Strafvollzugs in Preussen nach 1850* (Frankfurt: Verlag Roter Stern, 1974). The dearth of historical work on German prisons is reflected in Norval Morris and David Rothman, eds., *Oxford History of the Prison* (Oxford: Oxford University Press, 1995), and Norbert Finzsch and Robert Jütte, eds., *Institutions of Confinement: Hospitals, Asylums and Prisons in Western Europe and North America, 1500–1950* (Cambridge: Cambridge University Press, 1996).

book is meant to lay part of the groundwork for my own forthcoming history of penal reform and, hopefully, for further research in other areas of German criminal justice history.

Beyond criminal justice, the history of German criminology is also relevant to larger issues in modern German historiography. For a long time, the so-called *Sonderweg* school of German history maintained that Germany underwent an incomplete process of modernization that deviated from the normal path of Western development and therefore explained the Nazi regime as the result of the survival of premodern and antimodern features in German society.[17] Since the 1980s, however, historians critical of the *Sonderweg* approach have called attention to the modern features of German society, starting in the imperial period (1871–1918), and to the modern aspects of Nazi ideology and politics.[18] For the Weimar and Nazi periods, this new approach is perhaps best exemplified by the work of Detlev Peukert, who argued that Nazism "demonstrated, with heightened clarity and murderous consistency, the pathologies and rifts of the modern civilising process."[19] More specifically, he suggested in a controversial essay on "the genesis of the 'final solution' from the spirit of science" that "what was new about the 'Final Solution' in world-historical

17. Hans-Ulrich Wehler, *Das deutsche Kaiserreich, 1871–1918* (Göttingen: Vandenhoeck, 1973), translated as *The German Empire* (Leamington Spa: Berg, 1985); Ralf Dahrendorf, *Society and Democracy in Germany* (New York: Norton, 1967).

18. On the nineteenth century and Imperial Germany, see David Blackbourn and Geoff Eley, *The Peculiarities of German History* (Oxford: Oxford University Press, 1984). The relevance of Blackbourn and Eley's arguments concerning Imperial Germany for the genesis and character of Nazism is explored in Geoff Eley, "German History and the Contradictions of Modernity," in *Society, Culture and the State in Germany, 1870–1930*, ed. Eley (Ann Arbor: University of Michigan Press, 1996), 67–103. On the debate over the modernity of the Nazi regime, see Norbert Frei, "Wie modern war der Nationalsozialismus?" *Geschichte und Gesellschaft* 19 (1993): 367–87; Axel Schildt, "NS-Regime, Modernisierung, Moderne: Anmerkungen zur Hochkonjunktur einer andauernden Diskussion," *Tel Aviver Jahrbuch für deutsche Geschichte* 23 (1994): 3–22; Mark Roseman, "National Socialism and Modernization," in *Fascist Italy and Nazi Germany*, ed. Richard Bessel (Cambridge: Cambridge University Press, 1996), 197–229; Michael Prinz and Rainer Zitelmann, eds., *Nationalsozialismus und Modernisierung*, 2d ed. (Darmstadt: Wissenschaftliche Buchgesellschaft, 1994). For a general assessment of modernization theory in German historiography, see Thomas Mergel, "Geht es weiterhin voran? Die Modernisierungstheorie auf dem Weg zu einer Theorie der Moderne," in *Geschichte zwischen Kultur und Gesellschaft: Beiträge zur Theoriedebatte*, ed. Mergel and Thomas Welskopp (Munich: Beck, 1997), 203–32.

19. Detlev Peukert, *Volksgenossen und Gemeinschaftsfremde* (Cologne: Bund-Verlag, 1982), 296, translated as *Inside Nazi Germany* (New Haven: Yale University Press, 1987), 248; see also Peukert, *Die Weimarer Republik* (Frankfurt: Suhrkamp, 1987), translated as *The Weimar Republic* (New York: Hill and Wang, 1992).

terms was the fact that it resulted from a fatal racist dynamism present within the human and social sciences."[20] Although this formulation could be interpreted to mean that the Holocaust was the logical result of modern science,[21] in other writings Peukert made it clear that his "view that [Nazism] was one of the pathological developmental forms of modernity does not imply that barbarism is the inevitable logical outcome of modernization" but was meant to "call attention to the rifts and danger-zones which result from the modern civilizing process itself, so that the opportunities for human emancipation which it simultaneously creates can be the more thoroughly charted."[22] In other words, Peukert was challenging historians to abandon the normative conception of modernization, which associated modernity with "progress," in favor of a properly historical approach that takes into account both the emancipatory and repressive potentials of modernization.

It is this new historiographical focus on the ambiguities of modernity rather than the premodern or antimodern features of German society that gives this book broader relevance to the major issues of modern German history. Although the definitions of "modernization" and "modernity" remain controversial, few would deny that the development of nineteenth- and twentieth-century science was a key part of the modernization process. Hence the history of science—in this case the science of criminology—is a good starting point for examining the ambiguous implications of modernity. This book is not arguing that modern science was or is inescapably dangerous and repressive or that the Nazi regime as a whole is best understood as a modernizing regime. What I am arguing is that the modern sciences, especially medicine and criminology, were not exclusively progressive in their social implications but also had a dark side, an extremely repressive potential, and that these sciences played a significant role under the Nazi regime. At the same time, I have also made every effort not to let the Nazi experience overshadow the history of criminology.

The issue of the role of science under the Nazi regime brings us to the history of German medicine. Like the literature on criminal justice, most of the growing historical literature on German medicine, psychiatry, and eugenics focuses

---

20. Detlev Peukert, "Die Genesis der 'Endlösung' aus dem Geist der Wissenschaft," in *Max Webers Diagnose der Moderne* (Göttingen: Vandenhoeck, 1989), translated as "The Genesis of the 'Final Solution' from the Spirit of Science," in *Nazism and German Society*, ed. David Crew (London: Routledge, 1994), 274–99.

21. For such a critique of Peukert, see Michael Burleigh, *Ethics and Extermination: Reflections on Nazi Genocide* (Cambridge: Cambridge University Press, 1997), 180.

22. Peukert, *Volksgenossen und Gemeinschaftsfremde*, 296; *Inside Nazi Germany*, 249.

on the Nazi period.[23] But although it is of recent origin—most of it published during the past decade—it has far surpassed the literature on criminal justice in size and scope and includes a substantial amount of work on earlier periods. Without wishing to oversimplify a complex literature, I would argue that recent work on the history of German medicine and eugenics is characterized by two main arguments. First, much of this work has shown that Nazi anti-Semitism and the murder of the European Jews were part of a larger vision of biological politics that also targeted other groups perceived as "biologically inferior," including Gypsies, the mentally ill, the handicapped, homosexuals, persons labeled "asocial," and potentially anyone whose deviance was attributed to a "genetic defect." Hence the sterilization of persons with supposed "genetic diseases," the murder of the handicapped in the "euthanasia" program, and finally the murder of the Jews and Gypsies in the death camps must all be understood as connected components in the larger Nazi project of a "racial state."[24] And the German medical profession played a much larger role in

23. For good overviews of this literature, see *Medizin im Nationalsozialismus* (Munich: Oldenbourg, 1988); Achim Thom and Genadij Caregorodcev, eds., *Medizin unterm Hakenkreuz* (East Berlin: Verlag Volk und Gesundheit, 1989); Thomas Maretski, "The Documentation of Nazi Medicine by German Medical Sociologists: A Review Article," *Social Sciences and Medicine* 29 (1989): 1319–32; Norbert Frei, ed., *Medizin und Gesundheitspolitik in der NS-Zeit* (Munich: Oldenbourg, 1991); Michael Burleigh, " 'Euthanasia' in the Third Reich: Some Recent Literature," *Social History of Medicine* 4 (1991): 317–28; Franz-Werner Kersting, Karl Teppe, and Bernd Walter, eds., *Nach Hadamar: Zum Verhältnis von Psychiatrie und Gesellschaft im 20. Jahrhundert* (Paderborn: Schöningh, 1993); Hans-Walter Schmuhl, "Rassismus unter den Bedingungen charismatischer Herrschaft," in *Deutschland, 1933–1945*, ed. Karl-Dietrich Bracher, Manfred Funke, and Hans-Adolf Jacobsen, 2d ed. (Düsseldorf: Droste, 1993), 182–97; Geoffrey Cocks, "German Psychiatry, Psychotherapy, and Psychoanalysis during the Nazi Period: Historiographical Reflections," in *Discovering the History of Psychiatry*, ed. Mark Micale and Roy Porter (New York: Oxford University Press, 1994), 282–96; Paul Weindling, "Understanding Nazi Racism: Precursors and Perpetrators," in *Confronting the Nazi Past*, ed. Michael Burleigh (New York: St. Martin's, 1996), 66–83; Manfred Berg and Geoffrey Cocks, eds., *Medicine and Modernity: Public Health and Medical Care in Nineteenth- and Twentieth-Century Germany* (Cambridge: Cambridge University Press, 1997). The most recent survey of the history of German psychiatry is Dirk Blasius, *"Einfache Seelenstörung": Geschichte der deutschen Psychiatrie, 1800–1945* (Frankfurt: Fischer, 1994).

24. Benno Müller-Hill, *Tödliche Wissenschaft: Die Aussonderung von Juden, Zigeunern und Geisteskranken, 1933–1945* (Reinbek: Rowohlt, 1984), translated as *Murderous Science: Elimination by Scientific Selection of Jews, Gypsies, and Others, Germany, 1933–1945* (Oxford: Oxford University Press, 1988); Gisela Bock, *Zwangssterilisation im Nationalsozialismus* (Opladen: Westdeutscher Verlag, 1986); Hans-Walter Schmuhl, *Rassenhygiene, Nationalsozialismus, Euthanasie* (Göttingen: Vandenhoeck, 1987; 2d ed., 1992); Robert Proctor, *Racial Hygiene: Medicine under the Nazis* (Cambridge, Mass.: Harvard University Press, 1988); Michael Burleigh and Wolfgang Wippermann, *The Racial State: Germany, 1933–1945* (Cambridge: Cambridge

implementing this project than had previously been assumed.[25] Second, studies tracing the development of eugenics back to its turn-of-the-century origins have demonstrated that the eugenics movement had become a powerful force, with widespread support in the medical profession, before 1933 and that the supporters of eugenics did not come only from the political right but from a wide political spectrum, including liberals and socialists.[26]

Both of these arguments form an important part of the historiographical context of this book. On the one hand, this book seeks to show that criminals, too, were targets not just of criminal justice but of the biological politics of the Nazi racial state, most notably through schemes for the sterilization of criminals. On the other hand, efforts to provide both a biological explanation and solution to the crime problem dated back to the origins of criminology in the late nineteenth century and were not intrinsically connected with Nazi ideology. This book therefore seeks to show that the connection between criminological research and Nazi biological politics was more complicated than has often been assumed. Given the lack of research on the history of criminology, recent works on the Nazi racial state have often, not unreasonably, assumed that the crude genetic or even racial explanations of criminal behavior encountered among Nazi officials, doctors involved in the euthanasia program, or high-ranking police officials reflected the state of criminological research in the Nazi era.[27] By

---

University Press, 1991); Götz Aly, Peter Chroust, and Christian Pross, *Cleansing the Fatherland: Nazi Medicine and Racial Hygiene* (Baltimore: Johns Hopkins University Press, 1994); Michael Burleigh, *Death and Deliverance: "Euthanasia" in Germany, c. 1900–1945* (Cambridge: Cambridge University Press, 1994); Henry Friedlander, *The Origins of Nazi Genocide: From Euthanasia to the Final Solution* (Chapel Hill: University of North Carolina Press, 1995); Michael Zimmermann, *Rassenutopie und Genozid: Die nationalsozialistische "Lösung der Zigeunerfrage"* (Hamburg: Christians, 1996).

25. See especially Michael Kater, *Doctors under Hitler* (Chapel Hill: University of North Carolina Press, 1989).

26. Sheila Faith Weiss, *Race Hygiene and National Efficiency: The Eugenics of Wilhelm Schallmayer* (Berkeley: University of California Press, 1987); Weiss, "The Race Hygiene Movement in Germany, 1904–1945," in *The Wellborn Science: Eugenics in Germany, France, Brazil and Russia*, ed. Mark Adams (New York: Oxford University Press, 1990), 8–68; Peter Weingart, Jürgen Kroll, and Kurt Bayertz, *Rasse, Blut und Gene: Geschichte der Eugenik und Rassenhygiene in Deutschland* (Frankfurt: Suhrkamp, 1988); Paul Weindling, *Health, Race and German Politics between National Unification and Nazism, 1870–1945* (Cambridge: Cambridge University Press, 1989); Jochen-Christoph Kaiser, Kurt Nowak, and Michael Schwartz, eds., *Eugenik, Sterilisation, "Euthanasie": Politische Biologie in Deutschland, 1895–1945* (Berlin: Buchverlag Union, 1992); Michael Schwartz, *Sozialistische Eugenik: Eugenische Sozialtechnologien in Debatten und Politik der deutschen Sozialdemokratie, 1890–1933* (Bonn: Dietz, 1995).

27. Burleigh and Wippermann, *Racial State*, 167; Wagner, *Volksgemeinschaft ohne Verbrecher*, 265; Proctor, *Racial Hygiene*, 204–5; Friedlander, *The Origins of Nazi Genocide*, 3, 23, 252.

contrast, my research demonstrates that a significant portion of criminological research during the Nazi era was not characterized by such crude genetic or racial determinism but by a complex tension between hereditarian assumptions and increasing methodological and conceptual sophistication.

The role of scientists under the Nazi regime is a difficult and sensitive subject. I therefore wish to make it clear from the outset that my insistence on a more complex picture of criminology under the Nazi regime is not meant to advance an apologetic agenda or to promote a myth of apolitical or innocent scientists. On the contrary. For if the actions of Nazi era eugenic policy makers and practitioners, including some criminologists, were not in fact supported by the findings of mainstream criminological research, the moral responsibility of these practitioners and criminologists is even greater.

One of my main objectives in this book is to move beyond two master narratives about medicine and science under the Nazi regime. The first of these assumes that science is fundamentally progressive and argues that science and medicine were "perverted" by the Nazis.[28] The second narrative, by contrast, portrays modern science and medicine as major contributors to the Holocaust and sometimes comes close to presenting the Holocaust as a logical outcome of certain strands of modern science.[29] Seeking to avoid both of these extremes, I contend that criminology was inherently ambivalent in its political implications, full of both emancipatory and repressive potential. More specifically, I argue that the development of criminology from the late nineteenth century through the Nazi regime was characterized by a continuing tension between hereditarian biases and a dynamic of increasing scientific sophistication that consistently challenged these biases by revealing the complexity of the interaction between heredity and environment. Finally, I seek to demonstrate that this tension inherent in criminological research prevented criminology from becoming completely Nazified during the Nazi regime.[30]

Since the increasing sophistication of criminal-biological research made the goal of identifying a group of "genetic" criminals ever more elusive, the issue of

28. See, for instance, Müller-Hill, *Tödliche Wissenschaft*, translated as *Murderous Science*; Robert Jay Lifton, *The Nazi Doctors* (New York: Basic Books, 1986).

29. Peukert, "Die Genesis der 'Endlösung,' " 102–21, translated as "The Genesis of the 'Final Solution,' " 274–99; Mario Biagioli, "Science, Modernity and the 'Final Solution,' " in *Probing the Limits of Representation: Nazism and the "Final Solution,"* ed. Saul Friedlander (Cambridge, Mass.: Harvard University Press, 1992), 185–205.

30. For similar arguments for other fields of science, see Kristie Macrakis, *Surviving the Swastika: Scientific Research in Nazi Germany* (New York: Oxford University Press, 1993); Pamela Potter, *Most German of the Arts: Musicology and Society from the Weimar Republic to the End of the Third Reich* (New Haven: Yale University Press, 1998).

sterilizing criminals was far more contested—both before and after 1933—than the sterilization of various categories of the mentally ill. While the Nazi sterilization law and Nazi sterilization policy have usually been seen as a triumph for eugenicists, the history of sterilization policy concerning criminals reveals that in some areas eugenic hard-liners faced opposition that limited and sometimes even thwarted their ambitions. In short, my examination of the impact of criminology on eugenic policy suggests that in at least one important area Nazi "biological politics" left more room for disagreement and contention than has often been assumed.

The book's long chronological sweep has entailed several thematic limits. First, readers should not expect this history of criminology to include a full history of penal policy or penal reform. Although it could be argued that all aspects of penal policy were in some way connected with criminology, for the purposes of this volume I have had to be more selective. Hence this study focuses on those penal policy questions most directly connected with biological explanations of criminal behavior, namely, how to treat "abnormal" offenders and whether to impose eugenic measures on criminals. Readers interested in more information about penal policy and penal reform will find a comprehensive account of German penal reform from the Empire to Nazi Germany in my forthcoming book on penal reform.[31]

Second, although several chapters examine the reception of criminological theories among jurists, psychiatrists, Reichstag deputies, and officials who participated in debates on penal and eugenic policy, the book does not provide a systematic survey of views on criminal behavior among the public or among professionals not engaged in criminal-biological research. Third, I do not discuss the specialized literature on juvenile delinquents. Research on juvenile delinquents and "wayward youth" constituted a separate field of inquiry with its own specialized journals and associations that was quite distinct from general criminology from the very beginning of criminological research. Since research on juveniles has received considerable attention as part of the history of youth welfare and juvenile justice, readers interested in this subject can turn to a well-developed historical literature.[32]

Fourth, the Nazi persecution of racial minorities plays only a very limited role in this study. To be sure, since this book is concerned with criminological efforts to explain *ordinary* criminal behavior (property crime and violent crime) in biological terms, it will address the question of whether criminologists re-

---

31. On penal reform in Imperial Germany, see Wetzell, "Criminal Law Reform."
32. See literature cited earlier in this chapter.

garded ethnic minorities, namely Jews and "Gypsies" (Sinti and Roma), as somehow "racially predisposed" to criminal behavior. But it will not examine the Nazis' use of the criminal justice system for the purpose of persecuting racial minorities.[33]

Finally, for analogous reasons, the important issue of the legal treatment of male homosexuality, which the German penal code criminalized throughout the period under investigation, has been left out of the following account. To be sure, with regard to homosexuality, too, biological explanations and brutal medical "remedies" played an increasing role. The point, however, of such theories was not that homosexuals were predisposed to commit property or violent crimes but that they were biologically predisposed toward a sexual behavior that happened to be criminalized under the German penal code. Criminologists were fully aware that the cases of men convicted for homosexuality were totally different from those of the mass of "regular" (property and violent) criminals and that any biological explanation of their sexual behavior differed from biological explanations of general criminal behavior. Fortunately, on this subject, too, the interested reader can consult recent historical studies.[34]

The first chapter provides a brief overview of early nineteenth-century efforts to study crime with the tools of social or medical science and then places the late nineteenth-century origins of German criminology in the historical context of Cesare Lombroso's theory of the "born criminal" and the rise of a new penal reform movement in Imperial Germany. The second chapter examines how the German reception of Lombroso's theory resulted in the development of "criminal psychology" as a recognized scientific field in German psychiatry in the period 1880–1914, and the third chapter treats efforts to apply the results of criminal-psychological research to penal policy in the same period. The next two chapters discuss the development of criminology during the Weimar years. Chapter 4 focuses on "criminal-sociological" research on the

33. On "race defilement," see Robert Gellately, *The Gestapo and German Society: Enforcing Racial Policy, 1933–1945* (Oxford: Clarendon Press, 1990).

34. Hans-Georg Stümke and Rudi Finkler, *Rosa Winkel, Rosa Listen: Homosexuelle und "gesundes Volksempfinden" von Auschwitz bis heute* (Reinbek: Rowohlt, 1981); Burkhard Jellonnek, *Homosexuelle unter dem Hakenkreuz* (Paderborn: Schöningh, 1990); *Die Geschichte des Paragraphen 175: Strafrecht gegen Homosexuelle* (Berlin: Verlag Rosa Winkel, 1990); Geoffrey Giles, " 'The Most Unkindest Cut of All': Castration, Homosexuality and Nazi Justice," *Journal of Contemporary History* 27 (1992): 41–61; Frank Sparing, ". . . wegen Vergehen nach Paragraph 175 verhaftet": Die Verfolgung der Düsseldorfer Homosexuellen während des Nationalsozialismus (Düsseldorf: Grupello, 1997); Claudia Schoppmann, *Nationalsozialistische Sexualpolitik und weibliche Homosexualität*, 2d ed. (Pfaffenweiler: Centaurus, 1997); Centrum Schwule Geschichte, ed., *"Das sind Volksfeinde!" Die Verfolgung von Homosexuellen an Rhein und Ruhr, 1933–1945* (Cologne: Emons, 1998).

social causes of wartime crime, whereas Chapter 5 deals with the varieties of increasingly sophisticated criminal-biological research during the Weimar era. Chapter 6 examines the development of criminology under the Nazi regime. The final chapter discusses the reception and application of criminological research in the Weimar and Nazi years through the lens of Weimar debates over the sterilization of criminals and Nazi sterilization policy with regard to criminals.

CHAPTER ONE

THE ORIGINS OF MODERN CRIMINOLOGY

German criminology emerged as a recognized scientific field in the last quarter of the nineteenth century as a result of three interconnected developments: the emergence of a new German penal reform movement, the publication and reception of Cesare Lombroso's theory of the "born criminal," and an increasing interest in criminological questions among German psychiatrists. First, however, I will provide a brief survey of criminological research in the first three-quarters of the nineteenth century because some familiarity with this background is essential for properly assessing the developments that took place at the end of the century. On the one hand, the existence of medical-biological explanations of crime earlier in the nineteenth century shows that Lombroso was not the first to advance such an explanation. On the other hand, the substantial amount of work in "moral statistics" and on the subculture of professional criminals demonstrates that nineteenth-century researchers paid far more attention to social than to biological factors in crime. Only if this is understood can one appreciate the drastic shift in emphasis from social to medical-biological explanations of crime that occurred at the end of the nineteenth century.

Before setting out on this brief survey, I should point out that the origins of criminology are a matter of debate. Some scholars regard the psychiatrist Lombroso, whose book on the born criminal appeared in 1876, as the founder of criminology,[1] while others argue that modern criminology originated with Ce-

---

1. David Matza, *Delinquency and Drift* (New York: Wiley, 1964), 3; David Garland, *Punishment and Welfare: A History of Penal Strategies* (Aldershot: Gower, 1985), 77; Pasquale Pasquino, "Criminology: The Birth of a Special Knowledge," in *The Foucault Effect: Studies in Governmentality*, ed. Graham Burchell, Colin Gordon, and Peter Miller (Chicago: University of Chicago Press, 1991), 235–50.

sare Beccaria's treatise on penal reform more than a century earlier.[2] Still others propose that the origins of criminology are to be found in the work of early nineteenth-century moral statisticians[3] or nineteenth-century psychiatrists.[4] To decide the question of origins, one must first settle on a definition of the term "criminology." This is best done by determining its place among what we might call the "penal sciences," which the German penal reformer Franz von Liszt divided into three main branches: a pedagogical-practical branch concerned with training criminal lawyers and judges, consisting of criminal jurisprudence (the study of criminal law) and criminalistics (or forensics: scientific methods of gathering evidence); a scientific branch "concerned with the causal explanation of crime (criminology) and punishment (penology)"; and a political branch concerned with improving penal legislation (penal policy).[5] In accordance with this classification, the term "criminology" will be used here to denote the scientific study of the causes of crime. This definition differs from a broader one that includes penology and penal policy in the subject of criminology[6] and a narrower one that conceives of criminology as the study of *criminals* (rather than crime).[7]

If criminology is thus defined as the scientific study of the causes of crime, it follows that the liberal penal reformers of the late eighteenth and early nineteenth centuries—Cesare Beccaria in Italy, Sir Samuel Romilly, John Howard, and Jeremy Bentham in Britain, Paul Johann Anselm von Feuerbach in Bavaria—who are sometimes referred to as the "classical school of criminology"[8]

2. The following collections start with Beccaria: Hermann Mannheim, ed., *Pioneers in Criminology*, 2d ed. (Montclair: Patterson Smith, 1972); Piers Beirne, *Inventing Criminology: Essays on the Rise of "Homo Criminalis"* (Albany: State University of New York Press, 1993); Piers Beirne, ed., *The Origins and Growth of Criminology: Essays on Intellectual History, 1760–1945* (Aldershot: Dartmouth, 1994).

3. Alfred Lindesmith and Yale Levin, "The Lombrosian Myth in Criminology," *American Journal of Sociology* 42 (1937): 653–71; Achim Mechler, *Studien zur Geschichte der Kriminalsoziologie* (Göttingen: Schwartz, 1970).

4. Laurent Mucchielli, ed., *Histoire de la criminologie française* (Paris: L'Harmattan, 1994).

5. Franz von Liszt, "Die Aufgaben und die Methode der Strafrechtswissenschaft," in *Strafrechtliche Aufsätze und Vorträge*, 2 vols. (Berlin: Guttentag, 1905), 2:296; the essay was first published in 1899. Liszt's term for what I have called the penal sciences was "gesamte Strafrechtswissenschaft."

6. For such a larger definition, see Clarence Jeffery, "The Historical Development of Criminology," in *Pioneers in Criminology*, ed. Mannheim, 458–88.

7. Such a definition underlies David Garland's conception of the "criminological programme" in his "The Criminal and His Science," *British Journal of Criminology* 25 (1985): 109–37; and in Garland, *Punishment and Welfare*.

8. Terms such as "classical school" (of criminology) and "classical criminology" are used (with reference to Beccaria) in Jeffery, "Historical Development," 459; Beirne, *Inventing Crim-*

were not really criminologists in this sense because they were concerned with penal policy rather than the causes of crime.[9] Instead, my survey of nineteenth-century criminological research will focus on three groups of researchers who did investigate the causes of crime: physicians who advanced medical explanations of criminal behavior; "moral statisticians" who analyzed criminal statistics; and police officials and others who did fieldwork investigating the "breeding grounds" of crime and the subculture of "professional criminals."

Following this survey, the second half of the chapter will examine two of the factors that facilitated the development of criminology into a recognized scientific field at the turn of the century: Lombroso's theory of the born criminal and the emergence of a new German penal reform movement. The increasing interest in medical explanations of crime among turn-of-the-century German psychiatrists will form the subject of the next chapter.

Medical Explanations of Crime

Among nineteenth-century medical explanations of criminal behavior, three were particularly influential: Franz Joseph Gall's phrenology, Etienne-Jean Georget's "homicidal monomania," and James Prichard's "moral insanity." Gall began his work on the anatomy of the brain in Vienna, where he practiced medicine from 1785 to 1805. When his anatomical work was attacked as irreligious in 1805, he left Vienna, spent two years teaching at various German universities, and finally settled in Paris, where he taught until his death in 1828. His studies of brain anatomy led Gall to develop the theory that human behavior was regulated by twenty-seven different "faculties" or "propensities," each located in a particular part of the brain. In addition, he believed that the exterior bone structure of the skull indicated which of these propensities were highly developed and which were atrophied in any particular individual. Three of these propensities could give rise to criminal behavior if they were highly developed: greed, which could lead to theft; the instinct of self-defense, which

inology, 4; Philip Jenkins, "Varieties of Enlightenment Criminology," in Origins and Growth of Criminology, ed. Beirne, 79.

9. This point is made by Garland in Punishment and Welfare, 14. It is implicit in Leon Radzinowicz, Ideology and Crime (New York: Columbia University Press, 1966), which credits Beccaria with an important role in formulating the "liberal doctrine of criminal law" that gave rise to the "classical school of criminal law," not of criminology. For the most ambitious effort to demonstrate that Beccaria's treatise did contain "a very rudimentary attempt to forge some key concepts of an embryonic criminology," see Piers Beirne, "Toward a Science of Homo Criminalis: Cesare Beccaria's Dei delitti e Delle Pene (1764)," in Beirne, Inventing Criminology, 11–64.

could lead to violent fights; and the "carnivorous instinct" (*l'instinct carnassier*), which could lead to murder.[10] On his travels through Germany in 1805, Gall visited several prisons and found the faculty of greed well developed in all the thieves, whom he was reportedly able to pick out by the shape of their skulls.[11]

Although some criminal jurists regarded Gall's phrenology as a serious threat to the notion of legal responsibility, Gall insisted that an individual's propensities merely inclined behavior in certain directions but did not determine it, thus leaving the notions of free will and legal responsibility intact. Nor did Gall claim that his theory accounted for all crimes. Instead, he distinguished between crimes that resulted directly from well-developed propensities (such as for theft, fights, or murder) and crimes that resulted from circumstances without such propensities. Because he believed that criminals from propensity were more likely to become recidivists, Gall suggested that an offender's sentencing should take into account the results of a phrenological examination (*cranioscopie*) so that criminals from propensity could be given longer prison sentences.[12] Not surprisingly, contemporary courts remained skeptical and did not introduce phrenological examinations.[13]

Gall did, however, develop a following among the French medical profession. A few years after his death, in 1831 some of his followers founded the Phrenological Society of Paris, which continued to promote a medical approach to crime. Although Gall himself had been pessimistic about rehabilitating persons with pronounced propensities for theft or murder, the next generation of phrenologists strongly believed in the possibility of reeducation. They stressed that normal and "criminal" traits did not differ in kind but only in degree. Since theft and normal acquisitiveness, for example, derived from the same basic propensity, environmental influences might redirect the propensity away from crime.[14] Phrenology flourished in the middle of the nineteenth century but

10. Georges Lanteri-Laura, "Phrénologie et criminologie au début du XIXème siècle: Les idées de F. J. Gall," in *Histoire de la criminologie française*, ed. Mucchielli, 21–23; see also Michael Hagner, *Homo cerebralis: Der Wandel vom Seelenorgan zum Gehirn* (Berlin: Berlin Verlag, 1997), 89–129.

11. Dr. *Joseph Galls Besuche in den merkwürdigen Gefängnissen von Preussen und Sachsen* (Deutz, 1805), quoted in Abraham Baer, *Der Verbrecher in anthropologischer Beziehung* (Leipzig: Thieme, 1893), 412.

12. Lanteri-Laura, "Phrénologie et criminologie," 23–27.

13. Ibid., 26.

14. Marc Renneville, "Entre nature et culture: Le regard médical sur le crime dans la première moitié du XIXème siècle," in *Histoire de la criminologie française*, ed. Mucchielli, 31–32.

gradually became discredited in the latter half of the century. By the 1870s, when Lombroso developed his theory of the born criminal, the mainstream of the medical profession had rejected Gall's ideas.[15] Nevertheless, Gall's phrenology played an important role in preparing the ground for Lombroso's theories. Although Lombroso never posited the causal connection between criminal behavior and the shape of the criminal's skull that Gall had postulated, Gall helped to popularize the notion that many criminals committed their crimes as a result of innate propensities.

At the same time that Gall was developing his phrenological theories, French psychiatrists developed another medical explanation of crime. At the very beginning of the nineteenth century, Philippe Pinel, the French pioneer of psychiatry, abandoned the view that madness necessarily involved an intellectual disturbance and advanced the concept of *manie sans délire* or *manie raisonnante*, a partial insanity that left the patient's intellectual powers intact. Developing this concept further, Pinel's student Jean-Etienne Esquirol introduced the notion of "monomania" to denote "a single pathological preoccupation in an otherwise sound mind." In 1825, Etienne-Jean Georget, a student of Esquirol's, used this concept to challenge several judicial verdicts by arguing that the accused had suffered from "homicidal monomania." After sparking considerable controversy, the notion of homicidal mania became widely accepted among the most influential circles of French psychiatry, holding sway for more than two decades before being attacked and then quickly abandoned in the early 1850s.[16]

In the meantime, in 1835, the British psychiatrist James Prichard coined the term "moral insanity," which outlived and eventually replaced the notion of monomania. Strongly influenced by Pinel and Esquirol, Prichard distinguished between two types of insanity: one affecting the intellect and the other affecting emotions and will. The latter he called moral insanity.[17] According to Prichard, a morally insane person was "incapable not of talking or reasoning upon any subject proposed to him—for this he will often do with great shrewdness and

15. Lanteri-Laura, "Phrénologie et criminologie," 27.

16. Jan Goldstein, *Console and Classify: The French Psychiatric Profession in the Nineteenth Century* (Cambridge: Cambridge University Press, 1987), 152–96; quote p. 155.

17. Roger Smith, *Trial by Medicine: Insanity and Responsibility in Victorian Trials* (Edinburgh: Edinburgh University Press, 1981), 38–40; Henry Werlinder, *Psychopathy: A History of the Concepts* (Uppsala: University, 1978), 36–40; Fritz Berthold, "Die Entwicklung der moral insanity und der heutige Stand der Zurechnungsfähigkeit" (J.D. dissertation, University of Erlangen, 1937), 38–39.

volubility—but of conducting himself with decency and propriety in the business of life. His wishes and inclinations, his attachments, his likings and dislikings have all undergone a morbid change."[18] Such a condition did not necessary lead to criminal behavior, but it could. As Prichard observed, "There is scarcely an act in the catalog of human crimes which has not been imitated . . . by this disease."[19]

Prichard's moral insanity soon found its way into the French and German psychiatric vocabulary. But while Prichard's term originally designated emotional-volitional disorders in general, in France and the German states moral insanity took on a more specific meaning, referring to violent, immoral, and criminal behavior that was attributed to an isolated defect of the "moral sense." In the 1840s the French psychiatrist Bénédict-Augustin Morel introduced Prichard's concept to the French as "folie morale." By the 1860s it had supplanted the French diagnosis of monomania and been incorporated into Morel's influential degeneration theory.[20] In German-speaking Europe the reception of Prichard's concept was complicated by the fact that most German psychiatrists believed in the unity of mental faculties and hence rejected the notion that an individual's moral sense could be disturbed without his intellectual faculties being affected. But while some dismissed Prichard's concept, others used the term "moral insanity," or *moralischer Schwachsinn*, to refer to cases of mental illness that seemed primarily, but not exclusively, to affect an individual's moral sense.[21] Moral insanity, however, was generally regarded as a rare disorder and could therefore explain only a limited number of crimes.

Gall's phrenology, Georget's homicidal monomania, and Prichard's moral insanity demonstrate that Lombroso was by no means the first to advance a medical-biological explanation of crime. And although only the notion of moral insanity survived into the late nineteenth century, there can be no doubt that all three theories helped to prepare the ground for Lombroso by popularizing medical theories of crime.

18. James Prichard, *A Treatise on Insanity and Other Disorders Affecting the Mind* (London: Sherwood, Gilbert, and Piper, 1835), 4, quoted in Smith, *Trial by Medicine*, 38.

19. James Prichard, *On the Different Forms of Insanity in Relation to Jurisprudence* (London: Bailliere, 1842), 88, quoted in Smith, *Trial by Medicine*, 39.

20. Jean-Christophe Coffin, "La 'folie morale': Figure pathologique et entité miracle des hypothèses psychiatriques au XIXème siècle," in *Histoire de la criminologie française*, ed. Mucchielli, 89–106.

21. See Stolz, "Gedanken über moralisches Irresein (moral insanity)," *AZP* 33 (1877): 732–44. See also Knop, "Über Moral Insanity," *AZP* 31 (1875): 697–704, which strongly opposes the concept; and Berthold, "Entwicklung," 41–42.

Moral Statistics

For the systematic explanation of crime, the work of nineteenth-century "moral statisticians" was far more important than that of medical doctors. The two pioneers in this area were Lambert Adolphe Jacques Quetelet, a Belgian astronomer, and André-Michel Guerry, a lawyer at the royal court in Paris.[22] Both of them published their first analyses of criminal statistics in the early 1830s, just a few years after the French government started publishing official crime statistics in 1827. Their work was an attempt to apply the empirical approach of the natural sciences to the study of society. Their main finding was that the number of recorded crimes remained virtually constant from year to year. As Quetelet put it in a famous passage: "The share of prisons, chains, and the scaffold appears fixed with as much probability as the revenues of state. We are able to enumerate in advance how many individuals will stain their hands with the blood of their fellow creatures, how many will be forgers, how many poisoners, pretty nearly as one can enumerate in advance the births and deaths which must take place."[23] In addition, Quetelet and Guerry concluded that the commonly accepted theory that crime was caused by poverty or lack of education was not supported by their statistical findings. Instead, they found that the two most significant factors determining a person's statistical "propensity toward crime" (*penchant au crime*) were age and sex. The propensity for crime was highest between ages twenty-one and twenty-five and four times higher for men than for women.

Quetelet, who was bolder in drawing conclusions from his findings than Guerry, argued that society bore substantial responsibility for the crimes committed in its midst. "The crimes which are annually committed," he wrote, "seem to be a necessary result of our social organization . . . society prepares crime, and the guilty are only the instruments by which it is executed."[24] Some of Quetelet's critics interpreted these remarks as an attack on free will, unleashing an acrimonious debate on the subject that lasted for decades. Others

22. The following section on Guerry and Quetelet is based on Lindesmith and Levin, "Lombrosian Myth"; Radzinowicz, *Ideology and Crime*, 29–38; Mechler, *Studien*, 6–54; Piers Beirne, "The Rise of Positivist Criminology: Adolphe Quetelet's 'Social Mechanics of Crime' " and "The Social Cartography of Crime: A. M. Guerry's *Statistique Morale* (1833)," in Beirne, *Inventing Criminology*, 65–141; Jacques Van Kerckwoorde, "Statistique morale et statistique criminelle au XIXème siècle," in *Histoire de la criminologie française*, ed. Mucchielli, 253–68.

23. Quetelet, *Research on the Propensity for Crime at Different Ages*, quoted in Beirne, *Inventing Criminology*, 82.

24. Quetelet, *A Treatise on Man* (1842), quoted in Beirne, *Inventing Criminology*, 88.

thought Quetelet's talk of "social physics" indicated that he considered a nation's annual "budget of crime" forever fixed, but this was not the case.[25] "Since crimes . . . seem to be the necessary result of our social organization," Quetelet explained, "and since their number cannot be reduced without their causes being changed, it is the legislator's task to recognize these causes and eliminate them as far as possible. It is the legislator who fixes the budget of crime."[26] Thus, far from regarding the statistical regularities he had uncovered as a natural law, Quetelet argued that the "budget of crime" was determined by social conditions that could be changed through legislation.

Quetelet and Guerry also laid the groundwork for future analyses of criminal statistics by establishing some methodological and theoretical principles. First, if crime was analyzed in the aggregate with statistical methods, it appeared not as a random phenomenon but as one with certain regularities; it was these regularities that made further analysis meaningful. Second, by breaking down aggregate crime figures geographically, chronologically, and by key characteristics (primarily gender and age) of the offender, one could detect differences in the average "propensity toward crime" between different regions, chronological periods, and sections of the population. Third, such differentials in crime rates made it possible to test certain explanations of crime by correlating these differentials with other statistical data (such as the wealth or education level of a geographic region). Finally, the remarkable regularities in the propensity toward crime of any given population suggested that crime was not a random individual act but strongly influenced by a variety of statistically measurable factors, including social factors, so that society bore significant responsibility for crime.

In German-speaking Europe, the pioneering work of Quetelet and Guerry was continued and further developed by Georg von Mayr, chief of the Bavarian statistical office, and Alexander von Oettingen, professor of theology in Dorpat (now Tartu), both of whom published their first works on "moral statistics" in the 1860s. In 1867 Mayr published a detailed analysis of Bavarian crime statistics for the period 1835–61, which represented some advances over the work of

25. On the reception of Quetelet, see Beirne, *Inventing Criminology*, 92–97; Mechler, *Studien*, 36–54; Karl-Heinz Hering, *Der Weg der Kriminologie zur selbständigen Wissenschaft* (Hamburg: Kriminalistik Verlag, 1966), 145–67; Rudolf Wassermann, "Die Entwicklung der Kriminalstatistik von Quetelet bis G. von Mayr," *Annalen des Deutschen Reiches für Gesetzgebung, Verwaltung und Volkswirtschaft* (1911): 81.

26. Quetelet, "Sur la possibilité de mesurer l'influence des causes qui modifient les éléments sociaux" (1832), quoted in Mechler, *Studien*, 33.

the Belgian-French school.[27] First, Mayr based his statistics on the number of reported crimes, which he regarded as a more accurate measure of the actual incidence of crime than the number of convictions, which Quetelet and Guerry had used.[28] Second, Mayr called attention to the fluctuation of crime rates over time. Because French crime rates had been more or less constant during the years on which their original analyses were based (1825–30), Quetelet and Guerry had paid little attention to annual fluctuations. By contrast, Mayr argued that the significant annual fluctuations that he was able to document demonstrated that the remarkable regularities of criminal statistics did not reflect a natural law (a position often falsely attributed to Quetelet) but the impact of social conditions that were subject to change.[29]

Convinced that most thefts, which made up the lion's share of all crime, were motivated by the desire to obtain foodstuffs, Mayr hypothesized that rises in theft might be caused by increases in food prices. Using the price of grain as a rough index of food prices, he was able to demonstrate that the fluctuations of grain prices and property crime were so closely correlated that "every *Sechser* [Bavarian equivalent of a nickel] by which the price of grain increased resulted in one additional theft per 100,000 population" in the period 1835–61. In addition, Mayr demonstrated that increases in grain prices were correlated with decreases in violent crime. He explained this by arguing that increased difficulties in obtaining food provided less occasion for brutality and unrestrained sexual desire, which he considered the prime motives of violent crime.[30]

Only one year after Mayr's work appeared, the theology professor Alexander von Oettingen published his treatise *Moralstatistik* (1868).[31] Whereas Mayr's study was an original analysis of unpublished Bavarian statistical data on crime, Oettingen's tome was a wide-ranging synthesis on the larger topic of moral statistics, that is, not just crime rates but statistics on births, deaths, marriages, and suicides, based on the published statistics of different states, including France, England, Russia, and several German states. Going through three editions between 1868 and 1882, Oettingen's book was the standard survey of

27. Georg von Mayr, *Statistik der gerichtlichen Polizei im Königreiche Bayern und in einigen anderen Ländern*, vol. 16 of *Beiträge zur Statistik des Königreichs Bayern* (Munich: Statistisches Bureau, 1867). Mayr's work on criminal statistics continued for fifty years, culminating in his *Statistik und Gesellschaftslehre*, vol. 3, *Moralstatistik mit Einschluß der Kriminalstatistik* (Tübingen: Mohr, 1917).

28. Mayr, *Statistik der gerichtlichen Polizei*, 2.

29. Ibid., iv–v.

30. Ibid., 41–43.

31. Alexander von Oettingen, *Die Moralstatistik* (Erlangen: Deichert, 1868).

moral statistics in German-speaking Europe during the 1870s and 1880s. The sections on crime provided an up-to-date version of the statistical breakdowns that Quetelet, Guerry, and Mayr had pioneered: comparisons between different regions; periodic fluctuations of crime correlated with grain prices; crime rates by sex, age, occupation, and religion.[32]

While Mayr's tone was one of dispassionate statistical analysis, Oettingen was torn between two different approaches to his subject. On the one hand, he showed considerable methodological sophistication, which led him to call for restraint in interpreting the meaning of criminal statistics. Drawing any conclusions from the long-term movement of crime rates, he cautioned, was problematic because changes in crime rates might reflect changes in penal legislation or policing rather than any actual increase or decrease in crime. Likewise, comparisons between the crime rates of different countries were generally misleading because of differences in penal codes and policing.[33] By the third edition of 1882, this commitment to interpretive restraint had turned Oettingen into an outspoken critic of authors who saw increases in the German crime rate in the 1870s as evidence of a failing criminal justice system or the "increasing moral corruption" of the population. Far from necessarily reflecting a moral decline, Oettingen countered, "high crime rates [could] also be . . . a sign of advancing civilization, stricter penal legislation and a conscientious power of repression, and therefore derive from ethical motives."[34]

Despite this call for interpretive caution, however, Oettingen argued that moral statistics reflected the "communal ethos" and demonstrated the "collective guilt" (*Collectivschuld*) of society.[35] This argument was reminiscent of Quetelet's remarks but with a strong religious inflection. According to Oettingen, the remarkable regularities in aggregate crime rates demonstrated a permanent "disposition toward crime" deriving from "an inner egotistical inclination of the will" that could not "be limited to a mere fraction of the population," because "everyone contribute[d]." "For the seed of a loveless disposition, the desire for theft and murder which reveals itself in the finer nuances of greed and hate, is growing in every heart; . . . and in the cases of actual criminal individuals, it is the temptation and adversity of external circumstances that brings the same evil seed to flower which resides in all members of the [social] organism." In such cases, it was therefore "pharisaical self-

32. Ibid., 671–762, 878–900.
33. Ibid., 699, 702, 706–7.
34. Oettingen, *Die Moralstatistik*, 3d ed. (Erlangen: Deichert, 1882), 441–43.
35. Oettingen, *Moralstatistik*, 1st ed., 677, 716, 878.

deception and self-conceit" to "ignore the shared responsibility and guilt [*Mit-schuld*] which everyone bears as a member of society."[36]

For Oettingen, then, the "propensity for crime" referred not just to a statistical average but to a universal latent trait rooted in the sinful nature of man. Furthermore, Oettingen suggested that the basic motivating force behind crime was "the egotism that modern economists [were] idealizing as the main lever of healthy economic development," thus creating a disturbing connection between the roots of crime and mainstream bourgeois values.[37] When his insistence on the collective guilt of society led a leading jurist to accuse him of exculpating the individual criminal, Oettingen responded by distinguishing between moral and legal responsibility.[38] "By attributing moral responsibility to the community, we are not . . . exculpating the individual. We are merely aware . . . that the legitimate and necessary juridical sanction is never completely congruent with the moral judgment." The task of moral statistics was precisely to "reveal the moral collective guilt of society" that existed "alongside the juridically determined personal guilt of the individual criminal" in the "system of causes and motives" associated with crime. For it was the "ethical, intellectual and economic sphere of the surrounding society" that "create[d] the atmosphere in which the poisonous fruits [of crime] ripen[ed]."[39] As we shall see, the powerful sense of society's collective responsibility for crime that permeated Oettingen's work on moral statistics was largely lost during the subsequent development of criminology.

Studies of the "Criminal Classes"

A final group of social investigators took a different approach to studying crime as a social phenomenon. Whereas moral statisticians regarded crime as a product of society as a whole, this group saw crime as a phenomenon that was concentrated in certain social groups and locations. To be sure, moral statisticians, too, divided the general population into smaller units (by region, gender, or age) and found that certain groups had higher criminal propensities than others. But these were large social groups in which delinquents remained a small minority. The last set of investigators, by contrast, studied smaller social groups in which crime was supposedly endemic. And they did so not primarily

36. Ibid., 689; see also 890–91.
37. Ibid., 673.
38. Wilhelm Wahlberg, *Das Princip der Individualisirung in der Strafrechtspflege* (Vienna: Carl Gerold's Sohn, 1869).
39. Oettingen, *Moralstatistik*, 3d ed., 451, 454; see also 440.

through statistics but through direct observation. One of the pioneers in this tradition was Honoré-Antoine Frégier, an administrative police official in Paris, whose 1840 study presented a "moral topography" of the Parisian subculture of vagrants, beggars, prostitutes, cheats, and thieves that he collectively described as the city's "dangerous classes." In Frégier's analysis, crime was primarily a product of the vices of the poor: gambling, drinking, sexual excess, and above all idleness. As a remedy he recommended providing employment and fostering a strong work ethic and healthy morals.[40]

Two decades later, in 1861–62, the British journalist Henry Mayhew published a similar study of London's underworld. Mayhew regarded the division between "workers" and "nonworkers" as the most important social divide and argued that "those that will not work" were vagrants, beggars, cheats, thieves, and prostitutes, the same groups that Frégier had labeled as "dangerous classes." Although he recognized the importance of bad upbringing, poverty, and lack of education, Mayhew, like Frégier, regarded these people's refusal to work as the most important cause of crime. Furthermore, Mayhew established a distinction between "professional" criminals, who made a career of crime as a way of earning a living, and "casual" offenders, who committed crimes because of "the temporary pressure of circumstances."[41] The former category also formed the subject of Friedrich Christian Benedikt Avé-Lallement's monumental study of German *Gaunertum* that appeared at about the same time. Avé-Lallement used the term *Gaunertum* to refer to professional criminals as a subculture characterized by their own special language and other distinctive forms of communication. Like Frégier and Mayhew, he argued that unemployment and idleness were key factors leading to a life of crime.[42]

40. Mechler, *Studien*, 123–27; Radzinowicz, *Ideology and Crime*, 38–42. Frégier's major work was *Des classes dangereuses de la population dans les grandes villes, et des moyens de les rendre meilleurs*, 2 vols. (Paris: Bailliere, 1840). See also Louis Chevalier, *Classes laborieuses et classes dangereuses à Paris pendant la première moitié du XIXe siècle* (Paris: Plon, 1958).

41. Leon Radzinowicz and Roger Hood, *A History of English Criminal Law and Its Administration from 1750*, vol. 5, *The Emergence of Penal Policy* (London: Stevens and Sons, 1986), 77–84.

42. Peter Becker, "Vom 'Haltlosen' zur 'Bestie': Das polizeiliche Bild des Verbrechers im 19. Jahrhundert," in *"Sicherheit" und "Wohlfahrt": Polizei, Gesellschaft und Herrschaft im 19. und 20. Jahrhundert*, ed. Alf Lüdtke (Frankfurt: Suhrkamp, 1992), 97–131, esp. 102–4; Becker, "Une sémiotique de l'escroquerie: Le discours policier sur l'escroc au XIXe siècle," *Déviance et Société* 18 (1994): 155–70; Richard Evans, *Tales from the German Underworld: Crime and Punishment in the Nineteenth Century* (New Haven: Yale University Press, 1998), 151–59. Avé-Lallement's major work was *Das deutsche Gaunerthum in seiner social-politischen, literarischen und linguistischen Ausbildung zu seinem heutigen Bestande*, 4 vols. (Leipzig: Brockhaus, 1858–62).

In this literature on the "criminal classes," three central themes emerge, which are characterized by certain interpretive tensions. Regarding the issue of work and idleness, most writers on the criminal classes agreed that a "habitual indisposition to labor" (Mayhew) was a crucial factor in the etiology of crime but also argued that many thieves and con men treated crime as a profession.[43] Although these two observations appear contradictory, both became almost axiomatic tenets in late nineteenth-century criminology. The second theme concerns the perceived connections between crime, poverty, and other social ills. Sometimes such connections were interpreted as evidence of an underlying moral failing of individuals in the "dangerous classes." At other times, however, the connection between crime and poverty gave rise to the conclusion that crime was at least partly a result of social causes. Finally, there was the issue of the relationship of the criminal classes to the larger society. Here, too, the literature was characterized by a certain tension. The very terms used (dangerous classes, criminal class, *Gaunertum*) suggested that crime was the product of a separate social stratum. And as Leon Radzinowicz has written, it undoubtedly "served the interests and relieved the conscience of those at the top to look upon the dangerous classes as an independent category, detached from the prevailing social conditions."[44] Yet most commentators on the subculture of professional crime also acknowledged that this subculture was part of, and influenced by, the larger society. Both Mayhew and Avé-Lallement explicitly dismissed the notion that criminals could be recognized by the shape of their skull or other aspects of their physiognomy.[45] Frégier suggested that raising wages and improving working conditions might reduce the size of the "dangerous classes."[46] And Avé-Lallement criticized the police for regarding German *Gaunertum* as an isolated phenomenon connected with Gypsies and Jews and insisted instead that the development of professional crime had always depended on "the evolution of social and political conditions."[47]

By the 1870s a variety of investigators had made major contributions to the

43. Becker, "Vom 'Haltlosen' zur 'Bestie,' " 103.

44. Radzinowicz, *Ideology and Crime*, 38.

45. "But crime is an effect with which the shape of the head and the form of the features appear to have no connection whatsoever" (Mayhew, *The Criminal Prisons of London* [London, 1862], 413, quoted in Mechler, *Studien*, 96). "The *Gauner* is and remains lost for the ethnographer. His appearance does not differ from that of the ordinary everyday person, as nature created him, even if illness, passion, or sin have perhaps deformed his appearance" (Avé-Lallement, *Gaunerthum*, 2:5, quoted in Becker, "Une sémiotique de l'escroquerie," 163); Evans, *Tales of the Underworld*, 153.

46. Mechler, *Studien*, 125.

47. Avé-Lallement, *Gaunerthum*, quoted in Oettingen, *Moralstatistik*, 1st ed., 674.

scientific study of the causes of crime. At the beginning of the nineteenth century Gall's phrenology presented a biological explanation of crime. Although phrenology was discredited by midcentury, Prichard's concept of moral insanity became widely accepted as the century progressed. But while phrenology had claimed to explain a considerable proportion of crimes, moral insanity was considered a rare disorder, so that the explanatory scope of medical theories of crime was considerably diminished by midcentury.

As a result, moral statistics and studies of the criminal classes played a far greater role than medical theories in laying the foundations of criminology during the middle decades of the nineteenth century. Although moral statisticians commented on the role of *individual* factors (such as gender and age) in crime, none of them characterized criminals (or any subset of criminals) as *biologically* different from the general population. On the contrary, most moral statisticians emphasized the powerful influence of social factors on crime. Even analysts of the criminal classes, who placed more emphasis on individual moral failings such as an indisposition to labor, did not give such traits a biological or medical interpretation and often acknowledged that social factors played an important role in fostering such criminal classes. On balance, then, the research of nineteenth-century investigators into the causes of crime did far more to stress the role of social factors in crime than the role of individual, let alone biological-medical factors. This must be remembered in order to appreciate how much Lombroso's theories shifted criminologists' emphasis from social to individual-biological factors at the end of the nineteenth century.

Lombroso's Theory of the "Born Criminal"

In the last quarter of the nineteenth century the development of criminology into a recognized scientific field was strongly influenced and greatly accelerated by three developments common to most of western Europe: the publication and dissemination of Lombroso's theory of the "born criminal"; the rise of a new penal reform movement that called for criminological research; and increasing interest in criminological questions among psychiatrists.

Cesare Lombroso was an Italian physician who began his medical career as a military doctor in the Piedmontese army. He developed an interest in psychiatry and became head of the psychiatric ward in the hospital of Pavia in the mid-1860s. In 1876 he was appointed to a professorship at the University of Turin, where he taught until his death in 1909, holding chairs in forensic medicine, psychiatry, and eventually criminal anthropology. In 1876 Lombroso published *L'uomo delinquente* (Criminal man), the book that made him famous. In it he claimed to have identified "criminal man" as a distinct anthropological type. Based on anthropometric measurements of prison inmates, postmortem examinations of their skulls, and psychological observations, Lombroso argued that criminals were characterized by distinct features, including a smaller skull with certain traits found among animals, a taller body, handle-shaped ears, insensitivity to pain, acute eyesight, and left-handedness. Interpreting these characteristics as signs of a biological throwback to an earlier state of evolution, Lombroso concluded that the criminal was "an atavistic being who reproduces in his person the ferocious instincts of primitive humanity and the inferior animals."[48]

Whereas Lombroso's idea of measuring criminals' bodies and skulls derived from the anthropometric practices of contemporary physical anthropology, his interpretation of these characteristics as atavistic reflected the influence of Charles Darwin, who just a few years earlier had written: "With mankind, some of the worst dispositions, which occasionally without any assignable cause make their appearance in families, may perhaps be reversions to a savage state, from which we are not removed by very many generations. This view seems indeed recognized in the common expression that such men are the black sheep of the family."[49]

Lombroso's book was an odd assortment of statistical data on physical measurements, psychological observations, anecdotal information, speculative conclusions, and bizarre suggestions for the reform of criminal justice. Its eclectic

48. Cesare Lombroso, *L'Uomo delinquente* (Milan, 1876). There is no English translation; for this section I have used the German translation *Der Verbrecher (homo delinquens) in anthropologischer, ärztlicher und juristischer Beziehung*, trans. M. Fränkel, 2 vols. (Hamburg: Verlagsanstalt, 1887–90), and Lombroso, "Über den Ursprung, das Wesen und die Bestrebungen der neuen anthropologisch-kriminalistischen Schule in Italien," *ZStW* 1 (1881): 108–29. The quote is from Lombroso, "Introduction" to Gina Lombroso-Ferrero, *Criminal Man according to the Classification of Cesare Lombroso* (1911; rpt., Montclair: Patterson Smith, 1972), xxv. On Lombroso, see Marvin E. Wolfgang, "Cesare Lombroso," in *Pioneers in Criminology*, ed. Hermann Mannheim, 2d ed. (Montclair: Patterson Smith, 1972), 232–91; Stephen Jay Gould, *The Mismeasure of Man* (New York: Norton, 1981), 122–45; Gerd Ochs, "Die Lehre Lombrosos: Darstellung, Genealogie und Kritik der positiven Strafrechtslehre" (J.D. diss., University of Frankfurt, 1957); Daniel Pick, *Faces of Degeneration* (Cambridge: Cambridge University Press, 1989), 109–52; Mariacarla Gadebusch Bondio, *Die Rezeption der kriminalanthropologischen Theorien von Cesare Lombroso in Deutschland von 1880–1914* (Husum: Matthiesen, 1995), 18–51; Peter Becker, "Der Verbrecher als 'monstruoser Typus': Zur kriminologischen Semiotik der Jahrhundertwende," in *Der falsche Körper: Beiträge zu einer Geschichte der Monstrositäten*, ed. Michael Hagner (Göttingen: Wallstein, 1995), 147–73; Becker, "Physiognomie des Bösen: Cesare Lombrosos Bemühungen um eine präventive Entzifferung des Kriminellen," in *Der exzentrische Blick: Gespräche über Physiognomik*, ed. Claudia Schmölders (Berlin: Akademie Verlag, 1996), 163–86.

49. Charles Darwin, *The Descent of Man and Selection in Relation to Sex* (1871), 1:173, quoted in Radzinowicz and Hood, *History of English Criminal Law*, 5:6.

character only became more pronounced with each new edition. By the second edition of 1878 the book had doubled in length, as Lombroso added material on issues ranging from tattooing to suicide to the influence of the climate. While Lombroso had initially characterized the born criminal as a throwback to an earlier evolutionary stage rather than the product of a disease process, in later editions he began to link the born criminal to a variety of pathological conditions. In the third edition of 1884 he incorporated Prichard's concept of moral insanity by arguing that the atavistic born criminal was also "morally insane." In later editions he added that born criminals manifested signs of degeneration and epilepsy.[50] In short, Lombroso's atavism thesis was gradually supplemented by a series of psychiatric diagnoses, so that the etiology of the born criminal became ever more complex.

Later editions also complicated the picture by introducing new types of criminals, such as "occasional criminals" and "criminals of passion." While the first edition had suggested that all offenders were born criminals, the introduction of these new types allowed Lombroso gradually to reduce his estimate of the proportion of born criminals to about a third of all criminals. Finally, Lombroso's suggestions for the punishment of born criminals were no less eclectic and contradictory. On the one hand, he endorsed the death penalty as the best means of eliminating individuals whose criminal behavior was rooted in their biological constitution. On the other hand, he wondered whether the born criminal's antisocial energies could not be redirected to socially useful purposes. Bloodthirsty individuals, for instance, might be encouraged to become butchers or soldiers. For other criminals, Lombroso recommended preventive measures and indeterminate punishment.[51]

Since Lombroso was by no means the first to advance a biological theory of criminal behavior, the extraordinary impact of his work calls for explanation. Some features of his own work help to explain its impact. First, Lombroso's theory was far more ambitious than the theory of moral insanity, which was the only widely accepted medical-biological explanation of crime at the time. Whereas moral insanity was considered a rare condition, Lombroso initially claimed that the vast majority of criminals were born criminals. Second, Lombroso devoted enormous energy to propagating his theory of the born criminal: he wrote an entire book on the subject, updated and expanded his work in no fewer than five new editions over two decades, and disseminated his ideas in a continuous stream of other publications. Third, Lombroso's eclecticism and his

---

50. Lombroso, *Der Verbrecher*, 1:xix–xx; Gadebusch Bondio, *Rezeption*, 38–40.
51. Wolfgang, "Lombroso," 268, 279; Ochs, *Lehre Lombrosos*, 41.

constant incorporation of new medical theories assured him continued influ-ence. Each new edition confronted his critics with new modifications of his theory, making it impossible to mount a definitive refutation. Finally, Lom-broso was extremely successful in finding effective supporters and allies, espe-cially among reform-minded Italian jurists, including Enrico Ferri and Raffaele Garofalo. With them he founded a new academic journal,[52] which served as a public forum for what came to be known as the "Positive School" of criminal law and anthropology.[53]

Of course, the impact of Lombroso's ideas in the rest of Europe had at least as much to do with conditions in each country as with Lombroso and the Italian school. Although this study will focus on German developments, the late nineteenth-century birth of criminology was in many respects a general west-ern European phenomenon, taking place in Italy, France, Germany, and to a lesser extent Britain, among other countries. Above all, the reception of Lom-broso in each country depended on the degree to which criminal jurists and penal reformers, on the one hand, and the medical profession, on the other, were interested in criminological questions. We shall see that in Germany both groups showed considerable interest in criminological issues. In the remainder of this chapter we will examine how German criminal jurists became interested in criminology. In the next chapter we will look at the growing interest in criminological questions among German psychiatrists.

The German Penal Reform Movement

At first glance, the proposition that the reception of Lombroso's theories de-pended on the degree to which criminal jurists were interested in criminological issues may sound odd. Have not criminal jurists always been interested in criminological questions? To understand the changes taking place in the late nineteenth century, it is crucial to realize that for the first three-quarters of the nineteenth century the answer to this question was "no." Note that among all the criminological investigators discussed so far there was only one lawyer (Guerry).

Even the famous penal reformers who reformed criminal justice in the late eighteenth and early nineteenth centuries showed little interest in criminologi-cal issues. Although such men as Cesare Beccaria in Italy and Paul Johann Anselm Feuerbach in Bavaria did, of course, take an occasional interest in the

52. *Archivio di Psichiatria, Scienze Penali e Antropologia Criminale* (1880–).
53. Gadebusch Bondio, *Rezeption*, 42–43.

causes of crime, their works focused almost entirely on the legal issues of penal reform and made no significant contribution to the development of criminology.

Their lack of sustained interest in the etiology of crime becomes less surprising when one considers their penal and political ideologies. Most of the late eighteenth- and early nineteenth-century penal reformers were liberals who sought to protect the individual from the state by restricting the state's penal powers. They sought to achieve this goal by establishing a system of legally fixed punishments that would curtail judicial discretion and ensure that everyone received the same punishment for the same offense. If the political appeal of a system of fixed punishments lay in its promise to eliminate judicial arbitrariness, its appeal from the penal policy perspective was that by making the catalog of crimes and punishments public it promised to exert a powerful deterrent effect. The reformist system of fixed punishments was firmly linked to the idea of deterrence, that is, to the notion that if the punishment for a given offense outweighed its potential benefits, most people would be discouraged from committing such an offense. Of course, this strategy depended on the assumption that most people were autonomous and rational individuals who calculated the consequences of their actions in advance. This assumption derived from the liberal ideology of the reformers, rather than any empirical investigation of how people came to commit crimes.[54]

The political and penal ideology of the late eighteenth- and early nineteenth-century penal reformers explains why they showed so little interest in criminological research into the causes of crime. Their penal strategy of deterrence shows that the reformers thought they knew why people committed crimes: most offenders believed that they would derive benefits from committing their crimes. Therefore, the reformers hoped that a system of fixed punishments prescribed by law would convince most people that the disadvantages of punishment would outweigh any advantages to be gained from the crimes they might be contemplating. The reformers' liberal view of human nature made empirical research on the causes of crime appear unnecessary. On the contrary, any investigation into environmental or biological constraints on individual behavior could only undermine their liberal conviction that individuals were autonomous actors in full control of their own actions. The situation was no different for nineteenth-century jurists who saw the main purpose of punishment as retribution rather than deterrence. For retribution was based on the

54. Cesare Beccaria, *On Crimes and Punishments and Other Writings* (Cambridge: Cambridge University Press, 1995; originally pub. 1764); Eberhard Schmidt, *Einführung in die Geschichte der deutschen Strafrechtspflege*, 3d ed. (Göttingen: Vandenhoeck, 1964), 218–19, 232–46; Radzinowicz, *Ideology and Crime*, 5–28 (which differs on the role of deterrence).

assumption that individuals were morally responsible for their actions, another assumption that was independent of any empirical knowledge about the causes of crime. Thus neither the great penal reformers nor nineteenth-century re-tributivists showed much interest in criminological issues because their penal ideologies had no need for criminological research.

Only in the last quarter of the nineteenth century did the attitude of penal reformers toward criminological issues change. A new generation of reformers in several European countries called for changes in penal policy whose realization was to depend on criminological knowledge.[55] In Germany Franz von Liszt, a young professor of criminal law, initiated a penal reform movement in the 1880s that challenged all the major strands of nineteenth-century penal philosophy and practice. His reform proposals met with resistance, but they also quickly found considerable support, especially among younger professors and students of criminal law, as well as among lawyers and judges. By starting a new journal, setting up his own institute at the University of Halle and later in Berlin, and, finally, in 1889, founding the International Union of Penal Law (Internationale Kriminalistische Vereinigung), Liszt provided his movement with a strong institutional basis. By the end of the 1880s, he had given shape to a "modern school of criminal law," leading a growing movement for the reform of the criminal justice system.[56]

Liszt based his critique of the German criminal justice system on two main

55. On France, see Robert Nye, *Crime, Madness and Politics in Modern France* (Princeton: Princeton University Press, 1984); Gordon Wright, *Between the Guillotine and Liberty: Two Centuries of the Crime Problem in France* (New York: Oxford University Press, 1983); Ruth Harris, *Murders and Madness: Medicine, Law, and Society in the Fin de Siècle* (Oxford: Clarendon Press, 1989). On Britain, see Martin Wiener, *Reconstructing the Criminal: Culture, Law, and Policy in England, 1830–1914* (Cambridge: Cambridge University Press, 1990); David Garland, *Punishment and Welfare: A History of Penal Strategies* (Aldershot: Gower, 1985); Radzinowicz and Hood, *History of the English Criminal Law*, vol. 5.

56. Born in Vienna in 1851, Liszt held chairs in criminal law in Giessen (1879–82), Marburg (1882–89), Halle (1889–99), and, finally, from 1899 until his death in 1919, in Berlin. On Liszt, see Eberhard Schmidt, *Einführung in die Geschichte der deutschen Strafrechtspflege*, 3d ed. (Göttingen: Vandenhoeck, 1964), 357–86; Richard Wetzell, "Criminal Law Reform in Imperial Germany" (Ph.D. diss., Stanford University, 1991); Monika Frommel, "Internationale Reformbewegung zwischen 1880 und 1920," in *Erzählte Kriminalität: Zur Typologie und Funktion von narrativen Darstellungen in Strafrechtspflege, Publizistik und Literatur*, ed. Jörg Schönert (Tübingen: Niemeyer, 1991), 467–95. Liszt's new journal was the *Zeitschrift für die gesamte Strafrechtswissenschaft*. On the Internationale Kriminalistische Vereinigung (French name: Union Internationale de Droit Pénal; usually translated as International Union [or Association] of Penal Law), see Elisabeth Bellmann, *Die Internationale Kriminalistische Vereinigung* (Frankfurt: Peter Lang, 1994); Leon Radzinowicz, *The Roots of the International Association of Criminal Law and Their Significance: A Tribute and Reassessment on Its Centenary* (Max-Planck-Institut für ausländisches und internationales Strafrecht, 1991).

arguments. First, he pointed to the rising proportion of recidivists as evidence that the existing criminal justice system was ineffective. Second, he underscored the importance of this failure by insisting that the purpose of punishment did not lie in retributive justice but in protecting society against crime. For Liszt, punishment was not to serve a moral but a social purpose. Although the same point had been made by the late eighteenth- and early nineteenth-century reformers, Liszt disagreed with them over how the goal of protecting society should be achieved. Whereas the earlier reformers had seen the purpose of punishment as deterring the general public, Liszt saw it as individual behavioral prevention, that is, modifying or controlling the behavior of the individual criminal to prevent him or her from committing further crimes. Consequently, Liszt demanded that punishments should no longer depend on the legal offense (the principle of deterrence) or on the offender's individual degree of guilt (the principle of retribution) but on the future danger posed by the individual criminal. Depending on the severity of this danger, the punishment could take the form of rehabilitation, release on probation, or indefinite detention.[57]

If the earlier generation of reformers had sought to protect the individual from the state by limiting the state's penal powers, Liszt was concerned with better protecting society against crime by extending the state's punitive powers. This did not mean that Liszt and his fellow reformers wanted to dismantle the guarantees for individual liberty that the earlier generation had won. Liszt, too, adhered to the principle that all *crimes* had to be defined by law. But because he was interested in effective behavioral prevention, he did abandon the principle that all *punishments* must also be fixed by law. For if punishments were to prevent the individual criminal from committing future crimes, they could not be fixed by law or even determined in advance by a judge but had to depend on the criminal's progress during the administration of punishment.

It was the change in focus from the offense to the offender that led Liszt and his fellow penal reformers to broaden their vision beyond criminal jurists' traditional concern with jurisprudence and to become interested in criminological questions. By assigning punishment the purpose of preventing convicted offenders from committing future crimes, Liszt's "modern school of criminal law" not only called for the individualization of punishments but raised the question of the proper *content* of punishment. The purpose of punishment was

---

57. Liszt's seminal programmatic essay was "Der Zweckgedanke im Strafrecht" (1882), reprinted in his *Strafrechtliche Aufsätze und Vorträge*, 1:126–79. See also his "Kriminalpolitische Aufgaben" (first published 1889–92), ibid., 1:290–467.

no longer to inflict the "just measure of pain" but to modify the future behavior of the offender. How best to accomplish this goal was an open question. Clearly, the search for the best method of individualized prevention had to be based on some knowledge of what caused individuals to commit crimes in the first place. This is why Liszt and his fellow reformers became interested in criminological research. At the same time, the reformers' interest in scientific research on the causes of crime was fueled by the decline of the classic liberal image of man. For the social problems of an industrialized society and the obvious failure of general deterrence had eroded the liberal assumption that most people were autonomous and rationally calculating individuals. Unlike the earlier generation of penal reformers, Liszt and his "modern school" believed that individual actions, including crimes, were significantly constrained by both the environment and the personality of the individual. As Liszt put it in a famous formulation, "Crime is the product of the characteristics of the offender at the time of the crime and the external circumstances surrounding him at that time."[58]

In short, the penal reformers became interested in criminological research on the causes of crime because they thought that a proper understanding of these causes was necessary to discover the most effective means of preventing offenders from committing future crimes. Criminological research, they believed, ought to provide the foundation for penal policy. Strictly speaking, this view would have obliged the reformers to postpone detailed reform proposals until criminological research had thrown sufficient light on the causes of crime. In actuality, however, Liszt and his fellow reformers did not put the elaboration of their reform proposals on hold until criminological research had fully elucidated the causes of crime but proposed a detailed set of reforms that were as yet unsupported by criminological research. In particular, Liszt had specific ideas about the major categories of criminals and the penal measures appropriate for each.

Liszt began with the premise that punishment could serve three different purposes: the rehabilitation, deterrence, or incapacitation of an offender (through incarceration—Liszt saw no need for the death penalty). Deducing that "there must be three categories of criminals that correspond to these three forms of punishment," he recommended rehabilitation for those criminals who were both in need of and capable of rehabilitation; deterrence for those not in need of rehabilitation; and incapacitation for those incapable of rehabilitation. Elaborating on these categories, he argued that a large proportion of repeat

58. Liszt, "Die Aufgaben und die Methode der Strafrechtswissenschaft," in *Aufsätze und Vorträge*, 2:290.

offenders were "incorrigibles" who could be prevented from committing future crimes only by being incapacitated,[59] by means of indefinite detention, most likely for life. By contrast, "habitual" repeat offenders who appeared corrigible should receive an indeterminate prison sentence from one to five years, the length depending on the progress of rehabilitation. Finally, first-time offenders who appeared to be "occasional" criminals were not in need of rehabilitation but of deterrence. Since a prison term presented the danger of further criminalizing them, the best way to deter such criminals from committing further crimes was to suspend their sentences under a probation system.[60]

Thus, even though Liszt and his fellow reformers called for criminological research to provide a scientific basis for penal policy, they advocated a particular set of penal policies before such research could be conducted. This paradox provides a critical perspective on the reformers' claim that they were placing penal policy on a scientific foundation and alerts us to the fact that their proposals were based on several unsupported assumptions. Most important, the reformers assumed that the best way to prevent offenders from offending again was to transform or incapacitate them through individualized penal sanctions, rather than transforming the society around them. They also assumed that the key to an effective penal policy was to categorize offenders and to individualize punishment according to their personal characteristics. Finally, they assumed that it was crucial to distinguish "occasional" from "habitual" criminals and that a substantial portion of the latter were "incorrigibles."

Understanding the tension between the reformers' ambition to place penal policy on a scientific footing and the reality of unsupported assumptions is important for the purposes of this study because the reformers' proposals and their underlying assumptions also shaped the subsequent course of German criminology. For the penal reformers' focus on transforming or incapacitating the offender helped to steer criminological research away from the social causes of crime and toward investigating the personalities of offenders, the classification of offenders, and possible methods of distinguishing between corrigibles and incorrigibles.

The fact that the penal reformers helped to push criminologists to focus on the personalities of criminals rather than the social causes of crime was somewhat ironic because Liszt himself was convinced that the social causes of crime were far more important than any individual factors. Because of the importance of these social factors, Liszt argued, social policy measures (*Sozialpolitik*) were a

59. Liszt's term was "unschädlichmachen."
60. Liszt, "Der Zweckgedanke im Strafrecht," 163–73.

far more effective means of combating crime than penal sanctions that "only targeted individuals but could never transform social conditions." The construction of subsidized public housing, for instance, was likely to do more to reduce many forms of crime than "a dozen new criminal laws." However, most measures of social legislation did not fall into the purview of penal policy (*Kriminalpolitik*), which was the area in which Liszt, as a criminal jurist and penal reformer, concentrated his efforts. Thus, even though Liszt recognized that punishment was a less effective means of combating crime than social policy, his reform proposals focused on the individualization of punishment.[61] And as an unintended consequence, the newly developing field of criminology would likewise tend to neglect the social causes of crime by concentrating on the personality of the offender.

Liszt's contribution to the birth of criminology as a recognized field was in the nature of an impresario rather than a performer. He wrote widely on penal policy but did not himself undertake criminological research. He highlighted the importance of criminological research as the scientific foundation of penal policy and made criminology an integral part of the larger field of "penal science." Dissatisfied with the narrow focus on criminal jurisprudence among professors of criminal law at German universities, Liszt coined the new term *gesamte Strafrechtswissenschaft* ("comprehensive penal science") to designate a broader approach to the study of criminal justice that would combine criminal jurisprudence, criminology, penology, and penal policy.[62] This broader vision of penal science took concrete shape in several projects that helped to provide forums for criminological research. In 1881 Liszt founded the *Zeitschrift für die gesamte Strafrechtswissenschaft*, a journal designed to bring together jurisprudential, policy-oriented, and criminological research under the common rubric of a comprehensive penal science. The journal's first issue contained articles by Lombroso and the criminal statistician Oettingen.[63] When it became difficult to maintain this interdisciplinary focus in the *Zeitschrift*, Liszt cooperated with the psychiatrist Gustav Aschaffenburg to found and edit the *Monatsschrift für Kriminalpsychologie und Strafrechtsreform* (1904–), which became Germany's pre-

61. Liszt, "Über den Einfluß der soziologischen und anthropologischen Forschungen auf die Grundbegriffe des Strafrechts," in *Aufsätze und Vorträge*, 2:83 (first published in 1893); Liszt, "Das Verbrechen als sozialpathologische Erscheinung," ibid., 2:234–36 (first published 1898); Liszt, "Die Aufgabe und die Methode der Strafrechtswissenschaft," ibid., 2:295 (first published 1899).

62. Liszt, "Die Aufgaben und die Methode der Strafrechtswissenschaft," 296.

63. Lombroso, "Über den Ursprung"; Alexander von Oettingen, "Über methodische Erhebung und Verwerthung criminalstatistischer Daten," *ZStW* 1 (1881): 414–38.

mier journal of criminology. The connection between criminology and penal reform reflected in that journal's title also took concrete shape in the Internationale Kriminalistische Vereinigung (IKV; International Union of Penal Law) that Liszt founded together with Belgian and Dutch penal reformers. Although most of its members were criminal jurists, the IKV also included a significant number of psychiatrists engaged in criminological research. And both the IKV's international conferences and the more frequent meetings of its German chapter regularly included reports and discussions on criminological research. In summary, even though Liszt and most of the criminal jurists involved in the reform movement did not engage in criminological research themselves, their conviction that criminology ought to provide the basis of penal policy helped to create both a demand and a forum for criminological research. Most of this research was carried out by German psychiatrists who were reacting to Lombroso's theories of the born criminal. Their reception of Lombroso and the development of a German "criminal psychology" forms the subject of the next chapter.

CHAPTER TWO

FROM CRIMINAL ANTHROPOLOGY TO CRIMINAL PSYCHOLOGY, 1880–1914

Although Liszt and other criminal jurists committed to penal reform stressed the importance of criminological research, they did not themselves engage in it. This task was mainly undertaken by German medical doctors, especially psychiatrists. To be sure, criminal statisticians, like Oettingen, Mayr, and a handful of others, continued their work in criminal statistics. On the whole, however, German social scientists, including those in the newly emerging discipline of sociology, showed remarkably little interest in criminological questions. By contrast, the German medical community developed considerable interest in criminological questions in the course of the 1880s and 1890s for at least two reasons. First, Lombroso's theory of the born criminal confronted the German medical profession with a biological theory of crime to which it felt compelled to respond. Second, the German doctors' willingness to address criminological questions was facilitated by their long-standing contact with the criminal justice system as forensic psychiatrists in the courts and prison doctors in the correctional system. Before examining their reception of Lombroso, I shall therefore briefly discuss the state of German forensic psychiatry and the role of doctors in German prisons.[1]

1. Germany's physical anthropologists had little use for Lombroso. Rudolf Virchow publicly attacked Lombroso and dismissed his claims about the physical characteristics of the born criminal as false. See Virchow, "Über Criminalanthropologie," *Correspondenz-Blatt der Deutschen Gesellschaft für Anthropologie, Ethnologie und Urgeschichte* 27 (1896): 157–62; Cesare Lombroso, "Virchow und die Kriminalanthropologie," *Die Zukunft* 16 (29 August 1896): 391–96; Benoit Massin, "From Virchow to Fischer: Physical Anthropology and 'Modern Race Theories' in Wilhelmine Germany," in *Volksgeist as Method and Ethic: Essays on Boasian Ethnography and the German Anthropological Tradition*, ed. George Stocking (Madison: University of Wisconsin Press, 1996), 139.

Psychiatrists, Prison Doctors, and the Reception of Lombroso

Forensic psychiatry's role in the courtroom was based on the principle that insane offenders should not be punished. German criminal codes had recognized this principle as early as the sixteenth century. This recognition, however, did not immediately give medical doctors a part in courtroom proceedings because it was long assumed that laypeople were perfectly competent to judge a defendant's sanity. Even at the end of the eighteenth century, when doctors were beginning to be consulted in such cases, the philosopher Immanuel Kant demanded that defendants whose sanity was in doubt be referred to the philosophical rather than the medical faculty of the university. By the first half of the nineteenth century, however, German courts were calling on medical doctors with increasing regularity, and forensic psychiatry played a prominent role in the development of psychiatry as a new medical specialty.[2]

By the 1870s, it was standard procedure to call in a medical doctor if a defendant's mental condition was in doubt, even though that doctor was not necessarily a psychiatrist. The medical expert's opinion, however, was not binding on judge or jury and was sometimes disregarded. Many German psychiatrists resented the often hostile attitude of judges and juries and charged that a great number of insane offenders were unjustly convicted. In an 1886 study the Berlin psychiatrist W. Sander claimed that of 144 offenders whose insanity at the time of their trial appeared certain, only 38—roughly a quarter—had been recognized as insane. In many cases the issue of insanity had not even been raised. "If you have the misfortune that your brain falls ill and incidentally lets you commit a punishable act," Sander concluded, "the odds are 3 to 1 that in addition to the misfortune of the disease and the attendant physical and material misery, you and your family will lose your honor, too."[3]

2. On the history of forensic psychiatry, see W. Weygandt, "Die Entwicklung der gerichtlichen Psychiatrie und Psychologie," *MKS* 8 (1911): 209–20; Hans-Georg Güse and Norbert Schmacke, *Psychiatrie zwischen bürgerlicher Revolution und Faschismus*, 2 vols. (Kronberg: Athenäum, 1976), 2:205–15; Doris Kaufmann, "Boundary Disputes: Criminal Justice and Psychiatry in Germany, 1760–1850," *Journal of Historical Sociology* 6 (1993): 276–87; Kaufmann, "Psychiatrie und Strafjustiz im 19. Jahrhundert: Die gerichtsmedizinischen Gutachten der medizinischen Fakultät der Universität Tübingen, 1770–1860," *Medizin, Gesellschaft und Geschichte. Jahrbuch des Instituts für Geschichte der Medizin der Robert Bosch Stiftung* 10 (1991): 23–39; Kaufmann, *Aufklärung, bürgerliche Selbsterfahrung und die "Erfindung" der Psychiatrie in Deutschland, 1770–1850* (Göttingen: Vandenhoeck, 1995), 305–34; Regina Schulte, *Das Dorf im Verhör: Brandstifter, Kindsmörderinnen und Wilderer vor den Schranken des bürgerlichen Gerichts* (Hamburg: Rowohlt, 1989), 91–117.

3. W. Sander and Alfred Richter, *Die Beziehungen zwischen Geistesstörung und Verbrechen: Nach Beobachtungen in der Irrenanstalt Dalldorf* (Berlin: Fischer, 1886), 162–64. For a polemic

German doctors and psychiatrists did not deal with mentally ill offenders only as expert witnesses in the courtroom. As part-time or full-time prison doctors, they also encountered them in the prisons. When prison doctors began to take an interest in psychiatry, they found the incidence of mental illness to be much higher among prisoners than among the general population. In the mid-1870s some reported the proportion of insane prisoners to be as high as 5 percent.[4] As doctors and prison administrators became increasingly sensitive to the problem in the late 1870s and early 1880s, these estimates of insanity among prison inmates kept rising. An 1880 report by the Prussian Ministry of Interior, for instance, stated that the number of insane inmates in its prisons had doubled in the course of one year.[5]

Once a prisoner was diagnosed as mentally ill, he was usually transferred to an insane asylum. Therefore, insane asylums held not only people who had been acquitted or exempted from prosecution on grounds of insanity but a much greater number of convicted criminals who had been transferred from prisons. As a result, in some asylums the proportion of inmates with criminal records reached 5 to 15 percent, leading some psychiatrists to conclude that the mentally ill were from five to twenty-five times more likely to come into conflict with the law than a member of the general population.[6]

In principle, both the legal and the medical professions distinguished two groups: first, criminal lunatics or the criminally insane (*verbrecherische Irre*), that is, people who had committed criminal acts in a state of insanity, and second, insane criminals (*irre Verbrecher*), offenders who had become insane after the commission of their crime, usually in prison. Naturally, the detection of someone's insanity in prison did not mean that the person was not insane when he or she committed the crime, so that the actual proportion of the two groups was hard to determine. Asylum doctors in Dalldorf near Berlin estimated that as many as 75 percent of insane criminals transferred from prisons had been insane at the time of their crime.[7] Still, no one doubted that some criminals did become mentally ill during their prison terms. Some doctors even advanced the notion of a "prison psychosis" (*Gefängniswahn*); others insisted

on judicial disregard for psychiatric experts, see Prof. Liman, "Bemerkungen betreffend Dr. W. Sanders und Dr. A. Richters Werk über die Beziehungen zwischen Geistesstörung und Verbrechen," *Gerichtssaal* 39 (1887): 81–86.

4. "Geisteskranke in Strafanstalten," *AZP* 31 (1875): 649.

5. "Irre in Strafanstalten," *AZP* 37 (1881): 315.

6. W. Sommer, "Beiträge zur Kenntnis des kriminellen Irren," *AZP* 40 (1884): 110; Sander and Richter, *Die Beziehungen*, 134; Dirk Blasius, *"Einfache Seelenstörung": Geschichte der deutschen Psychiatrie, 1800–1945* (Frankfurt: Fischer, 1994), 96–97.

7. Sander and Richter, *Die Beziehungen*, 162.

that the mental illnesses of prisoners were no different from those of other people.[8]

Given the disproportionately high incidence of insanity in prisons and of criminality in insane asylums, some psychiatrists and prison doctors began to speculate whether a causal connection existed between crime and insanity. Some suggested that crime and insanity might share a common biological basis. Thus the question Lombroso sought to answer was already on the minds of some German psychiatrists, and in this basic sense Lombroso spoke to a current issue. Pre-Lombrosian forensic psychiatry, however, was concerned with the insane offender as an *exceptional* phenomenon, while Lombroso proposed a *general* link between abnormality and criminal behavior. This was the key difference between forensic psychiatry and the emerging field of criminal psychology. Furthermore, before the reception of Lombroso, forensic psychiatry investigated only the connection between crime and mental illness. No German prison doctor or psychiatrist was measuring criminals' skulls. In this respect, too, Lombroso's notion of the born criminal as an anthropological type with physical characteristics was radically new.

Most German psychiatrists probably first learned about Lombroso in 1878, two years after the Italian publication of his book, when a small notice in the *Allgemeine Zeitschrift für Psychiatrie* gave a brief summary of his findings.[9] The first critical assessment of Lombroso's work in Germany appeared only in 1885, when the psychiatrist Emil Kraepelin reviewed the third edition of *L'uomo delinquente* for Liszt's *Zeitschrift*.

Still at the beginning of his career in 1885, Kraepelin eventually became one of the most influential figures in the history of psychiatry. After receiving his

---

8. See, for example, Sommer, "Beiträge zur Kenntnis des kriminellen Irren," 138.

9. Fränkel, "Verbrecherschädel," *AZP* 34 (1878): 403–4. The legal journal *Gerichtssaal* published a more extensive summary a year later: Kornfeld and Garofalo, "Zur Criminalpsychopathologie," *Gerichtssaal* 31 (1879): 348–60. Shortly thereafter, in 1881, the first issue of Liszt's *Zeitschrift für die gesamte Strafrechtswissenschaft* carried an article by Lombroso himself: "Über den Ursprung, das Wesen und die Bestrebungen der neuen anthropologisch-kriminalistischen Schule in Italien," *ZStW* 1 (1881): 108–29. The *Zeitschrift* did not carry any more articles by Lombroso in subsequent years, probably to distance its own reform efforts from those of the Italian school. The well-established *Archiv für Strafrecht und Strafprozeß*, however, carried articles by Lombroso at regular intervals from 1882 to 1889, demonstrating that Lombroso's ideas were still perceived as meriting discussion in the mainstream of the German legal community during the 1880s: Lombroso, "Geschlechtstrieb und Verbrechen," *ASS* 30 (1882): 1–29; "Das Verbrechen in den Kinderjahren," *ASS* 32 (1884): 1–33; "Das politische Verbrechen vom anthropologischen Gesichtspunkt aus betrachtet," *ASS* 34 (1886): 54–60; "Die neuen Entdeckungen auf dem Gebiete der kriminalen Anthropologie im Jahre 1887," *ASS* 37 (1889): 36–47.

M.D. in 1878 and working as a research assistant and asylum psychiatrist for a while, Kraepelin was appointed to a chair in psychiatry at the University of Dorpat (now Tartu) in 1886 at the age of thirty, before moving on to prestigious professorships at Heidelberg (1891–1903) and Munich (1903–24). In 1883 he published the first edition of the psychiatry textbook that soon became the standard text in the field, going through eight editions over the next thirty years. The book's new classification of mental illnesses, which was based on the course and outcome of an illness rather than its presumed causes, became widely accepted and quickly established Kraepelin as the dean of German psychiatry. In fact, Kraepelin's division of serious mental illnesses into two basic forms, manic depression and schizophrenia, which he called dementia praecox, established the fundamental categories for the classification of mental disorders that is still followed today. Because of his reputation, Kraepelin trained many of the most important figures among the next generation of German psychiatrists, many of whom we will encounter in the following pages.[10]

In 1880 the young psychiatrist published a provocative book, his first, in which he called for the medicalization of criminal justice. Anticipating some of Liszt's ideas, Kraepelin proposed that the practice of fixed prison sentences be abolished in favor of indefinite detention in institutions modeled on insane asylums. Because he regarded both criminals and lunatics as the necessary products of heredity and milieu and considered the line between mental illness and "normality" difficult to draw, Kraepelin also recommended that the distinction between those who were legally responsible and those who were not should be dropped. Finally, Kraepelin rejected retribution in favor of social

10. On Kraepelin, see Edward Shorter, *A History of Psychiatry* (New York: Wiley, 1997), 100–109; Kurt Kolle, "Emil Kraepelin," in *Große Nervenärzte*, ed. Kurt Kolle (Stuttgart: Thieme, 1956), 1:175–86; Bernard Pauleikhoff, "Emil Kraepelin," in *Das Menschenbild im Wandel der Zeit: Ideengeschichte der Psychiatrie und der klinischen Psychologie* (Hürtgenwald: Pressler, 1983), 2:320–51; Paul Hoff et al., "Kraepelin," in *A History of Clinical Psychiatry*, ed. Roy Porter and German Berrios (New York: New York University Press, 1995), 261–301; Emil Kraepelin, *Lebenserinnerungen* (Berlin: Springer, 1983); Eric Engstrom, "Emil Kraepelin: Psychiatry and Public Affairs in Wilhelmine Germany," *History of Psychiatry* 2 (1991): 111–32; Engstrom, "Kulturelle Dimensionen von Psychiatrie und Sozialpsychologie: Emil Kraepelin und Willy Hellpach," in *Kultur und Kulturwissenschaften um 1900 II: Idealismus und Positivismus*, ed. Gangolf Hübinger, Rüdiger vom Bruch, and Friedrich Wilhelm Graf (Stuttgart: Steiner, 1997), 164–89; Paul Hoff, *Emil Kraepelin und die Psychiatrie als klinische Wissenschaft* (Berlin: Springer, 1994); Mariacarla Gadebusch Bondio, *Die Rezeption der kriminalanthropologischen Theorien von Cesare Lombroso in Deutschland von 1880–1914* (Husum: Matthiesen, 1995), 182–99; Hans Gruhle, "Kraepelins Stellung zur Verbrechensbekämpfung," *AZP* 84 (1926): 205–15; Gustav Aschaffenburg, "Der Einfluss Kraepelins auf die Kriminalpsychologie und Kriminalpolitik," *AZP* 87 (1929): 87–95.

protection as the sole purpose of criminal justice and suggested that the morally charged concept of punishment be discarded in favor of the morally neutral notion of "protective measures." In short, Kraepelin was recommending that the criminal justice system operate on the same principle as the insane asylum. Although his ideas were much too radical to garner any support, a more moderate version survived in Liszt's call for the individualization zur of punishments. Most important, Kraepelin's book on penal reform was the first sign of his lifelong interest in criminological questions and his conviction that psychiatry held the key to solving the crime problem through the medicalization of criminal justice. It was therefore not surprising that Kraepelin took an early interest in Lombroso's work and soon played an influential role in the development of German "criminal psychology."[11]

Kraepelin's 1885 review was of the third Italian edition (1884) of *L'uomo delinquente*, in which Lombroso had introduced a more complex classification of criminal types, reduced the proportion of born criminals to about 40 percent of all offenders, and described the condition of the born criminal not only as atavistic but as identical with "moral insanity." Kraepelin's review was generally positive. Although he cautioned that Lombroso's account of the born criminal's physiological characteristics must be considered provisional, he did not question the notion of the born criminal itself. Rather, he suggested that this category should be broken down into different subtypes: "a habitual thief," he proposed, "will presumably have a different somatic constitution from a robber or confidence man." Kraepelin did, however, reject Lombroso's claim that the born criminal's physical characteristics could provide valuable evidence in individual cases and insisted that all one could reasonably assert was "the relative frequency of the coincidence of certain physical characteristics with the disposition toward crime." In individual cases, he cautioned, physical characteristics were irrelevant, and only a psychological analysis of the offender's personality could reveal whether he or she was a "born criminal."[12]

Kraepelin also disagreed with Lombroso's atavism thesis. Pointing out that nature continually produced individuals with widely differing degrees of perfection, Kraepelin held that this was an entirely sufficient explanation for the appearance of mentally defective individuals, including those with a "criminal disposition" (*Verbrechernaturen*). He therefore saw no need to introduce the atavism hypothesis, especially since he was inclined to think that the factors at

---

11. Emil Kraepelin, *Die Abschaffung des Strafmaßes: Ein Vorschlag zur Reform der heutigen Strafrechtspflege* (Stuttgart: Enke, 1880).
12. Emil Kraepelin, "Lombrosos '*Uomo delinquente*,' " *ZStW* 5 (1885): 669–80.

work in the making of defective individuals were pathological. Moreover, Kraepelin found Lombroso's analogy between "primitive man" and the "born criminal" unconvincing. "Primitive man," Kraepelin argued, was located on a lower rung of a developmental series but fully capable of development, whereas the "born criminal" was in a defective state that blocked further development.[13] He concluded his review with a qualified but positive assessment of Lombroso:

> Even the elimination of Lombroso's remarks on the atavistic explanation of the criminal disposition would . . . not shake the fundamental theses of his work, even a great part of his observations and statistical data could be refuted by later findings without significantly diminishing the great importance of his *Uomo delinquente*. Its importance does not lie in the often debatable and fragmentary detail, but above all in the pathbreaking idea of regarding the criminal no longer as a loathsome monster from the standpoint of moral outrage, but as an object of scientific research, and to make his development, his personality, as well as his life and behavior the subject of careful study.[14]

By detaching the importance of Lombroso's work from its questionable particulars, Kraepelin was able to locate its significance in having opened up a new subject of research. Given Kraepelin's own call for a medical approach to criminal justice in his book on penal reform just five years earlier, this positive assessment of Lombroso was not surprising. But Kraepelin's conclusion ignored a crucial point. For between the details and the general point that the criminal ought to be studied scientifically, Lombroso's doctrine contained another assertion: that criminal behavior was a result of biological rather than social causes. In accepting this claim, Kraepelin ignored the problem that without Lombroso's "details," about which he, too, had doubts, this claim remained a mere assumption. As we shall see, however, the opinion that Lombroso was wrong about the born criminal's physical characteristics but right about the existence of born criminals became influential in the reception of Lombroso in the 1890s.

The year in which Kraepelin's review appeared (1885) also witnessed the First International Congress of Criminal Anthropology, which the Lombrosians convened in Rome. The French delegates to the congress disputed Lombroso's findings and called for a sociological interpretation of crime, but Lombroso's Italian school was in the majority and therefore able to steamroll French dissent. When the next congress met in Paris in 1889, the French had consolidated

13. Ibid., 678–79.
14. Ibid., 679–80.

their opposition and used their majority to subject Lombroso's anatomical determinism to relentless criticism. At the end of the congress, the French criminologist Gabriel Tarde was satisfied that Lombroso's criminal type had emerged "badly crippled, or rather reduced to the condition of a fading phantom."[15]

While the French were taking the lead in critically engaging the Lombrosian school in the second half of the 1880s,[16] Kraepelin's 1885 review remained the only sustained assessment of Lombroso in the German psychiatric community for another eight years, undoubtedly mainly because Lombroso's *L'uomo delinquente* did not appear in German translation until 1887–90.[17] Then, in 1893–94, four books on the question of the born criminal appeared.[18] Two of them defended Lombroso's theory. The other two rejected the notion of the born criminal and argued, instead, that many criminals were degenerates.

Degeneration Theory and Lombroso's German Critics

The medical concept of degeneration was introduced by the French psychiatrist Bénédict-Augustin Morel (1809–73) in 1857. Morel believed in the biblical account of creation and used the idea of degeneration to explain how the original human type created by God could have resulted in imperfect individuals. Degeneration theory also offered an explanation for the origins of mental illness. Assuming that acquired characteristics could be inherited, Morel wrote that "degenerations are pathological deviations from the normal human type that are hereditarily transmitted and evolve progressively toward decay."[19] The initial nonhereditary origins of the process of degeneration remained rather vague. Morel did indicate, however, that the process could be initiated by direct

15. Quoted in Gordon Wright, *Between the Guillotine and Liberty: Two Centuries of the Crime Problem in France* (New York: Oxford University Press, 1983), 122. On the congresses, see also Robert Nye, *Crime, Madness, and Politics in Modern France* (Princeton: Princeton University Press, 1984), 97–109; Gadebusch Bondio, *Die Rezeption*, 123–49.

16. See Marc Renneville, "La réception de Lombroso en France (1880–1900)," in *Histoire de la criminologie française*, ed. Laurent Mucchielli (Paris: L'Harmattan, 1994), 107–35; Laurent Mucchielli, "Hérédité et milieu social: Le faux antagonisme franco-italien," ibid., 189–214; Renneville, *La médecine du crime: Essai sur l'emergence d'un regard medical sur la criminalité en France* (Villeneuve d'Ascq: Presses Universitaires du Septentrion, 1997).

17. Cesare Lombroso, *Der Verbrecher (homo delinquens) in anthropologischer, ärztlicher und juristischer Beziehung*, trans. M. Frankel, 2 vols. (Hamburg: Richter, 1887–90); the French translation appeared the same year; no full English translation ever appeared.

18. See the books by Abraham Baer, Paul Näcke, Hans Kurella, and Julius Koch discussed below.

19. Quoted in Erwin Ackerknecht, *Kurze Geschichte der Psychiatrie*, 3d ed. (Stuttgart: Enke, 1985), 54.

physical causes such as intoxication (from alcohol, opium, and other poisons), by nervous disorders, or by social factors such as malnutrition and bad hygienic conditions. What was certain was that the condition of the descendants would progressively worsen: the first generation of a degenerating family might only be "nervous," the second would be neurotic, the third psychotic, and the fourth would be imbeciles and die out. By positing that one type of mental disorder could hereditarily give rise to a different and more serious one in the next generation (polymorphic heredity), Morel offered an explanation for almost all mental diseases. In addition, he claimed that degeneration was reflected in certain physiological and anatomical characteristics, called stigmata, which could include changes in the shape of the head, eyes, ears, or genitals. Morel was not totally pessimistic about the chances for recovery. Intermarriage with healthy families as well as improved social conditions, especially in sanitation, he thought, might reverse the degenerative process.

Morel's ideas quickly caught on not only in France, where they were further developed by Valentin Magnan, but also among such prominent German psychiatrists as Wilhelm Griesinger and Richard von Krafft-Ebing, and as a result, degeneration theory exerted a powerful influence on French and German psychiatry in the decades before the First World War. Degeneration theory appealed to psychiatrists for a variety of reasons. First, at a time when brain anatomy had failed to provide psychiatry with the somatic underpinning for which many had hoped, degeneration theory linked mental illness to clearly detectable physical signs. Second, because the process of degeneration manifested itself in changing symptoms over the course of several generations, degeneration theory could be used to explain almost any mental illness. Finally, since Morel regarded degeneration as a process of hereditary transmission that could be set in motion or accelerated by adverse environmental influences, degeneration theory offered the advantage of combining both genetic and environmental factors in a single explanatory theory.[20]

After psychiatrists such as Krafft-Ebing started to offer degeneration as an explanation for a wide variety of socially condemned behaviors, including

20. On degeneration theory, see Shorter, *History of Psychiatry*, 93–99; Ackerknecht, *Kurze Geschichte der Psychiatrie*, 53–56; Gunter Mann, "Dekadenz, Degeneration, Untergangsangst im Lichte der Biologie des 19. Jahrhunderts," *Medizinhistorisches Journal* 20 (1985): 6–35; Henry Werlinder, *Psychopathy: A History of the Concepts* (Uppsala: University, 1978), 56–66; Nye, *Crime, Madness and Politics*, 119–31; Ian Dowbiggin, "Degeneration and Hereditarianism in French Mental Medicine," in *The Anatomy of Madness: Essays in the History of Psychiatry*, ed. W. F. Bynum, Roy Porter, and Michael Shepherd (London: Tavistock, 1985), 188–232; Dowbiggin, *Inheriting Madness: Professionalization and Psychiatric Knowledge in Nineteenth-Century France* (Berkeley: University of California Press, 1991), 116–61.

crime, prostitution, and homosexuality, the concept quickly gained broader cultural currency. From the novelist Emile Zola, whose cycle of novels on the Rougon and Macquart families was meant to illustrate the inescapable power of hereditary degeneration, to the Hungarian writer Max Nordau, who diagnosed Europe's artistic elite as degenerate and looked to the working people for regeneration, many European intellectuals and journalists attributed a broad range of social ills to degeneration, which was frequently painted as a major threat to European civilization. Although the extremely vague notion of degeneration that was deployed in this broader cultural discourse differed greatly from the narrower medical meaning of the term, there can be little doubt that the wide dissemination of this discourse helped to pave the way for medical theories linking degeneration and crime.[21]

In the psychiatric community, the term "degenerate" tended to be applied to individuals who seemed to be afflicted with minor mental disorders that fell short of full-fledged insanity. In 1888, the German psychiatrist Julius Koch, director of the insane asylum in Zwiefalten in Württemberg, developed this aspect of degeneration theory by proposing a classification system for "all those mental irregularities, . . . be they hereditary or acquired, which do not represent mental illnesses, but . . . do not leave their bearer in full possession of his mental normality and capacity." Koch classified all these irregularities under the new rubric of *psychopathische Minderwertigkeiten* ("psychopathic defects," literally "inferiorities"), which he divided into three categories of increasing severity: the "psychopathic disposition," which represented "a recognizable mental infirmity"; the "psychopathic taint," characterized "by anomalies in excitability, a lack of harmony, an eccentric, contradictory self, peculiarities, primordial-instinctive impulses and outbursts and something periodic in their behavior"; and finally, "psychopathic degeneration," which was indicated "by a habitual mental weakness either mainly in the intellectual or mainly in the moral realm or in both."[22]

Although none of Koch's precise categories gained currency, the term *psycho-*

21. On the cultural dissemination of degeneration theory, see Arthur Herman, *The Idea of Decline in Western History* (New York: Free Press, 1996), 109–44; Daniel Pick, *Faces of Degeneration* (Cambridge: Cambridge University Press, 1989), 44–50; Nye, *Crime, Madness, and Politics*; Sander Gilman and J. Edward Chamberlin, eds., *Degeneration: The Dark Side of Progress* (New York: Columbia University Press, 1985); P. M. Baldwin, "Liberalism, Nationalism and Degeneration: The Case of Max Nordau," *Central European History* 13 (1980): 99–120.

22. Julius Koch, *Die psychopathischen Minderwertigkeiten* (Ravensburg: Otto Maier, 1891–93), 1, 13, 18, 110. Koch had first introduced the concept of "psychopathische Minderwertigkeiten" in his *Kurzgefaßter Leitfaden der Psychiatrie* (Ravensburg: Otto Maier, 1888). See also Werlinder, *Psychopathy*, 86–90.

pathische Minderwertigkeiten—or just *Minderwertigkeit* for short—gradually became established as the preferred designation for borderline mental disorders that had previously been referred to as cases of degeneration. Besides its terminological impact, Koch's treatise made two important contributions. By imposing classificatory order on the previously amorphous realm of minor mental irregularities, Koch helped to strengthen psychiatry's expansionist claim on the borderland of minor abnormalities that are now called "personality disorders." Furthermore, although most psychiatrists used the terms *minderwertig* and "degenerate" interchangeably in the pre-1914 era, Koch's diagnostic category of *psychopathische Minderwertigkeit* was only loosely linked to degeneration as an etiological theory and was therefore able to survive the gradual demise of degeneration theory in the postwar period.[23]

Starting in the early 1880s, some German psychiatrists and prison doctors turned to the concepts of degeneration and *Minderwertigkeit* to explain the statistical correlation between crime and insanity that they had begun to observe, arguing that both insanity and crime had their common breeding ground in degeneration. As evidence, they reported having found a high incidence of physical signs of degeneration among habitual criminals. But while they assumed that degeneration and insanity were linked by a biological process, they usually explained the link between degeneration and crime in sociological terms. Frequently convinced that the "struggle for existence" was becoming ever more burdensome, these authors contended that degenerate individuals found it difficult to compete and were therefore more likely to become delinquent. The link between degeneration and crime, in other words, was not intrinsic but environmental.[24]

This line of argument was pursued in the first sustained critique of Lombroso

---

23. On Koch and his place in the history of psychopathy and personality disorders, see Werlinder, *Psychopathy*, 88–89; German Berrios, "Personality Disorders: A Conceptual History," in *Personality Disorder Reviewed*, ed. Peter Tyrer and George Stein (London: Gaskell, 1993), 17–41; P. Pichot, "Psychopathic Behavior: A Historical Overview," *Psychopathic Behaviour: Approaches to Research*, ed. Robert D. Hare and Daisy Schalling (Chichester: Wiley, 1978); A. Lewis, "Psychopathic Disorder: A Most Elusive Category," *Psychological Medicine* 4 (1974): 133–40; H. Sass, S. Herpertz, and W. Ernst, "Personality Disorders," in *History of Clinical Psychiatry*, ed. Berrios and Porter, 633–55; Heinz-Peter Schmiedebach, "Zum Verständniswandel der 'psychopathischen' Störungen am Anfang der naturwissenschaftlichen Psychiatrie in Deutschland," *Der Nervenarzt* 56 (1985): 140–45.

24. Knecht, "Über die Verbreitung physischer Degeneration bei Verbrechern und die Beziehungen zwischen Degenerationszeichen und Neuropathien," *AZP* 40 (1884): 584–611; Sander and Richter, *Beziehungen zwischen Geistesstörung und Verbrechen*, 150; compare also Fränkel, "Über Degenerationserscheinungen bei Psychose," *AZP* 42 (1886): 76–82 (Fränkel had already been influenced by Lombroso).

in Germany. In a book titled *Der Verbrecher in anthropologischer Beziehung* (The criminal in anthropological perspective), published in 1893, Abraham Baer, doctor at the Plötzensee prison near Berlin, subjected Lombroso's anthropometric data on the born criminal to systematic scrutiny by testing it against statistical data on prisoners collected by himself and others. He concluded that none of the physical characteristics that Lombroso had attributed to the born criminal were particular to criminals and that, as a result, the born criminal did not exist. Instead, Baer interpreted these physical characteristics as stigmata of degeneration and insisted that "just as there are morally excellent people with severe stigmata of degeneration, so there are criminals with several convictions without any visible signs of degeneration." Baer did admit, however, that multiple recidivists and "incorrigibles," whom he called "genuine criminal characters" (*eigentliche Verbrechernaturen*), were especially likely to display a multitude of degenerative stigmata.[25]

In Baer's opinion, degeneration was frequent among criminals because most criminals were members of the lower classes, among which social conditions had made degeneration rampant. Concerning the question whether degeneration could promote criminal behavior, Baer also offered a sociological explanation. Quoting a colleague, he explained that "due to their reduced powers of nervous resistance, neuropathic [that is, degenerate] individuals are less well positioned in the struggle for existence than people with a normal nervous system; as a result, they are more likely to descend into poverty, to fall victim to excitement and passion, and in this respect one can assume a distant connection between neuropathic disposition and crime."[26]

Since Lombroso had come to equate the condition of the born criminal with moral insanity, Baer also addressed this issue. There was, he insisted, no "moral sense" as a localized organ of the brain and, consequently, no isolated defect of such an organ could occur. Instead, moral sentiments and behavior were tied to the development of an individual's general intelligence, so that disorders in the moral sphere were always symptoms of a general mental disorder that also affected the intellectual functions. Hence the main diagnostic criterion for distinguishing cases of insanity from mere "ethical depravity" lay in the presence of intellectual defects. Such cases of "moral imbecility" on the basis of mental illness were extremely rare, however. Baer also dismissed any attempt to label

25. Abraham Baer, *Der Verbrecher in anthropologischer Beziehung* (Leipzig: Thieme, 1893), 192, 382.
26. Ibid., 205, 248, 193.

such individuals as born criminals, asserting that they ought to be regarded as insane, not as criminals. In sum, Baer argued that the habitual criminal was not distinguished by any typical features but bore the same signs of degeneration that were common among the lower classes at large. The causes of crime, Baer concluded, were social, not biological: "Whoever wants to abolish crime must abolish the social ravages in which crime is rooted and grows."[27]

Baer's emphasis on degeneration and social causes found strong support in a book published the same year by Paul Näcke, a doctor at the Hubertusburg insane asylum near Leipzig in Saxony, who was soon to emerge as one of the most prolific writers in the field of criminal anthropology.[28] In addition to empirical challenges akin to Baer's, Näcke attacked Lombroso's entire enterprise on a general theoretical point: "Every people," he pointed out, "defines the concept 'crime' according to its current conventions of morality; the concept is thus not physiologically grounded in man, but . . . purely sociological. It therefore makes no sense to search for anthropological characteristics for a sociological concept."[29]

This said, Näcke agreed with Baer that a disproportionate number of habitual criminals—Näcke estimated more than half—were degenerate and concluded that both crime and insanity were rooted in a degenerate disposition. Whether this disposition would lead to psychosis or criminal behavior depended on the social milieu, which, Näcke insisted, "must be regarded as the decisive cause." If an individual had a degenerate disposition, "a carefree life, a fortunate temperament, good education [or a] higher intelligence" were likely to inhibit criminal behavior, whereas "bad upbringing, a bad example set by the parents, bad companionship, the many temptations of life, the increasingly difficult struggle for existence, insufficient mental gifts, malnutrition [or] all sorts of disease" were apt to hasten a descent into crime.[30] Considering how widely degeneration was spreading, Näcke was surprised that there was not more crime and insanity:

If we consider how much the genetic material [Keim] has more or less deteriorated in the broadest strata of the people, and not just the lower ones,

27. Ibid., 296–98, 411.

28. For biographical information on Näcke, see the obituaries by Kötscher in *AKK* 55 (1913): i–xx; and by Kellner in *AZP* 70 (1913): 984–88.

29. Paul Näcke, *Verbrechen und Wahnsinn beim Weibe. Mit Ausblicken auf die Criminal-Anthropologie überhaupt* (Vienna: Braumüller, 1894), 96. (The book actually appeared in October 1893; see Kötscher obituary.) See also the positive review by the retributivist Finger in *Gerichtssaal* 50 (1895): 378–85.

30. Näcke, *Verbrechen und Wahnsinn*, 157, 175, 178–79.

through depraving elements of all sorts that affected parents and ancestors, only one thing appears strange . . . : that there is not more crime, insanity and neurosis, especially since there are many occasions to provoke their outbreak. . . . Thus the latent disposition is so widespread that no one is protected against becoming criminal or insane as a result of powerful external factors.[31]

The "Born Criminal" Redefined

This emphasis on the social milieu as the decisive factor in the genesis of crime was sharply challenged by Hans Kurella, the German translator of many of Lombroso's works and Lombroso's most loyal follower in Germany. In his *Naturgeschichte des Verbrechers* (Natural history of the criminal), published in 1893, Kurella, a psychiatrist at the provincial insane asylum in Brieg, Silesia, and editor of the *Centralblatt für Nervenheilkunde und Psychiatrie*, defended Lombroso's thesis of the born criminal by incorporating various elements from degeneration theory and Darwinism. Drawing on Darwin's notion that every species naturally produced variations, Kurella argued that the born criminal was simply such a natural variation. This view, however, did not prevent him from also subscribing to Lombroso's atavism thesis. Thus he described the born criminal's physical characteristics, especially the shape of his skull, as "primatoid," indicating their similarity to features found in primates.[32]

But Kurella did not just insist that there were born criminals; he maintained that *all* criminal behavior was biologically determined and categorically rejected all sociological explanations of crime. Several years spent amid poor rural laborers in East Prussia had, he asserted, convinced him

that the most miserable wages, a lifelong diet of potatoes and sauerkraut, deep humiliation in hopeless dependence, contempt and squalor are not sufficient to make a criminal out of a normal human being. These conditions do, however, affect the crime rate in another way. As the effects of bad nutrition accumulate over generations, they cause a degeneration of the descendants of this wretched population, and it is from the degenerate children of these malnourished parents that criminals are recruited.[33]

31. Ibid., 178.

32. Hans Kurella, *Naturgeschichte des Verbrechers: Grundzüge der criminellen Anthropologie und Criminalpsychologie* (Stuttgart: Enke, 1893), 11–14; compare the reviews by Pelman in *AZP* 49 (1893): 300–301; Kirn in *AZP* 50 (1894): 403–12; and Finger in *Gerichtssaal* 49 (1894): 361–71. For a more detailed comparison of Kurella's and Lombroso's views, see Gadebusch Bondio, *Die Rezeption*, 104–18.

33. Kurella, *Naturgeschichte des Verbrechers*, 170.

Poverty, in other words, did not directly produce motives for criminal acts but only set in motion the biological process of degeneration, which could, after several generations, result in a "disposition toward crime" (*Verbrecheranlage*). What exactly constituted this biological disposition toward crime? Kurella acknowledged that moral sentiments such as pity or a sense of justice were not congenital. But, he argued, moral feelings were based on elementary emotions such as joy, pain, and fear, whose relative strength was predetermined by each individual's nervous system. The "criminal disposition" consisted of a particular set of extreme variations in the strength of these affects. Thus the fundamental task of criminal psychology was to investigate criminals' "individual affective disposition," while criminal anthropology would examine the connection between physiological abnormalities and the "absence, weakness or perversion of certain affects." These, according to Kurella, were the central problems, whose resolution, he admitted, still lay in the distant future.[34] Over the next two decades, Kurella promoted Lombroso's teachings through dozens of publications and his own translations of several of Lombroso's works.[35] Although Kurella's works were not without influence, he remained the only German author who defended Lombroso's notion of the born criminal as an atavistic being characterized by certain physical features.

More important for the development of German criminal psychology was another group of psychiatric authors. They, too, challenged Baer's and Näcke's emphasis on the milieu but without fully endorsing Lombroso's doctrine. In a lecture at the annual meeting of the Association of German Psychiatrists (Verein der deutschen Irrenärzte) in the fall of 1894, Robert Sommer, then still a lecturer (*Privatdozent*) in Würzburg but about to be appointed to the chair in psychiatry in Giessen the following year, charged that recent writers such as Baer and Näcke had confused two questions that should be sharply distinguished, namely "(1) whether there are born criminals; (2) whether this congenital moral abnormality expresses itself in significant morphological characteristics." Sommer agreed that Baer had indeed answered the second question by disproving Lombroso's claim that the born criminal displayed particular physical characteristics. But he insisted that this finding had no bearing on the

---

34. Ibid., 249–53.

35. See, for example, Cesare Lombroso, *Die Ursachen und die Bekämpfung des Verbrechens*, trans. Hans Kurella (Berlin: Bermuhler, 1902), and the following works by Kurella: *Die Grenzen der Zurechnungsfähigkeit und die Kriminalanthropologie* (Halle: Gebaür-Schwetschke, 1903); "Die soziologische Forschung und Cesare Lombroso," *MKS* 3 (1906): 398–409; *Cesare Lombroso als Mensch und Forscher* (Wiesbaden: Bergmann, 1910); "Zu Cesare Lombrosos Gedächtnis," *MKS* 7 (1910): 1–8.

first question. Baer's book, Sommer claimed, had been "misunderstood in important respects." In the "general jubilation over the refutation of Lombroso in the particulars" people had "missed the positive data that [Baer] has contributed to the theory that there are individual constitutions that endogenously tend toward crime." These positive data consisted of Baer's assertion that many criminals suffered from a "feeble intelligence." Hence, Sommer concluded, "the psychological analysis of recidivist criminals seems to amount to what has been asserted by Lombroso in a crude anatomical way . . . namely, that there are a number of individuals in whose cases inner disposition is far more important than external circumstances and who are therefore individuals with endogenous criminal constitutions (*endogene Verbrechernaturen*), even if one cannot establish a type in the anatomical sense."[36]

Independently of Sommer, Julius Koch, the author of the aforementioned work on *psychopathische Minderwertigkeiten*, took virtually the same position in a short treatise titled *Die Frage nach dem geborenen Verbrecher* (The question of the born criminal), published the same year (1894). Whereas Sommer's remarks on the topic had been brief, Koch drew on his classification of *psychopathische Minderwertigkeiten* (psychopathic abnormalities) to advance a more elaborate account of what amounted to a nonanatomical version of the born criminal. Koch divided habitual criminals into mentally healthy and mentally abnormal, "psychopathic" individuals. With respect to this last category, he then posed the crucial question whether "the psychopathy of such habitual criminals [merely] creates a general predisposition on the basis of which the milieu can provoke criminal behavior more easily," or whether there might not be "a psychopathic habitual criminal whose pathological constitution makes him disposed toward crime, and drives him to crimes with more or less compelling necessity." In answering this question, Koch agreed with Baer that there were psychopathic individuals whose criminal behavior was primarily caused by external circumstances. But, he argued, there was also a second group, "where the essential cause for habitual criminal behavior lies in the psychopathy itself, where there exists a pathological—congenital or acquired—moral debility and often even a positive inclination and drive toward crime." In short, there were "cases in which immanent pathological characteristics of the individual turn a person into a criminal."[37]

Although this category included cases of full-fledged insanity, Koch was most

36. Robert Sommer, "Die Criminalpsychologie," *AZP* 51 (1895): 782–803, esp. 783–86.
37. Julius Koch, *Die Frage nach dem geborenen Verbrecher* (Ravensburg: Otto Maier, 1894), 32–35. Compare the interesting, remarkably positive review by Näcke in *AZP* 52 (1896): 466–70.

interested in the intermediate cases of *"psychopathisch minderwertige* individuals, who, as a result of the quality of their nervous system, especially their brain, display moral weakness and an instinct toward evil . . . [or] just this instinct alone." Eager to distance himself from phrenology, Koch added that he did not, of course, believe that the brain contained an "organ of theft" or "ganglionic cells of morality, immorality, virtue [or] murder." But since the physical basis of mental processes remained mysterious, he was unable to provide a positive explanation, offering only the laconic remark that "the [biological] process in such matters is apt to be more complicated than one thinks." Contrary to Lombroso, however, Koch insisted that the criminal inclination could never occur in isolation but was always accompanied by other symptoms of mental pathology.[38]

Koch admitted that it would be difficult to demonstrate that a habitual criminal had become criminal not because of a general *minderwertige*, degenerate disposition but as a result of a specific moral weakness or "instincts directed toward the bad." Nevertheless, he suggested that a patient's past medical history would usually resolve the matter—exactly how remained unclear. Sometimes, however, the influence of the endogenous factor was crystal clear. How else was one to understand the cases of "children from the best families, growing up . . . in the most favorable milieu," who were nevertheless instinctively oriented toward the bad or the following cases?

> The most important evidence for my conception and the most instructive for me were certain cases where intellectually significant, ethically sensitive, psychopathic individuals gave me a deeper insight into their mental life. Right now I recall the picture of a highly gifted and highly educated man, whose innermost soul was revolted by any insincerity or dishonesty . . . whose thoughts and actions make him one of the noblest people I know, but who confessed to an instinctive inclination to commit small, senseless misappropriations, which no one would suspect him of. . . . I have encountered more than a few similar cases. Often the [patients] sense that something pathological is at play.[39]

Koch's case description shows that his understanding of the biological basis of criminal behavior was quite different from Lombroso's conception of the born criminal as a breed apart. Whereas Lombroso's born criminal served to distance the abnormal criminal from the normal rest of the population, Koch's notion of

38. Koch, *Die Frage*, 36–43, 21–22.
39. Ibid., 42.

a specific moral defect was able to explain immoral and criminal impulses in otherwise highly respectable people. Moreover, in Koch's scheme psychopathically *Minderwertige* with dispositions that involved a "specific stimulus to crime" (Koch generally preferred such paraphrases to the loaded term "born criminal") formed only one small, special category among the *Minderwertige* in general. Most *Minderwertige*, Koch reminded his readers, did not suffer from a moral defect, and many were morally impeccable people, a point that was all too soon forgotten as laymen began to use the term *Minderwertige* as a synonym for individuals who supposedly suffered from an endogenous inclination toward crime.[40]

Within less then two years, in 1896, Sommer's and Koch's challenge to Baer's and Näcke's emphasis on the milieu found another supporter in the psychiatrist Eugen Bleuler, then director of the insane asylum in Rheinau in Switzerland. Appointed to the prestigious chair of psychiatry at the University of Zurich and the directorship of the famous Burghölzli asylum in 1898, Bleuler quickly became one of the most prominent psychiatrists in German-speaking Europe, best known for refining Kraepelin's diagnosis of dementia praecox and giving it the name "schizophrenia."[41] Unlike Koch, who had maintained a somewhat critical stance toward Lombroso, Bleuler cast himself as Lombroso's defender. "It has become a dogma that the dogma of the born criminal has been thoroughly disproved," he wrote in his book *Der geborene Verbrecher* (The born criminal) (1896), "but this is absolutely not the case. Not a single valid argument has been advanced against Lombroso's conception. Baer and Näcke, too, have unwittingly proved the endogenous origins [of crime]." It did not matter that the atavism thesis remained unsupported or that Lombroso's "criminal type" could not yet be distinguished from degenerates in general. In Bleuler's estimation, "the essential element of [Lombroso's] doctrine is the assertion that . . . criminals differ physically and mentally from the average type of the healthy, honest individual," and this assertion, he insisted, was correct.[42]

"Moral depravity without other significant mental abnormalities" clearly oc-

40. Ibid., 45.

41. J. Klaesi, "Eugen Bleuler," in *Große Nervenärzte*, ed. Kolle, 1:7–16; Bernard Pauleikhoff, "Eugen Bleuler," in *Das Menschenbild im Wandel der Zeit*, 3:206–28.

42. Eugen Bleuler, *Der geborene Verbrecher: Eine kritische Studie* (Munich: J. F. Lehmann, 1896), 19–26. Compare the reviews by Näcke in *AZP* 53 (1897): 888–89 and by Finger in *Gerichtssaal* 52 (1896): 474–76. The cited passage alluded to a lecture by the Freiburg psychiatry professor Kirn, who had concluded a review of Baer's and Näcke's works with the statement: "Today the dogma of the born criminal has to be regarded as thoroughly discredited. Crime is in large part a consequence of social conditions" ("Über den gegenwärtigen Stand der Criminal-Anthropologie," *AZP* 50 [1894]: 705–13).

curred, but it was, Bleuler explained, interpreted in different ways. Some regarded this phenomenon as pathological and called it moral insanity; others, such as Lombroso, regarded it as a characteristic of an aberrant variation of the human species, "criminal man," whose genesis remained unexamined; a third group (Baer, Näcke) regarded it as an attribute that was produced by the milieu in normal and healthy people who thereby became criminals.[43] Bleuler began by examining the last position. How, he asked, could the milieu lead to moral depravity? His answer was revealing:

> In school, yes even in the street, where altruistic ideas and sentiments, for instance of honor and property, are present . . . there is always a sufficient stimulus for the development of moral notions which can suffice to protect the individual from crime. This explains why even under the most adverse circumstances criminals make up only a small part of a certain class of the people. But why does this smaller part succumb? Surely the most obvious answer is: because it is not as well organized [biologically] as the others. . . . We therefore have no other choice but to search for the predisposing cause for moral degeneration in criminal persons themselves.[44]

Bleuler's reasoning shows that his conception of an environmental explanation of crime was so narrow that it made the biological explanation inevitable. Since the general social conditions of the lower classes could not account for differences in individual behavior, Bleuler argued, these differences must result from biological factors. It does not seem to have occurred to him that important aspects of the environment could vary from individual to individual and therefore explain differences in behavior. The fact that Bleuler, one of the most influential psychiatrists of his time, could not conceive of a sophisticated environmental explanation of individual behavior reflects the strong preference for biological explanations among most late nineteenth-century psychiatrists.

Although criminals could not yet be distinguished from other degenerates by their physical characteristics, Bleuler maintained that they were set apart by "characterological attributes" such as "moral defects, a lack of inhibition, excessive drives, etc." While Bleuler admitted that criminal psychopathology could not yet describe the different "classes" of criminals in all their forms, one such class could already be defined, namely those characterized by a "defect of moral sentiments."[45] Anticipating the objection that the morality underlying

43. Bleuler, *Der geborene Verbrecher*, 26.
44. Ibid., 28–29.
45. Ibid., 1, 12–13.

those "moral sentiments" was not congenital but socially constructed, Bleuler explained:

> What the born criminal is lacking is not the laws to be instilled, but the possibility of making use of them in the same way as honest people. This defect can be congenital. Despite the best milieu the emotional resonance [Gefühlsbetonung] for all notions of good and bad ... can be lacking. Since it is primarily emotional resonance, not logical reasoning that determines our behavior, such people have to become criminals as a result of the congenitally defective organization of their brain, which does not allow for the development of ethical sentiments. . . . Those who conclude that there cannot be born criminals because morality is not inborn are guilty of the same fallacy as anyone trying to argue that because language is not inborn, no one can be born deaf.[46]

Having affirmed the existence of congenital "defects of moral sentiments," Bleuler raised the question of whether such defects could occur in isolation. Unlike Koch, Bleuler took the radical position that they could. There were, he claimed, "special functions of the cerebral cortex, which . . . determined the character and morality of the individual" and could, just like other mental capacities, such as memory, intelligence, and imagination, be subject to an isolated defect. Hence Bleuler fully endorsed the existence of moral insanity in the narrow sense of the term.[47]

Despite the primacy he accorded to biological factors, Bleuler acknowledged that the milieu could function as a trigger. For criminal behavior to occur, cases of a "highly developed criminal disposition" would require only a weak external impulse, while a less-developed disposition would require a stronger one. In principle, then, Bleuler accepted a spectrum of differently weighted combinations of biological and environmental factors, ranging from purely exogenous to purely endogenous cases. Not surprisingly, however, he asserted that exogenous cases were rare. Finally, he did not hesitate to make the extreme claim that "people with a considerable defect of this kind must, under whatever circumstances they live, become criminals."[48]

The appearance of Bleuler's book in 1896 concluded the remarkable series of books on criminal anthropology that began with the publication of Baer's critical study three years before, thus bringing to an end the first phase of the

46. Ibid., 20–21.
47. Ibid., 21, 23.
48. Ibid., 29, 31–34.

German reception of Lombroso. As we have seen, only Hans Kurella defended Lombroso's doctrine in its entirety. The rest of the books published between 1893 and 1896 fell into two categories. Baer and Näcke denied the existence of a born criminal and argued for the overwhelming influence of the milieu in triggering criminal behavior among a largely degenerate population. Sommer, Koch, and Bleuler, in contrast, maintained that although Lombroso was wrong about the born criminal's physical characteristics, there were indeed people who could be called born criminals in the sense that their criminal behavior was determined by an endogenous biological disposition.

Over the next two decades, from the mid-1890s to the outbreak of the First World War, the most influential exposition of the view that there were born criminals in this sense was to be found in the psychiatry textbook written by Emil Kraepelin, who had taken a strong interest in criminological questions from the outset of his career. Going through eight editions between 1883 and 1915, Kraepelin's *Psychiatrie* had established itself by the 1890s as the standard German textbook in psychiatry. Thanks to frequent revisions, its different editions also give us a good idea of the evolution of Kraepelin's ideas. The first through the sixth editions (1883–99) contained a section on "moral insanity," which Kraepelin defined as "the lack or weakness of those sentiments which counter the ruthless satisfaction of egotism."[49] This moral insanity or "moral feeblemindedness"[50] was attributed primarily to degeneration and treated as synonymous with Lombroso's born criminal.[51] While Kraepelin stressed that it was not currently possible to recognize moral insanity through physical characteristics, as late as 1899 he still expressed the hope that anthropological research might make it possible to identify such characteristics for various types of born criminals.[52]

In the 1904 edition, Kraepelin changed the section's heading from "Moral Insanity" to "The Born Criminal" and moved this section from the chapter on "congenital feeblemindedness" to a new chapter on "psychopathic person-

49. Kraepelin, *Psychiatrie: Ein kurzes Lehrbuch für Studirende und Ärzte*, 3d ed. (Leipzig: Abel, 1889), 568–69; 4th ed. (Leipzig: Abel, 1893), 670–73; 5th ed. (Leipzig: Barth, 1896), 799–802; 6th ed., 2 vols. (Leipzig: Barth, 1899), 2:583–86; Werlinder, *Psychopathy*, 79. The section on moral insanity remained virtually unchanged from the fourth through sixth editions.

50. Kraepelin used the terms *moralisches Irresein* and *moralischer Schwachsinn* interchangeably.

51. In the 4th edition (1893) Kraepelin did not list any of the older literature on moral insanity but gave only Lombroso's *Der Verbrecher*, Kurella, and Baer as sources and further reading on the subject.

52. Kraepelin, *Psychiatrie*, 6th ed., 1:585.

alities," which he defined as "mental deformities whose pathology was not recognized through changes from an earlier, healthy condition, but through their general deviation from the range of health," that is, the kind of personality disorders that Koch had called *psychopathische Minderwertigkeiten*.[53]

Kraepelin himself explained the significance of this change. For a long time, he charged, German psychiatrists had been unable to approach moral defects in the same dispassionate, scientific manner in which they approached intellectual ones. Caught in a moralistic stance toward moral disorders, they had insisted that a person's moral sense could not be defective unless the intellect was affected as well, and they had therefore classified "moral insanity" as a subtype of congenital feeblemindedness. "This approach," Kraepelin charged, "was influenced by considerations about the supposedly disastrous consequences that the doctrine [of moral insanity] would have for criminal justice."[54] Having determined that psychiatrists' linkage of moral and intellectual faculties "correspond[ed] to the principles that dominate our legislation rather than to the exigencies of psychiatric science,"[55] Kraepelin decided that there was in fact a "whole class of individuals" whose ethical faculties were disturbed without any *significant* intellectual defects, and therefore he removed moral insanity from its position as a subtype of feeblemindedness, which designated an intellectual defect.[56] By the next edition (1915) he had adopted the radical position that the "development of higher ethical faculties can . . . be subject to obstructions [*Hemmungen*] that do not affect the intellectual capacities" at all.[57] By claiming that defects in moral faculties could occur without the presence of any intellectual defects, Kraepelin was clearly vindicating the existence of born criminals characterized by "congenital ethical insensitivity."

Combining Biological and Social Explanations of Crime

While Kraepelin's textbook helped to popularize the notion of the born criminal, defined in terms of a moral defect, other developments strengthened the

53. In addition to born criminals, the psychopathic personalities included pathological liars, unstable personalities, and *Querulanten* (litigious personalities). See Kraepelin, *Psychiatrie*, 7th ed., 2 vols. (Leipzig: Barth, 1904), 2:xi, 796–97, 800, 815–41. The 8th edition changed the name of the category from "born criminal" to "die Gesellschaftsfeinde (Antisozialen)." Kraepelin, *Psychiatrie*, 8th ed. (Leipzig: Barth, 1909–15), 2076–2110.

54. Kraepelin, *Psychiatrie*, 7th ed., 1:817.

55. This wording is taken from Kraepelin, *Psychiatrie*, 8th ed., 2104.

56. Ibid. In the 1904 edition, Kraepelin still conceded that intellect and ethical faculties could never be completely independent.

57. Kraepelin, *Psychiatrie*, 8th ed., 2103, 2104.

explanation of criminal behavior pioneered by Baer and Näcke, who stressed the influence of environmental factors in leading degenerate *Minderwertige* onto a path of crime. One of these developments was the founding of a new journal devoted to covering the field of "criminal anthropology." The *Archiv für Kriminal-Anthropologie und Kriminalistik* was founded by the Austrian judge Hans Groß in 1898. More than sixty volumes of the *Archiv* appeared in the decade and a half before 1914. Having served as an examining judge and public prosecutor in the Austrian courts for thirty years, Groß had made a name for himself by publishing a handbook for examining judges which soon became the standard work on scientific methods of crime detection and, starting in 1899, earned him a rapid succession of professorial appointments at Austrian universities.[58]

That Groß used the term "criminal anthropology" in the journal's title, even though he rejected Lombroso's theory of the born criminal as an anthropological type, reflected the continuing influence of Lombrosian terminology. Although the term "criminal anthropology" continued to be used, "criminal psychology" gradually became the preferred term during the prewar years. The journal's title also indicated that it would cover "criminalistics," the study of scientific crime detection and the handling of scientific evidence—what we would call forensic science today—in which Groß himself was most interested. Although these two fields were quite distinct, Groß combined them because he saw both areas as part of a common research agenda that was to create the scientific basis for a comprehensive reform of the criminal justice system. Considering himself a member of Franz von Liszt's reformist school, Groß envisaged the creation of a new system of penal sanctions that would provide effective "psychological deterrents" (*Hemmungsvorstellungen*) to criminal behavior. To determine what form these deterrents should take, he had become interested in the psychological etiology of crime. But since the psychological origins of criminal behavior were difficult to uncover, Groß decided to start with the "phenomenological" task of examining crime in its external manifestations.

Groß entertained an interesting hypothesis about what the investigation of the external characteristics of crimes might reveal. The study of many crimes

58. Hans Groß (1847–1915) held professorships at the University of Czernowitz in the Bucovina (1899–1903), then in Prague (1903–5), and finally at Graz (1905–15). See Adolf Lenz, "Hans Groß: Gedenkrede," *ZStW* 37 (1916): 595–604; Roland Grassberger, "Hans Groß," in *Pioneers of Criminology*, ed. Hermann Mannheim, 2d ed. (Montclair: Patterson Smith, 1972), 305–17; *Geschichte der Rechtswissenschaftlichen Fakultät der Universität Graz*, vol. 3, *Strafrecht—Strafprozessrecht—Kriminologie* (Graz: Akademische Druck- und Verlagsanstalt, 1987), 33–56.

had convinced him that the commission of crimes often involved certain typical mistakes and made him wonder whether these mistakes indicated an inferior intellectual capacity on the part of criminals. Could it be that intellectual inferiority had made it difficult for them to earn an honest living and had therefore driven them to crime? Although he speculated that many criminals suffered from intellectual deficiencies, Groß did not believe in born criminals and rejected the notion that crime or criminals were in any way pathological. After all, his very hope to construct a system of effective psychological deterrents was predicated on the assumption that criminals functioned according to normal psychological patterns.[59]

The connection Groß had drawn between criminalistics and the field that was coming to be called criminal psychology was tenuous, however, and most of the *Archiv*'s articles proved unable to bridge the gap between the two fields. Although the *Archiv*'s coverage strongly favored criminalistics, over the years the *Archiv* carried scores of articles on forensic psychiatry, criminal psychology, and penal reform, covering such issues as the introduction of diminished responsibility, the role of psychiatric experts in the courts, homosexuality, juvenile delinquents, and proposals for preventive measures.

Almost all of the *Archiv*'s general articles on criminal psychology were written by Paul Näcke, who had an article in virtually every issue.[60] Since Groß was opposed to the notion of the born criminal, his recruitment of Näcke as his primary contributor for criminal anthropology made good sense. Although Näcke regarded the environment as the decisive cause of criminal behavior, he was by no means doctrinaire about this. On the contrary, throughout two decades of contributions, from his first book on the subject in 1893 until his death in 1913, Näcke remained extremely interested in the question of whether there might be endogenous or hereditary causes of criminal behavior. Anecdotal evidence from orphanages on the influence of heredity, for instance, engaged his serious attention, and he also became convinced that race was an important factor in criminal behavior.[61] Despite this recognition that heredity

59. Hans Groß, "Aufgabe und Ziele," *AKK* 1 (1898): 1–4; Groß, "Antrittsvorlesung," *AKK* 21 (1905): 169–83. See also Gadebusch Bondio, *Die Rezeption*, 153–66.

60. Among Näcke's more important contributions were "Degeneration, Degenerationszeichen und Atavismus," *AKK* 1 (1899): 200–221; "Drei kriminalanthropologische Themen," *AKK* 6 (1901): 261–72; "Die Hauptergebnisse der kriminalanthropologischen Forschung im Jahre 1901," *AKK* 9 (1902): 141–56; "Die Überbleibsel der Lombrososchen kriminalanthropologischen Theorien," *AKK* 50 (1912): 326–39. Näcke was also a regular contributor to Liszt's *ZStW*.

61. Paul Näcke, "Macht des persönlichen Faktors," *AKK* 9 (1902): 364–65; Näcke, "Rasse und Verbrechen," *AKK* 25 (1906): 64–73.

could play a part in causing criminal behavior, however, Näcke continued to maintain that "the [external] occasion is always necessary, and therefore one cannot speak of a 'born criminal.'" Although he admitted that degeneration could create a general predisposition toward crime, he insisted that "if the milieu is only halfway favorable, someone who is strongly predisposed toward crime can get through life without any trouble, while an unfavorable milieu will cause someone who shows only a small or even no disposition [toward crime] to go astray." Finally, he remained convinced that "most recidivists have certainly been more seduced and corrupted by the milieu than through individual factors."[62]

While Näcke's stream of articles in the *Archiv* steadily promoted the milieu-oriented explanation of criminal behavior, it did not really advance the field. The next major contribution was the work of a newcomer, Gustav Aschaffenburg. After studying medicine at several German universities, Aschaffenburg had spent the 1890s working under Emil Kraepelin, who was at that time professor and director of the psychiatric hospital in Heidelberg, where Aschaffenburg became associate director in 1894. During these years Kraepelin, who was himself engaged in systematizing the entire field of psychiatry, had directed Aschaffenburg's attention to criminal anthropology and encouraged him to write a synthesis. After a short term (1901–4) as head of the psychiatric ward at the prison in Halle, in 1904 Aschaffenburg was appointed professor of psychiatry at the Academy of Medicine in Cologne, where he remained for the rest of his career.[63]

In 1903 Aschaffenburg published the book that established him as Germany's foremost expert in criminology. Dedicated to Kraepelin, Aschaffenburg's *Das Verbrechen und seine Bekämpfung* (Crime and its repression) presented a systematic analysis of the causes of crime that was unprecedented in scope and sophistication. As a result, it became the standard work in German criminology and remained so for over thirty years, into the 1930s. Translated into English, the book also won its author an international reputation.[64] Al-

62. Näcke, "Macht des persönlichen Faktors," 365.
63. On Aschaffenburg, see Falk Busse, "Gustav Aschaffenburg (1866–1944)—Leben und Werk" (M.D. diss., University of Leipzig, 1991); Hans von Hentig, "Gustav Aschaffenburg," in *Pioneers of Criminology*, ed. Mannheim, 421–28, which contains personal reminiscences; Hans Gruhle and Rudolf Sieverts, "Zum Geleit," MKS 36 (1953): 1–5; L. Kanner, "In Memoriam: Gustav Aschaffenburg," *American Journal of Psychiatry* 101 (Nov. 1944): 427–28; Dorothea Seiffert, "Gustav Aschaffenburg als Kriminologe" (J.D diss., University of Freiburg, 1981).
64. Gustav Aschaffenburg, *Das Verbrechen und seine Bekämpfung: Kriminalpsychologie für Mediziner, Juristen und Soziologen, ein Beitrag zur Reform der Strafgesetzgebung* (Heidelberg:

though Aschaffenburg firmly rejected Lombroso's theory of the born criminal, his book was not conceived or structured as a critique of Lombroso. It was thus the first criminological work in a decade that was neither a refutation nor a defense of Lombroso. Aschaffenburg probably found it easier to emancipate himself from Lombroso because he belonged to a slightly younger generation, having entered the psychiatric profession only in the 1890s, when Lombroso was already under attack. To mark his distance from Lombroso's theories, Aschaffenburg consistently used the term "criminal psychology" (*Kriminal-psychologie*) instead of "criminal anthropology." Moreover, unlike many earlier books, Aschaffenburg's study did not begin with detailed craniometric and anthropometric examinations designed to refute Lombroso's claims. Most important, even though Aschaffenburg was a psychiatrist, the book offered a wide-ranging and evenhanded account of both social and individual factors in crime.

The first section of the book, on the "social causes of crime," was based on the pioneering work of moral statisticians such as Mayr and Oettingen, as well as the official crime statistics that the unified German state had been publishing since 1881. Using these sources, Aschaffenburg presented a comprehensive picture of the effects on crime rates of various social factors, including geographic location (city versus country), economic conditions, alcohol consumption, occupation, nationality, race, and religion. In general, Aschaffenburg identified two major movements in German crime rates over the preceding twenty years: first, a gradual increase in violent crimes such as battery, and second, periodic fluctuations in property crime, mostly theft. The first development Aschaffenburg attributed to the increased consumption of alcohol, backing up his case by correlating alcohol consumption and violent crime rates in different geographic areas and at certain times such as weekends and holidays. With regard to property crime, he endorsed Georg von Mayr's demonstration that the fluctuations in theft were directly correlated to changes in grain prices, observing, however, that it was not dire need but rather people's difficulty in adjusting their lives to the decrease in income that led them to crime. Aschaffenburg, who was Jewish, was especially careful in his examination of race and religion. He argued that the higher crime rates in Germany's eastern provinces, which some blamed on the Polish population, could be explained by the severe economic problems of the region. Likewise, he pointed out that the high propor-

Winter, 1903); 2d edition published in 1923; translated into English as *Crime and Its Repression* (Boston: Little, Brown, 1913).

tion of convictions of Jews for usury must be weighed against the high proportion of Jews engaged in commerce and trade. In short, Aschaffenburg offered plausible sociological explanations for both geographic and temporal variations in crime rates, which allowed him to reject the opinions that geographic variations were caused by racial differences or that temporal ones resulted from a general deterioration in the moral fiber of the nation.[65]

The sociological explanations, however, did not exhaust the etiology of crime. "The social causes," Aschaffenburg explained, "provide the impulse to crime, but while a great part of the people are able to maintain stability, another part succumbs, some faster, some slower. It is therefore necessary to examine in detail which of the individual's characteristics weaken its social resistance so much that the person becomes a criminal."[66] Aschaffenburg began the section on "individual causes of crime" by investigating the factor of heredity. He was willing to accept research findings showing that close to half of all criminals descended from criminal parents but pointed out that such statistics did not in any way prove the hereditary transmission of an "inclination to commit crimes" because parental criminality obviously provided children with a bad example and thereby constituted a powerful *environmental* factor affecting their future behavior. Regarding Lombroso's born criminal, Aschaffenburg drew on Baer's and Näcke's work to show that none of his supposed physical characteristics were specific to criminals: "The most important stigmata of degeneration, such as misshapen ears, . . . genital abnormalities . . . can all be found among healthy people. They are more numerous as we approach the degenerate mentally ill. Between the two stands the criminal." The fate of Lombroso's assertions under critical scrutiny, he suggested, had now become predictable: "Whenever a new phenomenon has come under criminal anthropological investigation, the same story repeats itself. First it is asserted that a certain type of anomaly is characteristic of the criminal; then it is demonstrated that the same phenomena are also found in nondelinquents, and finally one is left with the result that these anomalies are slightly more frequent among criminals."[67]

The book's section on the "individual causes of crime" provided the most systematic and sophisticated analysis of the interaction of biological and social factors in the etiology of crime published in the prewar years. Following the

---

65. Aschaffenburg, *Das Verbrechen*, 1st ed., 11–99, esp. 37–38, 40, 43, 84, 100.
66. The German term was *soziale Widerstandsfähigkeit* (ibid., 100).
67. Ibid., 102–3, 136–44.

lead of Baer and Näcke, Aschaffenburg argued that the frequency of degeneration among criminals was not surprising because "the overwhelming majority
of criminals come from those strata where need and misery reign, where poorly
nourished women have to consume their last energies in hard work even during
pregnancy." Thus the social environment was doubly responsible for criminal
behavior. Not only did dire need and the bad example of a morally depraved
milieu directly push many people into a career of crime, but the squalor of
lower-class life also led to a biological degeneration that rendered its victims
"socially unfit" (sozial unbrauchbar). Poverty, unhygienic living quarters, and
alcoholism were creating a generation of people who were unable to compete in
the "struggle for existence." Frequently far below average in their intellectual
abilities, some of these individuals were liable to succumb to the temptation of
crime.[68] Speaking from his own experience as a forensic psychiatrist, he related
that "after studying the [judicial] case files, I often expected to meet a rough,
brutal person, whereas I actually found a quiet, docile, even good-natured,
feebleminded person." Aschaffenburg stressed that those minderwertige degenerates who committed crimes did not do so because of some peculiar "moral
defect," let alone some active "drive to crime," but because they were altogether
"socially unfit," that is, unable to make an honest living, mostly because their
intellectual abilities were inferior.[69]

That Minderwertigkeit resulted mostly from social causes was ground for
optimism: "If we could remove all these people from the bad soil in which they
are rooted, if we could steel them through education and physical invigoration,
if we could protect them against the dangers of life, we would be able to save
them from ruin." But Aschaffenburg immediately tempered these prospects
with resignation: "These are utopias; life takes its course and crushes those who
cannot make a go of it."[70]

Of course, not all offenders fell into the category of "socially unfit" Minderwertige. In his classification of criminals, Aschaffenburg called this group "habitual criminals" and estimated that they constituted roughly half of all criminals. In contrast to habitual criminals who turned to crime as a result of
socioeconomic failure, Aschaffenburg distinguished a small group of "professional criminals" with an active inclination and commitment to crime. The
remaining half of all criminals was mostly made up of first-time offenders who
committed their crimes because of an unfortunate combination of circum-

68. Ibid., 144–45, 162.
69. Ibid., 45, 150, 164.
70. Ibid., 163.

stances: these were crimes resulting from negligence or recklessness, sudden bursts of passion, or a tempting opportunity.[71]

Aschaffenburg's book provided the first comprehensive synthesis of the social causes of crime and made an excellent case for their tremendous importance. It integrated criminal sociology and criminal psychology as mutually complementary approaches to the etiology of crime. Finally, in the section on the individual causes of crime, Aschaffenburg rejected the notion of an endogenous criminal disposition and supported Baer's and Näcke's position that criminal behavior was caused by social factors acting on a degenerate population. For Aschaffenburg, social causes led to biological degeneration; the resulting biological abnormalities severely handicapped its victims in social life; and this inferior social position—rather than any "moral defect" or "criminal inclination"—led some of them to criminal behavior. Going through three editions in two decades, Aschaffenburg's book quickly became the standard text in criminal psychology, thereby helping to counterbalance Kraepelin's defense of the born criminal with a theory that explained crime as the result of a complex interaction between biological degeneration and environmental factors.[72]

Within months of the appearance of his book, in early 1904, Aschaffenburg began publishing the *Monatsschrift für Kriminalpsychologie und Strafrechtsreform* (Monthly journal of criminal psychology and penal reform), which soon overshadowed Groß's *Archiv* and became the primary German journal in the field. While the first part of the title hastened the transition from "criminal anthropology" to "criminal psychology" as the preferred designation for medical research on the causes of crime, the title's reference to penal reform reflected Aschaffenburg's endorsement of Liszt's notion that criminology was supposed to provide the scientific foundation for penal reform. Aschaffenburg therefore asked Liszt to serve as an associate editor for the journal. Published monthly, the journal carried a wide, interdisciplinary variety of articles, mainly in five areas: criminal psychology: studies on degeneration or moral insanity, studies of certain types of offenders, such as sex offenders, vagabonds, homosexuals; criminal sociology: rare articles on social problems and criminal statistics; forensic psychiatry: trials of particular interest, reprints of psychiatric expert opinions, the situation of the forensic psychiatrist in court; the treatment of insane criminals and the criminally insane: reports on the current situation and

71. Aschaffenburg stated that about half of all *Zuchthausgefangene* were *sozial unrettbare* habitual criminals; since he did not indicate different proportions for regular *Gefängnisinsassen*, I have assumed that this proportion was meant to apply to all criminals, but the point remains unclear (ibid., 167–71).

72. For a different assessment, see Gadebusch Bondio, *Die Rezeption*, 199–219.

debates as to what kind of institution—penal or medical—they ought to be interned in; and legal reform proposals, especially those of interest to psychiatrists, such as the introduction of diminished responsibility and other preventive measures, which will be discussed in the next chapter.[73]

The articles published in the *Monatsschrift* in the decade between 1904 and 1914 and the proceedings of the Seventh International Congress for Criminal Anthropology, held in Cologne in October 1911, showed that German psychiatrists interested in the explanation of crime continued to be divided between those who defended a psychologized version of the born criminal and those who denied the existence of a criminogenic moral defect.[74]

Conclusion

The German reception of Lombroso coincided with two developments that expanded the scope of late nineteenth-century German psychiatry.[75] First, German psychiatry was extending its reach beyond the boundaries of full-fledged mental illness into the borderland of mental abnormalities that departed from the norm of mental health but did not constitute insanity: conditions that were referred to as *psychopathische Minderwertigkeiten* and attributed to degeneration (roughly what are termed "personality disorders" today).[76] Second, as psychiatry gained increasing recognition as a medical specialty, it came to play an expanded role in the criminal justice system.[77] The courts made more fre-

73. On the *Monatsschrift*, see Gadebusch Bondio, *Die Rezeption*, 174–80; Arno Pilgram, "Theorie der Kriminalitätsentwicklung—ein retardierter Spross der Kriminologie. Kritik der Kriminalitätsentwicklungstheorie am Beispiel der 'Monatsschrift für Kriminologie und Strafrechtsreform,' dem 'Zentralorgan' deutschsprachiger Kriminologie," in *Kriminalität in Österreich* (Vienna: Verlag für Gesellschaftskritik, 1980), 81–150.

74. Gustav Aschaffenburg and Dr. Partenheimer, eds., *Bericht über den VII. Internationalen Kongreß für Kriminalanthropologie* (Heidelberg: Winter, 1912); see especially Sommer's lecture, on page 270. On the debate in the *Monatsschrift*, see especially Robert Gaupp, "Über den heutigen Stand der Lehre vom 'geborenen Verbrecher,' " *MKS* 1 (1904): 25–42; Jakob Hartmann, "Über die hereditären Verhältnisse bei Verbrechern," *MKS* 1 (1904): 493–520; Richard Weinberg, "Psychische Degeneration, Kriminalität und Rasse," *MKS* 2 (1906): 720–30.

75. Much work remains to be done on the history of psychiatry in Imperial Germany. For general background, see Blasius, *Einfache Seelenstörung*, 61–115; Heinz-Peter Schmiedebach, "The Mentally Ill Patient Caught between the State's Demands and the Professional Interests of Psychiatrists," in *Medicine and Modernity: Public Health and Medical Care in Nineteenth- and Twentieth-Century Germany*, ed. Manfred Berg and Geoffrey Cocks (Cambridge: Cambridge University Press, 1997), 99–119.

76. See Eric Engstrom, "The Birth of Clinical Psychiatry: Power, Knowledge, and Professionalization in Germany, 1867–1914" (Ph.D. diss., University of North Carolina, 1997), 476–77.

77. See the literature on German forensic psychiatry cited earlier in this chapter.

quent use of forensic psychiatrists, and more prison doctors became interested in psychiatry. These prison doctors and forensic psychiatrists were soon reporting an inordinately high incidence of degeneration and insanity among criminals. Since the expansion of psychiatry also led to the "detection" of ever more cases of mental illness in the general population, it is not surprising that the intense scrutiny to which defendants and prisoners were subjected yielded even higher rates of mental illness or abnormality.

Having detected an unusual correlation between criminal behavior and mental abnormality in their own work, German psychiatrists and prison doctors took great interest in Lombroso's findings. Leaving aside the orthodox Lombrosian Kurella, the pioneers of German criminal psychology formed two main camps defending two different paradigms. The first group, including Kraepelin, Koch, and Bleuler, proposed what we might call the "Kraepelin paradigm": defending the notion of the born criminal but stripping him of his physical characteristics. Transforming Lombroso's atavistic anthropological type into a psychiatric category, this group maintained that there were people who committed crimes as a result of an endogenous moral defect. This view was challenged by a second group, who advanced what we might call the "Aschaffenburg paradigm." This group, including Baer, Näcke, and Aschaffenburg, denied the existence of born criminals, with or without physical characteristics. Although they conceded that widespread degeneration rendered many people intellectually inferior and socially unfit, they rejected the notion of an endogenous moral defect or criminal disposition and insisted that environmental factors always played a role in the etiology of crime. If degenerates were more likely to become criminal, this was not because their mental abnormalities were directly criminogenic but because these abnormalities often rendered them unable to make a living. Although Kraepelin's influential textbook defended his paradigm throughout the prewar years, Aschaffenburg's book and his editorship of the *Monatsschrift* as well as Näcke's stream of publications gradually established the Aschaffenburg paradigm as the predominant strand in the field.

This state of affairs did not differ much from the situation in France. While it is true that French doctors and jurists took the lead in criticizing Lombroso's theory of the born criminal at the International Congresses of Criminal Anthropology of the 1880s and 1890s, recent research has shown that the contrast between the supposedly sociological "French school" and the Lombrosian school has been overstated. Although the major figures of the French school, including Alexandre Lacassagne, Léonce Manouvrier, and Valentin Magnan, rejected Lombroso's theory of the born criminal as an atavistic anthropological type, they, too, saw a connection between criminal behavior and degeneration that very much resembled the Aschaffenburg paradigm. The question whether there was a French equivalent of the Kraepelin paradigm is more difficult, but at least one historian has argued that Lacassagne, too, subscribed to the "simplest biological determinism."[78]

The most striking feature of Lombroso's doctrine was the use of the born criminal's morphological characteristics as physical proof for the theory. What is remarkable about his reception is that even after Lombroso's physical evidence was refuted, proponents of the Kraepelin paradigm still defended the notion of the born criminal. To be sure, the lack of physical evidence did not disprove the idea that there might be a born criminal. But now the idea of the born criminal was completely unsubstantiated. When Bleuler, Koch, and Kraepelin maintained that the criminal behavior of certain people resulted from an organic moral defect, this was a mere assertion. Why, then, did they think this? Bleuler reasoned that since the environment was roughly the same for the mass of the poor, the fact that only a few became criminal could be explained only by individual biology. Since neither Koch nor Kraepelin offered a better explanation, we are left to conclude that their belief that immoral or antisocial behavior was caused by a biological defect reflected a fundamental preference for biological explanations over environmental ones, what some German scholars have termed "biologism" (*Biologismus*).[79] And yet one should not overstate the case for *Biologismus* as a general characteristic of late nineteenth-century German psychiatry because other psychiatrists, such as Näcke and Aschaffenburg, delivered balanced assessments of the interaction of biological and social factors.

Another point worth noting is that all the German proponents of the born criminal conceived of the criminal disposition as a moral defect (in the tradition of moral insanity) rather than as a positive drive toward crime (in the tradition of monomania).[80] This reference to a lack of morality was especially curious in

78. Mucchielli, "Hérédité et 'milieu social' " (quote from p. 121); Nye, *Crime, Madness, and Politics*, 97–131; Renneville, "La réception de Lombroso en France." See also Nye, "Heredity or Milieu: The Foundations of Modern European Criminological Theory," *Isis* 67 (1976): 335–55. For the interpretation criticized by Renneville and Mucchielli, see Pierre Darmon, *Médecins et assassins à la Belle Epoque: La médicalisation du crime* (Paris: Seuil, 1989).

79. See Gunter Mann, "Medizinisch-biologische Ideen und Modelle der Gesellschaftslehre des 19. Jahrhunderts," *Medizinhistorisches Journal* 4 (1969): 1–23; Mann, "Biologie und der 'Neue Mensch': Denkstufen und Pläne zur Menschenzucht im Zweiten Kaiserreich," in *Medizin, Naturwissenschaft, Technik und das Zweite Kaiserreich*, ed. Gunter Mann and Rolf Winau (Göttingen: Vandenhoeck, 1977), 172–88.

80. Here Koch, who spoke of both "sittliche Schwäche" and "ein positiver Hang und Trieb auf das Verbrechen," was a partial exception (Koch, *Die Frage*, 34).

an author like Kraepelin, who insisted that the medical and scientific approach to criminal behavior transcended moral evaluations. For the conceptualization of criminal behavior as the result of a defect suggested that moral behavior was somehow natural, normal, and inborn. Most psychiatric authors recognized that this idea of a natural moral sense contradicted the observation that moral conceptions differed from time to time and place to place. Bleuler, for instance, acknowledged that morality was socially determined and explained that by moral defect he meant that a person's very *capacity* for moral sentiments was missing. But he never examined whether criminals who supposedly suffered from a moral defect might just have had a *different* morality.

What did it mean to label criminal behavior as biologically abnormal? For some authors, like Bleuler, it might have been genuinely comforting to attribute criminal behavior to biological rather than social causes because this explanation relieved society of responsibility and distanced the supposedly abnormal criminal from the rest of society. For most authors, however, things were more complicated. Koch, for instance, related the case of a respectable patient who suffered from isolated criminal impulses. Moral defects, then, were not just something from which people who were "different" suffered but a problem that could strike anyone. This point was made even more forcefully by the proponents of the Aschaffenburg paradigm. In Näcke's eyes, degeneration was lurking everywhere. For these authors, degeneration was not a way of creating comfortable distance between the abnormal, lower-class degenerate and the honest citizen but a social problem that concerned everyone.

In the classic nineteenth-century model, a person could be either criminal or insane but never both. In the first case, the person would be held responsible and punished; in the second case, he or she would be treated. This binary distinction worked well as long as the mentally ill offender was considered an exceptional phenomenon. The idea of the born criminal destroyed it. Was the born criminal a criminal who should be punished or a mentally ill person who should be treated? Although Näcke and Aschaffenburg dismissed the notion of the born criminal, their contention that most criminals were degenerate and therefore often intellectually inferior created a similar problem. If these people suffered from mental deficiencies, could they be considered fully responsible for their actions? The medico-legal debate about this question forms the subject of the first part of the next chapter, which will also examine how the notion that most criminals were degenerate gave rise to new ways of thinking about the prevention of crime, including sterilization.

CHAPTER THREE

CRIMINOLOGY AND PENAL POLICY, 1880–1914

Having reviewed the development of criminological research from the 1880s to 1914 in the last chapter, we now turn to the implications of criminological research for penal policy. After a brief overview of Imperial Germany's criminal justice system and the penal reformers' agenda, I will examine the implications of criminological research for the fundamental issue of legal responsibility. The rest of this chapter will discuss the prewar debates on three issues that arose from the claim that many habitual criminals were *geistig minderwertig* (mentally deficient): Should *minderwertige* offenders receive punishment or medical treatment? Should *minderwertige* persons who appeared dangerous but had not committed a crime be subject to preventive detention? And, finally, should *minderwertige* criminals, or the *Minderwertige* in general, be sterilized?

Criminal Justice, Criminology, and the
Question of Legal Responsibility

It has been rightly pointed out that Imperial Germany's judicial system had a number of authoritarian and repressive features. Strict libel laws were used to restrict the freedom of the press. From 1878 to 1890 a special law outlawing Germany's Social-Democratic Party (SPD) made use of penal sanctions to combat the growth of the political party that seemed most threatening to those in power. And police ordinances regulating the public sphere attempted to curtail working-class activities.[1] While these repressive features were important, the fact that the government had to have recourse to a special law to combat the

---

1. Eric Johnson, *Urbanization and Crime: Germany, 1871–1914* (New York: Cambridge University Press, 1995), 15–51.

SPD indicates that the penal code did not easily lend itself to such political uses, just as the refusal of the parliament (Reichstag) to renew this law after 1890 indicates the degree to which mainstream political parties became averse to the use of penal sanctions for political purposes.

For the most part, Imperial Germany's criminal justice system bore distinctly liberal features. The Imperial German Penal Code (*Reichsstrafgesetzbuch*), which took effect in the Empire's first year of existence (1871), was modeled after the Prussian penal code of 1851. The Prussian code, in turn, had been strongly influenced by the French Code Pénal and the Bavarian penal code of 1813, which had been drafted by Germany's most famous early nineteenth-century penal reformer, Paul Johann A. Feuerbach. As a result of these influences, Imperial Germany's penal code was a classic liberal code in the sense that it reflected the desire of nineteenth-century liberals to limit the state's penal power. To protect citizens against arbitrariness, all crimes and punishments were fixed by the penal code. While all crimes were narrowly defined, the penal code left some room for judicial discretion by providing a range of punishments, with a statutory minimum and maximum, for each offense. Based on a penal philosophy that saw the main purpose of punishment as retribution and general deterrence, the entire penal code reflected the principle that the punishment should fit the crime without any regard to the person of the offender.[2]

Compared to those of France and Britain, the Imperial German Penal Code was moderate in its punishments. While British law allowed flogging for certain offenses well into the twentieth century, the German penal code abolished corporal punishment as a penal sanction, although corporal punishments continued to be practiced in some German prisons as a disciplinary measure until the First World War.[3] The French not only continued but extended the practice of penal transportation in the mid-1880s, but neither transportation nor forced labor figured as sanctions in the German code.[4] Only two offenses (premedi-

2. Eberhard Schmidt, *Einführung in die Geschichte der deutschen Strafrechtspflege*, 3d ed. (Göttingen: Vandenhoeck, 1964), 313–21, 343–45.

3. Leon Radzinowicz and Roger Hood, *History of the English Criminal Law and Its Administration*, vol. 5, *The Emergence of Penal Policy* (London: Stevens, 1986), 689–719; Richard Evans, *Tales from the German Underworld: Crime and Punishment in the Nineteenth Century* (New Haven: Yale University Press, 1998), 121–22.

4. Robert Nye, *Crime, Madness, and Politics in Modern France* (Princeton: Princeton University Press, 1984), 49–96; Gordon Wright, *Between the Guillotine and Liberty: Two Centuries of the Crime Problem in France* (New York: Oxford University Press, 1983), 129–52. On the use of transportation in various German states before German unification in 1871, see Evans, *Tales from the German Underworld*, 11–92.

tated murder and the assassination of the emperor or the heads of the federal states) carried the death penalty;[5] only a small number of offenses carried a penalty of life imprisonment; and the maximum for all other offenses was fifteen years in prison. Criminal procedure was based on the inquisitorial French model rather than the adversarial Anglo-American model. Thus each trial began with a preliminary investigation conducted by a judge, and during the trial expert witnesses were always court-appointed rather than hired by the parties. Compared to England and France, the use of juries was extremely limited. Jury trials were restricted to serious felonies such as murder and manslaughter. Most felonies were tried by courts composed of three professional and two lay judges (*Schöffen*). German judges therefore generally played a more important role in criminal justice than their English or French colleagues. Finally, unlike their counterparts in many countries, all German judges were professionally trained.[6]

The major criticism that German penal reformers, led by Franz von Liszt, directed at Germany's criminal justice system was that it was ineffective in protecting society against crime. The high proportion of recidivists, they argued, was proof that the fixed prison sentences prescribed by the penal code failed to prevent many offenders from committing new crimes after their release. Moreover, whereas the existing penal code reflected the twin goals of retribution and general deterrence, the reformers argued that the only purpose of punishment should be to protect society from crime. This goal, they explained, could best be achieved by a criminal justice system in which the punishment fit the criminal rather than the crime. They therefore proposed a system of individualized punishments, in which first-time offenders would receive suspended sentences for the purpose of specific deterrence; repeat offenders who seemed both in need of and capable of rehabilitation would be subject to a prison sentence for the purpose of rehabilitation; and repeat offenders who seemed incorrigible would be subject to indefinite detention for the sake of incapacitation.[7]

5. On the near abolition of the death penalty in the North German Reichstag of 1870, the history of the death penalty under the Imperial Penal Code, and the revival of abolitionist efforts in the 1890s, see Richard Evans, *Rituals of Retribution: Capital Punishment in Germany, 1600–1987* (Oxford: Oxford University Press, 1996), 329–484.

6. Johnson, *Urbanization and Crime*, 15–51; Nye, *Crime, Madness, and Politics*, 23–29; Clive Emsley, *Crime and Society in England, 1750–1900*, 2d ed. (London: Longman, 1996), 178–207.

7. Richard Wetzell, "Criminal Law Reform in Imperial Germany" (Ph.D. diss., Stanford University, 1991), esp. 43–83; Schmidt, *Einführung*, 357–81; also see my forthcoming history of penal reform from 1880 to 1945.

Although the principle of retributive justice and the system of fixed punishments were vigorously defended by the so-called classical school of criminal law, the reformers were able to convince most of the legal profession and the government that the existing penal code was in need of serious revision. In 1906 the government appointed an official reform commission, which published its first draft for a revised penal code in 1909 and was just completing its second draft, when the outbreak of the First World War cut short the reform effort. Although the commission's draft codes did not abandon the retributivist principles of the current code, they made some concessions to the reformers' demand for the individualization of punishment, which showed that the penal reform movement was making inroads into the legal profession.[8]

The most controversial issue raised by the penal reformers concerned the implications of criminological research for the question of individual legal responsibility, which threatened to undermine the very foundations of the existing penal code. The code's penal strategy of general deterrence was based on the assumption that most citizens were rational, autonomous actors who calculated the consequences of their actions, while its underlying ideology of retributive justice rested on the related assumption that offenders possessed free will and were therefore morally responsible for their actions. This was the reason why children under age twelve and insane persons were exempt from punishment in the German code, as in many others.[9] Criminological research, however, destroyed the notion of free will and the image of the rational, autonomous individual. And since the penal reformers wanted criminology to provide the scientific foundation for criminal justice, they endorsed this determinist view of criminal behavior.

But if there was no free will, what would happen to the notion of legal responsibility? While Liszt himself initially avoided addressing this potentially explosive topic, in 1892 his criminal law journal published an article by the penal reformer Hugo Appelius that spelled out the radical implications of criminological research for the question of legal responsibility. "Man," Appelius argued, "is the product of his descent, his upbringing, and the changing environments of his life to such a degree that these influences determine his actions with compelling force." Without free will, he concluded, no criminal could be held responsible for his acts, so that the received notions of guilt and legal responsibility were no longer tenable. Retribution had lost its justification, and the only legitimate purpose of punishment was the protection of society.

8. Wetzell, "Criminal Law Reform," 280–97; Schmidt, *Einführung,* 394–99.
9. Imperial German Penal Code, articles 51 and 55.

Needless to say, this article outraged the reformers' retributivist opponents, who saw their worst suspicions confirmed.[10]

The resulting controversy forced Liszt and the penal reformers' association, the Internationale Kriminalistische Vereinigung, to address the impact of criminological research on the question of legal responsibility. Over the next few years Liszt vacillated between two positions on this issue. On the one hand, he declared that criminological work had rendered the notion of legal responsibility untenable. Thus, in an 1896 lecture to the Third International Congress of Psychology, Liszt argued that "the distinction between the detention of incorrigible criminals and the institutionalization of dangerous insane persons is not only impracticable but also to be dismissed as a matter of principle." "Let the notions of crime and punishment live on in the creations of our poets as before," he concluded, "they do not stand up to the strict criticism of scientific knowledge. Thus the concept of punishment gives way to those of curative rehabilitation and preventive detention. The conceptual dividing line between crime and insanity gives way and falls—and with it . . . the concept of legal responsibility."[11]

Eliminating the notion of legal responsibility and the distinction between punishment and medical treatment did not pose a substantive problem for Liszt because he regarded the protection of society rather than retributive justice as the sole purpose of punishment. Since, in Liszt's scheme, offenders would be subject to whatever measures were necessary to prevent them from offending again, the question of whether they were legally or morally responsible for their actions was irrelevant. From a pragmatic standpoint, however, Liszt recognized that the elimination of legal responsibility was just not acceptable to the legal establishment or the German public at large. Therefore, in the same lecture just quoted, Liszt conceded that "the reigning legal-moral conceptions of the people undoubtedly demand a distinction between crime and insanity, prison and asylum."[12]

To preserve this distinction, Liszt felt compelled to rescue the notion of legal responsibility by redefining it without reference to free will. Initially, in 1892–93, Liszt proposed defining legal responsibility as "receptiveness to punishment" or the "capacity for normal reaction to motives." Since the purpose of

10. Hugo Appelius, "Die Reformbestrebungen auf dem Gebiete der Strafrechtspflege und das heutige Strafrecht," ZStW 12 (1892): 1–33. For a more detailed discussion, see Wetzell, "Criminal Law Reform," 173–81.

11. Franz von Liszt, "Die strafrechtliche Zurechnungsfähigkeit," ZStW 17 (1897): 70–84, reprinted in Liszt, Aufsätze und Vorträge, 2:214–29.

12. Ibid., 227.

punishment was to instill motivating ideas, he suggested, punishment should be applied only to those who were capable of responding to it.[13] A few years later, however, Liszt rejected this definition because it created problems in the cases of incorrigible criminals. Since these criminals were not receptive to rehabilitation, by Liszt's definition they would not be legally responsible. Furthermore, since psychiatric research had shown that mental health and mental illness were linked by a continuum of intermediate conditions, Liszt had developed doubts about the notion of normality contained in his criterion of "normal reaction to motives." As a result, in 1896 Liszt abandoned his earlier definition and proposed a formal, negative definition of legal responsibility, defining as legally responsible all persons who were not mentally ill or minors below a certain age.[14]

When the IKV took up the question of legal responsibility at its 1897 congress, some penal reformers called for the abolition of legal responsibility. Liszt, however, expressed concern that the elimination of legal responsibility, which would abolish the distinction between punishment and treatment, might go "too far in giving a unified [state] organ the right to impose both administrative and judicial measures."[15] He worried that the abandonment of legal responsibility would dissolve criminal justice in a larger system of administrative sanctions without any of the safeguards that judicial procedures guaranteed. Torn between the recognition that criminological research had fatally undermined the notion of legal responsibility and the fear that its abolition would spell the end of the criminal justice system with its procedural guarantees, German penal reformers subsequently abandoned the issue of criminology's general implications for legal responsibility in favor of pragmatic reform proposals that focused on the sentencing and punishment stages of criminal justice.

Having set aside the general issue of legal responsibility, the reformers focused on the individualization of punishments for different categories of offenders. Even in this context, however, the question of the implications of criminological research for penal reforms and the issue of legal responsibility reemerged, most acutely in the debates over the proper treatment of *minderwertige* offenders. For the reformers' call for the medical treatment of *minderwertige* criminals was inseparably connected with the question of whether their legal responsibility was somehow diminished.

13. Franz von Liszt, "Die deterministischen Gegner der Zweckstrafe," *ZStW* 13 (1893): 325–70, reprinted in Liszt, *Aufsätze und Vorträge*, 2:25–74, here esp. 42–45.

14. Liszt, "Die strafrechtliche Zurechnungsfähigkeit," 227–29.

15. Proceedings of the Seventh Hauptversammlung der IKV, Lisbon, 20–22 April 1897, *MIKV* 6 (1896–97): 474–75.

The Question of Diminished Legal Responsibility

By the late 1890s, the emerging psychiatric consensus that mental health and insanity were linked by a continuum of *geistige Minderwertigkeiten* (mental deficiencies) and that these were frequently found among criminals was beginning to affect judicial practice in Germany's courtrooms. The courts placed more defendants under psychiatric observation and were more likely than before to accept a psychiatrist's testimony that the accused was neither insane nor healthy, but *minderwertig*. In the decade between 1895 and 1905, the number of defendants placed under psychiatric observation by the Prussian courts nearly doubled.[16] Since *geistige Minderwertigkeit* seemed to diminish the defendant's responsibility, many courts considered it an extenuating circumstance and reduced the sentence accordingly in cases where the law allowed it. But as medical diagnoses of *Minderwertigkeit* became more frequent, making more criminals eligible for reduced sentences, the increasingly common lenience of the courts provoked public criticism.

This public criticism, which emerged in the 1890s, differed from the classic charge that psychiatrists were getting sane criminals acquitted on specious insanity defenses. For the public was gradually coming to accept the psychiatrists' claim of widespread mental deficiency among criminals. Yet this belief in the mental deficiency of many offenders only made the prospect of their release after a much-reduced sentence more upsetting. The legal system's treatment of *Minderwertige* was perceived as a problem because *minderwertige* criminals appeared to be simultaneously less responsible and more dangerous. Since retributive justice took into account only the reduction of responsibility, which

16. In the period 1895–97 an average of about 250 persons per year were placed under psychiatric observation by the Prussian courts; by the years 1904–5 this number had risen to about 500 per year. (These figures include actions by civil courts, which made up less than 10 percent of total cases in 1904–5.) Since the Prussian population grew by only 17 percent in this decade and the per capita crime rate remained constant, the 100 percent increase from 250 to 500 reflects an actual increase in the rate of psychiatric referrals per hundred court cases. See "Statistik über diejenigen Personen welche in den Jahren 1895–1897 bzw. 1898–1900 auf Grund des Par. 81 der Strafprozessordnung . . . in Folge Anordnung des Gerichts zur Vorbereitung eines Gutachtens über ihren Geisteszustand in öffentlichen Irrenanstalten beobachtet worden sind," *AZP* 60 (1903): 637–38; "Nachweisung derjenigen Personen, welche 1901–1903 auf Grund des Par. 81 der Strafprozessordnung . . . infolge Anordnung des Gerichts zur Vorbereitung eines Gutachtens über ihren Geisteszustand in öffentlichen und Privatirrenanstalten beobachtet worden sind," *AZP* 62 (1905): 123; same statistics for 1904–5 in *AZP* 63 (1906): 764–65; for 1906–8 in *AZP* 67 (1910): 172–73; for 1909–11 in *AZP* 70 (1913): 654–55. For a brief analysis of the 1895–1905 figures and figures for the population increase, see *AZP* 65 (1908): 854. For the German crime rate, see Eric Johnson, "The Roots of Crime in Imperial Germany," *Central European History* 15 (1982): table 1, 358.

led to reduced sentences, the justice system was perceived as operating at the expense of public safety.[17]

For years Liszt and his fellow reformers had been pointing to the high proportion of repeat offenders as evidence that fixed prison sentences were unable to prevent many convicts from committing new crimes. But their argument had failed to convince the legal profession, the general public, or the government to endorse the indefinite detention of repeat offenders. Now, however, the image of the mentally deficient offender provoked anxieties that the ordinary multiple recidivist had never evoked. The same people who had been content to see hardened repeat offenders released after limited sentences suddenly became worried about the release of *Minderwertige* who were only first-time offenders. The idea of pathological factors playing a role—no matter how slight—in criminal behavior proved far more unsettling to the public than sociological or statistical evidence on the high incidence of recidivism among "normal" offenders. Liszt and his fellow reformers were quick to seize this opportunity to advance their cause.

Because the mental condition of *Minderwertige* was impaired without qualifying as full-fledged insanity, the ensuing debates about their legal treatment revived an older debate about diminished responsibility (*verminderte Zurechnungsfähigkeit*). This earlier debate had turned on the question of whether the criminal code should supplement the binary distinction under which defendants were either legally responsible or irresponsible by reintroducing an intermediate category of partial responsibility, which had a long history in German law. Before German unification in 1871, the penal codes of most German states had recognized an intermediate state of diminished responsibility and granted those who qualified for this category reductions in their sentences. When the new Penal Code for the North German Confederation and subsequently for the unified Reich was prepared in 1869–71, the advisory medical commission strongly recommended that this category be included. But because the Imperial German Penal Code was closely modeled on the Prussian code, which contained no such category, the final version of the new code did not recognize diminished responsibility. Under the imperial code, forensic experts were forced to declare the defendant either fully responsible or not responsible at all. In practice, if they found the accused to be mentally deficient, they could mention this, and if the offense in question allowed for extenuating circumstances, judges might

17. Prominent court cases that provoked this public criticism included the Dippold and Arenberg trials. See Woldemar von Rohland, "Der Prozess Dippold: Eine juristische Betrachtung," *DJZ* 8 (1903): 486–88; Carl Pelman, "Bemerkungen zu dem Prozesse des Prinzen Prosper Arenberg," *MKS* 1 (1904): 60–63.

take it into consideration. But the psychiatric expert was still obliged to give a yes or no answer to the question of legal responsibility, and many felonies did not allow for extenuating circumstances.[18]

The majority of the psychiatric profession was unhappy with this situation from the start. The Association of German Psychiatrists took up the issue of diminished responsibility in 1887 and 1888 but decided not to petition the authorities because recent antipsychiatric comments suggested that government and parliament were hostile to psychiatric influence in the courtroom.[19] Barely ten years later, in the mid-1890s, Liszt's almost immediate success in launching a debate over the introduction of diminished responsibility reflected a changed climate, in which an increasing number of people began to think that the legal system's treatment of *minderwertige* offenders did not adequately protect the public.

In his aforementioned lecture at the International Congress of Psychology in Munich in 1896, Liszt called attention to the legal treatment of mentally deficient criminals by presenting a hypothetical scenario closely modeled on a recent case.[20] A teenage girl had killed a young child in her care so she could steal its earrings to get money for candy. The judges considered her legally responsible. But since she appeared to be suffering from mental deficiencies, they reduced her punishment to a couple of years in prison. The prison term, Liszt suggested, would not do anything to remedy her disturbed mental condition, and all too soon she would be "let loose" on society again "like a wild animal." In such cases, Liszt pointed out, the logic of retributive justice, which demanded lenience for those whose judgment was impaired, was diametrically opposed to society's need for protection. Liszt therefore demanded that if a mentally deficient offender had proven his or her dangerousness by committing a crime, he or she should be interned until the condition of dangerousness

18. On the legal history of the concept of diminished responsibility, see Wilhelm Kahl, "Gutachten über die strafrechtliche Behandlung der geistig Minderwerten," *Verhandlungen des siebenundzwanzigsten Deutschen Juristentages,* 4 vols. (Berlin: Guttentag, 1904), 1:138–84, esp. 152–55, 196–201; Alfred Gottschalk, ed., *Materialien zur Lehre von der verminderten Zurechnungsfähigkeit* (Berlin: Guttentag, 1904), 24–25, 112–21; F. Jolly, "Über geminderte Zurechnungsfähigkeit," *AZP* 44 (1888): 461–78; Albert Weingart, "Die verminderte Zurechnungsfähigkeit," *ZStW* 19 (1899): 136–39; Erardo Rautenberg, *Verminderte Schuldfähigkeit: Ein besonderer, fakultativer Strafmilderungsgrund?* (Heidelberg: Kriminalistik Verlag, 1984).

19. Jolly, "Über geminderte Zurechnungsfähigkeit"; "Bericht der Commission über den in der vorjährigen Sitzung gehaltenen Vortrag 'Über geminderte Zurechnungsfähigkeit,' " *AZP* 45 (1889): 524–47 (Report presented at the annual meeting of the Verein der deutschen Irrenärzte, Bonn, 16–17 September 1888).

20. Based on the Marie Schneider case. See Josef Metzger, "Zur Lehre von den Degenerationszeichen," *AZP* 45 (1889): 34.

had ceased. Since mentally deficient people were ill, they were to be exempt from punishment and interned in medical institutions. In fact, the measures Liszt recommended for mentally deficient offenders were no different from those he had recommended for all offenders: corrective rather than punitive treatment based on dangerousness rather than guilt. But while he knew that he could not implement these new principles for the entire criminal justice system, he hoped that they might be accepted for a category of offenders whose mental condition made them appear at once less responsible and more dangerous.[21]

Liszt's call for new provisions for the treatment of *minderwertige* offenders quickly sparked a series of debates and proposals. In 1898 the Forensic-Psychiatric Association of Dresden, a local society of lawyers and psychiatrists founded in 1894, produced the first draft law on diminished responsibility, which contained three main provisions. First, "offenders who at the time of the offense were in a state in which the [free] determination of their will was not excluded, but considerably limited" should benefit from the same reductions in sentences as juvenile offenders.[22] Second, because the "iron discipline" of German prisons harmed *Minderwertige*, they would serve their sentences in special institutions under the close supervision of a psychiatrist. Third, if an offender's condition of diminished responsibility was chronic and previous convictions made future offenses likely, the offender would remain interned beyond the end of the sentence for as long as there was a danger that he or she would commit future offenses. The association indicated that it expected a high proportion of "incorrigible multiple recidivists" to fall into this category.[23]

Contemporary German law and practice did not ignore the need to protect society against potentially dangerous lunatics, including those who were acquitted in a court of law. But this was a matter for the regional police authorities, who frequently took no action. What was new and significant about the Forensic-Psychiatric Association's proposal was the desire to have the mentally deficient subjected to the same measures as the insane and not to leave this matter to the police or to the medical authorities but to give the criminal court the means to press the matter before a guardianship court.[24]

21. Liszt, "Die strafrechtliche Zurechnungsfähigkeit," 222–25.
22. Proceedings of the Forensisch-psychiatrische Vereinigung zu Dresden's twenty-eighth meeting on 29 April 1897, thirtieth meeting on 17 June 1897, and thirty-ninth meeting on 30 June 1898, published in *AZP* 56 (1899): 442–47, 451–52.
23. Proceedings of the Forensisch-psychiatrische Vereinigung zu Dresden's thirty-ninth meeting on 30 June 1898 in *AZP* 56 (1899): 451–52; Georg Ilberg, "Über verminderte Zurechnungsfähigkeit," *AZP* 56 (1899): 474–84; Weingart, "Die verminderte Zurechnungsfähigkeit," 133–48.
24. On the problems of German administrative practice regarding acquitted *gemeingefähr-*

The Forensic-Psychiatric Association's proposal attempted to reconcile the potentially contradictory demands for retributive justice, medical treatment, and the protection of society. The retributivist concern with doing justice to the diminished guilt of *minderwertige* offenders found its expression in the proposed reduction of their sentences. The contradiction between punishment and medical treatment was formally resolved by combining both purposes in hybrid penal-medical institutions. And the protection of society was addressed by providing for the indefinite detention of *minderwertige* offenders who appeared to pose a permanent threat. The association's recommendation to punish, treat, and indefinitely intern the mentally deficient offender in a single hybrid institution shows the extent to which the boundaries between the administration of justice, the exercise of police powers, and medical treatment were becoming blurred.

The IKV Debate over the Treatment of *Minderwertige*

The publication of the Forensic-Psychiatric Association's proposal in major legal, psychiatric, and general periodicals in 1898–99 placed the issue of diminished responsibility and the treatment of *Minderwertige* on the agenda of various national associations, including the Association of German Psychiatrists, the Rheinisch-Westfälische Gefängnisgesellschaft (a prison reform association), and the association of penal reformers, the German section of the IKV.[25]

The German section of the IKV, which included jurists, police, and prison officials, as well as psychiatrists interested in penal reform, took up the issue of diminished responsibility at its annual meeting in Dresden in 1903. Here the question of how *minderwertige* criminals should be treated received three dif-

---

liche lunatics and *Minderwertige*, see Karl Krohne's comments in *MIKV* 12 (1905): 270; Felix Delbrück, "Zum Schutz der Gesellschaft gegen gemeingefährliche Geisteskranke und vermindert Zurechnungsfähige," *MKS* 1 (1904): 121–23.

25. The articles placed by the Dresden Association were Ilberg, "Über verminderte Zurechnungsfähigkeit," and Weingart, "Die verminderte Zurechnungsfähigkeit." On the annual meetings, see Wollenberg, "Die Grenzen der strafrechtlichen Zurechnungsfähigkeit bei psychischen Krankheitszuständen," *AZP* 56 (1899): 615–37 (lecture at the meeting of the Verein der deutschen Irrenärzte, Halle, 21–22 April 1899); Carl Pelman and Karl Finkelnburg, *Die verminderte Zurechnungsfähigkeit* (Bonn: Röhrscheid und Ebbecke, 1903) (lectures at the meeting of the Rheinisch Westfälische Gefängnisgesellschaft in 1902); Felix Delbrück, "Die vermindert Zurechnungsfähigen und deren Verpflegung in besonderen Anstalten," *MIKV* 10 (1902): 628–48 (lecture at the IKV Landesversammlung in Bremen in 1902). For other evidence of renewed interest in the topic, see Albert von Schrenck-Notzing, "Die Frage nach der verminderten Zurechnungsfähigkeit, ihre Entwicklung und ihr gegenwärtiger Standpunkt und eigene Beobachtungen," *AKK* 8 (1901): 57–83; Gerlach, "Zur Revision des deutschen Strafgesetzbuches," *AZP* 60 (1903): 673–83; Carl Pelman, "Strafrecht und verminderte Zurechnungsfähigkeit," *Politisch-Anthropologische Revue* 2 (1903–4): 63–72.

ferent answers. F. Leppmann, chief physician at the Moabit prison in Berlin and editor of the *Ärztliche Sachverständigen-Zeitung*, took the radical position that *minderwertige* offenders should not be punished at all but immediately placed in a medical institution for treatment and care until they were no longer considered dangerous. Leppmann insisted that this internment must take place outside the framework of the criminal justice system because "otherwise it could happen that instead of being sentenced to three years in a prison, someone will be sentenced to three years in an asylum. This would lead to a confusion of the public sense of law." By contrast, Dr. Delbrück, director of the Bremen insane asylum, defended the Forensic-Psychiatric Association's proposal that *minderwertige* offenders should be placed in special hybrid institutions where they would be subject to punishment and treatment simultaneously and, if they appeared prone to commit future crimes, to indefinite preventive detention. Finally, Liszt argued that punishment and treatment should be combined sequentially. The mentally deficient offender would first serve a reduced sentence, under medical supervision if necessary, but in a regular penal institution. Then, if the offender appeared dangerous, this punishment would be followed by internment in a medical asylum. The meeting endorsed Liszt's position and set up a small commission, including Leppmann, Delbrück, and Liszt, that was to prepare a draft law to be presented at its next annual meeting.[26]

While the IKV commission embarked on its work in the fall of 1903, a nationally publicized trial taking place in Bayreuth brought the problem of the legal treatment of *geistig Minderwertige* to public attention. A young boy had died as a result of months of cruel physical abuse by his tutor, a twenty-four-year-old student by the name of Dippold, who was brought to trial. A psychiatric examination suggested that the accused was *minderwertig* and this deficiency appeared to be the main reason why the court condemned him to only eight years of prison instead of the maximum sentence of fifteen.

Parts of the public were outraged, especially in conservative quarters, not because they doubted that the accused was in fact *minderwertig* but because the sentence seemed too light given the cruelty of the crime and the danger the culprit might pose in the future. In a prominent law journal, Woldemar von Rohland, a conservative retributivist law professor, criticized the verdict as much too lenient, even though he did not doubt that the accused suffered from a

26. Proceedings of the Ninth Landesversammlung der deutschen Gruppe der IKV in Dresden, 4–7 June 1903, in *MIKV* 11 (1904): 593–613. See also F. Leppmann, "Die Eigenart des heutigen gewerbsmässigen Verbrechertums," *MIKV* 9 (1901): 149–71 (lecture at the IKV Landesversammlung in Strassburg in 1900), and Delbrück, "Die vermindert Zurechnungsfähigen."

mental deficiency. Rohland argued that the brutality of the crime demanded the imposition of the maximum sentence, which should be further aggravated by hunger rations and corporal punishment. Finally, Rohland claimed that public demands for a more severe punishment in this case proved that the public's sense of justice was rooted in a strong belief in retribution rather than in the modern school's utilitarian idea of protecting society.[27]

Liszt responded by pointing out that it was precisely the logic of retributive justice that demanded lesser punishment for those whose mental capacities were impaired. The modern school, by contrast, determined punitive measures strictly on the basis of the individual's future dangerousness, without regard to past offenses or legal responsibility. Was not the courts' lenience in cases involving *Minderwertige* like Dippold the best evidence for the bankruptcy of retributive justice and the soundness of the social defensist approach? After all, Liszt argued, the fact that Rohland and the Bayreuth court disagreed on the correct punishment—the former pointing to the brutality of the deed, the latter to extenuating factors in the person of the criminal—showed that the retribution principle was unable to generate criteria for sentencing. Never one to mince words, Liszt concluded:

> Confidently, we may present everyone whom book-learning has not deprived of common sense with the choice: on the one hand we have the adherents of retribution, who keep a man like Dippold in prison for years, aggravate the sentence with corporal punishment and then, after the end of the sentence, let him loose on human society like a wild animal; on the other hand we have the adherents of protective punishment who incapacitate dangerous *Minderwertige* and thereby protect society from them and protect them from themselves.[28]

In the spring of 1904, by mandate of the IKV commission, Liszt published a draft law on diminished responsibility that spelled out the sequential solution

27. Rohland, "Der Prozess Dippold." For a prominent psychiatrist's view of the trial, see Paul Näcke, "Forensisch-psychiatrisch-psychologische Randglossen zum Prozesse Dippold, insbesondere über den Sadismus," *AKK* 13 (1903): 350–72. The psychiatric expert declared Dippold "geistig minderwertig" but legally responsible (ibid., 354). The court did not explicitly refer to the defendant's *Minderwertigkeit* as one of the extenuating reasons. Von Rohland therefore denied that it had played any role.

28. Liszt, "Nochmals zum Falle Dippold," *DJZ* 8 (1903): 541. Similar points were made by Liszt's former student Professor Eduard Kohlrausch in "Der Kampf der Kriminalistenschulen im Lichte des Falles Dippold," *MKS* 1 (1904): 16–25. For the rest of the controversy in the pages of the *DJZ*, see Carl Stooß, "Zum Falle Dippold," *DJZ* 8 (1903): 517–18, and Moritz Liepmann, "Vergeltungsstrafe und Zweckstrafe," *DJZ* 9 (1904): 93–98.

that he had proposed the previous year. All *minderwertige* offenders would first serve a reduced punishment; then those who appeared prone to commit further crimes would be subject to indefinite internment in a medical institution. Whereas previous proposals had restricted indefinite preventive detention to *Minderwertige* with several previous convictions, Liszt's draft dropped the recidivism requirement and extended this highly interventionist measure to all who were considered "dangerous," that is, likely to commit future crimes.[29] Even more drastically, Liszt's draft proposed to extend the imposition of preventive detention to *geistig Minderwertige* who had *not* committed any crime by making "proneness to commit crimes due to mental deficiency" a sufficient reason for the state to intern an individual.

It can be argued that this demand took the principle of social protection to its logical extreme. If society's protective measures should depend on an individual's future dangerousness, why wait until people had committed a crime? Because he was a liberal, however, Liszt was concerned about the threat that such a provision might pose to civil liberties and therefore proposed that preventive detention could be ordered only by a civil guardianship court in a regular court procedure declaring legal incompetence.[30]

When he presented his draft law to the annual meeting of the German section of the IKV in Stuttgart in June 1904, Liszt said that he expected that his proposal to extend preventive detention to nondelinquents would provoke lively controversy. In fact, however, this aspect of Liszt's proposal failed to arouse any opposition at all, thereby demonstrating the extent to which the penal reform community, including both jurists and psychiatrists, was willing to curtail individual rights in order to improve the protection of society. On the medical side, this attitude showed that many psychiatrists no longer saw their primary function as helping the sick individual but as protecting the health and

29. Subsequent discussions suggested that Liszt and others considered the majority of *minderwertige* offenders to fall into this "dangerous" category. See Karl Krohne's statement in *MIKV* 12 (1905): 269.

30. Franz von Liszt, "Vorentwurf eines Gesetzes betreffend die Verwahrung gemeingefährlicher Geisteskranker und vermindert Zurechnungsfähiger," *Ärztliche Sachverständigenzeitung* (15 January 1904 and 14 February 1904); Liszt, "Entwurf eines Gesetzes betreffend die Verwahrung gemeingefährlicher Geisteskranker und vermindert Zurechnungsfähiger," *MIKV* 11 (March 1904): 637–58; Liszt, "Schutz der Gesellschaft gegen gemeingefährliche Geisteskranke und vermindert Zurechnungsfähige," *MKS* 1 (1904): 8–15. See also Friedrich Oetker, "Entwurf eines Reichsgesetzes, betreffend die vorläufige Verwahrung und die Internierung gemeingefährlicher Geisteskranker und die Bestrafung, vorläufige Verwahrung und Internierung im Falle geminderter Schuldfähigkeit," *MIKV* 12 (1905): 58–75. Liszt and the IKV also organized a bibliography and anthology of materials on the issue that was published as Gottschalk, *Materialien zur Lehre von der verminderten Zurechnungsfähigkeit.*

safety of society as a whole.[31] Among the reformist criminal jurists, most of whom were liberals, this attitude reflected a similar shift from liberals' primary focus on individual liberty to a much greater concern with the protection of society. As Liszt's own concerns showed, this did not mean that the reformers were willing to abandon basic guarantees for civil liberty; it did mean that they were willing to give the state significantly more power.

The discussion of Liszt's proposals at the 1904 IKV meeting also revealed an interesting disagreement about the role of humanitarian considerations. Since retributivist critics often charged that the reformers' proposals reflected an excess of humanitarian concern for the criminal, Liszt saw his proposal as the perfect opportunity to demonstrate that the modern school was tougher on crime than the retributivists. His proposed measures against *Minderwertige*, he argued, intervened so deeply in people's lives that one could hardly speak of humanitarianism.[32] The meeting's second speaker, however, disagreed with Liszt and thereby revealed the existence of a self-consciously humanitarian tradition within the penal reform movement emanating from the prison reform movement. Karl Krohne, chief of the Bureau of Prisons in the Prussian Ministry of the Interior and a founding member of the IKV, argued that indefinite preventive detention of *minderwertige* offenders should indeed be seen as a humanitarian act of charity because

> our society treats these people cruelly. The poor relief administration tries to shove them off on the police, and vice versa; [left to their own devices] they commit a crime and are thrown into jail. The [local] poor relief administration is jubilant: they are behind bars . . . and the [central] justice administration has to bear the cost. . . . Out of prison, they become vagabonds and are soon thrown into a house of correction . . . they are shoved around so much that their condition deteriorates and they become more and more *minderwertig*.

Therefore, Krohne concluded, indefinite detention would indeed be more humane.[33]

The major point of dispute at the IKV's 1904 meeting concerned the question of whether habitual criminals should be eligible for the proposed provisions.

31. See Heinz-Peter Schmiedebach, "The Mentally Ill Patient Caught between the State's Demands and the Professional Interests of Psychiatrists," in *Medicine and Modernity: Public Health and Medical Care in Nineteenth- and Twentieth-Century Germany*, ed. Manfred Berg and Geoffrey Cocks (Cambridge: Cambridge University Press, 1997), 99–119.
32. Proceedings of the Tenth Landesversammlung of the Deutsche Landesgruppe of the IKV in Stuttgart, 25–28 May 1904, in *MIKV* 12 (1905): 264–86, esp. 267–68.
33. Ibid., 267–68.

Liszt's draft provisions were to apply if an offender's "legal responsibility is not excluded but considerably diminished," and his draft referred to the persons in question as "individuals with diminished responsibility."[34] Karl Krohne objected that the term "diminished responsibility" lacked a clear legal or medical definition and therefore proposed the use of the medical term *geistige Minderwertigkeit*. The special provisions under consideration should apply, he suggested, "if the offender was in a continuing state of *geistige Minderwertigkeit* that diminished his understanding of provisions of the penal code or his resistance against criminal actions." This suggestion provoked a strong objection from Liszt, who argued that Krohne's formulation would include habitual criminals, whose resistance to criminal impulses was undoubtedly reduced. But did anyone, Liszt asked, want habitual criminals to benefit from the provisions of the draft law, such as reduced punishments? Liszt made it clear that he did not.[35]

Gustav Aschaffenburg shared Liszt's objection and used his medical authority to confirm Liszt's hypothesis that a formulation in terms of *geistige Minderwertigkeit* would include habitual criminals:

A close intellectual examination and psychological analysis of our criminals shows us that almost all of them are intellectually inferior to the average general population, and often considerably so. We notice further that they are unstable and easily influenced . . . in short we cannot deny that all of them are *geistig minderwertig* in comparison with the healthy members of the same occupational groups. A question raised by the defense in this respect would therefore almost always have to be answered in the affirmative, but this is hardly what we want to achieve.[36]

Convinced that most habitual criminals were *minderwertig*, Aschaffenburg and Liszt tried to introduce subtle distinctions between two different kinds of *Minderwertigkeit* to exclude habitual criminals from the benefits of the proposed law. Aschaffenburg suggested that only truly "pathological" *Minderwertigkeit* should qualify for reduced sentences, while *Minderwertigkeit* resulting from bad upbringing or other social circumstances should not qualify. Liszt explained the distinction as follows:

We can imagine that there is diminished responsibility due to external influences, as a result of the [offender's] entire previous life, as a result of parental neglect in his childhood and youth, as a result of bad company into which he

34. Liszt, "Entwurf eines Gesetzes," 640.
35. Proceedings of the Tenth Landesversammlung, 268–69, 274.
36. Ibid., 275–76.

might have fallen as an adult, of the later conduct of his life, his many previous convictions, for instance. And if it was these external influences that gradually diminished his responsibility, if, that is, we are dealing with an incorrigible recidivist, then these are not the people I have in mind [as beneficiaries of the proposed law].[37]

Instead, the special provisions of his draft law would apply only to persons whose responsibility was diminished by "intrinsic influences," namely, as a result of a "congenital or acquired physiological and psychological condition."[38]

Since the notion of *Minderwertigkeit* was based on degeneration theory, which combined heredity and milieu as inextricable factors in the degeneration process, this distinction between pathological and nonpathological, or intrinsic and extrinsic, forms of *Minderwertigkeit* or diminished responsibility was fundamentally flawed. Most IKV members at the meeting seem to have sensed this problem and rejected Aschaffenburg's proposal to adopt the term "pathological *Minderwertigkeit*." Nevertheless, by rejecting Krohne's proposal to use the term *Minderwertigkeit* and endorsing Liszt's original formulation of diminished responsibility, the overwhelming majority of the assembly expressed agreement with Liszt's position that habitual criminals were to be excluded from the provisions of the law. The attempt to exclude habitual criminals was surprising because one would have thought that reformers like Liszt would have been eager to extend the innovations of the proposal to as large a category of criminals as possible. After all, the proposal basically reflected what they demanded for all criminals: indefinite detention based on dangerousness. Instead, we are left to conclude that the reformers remained caught in the logic of retribution and did not want the sentences of habitual criminals to be reduced. As a result, they attempted to reimpose notions of responsibility onto the medical paradigm of *Minderwertigkeit*. Members of the criminal underclass, whose *Minderwertigkeit* appeared as a result of their milieu, were to bear full responsibility for their mental deficiency and its consequences.

Liszt's proposal was unanimously adopted by the IKV assembly, which resolved to petition the upper and lower houses of the German parliament (Bundesrat and Reichstag) to prepare a new law on the basis of the draft.[39] Outside the IKV, however, Liszt's proposal met with two different kinds of criticism. The

37. Quote from Liszt explaining the limitation of his proposal to people "à responsabilité atténué par influences d'ordre intrinsèque" at the Tenth International Meeting of the IKV in Hamburg, 12–15 September 1905, as reported in the proceedings in *MIKV* 13 (1906): 474–75.
38. Ibid.
39. Proceedings of the Tenth Landesversammlung, 265–66, 285–86.

psychiatrist Eugen Bleuler, whose book on the born criminal was discussed earlier, attacked Liszt's proposal to subject *minderwertige* offenders to a reduced punishment before placing them in a medical institution. Liszt himself had admitted that this combination of punishment and treatment was an inconsistent compromise with retributivism, but he defended it as a necessary concession to the reigning popular conception of justice.[40] Bleuler, however, argued that the punishment would harm most mentally deficient offenders and therefore insisted that *Minderwertige* should not be punished at all but immediately treated as sick people and placed in an asylum. Since their permanent detention in a medical facility would protect society, Bleuler did not see why public opinion would be opposed to this solution.[41]

If the psychiatrist Bleuler criticized Liszt for not going far enough, the public prosecutor Hugo Högel questioned whether *Minderwertige* should be privileged at all. Högel agreed with the reformers that the distinction between sanity and insanity was not clear-cut and that there were many people whose intellect and willpower were underdeveloped. But why, Högel asked, should pathological mental deficiency be privileged over other extenuating circumstances such as enticement, need, occasion, or excitement? Högel was challenging the assumption that even minor mental pathologies justified a reduction in punishment that external circumstances such as dire need did not.[42] The fact that Högel was the only one to question this assumption throughout these debates demonstrates that the special status of insanity in the prevailing system of retributive justice still exerted a powerful effect on the penal reform movement. For in the existing retributive system the criminal could be exempt from legal responsibility and punishment only on grounds of mental disorder. External factors such as material need, no matter how serious, could never exempt the offender from responsibility but only diminish his guilt and reduce his sentence. Although one might have thought that the reformers' view that criminal behavior was determined by both biological and social factors would have led them to challenge the special status of mental pathology, they, too, continued to privilege the exculpatory potential of biological factors.

The Juristentag Debate over the Treatment of *Minderwertige*

In September 1904, the issue of the legal treatment of *minderwertige* offenders was taken up by the Twenty-seventh Deutscher Juristentag, the biennial meet-

40. Liszt, "Schutz der Gesellschaft gegen gemeingefährliche Geisteskranke."
41. Eugen Bleuler, "Zur Behandlung Gemeingefährlicher," *MKS* 1 (1904): 92–99.
42. Hugo Högel, "Die Behandlung der Minderwertigen," *MKS* 1 (1904): 333–40.

ing of the German legal profession. This in itself was a sign that the impact of criminal-psychological research had spread beyond the circle of penal reformers to the legal profession at large. For unlike the IKV, which was an organization of committed penal reformers, the Juristentag represented the entire German legal profession, many of whom were advocates of retributive justice opposed to Liszt's modern school. Before the meeting, Wilhelm Kahl, a colleague of Liszt's on the law faculty of the University of Berlin and a moderate retributivist, prepared a lengthy written report on the legal treatment of *Minderwertige*. Kahl agreed with the reformers that the goal of reform did not lie so much in reducing sentences for *Minderwertige*—although that would be part of it—but in individualizing punishment according to the special medical needs of the mentally deficient and, in many cases, supplementing their punishment with an indefinite detention that would combine medical treatment with the protection of society. Coming from a prominent, if moderate, member of the retributivist camp, this statement showed the extent to which mainstream legal circles had come to accept criminal psychology's claim that there was a high incidence of mentally deficient criminals and the reformers' call for preventive measures based on an offender's dangerousness.

Kahl's proposal was an implicit response to Bleuler and other critics of Liszt's IKV draft, who had charged that it was unacceptable first to imprison *Minderwertige* on the grounds that they were healthy enough to serve a regular sentence and then to intern them on the grounds that their medical condition posed a public threat. To avoid this contradiction Kahl proposed dividing *minderwertige* offenders into two categories: those who were capable of serving a regular prison sentence and not in need of additional detention; and those who were incapable of serving a regular sentence and also required indefinite preventive detention on account of their dangerousness and medical condition. The first category would serve their reduced sentences in a regular prison and then be released. The second category would immediately be placed in hybrid penal-medical institutions where they would remain as long as they appeared dangerous.[43]

The amalgamation of punishment and treatment for the second category was strongly criticized by the psychiatrist Leppmann, who reiterated the point he had made at the 1903 meeting of the IKV. Kahl's hybrid institutions, Leppmann charged in his report for the Juristentag, would create "second-class patients." That certain *minderwertige* offenders should, after having served their sentence,

---

43. Kahl, "Gutachten über die strafrechtliche Behandlung der geistig Minderwerten," 1:137–248, esp. 141, 199, 208, 233, 236, 247.

remain indefinitely interned in the same institution reflected a dangerous confusion of penal and medical measures. According to Leppmann, mentally deficient offenders should either immediately be placed in an insane asylum or at the very least serve their sentence in a penal institution and then be transferred to an asylum.[44]

Leppmann's insistence on a strict distinction between punishment and medical treatment was a mild criticism compared to the hostility toward criminal justice that was voiced by the two most prominent psychiatrists present at the Juristentag's meeting in Innsbruck. August Cramer, professor of psychiatry and director of the psychiatric hospital in Göttingen, frankly admitted that as a man of science he was a strict determinist and would like to see criminal justice and punishment totally abolished. Since this statement implied that all forms of deviance should be treated rather than punished, one would have expected Cramer to argue that *minderwertige* offenders should be exempt from punishment and immediately placed in medical institutions. On the contrary, however, Cramer insisted on a categorical distinction between delinquent and nondelinquent lunatics and strongly protested against Leppmann's suggestion that they be interned in regular insane asylums. "Is it not a slap in the face for modern science and its achievements," he asked, "if lunatics are to be interned in the same fashion as criminals?" If mentally deficient criminals were to be interned together with regular lunatics, this would not only reverse what little progress had been made in convincing the public that asylums were hospitals and not prisons but "would be a return to the dark ages."[45]

To some extent, the disagreement between Leppmann and Cramer reflected a conflict between different segments of the psychiatric profession. Prison psychiatrists like Leppmann hailed the transfer of *minderwertige* prisoners to insane asylums as a victory for psychiatry, while psychiatrists working in asylums and psychiatric hospitals, like Cramer, were naturally more ambivalent about these new arrivals. It was ironic that just at the moment when psychiatry's claim that *minderwertige* offenders ought to receive medical treatment rather than punishment was about to be recognized, psychiatrists like Cramer worried that this new category of deviants might taint psychiatric institutions with the stigma of criminality.

Emil Kraepelin, the other prominent psychiatrist speaking at the Juristentag, was not plagued by Cramer's worries about the public image of insane asylums.

44. F. Leppmann, "Gutachten über die strafrechtliche Behandlung der geistig Minderwerten," in *Verhandlungen des siebenundzwanzigsten Deutschen Juristentages*, 3:136–52.

45. *Verhandlungen des siebenundzwanzigsten Deutschen Juristentages*, 4:408–17. See also A. Finger's critical report in *Gerichtssaal* 65 (1905): 145–50.

Like Bleuler and Leppmann, Kraepelin attacked Kahl's combination of punishment and treatment in hybrid institutions as inconsistent and untenable. "Either [*minderwertige* criminals] are in need of special treatment, in which case it is only reasonable to apply this treatment from the outset, instead of administering a kind of sham punishment. Or one decides to punish them just like others, in which case one cannot justify detention after the sentence is served." Needless to say, Kraepelin advocated the first option.

After noting the similarity that the present proposals bore to some of the suggestions he had made in his book *Die Abschaffung des Strafmaßes* (On the abolition of fixed punishments) more then twenty-four years before, Kraepelin expressed confidence that the current reform proposals would set a trend toward a fundamental transformation of criminal justice. The nonpunitive approach from which full-fledged lunatics had first benefited and which was now being extended to *Minderwertige* would soon infuse all of criminal justice with a new spirit. "The more or less arbitrary boundary between full and diminished legal responsibility will become more and more blurred, and we will recognize how little responsibility any offender bears when we examine his descent, his congenital predisposition, his development, the influence of his environment, the events of his life, and his entire physical and mental personality." At that point, Kraepelin hoped, perhaps the idea of "replacing the fixed measure of pain with the free use of the state's powers in order to combat criminal inclinations in a given person" would triumph. The very fact that a psychiatrist could deliver such a speech at the foremost convention of the German legal profession and be received with applause showed how much the reformers had changed the climate since the first appearance of Liszt's and Kraepelin's provocative treatises almost twenty-five years earlier.[46]

In the discussion that followed, Kraepelin's objection to the conflation of treatment and punishment in Kahl's proposal found an unlikely ally in the retributivist A. Finger, professor of criminal law in Halle. Like Kraepelin, Finger argued for a clear-cut dichotomy: either the criminal act derived from a pathological disorder, in which case the offender was legally irresponsible and could not be punished, or the act was not caused by pathological factors, in which case the offender was legally responsible and would have to be sentenced to the full punishment. Insisting on this strict distinction, Finger rejected the notion of diminished responsibility. If the offender suffered from any pathological mental deficiencies whatsoever, he should bear no legal responsibility. *Minderwer-*

---

46. *Verhandlungen des siebenundzwanzigsten Deutschen Juristentages*, 4:418–34, quotes on 422, 431, 426.

tige offenders, he therefore argued, should not be punished but subjected to whatever preventive measures were necessary to protect society.

Although it seems odd, it was no accident that the retributivist Finger and Kraepelin, the radical critic of criminal justice, agreed that punishment and treatment were incompatible. Both took the meaning of the terms seriously. Kraepelin explained that punishment was by definition limited in time and could not be individualized, while medical treatment was by definition indefinite and highly individualized. Agreeing with this distinction, Finger feared that once the concept of punishment was filled with medical content, the door would be opened to a gradual medicalization of criminal justice. In Finger's view, the blurring of the boundaries between law, police, and medicine that was reflected in Kahl's hybrid penal-medical institutions might be much more dangerous than clear-cut concessions to medicine that left the boundaries intact.[47]

Finger's and Kraepelin's proposal that *minderwertige* offenders receive only medical treatment without any punishment was defeated at the Juristentag. Leppmann succeeded in convincing Kahl to drop the combination of punishment and treatment in hybrid penal-medical institutions. Instead, "dangerous" *minderwertige* offenders would serve their prison sentences before being indefinitely interned in an insane asylum. Adopted in this form, the Juristentag's proposal closely resembled Liszt's proposal that the German section of the IKV had accepted three months earlier. The recommendations of the Juristentag and the IKV did not result in immediate special legislation on the legal treatment of *Minderwertige* because the Reich Justice Ministry as well as the Prussian Justice Ministry opposed such legislation. The IKV petition included the immediate demand that all current *minderwertige* prisoners be placed under the supervision of a physician, who should, if necessary, be able to demand their removal from prison to an asylum.[48] When the Reich Justice Ministry solicited reactions to this proposal, the Prussian Ministry of Justice, which had authority over most of Prussia's prisons, responded that the notion of *geistige Minderwertigkeit* was not "sufficiently clarified" to serve as the basis for penal administration and that giving prison doctors authority over the treatment of prisoners would be an "unjustified deviation from established principles of administration."[49] Even

---

47. Ibid., 4:420–21, 439–40, 448–51, 454–56, 458–59, 462; A. Finger, "Über die 'geminderte Zurechnungsfähigkeit' und die strafrechtliche Behandlung der 'gemindert Zurechnungsfähigen,' " *Gerichtssaal* 64 (1904): 257–319.

48. IKV petition to the Bundesrat, 28 February 1905, ZStA Potsdam, Rep. RJM, 6077, Bl. 65–67.

49. Letter of the Preussischer Justizminister to the Reichs-Justizamt, 26 June 1905, ZStA Potsdam, Rep. RJM, 6077, Bl. 69.

though government officials remained skeptical, the IKV and Juristentag proposals for the introduction of diminished responsibility and the special treatment of *minderwertige* offenders did provide the basis for the relevant provisions of draft penal codes prepared by official penal reform commissions between 1906 and 1914 and again in the Weimar Republic. After the comprehensive penal reform failed, diminished responsibility was finally introduced as part of the Law against Dangerous Habitual Criminals passed under the Nazi regime in November 1933. This law allowed offenders with diminished responsibility to be interned in an insane asylum "if public safety requires it"; this medical internment would supersede the offender's sentence.[50]

The turn-of-the-century debates about the legal treatment of *Minderwertige* illustrate several important points. First, the Juristentag's endorsement of Kahl's proposals for the special treatment of *Minderwertige* demonstrates that both criminal psychology and Liszt's penal reform movement had had a significant impact on the mainstream of the German legal profession. Mainstream jurists had come to agree with criminal psychologists that *Minderwertigkeit* was a significant problem among criminals and with the penal reformers that *minderwertige* offenders should receive special treatment based on their individual dangerousness. Once a general consensus that *minderwertige* offenders ought to receive special treatment had been reached, the crucial question was what form this treatment should take. The discussion of this question was dominated by three conflicting demands: the logic of retributive justice demanded that persons whose responsibility was diminished by a mental disorder should receive a reduced sentence; the recognition of their mental disorder suggested that *Minderwertige* ought to receive medical treatment; finally, the conviction that *minderwertige* offenders were more likely to offend in the future called for their indefinite detention for the protection of society.

How these contradictory demands were negotiated is instructive. Even though the psychiatrists were conspicuously silent on the question of available therapies, to their credit, most psychiatrists, including Kraepelin, Bleuler, and Leppmann, categorically insisted that *Minderwertige* should receive medical treatment and be exempt from punishment. Most retributivist jurists, however, were unwilling to allow *Minderwertige* to evade all punishment. In this situation the position adopted by Liszt and his fellow reformers was revealing. Eager

50. Leopold Schäfer, Otto Wagner, and Josef Schafheutle, eds., *Gesetz gegen gefährliche Gewohnheitsverbrecher und über Maßregeln der Sicherung und Besserung* (Berlin: Vahlen, 1934). See especially the revised articles 42b and 51. See also Lothar Gruchmann, *Justiz im Dritten Reich, 1933–1940: Anpassung und Unterwerfung in der Ära Gürtner* (Munich: Oldenbourg, 1988), 838–43.

to compromise with the retributivists, they dropped the demand for medical treatment instead of prison and agreed to let *Minderwertige* serve a reduced prison sentence in return for retributivist agreement that "dangerous" *Minderwertige* would be subject to indefinite detention after serving their sentence. The nature of this compromise demonstrates that the reformers were almost solely concerned with the protection of society rather than the welfare of the individual. The sequential solution that was adopted—imprisonment followed by indefinite detention in an asylum—effectively exposed *minderwertige* offenders to the worst of both worlds: even though their mental disorder was not considered grave enough to exempt them from imprisonment, it was considered sufficiently serious to justify their indefinite internment. In the penal reformers' agenda, the results of criminal-psychological research were primarily used to justify the expansion of state intervention, not to transform the penal sanction into a therapeutic one.

Proposals for the Surveillance and Preventive Internment of *Minderwertige*

The proposals for the indefinite internment of dangerous *minderwertige* offenders that met with widespread support among the IKV and the Juristentag were not the only penal reform proposals arising from criminal psychology's "discovery" that many criminals were *minderwertig*. As we have seen, Liszt himself called for the preventive internment of *Minderwertige* who appeared dangerous, even though they had not committed a crime. Although this demand did not make its way into the proposal passed at the Juristentag, the idea was soon revived in other quarters. Calls for more radical crime prevention strategies, including the sterilization of *Minderwertige*, soon followed.

It is easy to see how people who thought criminal behavior was biologically determined might come up with new preventive and repressive solutions to the crime problem. But as the last chapter showed, those who endorsed the notion of a born criminal represented only one strand in the contested territory of German criminal psychology. Other criminal psychologists, like Aschaffenburg and Näcke, argued that even though a majority of criminals were degenerate, criminal behavior resulted primarily from social factors. Degenerates were especially likely to become criminal, not because they were intrinsically driven to crime but because their general mental inferiority made it difficult for them to make a living. But if some degenerates turned to crime because they were unable to survive economically, was not social legislation the best way to prevent this kind of crime? And if the reason that many people became degenerate in the first place lay in environmental factors such as poor hygiene, malnutrition, and alcoholism, was not the problem of degeneration best tackled by fighting these social ills?

Gustav Aschaffenburg took this approach when he addressed the question of crime prevention at the end of his 1903 survey of criminology. The best way to prevent crime, he argued, was to combat alcoholism, create alternatives to taverns by setting up people's reading halls, build public housing, provide public assistance for the sick, the poor, and the unemployed, and promote state education for wayward children. Aschaffenburg agreed with Liszt that once a crime had occurred, the purpose of punishment should not be retribution but the protection of society through indefinite internment with the goal of rehabilitation. Aschaffenburg even insisted that a criminal's degeneration did not diminish the hope for his or her rehabilitation because what appeared to be incorrigibility was "not a consequence of an inborn criminal disposition, but merely the inability, resulting from an often inadequate constitution and education, to live under the current social conditions without interfering with the rights of others." "Why," he asked, "should a constant effort not succeed in . . . slowly educating [such people]?" Aschaffenburg made only one proposal that emphasized the medical rather than the social causes of crime: his demand that *minderwertige* offenders be treated in hybrid penal-medical institutions. With this single exception, Aschaffenburg's suggestions for combating crime did not reflect the application of medico-biological insights but the view that crime was primarily a social phenomenon.[51]

The remainder of this chapter is about how some people failed to exercise Aschaffenburg's restraint. In these people's minds, criminal psychology's finding that many criminals were degenerate meant that biology was a significant factor in criminal behavior. In that case, they reasoned, it had to be possible to combat and, more important, prevent crime by tackling its biological basis. The first step was to move against *minderwertige* nondelinquents. If many criminals were *minderwertig*, would it not be wise to keep a close watch on all *Minderwertige* and to intern those who appeared dangerous before they had the chance to commit a crime?

Since the 1904 debates about the legal treatment of *Minderwertige* in the IKV

51. Gustav Aschaffenburg, *Das Verbrechen und seine Bekämpfung: Kriminalpsychologie für Mediziner, Juristen und Soziologen, ein Beitrag zur Reform der Strafgesetzgebung* (Heidelberg: Winter, 1903), 180–246, esp. 180–88, 241–43, quote on 233.

and at the Juristentag attracted considerable attention in the general press,[52] psychiatrists, lawyers, and others who had new proposals for crime prevention seem to have found it easy to publish them in newspapers. If Liszt had focused on the preventive internment of dangerous *Minderwertige*, others took the next logical step and called for the surveillance of all mentally deficient individuals. As early as 1903 a law professor by the name of Kuhlenbeck suggested that the police ought to keep an especially close watch on the relatives of criminals.[53] In 1904, Max Flesch, a professor of medicine, proposed that the medical exams in the schools be used to detect *geistige Minderwertigkeit* and that such information should be recorded in the students' records. Even more drastically, he called for the preventive internment of mentally deficient individuals even if they did not appear dangerous. Although Flesch acknowledged that many of these individuals might never become dangerous, he justified the measure by arguing that most of them were unfit for the "struggle for existence" that faced them in freedom, so that their internment was really in their own interest. A few years later the conservative *Kreuzzeitung* demanded general surveillance of all *Minderwertige* to prevent first-time offenses.[54]

In 1905, both a judge and a psychiatrist independently advanced the idea that the criminal record registries should be used to compile information on people's mental health. Since many criminals were mentally deficient, and since everyone agreed that it was important for the judge to be alerted to a defendant's mental deficiency, why not require doctors, hospitals, asylums, and schools to report mental deficiencies to the criminal record agencies so that all relevant information would be available at trial?[55] Four years later, these proposals received institutional backing in a petition from the German association of teachers at *Hilfsschulen*, special schools for what we would call students with learning disabilities. Demonstrating that the idea of a link between mental deficiency and crime had spread far beyond the legal and psychiatric commu-

---

52. See, for instance, "Wissenschaft gegen Parteihaß," *Vorwärts* no. 123 (28 May 1904), and "Volksrecht und Juristenrecht," *Vossische Zeitung* (31 May 1904), both clippings in ZStA, Rep. RJM, Nr. 6044, Bl. 119, 122.

53. L. Kuhlenbeck, "Das Strafrecht als soziales Organ der natürlichen Auslese," *Politisch-Anthropologische Revue* 1 (1902–3), 810.

54. Max Flesch, "Schutz den Schwachsinnigen: Kriminalanthropologische Bemerkungen," Beilage zur *Allgemeinen Zeitung* (München), Nr. 139, 20 June 1904, clipping in ZStA, Rep. RJM, Nr. 6078, Bl. 11–12; "Sicherungsanstalten für geistig minderwertige Verbrecher," *Neue Preussische Zeitung*, Nr. 57, 4 February 1909, clipping ibid., Bl. 59–60.

55. Matthaei, "Erweiterung des Strafregisters," *AKK* 18 (1905): 304–12; Hirschberg, "Wie ist es zu erreichen, daß der Geisteszustand des Angeklagten mehr als bisher berücksichtigt werde?" *MKS* 2 (1905): 512–14.

nities, the association explained that it considered all of its students mentally deficient and therefore likely to come into conflict with the law—not because of a criminal inclination but because of their general intellectual and moral deficiency. To ensure that the courts would take into account their students' mental deficiency, the association proposed that judges be obliged to examine the legal responsibility of all former students of *Hilfsschulen* and to solicit an expert opinion from the schools. So the courts would have the necessary information, the association petitioned the German government to adopt a regulation that the school records of all students in *Hilfsschulen* and in state compulsory education be included in the criminal register at the time of graduation.

Although such demands undoubtedly reflected the teachers' desire to bolster their status as professional experts, the petition was also motivated by their desire to ensure that their mentally deficient students would be granted extenuating circumstances. Remarkably, the teachers did not seem to worry that the inclusion of school records in the criminal registry might be a violation of their students' rights or that it might taint their students. Instead, it was the Prussian Ministries of Justice and of the Interior who pointed out that the inclusion of these students' files in the criminal record would create a negative association between state compulsory education, *Hilfsschulen*, and punishment and that a description of these students as mentally deficient in an official record could harm them later in life. Although the petition was rejected on these grounds, the Prussian Ministry of Justice did issue a regulation recommending that if the mental health of a defendant was in doubt, the courts should inquire if the defendant had attended a *Hilfsschule* and, if so, request his or her school records.[56]

In the fall of 1913, gruesome multiple murders committed by a Württemberg teacher, whose sanity was immediately cast into doubt, provoked renewed calls for the surveillance and internment of nondelinquent *Minderwertige*. A psychiatrist by the name of Dr. G. Zehden demanded that "dangerous" forms of mental deficiency be treated like a communicable disease: "Just as we have become used to reporting every case of a communicable disease such as smallpox . . . we should also insist that all persons who have been found to be suffering

---

56. Letter of the Vorstand des Verbandes der Hilfsschulen Deutschlands to the Reichskanzler, 9 August 1909, ZStA, Rep. RJM, Nr. 6077, Bl. 86–89; letter of the Prussian Justizminister to the Reichs-Justizamt, 8 September 1910, ibid., Bl. 118; letter of the Prussian Justizminister to the Prussian Minister des Innern and Unterrichtsminister, 20 November 1909, ibid., Bl. 119–21; Ministerialverfügung vom 11. November 1910, published in *Justiz-Ministerialblatt für die preussische Gesetzgebung und Rechtspflege* 72 (18 Nov. 1910): 402, reprinted in *MKS* 7 (1910), 565–66. See also the earlier articles by the director of the *Hilfsschule* in Braunschweig: H. Kielhorn, "Die geistige Minderwertigkeit vor Gericht," *MKS* 4 (1907): 165–76; "Straffälligkeit der geistig Minderwertigen," *MKS* 7 (1910): 106–9.

from a mental illness of a dangerous character must be reported [to the authorities] by their families or doctors to ensure permanent control and surveillance." The *Braunschweigische Landeszeitung* called for the indefinite preventive internment of all mentally unbalanced people whom their colleagues, neighbors, or family suspected of someday turning violent because it was "better to keep one healthy person under suspicion without cause than to let a dangerous mentally ill person run about at large."[57]

Proposals for Sterilization

An even more radical strategy than the surveillance or preventive internment of *Minderwertige* was to prevent such persons from having offspring so that the next generation would be spared a large number of potential criminals. This was the step from social defense to eugenics. In Germany, the sterilization of degenerates, and degenerate criminals in particular, was first proposed in 1899 by the psychiatrist Paul Näcke, whose forceful criticisms of Lombroso's theories were discussed in the previous chapter. The first German works on eugenics, by Wilhelm Schallmayer and Alfred Ploetz, had appeared just a few years earlier. They had warned their readers that the modern state's humanitarian support for the weak was undermining the process of natural selection and would therefore lead to the progressive degeneration of the population.[58] While Näcke was clearly influenced by Ploetz's book and shared his eugenic concerns, he did not think that the population was progressively degenerating at present. Sharply dismissing alarmists like the journalist Max Nordau,[59] Näcke argued that there was no evidence to show that mental illness, degeneration, or crime had in-

57. Dr. G. Zehden, "Schutz gegen gemeingefährliche Geisteskranke," *Braunschweigische Landeszeitung*, 24 and 25 Sept. 1913 (clipping in ZStA, Rep. RJM, Nr. 6078, Bl. 104–5); "Die Gefahren von Geisteskranken," *Braunschweigische Landeszeitung*, 17 Sept. 1913 (clipping ibid., Bl. 101).

58. Wilhelm Schallmayer, *Über die drohende physische Entartung der Culturvölker*, 2d ed. (Berlin: Heuser, 1895); Alfred Ploetz, *Die Tüchtigkeit unserer Rasse und der Schutz der Schwachen* (Berlin: Fischer, 1895). On the early history of German eugenics, see Peter Weingart, Jürgen Kroll, and Kurt Bayertz, *Rasse, Blut und Gene: Geschichte der Eugenik und Rassenhygiene in Deutschland* (Frankfurt: Suhrkamp, 1988), esp. 36–42, 73–79; Sheila Faith Weiss, "The Race Hygiene Movement in Germany, 1904–1945," in *The Wellborn Science: Eugenics in Germany, France, Brazil and Russia*, ed. Mark Adams (New York: Oxford University Press, 1990), 8–68; Paul Weindling, *Health, Race and German Politics between National Unification and Nazism, 1870–1945* (Cambridge: Cambridge University Press, 1989). On Schallmayer, see Sheila Faith Weiss, *Race Hygiene and National Efficiency: The Eugenics of Wilhelm Schallmayer* (Berkeley: University of California Press, 1987).

59. See P. M. Baldwin, "Liberalism, Nationalism and Degeneration: The Case of Max Nordau," *Central European History* 13 (1980): 99–120.

creased in recent times. On the contrary, he considered it virtually certain that better public hygiene and the general amelioration of social conditions had improved general health. In addition, he asserted, degeneration was held in check by the extinction of some degenerate bloodlines on the one hand and by an equally powerful process of regeneration, the continuous mixing of degenerate with healthy blood, on the other. Curiously, however, after having meticulously refuted the evidence for progressive degeneration, Näcke still worried whether the forces promoting degeneration might not come to dominate in the future. Nothing could make it clearer than this paradoxical twist in Näcke's argument that the fear of increasing degeneration derived from an irrational sense of unease that was unrelated to any actual evidence about the state of public health.[60]

How, then, Näcke asked, could degeneration be counteracted? Having always insisted on the importance of social factors in the genesis of degeneration and crime, he indicated that the most obvious remedy would be "the removal of all hygienic and social ills, because ultimately every [instance of] degeneration, which then becomes hereditary, is due to these factors." But although some progress had been made on this front, Näcke immediately cautioned that the social causes of degeneration could never be completely removed so that one would have to look to "radical remedies." Here Näcke examined four possible measures. First, certain groups of degenerates, including most criminals, could be legally barred from getting married; this measure, however, would not achieve its goal because it would not prevent illegitimate offspring. Second, degenerates could be interned for as long as they were fertile. Unconcerned about the cost to individual liberty, Näcke worried about the financial costs of such a program. But at any rate, he did not think that such a measure had any political chances, although he noted that the legal reformers' demand for indefinite detention would be of great help. Third, Näcke considered the propagation of birth control, which Ploetz had recommended, but observed that current birth control devices were too expensive to be affordable for the broader masses. Finally, Näcke concluded, the only remedy that remained was sterilization, which had recently been recommended by Italian and American authors. Since neither Schallmayer nor Ploetz had recommended sterilization, Näcke's 1899 article made him the first German advocate of sterilization. The German eugenics movement, which began to take organizational shape in 1904, did not formally endorse sterilization until the 1920s.[61]

60. Paul Näcke, "Die Kastration bei gewissen Klassen von Degenerirten als ein wirksamer socialer Schutz," AKK 3 (1899): 58–69. On sterilization in Germany before 1933, see Joachim Müller, Sterilisation und Gesetzgebung bis 1933 (Husum: Matthiesen, 1985).
    61. Näcke, "Die Kastration," 69–74; Weingart, Rasse, Blut und Gene, 166, 283–91.

Näcke endorsed vasectomy as a safe and efficient procedure for men but did not find any of the available operations for women safe enough to be practiced prophylactically, so he recommended that sterilization be limited to male degenerates. Considering the legal and moral side of the matter, Näcke thought that "individual rights always have to yield to the rights of the community" and that preventing the most degenerate elements from procreating was the state's "sacred duty." If the state exercised the right to intern criminals, lunatics, and lepers, often for the duration of their lives, he insisted, "this little operation represents only a minuscule interference with individual liberties."

In Näcke's scheme, those who should be subject to sterilization included habitual criminals ("but not those that offend again because of need"), those with "pronounced criminal natures" given to violence, and habitual sex offenders, but also nondelinquents, such as imbeciles, epileptics, incurable alcoholics, severe cases of neurasthenia and hysteria, and certain cases of chronic insanity. To make sterilization more palatable, Näcke suggested that it should be introduced gradually, initially limiting it to inmates of prisons and insane asylums. Only at a later stage should the measure be extended to degenerates among the general population, who presented a greater danger because they had more occasion to procreate. In conclusion, Näcke reported that a bill on the sterilization of recidivist criminals had been introduced and narrowly defeated in the state of Michigan in 1897. While he did not expect his proposal to pass in Germany during his lifetime, Näcke predicted—accurately, as it turned out—that the United States would be the first country to pass a sterilization law and that it would do so in the not too distant future.[62]

Näcke's advocacy of sterilization presents us with a curious problem, since one would have expected this proposal to come from someone who was convinced that heredity was a primary factor in criminal behavior, that hereditary characteristics were unchangeable, and that degeneration was steadily increasing. Näcke, however, held none of these views. He argued that even though many criminals were degenerates, the primary cause of criminal behavior lay in the milieu. He believed in the inheritance of acquired characteristics so that degeneration could be reversed by environmental factors. In fact, he explicitly

62. Näcke, "Die Kastration," 74–84, quotes on 84, 77, 78. On the history of sterilization in the United States, see Philip Reilly, *The Surgical Solution: A History of Involuntary Sterilization in the United States* (Baltimore: Johns Hopkins University Press, 1991), 41–55; James Trent, *Inventing the Feeble Mind: A History of Mental Retardation in the United States* (Berkeley: University of California Press, 1994), 184–224; Edward Larson, *Sex, Race, and Science: Eugenics in the Deep South* (Baltimore: Johns Hopkins University Press, 1995), 18–39; Nicole Hahn Rafter, *Creating Born Criminals* (Urbana: University of Illinois Press, 1997).

stated that the best remedy for degeneration would be the improvement of public sanitation. Finally, Näcke did not believe that degeneration was currently increasing.

Why, then, did he advocate sterilization? First, the evidence that public health was not currently degenerating could not outweigh Näcke's nagging fear that the forces promoting degeneration might still eventually overwhelm society, a fear that had obviously taken on a life of its own. Second, although Näcke believed that improved public sanitation offered an environmental solution to the problem of degeneration, he thought that such improvements would be slow and difficult to attain so that sterilization was by no means the only solution to the problem of degeneration, but a shortcut. Finally, Näcke was willing to impose the biological solution because he had no compunctions about curtailing individual liberties for the sake of public welfare.

Näcke's endorsement of sterilization despite his belief in a primarily environmental etiology of crime obviously represents an extreme case. Far from being an anomaly, however, his case displays two important features of early eugenic thought in heightened form. First, eugenics did not derive from any empirical finding (however subjective) that degeneration was on the rise but from the Social Darwinist assumption that society's curbs on natural selection must have adverse consequences. Second, the beginnings of eugenics preceded the triumph of the Mendel-Weismann paradigm that hereditary characteristics were immutable.[63]

Näcke's 1899 article failed to generate any immediate support for the idea of sterilization, which did not attract significant attention until 1907, when the state of Indiana passed a law providing for the sterilization of feebleminded individuals and "confirmed criminals."[64] Liszt's criminal law journal carried an article that evaluated the law positively and attributed its adoption in America to the fact that there "the individual is not valued as highly as in other *Kulturstaaten* [civilized states], and therefore the principle that the common welfare is more important than that of the individual is more easily realized there." The article seems to have provoked irritated letters, since Liszt and his fellow editors subsequently declared that the author's evaluation of the law reflected his own personal opinion.[65] The Frankfurt periodical *Die Umschau* reviewed the American law in a piece by a psychiatrist, Dr. Georg Lomer, who strongly endorsed what he called the "elimination" (*Ausmerzung*) of mentally deficient criminals

63. See Weingart, *Rasse, Blut und Gene*, 73–78, 85.
64. See Reilly, *Surgical Solution*, 43–44.
65. Max Lederer, "Die Kastration als sichernde Massnahme," *ZStW* 28 (1908): 446–48; editors' comments ibid., 560.

by means of sterilization. Countering humanitarian objections to such a policy, Lomer described mentally deficient criminals in dehumanizing terms: "To preserve these beasts in human form who inhabit the 'criminal wards' of our insane asylums with lenient laws while we mercilessly kill off every dog that has rabies is to show excessive conscientiousness and exaggerated moral scruples."[66] Aschaffenburg's *Monatsschrift* also carried a positive report on the American law.[67]

By 1911 the first German books on the sterilization of degenerates and criminals in the United States and in Switzerland had appeared.[68] In 1913, Hans Groß, the editor of the *Archiv für Kriminalanthropologie*, recommended the most extensive program of sterilization and castration with the argument that society was in a desperate situation:

> The constant deliberation about whether a given measure might damage the personality or independence [of the criminal] is only weak sentimentality. We have been talking about humanity toward criminals long enough; let us talk about humanity toward the rest of society; it is threatened by an alarmingly large number of degenerates and people with a criminal disposition, . . . survival is at stake . . . at this time it is permissible to use measures that might be regarded as extraordinary in calmer times.[69]

Groß called for the sterilization of people with a "pronounced criminal disposition" and of all who suffered from incurable, supposedly hereditary, diseases including epilepsy, tuberculosis, cancer, syphilis, and alcoholism. In addition, he called for castration not only of sex offenders but of all "violent, ineducable and intractable young people" who posed a threat to safety in the big cities and currently populated various correctional institutions.[70]

66. Georg Lomer, "Die Ausmerzung geisteskranker Verbrecher," *Die Umschau* Nr. 21, 23 May 1908 (Clipping, ZStA Potsdam, RJM 6078, Bl. 56–57).

67. P. Ziertmann, "Die Unfruchtbarmachung sozial Minderwertiger," *MKS* 5 (1909): 734–43. Näcke himself reported on American and Swiss sterilizations in "Über Kastration bei gewissen Entarteten," *AKK* 31 (1908): 174–76, and in "Die ersten Kastrationen aus sozialen Gründen auf europäischem Boden," *AKK* 32 (1909): 343–44.

68. Hans W. Maier, *Die nordamerikanischen Gesetze gegen die Vererbung von Verbrechen und Geistesstörung und deren Anwendung*, and Emil Oberholzer, *Kastration und Sterilisation von Geisteskranken in der Schweiz*, published together in *Juristisch-psychiatrische Grenzfragen*, vol. 8, nos. 1–3 (Halle: Marhold, 1911). Two years later this literature was supplemented by Geza von Hoffmann's more comprehensive and influential work *Die Rassenhygiene in den Vereinigten Staaten von Nordamerika* (Munich: Lehmann, 1913).

69. Hans Groß, "Zur Frage der Kastration und Sterilisation," *AKK* 51 (1913): 316–25, quote on 320.

70. Ibid., 324.

Far from being crackpots, Näcke and Groß were well-respected and influential representatives of criminal psychology and penal reform. Although there was no chance of a sterilization law passing in Imperial Germany and the leadership of the German eugenic community did not yet endorse sterilization, the campaign for sterilization was gaining support in the legal community. By the eve of the war, it was winning over prominent representatives of the retributivist school. In 1913 Josef Kohler, editor of the *Archiv für Strafrecht und Strafprozeß*, who generally maintained a critical and suspicious attitude toward criminal psychology, enthusiastically endorsed sterilization both as a way of preventing crime and as a general eugenic measure for improving public health. That same year the first legal dissertation on "sterilization and castration as a means of combating crime" appeared. It was sponsored by a retributivist law professor, Philip Allfeld at Erlangen University, and its young author strongly recommended the measure.[71]

The largest forum for the discussion of the sterilization question in the immediate prewar years was provided by the Seventh International Congress for Criminal Anthropology, which Aschaffenburg hosted in Cologne in 1911. There Hans Maier, a doctor working under Eugen Bleuler at the Burghölzli psychiatric clinic in Zurich, reported on recent sterilizations of delinquent *Minderwertige* in Switzerland and recommended the measure. Aschaffenburg disagreed. Although he endorsed the castration of sex offenders because it would allow for the release of people who would otherwise have to remain interned indefinitely, he opposed the sterilization of degenerates because he was skeptical about the role of heredity. Insisting that it was not at all clear whether the descendants of degenerates would necessarily suffer from the same condition, Aschaffenburg suggested that the merits of eugenic sterilization could be determined only after further research into the problem of heredity. His doubts were shared by others at the congress.[72] Nevertheless, the sterilization question was clearly to remain on the agenda. After examining the further development of criminology during the Weimar and Nazi years, we shall return to the sterilization issue in the final chapter.

71. Kohler's endorsements of sterilization are to be found in his review of the *Bericht über den 7. internationalen Kongress für Kriminalanthropologie in Köln, Okt. 1911* in *ASS* 60 (1913): 346 and in his review of Gerngross's book in *ASS* 61 (1914): 189; Friedrich L. Gerngross, *Sterilisation und Kastration als Hilfsmittel im Kampf gegen das Verbrechen* (Munich: Lehmann, 1913), was originally submitted as a legal dissertation at the University of Erlangen.

72. Gustav Aschaffenburg and Dr. Partenheimer, eds., *Bericht über den VII. Internationalen Kongreß für Kriminalanthropologie* (Heidelberg: Winter, 1912), 322–31, 392.

CHAPTER FOUR

CRIMINAL SOCIOLOGY IN THE WEIMAR YEARS

German criminology during the Weimar Republic was shaped by two opposing developments. On the one hand, the experience of the First World War and the accompanying surge in crime provided a powerful argument for the importance of the social causes of crime. On the other hand, the Weimar years saw an enormous increase in psychiatric research on criminal behavior that presented a strong case for biological explanations of crime. This chapter will examine the major studies of wartime crime and the development of a criminal sociology that elevated research on the social causes of crime to a new level of sophistication. The chapter's conclusion will provide a brief survey of the impact of criminological research on public attitudes, judicial practice, and penal reform under the Weimar Republic. The development of psychiatric research in what came to be known as "criminal biology" during the Weimar years forms the subject of the next chapter.

The most striking aspect of the development of the sociological study of crime in Germany before the Second World War is the virtual absence of sociologists or other social scientists working on the subject. The *Handwörterbuch der Soziologie* (Handbook of sociology), published in 1931, contained entries on a wide range of social phenomena from "the proletariat" to "the modern family" to "music," but nothing on crime. The prominent sociologist Ferdinand Tönnies was an exception. In 1895 he had published a brief article on "crime as a social phenomenon," in which he called for empirical research on professional criminals (*Gauner*). But he seems to have been unable to interest many of his students in the subject, and his own studies on crime in Schleswig-Holstein were minor contributions that did not significantly advance the field.[1] Since sociolo-

1. Alfred Vierkandt, ed., *Handwörterbuch der Soziologie* (Stuttgart: Enke, 1931). The Handwörterbuch contained a highly theoretical entry on the "sociology of law," which briefly

gists showed almost no interest in the subject, the sociological study of crime was generally regarded as synonymous with criminal statistics and left to stat-isticians. This had a strong influence on the development of the field. While American sociologists, for instance, were conducting detailed case studies of delinquents in the 1920s,[2] in Germany the sociological study of crime was confined to assembling and interpreting large-scale aggregate crime statistics. For a long time, this state of affairs severely limited the kinds of questions that German criminal sociology asked.

Germany's official crime statistics broke down the aggregate crime figures by year and geographic region, as well as by the criminal's age, gender, occupation, and religion.[3] Making use of this statistical material, German statisticians and jurists interested in criminal statistics focused on variations in crime rates between different time periods, geographic regions, and categories of people, which they sought to explain by correlating them with other statistical vari-ables. Two such correlations became widely accepted. The first was the chrono-logical correlation between the rate of property crime and economic conditions, which was first pointed out by Georg von Mayr in 1867, using the price of grain as an economic indicator.[4] The second was the geographic correlation between violent crime and alcohol consumption. Here it was argued, most comprehen-sively by Aschaffenburg in 1903, that the high rates of violent crime in certain German regions were explained by higher rates of alcohol consumption in these areas.[5]

Much of the work on criminal statistics during the Weimar years refined these two correlations, especially the economic one. Instead of grain prices, analysts chose economic indicators more appropriate to an industrial economy, such as wholesale prices for foodstuffs or industrial goods, nominal or real wages, or rates of unemployment; they established the correlation not just for

referred to penal policy. Ferdinand Tönnies, "Das Verbrechen als soziale Erscheinung," *Archiv für soziale Gesetzgebung und Statistik* 8 (1895): 329–44; and his *Uneheliche und verwaiste Verbrecher: Studien über das Verbrechertum in Schleswig-Holstein* (Leipzig: Wiegandt, 1930).

2. See, for example, William Healy, *The Individual Delinquent: A Textbook of Diagnosis and Prognosis for All Concerned in Understanding Offenders* (Boston: Little, Brown, 1915); Sheldon Glueck and Eleanor Glueck, *Five Hundred Criminal Careers* (New York: Knopf, 1930).

3. See Helmut Graff, *Die deutsche Kriminalstatistik: Geschichte und Gegenwart* (Stuttgart: Enke, 1975).

4. Georg von Mayr, *Statistik der gerichtlichen Polizei im Königreiche Bayern und in einigen anderen Ländern,* vol. 16 of *Beiträge zur Statistik des Königreichs Bayern* (Munich: Statistisches Bureau, 1867), 40–42.

5. Gustav Aschaffenburg, *Das Verbrechen und seine Bekämpfung: Kriminalpsychologie für Mediziner, Juristen und Soziologen, ein Beitrag zur Reform der Strafgesetzgebung* (Heidelberg: Winter, 1903), 55–72.

property crime or theft but for other categories of offenses such as receiving stolen property, robbery, arson, and abortion; and they demonstrated these correlations for the most recent data [6] The basic effect of all this work, however, was to confirm well-known arguments rather than adding anything new.

"A Giant Experiment":
Studies of Crime during the First World War

The major impetus for innovative work in criminal sociology came from the First World War and its dramatic impact on crime. Seizing on the war as a perfect test case for studying the effect of major changes in social conditions on crime, two professors of criminal law, Franz Exner and Moritz Liepmann, wrote comprehensive studies of crime during the war and postwar periods. Both Exner and Liepmann had studied with Liszt (Liepmann in the 1890s, Exner a decade later) and participated in his famous Kriminalistisches Seminar, which exerted a formative influence on their careers. Liepmann became a full professor in Kiel in 1902 and accepted a chair at the newly founded University of Hamburg in 1919. By the Weimar years, Liepmann's academic interests focused entirely on penal policy rather than criminal jurisprudence. A vocal opponent of the death penalty, he played key roles in the Internationale Kriminalistische Vereinigung and the prison reform movement. Finished just before his death in 1928, *Krieg und Kriminalität in Deutschland* (War and crime in Germany, published posthumously in 1930) was his last work.[7] Franz Exner was born in Vienna and began his career in Austria, with professorships in Czernowitz (1912) and then Prague (1916), before moving to Tübingen and then to Leipzig in the early 1920s. His early publications dealt with criminal jurisprudence, legal philosophy, and penal policy. *Krieg und Kriminalität in Österreich* (War and crime in Austria), which appeared in 1927 when its author was in his mid-

6. See Erwin Höpler, "Wirtschaftslage—Bildung—Kriminalität," *Archiv für Kriminologie* 76 (1924): 81; Woytinski, "Kriminalität und Lebensmittelpreise," *ZStW* 49 (1928): 647–75; Ernst Roesner, "Der Einfluß von Wirtschaftslage, Alkohol und Jahreszeit auf die Kriminalität," in *Bericht der Zentralstelle für das Gefangenenfürsorgewesen der Provinz Brandenburg* (Berlin, 1931); Roesner, "Die Ursachen der Kriminalität und ihre statistische Erforschung," *Allgemeines statistisches Archiv* 23 (1933): 19–35; Roesner, "Kriminalstatistik" and "Wirtschaftslage und Straffälligkeit," in *Handwörterbuch der Kriminologie*, ed. Alexander Elster and Heinrich Lingemann (Berlin, 1933–36), 2:27–54 and 2:1079–1116.

7. Moritz Liepmann, *Krieg und Kriminalität in Deutschland*, Wirtschafts- und Sozialgeschichte des Weltkrieges, Deutsche Serie (Stuttgart: Deutsche Verlagsanstalt, 1930). On Liepmann, see his entry in the *Neue Deutsche Biographie* and Ruth Hüser-Goldberg, "Das kriminalpolitische Programm von Moritz Liepmann (1869–1928)" (J.D. diss., University of Hamburg, 1974).

forties, reflected a permanent shift in Exner's interests toward criminology and marked the beginning of his career as interwar Germany's most prominent criminologist.[8]

Providing a detailed analysis of German and Austrian crime over a ten-year period (1914–24), Exner's and Liepmann's work was not only unprecedented in scale but also methodologically innovative because both men enriched their statistical material with sociological explanations of changes in crime patterns that went far beyond statistical correlations. Both authors demonstrated considerable sophistication in the analysis of statistical data and an awareness of the various pitfalls involved. Thus they noted that more crimes were likely to have gone unreported and more criminals undetected during the turbulent war and postwar period, so that declines in the figures for criminal convictions must be interpreted with caution, while statistical increases in crime became more significant. They also pointed out that the absolute crime figures (which counted only civilian convictions) were misleading unless corrected for the number of men serving in the military. Since this fluctuating number could not be ascertained, they resorted to calculating crime rates for groups that were not affected by conscription, such as women, youth, and men over age fifty.[9]

Agreeing that overall crime figures were almost meaningless, both authors offered a detailed breakdown of crime patterns by examining different categories of offenses and offenders, mainly women and youth. The two most important categories of offenses in both studies were violent offenses (mainly battery and homicide) and property offenses (mainly theft). Exner and Liepmann reported a strong decline in cases of battery during the war and generally lower numbers after the war for both Austria and Germany. Although the wartime decline in absolute numbers was in part due to the military draft, the authors showed that the number of battery convictions also declined among groups not subject to the draft, such as older men and women, and attributed this decline primarily to malnutrition and reduced alcohol consumption.[10]

Homicide figures presented a different picture. Here the war years showed only a slight decline, which was explained by the effect of the military draft. After the war, however, homicide convictions increased drastically, by about 50 percent in Austria and by more than 100 percent in Germany. Exner at-

8. Franz Exner, *Krieg und Kriminalität in Österreich*, Wirtschafts- und Sozialgeschichte des Weltkrieges, Österreichische und Ungarische Serie (Vienna: Holder-Pichler-Tempsky, 1927). For information on Exner, see his entry in the *Neue Deutsche Biographie* and his obituary in *Jahrbuch der Bayerischen Akademie der Wissenschaften* (1944–48), 140–46.

9. Exner, *Krieg*, 5–7; Liepmann, *Krieg*, 5–12.

10. Exner, *Krieg*, 90–95; Liepmann, *Krieg*, 39–40.

tributed the postwar increase in homicide to the brutalizing effect of a war whose slaughter devalued human life. Liepmann cautioned that without case studies, such psychological explanations remained speculative and stressed that the war had increased the number of firearms in circulation. Since Germany, which had retained capital punishment, had a higher homicide rate than Austria, which had abolished it, Liepmann also concluded that the death penalty had no impact on the homicide rate.[11]

If the war had, with the exception of postwar homicides, led to a general decline in violent offenses, it had the opposite effect on property crime. After dropping slightly during the first year and a half of war, Austrian thefts exceeded prewar levels by 1916, reached three times the prewar level in 1918, and culminated at eight times that level in 1920. And since these absolute figures for the civilian population did not take military conscription into account, the civilian crime rate had actually increased even more sharply.[12] The picture for Germany was similar. Among those who stayed home (youth, women, older men), theft doubled during the course of the war. After the war, thefts increased even further, reaching almost four times the prewar level in 1923 before falling off to prewar levels again in 1925.[13] The proportion of women, youth, and first-time offenders among those convicted of property crime increased greatly during the war.[14]

Both studies confirmed the view that major rises in property crime were caused by deteriorating economic conditions. To document what he called the "mass immiseration" of the war and early postwar years, Exner provided extensive data on food rationing, the soaring prices of essential foodstuffs, and the decline of real wages. Using these data, Exner demonstrated that the number of Viennese thefts rose and fell in inverse proportion to the level of real wages. Between 1915 and 1919 thefts more than doubled as the real wages of unskilled Viennese metal workers plummeted to 31 percent of their prewar level. When real wages rose again from 1920 to 1923, thefts declined just as sharply.[15]

Exner's understanding of how economic privation led to property crime was anything but simplistic. He had little patience with critics who dismissed economic explanations of wartime crime because many wartime thieves who came to trial were not destitute.[16] This objection, Exner insisted, did nothing to

11. Exner, *Krieg*, 95–97; Liepmann, *Krieg*, 35–38.
12. Exner, *Krieg*, 60–62.
13. Liepmann, *Krieg*, 55–59.
14. Exner, *Krieg*, 64–73.
15. Ibid., 74–84.
16. Höpler, "Wirtschaftslage—Bildung—Kriminalität."

weaken the economic explanation of property crime because the link between crime and economic conditions was often indirect. To be sure, some thefts were the direct result of hunger and cold, and Exner provided data on malnutrition to support that claim. More important, however, were the indirect effects of an economic downturn. First, people who were not starving might be tempted to steal when economic conditions deprived them of things to which they had become accustomed. Second, even people who were not in economic difficulties might become delinquent if the general economic need presented them with opportunities or temptations that were hard to resist. Thus many young people were tempted to steal because they were employed in unsupervised positions of trust as a result of the wartime labor shortage, while others could not resist stealing easily accessible things—metal door knobs, for example—that had suddenly acquired great value because of wartime shortages.[17] Although Liepmann supplemented the economic explanation with a psychological account of how conditions of life at the front and the home front gradually eroded the boundary between legal and illegal acts, he agreed with Exner that the causes for the increase in property crime lay "not in the psychological effects of armed conflict, but in the economic consequences of the war."[18]

Since Exner and Liepmann found that the proportion of women and youth among offenders had greatly increased during the war, both writers devoted special sections to these two groups. In Germany and Austria the proportion of female offenders soared from about 15 percent before the war to approximately 40 percent in 1918, returning to prewar levels in the mid-1920s. Between 1918 and 1922, Austria's female theft rate was higher than the male theft rate before the war. In absolute terms, the number of Austrian female offenders increased sixfold between 1913 and 1920. Most committed property offenses, mainly theft.[19]

In explaining this tremendous surge in female crime, Liepmann and Exner made two references to specifically female characteristics. Liepmann argued that most female homicides would have to be explained by "erotic and affective disturbances" such as jealousy or responses to wife-beating, while Exner mentioned women's "sexual privations" during the war as a criminogenic factor.[20] With these exceptions, however, Exner and Liepmann generally explained the surge in female crime as a result of the wartime changes in women's social position. Relating the "masculinization" of female crime to the masculinization

17. Exner, *Krieg*, 86–88.
18. Liepmann, *Krieg*, 59–62, 69.
19. Ibid., 131–35, 156; Exner, *Krieg*, 146–57.
20. Liepmann, *Krieg*, 137; Exner, *Krieg*, 147.

of women's social position, they argued that as women entered the workforce in large numbers and often assumed responsibility for feeding their families, they became subject to the same pressures and temptations that had led many men to property crime. Moreover, women took on these responsibilities at a time of particular economic duress. By referring readers to their previous discussions of the economic etiology of property crime, both authors suggested that the motivations and psychology of most female offenders did not differ from those of their male counterparts.[21]

The second social group that accounted for a disproportionate share of the wartime increase in crime was youth. In Germany, the share of minors (under age eighteen) among all civilian offenders increased from about 10 percent before the war to almost 30 percent in 1917. Although this increase partly reflected the change in the age structure of the civilian population resulting from the draft, it was also caused by a disproportionate surge in the number of juvenile offenders. Compared to prewar levels, the number of German juvenile delinquents doubled, peaking in 1918; its Austrian equivalent quadrupled, peaking in 1920. While the numbers of male and female juvenile delinquents grew at about the same rate, boys accounted for roughly 85 percent of the total. Once again, the overwhelming majority of offenses were against property, mainly theft.[22]

In accounting for the rise in juvenile delinquency, Exner and Liepmann offered their fullest sociological explanation of criminal behavior. Both authors offered thorough accounts of wartime changes in the medical, pedagogical, and economic aspects of the lives of German and Austrian youths, including malnutrition, the effect of absent fathers and working mothers, the disintegration of schooling, and the change from supervised apprenticeships to unsupervised factory labor. The combination of wartime privations, a lack of supervision, and new temptations at work and in the streets led many youths to become "wayward" and, in some cases, to steal. Although Exner and Liepmann described the cumulative effects of these social changes in terms of waywardness (*Verwahrlosung*), they did not conceive of this waywardness as an individual moral failing but as a social phenomenon. Thus Liepmann emphatically rejected not only "self-righteous moralizing judgments" but also "the urge to search for personality defects or a particular motivation of the individual offense." "There are no wayward children," he insisted, "only wayward conditions."[23]

21. Exner, *Krieg*, 146–47, 153; Liepmann, *Krieg*, 159–62.
22. Liepmann, *Krieg*, 97–100; Exner, *Krieg*, 167–72.
23. Exner, *Krieg*, 172–93; Liepmann, *Krieg*, 79–97.

Exner's and Liepmann's studies of wartime crime made three major contributions to criminology and the public discourse on crime during the war. First, their work served as a corrective to contemporary commentators who attributed the bulk of the increase in crime either to a general "moral decline" in German society or to a moral failing on the part of individual offenders.[24] By explaining the wartime surge in crime as the result of "economic crises and social upheavals," Exner and Liepmann firmly rejected this moralizing approach. "Just as in the fight against human diseases and economic crises, we only make progress . . . once we concentrate on the sober investigation of facts, causes and consequences and eliminate moralizing judgments and pathos," wrote Liepmann. "We will only conquer crime . . . if we ruthlessly exclude indignation, vehemence, and fear from our evaluation and treatment of this phenomenon and make causes and effects the only measures of our work."[25]

Second, Exner's and Liepmann's analyses strengthened the case for the importance of social rather than individual-biological causes of crime. Regarding the war as a gigantic "experiment" testing the influence of social factors on crime, both Exner and Liepmann explicitly saw their books as important contributions to the debate over whether the causes of crime lay primarily in the personality of the offender or in the social environment. Since the war had drastically transformed social conditions but had presumably left people's individual personalities untouched, Exner and Liepmann concluded that the wartime increase in crime provided the strongest possible evidence "for the great importance of all social factors" in explaining crime.[26] These "social factors," they insisted, included not just economic conditions but many other aspects, such as malnutrition, alcohol consumption, family life and schooling, working conditions, and even the psychological effects of the wartime atmosphere.

Finally, Exner's and Liepmann's work made a strong case for the primary importance of economic conditions among the social factors that influenced crime.[27] Although the economic argument was hardly new, Liepmann and Exner provided a more comprehensive and sophisticated analysis of the impact of economic conditions than any of their predecessors. Whereas most earlier studies were limited to demonstrating statistical correlations between the rate of property crime and certain economic indicators, Exner and Liepmann provided causal explanations of why and how poor economic conditions led to property

---

24. Höpler, "Wirtschaftslage—Bildung—Kriminalität"; see also the characterization of the political, pedagogical, and criminological literature in Liepmann, *Krieg*, 165.

25. Liepmann, *Krieg*, 165–66; Exner, *Krieg*, 200–201.

26. Exner, *Krieg*, 2–3, 197–201; Liepmann, *Krieg*, 163–65.

27. Exner, *Krieg*, 201.

crime. Furthermore, Exner in particular broadened the scope of economic explanations of crime by showing that the effect of economic need on crime was not limited to the obvious cases of theft from hunger but included the far larger number of cases in which a general economic crisis provided new criminal opportunities or temptations for people who were not in dire need themselves. Thus the theft of easily accessible objects that suddenly acquired great value because of wartime shortages had to be attributed to the deterioration of economic conditions, regardless of the individual economic situation of the offender.[28]

The argument that the increase in crime was attributable specifically to the economic impact of the war rather than its other social effects was bolstered by a skillful comparative analysis. Exner showed that neutral states such as Holland and Sweden had also witnessed drastic wartime increases in property crime, whereas England, which took part in the war, had seen a sharp decline in property crime. The neutral states, Exner argued, saw a rise in crime because their economic situations deteriorated, while England was spared such a development because its economy did not suffer as much from the war. Hence the comparative findings confirmed the argument that the German and Austrian wartime increase in property crime did not result from the moral or psychological effects of military conflict but from economic conditions.[29]

Both Exner and Liepmann believed that their criminal-sociological studies allowed them to draw conclusions for penal policy. In a published lecture based on his book, Exner argued that "the best penal policy will always be a good social policy."[30] Both Exner and Liepmann welcomed the postwar changes in penal policy such as the Juvenile Justice Law, the reduction in short-term prison sentences, and the recognition that a proliferation of penal provisions was counterproductive.[31] While Exner was concerned to keep his book strictly scholarly in tone and therefore made his comments on penal policy in a separate lecture, Liepmann did not hesitate to turn his conclusion into a ringing endorsement of the reform policies of Liszt's modern school. This difference in style reflected a difference in the place these two books occupied in their authors' lives and careers. Whereas Liepmann's book was an excursion into criminal sociology by a jurist who was mainly interested in penal reform, Exner's book was the work of a jurist who was primarily interested in criminology.

28. See esp. ibid., 200–201.

29. Ibid., 203–8.

30. Franz Exner, *Krieg und Kriminalität: Vortrag gehalten anlässlich der Universitätsgründungsfeier am 3. Juli 1926 in Leipzig*, Kriminalistische Abhandlungen, no. 1 (Leipzig: Wiegandt, 1926), 14.

31. Liepmann, *Krieg*, 166–70; Exner, *Krieg und Kriminalität: Vortrag*, 14.

Franz Exner's Criminal Sociology

Although his monograph on wartime crime quickly established Exner as Germany's preeminent criminal sociologist, it marked only the beginning of his contributions to criminology. Exner did more than anyone else to encourage criminological research among jurists, especially the younger generation of legal scholars. He sponsored a large number of dissertations on criminological topics and started a series of criminological monographs, his Kriminalistische Abhandlungen, in which they could be published. This series was a great success, publishing over twenty volumes in its first ten years (1926–35) and another twenty before the war cut short publication in 1941. Most of the studies in this series fell into four categories: studies of particular aspects of crime during the First World War (such as female crime, fraud); studies of certain groups of criminals (such as confidence men, thieves, murderers, child molesters); general studies of the influence of certain social factors on crime (such as wages, schooling, marriage); and case studies of groups of criminals to assess the relative weight of heredity and environment. In addition, Exner shaped the development of criminology by organizing the findings of criminal-sociological and criminal-biological research into a comprehensive synthesis. This effort began with Exner's article on "criminal sociology" in the *Handwörterbuch der Kriminologie* and culminated in his 1939 survey, which was the first comprehensive textbook of criminology since Aschaffenburg's 1903 survey.[32]

In his *Handwörterbuch* article Exner proposed a remarkably broad conception of criminal sociology, insisting that criminal sociologists should not only study the behavior of criminals but must also examine how state and society defined and reacted to crime. Criminal sociology in this wider sense would be divided into three areas: a "sociology of crime" in the narrow sense, which examined the actions of criminals; a "sociology of the prosecution of crime," which examined the actions of police, prosecutors, judges, and prison personnel; and a "sociology of social conceptions of crime," which examined society's (as opposed to the state's) conceptions, attitudes, and responses concerning crime. This broad conception of criminal sociology demonstrates Exner's awareness that crime was in part socially constructed.[33]

Exner had contributed to the "sociology of social conceptions of crime" in an

32. Exner, "Kriminalsoziologie," in *Handwörterbuch der Kriminologie*, ed. Alexander Elster and Heinrich Lingemann (Berlin: de Gruyter, 1933–36), 2:10–26; Exner, *Kriminalbiologie in ihren Grundzügen* (Hamburg: Hanseatische Verlagsanstalt, 1939), which is discussed in Chapter 6 below. See also Exner, "Kriminalistischer Bericht über eine Reise nach Amerika," *ZStW* 54 (1934): 345–93, 511–43.

33. Exner, "Kriminalsoziologie," 10–11.

article comparing the responses to crime of society and state and to the "sociology of criminal prosecution" in a book on the sentencing practices of German courts.[34] But since these two areas were still virtually uncharted territory, Exner limited his discussion in the *Handwörterbuch* to criminal sociology in the narrow sense, which he divided into a "general criminal sociology" that studied the development of crime in a particular geographic area and a "special criminal sociology" that studied the criminal behavior of particular categories of criminals (such as thieves, arsonists, burglars) and particular population groups (such as women, city dwellers, different occupations).

Exner defined criminal sociology in the narrow sense as "the science which seeks to describe crime as a social phenomenon and to understand crime in its dependence on social conditions [*in seiner gesellschaftlichen Bedingtheit*]."[35] According to Exner, the criminal sociologist should always take a comparative approach, seeking to explain not crime as such but variations in criminal activity: between different time periods, geographic areas, or groups of persons. Unlike most statisticians, Exner held that the criminal-sociological "explanation" for such variations should not just identify a statistical correlation between variations in crime and variations in another social factor but demonstrate a "meaningful connection" between the two by arriving at a "psychological understanding" (*Verstehen*) of the motivation for the type of crime in question. For this reason, the criminal sociologist had to have recourse to criminal-psychological methods but to apply them to an "average" person rather than a particular individual.[36]

Acutely aware that criminology suffered from a chronic vagueness of terminology, Exner was careful to define his terms. Since criminal sociologists were to understand crime "in its dependence on social conditions," he explained what he meant by "social conditions" or "environment," stressing three points. First, the environment was always specific to an individual, consisting only of that part of the general environment with which that individual was in contact. This point was important to counter a common criticism of social explanations of crime. Since many people lived in poverty but only some became criminal, the critics charged, criminal behavior could not be explained by environmental factors. By insisting that the environment varied from individual to individual, Exner invalidated this criticism. Second, by insisting that the environment included not just material conditions but also cultural, intellectual, and human

34. Franz Exner, "Gesellschaftliche und staatliche Strafjustiz," *ZStW* 40 (1919): 1–29; and his *Studien über die Strafzumessungspraxis der deutschen Gerichte* (Leipzig: Wiegandt, 1931).

35. Exner, "Kriminalsoziologie," 11–13.

36. Ibid.

factors such as the ideas, people, and institutions with which a person came into contact, Exner was able to refute the accusation that criminal sociologists took a "materialistic" or even Marxist approach that reduced everything to material and economic conditions.[37] Finally, Exner argued that a person's environment was always closely intertwined with his or her personality. The environment helped to shape an individual's personality, and this personality could also shape that individual's environment, through choice of occupation, for instance. This understanding of the interconnectedness of individual and social factors allowed Exner to overcome simplistic either/or positions in the heredity versus milieu debate.[38]

In Exner's analysis, an individual's environment was composed of four concentric circles corresponding to the domestic, occupational, local, and state environments. Under the domestic rubric he discussed the influence of parents, schooling, and marriage, drawing on several studies in his Kriminalistische Abhandlungen. These studies had shown that orphans, illegitimate children, children from broken homes, and truants in school were much more likely to become criminal than the average child. In addition, unmarried men and married women were more likely to become criminal.[39] Criminal behavior was also affected by a person's occupation, which not only determined economic position but could also present particular temptations or abilities conducive to crime. Regarding the local environment, Exner focused on differences between city and country (higher overall crime rate in cities but higher rate of battery in the countryside), but he also commented on the influence of local institutions or customs as illustrated by the fact that Germany's centers of alcohol production had the highest rates of battery.[40]

Most of Exner's analysis, however, was devoted to the environment at the level of the national state, which he divided into three aspects: culture and politics; the economy; and the judicial system. He was brief on cultural-political influences, mentioning as an example only the decrease in murders between the 1880s and 1914, which he attributed to the "progressive cultivation and civilization of the population." As one would expect, he cited the experience of the war as the strongest possible evidence for the "dependence of crime on the econ-

37. Exner, *Kriminalbiologie*, 31.
38. Exner, "Kriminalsoziologie," 15–16.
39. Tönnies, *Uneheliche und verwaiste Verbrecher*, 48; Manfred Hoffner, *Kriminalität und Schule*, Kriminalistische Abhandlungen, no. 17 (Leipzig: Wiegandt, 1932), 33–34; Hans Krille, *Weibliche Kriminalität und Ehe*, Kriminalistische Abhandlungen, no. 15 (Leipzig: Wiegandt, 1931), esp. 55–56.
40. Exner, "Kriminalsoziologie," 20–23.

omy." But Exner insisted that this dependence was highly complex and warned against three fallacies. Economic conditions must never be reduced to a single economic indicator (wages were irrelevant in times of high unemployment). It should not be assumed that bad economic times had a uniformly negative effect on crime (lowered alcohol consumption reduced personal violence). Finally, the effect of depressed economic conditions was not limited to crimes committed out of immediate personal need but included a large range of offenses that were made possible by or took advantage of the troubled economy.[41]

Exner noted that the effects of the judicial system on crime were often overestimated, by those who blamed high recidivism rates on the criminal justice system, but also underestimated, in criminal-sociological studies that ignored the impact of the judicial system. Primarily concerned about the latter problem, Exner sought to show the powerful effect of the criminal justice system on crime. The severity of punishments, he argued, made little difference. But the "degree of likelihood" that a criminal would be apprehended and punished exerted a strong effect on crime.[42] Thus the effectiveness of police and criminal procedure was clearly more important than substantive criminal law in controlling crime. Nevertheless, penal legislation and a rational system of punishments also played a significant role. Exner welcomed the replacement of short-term prison sentences by fines but criticized the lack of penal measures targeted at professional criminals. He also cautioned, however, that an excess of penal provisions was just as damaging as a shortage of them. The experience of wartime economic regulations had demonstrated that a proliferation of penal sanctions served only to undermine the authority of the law.[43]

Exner's work significantly advanced German criminal sociology. Besides clarifying the field's tasks and methods, Exner made two important contributions. First, he broadened the field of criminal sociology beyond the narrow confines of statistical work. Criminal sociologists, he insisted, were not to content themselves with identifying statistical correlations between variations in crime and another social factor but had to explain the psychological motivation connecting the two. Nor should they limit themselves to studying crime as a mass phenomenon but should examine the effect of social factors at the individual level as well. Second, Exner refined the concept of the environmental causes of

41. Ibid., 23–25.

42. This claim was confirmed by another Exner student who showed that the increasing lenience in sentencing between 1880 and 1932 coincided with long-term declines (or standstills) in almost all types of offenses. See Rupert Rabl, *Strafzumessungspraxis und Kriminalitätsbewegung*, Kriminalistische Abhandlungen, no. 25 (Leipzig: Wiegandt, 1936), 47.

43. Exner, "Kriminalsoziologie," 25–26.

criminal behavior in ways that allowed him to counter various criticisms of criminal sociology. Responding to the criticism that the environment could not account for individual differences of behavior, he insisted that the environment differed from individual to individual, which opened the way for a sophisticated analysis of social factors on the individual level. To counter charges of material-ism, he broadened the concept of the environment beyond economic conditions to include the full range of intellectual, cultural, political, and human factors that made up a criminal's social environment. Finally, Exner's demonstration that the influence of adverse economic conditions on crime was varied and complex greatly invigorated the economic explanation of crime.

Criminology and Criminal Justice in the Weimar Years

Although the experience of the wartime surge in crime reinvigorated the criminal-sociological branch of German criminology, as the next chapter will show, the Weimar Republic witnessed a flourishing of psychiatric research on crime that overshadowed environmental explanations of crime in the field of criminology. There is some evidence, however, that the enormous rise in crime during the war and early postwar years convinced a considerable section of society of the powerful impact of social and environmental factors on crime. Although documenting attitudes toward crime among the general population is difficult and falls outside the scope of this study, the treatment of crime and criminals in Weimar literature provides some information. A recent literary analysis of the image of the criminal in Weimar novels found that most por-trayed criminals as normal people whose criminal behavior was due to circum-stance rather than an abnormal personality, thus advancing a social explanation of crime that promoted sympathetic understanding for the criminal.[44]

Most of Weimar society also supported penal reform and the complete revi-sion of the penal code that had been initiated before the war. The fact that Germany's judicial institutions had survived the country's transition from a constitutional monarchy to a democratic republic virtually unchanged very likely increased public support for complete penal reform. If Germany's crimi-

44. Birgit Kreutzahler, *Das Bild des Verbrechers in den Romanen der Weimarer Republik* (Frankfurt: Peter Lang, 1987), 370, 374. On the artistic and literary depictions of sexual murder in particular, see Maria Tatar, *Lustmord: Sexual Murder in Weimar Germany* (Prince-ton: Princeton University Press, 1995). For a long-term perspective, see Jörg Schönert, ed., *Erzählte Kriminalität: Zur Typologie und Funktion von narrativen Darstellungen in Strafrechts-pflege, Publizistik und Literatur zwischen 1770 und 1920* (Tübingen: Niemeyer, 1991).

nal justice system had been out of date in 1914, many argued, it was surely out of date in a democratic welfare state that prided itself on its liberal, humanitarian, and enlightened approach to social problems. The legislative project of revising the penal code thus had significant support across much of the political spectrum, from the liberal Deutsche Volkspartei through the Catholic Center Party to the Social Democrats. Starting in the early 1920s, the Ministry of Justice established a reform commission that continued the work of the prewar commissions and produced a draft code that became the basis of parliamentary deliberations in 1927. Although a parliamentary committee spent countless hours amending the draft code over the next several years, the gradual dissolution of parliamentary government after 1930 eventually doomed the penal reform project to failure.[45]

Nevertheless, Weimar legislators, unwilling to wait for the lengthy process of comprehensive penal reform to take its course, passed partial reforms that they considered particularly urgent. The most important of these were the 1923 Law on Fines, which extended the use of fines in place of short-term prison sentences, and the Juvenile Justice Law, also passed in 1923, which raised the age of criminal responsibility from twelve to fourteen and promoted the use of correctional education instead of punishment for juvenile offenders between the ages of fourteen and eighteen.[46]

These reforms represented only one side of the penal reform agenda. The penal reformers' demand for the individualization of punishment called for more lenient punishment for some offenders and harsher punishment for others. While first-time offenders and juveniles were to benefit from suspended sentencing and educational measures, habitual offenders would be subject to indefinite detention. It was no coincidence that both the Law on Fines and the Juvenile Justice Law rendered criminal justice more lenient, for the liberal

45. Eberhard Schmidt, *Einführung in die Geschichte der deutschen Strafrechtspflege*, 3d ed. (Göttingen: Vandenhoeck, 1964), 405–8; Richard Evans, *Rituals of Retribution: Capital Punishment in Germany, 1600–1987* (Oxford: Oxford University Press, 1996), 493, 572–75. Also see my forthcoming history of German penal reform from 1880 to 1945.

46. Franz Exner, "Development of the Administration of Criminal Justice in Germany," *Journal of Criminal Law and Criminology* 24 (1933–34): 248–59; Schmidt, *Einführung*, 408–13. On the Juvenile Justice Law, see Edward Ross Dickinson, *The Politics of German Child Welfare from the Empire to the Federal Republic* (Cambridge, Mass.: Harvard University Press, 1996); Elizabeth Harvey, *Youth and the Welfare State in Weimar Germany* (Oxford: Clarendon Press, 1993); Detlev Peukert, *Grenzen der Sozialdisziplinierung: Aufstieg und Krise der deutschen Jugendfürsorge von 1878 bis 1932* (Cologne: Bund-Verlag, 1986); Gabriel Finder, "Education, Not Punishment: Juvenile Justice in Germany, 1890–1930" (Ph.D. diss., University of Chicago, 1997); and the voluminous literature on juvenile justice cited in the introduction.

political climate of the early Weimar years clearly favored the implementation of the lenient and humanitarian aspects of the penal reform agenda.

Most of the historical literature on the Weimar Republic's judiciary has focused on the political bias of the judges, who generally punished left-wing political criminals quite harshly, while treating right-wing political criminals with remarkable lenience.[47] This severity toward those perceived as political enemies might lead one to expect that Weimar judges also meted out stiff sentences to ordinary, nonpolitical criminals or at least to serious offenders. Just the opposite was the case. Like Weimar's penal legislation, the sentencing practices of the republic's criminal courts were marked by a trend toward increased lenience. This development was documented by none other than Exner, whose 1931 study of sentencing practices from 1882 to 1928 demonstrated that German courts had become more and more lenient over the entire fifty-year period.[48]

This trend toward milder punishments was most visible in the changing proportions of prison sentences and fines. In 1882, the first year for which national criminal statistics were available, prison sentences accounted for 75 percent and fines for 25 percent of all sentences. Thereafter, the proportion of fines increased steadily, reaching 50 percent in 1911, and, after a brief setback during the war and immediate postwar years, 70 percent in 1928. In addition, prison sentences became shorter over the same period. Since the penal code of 1871 had remained in effect throughout this period with only minor modifications,[49] these shifts in sentencing patterns were clearly the result of changing judicial practices rather than changing laws.[50]

In accounting for this phenomenon, Exner rejected two explanations that attributed the courts' increased lenience to deliberate changes in penal policy. According to the first explanation, the judiciary had been influenced by the penal reformers, who had long called for the replacement of short-term prison sentences (of a few days or weeks) by fines. Exner granted that the penal reformers' critique had undoubtedly influenced the judiciary but pointed out that this could not fully explain the changes in sentencing. For if this explana-

47. The classic historical account is Heinrich Hannover and Elisabeth Hannover-Druck, *Politische Justiz, 1918–1933* (Frankfurt: Fischer, 1966); the pattern was first documented by Emil Julius Gumbel, *Vier Jahre politischer Mord* (Berlin: Verlag der neuen Gesellschaft, 1922).

48. Exner, *Strafzumessungspraxis.*

49. The most important change of relevance here was the law on monetary fines of 1923. As Exner showed, however, this law had only a minor impact compared to the steady long-term increase in the proportion of fines over the 1882–1928 period.

50. Exner, *Strafzumessungspraxis,* 18–21.

tion were correct, the increase in fines would have resulted only in a reduction of short-term sentences. This, however, was not the case because there had been an additional shift from longer to shorter prison sentences, which clearly reflected a broader trend toward milder punishments.

To explain this trend, a second explanation suggested that the German judiciary's increasing lenience was a rational reaction to the gradual decline in German crime rates that had begun before the war and had, after a temporary increase in the war and immediate postwar years, continued under the Weimar Republic until the worldwide economic crisis struck in 1929–30. Why punish with severity if lenient punishments were sufficient to keep crime under control? But if this were the courts' reasoning, Exner objected, judges would have become more lenient only with offenses that were declining, not with those that were increasing. In fact, however, the trend toward lenience also affected offenses that were increasing, such as fraud or serious theft, so that this second explanation was also unsatisfactory.[51]

Having ruled out all penal policy explanations, Exner argued that the judiciary's increasing lenience was in fact attributable to the influence of criminological research that "regarded crime as the result of heredity, upbringing, and various other environmental influences." For "even if understanding . . . does not mean forgiving . . . this healthy and necessary striving for understanding has led with psychological necessity to more and more lenient . . . sentencing." Exner was not arguing that judges were reading and pondering criminological research and then acting on its penal policy implications. Rather, he contended that as criminological research filtered down into the general society, it had the "irrational" psychological effect of making people, including judges, more sympathetic toward the criminal and therefore more inclined toward milder punishments. Thus, increasing judicial lenience reflected a widespread popular attitude of "taking the side of the criminal" that resulted from a psychological rather than rational reception of criminological research.[52]

On the question of whether the judiciary's increased lenience was a good thing, Exner was of two minds. On the one hand, the fact that German crime rates had remained steady over the last fifty years and even decreased for some offenses seemed to vindicate the increasing lenience so that one could "only register with satisfaction that the courts have abandoned a judicial severity that has gradually became superfluous." On the other hand, however, Exner ob-

51. Ibid., 26–29.
52. Ibid., 28.

jected that judicial lenience was too indiscriminate and was especially concerned that the courts were showing undue lenience toward recidivist habitual criminals, who ought to be subject to more severe punishments.[53]

Not surprisingly, the subtleties of Exner's analysis were lost on the enemies of the Weimar Republic. As we shall see in Chapter 6, even though they themselves had benefited from it, the Nazis fiercely criticized the lenience of the Weimar courts and did not hesitate to blame it on the criminologists.

53. Ibid., 106, 103, 28.

CHAPTER FIVE

VARIETIES OF CRIMINAL BIOLOGY
IN THE WEIMAR YEARS

Despite the considerable advances in criminal sociology discussed in the previous chapter, research in this field was overshadowed by what came to be known as "criminal biology" during the Weimar years. The predominance of medico-biological over sociological research on the causes of crime that had begun with the late nineteenth-century reception of Lombroso was bolstered by an enormous expansion of psychiatric research on the causes of crime in the 1920s.

The great interest in criminological research among psychiatrists was closely connected to several broader developments in early twentieth-century German psychiatry. Most fundamentally, psychiatrists became increasingly concerned with the welfare and protection of society as a whole rather than the individual patient.[1] Moreover, psychiatric research on the connection between crime and mental abnormalities was part of psychiatry's expansion beyond full-fledged mental illness into the vast area of borderline abnormalities.[2] Both of these developments had begun in the prewar years, but they were greatly accelerated by the role that German psychiatry played in the war effort and therefore became more salient during the Weimar Republic.[3] In addition, psychiatric

1. Heinz-Peter Schmiedebach, "The Mentally Ill Patient Caught between the State's Demands and the Professional Interests of Psychiatrists," in *Medicine and Modernity: Public Health and Medical Care in Nineteenth- and Twentieth-Century Germany*, ed. Manfred Berg and Geoffrey Cocks (Cambridge: Cambridge University Press, 1997), 114, 118.

2. Henry Werlinder, *Psychopathy: A History of the Concepts* (Uppsala: University, 1978); German Berrios, "Personality Disorders: A Conceptual History," in *Personality Disorder Reviewed*, ed. Peter Tyrer and George Stein (London: Gaskell, 1993), 17–41; Heinz-Peter Schmiedebach, "Zum Verständniswandel der 'psychopathischen' Störungen am Anfang der naturwissenschaftlichen Psychiatrie in Deutschland," *Der Nervenarzt* 56 (1985): 140–45.

3. Paul Lerner, "Rationalizing the Therapeutic Arsenal: German Neuropsychiatry in World War I," in *Medicine and Modernity*, ed. Berg and Cocks, 121–48; Doris Kaufmann, "Science as

interest in criminological questions in the 1920s was closely connected to the burgeoning of research on the genetic causes of mental illness, which reflected the predominance of hereditarian thinking among psychiatrists. Finally, psychiatrists' interest in identifying the genetic factors in criminal behavior was related to their general enthusiasm for eugenics, which many began to see as a panacea not only for mental illness but for crime as well, a subject that is examined in Chapter 7.[4]

The expansion of psychiatric research on the causes of crime was accompanied by a change in terminology. Before the war Aschaffenburg had introduced the term "criminal psychology," which had gradually replaced "criminal anthropology" as the preferred designation of the field during the prewar period. After the war, "criminal psychology" gave way to "criminal biology," which quickly gained wide currency for designating medical research on the causes of crime. Finally, a general awareness that criminal biology formed part of a larger whole was reflected in the increasing use of the term "criminology" to refer to the larger field including both criminal biology and criminal sociology, although sometimes the term "criminal biology" was also used to refer to criminology as a whole.[5]

In discussing the development of German criminology and criminal biology in the 1920s, it must be remembered that neither criminology nor criminal biology achieved the status of academic disciplines during this period. Since 1904 German-speaking criminologists had their own professional journal, Aschaffenburg's *Monatsschrift für Kriminalpsychologie und Strafrechtsreform*, and in 1927 they founded a professional association, the Kriminalbiologische Gesellschaft. But there was only one German institution fully dedicated to criminological research: Theodor Viernstein's Kriminalbiologischer Dienst (Criminal-Biological Service) in Bavaria, founded in 1924, which gathered criminal-biological data on prison inmates.[6] Most criminal-biological research

---

Cultural Practice: Psychiatry in the First World War and Weimar Germany," *Journal of Contemporary History* 34 (1999): 125–44.

4. Peter Weingart, Jürgen Kroll, and Kurt Bayertz, *Rasse, Blut und Gene: Geschichte der Eugenik und Rassenhygiene in Deutschland* (Frankfurt: Suhrkamp, 1988), 188–366; Paul Weindling, *Health, Race and German Politics between National Unification and Nazism, 1870–1945* (Cambridge: Cambridge University Press, 1989), 399–439; Hans-Walter Schmuhl, *Rassenhygiene, Nationalsozialismus, Euthanasie*, 2d ed. (Göttingen: Vandenhoeck, 1992), 78–90.

5. Note the usage of *Kriminologie* in the title of the *Handwörterbuch der Kriminologie* (1933), as compared to the usage of *Kriminalbiologie* to refer to criminology as a whole in the name of the *Kriminalbiologische Gesellschaft*.

6. The Kriminalbiologischer Dienst is discussed in detail below. Its closest Austrian equivalent was Adolf Lenz's Kriminologisches Institut at the University of Graz. See *Geschichte der*

in Germany used data collected at the Central Record Office (Sammelstelle) of the Kriminalbiologischer Dienst, especially after it became associated with the prestigious Deutsche Forschungsanstalt für Psychiatrie (German Institute for Psychiatric Research) in 1930. In addition, there were a few university institutes, such as Moritz Liepmann's Seminar für Strafrecht und Kriminalpolitik in Hamburg, devoted to what we might call penal studies that included criminological research in their mission.[7] But there were no academic chairs or institutes of criminology. As a result, everyone doing criminological research was trained and working in other disciplines, primarily law and psychiatry.

With the exception of Theodor Viernstein, who was a prison doctor without special training in psychiatry, virtually all criminal-biological research in the interwar period was carried out by trained psychiatrists, most of whom held academic positions at universities and university clinics. The major figures in criminal-biological research included some of Germany's most prominent psychiatrists: Gustav Aschaffenburg, who was director of the university psychiatric clinic and professor of psychiatry at the University of Cologne and editor of the prestigious *Handbuch der Psychiatrie*; Kurt Schneider, who served as chief physician at Aschaffenburg's psychiatric clinic in Cologne and became director of the Clinical Section of the Deutsche Forschungsanstalt für Psychiatrie in Munich in 1931; Karl Birnbaum, who headed the psychiatric hospital in Berlin-Buch and taught as an adjunct professor at the University of Berlin; Johannes Lange, who headed the Clinical Section of the Deutsche Forschungsanstalt für Psychiatrie in Munich until his appointment as director of the psychiatric hospital of the University of Breslau in 1931; and Hans Gruhle, who worked at the psychiatric clinic of the University of Heidelberg. Except for Birnbaum, all were directly or indirectly connected with Emil Kraepelin and thus belonged to the so-called Munich school of German psychiatry. Aschaffenburg, Lange, and Gruhle had studied with Kraepelin; Schneider worked under Aschaffenburg for most of the 1920s; Lange and later Schneider worked at the Deutsche Forschungsanstalt für Psychiatrie in Munich, which Kraepelin had founded in 1917 and directed until his death in 1926.[8] There is little doubt that Kraepelin's

---

Rechtswissenschaftlichen Fakultät der Universität Graz, vol. 3, *Strafrecht—Strafprozessrecht—Kriminologie* (Graz: Akademische Druck- und Verlagsanstalt, 1987), 56–61.

7. Its Austrian equivalent was Graf Gleispach's Universitätsinstitut für die gesamte Strafrechtswissenschaft und Kriminalistik, renamed Universitätsinstitut für Kriminologie in 1934.

8. For a "genealogical chart" of the Munich school, see Kurt Kolle, ed., *Große Nervenärzte*, 2d ed. (Stuttgart: Enke, 1970), vol. 1, chart 1. On the Forschungsanstalt, see Matthias Weber, "Ein Forschungsinstitut für Psychiatrie: Die Entwicklung der Deutschen Forschungsanstalt für Psychiatrie in München zwischen 1917 und 1945," *Sudhoffs Archiv* 75 (1991): 74–89. For

own interest in criminological questions led him to direct many of his students toward criminal-biological research. Yet even those who had an abiding interest in criminal biology usually continued to do important work in other areas of psychiatry. Hence criminal biology did not become an obscure specialty but remained part of the mainstream of German psychiatry.

The first two sections of this chapter examine the institutionalization of criminal-biological research in Bavaria's Kriminalbiologischer Dienst and critical responses to it. After a brief section on two approaches located at opposite extremes of the spectrum of criminal-biological research (somatotyping and psychoanalytic theories of criminal behavior), the remainder of this chapter presents the three major strands of Weimar era criminal-biological research, all of which were connected to particular areas of general psychiatric research: first, Karl Birnbaum's and Kurt Schneider's research on links between crime and mental abnormalities, which was related to the new typology of "psychopathic personalities" developed by Schneider; second, research on the role of genetic factors in criminal behavior, which was part of psychiatric research on the genetic causes of mental illness conducted at the Deutsche Forschungsanstalt für Psychiatrie; and finally, Karl Birnbaum's and Hans Gruhle's research on criminal psychology, which was associated with the development of medical psychology and the study of personality known as *Persönlichkeitslehre* or *Charakterologie*. The reception and policy implications of Weimar criminal-biological research will be examined in Chapter 7, which looks at the debates over the question whether criminals should be sterilized and the responses to this issue in the bureaucracy and in parliament.

The Creation of Bavaria's Criminal-Biological Service

The introduction of criminal-biological examinations in Bavarian prisons was closely tied to Bavaria's adoption of the so-called progressive system of punishment in 1921. The progressive system was designed to give prisoners the opportunity and incentive to rehabilitate themselves by creating several progressively more lenient steps or levels of punishment in the prison. Since most Bavarian prisoners were held in communal confinement, the Justice Ministry feared that the negative influence of hardened criminals would undermine the attempt to rehabilitate potentially corrigible inmates and therefore decided to

---

biographical information on the individuals, see the sources cited for each individual later in this chapter.

exclude "incorrigible" inmates from the progressive system. This meant that incoming prisoners would have to be evaluated to determine whether they were corrigible or incorrigible.[9]

It was this new need to evaluate every incoming prisoner that provided the Bavarian prison doctor Theodor Viernstein with the long-sought opportunity to institutionalize criminal-biological examinations in Bavarian prisons. Working as a prison doctor at the Bavarian penitentiaries in Kaisheim and later Straubing since 1907, Viernstein believed that instead of simply providing inmates with needed medical care, prison doctors ought to contribute to criminological research by conducting systematic medical examinations of all prisoners.[10] He had been conducting such examinations from the beginning of his career, publishing his first findings in 1911.[11] After closely following the institutionalization of such examinations in Belgium's Service d'anthropologie pénitentiaire,[12] in 1922 Viernstein approached the Bavarian Ministry of Justice with a proposal to introduce regular "criminal-biological examinations" of all Bavarian prisoners on the basis of a questionnaire he had developed in Straubing. Viernstein offered two justifications for his proposal. First, his examinations would assist prison authorities in identifying the supposedly incorrigible inmates who were to be excluded from the new progressive system. Second, these same examinations could provide the basis for the implementation of eugenic measures made especially urgent by the effects of the recent war. "For us Germans," he told the ministry, "the thriving of the race must be one of the most important concerns of the present time, because vast masses of

9. Ministerialentschliessung of 3 November 1921, No. 57911, in *Der Stufenstrafvollzug und die kriminalbiologische Untersuchung der Gefangenen in den bayerischen Strafanstalten,* zusammengestellt im Auftrage des Bayerischen Staatsministeriums der Justiz, 3 vols. (Munich: n.p., 1926–29), 1:10–18; Ministerialentschliessung of 2 August 1922, No. 63798, ibid., 19–21.

10. Entschliessung vom 3. Juli 1907 (appointment as prison doctor at Kaisheim) and Entschliessung vom 1. Juli 1916 (transfer to Straubing), Personalakte Theodor Viernstein, File MInn 85264, BHStA.

11. Theodor Viernstein, "Ärztliche Untersuchungen an Kaisheimer Gefangenen," *Münchener Medizinische Wochenschrift* 58 (1911): 2322–25.

12. The Belgian Service was created in 1920 and was soon followed by the creation of a similar institution in Latvia. On the criminal-biological services in Belgium and Latvia, see Edmund Mezger, "Die Arbeitsmethoden und die Bedeutung der kriminalbiologischen Untersuchungsstellen," *Gerichtssaal* 103 (1933): 127–90; on Belgium, see also Werner Petrzilka, *Persönlichkeitsforschung und Differenzierung im Strafvollzug* (Hamburg: de Gruyter, 1930); for contacts between Viernstein and Neureiter (Latvia), see Ferdinand Neureiter, "Zu den biologischen Problemen im Strafvollzug," *Beiträge zur gerichtlichen Medizin* 6 (1924), and Viernstein's response in his "Entwicklung und Aufbau eines kriminalbiologischen Dienstes im bayerischen Strafvollzug," in *Stufenstrafvollzug,* 1:80.

valuable racial elements have been eliminated through the negative selection of the war."[13]

On the basis of Viernstein's proposals, the Bavarian Ministry of Justice provisionally introduced criminal-biological examinations in all its prisons in July 1923.[14] Six months later, it authorized the creation of a Criminal-Biological Central Record Office (Kriminalbiologische Sammelstelle) under Viernstein's direction that would gather the reports prepared in the different prisons.[15] Just as Viernstein was winning the support of the ministry, however, he encountered opposition among his medical colleagues at the fourteen other Bavarian prisons. Since staffing levels did not allow for the examination of every arriving prisoner, Viernstein had suggested that prison doctors examine every third or fourth arrival to guarantee random statistical sampling. His colleagues, however, wanted permission to selectively examine new inmates who appeared mentally abnormal so they could provide individual treatment. Although this might appear to be a minor disagreement, it actually represented a fundamental conflict over whether doctors should be primarily concerned with the welfare of their patients or the interests of society at large, in this case scientific research that would eventually help to protect society against crime. While Viernstein's colleagues continued to see their primary task as the provision of medical care for inmates, Viernstein sought to make the collection of data for scientific research the new priority. With the support of the ministry, Viernstein prevailed.[16]

To ensure that Viernstein's criminal-biological examinations were scientifi-

13. Viernstein to Bavarian Ministry of Justice, letters dated 29 October 1922, 25 February 1923, 28 February 1923, 19 April 1923, File MJu 22504, BHStA; Theodor Viernstein, "Einführung eines Stufensystems in den bayerischen Strafanstalten," *Zeitschrift für Medizinalbeamte* 35 (1922).

14. Ministerialentschliessung Nr. 32222 of 7 July 1923, with seven attachments, File MJu 22504, BHStA; also see prison directors' reports dated December 1923, on the implementation of the executive order in the same file; the *Entschliessung* (without the attachments) is reproduced in *Stufenstrafvollzug* 1:29.

15. Ministerialentschliessung Nr. 8633 of 27 February 1924, File MJu 22511, BHStA; also reproduced in *Stufenstrafvollzug*, 1:40–42.

16. Memorandum "Die erweiterte Zugangsuntersuchung" prepared "im Auftrage der Vereinigung der Strafanstaltsärzte," signed by Dr. Bauernfeind, 29 May 1924, File MJu 22511, BHStA; response by Viernstein, 29 June 1924, ibid.; memo "Die erweiterte Zugangsuntersuchung" prepared "im Namen der Vereinigung der Strafanstaltsärzte" signed by Dr. Bauernfeind, 13 July 1924, ibid.; "Denkschrift über die wissenschaftlichen Grundlagen für den Betrieb einer kriminalbiologischen Sammelstelle" by Viernstein, with cover letter dated 27 September 1924, which discusses a meeting between Viernstein and the other prison doctors on 19 July 1924, ibid. Viernstein's colleagues were also critical of his use of Ernst Kretschmer's physique types in his questionnaire.

cally sound, the Justice Ministry asked the Bavarian Medical Advisory Commission to evaluate his scheme. In a report written by Max von Gruber, who was professor of public health, president of the Bavarian Academy of Sciences, and a well-known eugenicist, the commission agreed with Viernstein's emphasis on the role of biology and heredity in human behavior and endorsed his scheme with great enthusiasm, suggesting only minor modifications.[17] With this scientific imprimatur, the Bavarian justice minister formally approved the permanent establishment of the Kriminalbiologischer Dienst in Bavarian prisons in April 1925.[18]

The great importance which both the Justice Ministry and prominent Munich academics attached to Viernstein's project manifested itself in a week-long training course for Bavarian prison doctors held that same month. Financed by the ministry and taught by Munich professors, the course instructed prison doctors in the techniques of anthropometric measurements and psychological exploration and provided general background in genetics, taught by the sober geneticist Hans Luxenburger, and eugenics, taught by the strident eugenicist Fritz Lenz.[19] Viernstein's Sammelstelle remained attached to the Straubing prison until 1930, when it become associated with the Genealogical-Demographic Section of the Deutsche Forschungsanstalt für Psychiatrie.[20]

To standardize the criminal-biological examinations to be conducted in all Bavarian prisons, Viernstein designed an elaborate ten-page questionnaire. Initially, he had intended that prison doctors would examine all incoming prisoners. But since there was usually only one doctor in each prison and the

17. Staatsministerium des Innern to Staatsministerium der Justiz, 19 January 1925, File MJu 22511, BHStA; Gutachten by Dr. Max von Gruber dated 19 December 1924, ibid.; Gutachten by Dr. Hermann Merkel, ibid. Gruber's Gutachten is reproduced as "Gutachten des Obermedizinal-Ausschusses im Staatsministerium des Innern," in *Stufenstrafvollzug*, 1:59–67.

18. Ministerialentschliessung Nr. 16716 of 26 April 1925, File MJu 22511, BHStA; see also "Gutachten über die endgültige Durchführung des kriminalbiologischen Dienstes," by Viernstein, with cover letter dated 16 January 1925, ibid.; the Entschliessung is also reproduced in *Stufenstrafvollzug*, 1:56–58.

19. "Bericht über den kriminalbiologischen Einführungskurs für die Strafanstaltsärzte," in *Stufenstrafvollzug*, 1:127–41. Ernst Rüdin was unable to attend and was replaced by Hans Luxenburger.

20. Viernstein to Ministry of Justice, 14 February 1927, File MJu 22512, BHStA; "Denkschrift betr. die Verlegung der bayerischen Kriminalbiologischen Sammelstelle nach München," by Viernstein, 1 January 1928, ibid.; Ministry of Justice to Ministry of Finance, 1 June 1928, ibid.; Ministry of Justice to Direktion des Zuchthauses Straubing, 28 June 1930, Personalakte Viernstein, File MInn 85264, BHStA. See also Viernstein, "Der Kriminalbiologische Dienst in bayerischen Strafanstalten," *MKS* 17 (1926): 1–7; Otto Kahl, "Die kriminalbiologische Untersuchung der Strafgefangenen in Bayern," *MKBG* 3 (1930): 18–20.

preparation of a full criminal-biological report took about four hours, it soon turned out that prison doctors could manage at most two examinations per week. As noted earlier, the two inmates to be examined each week were selected on a scheme that guaranteed random statistical sampling.[21] Starting in 1927, those incoming prisoners not subject to a full examination by the prison doctor were examined by nonmedical but university-educated prison personnel (administrators, prison chaplains, and teachers) according to a shorter questionnaire.[22] The initial report on each incoming prisoner was supplemented by follow-up reports at the time of release or, for the small number of long-term prisoners, in the third and each following year of detention.

The prisons forwarded a copy of each examination report to Viernstein's Central Record Office, which received about fifteen hundred full criminal-biological reports per year and, starting in 1928, approximately the same number of shorter, nonmedical reports each year, adding up to over ten thousand reports by 1930.[23] In addition, the existence of a criminal-biological report on a particular individual was noted in the criminal register to alert judicial authorities to the availability of criminal-biological information on that person. Thus, if a released Bavarian inmate committed another offense, the state prosecutor or judge in charge of the case could request a criminal-biological "expert opinion" (*Gutachten*) on the defendant from Viernstein's Central Record Office. In its first five years (1925–30), the Central Record Office issued a little over four hundred of these expert opinions, which were prepared on the basis of the criminal-biological reports in its files, usually by Viernstein. Unless Viernstein happened to have originally examined the inmate himself, he prepared these expert opinions solely from written reports without ever having met the inmate.[24]

21. Ministerialentschliessung of 26 April 1925, No. 16716, in *Stufenstrafvollzug*, 1:56–57; on conflicts over Viernstein's strict sampling instructions, see *Stufenstrafvollzug*, 1:59, 64, 76–77; the figure of four hours is Viernstein's estimate from *Stufenstrafvollzug*, 1:76.

22. Ministerialentschliessung of 14 December 1927, No. 54661, in *Stufenstrafvollzug*, 2:26–31.

23. Annual figures are averages calculated for the period 1925–30 (1928–30 for nonmedical reports) on the basis of 1930 totals reported in Kahl, "Kriminalbiologische Untersuchung," 20.

24. The Bavarian Justice Ministry asked state prosecutors to make use of criminal-biological reports as early as 1923 (Ministerialentschliessung of 22 October 1923, No. 46963, in *Stufenstrafvollzug*, 1:38–39); in 1926 it became mandatory for Bavarian prosecutors and judges to order criminal-biological expert opinions whenever the criminal register indicated their availability and a defendant's personal character seemed relevant to the case (Ministerialentschliessung of 11 October 1926, No. 46771, in *Stufenstrafvollzug*, 2:14–16); a good description of how Gutachten were requested and prepared is found in Hans Klare, *Das kriminalbiologische Gutachten im Strafprozeß* (Breslau: Schlettersche Buchhandlung, 1930), 72–78, 114, 121–24; the figure of four hundred is from Kahl, "Kriminalbiologische Untersuchung," 20.

Viernstein's questionnaire consisted of four main sections dedicated to genea-logical, sociological, psychological, and anthropometric information about the prisoner. The questionnaire began by asking the inmate about his parents and relatives to gather information about his heredity. Among other things, this sec-tion asked whether father or mother were criminal, alcoholics, or mentally ill, and what their general character and social behavior was, and included similar questions about other relatives. In the second section, the inmate was asked to provide information about his or her own life, including relations with parents, schooling, occupation, military service, earlier criminal offenses, and the in-mate's own account of the most recent offense. In the third section, the exam-iner was supposed to give a psychological assessment of the inmate both by observation and by asking questions. Here the examiner had to characterize the inmate's temperament, intelligence, forms of expression (speech, facial expres-sions, handwriting), and possible mental conditions (psychopathy or mental illness) by underlining the appropriate psychological characterizations in a kind of multiple-choice format.[25] For the purpose of assessing intelligence, some psychological tests, such as giving definitions or explaining a series of pictures, were included. In addition, inmates were asked about their attitudes toward themselves, their family, work, superiors, religion, politics, and other subjects. At the end of the psychological section, the examiner was asked to give a "provi-sional social prognosis" by categorizing the inmate as either corrigible or incor-rigible. The exam concluded with anthropometric measurements and a detailed physical description of the inmate, as well as two photographs.

The examination of an inmate usually took between one and one and a half hours; the preparation of a full written report took a total of about four hours. In addition to the exam, each prisoner was asked to write a short account of his or her life, and brief questionnaires about the inmate and his or her parents were sent to the police, school, and church authorities in the inmate's native city. Some inmates, of course, did not know the required information about parents, ancestry, or siblings. But although some were initially reluctant to reveal information, especially about their family, it appears that almost every-one cooperated after some prodding.[26]

---

25. The examiner was also asked to determine whether the inmate fit one of Ernst Kretsch-mer's somatotypes, which are discussed later in this chapter. The Bavarian prison doctors were critical of Kretschmer's typology; the Bavarian Obermedizinal-Ausschuß agreed with them and asked Viernstein to make this question optional and allow a psychological characterization not tied to Kretschmer's scheme; see *Stufenstrafvollzug*, 1:58–60, 64, 80–81.

26. An early version of the questionnaire is reproduced in Viernstein, "Biologische Pro-bleme im Strafvollzuge," *DZGGM* 3 (1924): 436–53; the 1925 version as well as the question-

The criminal-biological examinations' immediate practical purpose in the prison system was to determine whether an incoming prisoner should be considered corrigible or incorrigible, and therefore either eligible or ineligible for the progressive system. But while Viernstein naturally stressed this practical function in making his pitch to the Justice Ministry, he had broader and more ambitious goals. Above all, he saw the Criminal-Biological Service as a contribution to *Rassenhygiene* (the contemporary German term for eugenics). Eugenics, he explained, had two major tasks: to distinguish persons who furthered the race from those who harmed it and to promote an increase in the "racially beneficial" (*rasseförderlich*) and a decrease in the "racially harmful" (*rasseschädigend*) types. Every physician had the duty to contribute to eugenics for the well-being of the German people, but prison doctors could make a particularly important contribution because all criminals were "racially harmful" to some degree. Moreover, eugenics was perfectly compatible with criminal justice because both pursued the same "selective task" of "eliminating" persons considered harmful (*Schädlinge*) from the legal or racial standpoint.[27]

Although he generally considered criminals racially harmful, Viernstein also believed in the distinction between corrigible and incorrigible criminals. Giving this distinction a biological interpretation, he explained that criminals varied in the degree of their racial harmfulness. The role of prison doctors was to identify the "permanently harmful portion of the criminal population" to allow for its permanent segregation from society. Only such a biological classification could provide the necessary basis for the future policies that public safety and eugenics demanded: the permanent detention and sterilization of incorrigibles. But Viernstein's vision of the power of criminal biology did not stop at the prison walls. Assuming that criminal behavior was largely determined by heredity, he promised that criminal biology would identify "an entire stratum of

---

naires sent to police, parish, and schools are printed in *Stufenstrafvollzug*, 1:86–101, and in Viernstein, "Der kriminalbiologische Dienst," 10–17; for revisions to the questionnaire made in October 1926, see *Stufenstrafvollzug*, 2:9–13; the revised version in use since 1926 is reprinted in *Stufenstrafvollzug*, 3:36–44; the figure of one and a half hours for the actual exam is from Klare, *Das kriminalbiologische Gutachten*, 105; information about cooperation of inmates is from Kahl, "Kriminalbiologische Untersuchung," 24. The shorter questionnaire for nonmedical personnel, with three examples, is reproduced in *Stufenstrafvollzug*, 2:32–50.

27. The German word *Schädling* usually refers to destructive insects, vermin, parasites. Viernstein's view of criminal justice as a eugenic process of "social selection" was clearly influenced by Hans von Hentig's *Strafrecht und Auslese. Eine Anwendung des Kausalgesetzes auf den rechtbrechenden Menschen* (Berlin: Springer, 1914), which Viernstein cited. On Hentig's book, see Richard Wetzell, "Criminal Law Reform in Imperial Germany" (Ph.D. diss., Stanford University, 1991), 320–28.

the population, whose production of criminal personalities exerts a negative influence on socioeconomic conditions and on the hereditary substance of the race." By asserting that criminal biology could isolate the genetic pool from which criminals were recruited, Viernstein made the strongest possible claim for the power of criminal biology: that it would be able to prevent crimes as yet uncommitted by identifying individuals with a "criminal character" before they had had the chance to commit a crime.[28]

Viernstein's discussion of the eugenic tasks of criminal biology assumed what remained to be demonstrated. His argument that criminals must be racially harmful because crime harmed the race assumed that criminal *behavior* was biologically rooted in a criminal *person*. And his assertion that criminal biology would isolate a stratum of the population that "produced criminal personalities" implied that criminal behavior was hereditary. Remarkably, however, Viernstein admitted that the etiology of crime and the problem of the "influence of inherited characteristics on the development of personality" were open questions on which more research was needed. Convinced that heredity played an overwhelming role in criminal behavior, he apparently thought that research was needed only to show how, not whether, heredity affected personality and behavior.[29]

Besides its diagnostic and eugenic functions, Viernstein believed that the Criminal-Biological Service would help to prepare the ground for the "future German Penal Code" that would introduce the indefinite detention of incorrigible habitual criminals. Since this provision would require that criminals be evaluated at the time of sentencing, Viernstein proposed that judges order criminal-biological examinations to determine a defendant's corrigibility. To the objection that the introduction of biological criteria into the criminal trial would violate fundamental principles of justice, Viernstein responded by reiterating his view that "eugenics and criminal justice belong together: both serve the task of selection by suppressing those who harm the race and who are enemies of society."[30]

Viernstein reported his first research findings in a lecture on "types of the corrigible and incorrigible criminal," which he delivered at the first meeting of the Kriminalbiologische Gesellschaft, in Vienna, in the spring of 1927. The lecture included statistics based on Viernstein's criminal-biological examina-

---

28. Viernstein, "Entwicklung und Aufbau eines kriminalbiologischen Dienstes im Bayerischen Strafvollzug," in *Stufenstrafvollzug*, 1:69–70 (written in 1925); Viernstein, "Der Kriminalbiologische Dienst in bayerischen Strafanstalten," *MKS* 17 (1926): 4–5.

29. Viernstein, "Entwicklung und Aufbau," 70, and "Der Kriminalbiologische Dienst," 4.

30. Viernstein, "Entwicklung und Aufbau," 75, and "Der Kriminalbiologische Dienst," 5.

tions of roughly eight hundred male inmates of the Straubing prison. Of these, Viernstein considered 61 percent corrigible, 26 percent incorrigible, and 13 percent of uncertain prognosis. Assuming that the uncertain cases were evenly divided between corrigibles and incorrigibles, Viernstein arrived at an incorrigibility rate of 32 percent and observed that this figure was close to Lombroso's estimate for the proportion of born criminals. If prisoners were classified by type of offense, important variations emerged. The proportion of incorrigibles was low among violent offenders (10 percent), public-order offenders (5 percent), and sex offenders (21 percent), but extremely high for property offenders (51 percent).[31]

Viernstein's comments on the criteria for corrigibility and incorrigibility were disappointing. Since he had developed a detailed questionnaire for his criminal-biological examinations, one would have expected him to present a sophisticated formula that would take into account specific data on a criminal's personality, heredity, or previous life. But although Viernstein reiterated that "only the most comprehensive biological, mainly genetic-psychiatric, and environmental study of the individual" would allow criminal biologists to assess a criminal's corrigibility, the criteria that he offered were exceedingly vague. An offender's corrigibility, he proposed, depended on whether his criminal actions reflected his fundamental *Gesinnung. Gesinnung*, according to Viernstein's idiosyncratic definition, was "the fundamental emotional current, established by [a person's] store of ethical notions, with which [that person's] character . . . reacts to stimuli which require a supra-individual, altruistic response." If a criminal's crimes reflected a deeper antisocial *Gesinnung*, the criminal was incorrigible. The criminal biologist could grasp a criminal's *Gesinnung* only intuitively: understanding it was "less a matter of logical deduction than of . . . a sense [*Empfinden*] that one is dealing with a good or bad person, a sense that often cannot be explained."[32]

This explanation of the criteria for corrigibility was remarkable not only because it failed to make use of the detailed criminal-biological data that Viernstein was busy collecting but because it revealed the central role of moral categories in his ostensibly scientific work. Although Viernstein claimed to be investigating the problem of corrigibility as a "biologist" who did not "attach any moral judgment to [such] terms," his definition of *Gesinnung* simply

31. Theodor Viernstein, "Über Typen des verbesserlichen und unverbesserlichen Verbrechers," *MKBG* 1 (1927): 35–37; see also his "Typen des besserungsfähigen und unverbesserlichen Verbrechers (Selbstbericht)," in *Stufenstrafvollzug*, 2:168–81.

32. Viernstein, "Über Typen des verbesserlichen und unverbesserlichen Verbrechers," 50–53.

dressed up moral assumptions in biological language ("stimuli" requiring "altruistic responses"). His admission that he determined corrigibility through an intuitive assessment of whether the criminal was "good or bad" brought the moral categories underlying his approach into plain view.

Criticisms of the Criminal-Biological Service

Although Viernstein's position as head of Bavaria's Criminal-Biological Service gave him considerable influence in the criminological community,[33] the serious problems in his method of evaluating prisoners' corrigibility did not escape the notice of critical contemporaries. Most of this criticism came from prison reformers associated with Moritz Liepmann's Institute for Criminal Law and Penal Policy in Hamburg. In a widely read article on the progressive system as practiced in Bavarian prisons, published in 1926, Liepmann himself briefly criticized the role of Viernstein's Criminal-Biological Service. Although he had no objections to criminal-biological examinations, he charged that the Bavarian practice of separating corrigibles from incorrigibles lacked any scientific basis.[34] A year later Liepmann's criticism was followed up by Curt Bondy, former director of the juvenile prison in Hahnöfersand and now an adjunct professor (*Privatdozent*) at Liepmann's Institute in Hamburg.[35]

Bondy argued that corrigibility and incorrigibility (Bondy himself preferred the term "ineducability" [*Unerziehbarkeit*]) were relative rather than absolute concepts. Whether a prisoner was considered corrigible clearly depended on the pedagogical methods used in the process of rehabilitation. Highly critical of current rehabilitative methods, Bondy insisted that many who appeared incorrigible under current conditions could probably be rehabilitated with improved pedagogical methods. In addition, a criminal's corrigibility depended on the

---

33. Viernstein disseminated his ideas in numerous publications. Just for the period 1927–32, see Viernstein, "Über Typen des verbesserlichen und unverbesserlichen Verbrechers"; "Typen des besserungsfähigen und unverbesserlichen Verbrechers"; "Kriminalbiologie," in *Stufenstrafvollzug*, 3:7–50; "Die Kriminalbiologische Untersuchung der Gefangenen in Bayern," *MKBG* 3 (1930): 30–38; "Die kriminalbiologische Forschung in Bayern," *Monatsblätter des Reichszusammenschlusses für Gerichtshilfe* 6 (1931): 118–32; "Biologische Aufgaben in der Kriminalpolitik," *Eugenik* 1 (1930–31): 213–17; "Über Kriminalbiologie," *AZP* 98 (1932): 277–99; "Stufenstrafvollzug, Entlassenenfürsorge, Sicherungsverwahrung," *Monatsblätter des Reichszusammenschlusses für Gerichtshilfe* 7 (1932): 132–46, 166–76.

34. Liepmann, "Die Problematik des 'progressiven Strafvollzugs,' " *MKS* Beiheft 1, *Beiträge zur Kriminalpsychologie und Strafrechtsreform* (1926): 66.

35. On Bondy's role at Hahnöfersand and his pedagogical ideas, see Gabriel Finder, "Education, Not Punishment: Juvenile Justice in Germany, 1890–1930" (Ph.D. diss., University of Chicago, 1997), 167–91.

social environment in which he or she lived after being released from prison. A released inmate who committed further crimes and thus appeared incorrigible under difficult personal circumstances might not have offended again in a better environment. In short, a criminal's corrigibility depended largely on factors that lay outside of his or her personality. Since both current prison pedagogy and support for released convicts left much to be desired, the Bavarian practice of labeling certain incoming prisoners as incorrigible and excluding them from the progressive system was untenable.[36]

Besides calling into question the very notion of incorrigibility, Bondy also expressed doubts about the scientific soundness of Viernstein's criminal-biological examinations. Human genetics and criminal biology were still at such early stages of development that any practical application of their findings to individual cases was premature. But even if their scientific basis had been more secure, the Bavarian examinations were compromised because most Bavarian prison doctors lacked the psychiatric, genetic, and psychological training necessary for administering such examinations with any degree of reliability. In conclusion, Bondy made it clear that he was criticizing the use of criminal-biological examinations for determining the corrigibility of prisoners rather than criminal-biological examinations as such. Such examinations were a most welcome innovation, as long as their function was limited to contributing to scientific knowledge and aiding correctional officers in choosing the appropriate treatment for each criminal. At present, however, the Bavarians were "using inadequate methods to apply controversial and incomplete theories to [the] highly dubious concept" of incorrigibility.[37]

A few years later, Liepmann and Bondy's criticisms were followed up in a dissertation published by a Liepmann student, Werner Petrzilka, in 1930. If Bondy had mainly provided a conceptual critique of the notion of incorrigibility, Petrzilka offered a detailed institutional and methodological critique that cast serious doubts on all major parts of the criminal-biological examinations: the psychological evaluation was flawed because four hours were inadequate for assessing a prisoner's psychological profile and mental health; the sociological information was flawed because reports from the police, schools, and parish in a criminal's hometown were bound to be superficial and unreliable; and the information about the mental health of the criminal's parents and family was flawed because it was obtained from the prisoner himself, who could not possibly give an objective assessment. In short, the results of criminal-biological examina-

36. Curt Bondy, "Zur Frage der Erziehbarkeit," ZStW 48 (1927): 329–34.
37. Ibid.

tions were unreliable and had to be treated "with extreme caution." Since the examinations were unreliable, the separation of prisoners into corrigibles and incorrigibles lacked all justification.[38]

Similar points were made in another dissertation, which examined the expert opinions that Viernstein's Sammelstelle prepared for use in criminal trials of former Bavarian prisoners. Among other problems, Exner's student Hans Klare pointed out that Viernstein frequently based his expert opinions on the written reports of criminal-biological examinations conducted by other prison doctors without ever having met the criminal himself. Klare condemned this practice and suggested that the person preparing an expert opinion should always personally examine the criminal.[39]

Undeterred by these criticisms, the Criminal-Biological Service continued to classify incoming prisoners as corrigibles or incorrigibles. In a lecture at the 1930 meeting of the Kriminalbiologische Gesellschaft in Munich, Viernstein defended himself against his critics. Remarkably, he admitted that the determination of a criminal's "social prognosis" (that is, corrigibility) was not only an "essentially intuitive" judgment but one whose "scientific analysis and explanation was, without doubt, still lacking in many cases." Since these social prognoses were urgent, however, and future scientific work would undoubtedly confirm them, it was unnecessary to wait for "scientific verification."[40]

Viernstein also acknowledged Bondy's point that a prisoner's social prognosis depended not just on the prisoner's personality but also on his or her future environment. But their recognition of the environment's role led Viernstein and Bondy to different conclusions. Bondy thought that the environment's role undermined the very notion of incorrigibility and therefore called for improving the circumstances of released prisoners before labeling anyone as incorrigible. Viernstein, however, assumed that the environments of most released prisoners could not be changed and simply revised his definition of incorrigibility to include those who would become recidivists because of their future environment. A prisoner, he explained, could receive the prognosis of "incorrigible" either because of personal characteristics (such as emotional or ethical *Minderwertigkeit*) or because of "predictable adverse external circumstances" (such as alcohol, hardship, or unemployment) or a combination of both.[41] In other words, Viernstein had no qualms about calling for the permanent imprisonment of offenders who could most likely be prevented from offending again if

38. Petrzilka, *Persönlichkeitsforschung und Differenzierung*, 45–61.
39. Klare, *Das kriminalbiologische Gutachten*, 114–24.
40. Viernstein, "Kriminalbiologische Untersuchung der Gefangenen," 32.
41. Ibid., 34.

the adverse environment awaiting them upon their release could be changed. Although Viernstein's frankness in making this point was unusual, it illustrated a position shared by many criminal biologists. Like Viernstein, most criminal biologists focused on the biological causes of crime not because they subscribed to a rigid biological determinism that dismissed environmental factors but because they had convinced themselves that the social causes of crime were intractable.

Speaking in the fall of 1930, Viernstein used the economic depression to justify the exclusion of incorrigibles from the rehabilitative programs of the progressive system by presenting two new arguments. First, he declared that the limited financial resources of the state at a time of economic crisis made it imperative to restrict costly rehabilitation efforts to those who had the best chance of successful rehabilitation.[42] Second, he argued that devoting major resources indiscriminately to all criminals "would give incomprehensible preferential treatment to criminals at a time that imposed enormous burdens on the best members of the nation."[43] Not content to defend the Criminal-Biological Service against its critics, Viernstein also announced a drastically increased estimate of the proportion of incorrigibles among the prison population, which was based on a survey of approximately three thousand criminal-biological reports. Although three years earlier, in 1927, he had maintained that only a small minority of criminals were incorrigible, he now claimed that at least half of all prisoners were incorrigible.[44]

Not surprisingly, this controversial claim provoked a sharp response from Viernstein's critics. Once again, the attack emanated from the prison reformers associated with Moritz Liepmann at the University of Hamburg. Since Liepmann's death in 1930, the lead was taken by Rudolf Sieverts, Liepmann's successor and former *Assistent*, who in 1932 published a withering critique of Viernstein's incorrigibility figure, the Criminal-Biological Service, and Bavarian correctional policy. Like his mentor, Sieverts was a committed prison reformer who supported the introduction of pedagogical rehabilitation methods that was slowly getting under way in the 1920s. He was therefore particularly

42. Ibid., 35. This supports the argument made in Detlev Peukert, *Grenzen der Sozialdisziplinierung: Aufstieg und Krise der deutschen Jugendfürsorge von 1878 bis 1932* (Cologne: Bund Verlag, 1986), 296.

43. Viernstein, "Kriminalbiologische Untersuchung der Gefangenen," 35. This statement illustrates the argument made in Georg Rusche and Otto Kirchheimer, *Punishment and Social Structure* (New York: Columbia University Press, 1939).

44. Viernstein, "Kriminalbiologische Untersuchung der Gefangenen," 35, 31–32. The earlier estimate comes from Viernstein, "Über Typen des verbesserlichen und unverbesserlichen Verbrechers," 53.

distressed when German opponents of prison reform started citing Viernstein's increased estimate of incorrigibility as evidence that pedagogical prison reform had failed. Drawing on previous criticisms, Sieverts made a strong case that Viernstein's figure was based on unreliable data. How reliable could Bavarian criminal-biological examinations be when most Bavarian prison doctors lacked psychiatric training, and many examinations were conducted by nonmedical personnel such as administrators, teachers, or chaplains? The Criminal-Biological Service, he charged, was engaging in just the sort of "criminological dilettantism" that careful research was supposed to overcome.[45]

Sieverts was also disturbed by the conclusions regarding penal policy to which this pessimistic estimate was leading. Viernstein and the Bavarian prisons excluded "endogenous" prisoners from all rehabilitation efforts. But if half of all prisoners were indeed "endogenous criminals" with a high probability of recidivism, was it not imperative to give these prisoners special medical and pedagogical attention to ensure that they did not leave in worse, and hence more dangerous, condition than when they arrived? To drive this point home, Sieverts offered an interesting analogy. In medicine, he suggested, the finding that half of all prisoners suffered from a pathological condition "would give rise to a strong impulse for discovering appropriate methods of treatment," whereas Viernstein, who was, after all, a medical doctor, and the Bavarian prison authorities used this finding to justify a policy of total neglect for half of all prisoners. If the Bavarians wanted to give in to a widespread reactionary mood and abandon the reformist goal of differentiated pedagogical treatment for all prisoners, Sieverts protested, they should not abuse criminal biology to drape their decision in "a cloak of scientific justification."[46]

Viernstein's Criminal-Biological Service played an important role in the development of German criminal biology. First and foremost, it provided an institutional base and a unique collection of data on a large number of prisoners. As we shall see, many of the criminal-biological studies conducted in the 1920s and 1930s used the records of the Criminal-Biological Service. Second, Bavaria's Criminal-Biological Service provided a model that was soon emulated in

45. Rudolf Sieverts, "Gedanken über Methoden, Ergebnisse und kriminalpolitische Folgen der kriminal-biologischen Untersuchungen im bayrischen Strafvollzug," *MKS* 23 (1932): 588–601. See also the follow-up piece: Sieverts, "Gedanken über den kriminalbiologischen Dienst im bayrischen Strafvollzug: Ein Nachwort," *MKS* 24 (1933): 107–16.

46. Sieverts, "Gedanken über Methoden," 597, 598. For Viernstein's response, see his "Die Bekämpfung der Kriminalität vom bevölkerungspolitischen, erbbiologischen und rassenhygienischen Standpunkt," *Zeitschrift für Medizinalbeamte* 46 (1933): 532–48, also issued as a special reprint: E. Schütt and Viernstein, *Die Bekämpfung der Kriminalität vom bevölkerungspolitischen, erbbiologischen und rassenhygienischen Standpunkt* (Leipzig: Fischer, 1933).

other German states.[47] By 1930, criminal-biological examinations had been introduced in Württemberg, Saxony, Baden, and Prussia.[48] Finally, the Criminal-Biological Service's practical function in identifying incorrigibles and its role in laying the groundwork for a genetic population registry for eugenic purposes greatly appealed to the Nazis and would therefore play a key role in winning Nazi support for criminological research.

At the same time, the powerful public criticisms of the Criminal-Biological Service demonstrate that Viernstein's single-minded focus on the biological causes of crime and his pessimism with regard to corrigibility were not accepted by everyone in the criminological and penal reform communities. Although Viernstein's most vocal critics were jurists, the following sections will demonstrate that Viernstein's unsophisticated methodology and crude hereditarianism were not representative of psychiatric research on the causes of crime, most of which presented a far more complex picture of the interaction of biological and social factors in criminal behavior.

Psychoanalysis and Somatotyping

Two areas of research represented extremes on the criminal-biological spectrum. The first of these consisted of psychoanalysis and Adlerian *Individualpsychologie* ("individual psychology"). Both of these approaches rejected the dominant psychiatric paradigm that attributed abnormal behavior to congenital traits and explained criminal behavior as a manifestation of *acquired* psychological maladjustments. Adherents of *Individualpsychologie* attributed criminal behavior primarily to feelings of inferiority and discouragement (*Entmutigung*) resulting from childhood experiences,[49] while psychoanalytic authors explained

---

47. In the federal structure of the Weimar Republic prisons were administered by the states, so that the introduction of criminal-biological examinations was a matter for each state to decide.

48. Edmund Mezger, "Die Arbeitsmethoden und die Bedeutung der kriminalbiologischen Untersuchungsstellen," *Gerichtssaal* 103 (1933): 142–63; Friedrich von Rohden, *Einführung in die kriminalbiologische Methodenlehre* (Berlin: Urban, 1933); Rainer Fetscher, "Die Organisation der erbbiologischen Erforschung der Strafgefangenen in Sachsen," *BfG* 57 (1926): 69–75; Fetscher, "Aufgaben und Organisation einer Kartei der Minderwertigen," *MKBG* 1 (1927): 55–62; Fetscher, "Aus der Praxis einer Kartei," *MKBG* 2 (1928): 161–74; Fetscher, "Die wissenschaftliche Erfassung der Kriminellen in Sachsen," *MKS* 23 (1932): 321–35.

49. Alfred Adler, "Neurose und Verbrechen," *Internationale Zeitschrift für Individualpsychologie* (hereafter *IZI*) 3 (1924): 1–11; Adler, "Die kriminelle Persönlichkeit und ihre Heilung," *IZI* 9 (1931): 321–29; Special issue "Menschen vor dem Richter," *IZI* 9 (1931), issue 5, 321–407; Eugen Schmidt, "Verbrechen und Strafe," in *Handbuch der Individualpsychologie*, ed.

criminal behavior as the result of traumatic sexual experiences in childhood, an inner desire for punishment, or stunted personal development.[50] Since the German psychiatric profession maintained a generally hostile attitude toward psychoanalysis and *Individualpsychologie*, psychoanalytical and *individualpsychologisch* research on crime was thoroughly marginalized within mainstream criminal biology. At best, psychiatrists pursuing criminal-biological research conceded that psychoanalytic or *individualpsychologisch* explanations might apply in a few individual cases but denied their general validity.[51] Most psychiatrists, however, simply ignored psychoanalytic and *individualpsychologisch* approaches to criminal behavior.

While psychoanalytic explanations sought the causes of crime in exogenous factors, the other extreme in the spectrum of criminal-biological research was represented by the effort to establish correlations between criminal behavior and certain physical body types. In his influential book *Körperbau und Charakter* (Physique and character) of 1921, the psychiatrist Ernst Kretschmer claimed that there was a correlation between body type and temperament. Kretschmer's typology distinguished three main types of physique: the rotund "pyknic" type, the tall, thin "asthenic" type, and the muscular "athletic" type. According to Kretschmer, the asthenic and athletic types generally had a "schizothymic" temperament related to schizophrenia, while the pyknic type generally had a "cyclothymic" temperament related to manic depression. Kretschmer suggested that his system of somatotypes might be of use in criminal-biological

---

Erwin Wexberg (Munich: Bergmann, 1926), 2:150–79; Schmidt, *Verbrechen als Ausdrucksform sozialer Entmutigung: Eine einführende Betrachtung über das Werden und die Behandlung der kriminellen Persönlichkeit auf Grund der Erkenntnisse der modernen Psychologie* (Munich: Schweitzer, 1931); Gotthold Bohne, "Individualpsychologische Betrachtungen zu den Kapitalverbrechen der letzten Zeit," *DJZ* 33 (1928): 1502–7.

50. Theodor Reik, *Gedächtniszwang und Strafbedürfnis* (Vienna: Internationaler Psychoanalytischer Verlag, 1925); Franz Alexander and Hugo Staub, *Der Verbrecher und seine Richter* (Vienna: Internationaler Psychoanalytischer Verlag, 1929); Hans Coenen, *Strafrecht und Psychoanalyse* (Breslau: Schletter, 1929); Gotthold Bohne, "Psychoanalyse und Strafrecht," *ZStW* 47 (1926): 439–59; Fritz Wittels, *Die Welt ohne Zuchthaus* (Stuttgart: Hippokrates, 1928). See also Tilmann Moser, "Psychoanalyse und Strafrecht," in *Repressive Kriminalpsychiatrie* (Frankfurt: Suhrkamp, 1971), 226–36. For contemporary surveys and critiques, see Edmund Mezger, "Psychoanalyse und Individualpsychologie in der Strafrechtspflege," *Gerichtssaal* 102 (1932): 1–29; Johannes Nagler, "Anlage, Umwelt und Persönlichkeit des Verbrechers," *Gerichtssaal* 102 (1932): 429–45; Gotthold Bohne, "Bibliographie über die Verwertbarkeit der Tiefenpsychologie (Psychoanalyse und Individualpsychologie) im Strafrecht und Strafvollzug," *ZStW* 53 (1933): 395–402.

51. Karl Birnbaum, *Kriminalpsychopathologie und psychobiologische Verbrecherkunde*, 2d rev. ed. (Berlin: Springer, 1931), 226–29.

work.[52] Starting in the early 1920s, several psychiatrists and prison doctors, including Viernstein, investigated whether criminal behavior might be correlated with certain of Kretschmer's somatotypes. And, indeed, several studies found that most criminals belonged to the athletic and asthenic body types linked to a schizothymic temperament, while the rotund pyknic physique was rare among criminals.[53] Critics, however, pointed out that the pyknic type was rare in the general population as well and that the athletic and asthenic physiques were probably more common among the lower classes from which most criminals came. Whether the connections between physique and temperament that Kretschmer posited existed at all remained a controversial question throughout the Weimar years.[54]

The Search for Abnormal Character Traits:
From *Minderwertige* to "Psychopathic Personalities"

The continuity between medical research on the causes of crime before and after the First World War was strongest in the area of research devoted to the connection between crime and mental abnormalities. In the 1890s German prison doctors and psychiatrists had rejected Lombroso's notion of a born criminal with distinct physical characteristics but found that many criminals were *minderwertig*. The term derived from the work of the psychiatrist Julius Koch, who had coined the term *psychopathische Minderwertigkeiten* to describe borderline mental abnormalities.[55] In 1903, Gustav Aschaffenburg estimated that

52. Ernst Kretschmer, *Körperbau und Charakter* (Berlin: Springer, 1921); Kretschmer, "Biologische Persönlichkeitsdiagnose in der Strafrechtspflege," *DJZ* 31 (1926): 782–87. See also Kurt Schneider, "Körperbau und Charakter," *MKS* 12 (1921): 370–75; Edmund Mezger, "Zwanzig Jahre *Körperbau und Charakter*," *MKS* 33 (1942): 187–91. For an American perspective linking Kretschmer with Hooton's research in America, see Werner Landecker, "Criminology in Germany," *Journal of Criminal Law and Criminology* 31 (1940–41): 551–75.

53. Viernstein, "Einführung eines Stufensystems"; Rudolf Michel, "Körperbau, Charakter und Verbrechen," *Wiener Medizinische Wochenschrift* 75 (1925): 45–50; Friedrich von Rohden, "Körperbauuntersuchungen an geisteskranken und gesunden Verbrechern," *Archiv für Psychiatrie* 77 (1926): 151–63; Rohden, "Kriminalbiologische Untersuchungen an gesunden und geisteskranken Verbrechern," *DZGGM* 10 (1927): 620–33; Kurt Böhmer, "Untersuchungen über den Körperbau des Verbrechers," *MKS* 19 (1928): 193–209; Martin Riedl, "Über Beziehungen von geistig-körperlicher Konstitution zur Kriminalität und anderen Defekten," *MKS* 23 (1932): 473.

54. Böhmer, "Untersuchungen über den Körperbau," 197–203; Hans Gruhle, "Wesen und Systematik des biologischen Typus," *MKBG* 2 (1928): 19–20; Birnbaum, *Kriminalpsychopathologie*, 2d ed., 197–200.

55. Julius Koch, *Die psychopathischen Minderwertigkeiten* (Ravensburg: Maier, 1891–93). See Chapter 2.

roughly half of all criminals were *minderwertig*. For Aschaffenburg, *Minderwertigkeit* consisted in mental deficiencies in both the intellectual and the emotional-volitional realms, namely feeblemindedness (*Schwachsinn*) and a lack of psychological resilience or stability (*Haltlosigkeit*). The adherents of what we have called the "Aschaffenburg paradigm" believed that the causes of *Minderwertigkeit* and its connection with criminal behavior were primarily environmental. Following degeneration theory, they argued that the causes of *Minderwertigkeit* often lay in adverse environmental factors such as lack of prenatal care or malnutrition. And if *Minderwertigkeit* frequently led to crime, this was not because its bearers suffered from a "moral defect" but because their feeblemindedness and lack of resilience handicapped *Minderwertige* in economic life.[56]

In the Weimar period, criminal-biological thinking on mental abnormalities underwent several changes, including a change in terminology. Whereas prewar writers had shortened Koch's *psychopathische Minderwertigkeit* to *Minderwertigkeit*, postwar criminal biologists dropped the term *Minderwertigkeit* and used the adjective *psychopathisch* and its derivatives *Psychopathie* (psychopathy) and *Psychopathen* (psychopaths) to refer to borderline mental abnormalities. This change resulted from the sentiment that the terms *Minderwertigkeit* (literally, inferiority) and *Minderwertige* carried derogatory connotations of biological, moral, or social inferiority that were deemed inappropriate.[57] Although it seems strange to modern English-speakers, the switch to the terms "psychopath" or "psychopathic personality" was actually a conscious effort to replace the value-laden term *Minderwertigkeit* with a neutral, scientific-sounding term.[58] Since the English equivalents "psychopath" and "psychopathic" are strongly associated with antisocial behavior, it should be emphasized that in the interwar period the German terms *Psychopathie*, *Psychopathen*, and *psychopathisch* did not refer specifically to antisocial behavior but to the much broader area of mental abnormalities that late twentieth-century American psychiatrists call personality disorders.[59]

56. Gustav Aschaffenburg, *Das Verbrechen und seine Bekämpfung: Kriminalpsychologie für Mediziner, Juristen und Soziologen, ein Beitrag zur Reform der Strafgesetzgebung* (Heidelberg: Winter, 1903). See Chapter 2.

57. Karl Birnbaum, *Die psychopathischen Verbrecher: Die Grenzzustände zwischen geistiger Gesundheit und Krankheit in ihren Beziehungen zu Verbrechen und Strafwesen*, 2d rev. ed. (Leipzig: Thieme, 1926), 5.

58. Kurt Schneider, *Die psychopathischen Persönlichkeiten*, 2d ed. (Leipzig: Deuticke, 1928), 16; Birnbaum, *Die psychopathischen Verbrecher*, 2d ed., 5.

59. On Schneider's role in the history of the concept of "psychopathic" disorders in modern psychiatry, see Werlinder, *Psychopathy*; Berrios, "Personality Disorders"; P. Pichot, "Psycho-

Besides the change in terminology, Weimar research on *Psychopathie* also brought substantive changes. Most important, the prewar period's monolithic conception of *Minderwertigkeit* gave way to a typological approach that distinguished between a variety of "psychopathic personalities." This new approach was formulated most authoritatively in Kurt Schneider's book *Die psychopathischen Persönlichkeiten* (Psychopathic personalities), which first appeared in 1923.[60] Going through nine editions between 1923 and 1950, Schneider's book was one of the most influential works in twentieth-century German psychiatry and exerted a strong influence on criminal biology. After receiving his M.D. in 1912, Schneider took a position in Gustav Aschaffenburg's psychiatric clinic at the University of Cologne, where he worked for almost twenty years and also served as adjunct professor of psychiatry. In 1931, he was appointed to the prestigious positions of director of the Clinical Section of the Deutsche Forschungsanstalt für Psychiatrie and chief psychiatrist at the Munich City Hospital.[61]

The term "psychopathic personalities" had been introduced by Emil Kraepelin in the 1904 edition of his textbook, in which he had distinguished four types of psychopathic personalities: born criminals, pathological liars, querulous persons, and *Triebmenschen* (persons driven by a basic compulsion, including vaga-

---

pathic Behaviour: A Historical Overview," in *Psychopathic Behavior: Approaches to Research*, ed. Robert D. Hare and Daisy Schalling (Chichester: Wiley, 1978); Schmiedebach, "Zum Verständniswandel." For remarkable continuities between the concept of "psychopathic personalities" as discussed in this chapter and the current psychiatric category of "personality disorders" (including "antisocial personality disorder"), see *Diagnostic and Statistical Manual of Mental Disorders*, 3d ed. (Washington, D.C.: American Psychiatric Association, 1987), 335–58; Jeremy Coid, "Current Concepts and Classifications in Psychopathic Disorder," in *Personality Disorder Reviewed*, ed. Peter Tyrer and George Stein (London: Gaskell, 1993), 113–64; Herschel Prins, *Offenders, Deviants or Patients?*, 2d ed. (London: Routledge, 1995), 119–42.

60. Kurt Schneider, *Die psychopathischen Persönlichkeiten*, 1st ed. (1923); 2d ed. (1928); 3d ed. (1934); 4th ed. (1940); 5th ed. (1942); 6th ed. (1944); English translation: *Psychopathic Personalities* (London: Cassell, 1958).

61. On Kurt Schneider (1887–1967), see Bernard Pauleikhoff, "Kurt Schneider," in *Das Menschenbild im Wandel der Zeit* (Hürtgenwald: Pressler, 1987), 4:73–99; Dirk Blasius, "Die 'Maskerade des Bösen.' Psychiatrische Forschung in der NS-Zeit," in *Medizin und Gesundheitspolitik in der NS-Zeit*, ed. Norbert Frei (Munich: Oldenbourg, 1991), 279–83; Blasius, *"Einfache Seelenstörung": Geschichte der deutschen Psychiatrie, 1800–1945* (Frankfurt: Fischer, 1994), 159–60, 191–94, 201–4; K. P. Kisker, "Kurt Schneider," *Der Nervenarzt* 39 (1968): 97–98; H. Kranz, "In memoriam Kurt Schneider," *Archiv für Psychiatrie* 211 (1968): 1–6; H. J. Weitbrecht, "Kurt Schneider 80 Jahre—80 Jahre Psychopathologie," *FNPG* 35 (1967): 497–515; Matthias Weber, *Ernst Rüdin: Eine kritische Biographie* (Berlin: Springer, 1993), 163. Kurt Schneider should not be confused with his colleague Carl Schneider, professor of psychiatry in Heidelberg, who played a major role in the Nazi euthanasia program.

bonds, spendthrifts, and dipsomaniacs).[62] Disturbed that Kraepelin's typology resembled a list of socially undesirable forms of behavior rather than medical conditions, Schneider tried to avoid Kraepelin's value judgments by grounding his typology of psychopathic personalities in objective psychological criteria. He also tried to bring conceptual rigor to the slippery subject of mental abnormality by carefully defining his terms. Following Kraepelin, Schneider defined the term "personality" as referring only to a person's emotions and will, thereby excluding the intellect. Thus departing from Koch and Aschaffenburg, who had included feeblemindedness (*Schwachsinn*) as a characteristic of *Minderwertigkeit*, Schneider insisted that intellectual defects could never constitute an "abnormal personality." In defining the term "abnormal," Schneider rejected any normative "equation of the normal with what is healthy, functional or desirable" and opted for a purely quantitative conception of the norm as the statistical average, thus defining abnormal personalities simply as "variations" deviating from the "average" human personality.[63]

Despite Schneider's intention to provide an objective, statistical definition of abnormality, his definition suffered from a variety of problems. First, Schneider himself admitted that quantitative measurements were impossible in the realm of psychology and that his "average" was therefore an imagined one that could not be precisely determined. Second, if any deviation from the norm was considered abnormal, then the number of abnormal variations was infinite. But since no one could study an infinite number of abnormalities, how could this infinite number be reduced to a manageable number of abnormal personalities that could be studied? In response to this problem, Schneider proposed focusing on a limited subset, namely "those abnormal personalities who suffer from their abnormality or from whose abnormality society suffers."[64] Whereas general psychiatric usage had previously treated the terms "abnormal" and "psychopathic" personalities as synonyms, Schneider reserved the term "psychopathic personalities" for this subset, within which he distinguished ten major types. Avoiding Kraepelin's social and moral criteria, he defined these ten types

62. Emil Kraepelin, *Psychiatrie: Ein Lehrbuch für Studierende und Ärzte*, 7th ed., 2 vols. (Leipzig: Barth, 1904), 2:816–41.

63. Schneider, *Die psychopathischen Persönlichkeiten*, 2d ed., 1–2.

64. Ibid., 2. Note the strikingly similar formulation from a 1989 article on mental disorders: "Some generally accepted types of personality disorders are listed below. It is important to recognize that simply exhibiting the trait or even having it to an abnormal extent is not enough to constitute disorder—for that, the degree of abnormality must cause disturbance to the individual or to society" ("Mental Disorders," in *Encyclopaedia Britannica*, 15th ed. [Chicago, 1989], 23:965).

in purely psychological terms as hyperthymic (sanguine), depressive, insecure, fanatic, domineering, emotionally unstable, explosive, compassionless, weak-willed, and asthenic (nervous) psychopaths.[65]

After Schneider's careful efforts to avoid value judgments in his definition of abnormal personalities, the introduction of the "suffering of society" as a criterion for psychopathic personalities was surprising. Aware of the problem, Schneider explained that he had created the psychopathic category "not for scientific but for practical purposes" because it contained all those abnormal personalities which the psychiatrist encountered professionally. After all, abnormal individuals came to a psychiatrist's attention only if their abnormalities caused problems for them or the people around them. Schneider admitted that the "suffering of society" was a "totally subjective" and "teleological" criterion. But he denied that this presented a problem, since in "scientific studies" one could avoid the subjective category of psychopathic personalities and operate with the broader category of abnormal personalities. This attempt to finesse the problem of value judgments was clearly unsatisfactory, however, because Schneider's work actually had the effect of focusing attention on psychopathic personalities as the only mental abnormalities worthy of study.[66]

Although Schneider acknowledged that human personalities were affected by a variety of environmental and organic influences, he argued that abnormal personalities were always congenital and therefore usually hereditary.[67] But Schneider also noted that nothing was known about their mode of hereditary transmission, a position that he maintained throughout the interwar period. By characterizing abnormal personalities as congenital, Schneider was rejecting three other explanations: the common prewar view, found in Aschaffenburg, that mental abnormalities resulted from adverse environmental influences such as malnutrition; the psychoanalytic view that mental abnormalities resulted from a person's life experiences; and, finally, the view of degeneration theory that mental abnormalities formed part of a progressive disease process that could eventually lead to full-fledged mental illness. The rejection of these different views had somewhat contradictory implications. By rejecting the view that mental abnormalities could result from environmental influences or psychological experiences, Schneider was emphasizing the determining role of heredity. But by abandoning degeneration theory Schneider drew a sharp line

65. Schneider, *Die psychopathischen Persönlichkeiten*, 2d ed., 30–79.

66. Ibid., 3–4.

67. Congenital but nonhereditary abnormal personalities could result from intrauterine damage to the fetus or injuries at birth (ibid., 5).

between abnormality and mental illness, which suggested that abnormal personalities were far closer to normality than to mental illness. Schneider's rejection of the notion of degeneration also reflected a general waning of degeneration theory that began in the first decade of the twentieth century and led to its virtual eclipse by the end of the 1920s.[68]

While Schneider's book was the most influential general study of psychopathic personalities, the connection between psychopathy and criminal behavior received its most authoritative treatment in the work of Karl Birnbaum. After receiving his M.D. in 1905, Birnbaum began a lifelong career working in Berlin's municipal psychiatric hospitals in Herzberge and Buch, which culminated in his appointment as director of the Berlin-Buch Psychiatric Hospital in 1930, a position from which he was dismissed in 1933 because he was Jewish. Publishing more than a dozen books between 1909 and 1933, he was appointed lecturer (*Privatdozent*) in criminal psychology at the University of Berlin in 1923 and adjunct professor (*ausserordentlicher Professor*) in 1927. Birnbaum developed an early interest in criminal psychology when he was in charge of the high-security wards for criminal and dangerous inmates from 1908 to 1919.[69] His monograph on psychopathic criminals and his survey texts of forensic psychiatry and criminal biology quickly established him as a major figure in the field of criminal biology during the Weimar period.

First published in 1914 and issued in a revised edition in 1926, Birnbaum's book *Die psychopathischen Verbrecher* (Psychopathic criminals) reflected the shift from a monolithic conception of mental abnormality as *Minderwertigkeit* toward a typological approach that distinguished a variety of different psychopathic personalities. While the original 1914 edition had listed almost thirty different "psychopathic types," the 1926 edition had streamlined this typology into about a dozen major types, most of which were similar to Schneider's. Whereas

68. Edward Shorter, *A History of Psychiatry* (New York: Wiley, 1997), 97–98; Ian Dowbiggin, *Inheriting Madness: Professionalization and Psychiatric Knowledge in Nineteenth-Century France* (Berkeley: University of California Press, 1991), 162–71; Oswald Bumke, *Über nervöse Entartung* (Berlin: Springer, 1912).

69. Bernard Pauleikhoff, "Karl Birnbaum," in *Das Menschenbild im Wandel der Zeit* (Hürtgenwald: Pressler, 1987), 3:270–88; Hartwig Liedtke, "Karl Birnbaum: Leben und Werk" (M.D. diss., University of Cologne, 1982); F. Irro and P. Hagemann, "Karl Birnbaum: Versuch einer Würdigung der Lebensarbeit eines bedeutenden Psychiaters und zugleich ein verspäteter Nachruf," *Psychiatrie, Neurologie und medizinische Psychologie* 25 (1973): 117–23; biographical entries in *International Biographical Dictionary of Central European Emigres, 1933–1945*, 3 vols. (Munich: K. G. Saur, 1980–83), 2:111; and in D. Fischer, *Biographisches Lexikon der hervorragenden Ärzte der letzten fünfzig Jahre* (Munich: Urban und Schwarzenberg, 1932), 123.

Schneider's book was a general treatment of psychopathic personalities, which briefly mentioned each type's possible criminal propensities, Birnbaum's work was specifically devoted to the link between psychopathy and crime.[70]

Birnbaum claimed that psychopathic personalities were more frequent among criminals than among the general population, although he conceded that the proportion of psychopaths might be equally high among the lower social strata from which most criminals came. While the proportion of psychopaths among the general population was usually estimated at about 10 percent, their proportion among criminals had been estimated at between 5 and 30 percent, and Birnbaum trusted the higher figures.[71] To explain the disproportionate concentration of psychopaths among criminals, Birnbaum offered a general explanation of the connection between psychopathy and criminal behavior. According to Birnbaum, all psychopaths suffered from three basic deficiencies: their psychological reactions were out of proportion to the provoking stimuli (too weak or too strong); their character traits were not harmonized, so that strong drives often lacked the corresponding inhibitions; and they lacked mental resilience and balance, so that average stimuli could lead to a breakdown of normal mental functioning. All these deficiencies made it difficult for a psychopath to "adapt" to the demands of life.[72]

Although in some cases this inability to adapt led only to individual suffering, in many it led to antisocial behavior. The crimes of psychopaths "derive[d] directly from their individual nature, their entire personality." As a result, each psychopathic type was predisposed to particular kinds of crimes: the explosive type to crimes of passion, the pathological liar to fraud, and so on.[73] But although Birnbaum perceived an intrinsic link between psychopathy and crime, he also cautioned that a "psychopathic constitution" was by no means synonymous with antisocial behavior. On the contrary, some psychopaths displayed culturally and socially valuable character traits. In fact, the same psychopathic

---

70. Karl Birnbaum, *Die psychopathischen Verbrecher: Die Grenzzustände zwischen geistiger Gesundheit und Krankheit in ihren Beziehungen zu Verbrechen und Strafwesen* (Berlin: Langenscheidt, 1914); 2d rev. ed. (Leipzig: Thieme, 1926). Among his other major publications were *Kriminalpsychopathologie* (Berlin: Springer, 1921); *Kriminalpsychopathologie und psychobiologische Verbrecherkunde*, 2d rev. ed. (Berlin: Springer, 1931); *Handwörterbuch der medizinischen Psychologie* (Leipzig: Thieme, 1930). See also Karl Wilmanns, *Die sogenannte verminderte Zurechnungsfähigkeit* (Berlin: Springer, 1927).

71. Birnbaum, *Die psychopathischen Verbrecher*, 2d ed., 5–8. A year later, after a thorough review of the literature, the psychiatrist Karl Wilmanns estimated the incidence of psychopathy among "habitual criminals" to be as high as 50 to 75 percent (Wilmanns, *Die sogenannte verminderte Zurechnungsfähigkeit*, 74).

72. Birnbaum, *Die psychopathischen Verbrecher*, 2d ed., 10–15.

73. Ibid., 16–17.

constitution could give rise to either antisocial or social tendencies, depending on external influences. Only a minority of psychopaths were virtually doomed to commit crimes by the "endogenous" factor of their psychopathic constitution.[74] Of Schneider's ten psychopathic personalities, only two, compassionless (*gemütlose*) and weak-willed psychopaths, had high levels of criminal behavior; five exhibited some antisocial behavior; and three, including depressive, insecure, and asthenic psychopaths, hardly ever impinged on their environment.[75]

If psychopathic types with low criminal propensity committed a crime, this was either because exogenous influences had pushed them in an antisocial direction or because their primary psychopathic trait was combined with other traits that created a particularly criminogenic combination. Crowded living quarters, for instance, might lead an irritable or explosive psychopath to a violent outburst, while the temptations of the big city might lead the weak-willed type to theft.[76] A good example of criminogenic combinations of traits was provided in Schneider's discussion of the hyperthymic psychopath. According to Schneider, hyperthymic (i.e., hyperactive) psychopaths were fundamentally cheerful and active and therefore "usually useful, industrious and capable." But if their hyperthymic nature was combined with a "quarrelsome" trait, they were likely to insult others or get into fights; if it was combined with an "unstable" trait, they were apt to become vagabonds or beggars.[77] In sum, even though every psychopath's adaptive deficiencies carried a potential for antisocial behavior, only a very limited number of psychopaths actually became criminal because of particular combinations of traits or particular external influences.

Birnbaum and Schneider agreed, however, that there were two psychopathic types that had an extremely high propensity for criminal behavior. "Amoral psychopaths" (Birnbaum's term) had developed normal egoistic emotions but were deficient in "altruistic, social, and moral feelings," felt no emotional connection with the world around them, and lacked the "higher feelings" for "justice and truth, morality and decency, duty and honor." As a result, they were highly susceptible to criminal behavior of all sorts.[78] Concerned to avoid value-laden terms, Schneider called this type *gemütlos* (compassionless) but characterized it in essentially the same way, as lacking "compassion, shame, honor,

---

74. Ibid., 150–54.
75. Schneider, *Die psychopathischen Persönlichkeiten*, 2d ed., 35, 39, 49, 55, 61, 67, 69, 73, 75, 79.
76. Birnbaum, *Die psychopathischen Verbrecher*, 2d ed., 150–52.
77. Schneider, *Die psychopathischen Persönlichkeiten*, 2d ed., 30–35.
78. Birnbaum, *Die psychopathischen Verbrecher*, 2d ed., 54–65.

remorse, conscience."[79] Although Birnbaum thought that extreme cases of the amoral psychopath might be called born criminals, Birnbaum and Schneider agreed that not all *gemütlose* or amoral psychopaths had to become criminal. Especially if born into higher social strata and equipped with high intelligence, they could have successful careers.[80]

The second psychopathic type with a high propensity for crime was called *haltlos* (unstable or lacking resilience) by Birnbaum and *willenlos* (weak-willed; literally, "without will") by Schneider. According to Schneider, this type was characterized by a "lack of will" that made them vulnerable to external influences. In addition, Birnbaum argued that their emotions were characterized by a "hollowness" that made them unable to properly appreciate "important ideal values such as honor and morality, duty and responsibility, as well as material ones such as prosperity and health." *Haltlose* therefore ran a high risk of "social failure": their emotional hollowness might lead to an irresponsible, "pleasure-seeking" life; their lack of resilience might turn them into vagabonds and beggars; their weakness of will might cause them to be taken advantage of by "bad elements." In all of these cases the result was a continuous social decline that ended either in a "asocial-parasitic" existence (pimps, prostitutes, vagabonds) or an "antisocial-criminal" life (habitual thieves or burglars).[81]

Given Schneider's explicit effort to avoid value judgments in defining his psychopathic types, the value-laden nature of the preceding definitions is striking. Although Schneider thought he had banished value judgments by replacing Kraepelin's blatantly sociological and moral criteria with supposedly psychological ones, upon closer inspection his psychological criteria proved no less value-laden. By defining the *gemütlos* psychopath as lacking "compassion, shame, a sense of honor, remorse, and conscience," Schneider was clearly assuming that compassion and remorse were normal human characteristics. Yet this assumption was not based on statistical studies proving that the average person was compassionate but on the unexamined belief that a socially desirable trait like compassion must be biologically normal. The fact that even Schneider failed to escape this fallacy demonstrates that the conflation of social and biological norms was deeply ingrained in psychiatry.

As we saw in Chapter 2, prewar criminal psychologists propounded two different paradigms about the connection between crime and abnormality. While

79. Schneider, *Die psychopathischen Persönlichkeiten*, 2d ed, 69–73.

80. Birnbaum, *Die psychopathischen Verbrecher*, 2d ed., 62, 54–65; Schneider, *Die psychopathischen Persönlichkeiten*, 2d ed., 73.

81. Birnbaum, *Die psychopathischen Verbrecher*, 2d ed., 46–52; Schneider, *Die psychopathischen Persönlichkeiten*, 2d ed., 73–76.

the Kraepelin paradigm defended a revised version of the born criminal theory by arguing that many habitual criminals suffered from a "moral defect," the Aschaffenburg paradigm denied the existence of such a defect and argued that many habitual criminals were simply suffering from *geistige Minderwertig-keiten* that were found among noncriminals as well; if *Minderwertige* became criminal, it was because their feeblemindedness made it difficult for them to hold down a steady job. These two paradigms were characterized by three crucial differences. In the Kraepelin paradigm, the abnormality of habitual criminals (the moral defect) was congenital, specific to criminals, and directly criminogenic. In the Aschaffenburg paradigm, the abnormality of habitual criminals was usually acquired, common among noncriminals, and not directly criminogenic. The defenders of the "born criminal" posited a very close link between criminality and abnormality, while the Aschaffenburg camp saw only a loose connection between the two.

How did Birnbaum's and Schneider's work fit into this picture? In some respects, their work strengthened the connection between crime and abnormality. Like Kraepelin and other advocates of the born criminal, Birnbaum and Schneider regarded abnormal personalities as congenital, thereby linking criminal behavior to a person's heredity. In addition, Birnbaum insisted that the crimes of psychopaths "derived directly from their individual nature," thus tightening the connection between criminal behavior and a psychopath's individual abnormality. In other respects, however, Birnbaum's and Schneider's work weakened the connection between abnormality and crime. Most important, the term "psychopathic personalities" referred to general abnormalities that were neither specific to criminals nor directly criminogenic. Moreover, both Birnbaum and Schneider made it clear that psychopathic personalities became criminal only if different psychopathic traits came together in a particularly criminogenic combination or if certain environmental factors were present. Finally, Schneider's point that psychopathic personalities had no connection with mental illness, but were very close to normal variations of character, weakened the connection between crime and mental illness.

The Search for Genetic Factors

Most Weimar psychiatrists acknowledged that an individual's personality was not entirely hereditary but at least partly shaped by environmental influences. They therefore generally agreed that the role of heredity in criminal behavior was more limited and more complex than the role of personality. Since even the role of personality in criminal behavior was not yet fully understood, some psychiatrists recommended that it would be best to focus research on the role of personality in criminal behavior and leave aside the much thornier problem of genetic factors.[82] Most psychiatrists working in criminal biology, however, took an avid interest in the question of heredity, which was closely connected to their enthusiasm for eugenics.

Research on the role of heredity in criminal behavior dates back to the earliest years of German criminal anthropology, before the turn of the century. Very little was known about genetics, let alone human genetics, at this time. Without any knowledge about the physiological basis of heredity or modes of hereditary transmission, turn-of-the-century psychiatrists studied the role of heredity in insanity with statistical-genealogical methods, that is, by investigating the frequency of mental illness among a patient's relatives. The incidence of insanity among a person's relatives was called *erbliche Belastung* (literally, "hereditary burden").

Researchers interested in criminal behavior applied the same method to criminals, looking not just for mental illness but also for criminality in the family of a given criminal. The most widely cited study of this kind was published in 1904 by Jakob Hartmann, a psychiatrist working under Eugen Bleuler at the Burghölzli asylum in Zurich. Studying the extended families of two hundred Swiss prisoners, Hartmann found that 70 percent of these criminals were *erblich belastet*, that is, burdened with "hereditary abnormalities" among their relatives, with alcoholism in 30 percent, criminality or "abnormal characters" in 19 percent, mental illnesses in 15 percent, nervous illnesses in 5 percent, and suicides in 1 percent of the cases. Although the figure of 70 percent seemed considerable, its significance was greatly diminished by the fact that other studies had found no less than 60 percent *erblich Belastete* in the general population. Nevertheless, Hartmann concluded that the *erbliche Belastung* of his criminals was greater than that of normal people and almost as great as that of the mentally ill, which had been estimated at 78 percent.[83]

Such findings that many criminals were *erblich belastet* gave rise to three different theories about the role of heredity in criminal behavior. The high incidence of full-fledged mental illness among the relatives of criminals produced the theory that criminality might be genetically related to various types of mental illness. The high frequency of criminal behavior among the relatives of criminals led to the theory that some criminals might have inherited a "criminal dis-

82. Hans Gruhle, "Aufgaben der Kriminalpsychologie," *ZStW* 51 (1930–31): 476–77.
83. Jakob Hartmann, "Über die hereditären Verhältnisse bei Verbrechern," *MKS* 1 (1904–5): 493–520. For an earlier study, see E. Sichart, "Über individuelle Faktoren des Verbrechens," *ZStW* 10 (1890): 37–50.

position." Finally, the frequency of mental abnormalities (psychopathic traits) among the relatives of criminals gave rise to the theory that heredity played an indirect role in criminal behavior in the sense that some criminals might have inherited mental abnormalities which, although not directly criminogenic, could under certain external circumstances *contribute* to criminal behavior.

The first theory, which posited a genetic link between criminality and mental illness, was supported by several prewar studies. Some of these found an especially high incidence of schizophrenia among the families of criminals, suggesting that criminality was genetically related to schizophrenia.[84] Although this theory had some early critics, the proposition that criminal behavior had close genetic ties to mental illness, especially schizophrenia, was widely accepted into the 1930s, when it was discredited by a statistical study conducted by Friedrich Stumpfl, discussed in the next chapter.[85] The second theory, which argued that some criminals inherited a "criminal character," was also followed up in further research before the First World War. Examining the families of "amoral" criminals, the renowned psychiatrist Eugen Bleuler concluded that their "moral defect" was passed on from parents to children as a hereditary trait.[86] In 1914, the prison chaplain Carl Rath advanced the even bolder claim that criminality was inherited according to Mendelian rules. Examining fifteen hundred recidivists in the Siegburg prison, Rath found that in families with two criminal parents 87.5 percent of the sons had become criminal, whereas in families with one criminal parent 50.5 percent of the sons had become criminal, and concluded that criminality was a recessive Mendelian trait.[87]

But the notion that criminality was a genetic trait that could be passed on from

84. Gertrud Rinderknecht, "Über kriminelle Heboide," *ZGNP* 57 (1920): 35–70; Friedrich Meggendorfer, "Klinische und genealogische Untersuchungen über 'moral insanity,'" *ZGNP* 66 (1921): 208–31.

85. Johannes Lange, for instance, endorsed this theory in "Über die Anlage zum Verbrechen," in *Stufenstrafvollzug*, 2:144–45. For an early critical view, see Eduard Reiss, "Über erbliche Belastung bei Schwerverbrechern," *Klinische Wochenschrift* 1 (1922): 2184–87. The theory was later discredited by Friedrich Stumpfl, *Erbanlage und Verbrechen: Charakterologische und psychiatrische Sippenuntersuchungen* (Berlin: Springer, 1935); see Chapter 6 below.

86. Bleuler's study is summarized in Lange, "Über die Anlage zum Verbrechen," 146.

87. Carl Rath, *Über die Vererbung von Dispositionen zum Verbrechen: Eine statistische und psychologische Untersuchung* (Stuttgart: Spemann, 1914), 61–64. Rath's book was accepted as a doctoral dissertation by the Philosophical Faculty of the University of Bonn. On the rediscovery of Gregor Mendel's work and the flowering of Mendelian genetics at the turn of the century, see Weindling, *Health, Race and German Politics*, 230–39; Weingart, Kroll, and Bayertz, *Rasse, Blut und Gene*, 320–28; Jonathan Harwood, *Styles of Scientific Thought: The German Genetics Community, 1900–1933* (Chicago: University of Chicago Press, 1993), 34–36; Ernst Mayr, *The Growth of Biological Thought: Diversity, Evolution, and Inheritance* (Cambridge, Mass.: Harvard University Press, 1982), 727–38.

parents to children also met with immediate criticism. As early as 1903 Gustav Aschaffenburg had pointed out that criminal behavior among a criminal's parents or relatives was no proof of hereditary transmission. If children of criminal parents became criminal, this might well be because they learned such behavior from their parents and the criminal milieu in which they were raised. As Aschaffenburg noted, this criticism also invalidated the American studies of "crime families" like the Jukes, which interpreted the criminality of family members over several generations as evidence that their criminality was a hereditary trait.[88] Aschaffenburg concluded that there was no evidence to support the notion of a "hereditary criminal disposition" that could be passed on from parents to children. Definite evidence for genetic factors could be provided only by the "experiment of raising healthy children of criminal families in a decent environment without informing them of their descent, and observing whether criminal inclinations would nevertheless appear." Considering the obstacles facing such an experiment, Aschaffenburg thought it impossible to prove or disprove the existence of a hereditary criminal disposition. But, he argued, the notion of a genetic criminal disposition was "dispensable" because the bulk of criminal behavior was sufficiently explained by the combination of two well-documented factors: the adverse social milieu and the *Minderwertigkeit* of most criminals.[89]

By the Weimar years, Aschaffenburg's critical attitude had clearly prevailed. Those prewar studies that interpreted criminal behavior over several generations as evidence of a heritable criminal disposition were firmly dismissed by the major criminal biologists. Reviewing the existing literature on the role of heredity in crime in 1921, Karl Birnbaum agreed with Aschaffenburg that there was no evidence for the existence of a heritable criminal disposition.[90] A few years later, Johannes Lange and Hans Luxenburger of the Deutsche Forschungsanstalt für Psychiatrie reached the same conclusion.[91]

The criticisms of the notion of a hereditary criminal disposition voiced by

88. Richard Dugdale, *The Jukes: A Study in Crime, Pauperism, Disease, and Heredity* (New York: Putnam, 1877); see also Henry Goddard, *The Kallikak Family: A Study in the Heredity of Feeblemindedness* (New York: Macmillan, 1912). On the Juke and Kallikak studies, see James Trent, *Inventing the Feeble Mind: A History of Mental Retardation in the United States* (Berkeley: University of California Press, 1994), 70–72, 163–65; David Smith, *Minds Made Feeble: The Myth and Legacy of the Kallikaks* (Rockville: Aspen Systems, 1985); Diane Paul, *Controlling Human Heredity, 1865 to the Present* (Atlantic Highlands: Humanities Press, 1995), 43–44, 50–54; Philip Reilly, *The Surgical Solution: A History of Involuntary Sterilization in the United States* (Baltimore: Johns Hopkins University Press, 1991), 14–17.

89. Aschaffenburg, *Das Verbrechen und seine Bekämpfung*, 1st ed., 101–3.

90. Birnbaum, *Kriminalpsychopathologie*, 1st ed., 153.

91. Lange, "Über die Anlage zum Verbrechen"; Hans Luxenburger, "Anlage und Umwelt beim Verbrecher," *AZP* 92 (1930): 426.

Aschaffenburg, Birnbaum, Lange, and Luxenburger did not mean that these researchers thought that heredity played no role whatsoever in criminal behavior. Most of them gave some credence to the first theory, that some criminal behavior might be genetically connected to mental illness in the criminal's family. More important, all of them propounded what I call the "third theory," which argued that heredity often played an *indirect* role in crime. The reasoning behind this third theory was simple. While its proponents rejected the idea that anyone suffered from a hereditary criminal disposition, they believed that many criminals were indeed characterized by psychopathic abnormalities that frequently *contributed* to criminal behavior, even though they were not inherently criminogenic. Since heredity played a role in the etiology of these mental abnormalities, it followed that it also played an indirect role in the criminal behavior of abnormal criminals.

By the Weimar period, this third theory had clearly triumphed over the notion of a hereditary criminal disposition. Both Hans Luxenburger, one of the most highly regarded figures in human genetics (*Erbbiologie*) in the Weimar period, and Johannes Lange, soon to become Weimar's most prominent researcher on the role of heredity in crime, endorsed this theory in no uncertain terms. Both Lange and Luxenburger worked at the Deutsche Forschungsanstalt für Psychiatrie in Munich. Luxenburger was the senior researcher in its Genealogical-Demographic Section, headed by Ernst Rüdin, which conducted research on human genetics through statistical-genealogical methods.[92] Johannes Lange was often described as Emil Kraepelin's "favorite student." When Kraepelin founded the Forschungsanstalt in 1917, he appointed Lange codirector (with himself) of its Clinical Section, a position Lange continued to occupy as sole director after Kraepelin's death in 1926. In addition, Lange held concurrent positions as senior psychiatrist (*Oberarzt*) at the Munich City Hospital and as adjunct professor at the University of Munich. In 1930 he was appointed to a chair in psychiatry and the directorship of the psychiatric hospital at the University of Breslau. Lange took a special interest in criminal biology and had begun work on a twin study in the mid-1920s, using materials from the Bavarian Criminal-Biological Service, on whose scientific advisory board he served.[93]

92. On the Forschungsanstalt, Luxenburger, and Rüdin, see Matthias Weber, "Ein Forschungsinstitut für Psychiatrie," and Weber, *Ernst Rüdin: Eine kritische Biographie* (Berlin: Springer, 1993).

93. Hans Habel, "Die Bedeutung des Lebenswerkes von Johannes Lange für die Entwicklung der kriminalbiologischen Forschung," *MKS* 30 (1939): 1–9; Weber, *Ernst Rüdin*, 119, 146, 163.

As a result of the close association between the Forschungsanstalt and the Criminal-Biological Service, both Lange and Luxenburger were asked to deliver lectures on the role of genetics in crime to the service's continuing education seminars, which provide an excellent overview of their thinking on this difficult issue. In his 1927 lecture, Lange explicitly rejected the notion of a genetic criminal disposition but argued that genetic factors did contribute to the mental abnormalities of many criminals and thus played an indirect role in criminal behavior. Assuming that virtually all *habitual* criminals were psychopaths, Lange derived two conclusions from Schneider's and Birnbaum's work: first, habitual criminals did not represent a biologically homogeneous group but a diverse collection of different psychopathic personalities; second, the criminality of any individual criminal did not result from a single "criminal" character trait but from a particularly unfortunate combination of psychopathic traits. If habitual criminality derived from combinations of psychopathic traits, Lange concluded, then the role of heredity in crime was reduced to the role of heredity in the genesis of psychopathic abnormalities. Agreeing with Schneider that psychopathic abnormalities were generally hereditary, Lange argued that there were two possibilities for the hereditary transmission of criminogenic combinations of psychopathic traits. Either these combinations were passed on as a whole through "direct hereditary transmission," or they could be "newly created through the combination of negative but not yet criminogenic traits from both parents" (a process he called *Keimmischung*). Both of these possibilities, however, remained theoretical constructs because nothing was known about the modes of hereditary transmission for such traits.[94]

When Hans Luxenburger lectured on the same subject two years later, he concurred with Lange's views but was even more insistent on dispelling exaggerated notions of the power of heredity. With very few exceptions, such as eye color, he explained, what was transmitted through the process of biological inheritance was not "fixed characteristics" but "reactive potentials" (*Reaktionsbereitschaft*) that responded to external stimuli. Therefore, the actual manifestation of a particular trait in an individual was never the result of genetics alone but of an interaction between inherited potentials and environmental factors.

After debunking the general notion of purely genetic traits, Luxenburger addressed the special difficulties of studying criminal behavior. "Crime," he insisted, was "an arbitrarily defined sociological-juridical concept," subject to

94. Lange, "Über die Anlage zum Verbrechen." Except for the title, Lange used the term *verbrecherische Anlagen* in the plural to indicate that he was referring to criminogenic combinations of psychopathic traits rather than a unified hereditary criminal disposition.

changing definitions. Hence the existence of a genetic factor (*Anlage*) that
would predispose its bearer to "those phenomena and only those which were
subsumed under the concept crime" was a logical impossibility. It therefore
made no sense to speak of a "hereditary criminal disposition" (*Erbanlage zum
Verbrechen*).[95] There were, however, "certain specificities of character and temperament . . . that react with environmental stimuli in a way that can bring the
individual into conflict with the law." These Luxenburger referred to as hereditary "criminogenic preconditions" (*kriminogene Voraussetzungen*). Three
crucial differences distinguished Luxenburger's "criminogenic preconditions"
from the discarded notion of a hereditary criminal disposition. First, whereas
the latter was supposed to be a unified trait, an individual's criminogenic preconditions consisted of a combination of multiple traits, each of which was not
criminogenic in itself. Second, whereas the hereditary criminal disposition was
assumed to be the same for all criminals, criminogenic preconditions could vary
among different criminals. Finally, like any other genetic factors, these criminogenic preconditions were only "reactive potentials" whose actual manifestation always depended on environmental factors. "There are no pure hereditary
criminals and no pure milieu-criminals. Crime is a product of the interaction
between heredity and environment."[96]

Even though Lange and Luxenburger were convinced that heredity played an
important role in criminal behavior, their understanding of the role of heredity
was quite sophisticated. Far from propounding any kind of hereditarian determinism, Lange and Luxenburger stressed that the role of heredity in criminal
behavior was complex, indirect, and inextricably bound up with environmental
factors. Nor did their focus on heredity lead them to distance the biologically
"abnormal" criminal from the "normal" citizen. On the contrary, they argued
that the recognition of the biological and social forces at work should lead
to compassion rather than condemnation. As Lange put it, "The more one
comprehends the determining factors of [the criminal's] development and
nature . . . the easier it should become to recognize the human being in the
criminal." "The correctional officer, the teacher . . . the psychiatrist . . . must
learn to see [in the criminal] the unfortunate person in his predicament."[97]
Luxenburger concluded his lecture on a similar note: "Before the judgment seat
of nature, all of us are neither good nor evil . . . we are merely more or less
prepared, hereditarily and environmentally, for adapting to the norms estab-

95. Luxenburger, "Anlage und Umwelt beim Verbrecher," 418, 424, 426.
96. Ibid., 430–31, 436–38.
97. Lange, "Über die Anlage zum Verbrechen," 144.

lished by the other members of our species. . . . Good fortune obliges us to help those who are less fortunate, and helps us to pay our debt to fate, which made [social adaptation] . . . easier for us than for those we call criminals."[98]

By rejecting the notion of a hereditary criminal disposition and endorsing a more complex theory on the role of heredity in crime, criminologically oriented psychiatrists like Lange and Luxenburger greatly complicated their research agenda. Research could not focus on identifying a single genetic trait common to all criminals but had to take into account that hereditary criminogenic preconditions differed from individual to individual. Luxenburger therefore called for a criminal-biological "typology" as the next step in criminological research. Moreover, even in an individual case, a criminal's hereditary criminogenic preconditions did not consist of a single trait but of a combination of multiple "specificities of character," so that the researcher interested in genetic factors had to trace the hereditary transmission of multiple traits.

The first, highly speculative attempt at this type of research came from the psychiatrist Eduard Reiss. Reiss studied the families of over a hundred prisoners and tried to attribute the criminality of individual prisoners to the combination of character traits inherited from each parent. At the 1922 meeting of the German Association for Psychiatry, Reiss explained how certain combinations of inherited character traits could lead to criminal behavior: the criminality of a "remarkably brutal burglar characterized by megalomania, vanity, and pathological lying," for example, resulted from the combination of traits inherited from a "brutal and sensual father" and a "vain and arrogant mother with an excessive imagination," while the criminality of an "unreliable, irritable, and mendacious thief" could be attributed to the "mendacity" of the mother and the "pathological irritability" of the father. Reiss presented half a dozen such cases to demonstrate "the paramount importance of individual character traits or their combinations as the decisive moment for chronic criminality." Reiss's approach was particularly attractive because it could explain the appearance of a criminal in a hitherto "honest" family. But Reiss himself acknowledged that he could not prove the hereditary transmission of any of these traits and therefore admitted that his research remained speculative.[99]

At the 1927 meeting of the Association of German Correctional Officers (Verein der deutschen Strafanstaltsbeamten), the prominent psychiatrist Hermann Hoffmann held up Reiss's work as a model for future research because it contributed to the task of identifying the "building blocks" of human person-

---

98. Luxenburger, "Anlage und Umwelt beim Verbrecher," 438.
99. Reiss, "Über erbliche Belastung bei Schwerverbrechern."

ality, their relations to one another, and their genetic roots. Hoffmann was confident that cumulative data from criminal-biological examinations would reveal which combinations of character traits were especially common among different types of criminals. The ultimate goal of genetic research would be to "recognize the laws" by which the "crossbreeding" of particular parents produced certain kinds of offspring.[100]

The First Twin Study

Although Johannes Lange found Reiss's research suggestive, he also understood its basic methodological problem. Even if an individual shared certain traits with his or her parents, this was not proof of hereditary transmission because it was "impossible to distinguish the influences of the milieu from those of heredity."[101] Searching for a method that would allow him to distinguish between environmental and genetic factors, Lange came across the "twin method" and conducted the world's first twin study in the field of criminal biology. Published in 1929 and soon translated into English, this study made Lange the Weimar period's most prominent researcher on the role of heredity in crime.[102]

The twin method, first introduced by the British eugenicist Francis Galton in 1876,[103] consists of comparing a group of identical (monozygotic) twins with a group of fraternal (dizygotic) twins to determine whether identical twins are more likely than fraternal twins to share a particular trait known to be present in one of the twins. Twin pairs in which both partners share that particular trait are called concordant. The method assumes that the two types of twins differ only in their genetic similarity, namely, that identical twins share the same genetic makeup, whereas fraternal twins do not.[104] Therefore, according to the

100. Hermann Hoffmann, "Die erbbiologische Persönlichkeitsforschung und ihre Bedeutung in der Kriminalbiologie," *BfG* 58 (1927): 316–21.

101. Lange, "Über die Anlage zum Verbrechen," 146.

102. Johannes Lange, *Verbrechen als Schicksal: Studien an kriminellen Zwillingen* (Leipzig: Thieme, 1929), translated as *Crime and Destiny* (New York: Boni, 1930) and *Crime as Destiny* (London: Allen and Unwin, 1931). See also Lange's articles: "Psychiatrische Zwillingsprobleme," *ZGNP* 112 (1928): 283–87; "Leistungen der Zwillingspathologie für die Psychiatrie," *AZP* 90 (1929): 122–42; "Verbrechen und Vererbung," *Eugenik* 1 (1931): 165–73; "Kriminalität und Eugenik," *Medizinische Welt* 7, no. 22 (3 June 1933): 761–65.

103. Francis Galton, "The History of Twins as a Criterion of the Relative Powers of Nature and Nurture," *Fraser's Magazine* (1875): 566–76.

104. The method therefore assumes that the two types do not differ in the similarity of their environments; that is, that the environments of identical twins are no more similar than those of fraternal twins. Critics of the method challenge this assumption.

twin method, similar rates of concordance for both types of twins indicate that the trait in question is not genetic. Conversely, if all identical twins are concordant while most fraternal twins are not, this is seen as proof that the characteristic is genetic. Finally, if the concordance rate among identical twins falls short of 100 percent but is significantly higher than that of fraternal twins, this would indicate that the trait in question is strongly, but not exclusively, determined by genetic factors.[105]

Seeking to apply the twin method to shed light on the role of heredity in criminal behavior, Lange looked for pairs of twins in which at least one partner was convicted of a crime. Careful to avoid arbitrariness in the selection of his sample, he located all twins registered in the records of Bavaria's Criminal-Biological Service and all twins incarcerated in Bavarian prisons on a particular day. In addition, he checked for convicted twins among his own hospital patients and among the psychopaths studied by the Genealogical Department of the Deutsche Forschungsanstalt für Psychiatrie. From this sample of convicted twins, Lange selected all those cases in which the other twin was of the same sex, still living, and old enough to be convicted of a crime. Lange excluded different-sex twins because their concordance rates were likely to be affected by the well-known gender differential in crime rates. Following these criteria, Lange ended up with thirty pairs of twins (thirteen identical and seventeen fraternal) in which one partner was known to have been convicted of a crime. The study's results were as follows: among identical twins, the second twin was also convicted of a crime in ten (77 percent) of thirteen cases, whereas among fraternal twins the second partner was convicted in only two (12 percent) of seventeen cases. In short, identical twins were predominantly concordant, while fraternal twins were predominantly discordant. In accordance with the twin method, Lange therefore concluded that "heredity [*Anlage*] plays a predominant role among the causes of crime." Lange immediately added, however, that the results of the study, especially the discordance of about a quarter of identical twins, showed that environmental influences played a role as well.[106]

Going far beyond these aggregate figures, Lange's study included fairly complete accounts of the identical twins' lives and criminal careers based on per-

105. For a survey of twin research on criminality since Lange, see Karl Christiansen, "A Review of Studies of Criminality among Twins," in *Biosocial Bases of Criminal Behavior*, ed. Sarnoff Mednick and Karl Christiansen (New York: Gardner Press, 1977), 45–88. On the present state of twin research, see Lawrence Wright, *Twins and What They Tell Us about Who We Are* (New York: Wiley, 1997).

106. Lange, *Verbrechen als Schicksal*, 12–15.

sonal interviews as well as court and prison records. Drawing on these case studies, Lange wrote a long concluding chapter that added considerable nuance and complexity to his conclusions. If he had conducted a twin study on the role of heredity in an illness, Lange explained, the concordance figures would have spoken for themselves. Crime, however, was "not a purely biological phenomenon, inherent in the person of the criminal, but a social phenomenon, and therefore always subject to social conditions." For this reason, Lange felt the need to supplement the raw figures with a closer look at the interaction between genetic and environmental factors in individual cases.[107]

Lange's conclusion made it clear that when he spoke of "heredity" (*Anlage*) as a cause of crime he was not referring to some sort of "criminal character."[108] None of his criminal twins, Lange pointed out, had the sort of character that laypersons expected criminals to have. None of them would think of planning a major heist in the manner of professional criminals. None of them were "active criminals," that is, individuals whose egotism, lack of compassion, or cruelty doomed them to a life of crime. On the contrary, most of them were "good, gentle people." Lange was therefore certain that the "genetic factors" (*Anlagen*) involved in the twins' criminal behavior did not consist of a "criminal will"; beyond that, however, their nature remained largely unknown. As in his earlier lecture, Lange argued that the criminogenic genetic factors consisted of combinations of psychopathic traits that were not criminogenic in themselves but became so only in combination and under certain external circumstances. In addition, the number of cases in which both twins committed a great variety of offenses led Lange to speculate that all the various combinations of traits shared one key defect: a general "inability to resist basic drives" (*Widerstandslosigkeit gegenüber Triebregungen*). This defect, however, had nothing to do with a "criminal disposition," nor did it have to lead to criminal behavior.[109]

Lange's conclusion also relativized the role of heredity and highlighted the influence of the environment. Thus Lange reported that, with perhaps two exceptions, environmental factors played an "indispensable part" (*nicht fort-*

---

107. Ibid., 82–83.

108. Lange also addressed two possible objections to his hereditarian interpretation of the evidence: that the concordance between identical twins might be the result of reciprocal influences between them or similar psychological influences on both twins in early childhood. To the first objection he responded that in most of his cases reciprocal influences had been of minimal importance; to the second that twins were not always treated the same in childhood (ibid., 85–87).

109. Ibid., 89–91.

zudenken) in the criminal behavior of all his twins. In Lange's view, these criminogenic external influences included such diverse factors as economic conditions, regional customs, alcohol consumption, discrimination against former convicts, and the individual's socioeconomic position. To illustrate the role of these environmental factors, Lange mentioned the case of Karl Diener, who had fatally stabbed someone in an intoxicated state during an altercation in a Bavarian tavern. Diener's alcoholism, Lange explained, "was not his own doing, but resulted from the combination of his own hereditary constitution and our drinking customs." Likewise, Diener's carrying a knife reflected a general Bavarian custom. Even Diener's pulling his knife out in the course of the altercation had to be seen as a reflection of his lower-class social status, since a similarly intoxicated student, for instance, would never have pulled a knife but challenged his adversary to a duel. Another case that Lange used to illustrate the power of environmental influences was that of August Heufelder, who had turned to petty crime because he found it difficult to reenter economic life after years of military service and captivity as a prisoner of war during the First World War. After he was convicted and sent to prison, Heufelder found it impossible to find a job because of his criminal record. Although he was willing to make an honest living, social prejudice forced him back into a life of crime.[110]

Lange considered it "likely that many criminals become professional criminals in the same way [as Heufelder] . . . that is, because our society has no place for people of his character and history [of criminal convictions]." Lange did not hesitate to speak of the "responsibility of society" for crime in such cases. Like his mentor Kraepelin, he was also sharply critical of the widespread custom of excessive alcohol consumption, which played a significant role in the criminal behavior of many of the twins. "A society that tolerates, even promotes [alcoholism]," he charged, "has no legitimate right to interfere with the most serious sanctions in the lives of individuals who are not doing anything different from what everyone else is doing." It would be hard to find a stronger statement of society's responsibility for criminal behavior.[111]

In sum, Lange's concluding chapter presented a highly complex picture of the causes of criminal behavior. While the difference in concordance rates had initially led Lange to conclude that heredity played an "overwhelming" (*ganz überwiegende*) role in criminal behavior, his detailed qualitative analysis led him to conclude that "in addition to heredity, we see the great effect of external influences" as an "indispensable" factor in the genesis of criminal behavior in

110. Ibid., 91–92.
111. Ibid., 91–92, 94.

all cases.[112] At first glance, the two statements appear contradictory. How could Lange claim that heredity played an "overwhelming" role among the causes of crime while insisting that external influences were an "indispensable" factor in every case? The apparent contradiction is resolved if one realizes that when Lange pointed to heredity (*Erbanlage, Anlage*) as a criminogenic factor, he was not referring to a criminal disposition that doomed its bearers to a life of crime but to a combination of genetic traits (*Anlagen*) that could lead to criminal behavior under the influence of certain environmental factors. Lange's explanation of crime was multifactorial. On the one hand, he believed that the criminal behavior he observed would not have occurred without certain environmental factors such as alcoholism or the "current economic order"; on the other hand, he also believed that given these external factors, his concordant identical twins had committed crimes because they carried genetic traits that became criminogenic under these environmental conditions.

The best evidence that Lange endorsed a balanced rather than a narrowly hereditarian approach to crime appears in a crucial passage at the very end of his conclusion, in which Lange emphasized the similarities between criminals and "normal" persons:

> But in other respects, too, we must tear down the barriers that separate the good citizen from the "criminal." . . . We would only like to remind the reader that although many other psychopaths do not become antisocial in the sense of criminal behavior, they do become antisocial in a much more painful sense: nagging superiors who torment their employees, tyrants who make their families tremble, . . . these cannot be considered socially valuable individuals . . . and yet we are already deeply in the range of what is considered normal. But even if we think of actions which the legislator has declared illegal, how many people successfully avoid them? A young lady of my acquaintance, who has more money to spend on herself . . . than many large families, told me that it gives her particular pleasure to ride the streetcar without paying or at least to ride past the tariff zone for which she paid. All of us probably "ride beyond the tariff zone" on occasion, and we do it for the same reason that so many criminals commit their first offense; namely, because a dark impulse [*Laune*] gains the upper hand due to some lapse in our momentary or permanent social orientation. The difference that turns another person into a criminal depends only on the average strength of one's inhibitions [*Triebhemmung*]. . . . There is an uninterrupted continuum from

112. Ibid., 92.

the entirely normal to the pathological. The boundary is socially disastrous. That it is not exclusively determined by the degree of the anomaly [i.e., but also by external factors], therein lies the tragedy of so many criminal, but valuable individuals.[113]

This passage shows that even though Lange associated criminal behavior with genetic abnormalities, he also insisted that normality and abnormality were linked by a continuum and that environmental factors always played a role. Far from being a biological monster, Lange's habitual criminal was someone whose strength of inhibition happened to fall on the low end of the statistical range. Unlike Viernstein, who clothed his moral condemnation of criminals in biological language, Lange's biological understanding of habitual criminals led him to a nonjudgmental attitude toward criminals that was reflected in his penal policy recommendations. Since crime resulted from the interaction of genetic factors with environmental influences, Lange argued, "it makes no sense to administer retribution or to punish in the narrow sense of the word." Instead, Lange firmly endorsed the penal reformers' position that the only legitimate purpose of criminal justice was the "protection of society." Although some form of detention (*Freiheitsentzug*) would always remain the chief penal sanction, it had to be made more effective in rehabilitating inmates. To facilitate the reintegration of released prisoners into society, Lange called for abandoning the moral stigmatization of criminals in favor of a nonjudgmental attitude based on a scientific understanding of crime. Although society had to make a better effort to rehabilitate those who could be rehabilitated, Lange also believed that some criminals were incorrigible and would have to be permanently detained. To detect such persons as early as possible, it was imperative to subject all criminals to a thorough criminal-biological examination. Characteristically, however, Lange insisted that the permanent detention of incorrigibles take the "mildest" possible form. Finally, Lange also called for eugenic policies.[114]

We must seek to prevent people with active criminal genetic traits from being born. . . . Eugenic measures cannot rid us of those minor criminals who make up the majority of today's prison inmates. In these cases we are obviously dealing with the result of combinations of different genetic traits [*Keimmischungen*] that are necessary if we want to preserve the variety of individual characters that is a precondition for all cultural life. However, I do con-

113. Ibid., 94–95.
114. Ibid., 95–96.

sider it possible to prevent the intensive breeding [*Hochzucht*] of criminal genetic traits. But this will only be possible after we know much more than we know today. Our twin study only tells us that the traits [*Artung*] that lead to antisocial acts are formed through heredity. Regarding the particular mode of transmission of this set of traits, the twin method tells us nothing. If we want to further our knowledge in this respect . . . this will only be possible through the intensive study of families.[115]

In sum, while Lange clearly advocated eugenic measures as a way of combating crime, he also made it clear that the limited state of present knowledge did not allow such measures to be implemented in the foreseeable future.

To assess the broader significance of Lange's book, we must briefly examine its reception. On the most general level, there can be no doubt that in the ongoing debate over the relative importance of heredity and milieu as causes of crime Lange's book was perceived as tipping the scales in favor of heredity. But since I have stressed that Lange's views on the role of heredity were nuanced and complex, we must also ask whether Lange's audience understood the complexity of his views.

Among general psychiatrists not specializing in criminal-biological research the record was mixed. One psychiatrist reviewing the book claimed that Lange's study had proven that "heredity is everything, the environment . . . is virtually nothing."[116] But the sterilization debates that will be discussed in the final chapter provide considerable evidence that most Weimar psychiatrists understood that the role of genetic factors in criminal behavior was extremely complex and still posed an unsolved problem for scientific research.

Among psychiatrists specializing in criminal-biological research, most everyone appreciated that Lange had not identified a genetic criminal disposition and that the precise nature of the genetic factors whose importance he had highlighted remained unclear. Despite this consensus, specialists in criminal biology disagreed on the importance of Lange's study. Aschaffenburg, for instance, regarded Lange's twin study as "valuable evidence for the decisive importance of heredity,"[117] while other researchers took a much more skeptical

115. Ibid., 96.

116. Friedrich Meggendorfer, review of *Verbrechen als Schicksal*, by Johannes Lange, *Deutsche Zeitschrift für Nervenheilkunde* 108 (1929): 311–12. See also Fritz Lenz, review of *Verbrechen als Schicksal*, by Johannes Lange, *ARGB* 21 (1929): 335–36.

117. Gustav Aschaffenburg, "Kriminalanthropologie und Kriminalbiologie," *Handwörterbuch der Kriminologie*, ed. Alexander Elster and Heinrich Lingemann (Berlin: de Gruyter, 1933), 1:831.

position. The most coherent exposition of this critical attitude toward genetic research was found in the last major strand of Weimar criminal biology, to which we now turn.

Criminal Psychology

Kretschmer's somatotyping and Lange's genetic research shared the ambition of transcending a merely psychological approach and identifying the underlying *biological* causes of crime. Both of these approaches came under criticism from the criminal-psychological strand of Weimar criminal biology, which tried to redirect the focus of criminal-biological research away from the *biology* to the *psychology* of the criminal and from the study of *abnormal* criminals to the study of *all* criminals, be they normal or abnormal. This approach took shape in Karl Birnbaum's major work *Kriminalpsychopathologie und psychobiologische Verbrecherkunde* (1931) and the publications of the psychiatrist Hans Gruhle.[118] Since Birnbaum was a major figure in psychopathic research, it should be clear that the different strands of criminal biology outlined in this chapter must not be seen as mutually exclusive. Birnbaum's later work reflected a gradual broadening of his interests from abnormal to normal criminals. Gruhle, by contrast, was radical in his critique of the other approaches. Trained by Kraepelin, Gruhle spent most of his career (1905–34) at the psychiatric clinic of the University of Heidelberg. Whereas Birnbaum had become interested in criminal-biological issues through his work with the criminally insane in Berlin's psychiatric hospitals, Gruhle came to criminal biology through an early study of juvenile delinquents.[119] Although Gruhle did not write any further books on criminological topics, he influenced the development of criminal-biological research through a steady stream of articles and lectures.[120]

118. The jurist Erich Wulffen made similar arguments in his *Kriminalpsychologie: Psychologie des Täters* (Berlin: Langenscheidt, 1926).

119. Hans Gruhle, *Die Ursachen der jugendlichen Verwahrlosung und Kriminalität* (Berlin: Springer, 1912); Kurt Kolle, "Hans Gruhle," in *Große Nervenärzte*, ed. Kolle, 3:69–76; Bernard Pauleikhoff, "Hans Walter Gruhle," in *Das Menschenbild*, 4:51–72; entry for Gruhle in *Neue Deutsche Biographie* 7:209–10.

120. Gruhle, "Kriminalbiologie und Kriminalpraxis," *Kriminalistische Monatshefte* 2 (1928): 242; "Die Erforschung der Verbrechensursachen: Zum gleichnamigen Aufsatz des Grafen Gleispach," *MKS* 19 (1928): 257–68; "Wesen und Systematik des biologischen Typus," *MKBG* 2 (1928): 15–21; entries "Strafvollzug," "Verbrecher," and "geborener Verbrecher," in *Handwörterbuch der medizinischen Psychologie*, ed. Birnbaum, 586–90, 631–35, 635–37; "Aufgaben der Kriminalpsychologie," *ZStW* 51 (1930–31): 469–80; "Vererbungsgesetze und Verbre-

Birnbaum and Gruhle's desire to shift attention to the psychology of the criminal derived from their dissatisfaction with Kretschmer's somatotyping and current research on genetic factors in criminal behavior. In Gruhle's view, the search for "correlations between physique and criminal behavior" had been unsuccessful, and he dismissed the effort as "hopeless."[121] Birnbaum, too, concluded that researchers were "still very far from being able to identify certain constitutional types as characteristic of particular criminal personality types" and added that it was "doubtful that this will ever be possible."[122]

Birnbaum and Gruhle were no less critical of genetic research. Like most criminal biologists, they dismissed studies that presented criminal behavior in several generations of a family as evidence for genetic influence. "The presence of criminality in parents and children," Birnbaum insisted, "does not permit any genetic conclusions, since it might be genetically determined in one case, but environmentally determined in another."[123] But Birnbaum and Gruhle also expressed serious reservations about the methods and assumptions of current genetic research.[124] Although Birnbaum believed that Lange's twin study had indeed demonstrated "the existence of hereditary dispositions with an anti-social tendency," he pointed out that Lange's research had failed to provide any information on the nature or mode of transmission of genetic factors involved in criminal behavior. And since the twin method was not suited to providing answers to these questions, he recommended that criminal biologists focus on criminal psychology.[125]

Gruhle's critique of genetic research was more radical. Worried that Lange's twin study of 1929 might have given a dangerous boost to hereditarian theories, in 1932 Gruhle published a forceful article in which he attacked genetic research on crime as not only inconclusive but profoundly misguided. To begin with, Gruhle insisted that research on human heredity had to grapple with a great many uncertainties and complexities: the applicability of Mendelian rules to humans was doubtful; genetic traits were only potentials, whose actualization depended on external factors; since inherited characteristics could be recessive,

---

chensbekämpfung," *MKS* 23 (1932): 559–68; entries "Kriminalpsychologie," "Charaktero-logie," "Verbrechensursachen," "Vererbung," in *Handwörterbuch der Kriminologie*, 1:907–14, 200–207, 2:882–86, 904–9.

121. Gruhle, "Wesen und Systematik," 20.
122. Birnbaum, *Kriminalpsychopathologie*, 2d ed., 199.
123. Ibid., 206.
124. Ibid., 203–4.
125. Ibid., 206–8, 217.

many did not manifest themselves or would not be passed on to offspring; finally, for most mental illnesses, let alone psychological traits, the relation between dominance and recessiveness was not known.[126] Most important, Gruhle charged that "the overestimation of the hereditary argument blinds its supporters to the influences of tradition"—the transmission of behavior patterns through socialization.[127]

> If one reads the writings of criminals, observes the language and manners of factory girls when they think no one is watching them, or immerses oneself in the lives of juvenile delinquents, one will receive such a strong impression of the formative power of the group, the social stratum, the milieu, that one will regard it as artificial to make reference to hereditary factors to explain the lives of the younger generation. There is no need to eschew the thesis that it is more plausible to explain a person's behavior as a reaction to his situation in life than to explain it with a genetic factor that is intangible and cannot be proven.[128]

Gruhle's and Birnbaum's critique of criminal *biology* in the narrow sense led them to call for shifting attention to criminal *psychology*. To indicate this shift, Birnbaum coined the new term "criminal psychobiology" (*psychobiologische Verbrecherkunde*) to describe the general field of scientific research on criminals. Whereas the older field of criminal anthropology had its origins in physical anthropology, degeneration theory, and psychiatry, the new criminal psychobiology was to be closely allied with medical psychology and the study of personality known as *Persönlichkeitslehre* or *Charakterologie*.[129] Since *Persönlichkeitslehre* saw human beings as psychophysical units, criminal psychobiology would study both the role of psychological traits in criminal behavior (criminal psychology) and the possible physiological bases of such traits (criminal biology).[130] Of these two subfields, however, criminal psychology was clearly the more important, not only because genetic research and somatotyping had produced meager results but because, as Birnbaum wrote, "the deepest investigation of the physical foundations . . . of the criminal personality . . . can never provide what is most important: insight into the psychological state of

126. Gruhle, "Vererbungsgesetze und Verbrechensbekämpfung," 559–63; see also his later article "Vererbung."

127. Gruhle, "Vererbungsgesetze und Verbrechensbekämpfung," 565.

128. Ibid., 565.

129. Here Birnbaum was referring to such works as Hermann Hoffmann, *Das Problem des Charakteraufbaues: Seine Gestaltung durch die erbbiologische Persönlichkeitsanalyse* (Berlin, 1926); Kretschmer, *Körperbau and Charakter*. See also Gruhle, "Charakterologie."

130. Birnbaum, *Kriminalpsychopathologie*, 2d ed., 3–4, 191.

the criminal, into the psychological processes that motivated his offense."[131] "It has become fashionable," Gruhle concurred, "to focus research efforts on heredity and physique. These are wrong tracks [*Abwege*] that do not promise any results." Instead, researchers ought to be focusing their interest on the criminal's character.[132]

Even though Gruhle and Birnbaum called for studying the characters of criminals, they were sharply critical of the assumption that criminal behavior somehow reflected a uniform "criminal character." "The criminal," Birnbaum cautioned his readers, "does not represent a uniform human type."[133] Gruhle made the same point more forcefully:

It is grotesquely naive to deduce a criminal disposition (*Gesinnung*) or even a criminal character from the fact that someone has come into conflict with the law. The causes and reasons why someone might commit a crime are so incredibly diverse that only utter unfamiliarity with the personalities of criminals can explain why anyone would attribute tendencies toward crime to a person's character. Criminals acting from inclination, from weakness, from passion, from honor, from conviction are such indescribably different personalities that they do not have any traits in common. If a theoretician should get the idea that their common characteristic might be a lack of self-discipline or the lack of a tendency toward social integration, let him be advised that the latter has nothing to do with uniform character traits, and that the former does not characterize the "great" criminal: he exercises his profession with the utmost self-discipline. "The" criminal character does not exist.[134]

Besides criticizing the notion of a "criminal character," Gruhle and Birnbaum also debunked the assumption that most criminals were abnormal. As the author of the standard work on psychopathic criminals, Birnbaum had spent decades studying "abnormal" criminals. Yet when he explained his vision of a general psychobiology of the criminal, Birnbaum pointed out that psychopathic personalities were a minority among criminals and insisted that criminal psychobiologists must study the majority of normal criminals as well.[135]

Once again, Gruhle's critique was more radical. The search for the abnormal characteristics of criminals, he argued, had originated from a normative, value-

131. Ibid., 208.
132. Gruhle, "Aufgaben der Kriminalpsychologie," 476–77.
133. Birnbaum, *Kriminalpsychopathologie*, 2d ed., 192.
134. Gruhle, "Vererbungsgesetze und Verbrechensbekämpfung," 563.
135. Birnbaum, *Kriminalpsychopathologie*, 2d ed., 191–92.

laden notion of abnormality. Since "normal" citizens were law-abiding, those who violated the law had to be abnormal. When people turned to psychiatrists to verify this proposition, the psychiatrists detected psychopathic traits among many criminals. But since psychopathic personalities were frequently found among the general population, Gruhle argued, it was clearly wrong to draw a causal connection between psychopathic traits and criminal behavior. Only if the proportions of psychopaths among a large sample of criminals and among men of the same social stratum were known and compared could one determine whether psychopathy was a causal factor in crime. Gruhle noted that such data did not currently exist and doubted that any such causal connection would ever be found. In the meantime, Gruhle suggested, it was best to leave notions of normality versus abnormality out of criminal-biological research altogether.[136]

In addition to stressing the diversity and normality of most criminals, Birnbaum and Gruhle also argued that the character of each individual criminal was highly complex and dynamic. Criminal behavior could not be explained by reference to a general "criminal character" or a particular "criminogenic trait" but only by taking into account the interaction of different traits within a complex and changing personality.[137] Taking this approach, Birnbaum explained:

> The criminal personality is not just a mass of criminal, socially negative character traits, but a characterological complex in which all the different individual traits, socially positive and socially negative, socially indifferent and ambivalent ones, are joined into a whole. Generally speaking, it is not the . . . socially negative character of particular traits and much less a fixed, specifically criminal trait, but the particular combination of certain traits of differing social value, under a certain dominant character component, such as egotism, that gives the character a criminal tendency. . . . In this sense it must be emphasized that the characterization of certain traits as criminal is relative, and that hardly any character traits are absolutely criminal or absolutely noncriminal. Not just socially ambivalent, but even socially valuable traits . . . can become criminogenic in certain constellations.[138]

In short, the personalities of criminals were neither all bad nor dominated by a single criminal trait but as complex as everyone else's. To understand a person's criminal behavior, one had to understand all the different facets of that person's character and how they were interconnected. Hence the task of criminal psy-

136. Gruhle, "Verbrecher," 634; Gruhle, "Erforschung der Verbrechensursachen," 264.
137. Birnbaum, *Kriminalpsychopathologie*, 2d ed., 210–11. Also see Birnbaum, "Persön-lichkeitsforschung," *Handwörterbuch der Kriminologie*, 2:268–80; Gruhle, "Charakterologie."
138. Birnbaum, *Kriminalpsychopathologie*, 2d ed., 211.

chology was nothing less than assessing the criminogenic potential of all human character traits and their combinations.

Although Birnbaum and Gruhle sought to shift attention from criminal biology to criminal psychology, the study of criminal personalities still raised the question of the relative importance of genetic versus environmental influences. Birnbaum's views on this issue were contradictory because his sophisticated understanding of human character constantly got in the way of his hereditarian leanings. Thus his claim that congenital traits[139] were more important than acquired traits because they formed "the real endogenous core of the personality from which the drives toward antisocial behavior derive" was undermined by his own admission that acquired traits and environmental influences played a significant role in human character development and behavior.[140]

Gruhle addressed the question of the relative importance of congenital versus acquired traits by drawing a distinction between two main categories of criminals: the mass of criminals, who did not differ from the general population in their congenital traits; and a minority of criminals with congenital traits that doomed them to crime but only if they were members of the lower classes.

> If one wants to retain the notion of the "born criminal" at all, one can only define it as follows: a born criminal is someone whom nature has endowed with certain character traits (brutality, activity, energy, for instance) so that he has to end up committing crimes (primarily property crime) if he lives on the social level of the working class. If the same character had entered the world as a child of a well-situated, economically protected circle, he would most probably have been spared a criminal career. Thus membership in the proletariat is one of the primary conditions of crime.[141]

Gruhle added that there was a third group, whose congenital traits doomed them to crime in any social stratum; a certain kind of confidence man, for instance. But this group was extremely small and statistically insignificant.[142] Gruhle insisted, however, that the congenital traits of the vast majority of criminals were either criminologically irrelevant or relevant only in combi-

---

139. Birnbaum preferred the term "congenital" traits because he was aware of how little was known about human genetics. Although many congenital traits were probably genetic, Birnbaum pointed out that congenital traits could also be the result of external influences on fetal development (ibid., 213).

140. Ibid., 211–19, 221, 223.

141. Gruhle, "Erforschung der Verbrechensursachen," 258. See also Gruhle, "Geborener Verbrecher," 637, and Gruhle, "Kriminalpsychologie," 911.

142. Gruhle, "Erforschung der Verbrechensursachen," 258; Gruhle, "Kriminalpsychologie," 911. See also Gruhle, "Vererbung," 907, 908.

nation with membership in the lowest social stratum. In addition, Gruhle quali-fied the role of congenital traits in three ways. First, even those criminals whose congenital traits doomed them to crime on the social level of the proletariat did not form a homogeneous group; a wide variety of congenital traits could have this effect. Second, even congenital traits were not necessarily incorri-gible but frequently responded to educational measures. Finally, Gruhle saw no evidence whatsoever that these congenital traits were genetically trans-mitted and considered it far more likely that such traits were newly formed through the combination of various inherited traits that were not criminogenic in themselves.[143]

It is easy to see that Gruhle and Birnbaum's differentiated approach to the problem of criminal behavior greatly complicated the tasks of criminal-psychological research. If research could no longer be limited to the field of abnormality, which was psychiatrists' expertise, if criminals were a highly di-verse group, and if the personality of each criminal was highly complex and dynamic, then how were criminal psychobiologists to study their protean sub-ject? As we have seen, Gruhle and Birnbaum's answer was to call for a reorien-tation of the field. Instead of searching for the genetic or physiological bases of criminal behavior, researchers were to study the personalities of criminals. Furthermore, criminal biologists ought to abandon efforts to characterize "the criminal" as a uniform type and instead recognize the diversity of criminals. Both recommendations translated into a call for sober empirical studies of small groups of criminals with attention to their character and motives. Yet these recommendations were unable to counter criminal biologists' growing attrac-tion to genetic research.

Assessing the Different Trends in Weimar Criminal Biology

Overall, criminal biology in the Weimar years reflected two opposing trends: a trend to pathologize the criminal and to explain criminal behavior primarily as the result of biological abnormality, versus a competing trend to regard the criminal as biologically normal and to acknowledge the importance of social factors in explaining crime. Regarding the first trend, we find that many crimi-nal biologists not only treated a criminal's personality as a decisive crimi-nogenic factor but argued that this personality was pathological or abnormal. This approach was most pronounced in research on the psychopathic criminal.

143. Gruhle, "Kriminalpsychologie," 911; Gruhle, "Vererbung," 909; Gruhle, "Vererbungs-gesetze und Verbrechensbekämpfung," 566.

Although estimates varied, most researchers agreed that a large percentage of habitual, recidivist criminals were psychopathic personalities.

Criminal biologists' sophistication in defining normality and abnormality varied greatly. Whereas Kraepelin used highly subjective and value-laden notions of normality, Schneider sought to avoid this problem by defining the "norm" as a statistical average and "abnormal personalities" as deviations from that average. Schneider's definition of "psychopathic personalities" as "those abnormal personalities who suffer from their abnormality or whose abnormality makes society suffer," however, reintroduced social value judgments and ended up reinforcing the connection between abnormality and antisocial behavior. Despite Schneider's efforts to construct his psychopathic types on the basis of objective psychological criteria, categories like his *gemütlose* (compassionless) or *willenlose* (weak-willed) psychopaths also reflected value judgments. Likewise, Birnbaum argued that psychopathic *Haltlosigkeit* (lack of resilience) manifested itself in the "inability to properly emphasize important values such as honor and morality, duty and responsibility."[144] Although criminal biologists insisted that criminal behavior as such could never be regarded as evidence of a criminal's abnormality, they were clearly inclined to interpret deviations from social norms as deviations from biological norms. In short, criminal biologists "medicalized" moral categories in such a way that social deviance became evidence of mental abnormality.

Most Weimar criminal biologists also regarded abnormal character traits as congenital and, therefore, in most cases hereditary.[145] This view marked a change from the prewar years, when most psychiatrists had subscribed to the theory of degeneration, which attributed such abnormalities to a combination of genetic and environmental factors. The abandonment of degeneration theory paved the way for Schneider's hereditarian position that psychopathic personalities were always congenital. But though Schneider and Birnbaum believed that psychopathic personalities were always congenital, they did not claim that criminal behavior was determined by heredity because whether or not a psychopathic personality committed a crime always depended on environmental factors. Therefore the question of the relative weight of heredity and environment in criminal behavior remained open. Lange's twin research was meant to address this question, and there can be no doubt that his results were widely regarded as proof that heredity played a preponderant role in criminal behavior.

---

144. Schneider, *Die psychopathischen Persönlichkeiten*, 2d ed., 1–5, 69–70, 73–75; Birnbaum, *Die psychopathischen Verbrecher*, 2d ed., 46.

145. The exceptions were damage to the germ (embryo), the fetus, and injury at birth.

Finally, the trend to pathologize the criminal was manifested in the persistence of the notion of the born criminal. The prewar reception of Lombroso had resulted in a split between the proponents of the Aschaffenburg paradigm, who rejected the notion of the born criminal entirely, and the adherents of the Kraepelin paradigm, who defended a psychiatric version of the born criminal defined in terms of moral insanity or a moral defect. In the Weimar years, this psychiatric version of the born criminal was transformed into the psychopathic type that Schneider called *gemütlos* (compassionless) and Birnbaum called "amoral." To be sure, Schneider and Birnbaum pointed out that compassionless/amoral psychopaths were not necessarily doomed to a life of crime. If born into a wealthy family, for instance, their lack of scruples might result in economic success. Furthermore, whereas Lombroso had claimed that born criminals accounted for a third of all criminals, Schneider and Birnbaum regarded the amoral/compassionless psychopath as extremely rare. Nevertheless, Schneider and Birnbaum admitted that the compassionless/amoral psychopath came closest to the born criminal.[146] As a result, the two were often treated as synonymous and the notion of the born criminal lived on. And the mere survival of the concept allowed others to insist that, errors in detail notwithstanding, Lombroso's theories contained an important kernel of truth: that in the most severe cases crime was indeed the result of biological abnormality.[147]

On the other hand, Weimar criminal biology also witnessed a countervailing trend in the direction of treating criminals as biologically normal and acknowledging the important role of environmental factors. Above all, this trend manifested itself in the gradual disintegration of the notions of "the criminal" or "the criminal character" as biological entities. In every area of research, criminal biologists arrived at the conclusion that there was no such thing as "the criminal." To be sure, this trend had begun with the first German studies refuting the existence of Lombroso's born criminal. But in the prewar period Aschaffenburg had still described about half of all criminals as *geistig minderwertig*, that is, as a unified group with certain characteristics. By the Weimar period, however, not only the notion of "the criminal" but even more restricted concepts such as the "psychopathic criminal" or the "habitual criminal" became dissolved into a myriad of different "psychopathic personalities" or "types."

The notion of a "criminal character" or "criminal disposition" had become untenable because criminal biologists had become convinced that, first, criminal

146. Schneider, *Die psychopathischen Persönlichkeiten*, 69–73; Birnbaum, *Die psychopathischen Verbrecher*, 53–55, 62, 154–55.

147. See, for example, Friedrich von Rohden, "Lombrosos Bedeutung für die moderne Kriminalbiologie," *Archiv für Psychiatrie und Nervenkrankheiten* 92 (1930): 140–54.

behavior could result from a great variety of different motivations and character traits; second, criminal behavior arose from complex combinations of different character traits that were not "criminal" in themselves; and finally, since character traits were only potentials, criminal behavior was always the result of personal and environmental factors. In short, the causes of criminal behavior were seen to be as diverse and complex as the causes of all other human behavior. As a result, the criminal began to look more and more like any other normal human being, and criminal biology became inextricably bound up with the general study of human behavior, psychology, and genetics. But since the consensus was that all these fields were still in early stages of development, the goal of understanding criminal behavior, let alone prognosticating an offender's dangerousness or corrigibility, became more elusive than ever. Ironically, the increasing sophistication of criminal biologists had made their goal harder to reach.

The disintegration of the notion of a criminal disposition also complicated the question of heredity and made the implications of Lange's twin research much less clear-cut. At first glance, Lange's finding that identical twins had a high (77 percent) concordance rate, whereas fraternal twins had a low one (12 percent), seemed to suggest that heredity played an overwhelming role in criminal behavior. But if there was no such thing as a criminal disposition, what exactly was being passed on through heredity? Lange himself admitted that his research shed no light on the nature of the genetic factors that predisposed its bearers to antisocial behavior. Recognizing that character traits were only potentials, he also conceded that the criminal behavior of his concordant identical twins was not determined by heredity alone but by external influences as well. The same point was driven home by the very existence of discordant identical twins (23 percent), which, Lange acknowledged, could be explained only by environmental factors.[148]

Thus the widespread inclination to explain criminal behavior as the result of genetic abnormalities was tempered by the recognition that criminal behavior was as diverse and complex as all human behavior and always subject to environmental influences. As a result, Weimar criminal biologists recognized the futility of approaching heredity and milieu as alternative explanations and concluded that both factors played a role in criminal behavior. Yet the recognition of both factors allowed for differences in emphasis. Some criminal biologists, like Birnbaum and Gruhle, did not tire of pointing out that even persons with potentially criminogenic psychopathic personalities did not usually be-

148. Lange, *Verbrechen als Schicksal*, 82–83, 90–92, 96.

come criminal unless, as Gruhle put it, "fate put them in this world as members of the proletariat."[149] Others, however, presented heredity as the decisive factor. In an article assessing the state of criminal biology at the very end of the Weimar period, Gustav Aschaffenburg indicated that the criminal-biological work of the Weimar years had convinced him that, even though the environment played a role, the "ultimately decisive" factor was the criminal's personality and that this personality was "overwhelmingly" a matter of heredity. While he acknowledged that an individual's personality was affected by environmental factors, he argued that heredity provided a "fixed framework" that set sharp limits on external influences.[150]

Although Aschaffenburg felt confident in stressing the importance of personality and heredity, he admitted that criminal-biological research was still in its early stages. The increasing sophistication of criminal-biological research and the resulting disintegration of the notion of a criminal disposition had so complicated the questions under investigation that progress became ever more elusive. Summarizing the state of the field in 1932, Aschaffenburg therefore concluded that criminal biology was "far from possessing reliable methods for examining and evaluating the personality of the criminal"; that research on human heredity met with "almost insurmountable difficulties" and would therefore be slow to produce reliable results; and that it was "currently impossible to differentiate between corrigibles and incorrigibles with criminal-psychological methods."[151] In short, Aschaffenburg acknowledged that after about forty years of research—thirty years after his landmark synthesis of 1903—criminal biology was still a science in its infancy.

The next chapter traces the development of criminology during the Nazi regime. The reception and implications of criminal-biological research for penal and eugenic policy during both the Weimar and Nazi years will be discussed in the final chapter.

149. Gruhle, "Wesen und Systematik," 21.
150. Aschaffenburg, "Kriminalanthropologie und Kriminalbiologie," 830–32.
151. Ibid., 825, 828, 840.

CHAPTER SIX

CRIMINOLOGY UNDER THE NAZI REGIME

Criminology and Nazism

When the National Socialists came to power in January 1933, their future attitude toward criminology was an open question. Nazi pronouncements on crime
and criminal justice during the Weimar years suggested that the party held a
contradictory attitude toward criminology. For although the Nazis themselves
subscribed to a biological approach to crime that drew on criminal-biological
research, activist Nazi jurists were frequently hostile to criminology. These
jurists attacked Weimar criminal justice as excessively lenient and blamed the
supposed "emasculation" (*Verweichlichung*) of criminal justice on the liberalism and misguided humanitarianism of Weimar penal reformers and criminologists. The criminological interest in "understanding" the personality of
the criminal, they charged, had undermined the notion of individual responsibility and therefore led to more and more lenient punishments that compromised society's defense against crime. Instead, they called for a "tough on
crime" policy of harsh retributive punishment that had no use for criminological considerations.[1]

While it was indeed true that the criminal courts had become more lenient
over the Weimar years, as Franz Exner showed in his 1931 study of the subject,
this trend had begun in the 1880s, long before the Weimar Republic. Although
Exner, too, attributed this trend to the influence of criminology, he insisted that
the increase in lenience reflected an "irrational" psychological response to criminology's new focus on the social and biological determinants of crime, rather

---

1. Georg Dahm and Friedrich Schaffstein, *Liberales oder autoritäres Strafrecht?* (Hamburg:
Hanseatische Verlagsanstalt, 1933), 13, 15; see also Franz Exner's response to such criticisms
in "Aufgaben der Kriminologie im neuen Reich," *MKS* 27 (1936): 3.

than a rational penal policy response to the specific results of criminological research. For even though criminological research had suggested that habitual offenders should be subject to additional protective measures, the increasing lenience of the courts was general and indiscriminate.[2]

Although they were important, Nazi jurists' attacks on criminology as the root cause of the emasculation of Weimar criminal justice represented only one aspect of the National Socialist attitude toward criminology. For the Nazis' inclination toward a biological view of human society and their enthusiasm for eugenics drew them toward criminal-biological research. Already in 1925 Nazi deputies in the Prussian diet called for the sterilization of "hereditarily tainted" criminals.[3] Hitler himself, in a speech to the 1929 Nazi Party Congress in Nuremberg, called it outrageous that "criminals are allowed to procreate" and demanded drastic eugenic measures. In his *Der Mythus des 20. Jahrhunderts* (Myth of the twentieth century), Alfred Rosenberg, the party's chief ideologist, called for the sterilization of recidivist criminals, and Hans Frank, head of the Nazi Party's legal office and leader of the Nazi lawyers' association, demanded the "ruthless elimination of the procreation of criminal characters."[4] Although the Nazis were clearly oblivious to the complexities of criminal-biological research, these hereditarian and eugenicist views suggested that they would be sympathetic to the enterprise of criminal biology.

Since the Nazi penchant for hereditarianism and Nazi criticisms of Weimar criminal justice implied diametrically opposed attitudes toward criminology, the new regime's attitude toward this field could have taken either a positive or negative turn. Prominent criminologists seem to have understood the dangers and opportunities that this situation presented. Eager to gain the support of the new government, they sought to make criminology appealing by dissociating criminology from the supposed failures of Weimar criminal justice and capitalizing on the Nazis' predilection for a biological view of society.

The first strategy was already evident in Gustav Aschaffenburg's first publication after the Nazi seizure of power. In a lead article in the *Monatsschrift für Kriminalpsychologie* that appeared in the spring of 1933, Aschaffenburg set out

2. Franz Exner, *Studien über die Strafzumessungspraxis der deutschen Gerichte* (Leipzig: Wiegandt, 1931). For a detailed discussion of this study, see Chapter 4 above.

3. Gisela Bock, *Zwangssterilisation im Nationalsozialismus* (Opladen: Westdeutscher Verlag, 1986), 24.

4. Hitler speech, *Völkischer Beobachter* 42/181 (7 August 1929); Alfred Rosenberg, *Der Mythus des 20. Jahrhunderts* (Munich: Hoheneichen, 1930), 545; Hans Frank in *National-sozialistische Monatshefte* 1 (1930): 298; all quoted in Bock, *Zwangssterilisation*, 24–25.

to rebut the charge that the medical-scientific study of crime had contributed to the emasculation of criminal justice. While he agreed that Weimar criminal justice had indeed become unduly lenient, he denied that psychiatrists bore any responsibility for this development by disputing the assumption that psychiatrists always placed the interests of their patients above those of society. On the contrary, he insisted, psychiatrists routinely "deprive[d] patients of their freedom of movement in order to protect the public" and were thus well aware that "the interests of the patient must come second to the general welfare." Hence, when psychiatrists had taken an interest in crime and penal reform, they had naturally placed public safety first. Applying psychiatric principles to criminal justice, they had simply advocated that "curable" offenders be treated and that those who could not be cured be "permanently remove[d] from society." If indefinite preventive detention had failed to become law and judges were extending lenient sentences and probation to undeserving offenders, this was hardly the fault of psychiatrists and penal reformers. Although Aschaffenburg's article refuted Nazi attacks on criminologists and penal reformers, it was also meant as a conciliatory gesture toward activist Nazi jurists. If Nazi jurists demanded tough measures against crime, Aschaffenburg was suggesting, there was no reason to quarrel because psychiatrists and penal reformers made the same demand.[5]

At the first conference of criminologists under the Nazi regime in June 1933, Adolf Lenz offered a similar defense of criminology but went considerably further and fully endorsed the Nazi seizure of power. In his opening speech to the convention of the Criminal-Biological Society (Kriminalbiologische Gesellschaft) in Hamburg, Lenz, the society's Austrian chairman, hailed the Nazi seizure of power as a positive development that sought to "elevate the fragmented life of our state to the unity, dignity and superiority that it deserves." What was more, he echoed Nazi criticisms of criminal justice in stereotypical Nazi language, complaining that the previous "liberalistic-individualistic period" had led to "signs of disintegration in criminal justice and the prison system." Seeking to distance criminology from this sad decline, Lenz rejected "the opinion that the uncovering of criminogenic causes in heredity and environment must always lead to a more lenient judgment of the criminal." On the contrary, he insisted, "the finding that socially, legally or ethically inferior [minderwertige] dispositions played a role in a crime" must always lead to a "stricter judgment," presumably because "ethically inferior" criminals posed a

5. Gustav Aschaffenburg, "Neue Horizonte?" MKS 24 (1933): 158–62.

greater danger to society. In agreement with Nazi judicial activists, Lenz thus called for "severe punishments" to defend the legal order.[6]

Although Aschaffenburg's and Lenz's interventions were clearly calculated to integrate criminology into the Nazi penal policy agenda, their insistence that criminologists had not promoted a more lenient penal policy contained an important element of truth. As we saw in earlier chapters, criminologists and penal reformers were not primarily motivated by humanitarian concern for the criminal but by a desire to protect society more effectively. If habitual criminals were regarded as abnormal, this meant that they were more dangerous and should therefore be subject to intensive individualized treatment in the form of an indeterminate sentence, which was hardly more lenient. Moreover, even though criminologists and penal reformers called for an essentially therapeutic rather than retributive approach to punishment, they also believed in the existence of incorrigible criminals for whom they demanded the harshest of all punishments, indefinite detention. In this sense, then, Aschaffenburg and Lenz were right in believing that most criminologists had not purposely promoted judicial lenience.

If Lenz's and Aschaffenburg's main concern was to distance criminology from the supposed emasculation of Weimar criminal justice and to bring it into line with the Nazi demand for a harsher penal policy, others made their pitch for criminology by connecting it with Nazi biological and eugenic politics. As Franz Exner put it, at a time when "biological facts and considerations" played an unprecedented role in German politics and legislation, criminal biology should gain in importance.[7] Theodor Viernstein made the most compelling case for the connection between criminal biology and Nazi eugenic policy. In a lecture to the Association of Public Health Officials (Deutscher Medizinalbeamtenverein) in September 1933, on "the fight against crime from the perspective of population policy, genetics, and eugenics," Viernstein argued that the criminal-biological examinations of prisoners that he was administering in Bavaria provided a model for conducting a national biological survey to classify the entire population according to its genetic value, which would lay the groundwork for implementing a comprehensive eugenic policy.[8]

---

6. Adolf Lenz, "Begrüssungsansprache," *MKBG* 4 (1933): 16–19.

7. Exner, "Aufgaben der Kriminologie im neuen Reich," 3.

8. Theodor Viernstein, "Die Bekämpfung der Kriminalität vom bevölkerungspolitischen, erbbiologischen und rassenhygienischen Standpunkt," *Zeitschrift für Medizinalbeamte* 46 (1933): 546. See also Viernstein, "Erbwertliche Erforschung und Beurteilung abgrenzbarer Bevölkerungsschichten," in *Erblehre und Rassenhygiene im völkischen Staat*, ed. Ernst Rüdin

Four years later, at the 1937 meeting of the Criminal-Biological Society, Viernstein, who had joined the Nazi Party earlier that year and been elected to the society's chairmanship, expanded his claims for the social importance of criminal biology.[9] In the context of Nazi eugenic policy, he argued, "criminal biology necessarily acquires new importance outside the criminal justice system because it provides a scientifically based treatment for a definable stratum of the population that is, at least in part, not only socially detrimental, but also genetically and racially harmful and must therefore be subjected to systematic elimination [*Ausschaltung*]." (Although the reference to elimination sounds murderous, Viernstein was clearly referring to sterilization.) In the new Nazi state, "the decisions of the criminal biologist" played a role in "the sterilization of genetically diseased persons, the granting of marriage loans and child support payments, . . . and [the administration] of National-Socialist welfare." Clearly, Viernstein was seeking to bolster Nazi support for criminal-biological examinations of prisoners by arguing that they could provide not only a "social prognosis" of the prisoner's corrigibility but an assessment of the criminal's "genetic health" that would be helpful in implementing eugenic measures.[10]

By the time of Viernstein's 1937 speech, the strategy of linking criminal biology to the broader eugenic agenda of the Nazi state was already bearing fruit. Apparently convinced by such arguments, the Nazi regime showed unprecedented support for criminal biology by expanding the Bavarian system of criminal-biological examinations to the national level. Because in the Weimar Republic the administration of prisons fell under the jurisdiction of the individual states, the Bavarian model of criminal-biological examinations had been disseminated in a piecemeal fashion. By the end of the republic, criminal-biological examinations had been introduced in a handful of other states (*Länder*), including Saxony, Baden, Württemberg, and Prussia.[11] This situation changed under the Nazi regime, as the Reich Ministry of Justice took over the justice ministries

---

(Munich: Lehmann, 1934), 333–47; Viernstein, "Stellung und Aufgaben der Kriminalbiologie im Hinblick auf die nationalsozialistische Gesetzgebung," *DZGGM* 26 (1936): 3–16.

9. Viernstein applied for Nazi Party membership in June 1937, which was granted and backdated to 1 May 1937. BDC, NS-Ortskartei, A-3340-MFOK-X0066.

10. Theodor Viernstein, "Schlußansprache," *MKBG* 5 (1937): 120.

11. Ferdinand von Neureiter, "Die Organisation des kriminalbiologischen Dienstes in Deutschland," *MKBG* 5 (1937): 22; *Justizministerialblatt für die preussische Gesetzgebung und Rechtspflege* 92 (1930): 266. In 1930 the examinations were introduced in only nine of forty-six Prussian prisons, and even then the actual implementation of the testing regime was slow until 1935.

of all the states, a process that was completed by early 1935.[12] Using its newly acquired powers, in January 1935 the Reich Ministry of Justice expanded the regime of criminal-biological examinations from a handful of Prussian prisons to all Prussian prisons with a full-time prison doctor, and in January 1937 it made criminal-biological examinations mandatory for all juvenile inmates throughout Germany.[13] Finally, in November 1937, the Ministry of Justice established a national Criminal-Biological Service with criminal-biological examination centers in seventy-three prisons and nine regional record offices reporting to a national Criminal-Biological Research Office (Kriminalbiologische Forschungsstelle) at the Reich Health Office (Reichsgesundheitsamt).[14]

The national Criminal-Biological Service was charged with investigating both the prisoners' "genetic traits" and the "shaping of their personality by life." The examinations were to follow a standardized questionnaire that was patterned after the Bavarian model and adapted to the guidelines of the International Penal and Prison Commission in Bern, reminding us that criminal-biological examinations were very much an international project.[15] Although the creation of a Criminal-Biological Service at the national level aimed at examining every prisoner, it stopped short of achieving this goal because only prisons with full-time doctors (about two-thirds of all prisons) were ordered to establish "criminal-biological examination centers" and none of them received any additional staff. Because of this understaffing, examinations in most prisons were limited to certain categories of incoming prisoners, including juveniles, long-term prisoners, and prisoners sentenced to special preventive measures. Nevertheless, the establishment of the national Criminal-Biological Service significantly expanded the number of criminal-biological examinations.[16]

On the most basic level, the national Criminal-Biological Service was supposed to play a role in the criminal justice system. The results of individual examinations were to serve as the basis for "criminal-biological evaluations"

12. Lothar Gruchmann, Justiz im Dritten Reich, 1933–1940: Anpassung und Unterwerfung in der Ära Gürtner (Munich: Oldenbourg, 1988), 105, 111.

13. Neureiter, "Die Organisation," 22–23; "Allgemeine Verfügung des Reichsministers der Justiz vom 22. Januar 1937," Deutsche Justiz 99 (1937): 97.

14. "Allgemeine Verfügung des Reichsministers der Justiz betreffend Einrichtung eines kriminalbiologischen Dienstes im Bereich der Reichsjustizverwaltung vom 30. November 1937," Deutsche Justiz 99 (1937): 1872; "Durchführungsverordnung zur AV. des RJM vom 30. November 1937," ibid.; both reprinted in Ferdinand von Neureiter, "Der kriminalbiologische Dienst in Deutschland: Text und Erläuterung der AV. des Reichsjustizministers vom 30. November 1937," MKS 29 (1938): 65–68; and in Neureiter, Kriminalbiologie (Berlin: Heymanns, 1940), 74–77.

15. Neureiter, "Der kriminalbiologische Dienst," 65, 73.

16. Ibid., 65–67, 69–70.

to be presented in court at sentencing hearings.[17] In addition, however, the Criminal-Biological Service was assigned several functions in the administration of Nazi eugenic policy. First, it was to assist in the data collection for a national survey of genetic health by forwarding the results of every criminal-biological examination to the Reich Health Office.[18] Second, it was to aid health authorities in identifying criminals to be targeted for individual eugenic measures. Prison authorities were ordered to report any prisoners who might be suffering from any of the "genetic diseases" enumerated in the 1933 sterilization law to the health authorities, who would then initiate sterilization proceedings (discussed in detail in Chapter 7).[19] Furthermore, the results of each criminal-biological examination were to be reported to the Public Health Offices (Gesundheitsämter) in the criminal's birthplace and city of residence,[20] so that if a former prisoner sought a marriage license, local health authorities could use his criminal-biological records to assess whether he suffered from mental defects that barred him from marriage according to the Marriage Health Law of 1935.[21] Finally, if the criteria for sterilization were ever expanded, local health authorities would be able to examine the records of former criminals in their district to determine if they met the new criteria. While a full discussion of the relationship between criminology and Nazi eugenic policy will be deferred until the next chapter, there can be no doubt that the creation of a national Criminal-Biological Service was in large part motivated by its utility for Nazi eugenic policy. In this sense, the strategy of gaining Nazi support for criminal biology by highlighting its connection to eugenic policy was indeed successful.

17. Ibid., 65. Since a criminal had to enter prison to undergo a criminal-biological examination, this information would be available only at the trials of repeat offenders.

18. Ibid., 66, 68, 71. On the project of a "erbbiologische Bestandsaufnahme des deutschen Volkes," which had collected data on ten million people by 1942, see Viernstein, "Erbwertliche Erforschung"; E. Schütt, "Die erbbiologische Bestandsaufnahme," *Der öffentliche Gesundheitsdienst,* ser. B, 2 (1936): 241; E. Schütt, "Erläuterungen zur erbbiologischen Bestandsaufnahme," ibid., ser. A, 2 (1936): 255; Karl Heinz Roth, "Erbbiologische Bestandsaufnahme—Ein Aspekt ausmerzender Erfassung vor der Entfesselung des 2. Weltkrieges," in *Erfassung zur Vernichtung: Von der Sozialhygiene zum Gesetz über Sterbehilfe,* ed. Roth (Berlin: Verlagsgesellschaft Gesundheit, 1984), 57–100; Peter Weingart, Jürgen Kroll, and Kurt Bayertz, *Rasse, Blut und Gene: Geschichte der Eugenik und Rassenhygiene in Deutschland* (Frankfurt: Suhrkamp, 1988), 485–94.

19. Erlass des Reichsministers der Justiz betreffend Unfruchtbarmachung erbkranker Verbrecher vom 15. Dezember 1933, reprinted in Arthur Gütt, Ernst Rüdin, and Falk Ruttke, *Gesetz zur Verhütung erbkranken Nachwuchses* (Munich: Lehmann, 1934), 175.

20. Neureiter, "Der kriminalbiologische Dienst," 66, 68, 71.

21. On the Marriage Health Law, see Chapter 7.

Anti-Semitism

If the Nazis' biological worldview furthered support for criminal-biological examinations, its anti-Semitic component also spelled the end of the careers of Jewish criminologists. Karl Birnbaum, who was fifty-five years old in 1933 and had become director of the municipal psychiatric hospital Berlin-Buch in 1930, was dismissed in 1933 under the provisions of the Law for the Restoration of a Professional Civil Service, which purged Jews from civil service positions. He emigrated to the United States in 1939, where he died in 1950.[22]

Gustav Aschaffenburg, who was sixty-seven years old in 1933, qualified for an exemption under the 1933 civil service law but was pressured into retiring from his positions as professor and director of the psychiatric clinic at the University of Cologne in March 1934. He was able to retain the editorship of his *Monatsschrift für Kriminalpsychologie* for another year and a half. When the journal's publisher urged greater caution in 1934, Aschaffenburg's coeditor, Hans von Hentig, who was not Jewish but was politically opposed to the Nazis, resigned. By 1935, anti-Semitic pressures had become so great that Aschaffenburg was forced to give up the editorship of the journal that he had founded thirty years earlier. Starting in 1936, the journal was coedited by Franz Exner, Johannes Lange, and Rudolf Sieverts, who remained in close contact with Aschaffenburg until Lange was denounced to the Gestapo for this contact. When the three new editors considered resigning in protest against Aschaffenburg's being barred from publishing in the journal he had founded, Aschaffenburg asked them to stay on to prevent the journal from falling into the hands of party hacks. In his 1935 farewell editorial, Aschaffenburg cited his seventieth birthday as the ostensible reason for transferring the journal's editorship to "younger colleagues" and once again defended criminologists and penal reformers against the charge that they were responsible for the excessive lenience of Weimar criminal justice. Insisting that criminologists and reformers had always put the protection of society first, he described the goal of penal reform in typical Nazi terminology as "freeing the *Volksgemeinschaft* [national community] from *Schädlinge* [harmful elements, para-

---

22. Hartwig Liedtke, "Karl Birnbaum: Leben und Werk" (M.D. diss., University of Cologne, 1982), 58–60, 67–75; F. Irro and P. Hagemann, "Karl Birnbaum—Versuch einer Würdigung der Lebensarbeit eines bedeutenden Psychiaters und zugleich ein verspäteter Nachruf," *Zeitschrift für Psychiatrie, Neurologie und medizinische Psychologie* 25 (1973): 117; Bernard Pauleikhoff, "Karl Birnbaum," in *Das Menschenbild im Wandel der Zeit* (Hürtgenwald: Pressler, 1987), 3:270; D. I. Fischer, ed., *Biographisches Lexikon der hervorragenden Ärzte der letzten fünfzig Jahre* (Munich: Urban und Schwarzenberg, 1932), 123; *International Biographical Dictionary of Central European Emigrés, 1933–1945*, 2:111.

sites]."[23] In 1939 Aschaffenburg emigrated to Switzerland and later to the United States, where he lectured at Johns Hopkins University in Baltimore before his death in 1944.[24]

While Aschaffenburg's use of Nazi terminology reflected his desire for accommodation with "tough-on-crime" Nazi jurists, it also shows that even in late 1935, after the passage of the Nuremberg Laws, Aschaffenburg does not seem to have seen any connection between the biological approaches to crime that he had pioneered and the anti-Semitism that would drive him out of the country a little over two years later. To be sure, Aschaffenburg's failure to perceive this connection can be seen as evidence of errors of judgment: an underestimation of the seriousness of Nazi anti-Semitism and a failure to understand that the Nazis regarded criminal biology and anti-Semitism as complementary parts of a eugenic-racial policy designed to rid the *Volksgemeinschaft* of "biologically inferior" elements. Just as important, however, Aschaffenburg's failure to connect criminal biology to the racist and anti-Semitic components of Nazi ideology also demonstrates that it is wrong to assume that criminal biology and racism (including anti-Semitism) were intrinsically connected. Just as Aschaffenburg and Birnbaum did not see their work as contributing to anti-Semitism, many German Jewish doctors endorsed eugenics without much worry that this might promote anti-Semitism. While some criminologists did indeed hold racist prejudices against Jews and other groups, the criminal-biological project focused primarily on individual, as opposed to racial, characteristics of biological abnormality. Although the anti-Semitic wing of the eugenics movement and the Nazis demonstrated that eugenics and criminal biology could be linked to a racist and anti-Semitic agenda, it is important to remember that this connection was by no means inevitable.

In the fall of 1936 the academic division of the Nazi Association of Lawyers (Rechtswahrerbund) organized a conference titled "Jews in Legal Studies" (*Das Judentum in der Rechtswissenschaft*), which featured a series of extremely anti-Semitic lectures, including a lecture on "Jews and crime" and another on "Jews in criminal psychology," all of which were published.[25] The lecturers

23. Gustav Aschaffenburg, "Rückblick und Ausblick," MKS 26 (1935): 531–35.

24. Falk Busse, "Gustav Aschaffenburg: Leben und Werk" (M.D. diss., University of Leipzig, 1991), 8–10; Hans von Hentig, "Gustav Aschaffenburg," in Pioneers in Criminology, ed. Hermann Mannheim, 2d ed. (Montclair: Patterson Smith, 1972), 421–28; "Vorwort," MKS 27 (1936): 1; "Gustav Aschaffenburg zum siebzigsten Geburtstag," MKS 27 (1936): 294; L. Kanner, "In Memoriam: Gustav Aschaffenburg," American Journal of Psychiatry 101 (1944): 427–28; Hans Gruhle and Rudolf Sieverts, "Zum Geleit," MKS 36 (1953): 1–5.

25. Das Judentum in der Rechtswissenschaft: Ansprachen, Vorträge und Ergebnisse der Tagung der Reichsgruppe Hochschullehrer des NSRB am 3. und 4. Oktober 1936, 8 vols. (Berlin:

on both of these topics were marginal figures in the field of criminology, per-haps because the organizers were unable to get major criminologists to par-ticipate. The lecture on Jews and crime, delivered by Johann von Leers, a lec-turer at the Hochschule für Politik in Berlin, consisted of a historical discussion of the role of Jews in organized brigandry from the mid-sixteenth to the early nineteenth centuries that culminated in the conclusion that the Jews were a "criminal counter-race" whose conception of God bore "genetically criminal features."[26]

The lecture on Jews in criminal psychology was delivered by Max Mikorey, a senior staff physician at the Psychiatric Clinic in Munich and a member of the Academy of German Law. Mikorey argued that the "Jewish people" (*Judentum*) had developed an "internal" and an "external" criminal psychology. In their internal criminal psychology, as recorded in the Talmud and the Pentateuch, the Jews took a harsh retributive attitude toward crime. Since Jehovah was a wrathful God who exacted harsh punishment, "in rootless Jewry's eternal state of war against all other peoples, the criminal in their own ranks [was] met with the severity of martial law." But whereas internal Jewish criminal psychology sought to protect the Jewish people against crime, external Jewish criminal psychology, which was propagated in the countries in which Jews lived, was a "weapon in the fight of emancipated Jewry for political power." The psycho-logical analysis of crime was designed to relativize crime and make it appear harmless in order to sabotage the foreign state's power to punish. "Behind the phraseology of humanitarianism, justice, and scientific knowledge, Jewish criminal psychology formulated . . . its veto against the punitive power [*Straf-hoheit*] of its host peoples [*Wirtsvölker*]."[27] Because a nation's attitude toward crime was closely connected to its resistance to the ambitions of foreign races, this attack on a country's punitive power would ultimately undermine its re-sistance to Jewish ambitions and thereby open the way for the Jewish ascension to power.[28]

According to Mikorey, the "political history" of this external Jewish criminal

---

Deutscher Rechts-Verlag, 1936); Horst Göppinger, *Juristen jüdischer Abstammung im "Dritten Reich,"* 2d ed. (Munich: Beck, 1990), 153–63.

26. Johann von Leers, "Die Kriminalität des Judentums," in *Das Judentum in der Rechtswis-senschaft*, vol. 3, *Judentum und Verbrechen* (Berlin: Deutscher Rechtsverlag, 1936), 5–60. On Leers, see Göppinger, *Juristen*, 155.

27. One of the tract's most vicious features was Mikorey's description of the relationship between Jews and the peoples among which they lived as that of a parasite to its "host" (*Wirt*).

28. Max Mikorey, "Das Judentum in der Kriminalpsychologie," in *Das Judentum in der Rechtswissenschaft*, vol. 3, *Judentum und Verbrechen*, 61–67.

psychology unfolded in three phases. The first blow against the state's punitive power was struck by the theory of the born criminal advanced by the Jewish criminologist Lombroso. The problem was not that Lombroso was somehow soft on crime. Mikorey admitted that Lombroso knew no "sentimental pity for the criminal" and had even suggested that born criminals be incapacitated through lifelong imprisonment or the death penalty. But according to Mikorey, the fact that the born criminal was an atavistic anthropological type destined to a life of crime meant that he could not be judged by the standards of classic criminal law based on free will. As a result, the state's punitive power was deprived of a key element, which had also served as a barrier to Jewish political aspirations: its "moral-political pathos." After initial successes, Lombroso's theories were soon abandoned because the "tactical situation of political Judaism" was changing. In the early 1870s, when Lombroso had written his famous book, there had been no danger that the notion of a "criminal race" might promote racial anti-Semitism because a general ideology of equality still held sway. After the wave of anti-Semitism that followed the depression of the 1870s, however, Mikorey argued, it became clear that the idea of the born criminal could become an anti-Semitic weapon, and Jewish criminal psychology therefore quickly abandoned it. According to Mikorey, "The following retreat of Jewish criminal psychology from Lombroso's indefensible and dangerous positions across the icy heights of statistics into the camp of Marxist world revolution [was] one of the greatest masterworks of Jewish strategy."[29]

In its next phase, Jewish criminal psychology concentrated on criminal statistics, which shifted the focus from biological and racial to social explanations of crime. Slowly, the responsibility for crimes was transferred from the individual to society. Mikorey presented Gustav Aschaffenburg as the "typical representative" of this approach, although he admitted that Aschaffenburg had always remained a sober analyst who had never promoted the "corrupting tendencies" of "Jewish Marxism." Jewish defense lawyers, demagogues, writers, and journalists, however, had effectively promoted a Marxist version of this sociological criminal psychology. "Not the Jewish criminal psychology of university lecture halls or theoretical treatises, but this demagogical psychology of crime was the most dangerous blow against the punitive power and integrity of the state." Finally, in the last phase, this Marxist Jewish criminal psychology was "ideally supplemented" by Freud's psychoanalysis and Adler's "individual psychology." By arguing that every individual harbored potential criminal tendencies, Freud

29. Ibid., 68–73.

and Adler destroyed the "sense of moral distance" between normal citizen and criminal that should undergird every criminal justice system.[30]

Mikorey's tract presented an anti-Semitic version of the charge that criminology was responsible for the supposed emasculation of the criminal justice system. The feat of presenting the entire development of criminology as a Jewish conspiracy was achieved by simply ignoring the contributions of non-Jewish figures. If the major charge was that Jewish criminal psychology had undermined the moral foundations of criminal justice, what about Kraepelin, who had advocated the replacement of a morally grounded criminal justice system by medical treatment? What about Liepmann and Exner's contribution to the sociological explanation of crime? Furthermore, by attacking both the biological and the sociological strands of criminology as the products of a Jewish conspiracy, Mikorey had effectively demolished the entire field. Finally, if Mikorey charged Lombroso with undermining the notion of free will, on which criminal justice was based, the same criticism applied to the more recent varieties of criminal-biological and genetic research, even though Mikorey carefully omitted them from his account. For these reasons, it is hardly surprising that Mikorey's critique of "Jewish criminal psychology" was not followed up by the psychiatrists and jurists working on criminological questions during the Nazi years.

The Search for Genetic Factors Continued

Evidence from a variety of historical studies suggests that many people in Nazi Germany endorsed genetically determinist or racist explanations of criminal behavior. In their study of the Nazi racial state Michael Burleigh and Wolfgang Wippermann have argued that in "the Nazis' view of the world, 'asocial' and criminal behavior was not determined by either individual choice or the social environment, but rather was innate and hence heritable." Patrick Wagner has shown that by the late 1930s, the police leadership in the Reichskriminal-polizeiamt had come to regard "professional and recidivist crime as a genetically produced phenomenon." Other studies have demonstrated that some doctors and others involved in the persecution and eventual murder of the handicapped, Jews, and Gypsies claimed that these groups were characterized by "criminality" as a racial characteristic. Thus Robert Proctor has argued that Nazi medical leaders believed that "Jews were racially disposed to commit crime." And Henry Friedlander has shown that "race hygiene had always linked the

30. Ibid., 73–82.

handicapped to criminal and antisocial behavior"; that researchers on Gypsies claimed that "gypsies as a group were degenerate, criminal, and asocial and that this condition was hereditary"; and that "the Nazi killers used the language of Lombroso to target . . . gypsies and the handicapped."[31]

In short, there is considerable evidence that police officials subscribed to genetic explanations of crime and that a substantial number of medical doctors, especially those involved in the persecution and killing of Jews, Gypsies, and the handicapped, regarded those groups as racially predisposed toward crime. The question to what extent such views were representative of the medical profession in general or German society as a whole falls outside the scope of this study, although the discussion of the reception of criminological research in Weimar and Nazi sterilization debates in the next chapter will throw some light on this matter. This chapter, by contrast, will focus on the development of criminology as a specialized field of research and therefore examine the question to what extent *specialists in criminology* came to endorse genetically determinist explanations of crime during the Nazi period.

Friedrich Stumpfl's Family Study

The most important and influential research in criminal biology during the Nazi regime was the work of Friedrich Stumpfl. The son of a high-ranking official in the Austrian Foreign Ministry, Stumpfl had studied medicine and anthropology in Vienna. When Johannes Lange left the Deutsche Forschungsanstalt für Psychiatrie in Munich to accept a position as full professor and chief of the psychiatric clinic in Breslau in 1930, Stumpfl was hired to continue criminal-biological research at the Forschungsanstalt. Specifically, Stumpfl was asked to carry out a research project devised by Ernst Rüdin, head of the Forschungsanstalt's Genealogical-Demographic Department and, since 1931, director of the Forschungsanstalt as a whole.[32] This project called for comparing a group of multiple recidivists with a group of one-time offenders. After four

31. Michael Burleigh and Wolfgang Wippermann, *The Racial State: Germany, 1933–1945* (Cambridge: Cambridge University Press, 1991), 167; Patrick Wagner, *Volksgemeinschaft ohne Verbrecher: Konzeptionen und Praxis der Kriminalpolizei in der Zeit der Weimarer Republik und des Nationalsozialismus* (Hamburg: Christians, 1996), 265; Robert Proctor, *Racial Hygiene: Medicine under the Nazis* (Cambridge, Mass.: Harvard University Press, 1988), 204–5; Henry Friedlander, *The Origins of Nazi Genocide: From Euthanasia to the Final Solution* (Chapel Hill: University of North Carolina Press, 1995), 3, 23, 252.

32. Matthias Weber, *Ernst Rüdin: Eine kritische Biographie* (Berlin: Springer, 1993), 163, 173; Weber, "Ein Forschungsinstitut für Psychiatrie: Die Entwicklung der Deutschen Forschungsanstalt für Psychiatrie in München zwischen 1917 und 1945," *Sudhoffs Archiv* 75 (1991): 84.

years of full-time research, Stumpfl published his results in 1935 in a book titled *Erbanlage und Verbrechen: Charakterologische und psychiatrische Sippenuntersuchungen* (Heredity and crime: Characterological and psychiatric family studies).[33]

Stumpfl's study was designed to pick up where Lange's 1929 twin study had left off. Lange claimed to have demonstrated that heredity played a predominant role in the etiology of criminal behavior but acknowledged that his study provided no information about the nature of the genetic factors involved. Stumpfl sought to make progress on precisely this issue. He started with the hypothesis that the criminal behavior of habitual, recidivist criminals had genetic origins, whereas that of occasional, one-time offenders did not. To test this hypothesis, Stumpfl proposed to investigate whether the extended families of a group of recidivists showed a higher incidence of criminal behavior than the families of one-time offenders. If so, a genetic explanation was at least plausible, and the study could then proceed to compare the genetic traits of the recidivists and their families with those of the one-time offenders and their families, who would function as a control group. If certain traits were much more frequent among recidivists and their families than they were in the control group, it could be argued that these traits were the genetic criminogenic traits implicated in recidivist criminal behavior. This only left the question of what traits to look for. Since criminal-biological research had long posited that crime was connected with psychopathy and perhaps even with mental illness, Stumpfl chose to investigate the incidence of both mental illnesses and psychopathic traits.

With this research plan in mind, Stumpfl assembled his two study groups: 195 male recidivists from the files of the Bavarian Criminal-Biological Service who had been convicted and sentenced to prison terms at least five times and 166 male one-time offenders who had been sentenced to a prison term of at least three months and had been free of convictions for at least fifteen years since. For information on the recidivists Stumpfl relied mostly on their criminal

33. Friedrich Stumpfl, *Erbanlage und Verbrechen: Charakterologische und psychiatrische Sippenuntersuchungen* (Berlin: Springer, 1935). Some of the study's findings were published in earlier articles: "Die kriminelle Familie," *Volk und Rasse* 8 (1933); "Erbanlage und Verbrechen," *ZGNP* 145 (1933): 283–326; "Die kriminellen Verwandten," *AfK* 93 (1933): 80–86; "Grundlagen und Aufgaben der Kriminalbiologie," in *Erblehre und Rassenhygiene im völkischen Staat*, ed. Ernst Rüdin (Munich: Lehmann, 1934), 317–32. See also Karl Schnell, *Anlage und Umwelt bei 500 Rückfallsverbrechern*, Kriminalistische Abhandlungen, no. 22 (Leipzig: Wiegandt, 1935); Albert Schmid, *Anlage und Umwelt bei 500 Erstverbrechern*, Kriminalistische Abhandlungen, no. 24 (Leipzig: Wiegandt, 1936).

records, but he conducted personal interviews with most of the one-time offenders. In addition, he personally visited more than 1,700 relatives, gathering information on a total of over 18,000 persons.[34]

Stumpfl's findings confirmed his initial hypothesis regarding criminal behavior. The incidence of criminal convictions among the relatives of recidivists was substantially higher than among the relatives of one-time offenders: 37 percent versus 10 percent for brothers; 17.5 percent versus 5 percent for male cousins; 28 percent versus 4 percent for fathers. Given the high concentration of criminals in the extended families of the recidivists, a genetic explanation of their criminal behavior was at least plausible, and Stumpfl's search for potential criminogenic genetic factors could proceed.[35]

Regarding mental illness, Stumpfl found that the extended families of the recidivists had no more schizophrenics, manic-depressives, or epileptics than the families of one-time offenders and that the incidence of mental illness in both groups was no higher than in the larger population. He therefore concluded that there was no evidence for a biological connection between criminal behavior and any of the major types of mental illness (psychoses): schizophrenia, manic depression, epilepsy. Thus a major variant of the genetic explanation of crime, which had been widely accepted for more than half a century, was finally discredited.[36]

Stumpfl's investigation of psychopathic traits revealed that all except two of the recidivists but only about 15 percent of one-time offenders were "psychopathic." The extended families of the two groups showed a similar contrast, with a high incidence of psychopaths among the families of recidivists (31 percent among fathers, 34 percent among siblings) compared to much lower figures among the families of one-time offenders (7 percent among fathers and siblings). Using Kurt Schneider's typology of psychopathic personalities, Stumpfl determined that three types of psychopathic traits were especially prevalent among the recidivists: 58 percent were *willenlos* (weak-willed), 49 percent were *gemütlos* (compassionless), and 30 percent were hyperthymic (hyperactive); overall, 72 percent of the recidivists displayed one or more of these three traits. These findings led Stumpfl to conclude "that certain character traits and abnormalities in combination with others bring about severe recidivist criminality and must therefore be considered genuine causes of crime." In addition,

---

34. Stumpfl, *Erbanlage und Verbrechen*, iii–iv, 1–4.
35. Ibid., 4–42, 284–88; see also Stumpfl, "Erbanlage und Verbrechen."
36. Stumpfl, *Erbanlage und Verbrechen*, 43–44, 47, 288–93.

Stumpfl regarded the elevated incidence of the same psychopathic traits among the recidivists' relatives as evidence that "these character traits are genetically transmitted to offspring and are responsive to external influences only to a very limited degree." In short, there were "genetic" connections "between serious [recidivist] criminality and certain forms of psychopathy."[37]

Although his hereditarian bias was plain, Stumpfl understood that many of his findings were potentially amenable to milieu-oriented explanations. This issue was made especially acute by Stumpfl's admission that the average child-hood environment of his recidivists was distinctly worse than that of one-time offenders: many were illegitimate children, born into the lowest social stratum, often abused by their parents, sometimes even forced to beg or steal. Neverthe-less, Stumpfl insisted, it would be wrong to attribute their criminality simply to their environment because the most important feature of this environment was the parents, and parents affected their children not just through their example but also through their heredity. This formulation led him to concede, however, that "heredity and environment form[ed] an interwoven web" that could not be disentangled. But later in the text he once again claimed priority for heredity, arguing that "in the final analysis, the finding that recidivists generally grew up in much worse environmental conditions than one-time offenders points back to their genetic defects, since these environmental conditions are primarily determined by the quality of the parents and are an indication of genetic defects in them."[38]

Having thus dismissed the role of childhood environment as a by-product of parental genetic quality, Stumpfl concluded that the clusters of psychopathic traits among recidivists were "genuine causes of crime" and that his recidi-vist criminals were thus "genetically determined criminal personalities." But Stumpfl was too sophisticated to maintain that genetic character traits were immune to external influences and acknowledged that genetic character traits were "malleable," that is, responsive to environmental influences, although some were likely to be more malleable than others. Stumpfl argued that deter-mining the extent of malleability for various psychopathic character traits was an important area for future research because only such research could answer the crucial question to what extent genetic psychopathic traits could be modi-fied through pedagogical measures to prevent crime.[39]

37. Ibid., 131–54, 237–48, 293–98.
38. Ibid., 32, 38.
39. Ibid., 297, 235–37.

Stumpfl's Twin Study

Convinced that twin studies offered the best method for determining the malleability of genetic traits, Stumpfl conducted a study of twins that was designed
to improve on Lange's pioneering 1929 work. Published in 1936 under the title
Die Ursprünge des Verbrechens (The origins of crime), Stumpfl's twin study is of
interest both because its results differed from Lange's and because it showed an
evolution of Stumpfl's views on the role of heredity and environment.[40]

Stumpfl's study was based on a sample of thirty-two pairs of male twins
(seventeen fraternal and fifteen identical twins), in which at least one twin in
every pair had a criminal record.[41] In accordance with the twin method, Stumpfl
was looking for a difference in concordance rates between identical and fraternal twins, with concordance defined as the criminality of both twins. Compared
to Lange's figures, Stumpfl's results were disappointing. Lange had found that
77 percent of his identical twins versus only 12 percent of his fraternal twins
were concordant, a difference of 65 percentage points that demonstrated the
power of heredity. Stumpfl, by contrast, found that only 60 percent of his identical as opposed to 41 percent of his fraternal twins were concordant, a difference of less than 20 percentage points, which, he acknowledged, was "minor."
To explain the discrepancy between his and Lange's results, Stumpfl subjected
Lange's study to critical scrutiny and argued that Lange's results had been
distorted. In addition, he reported that the concordance rates in a preliminary
report of a twin study being conducted by Heinrich Kranz (63 percent among
identical versus 46 percent among fraternal twins) were very close to his own.[42]

---

40. Friedrich Stumpfl, *Ursprünge des Verbrechens: Dargestellt am Lebenslauf von Zwillingen*
(Leipzig: Georg Thieme, 1936). See also Heinrich Kranz, *Lebensschicksale krimineller Zwillinge*
(Berlin: Springer, 1936), which also found only a small difference in concordance rates be-
tween identical and fraternal twins (66 percent versus 54 percent).

41. With an initial sample of 550 pairs of twins with at least one convicted partner, Stumpfl
could have outdone Lange's study by the sheer size of his sample. But for practical reasons (he
had to visit each twin for a personal examination), Stumpfl restricted his sample to the 65
twins residing in Bavaria. From this sample he then excluded the 28 opposite-sex twins
because of the overwhelming effect of gender on crime. Leaving aside the tiny sampe of five
female same-sex twins, Stumpfl thus ended up with a core sample of 32 pairs of male twins
that was no larger than Lange's (ibid., 16–18).

42. Ibid., 18–23; Johannes Lange, *Verbrechen als Schicksal: Studien an kriminellen Zwillingen*
(Leipzig: Thieme, 1929), 15; Heinrich Kranz, "Die Kriminalität bei Zwillingen," *Zeitschrift für
induktive Abstammungs- und Vererbungslehre* 70 (1933): 67. Stumpfl reported his results in the
form of discordance (rather than concordance) rates. Stumpfl argued that Lange's results had
been distorted by two problems: Lange had not studied the fraternal twins as thoroughly as
the identical twins and had therefore probably missed some criminal records; two pairs of

Although Stumpfl's findings seemed to suggest that the role of heredity was minor after all, he was too much of a hereditarian to let matters rest there. Drawing on the distinction between recidivists and one-time offenders in his earlier study, he proceeded to distinguish between "serious" and "minor" forms of criminality among his identical twins. Once this distinction was made, it emerged that male recidivist identical twins were concordant in eight out of nine cases (89 percent), whereas male nonrecidivist identical twins were concordant in only one out of six cases (17 percent). Since the single discordant case among the identical recidivist twins involved a twin who had become criminal later in life, Stumpfl concluded that except for cases with a late onset of criminal behavior (Spätkriminelle), male "identical twins who are characterized by serious criminality are completely concordant in regard to crime."[43]

Rather surprisingly, Stumpfl immediately relativized the significance of this finding by providing a remarkable analysis of the methodological problems and limitations of psychological twin research. The underlying principle of twin research, that is, the idea that differences in concordance rates between identical and fraternal twins demonstrated the importance of heredity, was based on the assumption that the environments of identical twins were no more similar than the environments of fraternal twins. Stumpfl argued that although this assumption held for somatic twin research, it was not valid for psychological research. Among fraternal twins growing up together, the same external event might harm the psychological development of one twin, while remaining irrelevant for the other because their different hereditary character structures could cause them to experience the same event differently. Identical twins, by contrast, always experienced an external event in the same way because they shared the same character structure. Hence the environmental influences acting on identical twins growing up together were in fact more similar than those of fraternal twins growing up together. Therefore, Stumpfl concluded, the complete concordance among his identical twins, as opposed to the much lower concordance among fraternal twins, did not constitute conclusive evidence of the influence of heredity.[44]

Stumpfl's recognition of these methodological problems led him to abandon the hereditarianism of his earlier book in favor of a more complex understanding of the interaction of heredity and environment. This was especially evident

---

identical twins that Lange regarded as concordant had not been judicially convicted. With these corrections, Lange's concordance rates approached Stumpfl's.

43. Stumpfl, Ursprünge des Verbrechens, 93–98. A small sample of three pairs of female recidivist identical twins showed a lower concordance rate (two out of three).

44. Ibid., 127–31.

in his discussion of the different causes of what he called "serious criminality" (*Schwerkriminalität*), recidivist criminal behavior that manifested itself before age twenty-five. Whereas Stumpfl had previously attributed recidivist criminality exclusively to hereditary psychopathic traits, he now added that it could also result from a "puberty crisis" or a permanent "psychological deformation" sustained during childhood as a result of external factors such as abuse or exposure to an immoral milieu. He also acknowledged that his twin research was unable to determine whether a person's recidivist criminality resulted from hereditary psychopathic traits or a psychological deformation.[45]

But according to Stumpfl, the inability to determine whether recidivist criminality was caused by genetic or environmental influences was not a problem because the only question that mattered was whether any given recidivist criminal was amenable to corrective influences (*beeinflussbar*), that is, "whether a reintegration into the community [was] possible." "In all cases that reveal themselves as recidivist criminals and do not make up for this shortcoming through useful and reliable work in a company or through dutiful and brave conduct in the military," Stumpfl suggested, "eugenic measures [were] called for in the interest of the common good." On the other hand, "recidivists who are amenable to external influences and have . . . shown themselves to be valuable human beings in some important areas, must . . . not be eliminated through eugenic measures."[46]

Although Stumpfl was tempted to link the question of corrigibility to the distinction between genetic and environmental causes, he had to acknowledge that such a link did not exist. In the end, therefore, "a distinction between recidivists who can be reintegrated into the community and those who cannot can never be made schematically, but must always be left to life itself, and can only be reached through an evaluation of the entire personality in each individual case."[47] This vague formulation revealed that Stumpfl's research on genetic factors had failed to produce new guidelines for assessing a criminal's corrigibility. Stumpfl's references to recidivists proving themselves valuable members of the community "in a company" or "in the military" suggested that the real test of corrigibility lay in the empirical observation of social behavior that amounted to a tautology: if a criminal could be integrated, then he was corrigible.

---

45. Ibid., 147–61, 164, 131, 146, 169. "The boundaries between serious criminality [Schwerkriminalität] from psychological deformation [seelischer Verbildung] . . . and serious criminality from genetic disposition [erblicher Veranlagung] cannot usually be established by twin research" (131).

46. Stumpfl, *Ursprünge des Verbrechens*, 146, 151.

47. Ibid., 152.

Despite all these qualifications, Stumpfl recommended the sterilization of all incorrigible recidivists.[48] Since he had acknowledged that it was impossible to determine whether any given case of recidivist criminality was caused by genetic or environmental factors and that the distinction between corrigibles and incorrigibles was by no means congruent with the distinction between environmental and genetic cases, this recommendation made no sense. For if the criminal behavior of an incorrigible recidivist could have resulted from environmental factors, what justification was there for sterilizing him? Certainly not a genetic one. Stumpfl's views on eugenic measures against criminals were not keeping pace with the evolution of his scientific views. As the next chapter will show, Stumpfl was typical of a number of criminal biologists who endorsed eugenic measures for criminals against their better scientific judgment.

Stumpfl's studies advanced criminal-biological research in a variety of ways. His finding that the families of recidivists showed no increased incidence of mental illness refuted the long-standing theory of a genetic connection between mental illness and criminal behavior. At the same time, his findings of widespread psychopathy among recidivists and their families reinforced the view that many habitual criminals were psychopaths. Concerning the key question of genetic versus environmental causes of crime, Stumpfl's work sent contradictory messages. On the one hand, in his first book, Stumpfl asserted that the clusters of psychopathic traits found among recidivist criminals were "genuine causes of crime" and that the recidivist criminal was a "genetically determined criminal personality." His twin study claimed to have confirmed this finding.[49] On the other hand, Stumpfl demonstrated unprecedented methodological sophistication, which obliged him to qualify his hereditarian claims. This was especially evident in his second book, the twin study, in which he conceded, first, that recidivists could become criminal as a result of milieu-induced "psychological deformations" rather than genetic traits; and second, that because of the greater similarity of the environments of identical as compared to fraternal twins, differences in concordance rates could not be regarded as proof of the influence of genetic factors, as Lange had previously assumed.

There is no doubt that Stumpfl's books, published in 1935 and 1936, were the most important and influential books published in the field of criminal biology in the 1930s. In addition, Stumpfl disseminated his views in numerous lectures and articles published between 1936 and 1939, when he left the Deutsche Forschungsanstalt für Psychiatrie in Munich for a professorship at the Univer-

48. Ibid., 146, 174.
49. Ibid., 160.

sity of Innsbruck and turned to other research topics. (In 1939 he also applied for membership in the Nazi Party, which was granted in 1941.)[50] Between 1936 and 1939 he published a dozen articles in the major journals in criminology, criminal law, and psychiatry; he delivered lectures at meetings of the Association for Forensic Psychology and Psychiatry (April 1937) and of the Criminal-Biological Society (October 1937); he prepared a report for the international Criminological Congress in Rome (October 1938); and he contributed a chapter on crime and heredity to the major handbook of human genetics.[51] All this made Stumpfl the most prolific and very likely the most widely read writer on criminal-biological matters in the second half of the 1930s.

Although Stumpfl's lectures and writings between 1936 and 1939 exhibited the same tension between hereditarian claims and a reluctant acknowledgment of the role of environmental factors as his books, one can detect an increasing concern to alert readers to unresolved questions, the methodological limitations of twin research, and the complexity of the interaction of genetic and environmental factors. Thus Stumpfl made an effort to dispel simplistic hereditarian interpretations of the twin studies conducted by Lange and himself. "The results" of twin studies, he cautioned, "were often incorrectly interpreted as if crime [were] an unavoidable fate."[52] To root out such simplistic views, Stumpfl made a conscious effort to present the results of his twin study in a differentiated way. To be sure, he still claimed that his twin studies had demonstrated that

50. Weingart, Kroll, and Bayertz, *Rasse, Blut und Gene*, 439; BDC, NSDAP-Ortskartei, A-3340-MFOK-W-0074.

51. Friedrich Stumpfl, "Kriminelle Psychopathen: Ein kritischer Beitrag zur Frage des 'moralischen Schwachsinns,'" *Der Erbarzt* 3 (1936): 134; "Kriminalbiologische Forschung und der Vollzug von Strafen und sichernden Massnahmen," *Gerichtssaal* 108 (1936): 338–61; "Untersuchungen an kriminellen und psychopathischen Zwillingen," *Der öffentliche Gesundheitsdienst* 2 (1936); "Die Vererbung des Charakters," in *Die Persönlichkeit im Lichte der Erblehre* (Leipzig: Teubner, 1936); "Erbanlage und Verbrechen: Eine Erwiderung auf die Bemerkungen von Prof. Lange und Prof. Exner, sowie Prof. H. Mayer," *MKS* 28 (1937): 92–98; "Vortrag auf der Jahresversammlung der Vereinigung für gerichtliche Psychologie und Psychiatrie am 17.4.1937," *Deutsches Recht* 7 (1937): 336; "Psychopathenforschung und Kriminalbiologie: Erbbiologische Ergebnisse, 1933–1937," *FNPG* 9 (1937): 167–76; "Über Erbforschung an Rechtsbrechern," *MKBG* 5 (1937): 111–15; "Über kriminalbiologische Erbforschung," *AZP* 107 (1938): 38–63; "Verbrechen und Vererbung," *MKS* 29 (1938): 1–21; "Psychopathenforschung unter dem Gesichtspunkt der Erbbiologie, 1937–1939," *FNPG* 11 (1939): 409–16; "Gutachten zum Thema: Studium der Persönlichkeit des Verbrechers," in *Römischer Kongreß für Kriminologie* (Berlin: Decker's Verlag, 1939), 217–27; "Kriminalität und Vererbung," in *Handbuch der Erbbiologie des Menschen*, ed. Günther Just, vol. 5, pt. 2 (Berlin: Springer, 1939), 1223–74.

52. Stumpfl, "Über kriminalbiologische Erbforschung," 55; "Über Erbforschung an Rechtsbrechern," 113.

"the criminal with a pronounced tendency to recidivism [was] genetically pre-disposed toward crime."[53] But he also pointed out that the criminogenic genetic traits involved were only potentials, whose actualization depended on environmental factors. He therefore ceased describing the psychopathic traits that he found among recidivist criminals as "genuine causes of crime" (the formulation of his 1935 book)[54] and characterized them instead as a kind of fertile "top-soil in which criminality can develop more easily," but only if certain environmental factors were present.[55]

Stumpfl's view that most recidivist criminals were genetically predisposed toward crime and his view that criminogenic genetic traits were only potentials dependent on environmental factors led him in different directions. His belief in a link between recidivist criminality and certain genetic traits led him to develop the theory that "the rate of criminal activity in a segment of the population" was an indicator of the "character and personality structure" in that population, in other words, that a population's rate of criminal activity was a measure of its genetic quality. What is more, he claimed that psychopathic abnormalities became ever more concentrated "in the lowest social strata."[56]

This remarkable claim derived from Stumpfl's "biological law of partner selection," according to which persons with similar character traits were sexually attracted to one another, so that a man with certain psychopathic traits was likely to marry a woman with similar traits.[57] Having originally developed this theory to explain the high rates of psychopathy and criminality among the wives of the recidivists,[58] Stumpfl now claimed that his "biological law of partner selection" demonstrated that criminality was part of a process of "sedimentation" (Verschlackung, literally "scorification") through which certain psychopathic traits became concentrated in the extended families that made up the lowest stratum of the population, such as vagabonds and big-city riffraff. Making a huge leap, Stumpfl then asserted that "this natural law . . . surrounds every race . . . with a natural protective rampart, which unconsciously protects it from degeneration. Where this protective rampart is still intact, it must not

53. Stumpfl, "Kriminalbiologische Forschung und der Vollzug," 340; "Kriminalität und Vererbung," 1232.

54. Stumpfl, Erbanlage und Verbrechen, 297.

55. Stumpfl, "Über kriminalbiologische Erbforschung," 42; "Kriminalität und Vererbung," 1229, 1238.

56. Stumpfl, "Kriminalität und Vererbung," 1229, 1238, 1264–68.

57. Stumpfl, "Über kriminalbiologische Erbforschung," 48–53; "Kriminalität und Vererbung," 1237–38.

58. Stumpfl, Erbanlage und Verbrechen, 20–31, 287.

be endangered."[59] Drawing on Robert Ritter's research on Gypsies, Stumpfl deduced that "maintaining the purity of the gypsy race [was] in the interest of the state."[60] Although such racist conclusions were rare in Stumpfl's writings, they show that even Stumpfl, who acknowledged the complex interaction of heredity and environment in the etiology of criminal behavior, was unable to resist crude hereditarian and racist theories about marginal social or ethnic groups.

At the same time, however, Stumpfl's recognition that the actualization of criminogenic genetic traits depended on external factors led him to emphasize the importance of environmental influences in penal policy. "The results of twin studies," he cautioned, "must not lead us to abandon educative measures in the combat against crime. On the contrary." Regarding the ratio of corrigibles to incorrigibles, Stumpfl cited the results of a study by the American criminologist William Healy, who found only 20 percent incorrigibles in a sample of recidivist juvenile delinquents. Reporting that his own experience confirmed these estimates, Stumpfl stressed that even among recidivists those who could be "transformed into useful members of the nation" outnumbered incorrigibles by "two to three times." The realization that "not everyone who entered a criminal career can be regarded as biologically or ethically inferior," he concluded, ought to be "a great incentive for measures of positive eugenics and education."[61]

Alas, he had to admit that the problem of distinguishing corrigibles from incorrigibles was still "very far from being resolved," as was the question of the best methods of treatment. Although he claimed that his studies had laid a "general scientific foundation for prognoses of recidivism," his only practical recommendation was that such prognoses be based on a "holistic evaluation of the personality" that took into account both "the genetic foundations of the personality and its developmental possibilities."[62] If the vagueness of this advice showed that his research was of little practical use, Stumpfl's admonition to evaluate not just genetic factors but the range of "developmental possibilities" was significant because it reflected his recognition that the interaction of genetic factors with environmental forces was crucial. For the same reason, Stumpfl concluded his later articles not with a call for more research on heredity but with a call for work in "developmental psychology," to allow for a better under-

59. Stumpfl, "Kriminalität und Vererbung," 1223, 1238; "Über kriminalbiologische Erbforschung," 55; "Über Erbforschung an Rechtsbrechern," 113.
60. Stumpfl, "Über kriminalbiologische Erbforschung," 53.
61. Ibid., 59–60.
62. Stumpfl, "Über Erbforschung an Rechtsbrechern," 114; "Kriminalbiologische Forschung und der Vollzug," 347, 357–58; "Kriminalität und Vererbung," 1271.

standing of the "unfolding of genetic traits" under the influence of "experiences" triggered by external factors.[63]

The Search for Genetic Factors Criticized

Stumpfl's work met with a remarkably critical reception. Upon the publication of Stumpfl's family study, the premier criminology journal, the *Monatsschrift für Kriminalpsychologie*, published a lengthy review article by Lange and Exner that raised major critical questions. Lange, for instance, doubted whether Stumpfl could have accurately diagnosed psychopathic traits among the criminals' relatives, given the large numbers and his limited contact with them during a brief visit.[64] Exner criticized Stumpfl for not breaking down his group of recidivists into smaller, more coherent categories. After all, thieves, violent criminals, sex offenders, and political offenders were likely to differ greatly in their characteristics, so that treating all recidivists as a homogeneous category was likely to result in misleading conclusions.[65]

Besides Lange, who died in 1938, and Exner, who elaborated on his criticisms in his survey of criminology (discussed below), Stumpfl's most prominent critics included the jurist Hellmuth Mayer and the psychiatrist Hans Gruhle. Mayer was a professor of law at the University of Rostock, a member of the official committee charged with revising the penal code, and a member of the working group on criminal justice of the Nazi lawyers' organization (NS-Rechtswahrerbund).[66] Since Mayer disseminated his criticisms of Stumpfl's work in a variety of venues, including his textbook of criminal law (1936), a lecture delivered to the Nazi lawyers' organization, an article in a premier legal journal, and a published report for the Criminological Congress in Rome (1938), it is very likely that his criticisms reached a large audience of criminologically oriented jurists.[67] Whereas Mayer was closely allied with the Nazis, Gruhle's appointment to a chair in psychiatry in 1934 was vetoed by Nazi

63. Stumpfl, "Verbrechen und Vererbung," 21; "Kriminalität und Vererbung," 1271.

64. Johannes Lange, "Bemerkungen zu Stumpfl: *Erbanlage und Verbrechen*. Psychiatrische Bemerkungen," *MKS* 27 (1936): 329–36.

65. Franz Exner, "Bemerkungen zu Stumpfl: *Erbanlage und Verbrechen*. Kriminalistische Bemerkungen," *MKS* 27 (1936): 336–39.

66. Strafrechtliche Arbeitsgemeinschaft der Reichsfachgruppe Hochschullehrer im NS-Rechtswahrerbund.

67. Hellmuth Mayer, *Das Strafrecht des deutschen Volkes* (Stuttgart: Enke, 1936), 37–46, 143–59; "Kriminalpolitik als Geisteswissenschaft," *ZStW* 57 (1937): 1–27; "Gutachten zum Thema: Studium der Persönlichkeit des Verbrechers," in *Römischer Kongreß für Kriminologie* (Berlin: Decker, 1939), 188–92.

political authorities because they considered him politically unreliable. Suddenly unemployed, Gruhle went through difficult times until he was appointed director of the insane asylum Zwiefalten in Württemberg in 1936.[68] Despite this professional setback, Gruhle was regularly asked to write reviews of the criminal-biological literature for several of the most important journals in criminal law and psychiatry.[69] Since Gruhle's political difficulties and critical attitude toward criminal-biological research were well known, the fact that the editors of these journals continued to commission review articles from him suggests that they were sympathetic to his scientific if not his political views. In any event, both Mayer and Gruhle were well positioned to reach a large audience among jurists and psychiatrists interested in criminology.

My discussion of the criticisms of Stumpfl's work will be divided into three parts, respectively addressing the problematic nature of, first, the concept of psychopathy; second, the evidence for the inheritance of psychopathic traits; and third, the connection between psychopathic traits and criminal behavior. These criticisms are worth a closer look because they show that even during the Nazi period, which is usually associated with the crudest forms of biological determinism, prominent and influential members of the criminological community were very articulate in criticizing the weaknesses of biological and genetic explanations of criminal behavior.[70]

Psychopathy: A Problematic Concept

One of the claims that immediately drew critical attention was Stumpfl's assertion that all but two of the almost two hundred recidivists in his sample were psychopaths. When Exner read that Stumpfl had, following Schneider, defined psychopaths as "abnormal personalities who suffer from their abnormality or who disturb society as a result of their abnormality,"[71] he complained that

---

68. Kurt Kolle, "Hans W. Gruhle," in *Große Nervenärzte*, ed. Kolle (Stuttgart: Thieme, 1963), 3:69; Bernard Pauleikhoff, *Das Menschenbild im Wandel der Zeit: Ideengeschichte der Psychiatrie und der klinischen Psychologie*, 4 vols. (Hürtgenwald: Pressler, 1983–87), 4:51.

69. Gruhle, "Literaturbericht: Gerichtliche Psychiatrie und Kriminalpsychologie," *ZStW* 54 (1934): 502–9; "Literaturbericht: Kriminalpsychologie," *ZStW* 55 (1935): 483–94; "Literaturbericht: Kriminalbiologie," *ZStW* 58 (1938): 146–66; "Kriminalitätsgeographie," *MKS* 29 (1938): 277–88; "Antlitz, Gestalt, Haltung, Gebaren des Verbrechers," *MKS* 30 (1939): 215–34; "Sammelreferat über Kriminalitätsgeographie," *MKS* 31 (1940): 265–69; "Literaturbericht: Kriminalbiologie," *ZStW* 61 (1941): 556–69; "Forensische Psychiatrie und Kriminalpsychologie der Jahre 1938 und 1939," *AZP* 119 (1942): 298–336; "Die Erforschung und Behandlung des Verbrechers in den Jahren 1938 bis 1940," *FNPG* 14 (1942): 123–68.

70. Compare Mayer, "Kriminalpolitik," 16.

71. Stumpfl, *Erbanlage und Verbrechen*, 137; Kurt Schneider, *Die psychopathischen Persönlichkeiten*, 2d ed. (Leipzig: Deuticke, 1928), 3.

according to this definition every multiple recidivist was a psychopath.[72] Stumpfl defended himself by stressing that not everyone who disturbed society but only those who displayed "character abnormalities" qualified as psychopathic.[73] But Mayer pointed out that Stumpfl's definitions of character abnormalities were replete with moral criteria. Thus Stumpfl had characterized *gemütlose* psychopaths as lacking "the ability to love, a sense of honor, compassion, shame, faithfulness, conscience."[74] According to this definition, Mayer observed, "every morally reprehensible person [was] by definition a psychopath." Mayer also cited Stumpfl's own assertion that recidivist criminality implied the presence of psychological abnormalities as evidence that Stumpfl was treating recidivism as a symptom of abnormality, so that psychopathy was in fact nothing but a label for "ethically reprehensible" persons. Since most people assumed that "psychopathy" referred to a "particular pathological condition that the physician can recognize through particular scientific characteristics," Mayer concluded, the term was highly misleading and ought to be dropped from any discussion of criminal behavior.[75]

Gruhle, too, was critical of Stumpfl's notion of psychopathy but did not wish to jettison the concept altogether. Instead, he insisted that the term "psychopathy" ought to be "value-free," which meant that psychopathy ought to be defined not by reference to "culturally mediated behaviors," such as criminal behavior, but only by reference to formal or "empty" psychological characteristics. Although most authors claimed to be adhering to a value-free definition of psychopathy, Gruhle charged, they often violated this principle by conflating "moral and psychological considerations" in their diagnoses. According to Gruhle, it was such a conflation that had led Stumpfl to diagnose 99 percent of his recidivists as psychopathic, even though "most habitual criminals act[ed] out of normal motives." But even if a criminal had genuine psychopathic traits, it was wrong to assume that these traits always played a criminogenic role. For in reality, Gruhle argued, a criminal's psychopathic traits were most often unrelated to his criminal behavior, and one should speak of "psychopathic criminals" only if such a connection could be established.[76]

72. Exner, "Bemerkungen zu Stumpfl," 338.

73. Stumpfl, "Erbanlage und Verbrechen: Eine Erwiderung," 96; "Kriminalbiologische Forschung und der Vollzug," 351; "Psychopathenforschung unter dem Gesichtspunkt der Erbbiologie," 414.

74. Stumpfl, *Erbanlage und Verbrechen*, 139, quoted in Mayer, "Kriminalpolitik," 18.

75. Mayer, "Kriminalpolitik," 18–20; Mayer, *Strafrecht des deutschen Volkes*, 45.

76. Gruhle, "Erforschung und Behandlung," 125–26, 133–35.

Gruhle's views received authoritative support from the man who had coined the standard definition of psychopathy, Kurt Schneider, who had succeeded Lange as director of the Clinical Section of the prestigious Deutsche Forschungs-anstalt für Psychiatrie in Munich in 1931. In an important article for the criminological *Monatsschrift*, Schneider expressed concern that his well-known definition of psychopathic personalities as "abnormal personalities who suffer from their abnormality or from whose abnormality society suffers" had given rise to misunderstandings. Acutely aware that "society's suffering" was a value-laden concept, Schneider stressed that this criterion was used only to define a subset of "abnormal personalities" for purely practical purposes since these were the cases likely to come to the psychiatrist's attention. "Abnormal personalities," however, were defined as deviations from a purely statistical norm, and for scientific purposes it was this "value-free" category of "abnormal personalities" that was decisive. If some researchers "simply label[ed] asocials, troublemakers, criminals, everyone from whom society suffers, as psychopaths," Schneider insisted, they were "slipping into a sociological, even political concept of psychopathy that ha[d] nothing to do with" his definition.[77] Gruhle's and Schneider's interventions demonstrate that prominent psychiatrists with criminal-biological interests were remarkably aware of the danger of conflating moral and medical categories and misinterpreting culturally conditioned behaviors as congenital character traits.

Challenging the Evidence for the Inheritance of Criminogenic Traits

The second issue on which the critics focused was Stumpfl's claim that the criminogenic traits involved in recidivist criminality were hereditary. Both Mayer and Gruhle pointed out that the elevated incidence of criminality and psychopathy in the families of recidivists provided no proof of hereditary transmission because both could just as easily be explained as the results of a shared environment. In a trenchant remark, Gruhle charged that Stumpfl's family study had not produced any new evidence but simply reinterpreted a familiar set of facts in a hereditarian way reflecting "the extent to which today's belief in the overwhelming importance of heredity differs from earlier views":

Formerly it was said that it was not surprising if the child of a criminal became a criminal, since it grew up in a milieu which directed the child onto this path of life, just as . . . the environment of a pastor's home led at least one

77. Kurt Schneider, "Über Psychopathen und ihre kriminalbiologische Bedeutung," *MKS* 29 (1938): 355, 356.

of the sons to become a pastor. Today the cause [of this phenomenon] is thought to lie in the genetic substance that father and son share. . . . Thus Stumpfl's studies . . . reflect the same decline of the milieu theory which it has suffered in politics, sociology, everywhere. One should note that it is usually the same facts that are being reported but their interpretation has changed ideologically [weltanschaulich].[78]

Mayer and Gruhle found Stumpfl's twin study no more convincing than his family study. Mayer provided an impressive list of the flaws in Stumpfl's twin study and twin research generally: the number of twins was too small to justify general conclusions; the determination whether twins were monozygotic (identical) was often dubious; the difference in concordance rates between identical and fraternal twins was too small to be significant; and the concordance rates were probably skewed because researchers were more likely to come across concordant pairs, since in those cases both partners had come into contact with the criminal justice system. Finally, the basic premise of twin research, that identical twins shared both heredity and environment, whereas fraternal twins shared the same environment only, was flawed. Fraternal twins did not share the same environment because they were likely to be treated quite differently by their parents, whereas identical twins were treated the same.[79] Gruhle supplemented Mayer's detailed critique with a more fundamental one:

"Heredity and crime" is roughly equivalent to "heredity and handicrafts," "heredity and civil service" because all three behaviors are cultural behaviors. There is no reason to assume that cultural behaviors are heritable. There is reason, even evidence, to assume that vital forms and functions, that is, those connected with the body, are hereditary. This includes psychological forms of behavior, insofar as they are empty, that is, not connected with the cultural realm. Brutality, lack of emotions, . . . lethargy . . . can be inherited. But their heritability does not indicate in which areas of culture those characteristics or tendencies will manifest themselves. . . . A person who has inherited an excessive impulsiveness will more easily come into conflict under today's cultural conditions. A genetically brutal fellow is more likely to fall into crime, especially violent crime. . . . [But these] connections between certain genetic psychological traits and specific cultural behaviors . . . are loose and strongly determined by environment and fate.[80]

78. Gruhle, "Literaturbericht: Kriminalbiologie," ZStW 58 (1938): 148–49.
79. Mayer, "Kriminalpolitik," 24–26.
80. Gruhle, "Erforschung und Behandlung," 127.

The Complex Connection between Character and Criminal Behavior

Finally, Stumpfl's critics suggested that even if one were to accept that virtually all of Stumpfl's recidivists and a considerable proportion of their relatives did indeed display psychopathic character traits and that these psychopathic traits were indeed hereditary, there remained the crucial question of whether these traits were in fact criminogenic, as Stumpfl claimed. Both Gruhle and Mayer argued that they were not. Gruhle insisted that genetic character traits were always of a "formal" or "empty" nature and therefore were never directly connected to specific culturally conditioned behaviors such as crime. Mayer made the same case even more pointedly: "All traits are in themselves good, even the one-sided traits, which are necessary for certain tasks in life. Every trait suffers from the dark side of its advantages. Only certain congenital personalities are protected against the fate of becoming a recidivist criminal: absolutely boring persons who do not amount to much."[81]

Most important, Mayer criticized Stumpfl for assuming that crime reflected abnormal psychological traits instead of considering that it might be a "normal psychological reaction, a normal product of social activity." In Mayer's view, the criminogenic effect of psychopathic traits could be determined only after one addressed the question of "whether there [were] social conditions . . . under which recidivist crime [was] . . . a normal psychological reaction."[82] And such conditions, Mayer maintained, did indeed exist in what Mayer called the stratum of "pariahs":

> This term is meant to convey that this is a stratum of the population that stands outside the dominant social value system. . . . We are therefore not dealing with . . . [the argument] that an individual is culturally unfit either as a result of biological defects or a bad upbringing. Such an approach views social deviance too much as an individual fate or even an individual failure. Instead, it must be recognized that the empirical validity of the social value system does not reach all groups of the population equally.[83]

For anyone growing up in this stratum of the population—including beggars, vagrants, habitual thieves, con men, fences, prostitutes, and pimps—whom Mayer distinguished sharply from members of the working class,[84] certain forms of crime (mainly property crime) were perfectly normal forms of behavior and therefore required no "psychopathic" explanation.

81. Mayer, "Kriminalpolitik," 21.
82. Ibid., 16, 21.
83. Mayer, *Strafrecht des deutschen Volkes*, 146–47; see also his "Kriminalpolitik," 15, 22.
84. Mayer, *Strafrecht des deutschen Volkes*, 147, 152–53.

In addition, Mayer offered one other "normal-psychological" explanation for "falling into a career of chronic crime." If someone's personality was not suitable for the "social tasks" posed by his or her particular environment, this person was more likely to become criminal. "If one studies the courses of criminals' lives, one often gets the impression that above all, it is strong-willed and imaginative, *above-average* persons facing only the option of the unskilled laborer, who are especially at risk." By contrast, "those who [were] obedient and demand[ed] nothing from life, pedants and absolute bores, [were] in relatively little danger" of becoming criminal.[85] In short, Mayer rejected Stumpfl's biological explanation of recidivist crime in favor of an environmental one. But instead of focusing on economic factors, Mayer's environmental explanation stressed the existence of alternative value systems in certain parts of the population.

Mayer also provided a fundamental critique of criminal biology and of criminology in general. According to Mayer, criminology "lacked a coherent scientific subject" because crime was a purely legal concept. "If one removes the juridical label, there remain only a number of extremely diverse actions that have no biological, psychological or sociological unity." But if crime was a strictly legal category, then the only proper way to study the subject was from the point of view of penal policy (*Kriminalpolitik*), which was a branch of the humanities, rather than criminology, which conceived of itself as a science. Penal policy, Mayer argued, was mainly a matter of "social psychology," that is, of understanding the "normal psychological patterns of social life." Only once these normal psychological patterns were known did it make sense to interpret criminal behavior "biologically or psychiatrically." The medical sciences could at best play a subordinate role. If certain "psychological phenomena" were associated with certain "biological conditions," this information could prove useful for penal policy because it offered the possibility of prognoses of future behavior. This was indeed the case for full-fledged mental illnesses but not for the mass of "healthy or even psychopathic" persons. "How little scientific findings [did] to promote the understanding of criminal behavior [was] demonstrated by the average criminal-biological report," which, according to Mayer, provided nothing beyond "sociological and general psychological statements."[86] As an active member of the Nazi lawyers' organization and a member of the official commission on revising the penal code, Mayer certainly viewed himself, and was perceived by others, as a Nazi jurist. His views, which were as critical of criminal biology as anything written during the Weimar years, demonstrate

---

85. Emphasis added. Mayer, "Kriminalpolitik," 22–23; *Strafrecht des deutschen Volkes,* 46.
86. Mayer, "Kriminalpolitik," 1–6.

that it would be a mistake to assume a natural affinity between Nazi jurists and criminal biology.

Combining Criminal Biology and Sociology: Two Syntheses

Edmund Mezger's Survey

Not all jurists were as skeptical of the notion of a "scientific criminology" as Mayer. In fact, the two major surveys of criminology produced during the Nazi period were written by jurists. The first was Edmund Mezger's survey of 1934. Mezger started out as an associate professor in Tübingen in 1921 and held chairs in criminal law first in Marburg (1925–32) and then in Munich (1932–51). Widely published, Mezger was one of Germany's most prominent professors of criminal law. Held in high regard by the Ministry of Justice, he served on the official penal reform commission (1934–36), was consulted by the ministry on several occasions, and was asked to preside over one of the sections of the International Criminological Congress in Rome in 1938. He became a member of the Nazi Party in 1937.[87]

Mezger's 1934 survey *Kriminalpolitik auf kriminologischer Grundlage* (Penal policy on a criminological basis) was disappointing in its substance.[88] Despite its title, the book did not develop a comprehensive penal policy based on criminological research. Nor was it a useful textbook of criminology. For unlike Aschaffenburg's classic work of 1903 or Exner's later volume of 1939, Mezger's book did not pull together existing research to provide a systematic account of the causes of crime but provided only a relatively superficial review of the literature. In the absence of a synthesis or original criticism, the book's interest lies in Mezger's attitude toward the different approaches, his remarks on penal policy, and the section on his own "dynamic conception of crime." Mezger's criminological views are of particular interest because, as a jurist with strong sympathies for the Nazi regime and an interest in criminology, the author was pulled in three different directions: as a criminologist, he believed that criminology provided important insights into the causes of crime and sought to apply its findings to penal policy; as a jurist who took a moderate position in the debate between reformers and retributivists, he agreed with the reformist demand for individualized punishments but sought to safeguard the notion of individual legal responsibility; finally, as a strong supporter of the Nazi regime,

---

87. Entry on Mezger in *Neue Deutsche Biographie*. The information on NSDAP membership is from BDC, NSDAP-Ortskartei, A-3340-MFOK-O-0072.

88. Mezger, *Kriminalpolitik auf kriminologischer Grundlage* (Stuttgart: Enke, 1934).

he sought to bring his penal policy recommendations into line with Nazi ideology, especially its racial aspect. These three goals were often at cross-purposes.

Mezger regarded social explanations of crime as a serious threat to the principle of individual responsibility. "In its final consequences," he wrote, "the sociological conception of crime [spells] the end of individual responsibility . . . and thus the end of all culture" and was therefore unacceptable to the "total state," Mezger's term for the Nazi state. The "biological conception of crime," by contrast, was of great importance for the penal policy of the total state because it provided "an indispensable basis for recognizing the racial [*rasse- und blutmässigen*] characteristics of the individual criminal and for treating the individual accordingly."[89]

Despite this general bias in favor of criminal biology and against criminal sociology, Mezger's review of the different approaches and his own "dynamic" conception of crime painted a more complex and balanced picture. In the section on sociological approaches, Mezger acknowledged that crime could not be adequately understood "without the most thorough investigation of the social factors of crime" and that a "good social policy [was] often the best penal policy." In his discussion of criminal-biological research, he pointed out that the principles of psychiatric-genetic research on mental illnesses could not simply be applied to criminality because crime was a complex product of endogenous and exogenous factors.[90] In the section on his own dynamic conception of crime, finally, he explained that both personality and environment were "dynamic" factors that were constantly developing and changing in interaction with each other. A "latent criminality," he insisted, was present in all humans. Whether it became manifest depended on the interaction of personality and environment. Therefore, one-sided biological or environmental theories of crime had to be rejected, and the criminologist had to pay equal attention to the criminal's personality and environment.[91] In sum, careful study of the criminological literature had led even a jurist with a strong bias against sociological and in favor of biological theories of crime to arrive at a relatively balanced view of the influence of biological and environmental factors on crime.

89. Ibid., 172–73, 138.

90. Ibid., 172–73, 109–10.

91. Ibid., 177, 179, 189–90. For Mezger's first presentation of his "dynamic conception of crime" in 1927–28, see his *Moderne Strafrechtsprobleme* (Marburg: Elwert, 1927), 26–31, and his "Konstitutionelle und dynamische Verbrechensauffassung," *MKS* 19 (1928): 385–400. In both pieces, but especially in *Moderne Strafrechtsprobleme*, Mezger explicitly mentioned the psychoanalytic origins of his "dynamic" approach. Under the changed political circumstances of 1933–34, Mezger's *Kriminalpolitik* made no more mention of this.

Although Mezger's book was written with the clear intention of making criminological research useful to the Nazi state, its 1934 publication date meant that it reflected Mezger's evaluation of the criminological research of the Weimar era. To evaluate his reception of criminological research during the Nazi regime, we must turn to the survey's second edition of 1942 and a 1938 paper for the Criminological Congress in Rome, both of which showed an increased sophistication in the analysis of biological factors and greater insistence on the role of environmental ones. Thus in the 1942 edition, Mezger explicitly rejected any notion of "criminal genetic traits" (*kriminelle Anlage*). The only claim that could be made, he insisted, was that there were "hereditary traits whose bearers become criminal with an increased probability," but whether such a person would actually commit a crime depended on external circumstances.[92] The 1942 edition also reported that the "intensified genetic research" of recent years had "thrown into sharp relief" the importance of social factors by demonstrating that "criminality is not at all solely determined by genetic factors, and can therefore be positively affected through environmental influences, even in some cases where certain genetic defects [were] present."[93] Remarkably, then, Mezger's comments at the Rome conference and the survey's 1942 edition show that between 1934 and 1942 Mezger arrived at an even greater appreciation of the role of environmental factors and the limits of biological factors in crime.

For the same reason, Mezger's comments on the role of "race" in crime were relatively moderate. In the first edition (1934), Mezger stressed the crucial importance of race in principle but cautioned that the extent to which the criminal behavior of the Jewish population was due to racial rather than social factors remained an open question.[94] In the 1942 edition, this position remained unchanged. For after asserting that race "exerts an influence on criminal behavior," Mezger added that "in reality" the racial factor was "interwoven with social factors in an inextricable fashion" because "race does not just determine [a person's] criminal activity, but his whole social position within the community, which in turn has criminological effects of its own." In this context, Mezger explicitly criticized past studies of Jewish criminality for confusing race and religion and therefore missing the fact that religion often affected people's

92. Mezger, *Kriminalpolitik auf kriminologischer Grundlage*, 2d ed. (Stuttgart: Enke, 1942), 118–19.

93. Ibid., 166, 241. For similar comments, see Mezger, "Gutachten zum Thema: Studium der Persönlichkeit des Verbrechers," in *Römischer Kongreß für Kriminologie*, 197. See also Mezger, "Die künftigen Aufgaben kriminologischer Arbeit," ibid., 83–91.

94. Mezger, *Kriminalpolitik*, 1st ed., 144.

social position more than race. The only mention of Gypsies was a reference to an older literature on the criminality of Gypsies (referring to a work of 1922).[95] Thus, although Mezger supported the general assertion that race affected criminality, he also stressed that it was virtually impossible to disentangle racial and social factors in practice. Given the contemporary context of Nazi racist attitudes toward Jews and Gypsies, Mezger's position on the role of race in crime therefore appears comparatively moderate. This assessment is confirmed by the fact that a contemporary reviewer severely criticized Mezger's book for its neglect of the role of race and especially the "Jewish and gypsy question."[96]

Mezger's penal policy recommendations for the new Nazi state consisted of two guiding principles: "restoring the responsibility of the individual vis-à-vis the national community" and "excluding elements that are harmful to nation or race" from the national community.[97] What interests us here is Mezger's claim that these penal policy recommendations were based on the results of criminological research. As far as "restoring the responsibility of the individual" was concerned, it was hard to see how criminological research could possibly strengthen it. Although Mezger was worried about the exculpatory implications of environmental explanations of crime, he himself argued that cases where "an individual offended under the influence and pressure of extraordinary environmental circumstances" should be treated with "far-reaching lenience."[98] Since sociological and biological research was clearly eroding legal responsibility, Mezger's reassertion of the principle of individual responsibility was not an attempt to implement but to limit the impact of criminological research.[99]

In analyzing Mezger's second maxim of "excluding elements harmful to nation or race" from the "national community," one should distinguish between those considered "racially harmful" (*rasseschädlich*) and those considered "harmful to the nation" (*volksschädlich*).[100] As far as the latter category was

95. Mezger, *Kriminalpolitik*, 2d ed., 146–47.

96. A. Harasser, review of *Kriminalpolitik auf kriminologischer Grundlage*, 2d ed. (1942), by Edmund Mezger, *ARGB* 36 (1942): 240–42.

97. Mezger, *Kriminalpolitik*, 1st ed., 203.

98. Ibid., 173.

99. In the first edition Mezger seemed to oppose the introduction of "diminished responsibility," but after the 1933 Law on Habitual Criminals introduced diminished responsibility, Mezger took the view that psychopaths were eligible for it. See Mezger, *Kriminalpolitik*, 1st ed., 65–66; *Kriminalpolitik*, 2d ed., 65; "Zum Begriff des Psychopathen," *MKS* 30 (1939): 190–92.

100. Mezger, *Kriminalpolitik*, 1st ed., 203. Compare similar passage in *Kriminalpolitik*, 2d ed., 238. Reference to "rasseschädliche Elemente" was dropped in the second edition.

concerned, Mezger's maxim merely stated the obvious, since virtually any penal policy seeks to remove from society those who harm it. As far as "racially harmful elements" were concerned, the context indicated that this was a reference to sterilization. But since, in Mezger's own estimation, genetic factors were never the sole determinant of criminal behavior, any plan to sterilize criminals seemed to lack justification. And indeed, even in the second edition of 1942, Mezger did not call for the sterilization of any category of criminals but only noted that the eugenic sterilizations of feebleminded persons included some criminals.[101]

Finally, Mezger tried to link penal policy to criminology by arguing that criminal-biological research provided the criminal justice system with the ability to recognize an offender's biological characteristics ("personality type") and to treat the individual criminal accordingly, both in sentencing and in the administration of punishment.[102] But even in the 1942 edition, Mezger admitted that the goal of establishing a typology of "personality types" among criminals remained unattained; in fact, he thought that even the distinction between normal and psychopathic criminals was often dubious.[103]

Summarizing the relationship of Mezger's penal policy to criminology, then, we find that Mezger's principle of individual responsibility was actually being eroded by criminological research. His call for eugenic measures was undermined by his own recognition that no one's criminality was determined by genetic factors alone. And the recommendation that penal treatment be based on criminals' biological characteristics remained an abstract demand because current research did not yet allow for the diagnosis of biological types.

Franz Exner's Synthesis

If Mezger's book was little more than a survey of the existing criminological literature, Franz Exner's *Kriminalbiologie*, published in 1939, sought to provide a systematic account of the causes of crime on the basis of existing research.[104] As the first synthesis of criminology since Aschaffenburg's classic work of

101. Mezger, *Kriminalpolitik*, 2d ed., 269–73. See the discussion of sterilization in Chapter 7.

102. Mezger, *Kriminalpolitik*, 1st ed., 138; *Kriminalpolitik*, 2d ed., 240. It is characteristic and significant that Mezger moderated his language from the first edition ("rassen- und blutmässigen Bedingtheiten des einzelnen Kriminellen") to the second one ("Persönlichkeitstypen zu finden, denen bestimmte Behandlungstypen zugeordnet werden können").

103. Mezger, *Kriminalpolitik*, 2d ed., 67, 240.

104. Franz Exner, *Kriminalbiologie in ihren Grundzügen* (Hamburg: Hanseatische Verlagsanstalt, 1939); 2d ed. (Hamburg: Hanseatische Verlagsanstalt, 1944); 3d ed. under the title *Kriminologie* (Berlin: Springer, 1949); Spanish translation: *Biologia Criminal* (Barcelona: Bosch, 1946); Italian translation: *Criminologia* (Milan, 1953).

1903, Exner's book was the most important criminological work published in Germany in the interwar period. Exner was a professor of criminal law who had turned to criminal-sociological research in the mid-1920s. As a professor in Leipzig and since 1933 in Munich, he assigned many of his law students dissertations on criminological topics, which he used for his own criminological synthesis. Many of these legal dissertations were published in the Kriminalistische Abhandlungen (47 volumes, 1926–41), edited by Exner, Germany's only publication series dedicated exclusively to criminological topics. In 1934 he traveled to America to familiarize himself with American criminology and criminal justice. When Aschaffenburg was forced to give up his editorship of the *Monatsschrift für Kriminalpsychologie* in 1936, Exner became one of its coeditors. His publications and activities made Exner the most important figure in German criminology in the 1930s. Unlike his Munich colleague Edmund Mezger, who unequivocally aligned himself with the Nazi regime, Exner avoided explicit political comments in his writings and appears not to have joined the Nazi Party.[105]

Exner's book was entitled *Kriminalbiologie,* but he used the term to refer to the entire field of criminology, which he defined as "the study of crime as a phenomenon in the life of the nation and in the life of the individual."[106] The book began with a general section on heredity and environment, in which Exner emphasized the interaction of both according to two basic principles. Since genetic factors were only potentials, "what becomes of [a person's] heredity [*Anlage*], depends, within a certain range determined by it, on the environment." Likewise, "what kind of environment and how an environment affects a person depends, within a range determined by the environment, on [the person's] heredity." The criminologist always had to take both factors into account. Exner also cautioned that general statements about the relative importance of heredity and environment in criminal behavior could not be made because "the investigation of individual criminals and different criminal types is bound to arrive at totally different results in this regard."[107]

In accordance with Exner's definition of criminology as the study of crime as both a collective and an individual phenomenon, the book was divided into a first part on "crime in the life of the national community" and a second part on "the offender." Furthermore, to consider both biological and environmental

105. Entry on Exner in *Neue Deutsche Biographie.* The NSDAP *Ortskartei* in the BDC records does not show an entry for a Franz Exner with his birthdate.

106. Exner, *Kriminalbiologie,* 1st ed., 11, 20.

107. Ibid., 27–44, esp. 39, 44. This section was based on Johannes Lange and Franz Exner, "Die beiden Grundbegriffe der Kriminologie: Anlage und Umwelt," *MKS* 27 (1936): 353–74.

factors, the first part was divided into separate sections on "ethnic character" (*Volkscharakter*) and the "environment of the nation," while the second part was split into sections on the "person of the offender" and the "offender's environment."

In his chapter on "ethnic character and crime," Exner addressed the question of how the characteristics of a particular race or ethnic group affected criminal behavior by analyzing crime rates among African Americans, Germany's Polish minority up to 1918, and German Jews. Convinced that "the Germans [were] not a racially homogeneous nation" and that German regional populations differed in their racial character, Exner also compared the crime rates of different German regions. He did not study Gypsies. With characteristic methodological sophistication, Exner began by considering possible environmental explanations for elevated crime rates among certain groups, such as discriminatory treatment of African Americans by law enforcement and higher rates of alcohol consumption in the wine-producing Palatinate. Nevertheless, in every case Exner concluded that the differences in crime rates between particular groups or regions were not adequately explained by environmental factors alone and must therefore be attributable at least partly to racial or ethnic differences. This did not mean that the "racial characteristics" that contributed to elevated crime rates consisted of a "predisposition to criminal behavior." Thus Exner partially attributed the elevated crime rate of African Americans to a "genetic inability to adapt to the changed living conditions in the United States" and the higher rates of violent crime in Bavaria to a more impulsive Bavarian temperament. Since crime rates were lowest in the northwest of Germany, where the "Nordic race" was supposedly purest, Exner did raise the possibility of a "connection between Nordic race and a lower crime rate" but stressed that this remained an uncorroborated hypothesis.[108]

In the section on German Jews, Exner reported that Jews had a lower crime rate than Christians for certain offenses, such as violent crimes and theft, and a higher one for others, such as fraud and embezzlement. Rejecting sociological explanations as insufficient, Exner then offered a racial explanation of the differences. "The picture of Jewish criminality," he wrote, "coincides with the basic features of Jewish nature. Just as Jews are in their social behavior more active with their heads rather than their hands, so it is in their antisocial behavior. . . . In social as in antisocial matters, he [the Jew] is dominated by the strongest acquisitive drive and ruthlessly pursues his material interests." After having

---

108. Exner, *Kriminalbiologie*, 47–71. This chapter was based on Exner, "Volkscharakter und Verbrechen," *MKS* 29 (1938): 404–21.

provided racial explanations for the difference in crime rates between different German regions, Exner was arguing that Jewish criminality was different from that of Christians—not that Jews were more criminal or that all Jews were biologically predisposed to commit crimes. Nevertheless, his analysis of Jewish crime rates was clearly anti-Semitic.[109]

In line with Exner's personal expertise in criminal sociology, the section on "the nation's environment" was far more extensive than the brief chapter on the role of "ethnic character" and consisted of separate chapters on the role of the natural, economic, cultural, and political environments. In this section Exner explicitly addressed the opinion, "heard repeatedly," that the passage of racial and eugenic laws and the Law on Habitual Criminals showed that "the new German state" focused on the role of heredity and that criminological research on environmental factors was therefore unlikely to have any impact on public policy. Clearly concerned about such views, Exner attacked them as wrongheaded because the Nazi state also emphasized education. "Never has there been as much discussion of education as in the last few years." Since education meant guidance through environmental influence, he argued, criminal-sociological research was more important than ever before. Nevertheless, he acknowledged that the impact of economic conditions on crime was seriously underestimated in Nazi Germany.[110] This suggests that Exner did perceive a certain neglect of environmental factors and saw his detailed exposition of environmental causes as a means of correcting this imbalance.

Exner began by pointing out that since the population's genetic makeup was relatively constant, any significant change in national crime rates was of necessity attributable to environmental factors. In his chapter on the economic environment, Exner reaffirmed the crucial role of economic conditions and gave a detailed statistical account of the influence of fluctuations in prices, income, unemployment, and monetary value (inflation) on German crime rates that reflected the sophistication of his study of Austrian crime during the First World War. Most interesting among the environmental chapters were Exner's comments on the impact of penal policy. Drawing on his earlier study of sentencing practices, he demonstrated that the common assumption that harsher punishments were a more effective deterrent to crime was mistaken. Between 1880 and 1933 the sentencing practices of German courts had become more lenient, yet the crime rate had generally declined, suggesting that sentencing practices had no effect on crime. Indeed, experience had shown that the severity

---

109. Exner, *Kriminalbiologie*, 67–71, 35–44, 149–269.
110. Ibid., 72, 87.

of punishment played only a minor role in a criminal's considerations before committing a crime; far more important was the likelihood of his apprehension and conviction. While some attributed the further decline in crime since 1933 to an increased toughness in sentencing, Exner very much doubted this. By contrast, he stressed that positive social policy measures always had a strong effect on crime by reducing the rate of theft.[111]

The book's second half was devoted to "crime as a phenomenon in the life of the individual," that is, the "offender" (*Täter*). In an opening chapter on the role of heredity, Exner stressed that an offender's "personality" was by no means synonymous with his or her "heredity" (*Anlage* or *Erbgut*). To be sure, a person's personality was strongly influenced by his or her "heredity"; but the "development of the personality [was] also determined by the environment." In addition, the criminal act itself was "always a reaction to environmental impressions." "This creates a knot of hereditary and environmental influences that can never be disentangled, neither in general, nor in any particular case." Therefore, Exner warned, the commonly used term "genetic criminal disposition" (*verbrecherische Anlage*) was extremely problematic and could be used only in a very restricted meaning, namely, to signify that "based on his heredity, a person has from the outset developed in a certain direction that allows character traits to develop that, according to general experience, are likely to lead their bearer onto the path of crime."[112]

Even if one used the term in this restricted sense, Exner stressed that several caveats should be borne in mind. First, since the concept of crime was legally defined and therefore "depend[ed] on time and place," a person who had a "criminogenic disposition" in present-day Germany might not possess it under another legal system. Someone who was "genetically homosexual," for instance, might be said to possess a "criminogenic disposition" in Germany but not in Italy. Second, a criminogenic disposition must not be thought of "as a biological entity comparable to a genetic predisposition for a certain disease" because a criminogenic disposition resulted from a combination of many genetic factors (potentials), none of which were criminogenic in themselves; furthermore, the nature of the criminogenic combination differed from individual to individual. Third, because any criminogenic disposition arose from a multitude of genetic factors that were inherited separately, it was not genetically transmitted as a whole. Hence parents might possess such a disposition, whereas their offspring did not and vice versa. Finally, the concept of a criminogenic genetic disposition

111. Ibid., 72, 86–112, 138–39.
112. Ibid., 149–51.

was always based on the assumption of "typical" or average external conditions. Because of the role of external conditions, one might distinguish different degrees of "criminogenic disposition": if someone became criminal despite favorable external conditions, one could assume a high degree of criminogenic disposition; if external conditions were normal, a lower degree of criminogenic disposition; if external conditions were bad, a still lower degree, to the point that one could not speak of criminogenic disposition at all. In sum, Exner defined the term "criminogenic disposition" with an unprecedented sophistication that took into account the interaction of environment and heredity.[113]

Having established the complexity of the role of genetic factors in crime, Exner went on to provide a critical review of the three major research methods used to study this problem. The first method, studies of individual "crime families" like the Jukes and the Kallikaks, were quickly dismissed, both because the recurrence of crime from generation to generation might well be the result of environmental influences and because these families were extreme cases whose uniqueness ruled out general conclusions. Second, Exner reviewed "statistical family studies" (by Stumpfl and others) that investigated the incidence of mental illness, criminality, alcoholism, and psychopathy among the parents and families of criminals. Here Exner endorsed Stumpfl's finding that the families of criminals showed no unusual incidence of mental illness (psychoses). But he dismissed reports of elevated rates of criminality among criminals' parents as inconclusive because "the children of criminals usually grew up in a very bad environment," so that "it remain[ed] unclear to what extent their own criminal career [was] due to this environment or their heredity." The same objection, he argued, applied to the role of alcoholism in a criminal's family. Only in the case of psychopathy was Exner convinced that statistical family studies had indeed provided evidence for the role of genetic factors in criminal behavior. Although he noted the lack of reliable figures on the incidence of psychopathy in the general population, he concluded that the abnormally high proportion of psychopaths among the parents of recidivists reported by Stumpfl and others had indeed demonstrated a "genetic connection between psychopathy and [recidivist] criminality."[114]

Finally, Exner offered a careful assessment of the twin research conducted over the past decade. Lange's initial twin study had reported such high concordance rates for identical twins and such low ones for fraternal twins that some people "had drawn the premature conclusion that genetic factors were abso-

113. Ibid., 150–53.
114. Ibid., 153–64.

lutely decisive" in criminal behavior.[115] This conclusion, however, he noted, conflicted not only with Lange's own, much more cautious interpretation but with the results of subsequent research, which found a much narrower gap in concordance rates. To present these results, Exner compiled the findings of the twin studies by Lange, Stumpfl, Heinrich Kranz, and the Dutchman A. M. Legras, and calculated the cumulative concordance rates for the combined samples, which yielded a 71 percent concordance rate for identical twins as opposed to 38 percent for fraternal twins. While this difference in concordance rates showed that genetic factors played an important role in criminal behavior, the fact that nearly a third of identical twins were discordant demonstrated that environmental factors also mattered. Although Exner was aware of the criticisms leveled against twin research, he did not think that these completely invalidated such research. Most important, Exner argued, the results of the twin studies did not really solve any problem but posed one: "How are we to understand why identical twins . . . behave in part concordantly and in part discordantly with regard to crime?"[116]

Statistical family studies and twin studies, Exner concluded, had demonstrated that genetic factors played a "prominent role among the causes of crime." Therefore purely environmental explanations, whether of a materialist or psychoanalytic variety, were clearly refuted. At the same time, however, purely genetic explanations were refuted as well because the existence of discordant identical twins (amounting to about a third of all cases) clearly demonstrated that genetic factors did not always play a decisive role. The importance of genetic factors, Exner suggested, was most likely different for different groups of criminals. Although past studies showed that genetic factors played a more frequent role among recidivists than among occasional offenders, recidivist criminality was not always attributable to criminogenic genetic factors. Hence the problem of "identifying those groups of criminals in which genetic factors play a practically decisive role" remained an "unresolved task" for future research.[117]

Research on "Asocials"

Not all criminological research conducted in the Third Reich was as sophisticated as that of Stumpfl and his critics or of Exner and Mezger. The most important instance of a crudely deterministic, hereditarian, and racist approach to the crime problem was the research on "asocials" conducted by Robert Ritter.

115. Ibid., 167.
116. Ibid., 164–74.
117. Ibid., 174–77.

Born in 1901 as the son of a naval officer, Ritter served in one of the right-wing free corps after the revolution of 1918–19, then studied medicine and received his M.D. in 1930. After working for two years in French and Swiss hospitals, he accepted a position as a psychiatrist in the youth ward of the psychiatric clinic of the University of Tübingen in 1932. There he began research on the "asocial" inhabitants of a poor neighborhood on the outskirts of Tübingen, which resulted in a book that he submitted for his *Habilitation*[118] in 1936 and published under the title *Ein Menschenschlag* the following year.[119] Shortly after his *Habilitation*, in late 1936, Ritter was appointed director of the newly created Research Institute for Eugenics and Population Biology (Rassenhygienische und Bevölkerungsbiologische Forschungsstelle) of the Reich Health Office (Reichsgesundheitsamt) in Berlin, where he worked on establishing a comprehensive database that would register Sinti and Roma ("Gypsies") and other "vagrants" in Germany.[120] When the Reich Health Office set up a Criminal-Biological Research Institute (Kriminalbiologische Forschungsstelle) in 1937 to collect the reports on the criminal-biological examinations that had just been expanded to the national level, this institute was initially separate from Ritter's institute and headed by Ferdinand Neureiter.[121] But when Neureiter accepted a professorship in Strassburg in 1940, Ritter took over the Criminal-Biological Institute as well and the two institutes were merged. Finally, in late 1941, Ritter's connections with the German police led to his appointment as director of the newly established Criminal-Biological Institute of the Security Police (Kriminalbiologisches Institut der Sicherheitspolizei),[122] which conducted criminal-biological screenings of juvenile delinquents interned in several re-

118. In Germany the *Habilitation* is a postdoctoral academic qualification requiring a second scholarly monograph to be eligible for a professorship.

119. Robert Ritter, *Ein Menschenschlag: Erbärztliche und erbgeschichtliche Untersuchungen über die—durch 10 Geschlechterfolgen erforschten—Nachkommen von "Vagabunden, Jaunern, und Räubern"* (Leipzig: Thieme, 1937).

120. On the Forschungsstelle and Ritter's activities there, see Ute Brucker-Boroujerdi and Wolfgang Wippermann, "Die 'Rassenhygienische und Erbbiologische Forschungsstelle' im Reichsgesundheitsamt," *Bundesgesundheitsblatt* 32 (1989), Sonderheft (March 1989): 13–19; Herbert Heuß, "Wissenschaft und Völkermord: Zur Arbeit der 'Rassenhygienischen Forschungsstelle' beim Reichsgesundheitsamt," ibid., 20–24; Michael Zimmermann, *Rassenutopie und Genozid: Die nationalsozialistische "Lösung der Zigeunerfrage"* (Hamburg: Christians, 1996), 139–46; Zimmermann, *Verfolgt, vertrieben, vernichtet: Die nationalsozialistische Vernichtungspolitik gegen Sinti und Roma* (Essen: Klartext, 1989), 33–39.

121. On the Kriminalbiologische Forschungsstelle, see Neureiter, "Die Organisation des kriminalbiologischen Dienstes in Deutschland"; Neureiter, *Kriminalbiologie*, 7–20.

122. See Robert Ritter, "Das kriminalbiologische Institut der Sicherheitspolizei," *Kriminalistik* 16 (1942): 117–19.

education camps (*Jugendschutzlager*) and also worked on establishing a database of "asocial and criminal families."[123]

Most of Ritter's research activities between 1937 and 1945 focused on Gypsies, and his registration of Gypsies played a crucial part in their persecution, internment, and eventual murder in the camps of the Third Reich. The historical literature has discussed Ritter primarily in this context.[124] Nevertheless, Ritter's role as head of two criminal-biological institutes and the fact that he wrote about asocials and criminals who were not Gypsies warrants an examination of his views on crime and asocial behavior.

Ritter's views on asocial and criminal behavior can be traced back to his research on the population of a poor quarter near Tübingen. The famous studies of "crime families" such as the Kallikaks and the Jukes had traced the descendants of one criminal couple through several generations. Since this method had the disadvantage of neglecting the cumulative effects of intermarriage in every generation, Ritter approached his study from the opposite direction. In *Ein Menschenschlag* (1937) he examined the inhabitants of a poor neighborhood whom he labeled as "asocial" because they depended on welfare or lacked steady work and traced their ancestry through ten generations back to 1650. Unlike Stumpfl, Ritter did not conduct any personal medical examinations but based his study of the living population solely on their criminal records and welfare files; for information on their ancestors he relied on genealogical and other surviving records. Based on these sources, Ritter reported that the present population he was investigating was descended from "vagabonds, *Gauner* [habitual criminals], and robbers," who had formed a "Gaunergesellschaft" (society of criminals) in the seventeenth and eighteenth centuries. This *Gaunergesellschaft* was "not just a sociological phenomenon but the expression of a genetic fact, the existence of a *Vagabunden- und Gaunerschlag*," that is, a "genetic population" of

---

123. On Ritter's career, see Joachim Hohmann, *Robert Ritter und die Erben der Kriminalbiologie: "Zigeunerforschung" im Nationalsozialismus und in Westdeutschland im Zeichen des Rassismus* (Frankfurt: Peter Lang, 1991), 29–32, 133–37; Patrick Wagner, *Volksgemeinschaft ohne Verbrecher: Konzeptionen und Praxis der Kriminalpolizei in der Zeit der Weimarer Republik und des Nationalsozialismus* (Hamburg: Christians, 1996), 274–79, 378–84; Zimmermann, *Verfolgt, vertrieben, vernichtet*, 25–39; Zimmermann, *Rassenutopie und Genozid*, 125–55; Friedlander, *Origins of Nazi Genocide*, 249–50.

124. On the Nazi persecution of the Roma and Sinti ("Gypsies") and Ritter's role in it, see Zimmermann, *Rassenutopie und Genozid*; Friedlander, *Origins of Nazi Genocide*, 246–62; Sybil Milton, "The Holocaust: The Gypsies," in *Genocide in the Twentieth Century: An Anthology of Critical Essays and Oral History*, ed. William Parsons, Israel Charny, and Samuel Totten (New York, 1995), 209–64; Burleigh and Wippermann, *Racial State*, 113–30; Benno Müller-Hill, *Murderous Science: Elimination by Scientific Selection of Jews, Gypsies, and Others, Germany, 1933–1945* (Oxford: Oxford University Press, 1988), 57–62.

vagabonds and criminals. Over time, Ritter argued, the sociological structure of the *Gaunergesellschaft* had disappeared, but the biological *Menschenschlag* (genetic population), which he called "Jenischer Menschenschlag," remained. Observing that "neither wheel nor gallows . . . neither prisons nor workhouses . . . neither church nor school have been able to change this *Menschenschlag,*" Ritter concluded that its members were genetically destined for an asocial and criminal life and utterly incorrigible, and he frequently referred to them as "born criminals" and "born vagabonds."[125]

This last proposition was typical of Ritter's faulty reasoning. Since various punitive and educative measures had not curbed criminal and asocial behavior among this population, Ritter concluded that this behavior must be genetically determined. It does not seem to have occurred to him that the state's punitive and educative measures could have been outweighed by negative environmental influences reproduced from generation to generation. Although Ritter's study went beyond examining the descendants of a single criminal couple, it suffered from the same methodological flaws as the earlier studies of crime families. For Ritter's study, too, failed to address the objection that criminal behavior over several generations could be the result of environmental factors continuing or being reproduced from generation to generation rather than genetic factors. Since criminologists such as Aschaffenburg and Lange had long discredited studies of criminal families with exactly this argument, Ritter's study betrayed complete ignorance of the methodological progress made by mainstream criminological research. It is easy to see, however, that his crude biological determinism made Ritter the perfect candidate for the positions he was offered by the Reich Health Office and the police. For just as the eugenic hard-liners in the Reich Health Office were eager for a researcher who would lend scientific legitimation to racist stereotypes of Gypsies as genetically asocial and criminal, the leadership of the police welcomed an expert who argued that a significant portion of crime could be traced to specific population groups.

In 1940–42 Ritter published several short, programmatic articles, in which he generalized and further developed some of the findings of his case study of the "Jenischer Menschenschlag." In an article titled "Primitivity and Criminality" he argued that "in the midst of our society lives a large population group whose members have lived as vagabonds, thieves, cheats, and robbers for centuries." Studies of such "vagrant population groups" had "shown that there are psychological, characterological, [and] constitutional characteristics that are

125. Ritter, *Ein Menschenschlag,* esp. 51, 59, 60–61, 80, 86, 110, 111.

common to a large part of all criminal asocials," above all "primitivity and unsteadiness [*Unstetigkeit*]." Gypsies, Ritter contended, represented the purest type of the "primitive" because they were concerned only with satisfying present desires, had no desire to work, and had no sense for order and hygiene. Petty crime, such as begging, vagrancy, small thefts, and minor fraud, was an inextricable part of the Gypsies' way of life. Since neither punishment, education, welfare, nor settlement had been able to change their character, Gypsies and members of *Gaunerschläge* such as the Jenische had to be regarded as incorrigible. Having ruled out standard penal sanctions as ineffective, Ritter recommended that Gypsies, "asocial primitives," and "hereditary criminals" (*Verbrecher aus Erbanlage*) be subject to indefinite "preventive detention in workcamps or guarded closed settlements," which clearly legitimated the internment of Gypsies and other supposed "asocials" in concentration camps. Finally, to prevent their future propagation, he recommended that Gypsies, members of "asocial" families and "hereditary criminals" be sterilized, an injunction he repeated in a 1942 article with the telling title "genetic crime prevention" (*erbärztliche Verbrechensverhütung*).[126]

In an article on the "tasks of criminal biology" from 1941 Ritter developed his vision of a comprehensive nationwide "archive of asocial and criminal families" (*Sippen*) that would make it possible to determine the "genetic value" (*Erbwert*) of each individual and to "predict" which individuals were of a "criminal nature" (*Verbrechernatur*).[127] Since the creation of such a nationwide database was a difficult task, this type of crime prevention was clearly a vision for the future. When Ritter was appointed head of the newly created Criminal-Biological Institute of the Security Police in late 1941, however, he practiced his prognostic skills on juvenile delinquents and wayward youths who were sent to the youth reeducation camps (*Jugendschutzlager*) Uckermark and Moringen. At least fifty-two were sent to concentration camps as a result of negative "social prognoses." It is likely that many of them perished there.[128]

Another influential research project on asocials besides Ritter's was a work by Heinrich Wilhelm Kranz and Siegfried Koller titled *Die Gemeinschaftsunfähigen: Ein Beitrag zur wissenschaftlichen und praktischen Lösung des sogenannten "Asozialenproblems"* (Those incapable of [fitting into] the community: A

126. Ritter, "Primitivität und Kriminalität," *MKS* 31 (1940): 197–210; "Erbärztliche Verbrechensverhütung," *Deutsche Medizinische Wochenschrift* (22 May 1942): 535–39.

127. Ritter, "Die Aufgaben der Kriminalbiologie," *Kriminalistik* 15 (1941): 38–41.

128. Ritter, "Das kriminalbiologische Institut"; Wagner, *Volksgemeinschaft ohne Verbrecher*, 376–81.

contribution toward the scientific and practical solution of the so-called "problem of asocials"), which appeared in two parts in 1939 and 1941.[129] Heinrich
Wilhelm Kranz was a Nazi Party activist who managed to parlay offices he held
in Nazi organizations into a university professorship. Born in 1897, Kranz had
been a volunteer in the First World War and served in a student free corps unit
after the war. After receiving his M.D. in 1921, he worked in the ophthalmology
clinic of the University of Giessen, receiving his *Habilitation* in 1926, and entered private practice as an ophthalmologist in 1928. He joined the Nazi Party
in 1930, became a local SA leader, and organized courses on eugenics for the
Nazi Physicians' League. When the Nazi Party formed its Rassenpolitisches
Amt (Office for Racial Policy) in 1934, he became head of the regional branch
(*Gauamtsleiter*) of the Rassenpolitisches Amt in Hessen-Nassau. In this capacity, he set up an Institute for Genetic and Racial Research, which in 1937
became part of the University of Giessen, where Kranz was appointed associate
professor. In 1940 he was promoted to full professor and became president
(*Rektor*) of the University of Giessen. A year later he moved to a chair in
genetics and eugenics at the University of Frankfurt.[130]

Kranz's coauthor, Siegfried Koller, who was ten years Kranz's junior, was a
young specialist in medical statistics. He earned his Ph.D. with a statistical
study of blood types in 1930 at the age of twenty-two. In 1931 he received a
Rockefeller fellowship to set up a statistical department at the internationally
renowned Kerckhoff Institute for Cardiac and Circulatory Research in Bad
Nauheim, where he began to apply his knowledge of advanced statistical theory
to critique and refine the statistical methods used in human genetic research.
Shortly after the Nazi seizure of power in May 1933, Koller joined the Nazi
Party, and in 1934 he began his collaboration with Kranz. He helped Kranz to
secure a grant for his fledgling Institute on Genetic and Racial Research from

129. Heinrich Wilhelm Kranz and Siegfried Koller, *Die Gemeinschaftsunfähigen: Ein Beitrag
zur wissenschaftlichen und praktischen Lösung des sogenannten "Asozialenproblems,"* 2 vols.
(Giessen: Karl Christ, 1939, 1941).

130. Joachim S. Hohmann, "Fanatischer Nazi und Zigeunerforscher: H. W. Kranz," in
Hohmann, *Robert Ritter und die Erben der Kriminalbiologie,* 297–302; Weingart, Kroll, and
Bayertz, *Rasse, Blut und Gene,* 456–58; Helga Jakobi, Peter Chroust, and Matthias Hamann,
*Aeskulap & Hakenkreuz: Zur Geschichte der Medizinischen Fakultät in Gießen zwischen 1933 und
1945* (Giessen: Justus-Liebig-Universität, 1982), 130 ff. Kranz committed suicide in 1945. The
Heinrich Wilhelm Kranz (1897–1945) discussed here should not be confused (as has some-
times happened in the literature) with the psychiatrist Heinrich Kranz (1901–79) who worked
with Johannes Lange and wrote the twin study *Lebensschicksale krimineller Zwillinge* (Berlin:
Springer, 1936). On the second Kranz, see his autobiographical sketch "Heinrich Kranz," in
Psychiatrie in Selbstdarstellungen (Bern: Huber, 1977), 194–218.

the well-funded Kerckhoff Institute and studied medicine under Kranz, earning his M.D. in 1938. In the late 1930s Koller and Kranz collaborated on the research project on asocials that resulted in the publication of *Die Gemeinschaftsunfähigen*; its first volume appeared in 1939 under Kranz's name, its second volume in 1941 under both names. Since this was a large-scale statistical study characterized by the sophistication of its statistical methods, most of the book was undoubtedly the work of Koller, who was appointed as head of the Biostatistical Institute of the University of Berlin in March 1941.[131]

The point of departure for Kranz and Koller's study was their judgment that "psychiatry's attempts to solve the problem of asocials have been unsatisfactory" because psychiatrists had not been able to identify a medical diagnosis for asocial behavior. Research on psychopathic personalities, in particular, had failed to develop a satisfactory definition and diagnosis of psychopathy and was facing "insurmountable difficulties." Since jurists required a medical diagnosis as the basis for compulsory eugenic measures, psychiatry's failure to develop such a diagnosis for asocials had effectively stalled the implementation of a eugenic "solution" to the problem of asocials. This was why Kranz and Koller decided to adopt a nonpsychiatric and, as they called it, purely "sociological" approach to the subject of asocial behavior. This meant that, unlike Stumpfl, they did not conduct any medical, psychiatric, or characterological examinations of the asocial persons under investigation but based their study exclusively on official records documenting criminal or asocial behavior.[132]

They began their research with an initial group of 282 persons (219 men and 63 women) who had come to the attention of the authorities in a Hessian district within a five-year period, either through criminal convictions or through contacts with welfare, youth welfare, or employment offices (*Wohlfahrtsämter, Jugendämter, Arbeitsämter*). Kranz and Koller then used the records of the same agencies to gather information about the spouses and siblings of the initial group, their parents and their spouses' parents, and their children, for a total of about 5,800 persons in three generations.[133]

---

131. Götz Aly and Karl Heinz Roth, "Siegfried Koller," in Aly and Roth, *Die restlose Erfassung* (Berlin: Rotbuch, 1984), 96–115; Weingart, Kroll, and Bayertz, *Rasse, Blut und Gene*, 457–58. See also Klaus Scherer, "Aus dem Leben eines Wissenschaftlers," in Scherer, *"Asozial" im Dritten Reich: Die vergessenen Verfolgten* (Münster: Votum, 1990), 114–24, which contains an interview with Koller. Koller enjoyed a successful career after 1945, joining the Statistisches Bundesamt in 1953 and being appointed to a chair for medical statistics at the University of Mainz created for him in 1963, which he held until his retirement in 1978.

132. Kranz and Koller, *Die Gemeinschaftsunfähigen*, 2:10–11, 31, 33.

133. Ibid., 59–65; see also 1:10–18.

On the basis of these official records, all persons under investigation were classified as belonging to one of four categories: "criminal," in case of multiple criminal convictions; *gemeinschaftsuntüchtig* ("inept at [fitting into] the community") if official records showed them to be on welfare, without steady work (*arbeitscheu*), homeless, alcoholic, vagrants, beggars, itinerant peddlers, or prostitutes; "unremarkable" (*unauffällig*) if they had not attracted official attention at all; and "socially reliable" (*sozial bewährt*) if official records indicated that they were upstanding and productive members of the community. While the "unremarkable" and the "socially reliable" formed the larger category of the *Gemeinschaftsfähige* (those "capable of [fitting into] the community"), criminals and *Gemeinschaftsuntüchtige* were combined into the larger category of *Gemeinschaftsunfähige* (those "incapable of [fitting into the] community"), Kranz and Koller's preferred term for "asocials."[134] *Gemeinschaftsunfähige* were defined as persons who "according to their entire personality are not able to meet the minimal demands that the national community [*Volksgemeinschaft*] makes on their personal, social, and *völkisch* behavior."[135]

Everyone in the initial group of 282 persons was either criminal or *gemeinschaftsuntüchtig*. The collection and analysis of data focused on determining the proportions of the four categories mentioned among the initial group's relatives, including spouses, siblings, and their parents and children. Kranz and Koller found no significant differences between the families of criminals and those of *Gemeinschaftsuntüchtige* in this regard.[136] Their major finding was that the adult children of two asocial (*gemeinschaftsunfähig*) parents were asocial in 66 percent of cases, whereas the adult children of two *gemeinschaftsfähige* parents were asocial in only 9 percent and those of two "socially reliable" parents in only 5 percent of cases.[137]

Methodologically, two things were remarkable about Kranz and Koller's study. First, Koller's expertise in statistical methods frequently led him to acknowledge that differences in percentages that appeared to be significant were in fact statistically insignificant because they fell within the range of random statistical variation (*Zufallsbereich*).[138] Second, although they proposed that "the strong regularities found in our statistics could be explained by environ-

---

134. Ibid., 2:11–18, 59, 1:10–11.
135. Ibid., 2:16; compare also 1:10. "*Völkisch* behavior" meant behavior that took into account the welfare of the "national community" (*Volksgemeinshaft*) extolled by the Nazis.
136. Ibid., 2:65–74.
137. Ibid., 132, 106.
138. For examples, see ibid., 46, 51, 72–73, 93, 110.

mental influences only with great difficulty," Kranz and Koller conceded that "statistics on extended families [such as theirs] [did] not logically prove heritability, but could . . . also be explained through environmental circumstances."[139]

Having admitted that their own study could not logically prove the influence of heredity in asocial behavior, Kranz and Koller argued that such proof was in fact provided by twin studies. Once again, Koller's statistical sophistication greatly complicated their argument. Kranz and Koller focused on the twin study published in 1936 by Kranz's namesake Heinrich Kranz, a psychiatrist who had conducted his research under Johannes Lange at the University of Breslau. The problem was that Heinrich Kranz had found only a very small difference in the concordance rates concerning criminal behavior between identical and fraternal twins (66 percent versus 54 percent).[140] By redefining concordance in his sample to exclude one-time offenses but include sustained asocial behavior (rather than criminal behavior only), Kranz and Koller arrived at a much larger difference in concordance rates (65 percent for identical versus 33 percent for fraternal twins) but had to admit that even this difference was not statistically significant because it lay within the range of random statistical variation. They therefore decided to exclude from the sample four pairs of identical twins whose discordance was supposedly due to environmental differences. This manipulation violated the basic logic of the twin method but increased the concordance figure for identical twins. After further excluding all twins who grew up in an "asocial environment" from Kranz's sample, the authors finally brought the concordance figures to 76 percent versus 24 percent, thus yielding a statistically significant difference that proved "the decisive effect of genetic factors on the genesis of asocial behavior."[141]

Assuming that twin studies had proven the "decisive effect" of heredity on asocial behavior, this still left the question of what the genetic factors causing asocial behavior were. Here, too, Kranz and Koller's determination to prove the role of heredity was at odds with their methodological and conceptual sophistication. Asocial behavior, they argued, did not result from a single genetic trait

139. Ibid., 129; for similar statements, see 1:34, 2:39.

140. Heinrich Kranz, *Lebensschicksale krimineller Zwillinge* (Berlin: Springer, 1936).

141. Analogous manipulations of the data in Stumpfl's twin study yielded similar figures, but Kranz and Koller acknowledged that they were not statistically significant because of the small size of the sample. When the revised data from Kranz and Stumpfl's twin studies were combined, the concordance rates came to 78 percent for identical versus 24 percent for fraternal twins, yielding a difference that was once again statistically significant because of the larger size of the combined sample. See Kranz and Koller, *Die Gemeinschaftsunfähigen*, 2:41–52.

but from a "complex of interlocking genetic traits, whose interaction with environmental influences shape[d] . . . the asocial personality in ways that [were] not generally understood."[142] Asocial behavior was caused by a combination of several "individual defects" that were inherited separately. Because they were inherited separately, Kranz and Koller conceded, the specific combination that supposedly triggered asocial behavior in a parent was unlikely to be transmitted to his or her offspring. But, they insisted, the offspring of such parents were likely to suffer from other combinations of "genetic defects" that were just as likely to result in asocial behavior. In sum, they argued that asocial behavior over several generations of a particular population resulted from changing combinations of a large number of genetic defects endemic in that population, a view reflected in the strange formulation that the "genetic factors underlying asocial behavior" reflected "the participation of the entire 'underworld of genes' " found in a "lower stratum" (*Unterschicht*) of the national population.[143]

Even though they acknowledged, first, that there were "no clear boundaries" dividing this genetically defective "lower stratum" from the rest of the population, second, that their own study could not prove the role of heredity in asocial behavior, and third, that the exact nature of the genetic factors that supposedly caused asocial behavior remained unknown, Kranz and Koller concluded by calling for drastic eugenic measures to combat asocial behavior. What should the criteria for sterilization be? Psychopathy could not be added to the sterilization law because many psychopaths were not asocial; and a medical diagnosis that would permit the differentiation of asocial psychopaths from other psychopaths was not forthcoming.[144] While this situation had stumped other psychiatrists, Kranz and Koller proposed to dispense with medical diagnoses and to base the sterilization of asocials on purely sociological criteria. Concretely, they proposed a new law providing for the sterilization of persons whose inability to "satisfy the minimal demands that the national community made on their personal, social and *völkisch* behavior" marked them as "asocial" and who had two or more asocials among their close blood relatives. The decision to sterilize them would not depend on the medical diagnosis of a genetic defect but on the court's judgment whether they and two close blood relatives led "asocial" lives according to the law's definition.[145]

142. Ibid., 52.
143. Ibid., 52–55, 130–31.
144. Ibid., 135–45, esp. 140.
145. Ibid., 160–62. For a more detailed discussion of Kranz and Koller's sterilization proposals, see Chapter 7.

Although both Ritter's and Kranz and Koller's research on asocials fell outside the mainstream of criminological research, their work is important to
understand the full spectrum of criminological research under the Nazi regime
and especially in the late 1930s and early 1940s. Ritter's work was characterized
by a simplistic genetic determinism that ignored the conceptual and methodological advances of decades of criminological research. What is more, while the
racial dimension had remained peripheral in mainstream criminology, Ritter
based his entire criminological analysis on the crassest racial stereotypes of the
Roma and Sinti ("Gypsies"). Not surprisingly, Ritter's emphasis on race, his
genetic determinism, and his willingness to offer simple eugenic solutions en-
deared him to officials in the Reich Health Office and in the police leadership,
who hired him to head their research institutes. In this sense, one might say
that it was precisely the simplistic and methodologically backward quality of
Ritter's research that accelerated his career in the Third Reich.

Kranz and Koller's work presents us with a much more complicated picture.
For, on the one hand, their book was the product of increasing conceptual and
methodological sophistication. Both their frank acknowledgment that family
studies such as theirs failed to prove the influence of heredity on asocial behavior because they could not separate the influence of genetic and environmental factors and their view that asocial behavior did not result from a single
genetic trait but from combinations of different, separately inherited traits
reflected the most advanced criminological research of the time. Moreover,
Koller's knowledge of statistical methods, which included calculating the range
of random statistical variation for every analysis, was far more advanced than
that of Lange, Stumpfl, Exner, or any other criminologist. In this respect, then,
Kranz and Koller's work supports this chapter's argument that a trend toward
increasing conceptual and methodological refinement in criminological research continued during the Nazi era. What is more, Kranz and Koller understood that the increasing sophistication of criminal-biological research had
made the goal of identifying the biological or genetic factors in criminal behavior ever more elusive. They recognized that "psychopathy" remained too
vague a category to be helpful and that a medical diagnosis corresponding to
asocial behavior would not be forthcoming for a long time. This was why they
proposed the radical solution of basing the sterilization of asocial persons not on
an individual medical diagnosis but on purely sociological criteria, while justifying such a policy with a general assertion that heredity played a significant
role in asocial behavior.

On the other hand, Kranz and Koller's work provides the most extreme example of how a deeply ingrained hereditarianism can ride roughshod over the greatest methodological sophistication. Kranz and Koller's hereditarianism was closely linked to their belief in a eugenic solution to the crime problem and the "problem of asocials" that had to be implemented despite psychiatry's failure to identify the genetic factors that supposedly caused criminal and asocial behavior. In Kranz and Koller's case, hereditarianism and eugenics had become dogmas.

Conclusion

In conclusion, we find that the development of criminal biology and criminology in the Nazi period presents a complex picture that differs from what one might have expected in the Nazi racial state. Nazi leaders, police officials, doctors involved in the euthanasia program, and many others in Nazi Germany believed not only in genetically deterministic but often racist explanations of crime and characterized racial minorities like Gypsies and Jews as inherently criminal. Such views were also held by researchers on "asocials" and Gypsies, most notably Ritter, Kranz, and Koller, who exerted some influence on criminological research. There is some evidence that in the very late 1930s Stumpfl began to be influenced by such racist conceptions of crime. Moreover, as the first section of this chapter demonstrated, leading criminologists were eager to win Nazi support for criminology by stressing its usefulness for Nazi eugenic and penal policy.

On the whole, however, genetically deterministic and racist explanations of crime did not predominate in mainstream criminal biology and criminology. On the contrary, mainstream criminology in the Nazi era was characterized by a continuing process of increasing methodological sophistication. While Stumpfl's research at the Deutsche Forschungsanstalt für Psychiatrie continued the search for genetic factors in criminal behavior, it also reflected an increased awareness of the inherent limitations of the twin method that obliged Stumpfl to acknowledge the complexity of the interaction of heredity and environment.

Most remarkably, perhaps, many of the criticisms that have been leveled at research on the genetic causes of crime after 1945 were in fact articulated by contemporary critics like Gruhle, Mayer, and Exner during the Nazi years. Likewise, the two major surveys of criminology written by jurists reflected a relatively sophisticated and balanced approach to the etiology of crime. Both Mezger and Exner asserted that race played a role in criminal behavior and made explicitly anti-Semitic comments. But neither described Jews, Gypsies, or any other racial group as inherently criminal. Mezger's and Exner's textbooks also showed that some of the unintentionally antihereditarian implications of criminal-biological research were not lost on the jurists. Mezger, for instance, observed that recent twin research had actually highlighted the influence of environmental factors.

In conclusion, while this chapter has demonstrated that prominent criminologists openly appealed for Nazi support by offering criminology's services in the implementation of Nazi penal and eugenic policies, it has also shown that a considerable portion of mainstream criminological research in the Nazi era was not characterized by the crude genetic determinism and racism that pervaded so much of Nazi Germany. The latter finding supports the argument that a considerable amount of "normal science" continued under the Nazi regime, as has been suggested by other recent work in the history of German science.[146]

146. See Arleen Tuchmann, "Institutions and Disciplines: Recent Work in the History of German Science," *Journal of Modern History* 69 (1997): 300, 316, 317; Kristie Macrakis, *Surviving the Swastika: Scientific Research in Nazi Germany* (New York: Oxford University Press, 1993), 3–4, 199.

CHAPTER SEVEN

CRIMINOLOGY AND EUGENICS, 1919–1945

Having surveyed the internal development of criminology during the Nazi years, we must now ask what role criminological research played in penal and eugenic policy. Since most of the people involved in debating or carrying out these policies did not themselves specialize in criminology, this chapter also deals with the reception of criminological research among German jurists, doctors, politicians, and bureaucrats. While most of this chapter will focus on policy concerning the sterilization of criminals during the Weimar and Nazi years, we will begin with a general overview of Nazi penal policy.

Nazi penal policy was driven by two competing attitudes. On the one hand, the Nazis criticized the supposed "emasculation" of criminal justice during the Weimar years and blamed it on penal reformers and criminologists. In the Nazis' view, all penal reformers were liberals whose belief in individual rights led them to champion the rights of criminals at the expense of the protection of society. Furthermore, the Nazis charged, criminology's focus on the social and biological causes of crime had effectively relieved the criminal of individual responsibility and therefore undermined the moral foundation of criminal justice. As a result, Weimar penal reformers had, according to the Nazis, supplemented their liberal agenda with humanitarian concern for ameliorating the treatment of criminals. Having thus characterized Weimar penal reformers as "soft on crime," activist Nazi jurists called for harsher penal policies that would administer just retribution and place the protection of state and society above any liberal concerns for the rights of the accused. Dismissing rehabilitative efforts as motivated exclusively by humanitarian considerations, Nazi jurists demanded that imprisonment become unsparingly punitive again.[1]

1. Georg Dahm and Friedrich Schaffstein, *Liberales oder autoritäres Strafrecht?* (Hamburg:

But even as they blamed criminological research for undermining the moral foundation of criminal justice, the Nazis' own penchant for a racial-biological view of society made criminal-biological explanations of crime appealing to them. Prominent Nazi leaders' comments on criminals were frequently characterized by the crudest genetic determinism,[2] and the affinity between criminal biology and Nazi "biological politics" led the Nazi regime to support the creation of a national Criminal-Biological Service.

The Nazis' call for tough-minded retributive justice and their belief that most criminals were genetically defective were profoundly contradictory. To be sure, the pre-1933 penal reformers, too, had wrestled with and failed to resolve a similar contradiction. For even though Liszt and his fellow reformers had concluded that social and biological explanations of crime had rendered the notion of legal responsibility untenable in principle, they had refused to abolish legal responsibility. From the criminal's point of view, the reformers had combined the worst features of the judicial and medical approaches. For in the reformist scheme most "abnormal" offenders were still considered guilty but were then subjected to additional measures, such as indefinite detention, because of their abnormality.

But although the pre-1933 penal reform agenda and Nazi penal policy were both characterized by the same fundamental contradiction between a determinist view of crime and a refusal to recognize its exculpatory implications, there were two crucial differences. First, the reformers had completely rejected the notion of retributive justice. Second, they had called for a system of individualized punishments leading to longer sentences for some but lesser punishments for others. The Nazis, by contrast, affirmed their belief in retributive justice and sought to make punishments harsher for all offenders. Thus Nazi penal policy pushed the contradiction between regarding criminals as biolog-

---

Hanseatische Verlagsanstalt, 1933); Karl Siegert, *Grundzüge des Strafrechts im neuen Staate* (Tübingen: Mohr, 1934); Eberhard Schmidt, *Einführung in die Geschichte der deutschen Strafrechtspflege*, 3d ed. (Göttingen: Vandenhoeck, 1964), 425–30; Klaus Marxen, *Der Kampf gegen das liberale Strafrecht* (Berlin: Duncker & Humblot, 1975); see also Max Mikorey, "Das Judentum in der Kriminalpsychologie," in *Das Judentum in der Rechtswissenschaft*, vol. 3, *Judentum und Verbrechen* (Berlin: Deutscher Rechts-Verlag, 1936), 61–82 (discussed in the previous chapter).

2. Hitler speech in *Völkischer Beobachter* 42/181 (7 Aug. 1929); Alfred Rosenberg, *Der Mythus des 20. Jahrhunderts* (Munich: Hoheneichen, 1930); Hans Frank in *Nationalsozialistische Monatshefte* 1 (1930): 298; all quoted in Gisela Bock, *Zwangssterilisation im Nationalsozialismus* (Opladen: Westdeutscher Verlag, 1986), 24–27; Helmut Nicolai, *Die rassengesetzliche Rechtslehre* (Munich: Eher, 1932).

ically inferior and holding them fully responsible to much greater extremes than the penal reformers ever did. The Nazis made criminals suffer the worst consequences of both the retributive and determinist approaches to crime. For even as they exposed criminals to the full force of retribution through a tough-on-crime policy that abandoned time-honored liberal restraints on state power, they drew on biological explanations of crime to justify additional measures such as indefinite detention and sterilization.

Under the Nazis, too, attempts to achieve a comprehensive reform of the penal code failed.[3] Prominent among the Nazi changes in penal policy were two measures directed against "habitual" and "professional" criminals. The Law against Dangerous Habitual Criminals (Gesetz gegen gefährliche Gewohn-heitsverbrecher) of November 1933 made it possible to keep convicted "dangerous habitual criminals" in indefinite "preventive detention" (*Sicherungsverwahrung*) even after the end of their prison sentences.[4] Although the Nazis refused to admit it, this law simply implemented a long-standing demand of the pre-1933 penal reform movement, which had formed part of every draft penal code since the prewar years. The second Nazi measure directed against habitual and professional criminals, by contrast, marked a clear break not only with the penal reform tradition but with the basic principles of the rule of law. The Prussian ordinance on "preventive police custody" (*vorbeugende Polizeihaft*), also of November 1933, allowed the police to intern "professional criminals" in concentration camps for an indefinite period without a court order.[5]

Leaving aside the Nazi use of criminal justice against political enemies and racial and other minorities, Nazi penal policy directed against "ordinary" crime, that is, property crime and violent crime, was characterized by three main features: the dismantling of liberal restraints on the state's penal power, as reflected in the Nazi law that permitted the use of analogy in criminal law, which violated the principle that all crimes had to be defined in the penal code;[6] the increasing encroachment of the police on the traditional functions of the criminal justice

3. Lothar Gruchmann, *Justiz im Dritten Reich, 1933–1940: Anpassung und Unterwerfung in der Ära Gürtner* (Munich: Oldenbourg, 1988), 753–822.

4. Christian Müller, *Das Gewohnheitsverbrechergesetz vom 24. November 1933* (Baden-Baden: Nomos, 1997); Gruchmann, *Justiz im Dritten Reich*, 838–44; Gerhard Werle, *Justiz-Strafrecht und polizeiliche Verbrechensbekämpfung im Dritten Reich* (Berlin: de Gruyter, 1989), 86–107.

5. On the Prussian *Erlass*, see Patrick Wagner, *Volksgemeinschaft ohne Verbrecher: Konzeptionen und Praxis der Kriminalpolizei in der Zeit der Weimarer Republik und des National-sozialismus* (Hamburg: Christians, 1996), 199.

6. Gruchmann, *Justiz im Dritten Reich*, 847–63; Werle, *Justiz-Strafrecht*, 141–44.

system, as reflected in the internment of professional criminals in concentration camps without trial;[7] and an enormous increase in the use of the death penalty.[8]

What contribution did criminological research make to Nazi penal policy? Many aspects of Nazi penal policy were driven by the goal to make criminal justice harsher, ultimately to the point of state terror, and were not intrinsically connected to criminological research. For some measures, however, a biological characterization of the offender could be and was used as additional justification. Both of the aforementioned measures against habitual criminals, for instance, were clearly influenced by criminological research in the sense that criminologists played an important part in perpetuating the concept of the habitual criminal. But since this concept had played a key role in the penal reform movement since the beginning and was therefore largely independent of criminological research, the Nazi measures against habitual criminals did not really hinge on criminological research for their justification. The increased use of the death penalty presents us with a similar situation. On the one hand, the Nazis drew on a biological view of criminals as genetically defective to justify the increased application of the death penalty. During the Second World War, for instance, Hitler himself argued that military combat was exacting its highest toll among the "positive elements" of the population and that "negative elements" therefore had to be killed in larger numbers to restore balance.[9] On the other hand, however, the Nazis also justified all punishments, including capital punishment, in terms of retributive justice.[10]

While all of the Nazi penal policy measures discussed so far could be justified in terms of retributive justice alone, there was one aspect of Nazi penal policy that depended directly on criminal-biological research and therefore provides an ideal test case for examining its impact: the question of sterilizing criminals. Since the Nazi sterilization law of July 1933 and its implementation are best understood in the context of the sterilization proposals and debates that took place during the Weimar Republic, we will pick up the thread of this story there.

---

7. Werle, *Justiz-Strafrecht*, esp. 499–521; Wagner, *Volksgemeinschaft ohne Verbrecher*, 199–202, 258–62.

8. Richard Evans, *Rituals of Retribution: Capital Punishment in Germany, 1600–1987* (Oxford: Oxford University Press, 1996), 613–737.

9. Ibid., 696–710, Hitler quote on 702.

10. See, for example, August Schoetensack, "Strafe und sichernde Maßnahme," in *Denkschrift des Zentralausschusses der Strafrechtsabteilung der Akademie für deutsches Recht über die Grundzüge eines Allgemeinen Deutschen Strafrechts* (Berlin: Decker, 1934), 90–99; *Nationalsozialistische Leitsätze für ein neues deutsches Strafrecht*, Part 1 (n.p., 1935), 23–25. See also Gruchmann, *Justiz im Dritten Reich*, 790; Werle, *Justiz-Strafrecht*, 700–704.

Sterilization Debates among Weimar Psychiatrists, 1923–1933

According to most legal experts, sterilization was illegal in Imperial and Weimar Germany because it fell under the penal code's definition of bodily injury. The only exception consisted of sterilizations carried out for medical reasons, to preserve a patient's health.[11] As we saw in Chapter 3, the earliest proposals for sterilizing criminals dated back to the turn of the century. The sterilization of criminals and other "degenerates" was first proposed by Paul Näcke in 1899 but did not garner much support. The introduction of sterilization laws in several American states in the first decade of the twentieth century periodically revived discussion of the subject, but the majority of German psychiatrists, including the pioneers of criminal psychology, remained skeptical of sterilization throughout the prewar period.[12] Even the leaders of the German eugenics movement did not push for a sterilization law and gave priority to "positive eugenics" during the prewar period. Among Germany's major eugenicists only Ernst Rüdin advocated the sterilization of "mental defectives" before 1914.[13]

This situation changed after the First World War, which provided German eugenicists with new arguments for their demands. Some eugenicists now asserted that eugenic measures to improve the quality of the population had become more urgent than ever because the war had killed off "our genetically most valuable elements."[14] Others used postwar Germany's difficult economic situation to argue that the mentally ill imposed an unacceptable financial burden that could be lessened only by sterilizing the mentally ill and thus gradually reducing asylum populations. As a result of such arguments, in 1922, the main organization of the German eugenics movement, the German Society for

11. Joachim Müller, *Sterilisation und Gesetzgebung bis 1933* (Husum: Matthiesen, 1985), 52–53; Eduard Kohlrausch, "Sterilisation und Strafrecht," *ZStW* 52 (1932): 383–404.

12. Paul Näcke, "Die Kastration bei gewissen Klassen von Degenerirten als ein wirksamer socialer Schutz," *AKK* 3 (1899): 58–84. On the introduction of sterilization laws in the United States, see Philip Reilly, *The Surgical Solution: A History of Involuntary Sterilization in the United States* (Baltimore: Johns Hopkins University Press, 1991), 41–55. On the relations between the German and American eugenics movements before 1933, see Stefan Kühl, *The Nazi Connection: Eugenics, American Racism and German National Socialism* (New York: Oxford University Press, 1994), 13–26; Kühl, *Die Internationale der Rassisten: Aufstieg und Niedergang der internationalen Bewegung für Eugenik und Rassenhygiene im 20. Jahrhundert* (Frankfurt: Campus, 1997); Robert Proctor, *Racial Hygiene: Medicine under the Nazis* (Cambridge, Mass.: Harvard University Press, 1988), 97–101.

13. Müller, *Sterilisation und Gesetzgebung*, 48–49, 59–60.

14. Robert Gaupp, *Die Unfruchtbarmachung geistig und sittlich Kranker und Minderwertiger* (Berlin: Springer, 1925), 13.

Racial Hygiene, amended its platform to demand passage of a law that would legalize the voluntary sterilization of persons with genetic illnesses.[15]

It was not, however, the German Society for Racial Hygiene but the physician and district health officer Dr. Gerhard Boeters of Zwickau in Saxony who made sterilization a major topic of discussion among German doctors and jurists. In May 1923 Boeters presented the Saxon government with a memorandum in which he proposed that mentally ill persons be subject to compulsory sterilization and that criminals should "have their sentences reduced if they voluntarily undergo sterilization." Not content with petitioning the government, Boeters also mounted a public relations campaign to publicize his proposals. In January 1924, a widely circulated medical journal published his "Appeal to German Physicians" in which he warned that the "spiritual elite of the German people" was on the verge of perishing in a "flood of mentally and morally inferior elements." To avert this danger, Boeters called on the medical profession not only to support his campaign for a sterilization law but to take matters into their own hands by "searching out mental defectives" and sterilizing them. Through more than a dozen articles in medical periodicals and the popular press, Boeters succeeded in provoking a sustained public debate on sterilization among German physicians and jurists. Most intense in 1924–25, this debate took place in letters to the editor, lectures at professional meetings, and dozens of articles in professional journals and continued throughout the 1920s and early 1930s.[16] The response to Boeters's proposals for the sterilization of the mentally ill was mixed. Most physicians participating in the debate were sympathetic to eugenics and called for the legalization of voluntary eugenic sterilization but opposed Boeters's call for compulsory sterilization. A minority was more critical and insisted that the study of human

15. Ibid., 21; Müller, *Sterilisation und Gesetzgebung,* 57–60; Peter Weingart, Jürgen Kroll, and Kurt Bayertz, *Rasse, Blut und Gene: Geschichte der Eugenik und Rassenhygiene in Deutschland* (Frankfurt: Suhrkamp, 1988), 230–31, 254–66.

16. Gerhard Boeters, "Eingabe an die Sächsische Staatsregierung vom 21 Mai 1923," printed in Hans W. Maier, "Zum gegenwärtigen Stand der Frage der Kastration und Sterilisation," *ZGNP* 98 (1925): 206–7; Boeters, "Aufruf an die deutsche Ärzteschaft," *Ärztliches Vereinsblatt für Deutschland* 51, no. 1297 (9 Jan. 1924): 3–4; both are reprinted in Jochen-Christoph Kaiser, Kurt Nowak, and Michael Schwartz, eds., *Eugenik, Sterilisation, "Euthanasie": Politische Biologie in Deutschland, 1895–1945* (Berlin: Union, 1992), 95–96; Boeters, "Die Unfruchtbarmachung Geisteskranker, Schwachsinniger und Verbrecher aus Anlage," *Zeitschrift für Medizinalbeamte* 38 (1925): 336–41. On Boeters's initiatives, see also Müller, *Sterilisation,* 60–63, 68–72; Weingart, Kroll, and Bayertz, *Rasse, Blut und Gene,* 291–92; Paul Weindling, *Health, Race and German Politics between National Unification and Nazism, 1870–1945* (Cambridge: Cambridge University Press), 388–93.

genetics was not advanced enough to determine whether any mental illness was hereditary.[17]

Since we are interested in the impact of criminal-biological research on eugenic debates and policy, I shall focus on the debate over the sterilization of criminals rather than the mentally ill. Participants in this debate—mostly psychiatrists who did not specialize in criminal biology—were essentially divided into two camps: a majority that endorsed the sterilization of criminals in some form (usually only voluntary sterilization) and a minority that opposed the sterilization of criminals.

Advocates of sterilization faced greater difficulties in justifying the sterilization of criminals than that of certain categories of the mentally ill. Many German psychiatrists argued for sterilizing those suffering from certain mental illnesses because recent research had convinced them that some mental illnesses, especially schizophrenia, were attributable to genetic factors that were hereditarily transmitted.[18] Even advocates of sterilization, however, believed that the role of genetic factors in crime was far more complicated than their role in mental illness. Thus in a 1933 article on criminality and eugenics for the medical weekly *Medizinische Welt*, Johannes Lange cautioned his readers against drawing unwarranted conclusions from his twin study:

> According to the twin method one has to conclude that heredity [*Anlage*] is of unexpectedly great importance for a person's social behavior with regard to the penal laws. . . . One might think that with this result much has been achieved that is relevant for eugenics. If heredity is of such importance for the etiology of crime, one would make every effort to prevent the further spread of such negative criminogenic genetic traits [*Anlagen*]. Whoever draws this conclusion would show that he did not understand correctly. If an entire genetic constitution [*Gesamtanlage*] as such makes its bearer susceptible to coming into conflict with the penal code in one way or another, that does not mean that the hereditary structures relevant to the criminal actions are heritable as such and as a whole. . . . On occasion, criminogenic genetic constitutions can suddenly appear and disappear in very good [i.e., law-

17. Müller, *Sterilisation*, 60–68; Weingart, Kroll, and Bayertz, *Rasse, Blut und Gene*, 293–320; Weindling, *Health, Race and German Politics*, 388–93, 450–57.

18. See, for instance, Ernst Rüdin, "Psychiatrische Indikation zur Sterilisierung," *Das kommende Geschlecht* 5 (1929): 6; Johannes Lange, "Referat," in "Die Eugenik im Dienste der Volkswohlfahrt: Bericht über die Verhandlungen eines zusammengesetzten Ausschusses des Preußischen Landesgesundheitsrates vom 2. Juli 1932," *Veröffentlichungen aus dem Gebiete der Medizinalverwaltung* 38 (1932): 659–61.

abiding] families through an unfortunate combination of maternal and paternal hereditary traits [*Erbmischung*], and conversely, criminal parents may . . . have socially valuable offspring.[19]

Even those proponents of sterilization who did not specialize in criminal biology showed that they were aware of the complexity of the role of heredity in criminal behavior, which demonstrates that the sophistication of Weimar era criminal-biological research was not lost on the nonspecialist audience. Thus the prominent eugenicist Ernst Rüdin, who succeeded Kraepelin as director of the Deutsche Forschungsanstalt für Psychiatrie in Munich, where Lange's twin study had been conducted, acknowledged that "the study of the hereditary transmission of psychopathic traits . . . [was] not yet advanced enough to allow general conclusions" and rejected "one-sided personality theories" of crime, insisting that crime must be understood "as a product of the interaction of environment and personality."[20] Likewise, the psychiatrist Robert Gaupp explicitly recognized that studies of "criminal families" did not prove genetic transmission because "people have rightfully pointed out that . . . the milieu [also] promoted the continuation of crime and waywardness."[21]

But if the proponents of sterilization were aware that the role of heredity in criminal behavior was complex and that most criminal behavior was affected by environmental factors, how did they justify the sterilization of criminals? The answer lies in two patterns of argumentation that recurred throughout the pro-sterilization literature.[22] First, advocates of sterilization maintained that

19. Johannes Lange, "Kriminalität und Eugenik," *Medizinische Welt* 7, no. 22 (3 June 1933): 762–63. The same point is made in Lange, "Verbrechen und Vererbung," *Eugenik* 1 (1931): 170.

20. Ernst Rüdin, "Wege und Ziele der biologischen Erforschung der Rechtsbrecher mit besonderer Berücksichtigung der Erbbiologie," *MKBG* 3 (1930): 164, 167.

21. Gaupp, *Die Unfruchtbarmachung*, 25; see also Gaupp, "Die Unfruchtbarmachung geistig und sittlich Minderwertiger," *ZGNP* 100 (1926): 139–81. The same point was made by Rainer Fetscher: "The frequent occurrence of criminality in particular families can reflect a social situation as well as an endogenous one. Both factors probably play a role" (Fetscher, "Die Sterilisierung aus eugenischen Gründen," *ZStW* 52 [1932]: 414).

22. My analysis is based on the following interventions on the pro-sterilization side (all dealing with the sterilization of criminals) between 1924 and 1933: L. W. Weber, "Kastration und Sterilisation geistig Minderwertiger," *ZGNP* 91 (1924): 93–113; Gaupp, *Die Unfruchtbarmachung*; Gaupp, "Die Unfruchtbarmachung geistig und sittlich Minderwertiger"; Rüdin, "Psychiatrische Indikation zur Sterilisierung"; Rüdin, "Wege und Ziele"; Rüdin, "Schwangerschaftsunterbrechung und Unfruchtbarmachung, insbesondere bei sozialer und eugenischer Indikation," *MIKV* N.F. 6 (1932): 49–62; Hans Luxenburger, "Psychiatrische Erbprognose und Eugenik," *Eugenik* 1 (1931): 117–24; Luxenburger, "Zur Frage der Schwangerschaftsunterbrechung und Sterilisierung aus psychiatrich-eugenischer Indikation," *ZStW* 52 (1932): 432–

even though the precise role of heredity in crime remained unclear, criminal-biological research had proven a "general connection between heredity and crime" that was sufficient to justify the sterilization of at least some criminals.[23] Second, they called for making sterilization dependent on individual examinations. Whereas Boeters's proposal targeted *all* criminals for sterilization, most pro-sterilization psychiatrists conceded that the present state of research did not warrant the sterilization of all criminals or even groups of criminals (whether defined by offense, recidivism, or personal traits) but insisted that recent research did provide sufficient grounds for sterilizing individual criminals upon careful examination.

Proposals to make the sterilization of criminals dependent on individual examinations raised the question of what the criteria for sterilization should be. On this issue, the pro-sterilization camp can be divided into three main groups advancing different strategies for justifying and implementing the sterilization of criminals. The first group believed that individual examinations could determine whether a person's criminal actions resulted from genetic factors. Thus the psychiatrist L. W. Weber suggested that "habitual criminals" and "criminal psychopaths" be examined to determine "whether [their] antisocial or criminal activities derive mainly from [their] psychological personalities or from adverse environmental influences." If the examination revealed that a criminal's activities were "based on a particular set of negative traits likely to be transmitted to offspring," that criminal ought to be sterilized.[24]

This approach suffered from an obvious problem: if, as everyone admitted, neither the genetic traits involved in criminal behavior nor their mode of transmission were known, what evidence of genetic factors could such a "genetic

---

39; Luxenburger, "Zur Frage der Zwangssterilisierung," *Eugenik* 3 (1933): 76–79; Lange, "Verbrechen und Vererbung"; Lange, "Kriminalität und Eugenik"; Rainer Fetscher, "Die Sterilisierung aus eugenischen Gründen"; Fetscher, "Zur Theorie und Praxis der Sterilisierung," *MKBG* 4 (1933): 247–57; Fritz Lenz, "Zur Frage eines Sterilisierungsgesetzes," *Eugenik* 3 (1933): 73–76; A. Ostermann, "Zum Sterilisierungsgesetz," *Eugenik* 3 (1933): 137–40.

23. L. Stemmler, "Die Unfruchtbarmachung Geisteskranker, Schwachsinniger und Verbrecher aus Anlage," *AZP* 80 (1924): 461; see also Lange, "Verbrechen und Vererbung," 166–67, 169.

24. Weber, "Kastration und Sterilisation," 106–7. The author was director of the insane asylum in Chemnitz and should not be confused with F. A. Weber, who headed the Saxon Landesgesundheitsamt. For other examples of the same line of argument, see Stemmler, "Die Unfruchtbarmachung Geisteskranker"; Hans W. Maier, "Zum gegenwärtigen Stand der Frage der Kastration und Sterilisation," *ZGNP* 98 (1925): 200–219; Otto Kankeleit, "Künstliche Unfruchtbarmachung aus rassehygienischen und sozialen Gründen," *ZGNP* 98 (1925): 220–54; Gaupp, *Die Unfruchtbarmachung*. See also Rainer Fetscher, "Die Sterilisierung aus eugenischen Gründen," *ZStW* 52 (1932): 404–23.

examination" uncover? The only "genetic" information available at this time was genealogical. In the Bavarian criminal-biological examinations, for instance, a genealogical chart provided information about the incidence of "abnormal" or criminal behavior in the criminal's family. But a high incidence of criminal behavior in a criminal's family was inconclusive because, as almost everyone acknowledged, criminal behavior over several generations could be explained environmentally. A high incidence of "abnormal" traits or mental illness in the criminal's family was no more helpful because nothing definite was known about their connection with criminal behavior. It was therefore hard to see how individual examinations could provide evidence of genetic factors in criminal behavior that would justify a criminal's sterilization.

A second strategy, proposed by Johannes Lange, circumvented this problem by defining the criteria for sterilization differently. Lange was very careful in interpreting the results of his twin study. While he claimed to have shown that heredity played an important role in criminal behavior, he acknowledged that his study had not revealed the existence of a "criminogenic genetic trait." In Lange's view, the criminal behavior of the vast majority of habitual criminals did not derive from a heritable criminogenic trait but from an unfortunate combination of paternal and maternal psychopathic traits that became criminogenic only in this particular combination. Since the occurrence of such criminogenic combinations could not be predicted, and most psychopathic traits were harmless, Lange did not believe that general eugenic measures against psychopaths were warranted.[25]

But although Lange insisted that the sterilization of criminals could not be justified on the basis of genetic criminogenic traits, he did propose a general eugenic screening of all criminals. Whereas L. W. Weber wanted individual examinations to determine whether a person's criminal behavior was caused by genetic factors, Lange proposed individual examinations to detect hereditary mental abnormalities regardless of any connection with criminal behavior. If the individual examination revealed that a criminal was feebleminded, for instance, and his genealogical information suggested that this feeblemindedness was genetic, he would be recommended for eugenic sterilization without any claim that his *criminal behavior* was due to genetic causes. For although Lange appreciated the complexity of the role of genetics in criminal behavior, he shared the widespread conviction that many mental illnesses and abnormalities, including schizophrenia and most cases of feeblemindedness (*Schwachsinn*),

25. Lange, "Verbrechen und Vererbung," 170–73; Lange, "Kriminalität und Eugenik," 764.

were hereditary, and therefore had no qualms about sterilization in such cases. Thus Lange did not justify the sterilization of individual criminals on the basis of *criminogenic genetic defects* but on the basis of hereditary mental abnormalities or illnesses that occurred in both criminals and noncriminals and were undesirable from a eugenic point of view regardless of any criminogenic effect.[26]

The third strategy for justifying the sterilization of criminals was the boldest. If it was impossible to disentangle genetic and environmental influences, clearly the best strategy was to justify sterilization on both grounds. This argument was first advanced by Robert Gaupp, a prominent professor of psychiatry in Tübingen, who gave a lecture on sterilization at the annual meeting of the German Association for Psychiatry in 1925 that was later published and became a widely read book.[27] Gaupp acknowledged that environmental factors played a role in criminal behavior but insisted that this was not an argument against the sterilization of criminals. After all, the same environmental factors that might account for a person's criminal behavior were also likely to push that person's children into a life of crime. Therefore, the decision about whether a criminal should be sterilized ought not to depend on evidence of genetic criminogenic factors but on whether the *combination* of his "genetics, constitution, mental development" and his "milieu and economic situation" made it likely that his offspring would not be "mentally and morally adequate [*vollwertig*]." If this was the case, the criminal should be sterilized.[28]

Thus no one in the pro-sterilization camp endorsed Boeters's original proposal of encouraging *all* criminals to undergo voluntary sterilization by offering reduced sentences. Nor did anyone advocate the sterilization of any particular group of criminals, such as habitual criminals.[29] Instead, advocates of

26. Lange, "Kriminalität und Eugenik," 763–65; "Verbrechen und Vererbung," 168, 173; "Referat," 655–63. In addition to Lange, this approach was proposed by Rainer Fetscher in "Die Sterilisierung aus eugenischen Gründen," 414, 415; and in his "Zur Theorie und Praxis der Sterilisierung," 253.

27. On Robert Gaupp (1870–1953), see Bernhard Pauleikhoff, "Robert Gaupp," in *Das Menschenbild im Wandel der Zeit: Ideengeschichte der Psychiatrie und der klinischen Psychologie*, 4 vols. (Hürtgenwald: Pressler, 1983–87), 4:131–49.

28. Gaupp, *Die Unfruchtbarmachung*, 26; see also Gaupp, "Die Unfruchtbarmachung geistig und sittlich Minderwertiger." The same argument is made in Lenz, "Zur Frage eines Sterilisierungsgesetzes," 74; and in M. Staemmler, "Die Sterilisierung Minderwertiger vom Standpunkt des Nationalsozialismus," *Eugenik* 3 (1933): 106. Lange also mentions this argument at the end of his "Kriminalität und Eugenik," 765.

29. Hans Luxenburger called for the sterilization of all recidivist habitual criminals who were "psychopathic." This would still require an individual medical exam but not proof that their psychopathic traits caused their criminal behavior (Luxenburger, "Zur Frage der

sterilization insisted that the sterilization of criminals depend on individual examinations, although they differed on the criteria to be used. They also differed on whether the sterilization of criminals who met the criteria should be voluntary or compulsory. Some, like Gaupp, advocated compulsory sterilization; others, including Hans Luxenburger, called only for voluntary sterilization, while still others, including Rüdin and Lange, remained vague or undecided on this issue.[30]

Compared to the pro-sterilization camp, those who opposed the sterilization of criminals in the Weimar debates were a small group. If we use published articles and lectures at professional meetings as our measure, the pro-sterilization majority consisted of about a dozen psychiatrists, while only two psychiatrists[31] publicly opposed the sterilization of criminals. The first was Albert Moll, a prominent practitioner, well known for his work on human sexuality, who insisted in 1929 that there was "no scientifically grounded indication whatsoever" for the sterilization of criminals.[32] The second and more influential opponent was Hans Gruhle, the most important proponent of the criminal-psychological strand in Weimar criminal biology. In an article that was published in Germany's major criminological journal in 1932, when sterilization efforts were rapidly gaining momentum, Gruhle carefully reviewed the unresolved problems involved in studying the role of heredity in crime and concluded that there was no scientific justification for the sterilization of criminals.[33]

Gruhle started by pointing out that human heredity in general was highly complex and poorly understood. While certain basic "functional" characteristics, such as spontaneity, were most likely hereditary, it was unknown to what extent more specific character traits were determined by heredity or environment.[34] Thus even if a "criminal disposition" existed, there was no reason to

---

Schwangerschaftsunterbrechung"). To my knowledge, the first author to demand that all habitual criminals (to be legally defined) be sterilized—without any individual examination of their hereditary constitution—was M. Staemmler, a National-Socialist writing after the Nazi seizure of power, in early 1933 (Staemmler, "Die Sterilisierung Minderwertiger").

30. Luxenburger, "Psychiatrische Erbprognose und Eugenik"; Luxenburger, "Zur Frage der Schwangerschaftsunterbrechung"; Luxenburger, "Zur Frage der Zwangssterilisierung"; Lange, "Verbrechen und Vererbung"; Lange, "Kriminalität und Eugenik"; Rüdin, "Wege und Ziele"; Rüdin, "Schwangerschaftsunterbrechung und Unfruchtbarmachung."

31. And one jurist, Joseph Heimberger, "Sterilisierung und Strafrecht," *MKS* 15 (1924): 154–66.

32. Albert Moll, "Sterilisierung und Verbrechen," *Kriminalistische Monatshefte* 3 (1929): 121–26.

33. Hans Gruhle, "Vererbungsgesetze und Verbrechensbekämpfung," *MKS* 23 (1932): 559–68.

34. Ibid., 559–63.

assume that it was hereditary. Gruhle, however, did not believe that such a disposition existed. It was "grotesquely naive," he wrote, to "infer a criminal disposition, let alone a criminal character, from the fact that someone has come into conflict with the law." Stressing the importance of the working-class milieu for most criminals, Gruhle argued that it was far more plausible to explain a person's criminal behavior as the result of environmental factors rather than "elusive and unprovable" genetic ones. At most a very small minority of criminals were predisposed toward certain types of crime because of congenital character traits; and even in those cases such congenital traits need not be inherited.[35] Gruhle concluded that eugenic measures against criminals lacked all scientific justification:

> We do not know of a criminal character. We know of no character trait that predisposes its carrier toward crime, with the exception of a few very small groups (for instance, confidence men). We do know a number of different characterological structures that predispose their carriers toward crime on the level of the proletariat. About the heritability of these structures we know nothing. . . . The sterilization of any criminal as such—I am not speaking of feeblemindedness [*Schwachsinn*]—cannot be justified in any way, as long as one bases it on eugenic considerations.[36]

As the exception he made for feeblemindedness indicated, Gruhle's opposition to the sterilization of criminals did not reflect a general opposition to eugenic sterilizations. Gruhle supported eugenic sterilizations for mental abnormalities that he considered genetic but opposed the sterilization of criminals *as such* because he saw no evidence for the existence of criminogenic genetic factors.[37]

Gruhle's remark that the sterilization of criminals could not be justified "as long as one bases it on eugenic considerations" was meant to raise the issue of criminals' poor parenting skills as possible grounds for sterilization. Most criminals, Gruhle conceded, did not make good parents. "It is not accidental that so many juvenile delinquents come from alcoholic and criminal families: they came to know waywardness and antisocial behavior as their normal way of life

35. Ibid., 563–66.
36. Ibid., 566.
37. In this respect, Gruhle was in agreement with Lange's proposal for eugenic screenings of criminals. But although Gruhle believed that a substantial portion of criminals were feebleminded, he insisted that very few cases of feeblemindedness were genetic and concluded that eugenic sterilizations for feeblemindedness were rarely justified. See Hans Gruhle, "Schwachsinn, Verbrechen und Sterilisation," *ZStW* 52 (1932): 424–32.

from their earliest youth." Unlike the demand that criminals be sterilized for eugenic reasons, Gruhle noted, a proposal to sterilize those incapable of raising children was at least logically consistent. But Gruhle added two important reservations. First, this justification of sterilization in terms of parenting must not be conflated with the eugenic justification. Second, if a person's incapacity to raise children was to be sufficient grounds for sterilization, then this policy would have to be applied to everyone regardless of social status.[38] Although Gruhle did not explicitly take a position, the way in which he made this point suggested that he did not endorse such a policy: "Will people have the courage also to sterilize a severely hysterical woman unsuited for child rearing who comes from a good family? Will it suffice in the future merely to prove unfitness for child rearing in order for sterilization to be authorized? Is anyone ready to take the responsibility for the demographic, legal-philosophical, and other social consequences?"[39]

Weimar Bureaucrats and Politicians Respond, 1923–1933

The sterilization debate taking place in the medical community also affected Weimar's political decision makers. Since Boeters had originally presented his sterilization proposal as a memorandum to the Saxon government, the first official reaction came from the government in Dresden. Although Boeters's relentless publicity campaign eventually soured his relations with the authorities, the Saxon government initially treated his memorandum as a serious proposal, and in the fall of 1923 the Saxon Department of Public Health (Landesgesundheitsamt) solicited two expert opinions on the sterilization question and set up a special commission to study Boeters's proposals.[40]

Regarding the sterilization of criminals, the medical expert opinion by the Saxon psychiatrist L. Stemmler displayed the familiar features of the pro-sterilization argument. Although it had "not so far been possible to prove the hereditary transmission of criminal psychological dispositions, neither statistically nor by demonstrating a specific mode of hereditary transmission," the report insisted that it was nevertheless a "recognized fact that certain general psychological traits . . . that underlie antisocial tendencies are by their nature

38. Gruhle, "Vererbungsgesetze und Verbrechensbekämpfung," 567.
39. Ibid., 568.
40. F. A. Weber, "Die Unfruchtbarmachung Geisteskranker, Schwachsinniger und Verbrecher aus Anlage," *Zeitschrift für ärztliche Fortbildung* 22, no. 5 (1 March 1925): 152–55; Müller, *Sterilisation und Gesetzgebung*, 68–69; Weindling, *Health, Race and German Politics*, 389–91.

heritable" and that "there is a general connection between heredity and crime." These "facts," the report argued, justified the sterilization of violent criminals and sex offenders on a case-by-case basis if there was sufficient evidence of *erbliche Belastung*, that is, a high concentration of abnormal traits in the criminal's family. While the report recommended that prison doctors encourage such criminals to agree to voluntary sterilization for the time being, it also proposed that the new penal code should provide for the compulsory sterilization of criminals.[41]

Based on this report, in May 1924 the special commission of the Saxon Department of Public Health recommended the voluntary sterilization of persons with a variety of mental conditions, sex offenders, and "especially serious violent habitual criminals." Since most legal experts agreed that sterilizations, except those necessitated by medical reasons, were illegal under current law because they were legally considered bodily injuries (*Körperverletzung*), the commission proposed that the penal code's article on bodily injury be amended to exempt from punishment the voluntary eugenic sterilization of persons "who suffer or have suffered from a mental illness . . . or from a severe criminal disposition on which they have acted."[42] The Saxon Ministries of the Interior and of Justice accepted these recommendations and in July 1924 forwarded them to the Reich Justice Ministry with the request that it consider changing the penal code so as to legalize voluntary eugenic sterilizations of the mentally ill and "hereditary criminals" (*Anlageverbrecher*). Since this request involved a matter of public health, the Reich Justice Ministry asked the Reich Interior Ministry for its opinion on eugenic sterilization. The response of the Interior Ministry indicates that its bureaucrats were skeptical of current genetic research. Even though sterilization was practiced in America, they responded, it was not advisable to take official action on this issue "until the resolution of questions in genetic research." After this response, the Reich Ministry of Justice decided not to pursue the matter, and the proposal was shelved.[43]

Within less than four years, the Reich Ministry of Justice was faced with a similar proposal when the sterilization issue surfaced during the deliberations

41. Stemmler, "Die Unfruchtbarmachung Geisteskranker," 459–62. See also L. Stemmler, "Der Stand der Frage der Sterilisierung Minderwertiger," *Archiv für soziale Hygiene und Demographie* N.F. 1 (1925–26): 209–18.

42. The findings of the commission were reported in Weber, "Die Unfruchtbarmachung Geisteskranker"; Jenny Blasbalg, "Ausländische und deutsche Gesetze und Gesetzentwürfe über Unfruchtbarmachung," *ZStW* 52 (1932): 493; Müller, *Sterilisation und Gesetzgebung*, 68–69.

43. Saxon Ministries of Justice and Interior to RJM, 30 March 1925, Rep. 30.01, file 6094, p. 17, BA Abt. Potsdam; internal RJM memorandum, dated 1 February 1928, ibid., p. 24.

of the Reichstag committee in charge of the revision of the penal code in 1928–29. The new draft code under consideration by the committee provided for the indefinite "preventive detention" (*Sicherungsverwahrung*) of "dangerous habitual criminals," which would last until a court decided to release them.[44] In this context, in October 1928, several members of the Reichstag committee on penal reform, including the representatives of the conservative, Catholic Bavarian People's Party (BVP) and the two liberal parties, the German Democratic Party (DDP) and the German People's Party (DVP), introduced a motion to insert the provision that "the court may agree [to release a prisoner from preventive detention] especially if the detainee has undergone sterilization." The authors of the motion, who included former justice minister Erich Emminger (BVP), stressed that they called for voluntary rather than compulsory sterilization and justified their proposal by reference to the recent eugenic literature, the American sterilization laws, and studies showing a high incidence of "abnormalities" and criminality among the parents of juvenile delinquents.[45]

The representatives of the Reich Ministry of Justice on the Reichstag penal reform committee opposed this motion with three arguments: it was misguided to make sterilization a condition for release from preventive detention because the operation did not make the criminal any less dangerous; the criminal's consent under these circumstances could not be considered truly voluntary, so that the provision would actually introduce a veiled form of compulsory sterilization; finally, the current state of genetic research left many questions unresolved and therefore did not justify eugenic measures. Among the committee members, the representatives of the Catholic Center Party and the Communist Party concurred with the government in opposing the motion, and the DDP and BVP signatories of the motion changed their minds and withdrew their support. The representative of the conservative German National People's Party (DNVP) remained undecided. Only the Social Democratic (SPD) deputies supported the liberal DVP's motion with the remarkable argument that even though they agreed that sterilization really had no place as a condition of release from preventive detention, they would support the motion to signal their party's general support for eugenics. In the end, the committee decided to refer the

---

44. Articles 59–62, *Entwurf eines Allgemeinen Deutschen Strafgesetzbuchs*, dated 14 May 1927, *Verhandlungen des Reichstags*, 3. Wahlperiode (1924–27), Drucksache Nr. 3390. "Preventive detention" was unlimited but was to take place in renewable three-year terms.

45. *Verhandlungen des Reichstags*, 4. Wahlperiode (1928), 21. Ausschuß (Reichsstrafgesetzbuch), 14. Sitzung (30 October 1928), 9–11; see also Blasbalg, "Ausländische und deutsche Gesetze," 494–96; Erwin Höpler, "Sterilisierung und Strafrecht," *ARGB* 25 (1931): 208–10.

matter to a subcommittee, which never reported back because the legislative session ended prematurely when the Reichstag was dissolved and early elections were called in 1930.[46]

The fact that the 1928 motion was supported by the liberal DVP and the Social Democrats demonstrates that eugenics was by no means only a right-wing policy.[47] As if to confirm this point, it was the Social Democrats who introduced the next motion for the sterilization of criminals when another Reichstag committee worked on the revision of the penal code in early 1931. This time the Social-Democratic motion proposed that the draft code's "rehabilitative and preventive measures"[48] should be broadened to include the voluntary sterilization of habitual criminals. "A habitual criminal who poses a danger to public safety," the proposed article read, "can be sterilized with his consent if, according to a medical expert, there is a danger that his bad genetic characteristics [*schlechte Erbanlagen*] will reappear among his progeny." The Social Democrats justified their 1931 motion with the same references to the eugenic literature and U.S. sterilization laws that had been invoked in favor of the 1928 motion. In addition, however, they claimed that genetic research had made significant progress since 1928: "Two years ago, the problem of sterilization was described as not yet ripe for a decision. In the meantime the criminal-biological research institutes have discovered more material, and there is no doubt anymore that bad genetic traits [*schlechtes Erbgut*] create a disposition to commit crimes." Nevertheless, the Social Democrats apparently believed that genetic research was not advanced enough to justify compulsory sterilization and sought to make their proposal more appealing by surrounding it with several safeguards: sterilization would be limited to habitual criminals and would require the criminal's consent and a medical opinion.[49]

46. *Verhandlungen des Reichstags*, 4. Wahlperiode (1928), 21. Ausschuß (Reichsstrafgesetzbuch), 14. Sitzung (30 October 1928), 9–12, and 15. Sitzung (31 October 1928), 1–6.

47. On SPD support for eugenics, see Michael Schwartz, *Sozialistische Eugenik: Eugenische Sozialtechnologien in Debatten und Politik der deutschen Sozialdemokratie, 1890–1933* (Bonn: Dietz, 1995), esp. 271–74, 293–311. On SPD attitudes toward criminal biology, see Schwartz, "Kriminalbiologie und Strafrechtsreform: Die 'erbkranken Gewohnheitsverbrecher' im Visier der Weimarer Sozialdemokratie," in *Kriminalbiologie*, ed. Justizministerium des Landes Nordrhein-Westfalen (Düsseldorf, 1997), 13–68, which appeared after this manuscript was virtually finished.

48. Articles 55–64, "Entwurf eines Allgemeinen Deutschen Strafgesetzbuchs," *Verhandlungen des Reichstags*, 5. Wahlperiode (1930), Drucksache Nr. 395 (6 Dec. 1930). The proposed measures included detention in mental hospitals, workhouses, and detoxification centers and indefinite detention for habitual criminals.

49. *Verhandlungen des Reichstags*, 5. Wahlperiode (1930), 18. Ausschuß (Strafgesetzbuch),

Only the Nazi Party supported the Social-Democratic motion of 1931, whereas the representatives of all other parties on the Reichstag penal reform committee—including liberals (DVP, Staatspartei), conservatives, communists, Center Party, and BVP—opposed it. At least in part, this opposition was the result of a changed assessment of recent genetic research. Former justice minister Emminger of the Bavarian People's Party, who had cosponsored the 1928 sterilization motion,[50] reported that he had carefully followed publications in human genetics and eugenics since that time and had concluded that "genetic research on humans is only in its very early stages and will need generations to arrive at reliable results." After a closer look at the research had turned him into a skeptic, Emminger, like the Center Party deputies, opposed any form of sterilization, whether voluntary or compulsory.[51]

The committee's deliberations on the 1931 SPD motion were complicated by the fact that the draft penal code under discussion in 1931 already included a revised article on bodily injury (scheduled for discussion at a later date) that legalized voluntary eugenic sterilizations. While Emminger (BVP) and the Center Party deputies opposed this change, the other members of the committee—liberals, conservatives, and communists—supported the legalization of voluntary sterilization. The SPD motion therefore presented them with the question of whether to endorse an additional provision for the voluntary sterilization of criminals in the penal code's section on "preventive measures," and all of them decided that such a provision was both unnecessary and inappropriate.[52]

Most interesting was the position of the Reich Justice Ministry, which signified a major reversal. Both in its response to the Saxon government proposal of 1924 and in the 1928 deliberations of the Reichstag committee, the ministry had opposed the legalization of sterilization in any form with the argument that current genetic research failed to make a conclusive case for eugenic sterilization. Now, three years later, in 1931, the Justice Ministry continued to oppose compulsory sterilization but changed its position on voluntary sterilization. In response to the SPD motion, the Justice Ministry's representative told the committee that his ministry supported the proposed change in the definition of

---

11. Sitzung (6 Feb. 1931), 6–7; see also Blasbalg, "Ausländische und deutsche Gesetze und Gesetzentwürfe über Unfruchtbarmachung," 494–96; Höpler, "Sterilisierung und Strafrecht," 208–10.

50. In the course of the 1928 deliberations Emminger had withdrawn his signature from the motion because he had come to believe that sterilization, in men at least, could be reversed through another surgical procedure.

51. *Verhandlungen des Reichstags*, 5. Wahlperiode (1930), 18. Ausschuß (Strafgesetzbuch), 11. Sitzung (6 Feb. 1931), 6–7, 11–12.

52. Ibid., 11. Sitzung (6 Feb. 1931), 6–12, and 12. Sitzung (11 Feb. 1931), 1–3.

bodily injury that would legalize voluntary sterilization. On the motion to include the voluntary sterilization of criminals among the penal code's "protective measures," the ministry took a neutral position. Far from its earlier worry that such a provision might bring undue pressure to bear on prisoners, in 1931 the ministry's only concern was that it not be applied too narrowly.[53]

Opposed by everyone except the Nazis and the Justice Ministry, the motion was doomed to failure and was therefore withdrawn by its SPD sponsors. Further discussion on the legalization of voluntary sterilization was postponed until the discussion of the penal code's article on bodily injury, which took place in January 1932.[54] Over the objections of the Center Party and BVP, the majority of SPD and liberals voted to amend the article on bodily injury at that time.[55] The new article provided that consensual bodily injuries were illegal only if they violated public morals, a clause meant to legalize voluntary *eugenic* sterilizations but not sterilizations for contraceptive purposes.[56] The committee's work on the reform of the penal code was soon terminated by the 1932 Reichstag elections and the collapse of the Weimar Republic. Although the planned general reform of the penal code failed, the amended article on bodily injury was later passed into law by the Nazis by special legislation in the spring of 1933.

Even though the 1931 motion for the sterilization of criminals was defeated, its discussion in the Reichstag committee provides a valuable picture of party-political and official attitudes toward the sterilization of criminals at the end of the Weimar Republic. While there was widespread support for legalizing voluntary eugenic sterilization by reforming the article on bodily injury, only Social Democrats and Nazis supported the motion to include a special provision for the sterilization of habitual criminals in the penal code. The overwhelming majority, including communists, liberals, Catholics, and conservatives, rejected the introduction of sterilization measures specifically directed at criminals. The reasons for this position varied. The Center Party opposed all sterilizations largely for religious reasons. Others, including former justice minister Em-

53. Ibid., 11. Sitzung (6 Feb. 1931), 7–10, and 12. Sitzung (11 Feb. 1931), 1.

54. Ibid., 12. Sitzung (11 Feb. 1931), 3.

55. KPD, NSDAP, and DNVP had left the Reichstag committee by this time. In voting for the amendment in 1932 Chairman Wilhelm Kahl (DVP) had changed his mind. In 1925 he had opposed a similar amendment, proposed by the eugenicist Grotjahn, saying that he "could never allow the eugenic principle to be smuggled into penal law" (Müller, *Sterilisation und Gesetzgebung*, 73).

56. Ernst Rosenfeld, "Fünf Forderungen an die rechtliche Regelung der Sterilisation," *MKBG* 4 (1933): 261; remarks by Dr. Schäfer (RJM), ibid., 272–73; Bock, *Zwangssterilisation*, 55.

minger, had taken a closer look at the medical literature and found that the current state of genetic research simply did not justify sterilization. Some politicians, such as the liberal committee chairman Wilhelm Kahl (DVP) had formal, legal objections to the inclusion of voluntary sterilization among compulsory penal measures, whereas the communists feared that even a provision for "voluntary" sterilization of criminals might expose prisoners to undue pressure.[57] Although their reasons varied, a clear political majority refused to make laws that would make criminal behavior a criterion for sterilization.

If one compares the attitude of Weimar politicians and judicial officials toward sterilization with that of the psychiatrists discussed in the previous section, two things stand out. By 1931, the psychiatric profession's overwhelming support for voluntary eugenic sterilization in general had clearly won over the majority of political parties and even the Ministry of Justice, which had remained extremely skeptical through the late 1920s. Psychiatric proposals for the sterilization of *criminals*, however, were met with skepticism and rejected by most political parties. Even more remarkably, this skepticism seems to have increased in the later Weimar years, since several parties—including the liberal DDP and DVP as well as the Catholic BVP—who had supported a motion for the sterilization of criminals in 1928 rejected such a proposal in 1931. In short, even as most political parties came to support the legalization of voluntary eugenic sterilization, they became equally convinced that sterilization measures targeting criminals were not warranted. Although the idea of eugenics was conquering the political arena, the connection between genetics and crime remained too weak to justify the sterilization of criminals. This finding strongly suggests that the complexities of criminal-biological research discussed in previous chapters were successfully conveyed to a larger, nonspecialist audience.

The same dichotomy of support for eugenics in general but not for the sterilization of criminals was evident in the official draft for a sterilization law that was prepared by the Prussian Health Council (Landesgesundheitsrat) in the summer of 1932. By 1932, the advocates of eugenics were using the economic depression to lend greater urgency to their demands. At a time of severe government cutbacks, the argument that eugenic sterilizations would reduce the number of the mentally ill in state institutions undoubtedly increased support for sterilization.[58] Furthermore, it was now clear that the comprehensive reform of the penal code, which seemed to be moving closer to parliamen-

57. *Verhandlungen des Reichstags*, 5. Wahlperiode (1930), 18. Ausschuß (Strafgesetzbuch), 11. Sitzung (6 Feb. 1931), 11–12, and 12. Sitzung (11 Feb. 1931), 2–3.

58. For an example of the economic-fiscal argument, see the pro-eugenics motion of 20 January 1932 in the Prussian Staatsrat, quoted in Müller, *Sterilisation und Gesetzgebung*, 93.

tary passage in 1928–31, would be delayed indefinitely. The expectation that voluntary sterilization would be legalized through a general reform of the penal code had therefore vanished, and supporters of sterilization had to consider special legislation: either a law revising the penal code's article on bodily injury in a way that would legalize voluntary eugenic sterilization,[59] or a special "sterilization law" that would authorize sterilization for specific medical conditions. It was to consider such legislation that the Prussian Health Council held a conference on eugenics in the summer of 1932.[60]

At this conference the prominent Berlin law professor and legal reformer Eduard Kohlrausch argued that a special sterilization law was preferable to merely revising the penal code's article on bodily injury because such a law could enumerate specific illnesses and establish a standard administrative procedure for determining what qualified as a eugenic sterilization. He also offered an interesting analysis of the historical and political context of eugenic legislation. If current medical knowledge had been available, the eighteenth-century police state would have legalized *eugenic* sterilization regardless of consent. Nineteenth-century liberals, by contrast, would have decriminalized any consensual sterilization, whether it served eugenic purposes or not. The present "social state," which sought to balance individual and social needs, Kohlrausch argued, would have to require both consent and eugenic purpose as conditions for legalizing sterilization.[61] In accordance with Kohlrausch's recommendations, a special commission of the Prussian Health Council, which included Kohlrausch as well as Johannes Lange, drafted a special sterilization law, whose first article provided that "a person who suffers from hereditary mental illness, hereditary feeblemindedness [*Geistesschwäche*], hereditary epilepsy or another hereditary illness, or who is a carrier of pathological genetic traits, can be sterilized if the person consents and if according to medical science serious physical or mental genetic defects are to be expected among the person's progeny."[62]

59. The proposed change in the article on bodily injury (as contained in the 1930 draft for the penal code) would have legalized only voluntary *eugenic* sterilization; voluntary sterilizations for other reasons would have remained illegal. This was achieved by providing that consensual bodily injuries were still punishable if they violated "public morals" (*die guten Sitten*).

60. "Die Eugenik im Dienste der Volkswohlfahrt: Bericht über die Verhandlungen eines zusammengesetzten Ausschusses des Preußischen Landesgesundheitsrates vom 2. Juli 1932," *Veröffentlichungen aus dem Gebiete der Medizinalverwaltung* 38, no. 5 (1932): 631–740; Müller, *Sterilisation und Gesetzgebung*, 95–99.

61. "Die Eugenik im Dienste der Volkswohlfahrt," 670–82.

62. Ibid., 737.

Although consent was required, the formulation shows that the draft legalized eugenic sterilizations on a fairly extensive scale. It did not, however, include any provisions for the sterilization of criminals. This was all the more remarkable because many foreign sterilization laws (including American laws) that clearly served as models did mention antisocial behavior and criminals.[63] By contrast, the German drafting commission had, as one of its members pointed out, consciously decided to omit any mention of criminals and to define the target group strictly in medical-eugenic terms.[64] To be sure, both Kohlrausch and Lange indicated that the medical criteria of the sterilization law would undoubtedly apply to some criminals.[65] But once again, the scientific evidence on the connection between genetics and crime was judged insufficient to justify sterilization measures targeted at criminals.

During the fall of 1932 the Prussian Health Council's draft for a national sterilization law received public support from Germany's main physicians' associations. In November 1932, several physicians' representatives even asked the government to issue a sterilization law by emergency decree. By December 1932, the Reich Ministry of the Interior was seriously considering introducing such a law.[66]

The Nazi Sterilization Law of July 1933

On 30 January 1933, the Nazi seizure of power created an entirely new political situation. Past pronouncements by Hitler and other Nazis suggested that eugenics would be a matter of high priority for the new government. While most Weimar parties had come to support voluntary sterilization, the Nazi Party and the Nazi Physicians' League had long been pressing for compulsory eugenic sterilization.[67] In March 1933 the new Nazi government began preparing a sterilization law based on the Prussian draft.[68] In May 1933, even before the new

63. Reilly, *Surgical Solution*, 41–55; Proctor, *Racial Hygiene*, 97–101.

64. A. Ostermann, "Die Eugenik im Dienste der Volkswohlfahrt," *Eugenik* 2 (1932): 252, quoted in Müller, *Sterilisation und Gesetzgebung*, 99.

65. "Die Eugenik im Dienste der Volkswohlfahrt," *Veröffentlichungen aus dem Gebiete der Medizinalverwaltung* 38, no. 5 (1932): 667, 669, 681.

66. Müller, *Sterilisation und Gesetzgebung*, 101–3; Bock, *Zwangssterilisation*, 80–81.

67. Bock, *Zwangssterilisation*, 23–27. On the Nazi Physicians' League, see Michael Kater, *Doctors under Hitler* (Chapel Hill: University of North Carolina Press, 1989), 63–68; Proctor, *Racial Hygiene*, 65–74.

68. On the origins of the Nazi sterilization law, see Bock, *Zwangssterilisation*, 80–94; Müller, *Sterilisation und Gesetzgebung*, 105–22; Jeremy Noakes, "Nazism and Eugenics: The Background to the Nazi Sterilization Law of 14 July 1933," in *Ideas into Politics*, ed. R. J. Bullen,

draft for a sterilization law was finished, the government enacted a law amending the penal code that included the changes in the article on bodily injury that
had been recommended by the Reichstag committee on penal reform in early
1932. By providing that consensual bodily injuries were legal unless they violated public morals, this amendment legalized voluntary eugenic sterilizations,
while keeping voluntary sterilizations for contraceptive purposes illegal.[69]

In the meantime, preparations for a special sterilization law were proceeding
apace under the direction of Dr. Arthur Gütt, who became chief of the department of medical affairs (*Medizinalreferent*) in the Reich Ministry of the Interior
on 1 May 1933. Gütt was an outsider in the ministerial bureaucracy and the
eugenics movement. Until his appointment, he had been a district medical officer (*Kreisarzt*) in a town near Hamburg. But he had been active in right-wing
politics in the early 1920s, had joined the Nazi Party in September 1932, and
had, in February 1933, sent a memorandum on eugenic policy to Dr. Leonardo
Conti, the Berlin deputy of the Nazi Physicians' League and commissioner for
medical affairs in Prussia.[70] Conti evidently liked the memorandum and helped
to arrange for Gütt's appointment to his new post, which made Gütt coordina-
tor of Nazi eugenic policy.[71]

Gütt moved quickly and prepared a new draft for a sterilization law over the
course of May and June 1933. There is considerable evidence that in preparing
his draft Gütt called on the help of Ernst Rüdin, the director of the Deutsche
Forschungsanstalt für Psychiatrie, which sponsored Lange's and Stumpfl's
criminal-biological research and housed the Central Record Office of Bavaria's
Criminal-Biological Service. One of the major figures in the German eugenics

---

H. Pogge von Strandmann, and A. B. Polonsky (London: Croom Helm, 1984), 75–94; Weingart, Kroll, and Bayertz, *Rasse, Blut und Gene*, 464–80; Weindling, *Health, Race and German
Politics*, 522–25; Proctor, *Racial Hygiene*, 95–104.

69. Strafgesetzbuch, article 226a. See remarks by Dr. Schäfer (RJM) in *MKBG* 4 (1933):
272–73; Bock, *Zwangssterilisation*, 81–83.

70. On Conti, see Kater, *Doctors under Hitler*, 64–65.

71. On Gütt and his appointment, see Alfred Ploetz, "Lebensbild Arthur Gütts," *ARGB* 30
(1936): 279–83; Alfred Ploetz and Ernst Rüdin, "Ministerialdirektor Dr. Arthur Gütt 5 Jahre
Leiter der Abteilung für Volksgesundheit im Reichsministerium des Innern," *ARGB* 33
(1939): 88; Lemme, "Fünf Jahre Abteilung Volksgesundheit im Reichsministerium des Innern," ibid., 89–90; Cropp, "Fünf Jahre Abteilung 'Volksgesundheit' des Reichsministeriums
des Innern unter Leitung von Ministerialdirektor Dr. Arthur Gütt," *Der öffentliche Gesundheitsdienst* 4 (1938–39): 869–97; Ernst Rüdin, "Die Bedeutung Arthur Gütt's für die Erb- und
Rassenforschung und deren praktische Anwendung," *Der öffentliche Gesundheitsdienst* 4
(1938–39): 897–99; Noakes, "Nazism and Eugenics," 85–86; Weindling, *Health, Race and German Politics*, 523–24; Matthias Weber, *Ernst Rüdin: Eine kritische Biographie* (Berlin: Springer,
1993), 181.

movement, Rüdin was also among the most radical. Already during the Wei-mar years he had suggested that voluntary sterilization was only a step toward the ultimate goal of compulsory measures. Although the evidence for Rüdin's collaboration in the earliest stages of drafting the 1933 sterilization law is not conclusive, we do know that he helped to shape the law at a meeting of the Interior Ministry's board of experts (Sachverständigenbeirat) on "Population and Racial Policy" to whom Gütt presented his draft in early July 1933.[72]

Since the Enabling Act of March 1933 had transferred the Reichstag's legisla-tive powers to Hitler's cabinet, the final draft of the Law for the Prevention of Genetically Diseased Offspring (Gesetz zur Verhütung erbkranken Nach-wuchses), as the sterilization law was officially called, was presented directly to the cabinet for approval. The cabinet approved the law on 14 July 1933, but in order not to jeopardize Germany's impending concordat with the Catholic church, whose opposition to sterilization was well known, the public announce-ment of the law was postponed until 26 July. It took effect on 1 January 1934.[73]

It is instructive to compare the Nazi sterilization law with the 1932 draft of the Prussian Health Council. In one major respect, the Nazi law was more radical. While the Weimar draft had required the consent of the person to be sterilized, the law of 1933 introduced compulsory sterilization. In other re-spects, however, the Nazi law was more limited. The Weimar draft had autho-rized the sterilization of persons suffering from *any* hereditary illness if "seri-ous physical or mental genetic defects [were] to be expected among the person's progeny." The Nazi law, by contrast, greatly reduced the law's scope by limiting its application to nine illnesses that were specifically enumerated in the law (congenital feeblemindedness, schizophrenia, manic depression, hereditary epi-

---

72. On Rüdin, see Weber, *Ernst Rüdin*; and Dirk Blasius, "Die 'Maskerade des Bösen.' Psychiatrische Forschung in der NS-Zeit," in *Medizin und Gesundheitspolitik in der NS-Zeit,* ed. Norbert Frei (Munich: Oldenbourg, 1991), 271–74. Historians differ on Rüdin's precise role regarding the sterilization law. Weber argues that Rüdin did not participate in drafting the law but only in writing the published commentary (Weber, *Ernst Rüdin*, 181–83). By contrast, Gisela Bock (*Zwangssterilisation*, 84), Paul Weindling (*Health, Race and German Politics*, 524), and Joachim Müller (*Sterilisation und Gesetzgebung*, 106) all maintain that Rüdin participated in drafting the law. Whether or not Rüdin participated in the initial stages of preparation, his prominent role in the Sachverständigenbeirat seems to indicate that he did play a part in drafting the law. See also Blasius, *"Einfache Seelenstörung": Geschichte der deutschen Psychi-atrie, 1800–1945* (Frankfurt: Fischer, 1994), 154–57; Ploetz and Rüdin, "Ministerialdirektor Dr. Arthur Gütt"; Rüdin, "Die Bedeutung Arthur Gütts"; Alfred Ploetz, "Der Sachverstän-digenbeirat für Bevölkerungs- und Rassenpolitik," *ARGB* 27 (1933): 419. On the Sachverstän-digenbeirat, see Weingart, Kroll, and Bayertz, *Rasse, Blut und Gene*, 460–64.

73. Bock, *Zwangssterilisation*, 86–87.

lepsy, Huntington's chorea, hereditary blindness or deafness, serious heredi-tary physical deformities, and severe alcoholism).[74]

Like the Weimar draft, the Nazi sterilization law made no mention of crimi-nals. Although the Nazi seizure of power had allowed Gütt and Rüdin to over-rule Weimar era objections to compulsory sterilization, they had been unable to overcome the serious reservations about sterilization measures targeting crimi-nals. This was not for lack of trying. Although Gütt's initial draft of June 1933 has not survived, other memoranda indicate that this draft included "crimi-nogenic genetic traits" (*Verbrecheranlagen*) among the "hereditary diseases" that were to be subject to the sterilization law.[75] When this draft was circulated to other ministries, however, the Reich Ministry of Justice objected to the inclusion of criminals, arguing that criminals and the "genetically ill" should not be treated in the same law.[76] Gütt interpreted this objection to mean that the inclusion of criminals in a general sterilization law might be seen as giving sterilization a punitive character and agreed to remove any mention of crimi-nals from his draft.[77]

When the final draft of the law was discussed in the cabinet, however, it emerged that Hitler himself was eager to see "habitual criminals" sterilized. Although he apparently accepted the Justice Ministry's objections to including criminals in the sterilization law, Hitler ordered that the public promulgation of the sterilization law include an announcement that the revised penal code would include "provisions for the castration of sex offenders and the steriliza-tion of habitual criminals."[78] Hitler's enthusiasm for the sterilization of crimi-nals, in particular, was not surprising. The support for the sterilization of crimi-nals among Nazi deputies in the Reichstag committee on penal reform in the late Weimar years was not an isolated incident. Always supporting the most

74. *GRR*, 1st ed., 56. For a detailed comparison of the Nazi law and the Weimar draft, see Müller, *Sterilisation und Gesetzgebung*, 106–12.

75. Mention of criminals (later crossed out) in Gütt's draft for "Begründung," Rep. 15.01 (RMI), file 26248, pp. 285–86, BA Potsdam; *GRR*, 2d ed. (Munich, 1936), 64.

76. Letter from RJM to RMI dated 6 July 1933, Rep. 15.01 (RMI), file 26248, p. 249, BA Potsdam.

77. Gütt's draft for "Begründung," Rep. 15.01, file 26248, p. 289, BA Potsdam. The same reasoning for the exclusion of criminals from the sterilization law can be found in *GRR*, 2d ed., 64; "Es geht um die Zukunft unseres Volkes," *Völkischer Beobachter* (27 Feb. 1933), 2, quoted in Christine Makowski, *Eugenik, Sterilisationspolitik, "Euthanasie" und Bevölkerungspolitik in der nationalsozialistischen Parteipresse* (Husum: Matthiesen, 1996), 208; *Presseanweisung* of 19 July 1938, quoted ibid., 208–9.

78. Internal memo on the cabinet meeting by Gütt dated 14 July 1933, Rep. 15.01 (RMI), file 26248, p. 331, BA Potsdam; Bock, *Zwangssterilisation*, 87.

extreme eugenic agenda, prominent Nazis had long demanded the sterilization of criminals. In 1925 Nazi deputies in the Prussian diet had introduced a motion calling for the sterilization of "genetically defective criminals." In 1930 party ideologist Alfred Rosenberg had called for the sterilization of recidivist criminals in his *Mythus des 20. Jahrhunderts* (Myth of the twentieth century), and Hans Frank, head of the Nazi lawyers' association, had demanded that the reproduction of "criminal characters" be stopped.[79]

When Hitler called for provisions on the castration of sex offenders and the sterilization of habitual criminals to be included in the revised penal code, he was unduly optimistic about the prospects for comprehensive penal reform. Plans for a general revision of the penal code quickly became bogged down, and it was decided that new measures against sex offenders and habitual criminals would be introduced in a special law. The preparation of this new Law against Dangerous Habitual Criminals and on Rehabilitative and Preventive Measures (Gesetz gegen gefährliche Gewohnheitsverbrecher und über Maßregeln der Besserung und Sicherung) lay in the hands of the Reich Ministry of Justice. Even though Gütt worked for the Interior Ministry, he insisted on participating in the drafting of the law because he expected that it would implement the eugenic measures against criminals that had been left out of the sterilization law. By October 1933, the Justice Ministry had prepared a draft that provided, among other things, for the castration of dangerous sex offenders and the indefinite detention of habitual criminals but did not mention sterilization. When Gütt met with the responsible department chief from the Ministry of Justice, he made two demands: first, the new Law against Habitual Criminals should provide for the sterilization of "serious criminals" (*Schwerverbrecher*) by making them subject to the procedures of the sterilization law; second, the Justice Ministry should issue an executive order instructing prison authorities to report criminals who appeared to suffer from one of the "hereditary diseases" listed in the sterilization law to the Hereditary Health Courts.[80]

The Justice Ministry official in charge of preparing the law on habitual criminals, Leopold Schäfer, immediately promised to implement the second demand,[81] which was fulfilled in December 1933, when the Ministry of Justice issued a circular requesting that all courts, prosecutors, and prison officials

79. Bock, *Zwangssterilisation*, 24–25.
80. Gütt's minutes of meeting on 10 October 1933, Rep. 15.01 (RMI), file 26249, pp. 101–2, BA Potsdam.
81. Gütt's minutes of meeting on 10 October 1933, Rep. 15.01, file 26249, p. 105, BA Potsdam.

report criminals who might suffer from a "genetic disease" enumerated in the sterilization law to the Hereditary Health Courts for a sterilization hearing.[82] Gütt's request that the Law on Habitual Criminals provide for the sterilization of "serious criminals," however, was turned down. "The whole problem" of sterilization, Schäfer argued, was "still new," and "more experience [had] to be gathered." If, at some point in the future, "the sterilization of serious criminals should prove necessary, this matter should be addressed by amending the [sterilization law]," rather than the Law on Habitual Criminals or any part of the penal code.[83] Since this argument completely contradicted the position that the ministry had taken when it vetoed the inclusion of criminals in the sterilization law on the grounds that criminals and genetically diseased persons should not be treated in the same law, it certainly appears that the Justice Ministry was trying to prevent the sterilization of criminals with whatever arguments seemed opportune.

Gütt went along with the Justice Ministry's arguments because the ministry's declaration that the sterilization of criminals was a matter for the sterilization law rather than the penal code effectively gave him future jurisdiction over this issue. To make sure that the ministry did not change its mind again in the future, Gütt requested and received an official memorandum stating that the sterilization of criminals was a matter for the Ministry of the Interior.[84] In the official commentary accompanying the Law on Habitual Criminals the Ministry of Justice declared that "the task of protecting the nation from the inferior offspring of genetically diseased criminals lies in the area of eugenics, not criminal law. When the question becomes ripe for legislation, it will be addressed not in the penal code, but in an amendment to the Law for the Prevention of Genetically Diseased Offspring."[85]

In the crucial months of legislative activity in 1933 the Reich Ministry of Justice had, then, twice prevailed over Gütt. First, in the passage of the steriliza-

82. Reichsminister der Justiz to Landesjustizverwaltungen, dated 15 December 1933, Rep. 30.01 (RJM), file 5982, pp. 418–19, BA Potsdam; also reprinted in GRR, 1st ed., 175. In response to this circular, the justice ministries of most German states issued executive orders instructing their courts and prisons to report "genetically ill" criminals. See Erlass of Prussian Minister of Justice, dated 23 March 1934, Rep. 30.01 (RJM), file 5982, pp. 422–24, BA Potsdam; other Erlasse, ibid., 425ff.

83. Gütt's minutes of meeting on 10 October 1933, Rep. 15.01, file 26249, p. 103, BA Potsdam.

84. Internal memo by Gütt on meeting of 11 October 1933, Rep. 15.01, file 26249, pp. 97–98, BA Potsdam.

85. Begründung zum Gesetz gegen Gewohnheitsverbrecher, reprinted in GRR, 1st ed., 183.

tion law, and then in the formulation of the law on habitual criminals the Justice Ministry had successfully vetoed provisions for the sterilization of criminals.

Expanding the Definition of Feeblemindedness

Without any special provisions for them, criminals were to be treated the same as anyone else in the implementation of the sterilization law. Only if they suffered from one of the "hereditary diseases" enumerated in the sterilization law could they be sterilized. Criminals currently serving a prison term were at a disadvantage in one respect. Since prison authorities were instructed to report inmates suffering from the hereditary diseases listed in the sterilization law to the Hereditary Health Courts (Erbgesundheitsgerichte), prisoners were potentially subject to a more rigorous eugenic screening than normal citizens, although the shortage of medical personnel in prisons undoubtedly restricted such screenings to a minority of prisoners. If a prisoner's case came before a Hereditary Health Court, however, the court's decision was to be based strictly on the prisoner's medical diagnosis; the prisoner's crimes were not supposed to affect the outcome. Such was the legal situation created by the Justice Ministry's victories.

Even before the sterilization law took effect, however, Gütt and Rüdin sought to undermine the Justice Ministry's victory by reintroducing criminal behavior as a criterion in sterilization proceedings through the back door. Gütt and Rüdin were able to influence the implementation of the law in the Hereditary Health Courts because they coauthored (together with the jurist Falk Ruttke) an annotated edition of the sterilization law that became the standard legal and medical commentary on the law, used by everyone involved in sterilization proceedings. In fact, since Gütt was known to be the main author of the law, on which both Rüdin and Ruttke had collaborated, their commentary had almost official status. While the jurist Ruttke was responsible for the legal sections, Gütt and Rüdin wrote the medical commentary.[86]

Gütt and Rüdin were determined to sterilize as many criminals as possible. Although their commentary acknowledged that "the legislator" had decided not to include provisions for the "sterilization of habitual criminals" in the law, Gütt and Rüdin also indicated that they themselves had "no doubts" about the existence of "hereditary criminal traits" (Verbrecheranlagen).[87] Unfortunately, from their point of view, the psychiatric diagnosis most closely associated with

86. GRR, 1st ed. (1934); 2d ed. (1936).
87. GRR, 1st ed., 6, 215.

criminal behavior—psychopathy—had been omitted from the sterilization law's list of hereditary diseases. Of the nine diagnoses on this list, Gütt and Rüdin regarded "feeblemindedness" (*Schwachsinn*) as the most promising for "preventing the propagation of genetic criminal traits."[88]

Feeblemindedness was by far the most common diagnosis in German sterilization proceedings, accounting for more than half of all sterilizations.[89] The diagnosis of feeblemindedness referred to intellectual defects, which were often divided into three degrees of severity: debility, imbecility, and idiocy.[90] Despite the official claim that the sterilization law included only diseases whose "hereditary transmission" was "sufficiently researched," Gütt and Rüdin admitted that the hereditary transmission of congenital feeblemindedness was "not yet understood in all its details."[91] Nevertheless, both the sterilization law and the Gütt-Rüdin commentary sought to maximize the number of cases of feeblemindedness that would be subject to sterilization. First, the law provided for the sterilization of all persons suffering from "congenital" feeblemindedness. This presumed that congenital feeblemindedness was always hereditary, which was not necessarily the case, since congenital cases could also result from intrauterine or perinatal injuries. Second, since the law did not require that the case of feeblemindedness be "serious," the Gütt-Rüdin commentary insisted that even the slightest degree of feeblemindedness justified sterilization. Finally, and most insidiously, Gütt and Rüdin's commentary established the rule that feeblemindedness should always be considered congenital unless there was "certain proof" that it stemmed from exogenous causes, such as a head injury, thereby shifting the burden of proof to the defendant.[92]

Sterilizing feebleminded criminals would have been within the intent of the law if Gütt and Rüdin had adhered to the traditional medical definition of feeblemindedness. In fact, however, they significantly expanded the disease's definition. According to a long-standing psychiatric consensus, feeblemindedness referred only to defects in intelligence, whereas defects in the emotional-volitional realm of "character" fell under the diagnosis of psychopathy. This understanding of feeblemindedness as an intelligence defect was reflected in the administrative regulations for the implementation of the sterilization law,

88. Ibid., 174; *GRR*, 2d ed., 64.

89. Bock, *Zwangssterilisation*, 303.

90. Oswald Bumke, *Lehrbuch der Geisteskrankheiten*, 3d ed. (Munich: Bergmann, 1929), 188, quoted in Hans Fickert, *Rassenhygienische Verbrechensbekämpfung* (Leipzig: Wiegandt, 1938), 41, which also gives other references confirming this psychiatric consensus.

91. *GRR*, 1st ed., 61, 91.

92. Ibid., 56, 91, 93.

which introduced an intelligence test as a diagnostic tool in determining feeble-mindedness.[93] Abandoning this standard medical definition, Gütt and Rüdin expanded the definition of feeblemindedness to include persons who suffered from "disturbances in emotions, will, drives, [or] ethical sentiments"—even if their intelligence was not significantly retarded. Gütt and Rüdin thus incorporated all the classic symptoms of "psychopathic personalities" into their expanded definition of feeblemindedness. Since such emotional-volitional disturbances could not be detected in an intelligence test, they suggested that such "schematic" methods be supplemented with a more comprehensive examination, including an "examination of character [*Charakterprüfung*], success in school, occupation, and life, [and] behavior toward the legal order."[94] By making "disturbances in ethical sentiments" and "behavior toward the legal order" criteria for the diagnosis of feeblemindedness, Gütt and Rüdin were calling for the sterilization of criminals, regardless of whether a significant intelligence defect was present: "In the cases of many *Debile* [lowest grade of feeblemindedness], who are asocial or antisocial . . . one will therefore be able to recommend sterilization without any reservations, even if they are not inordinately retarded in the development of their intelligence. . . . Thus one will be able to sterilize many psychopaths, hysterics, criminals, prostitutes."[95]

In the second edition of their commentary, which appeared in 1936, Gütt and Rüdin became even bolder by announcing that "partial defects" in any "part of the total personality" qualified as feeblemindedness in the sense of the law and that it was "immaterial" whether "one academic opinion focuses more on the area of the intellect, and the other more on that of character."[96] They also formalized the first edition's general injunction to supplement the intelligence test with other evidence from the person's life by introducing a new diagnostic criterion called *Lebensbewährung*, which could be translated as "test of life" or "proving one's worth in life." This new criterion was supposed to be decisive in "borderline cases," in which the intelligence test revealed only "small deficiencies," and was explained as follows:

> With great probability feeblemindedness is present if the person concerned is unable to earn a living in a regular occupation or to integrate him or herself socially. Such feebleminded persons are conspicuous for the insufficient de-

93. The intelligence test is reproduced ibid., 76–78. See also Proctor, *Racial Hygiene*, 108–12; Michael Burleigh and Wolfgang Wippermann, *The Racial State: Germany, 1933–1945* (Cambridge: Cambridge University Press, 1991), 138–40; Bock, *Zwangssterilisation*, 313–20.
94. *GRR*, 1st ed., 94.
95. Ibid.
96. *GRR*, 2d ed., 119–20.

velopment and malformation of their moral notions and the inability to develop a proper understanding of the order of human society. Even if defects of intelligence in the usual sense can rarely be detected . . . such persons are nevertheless feebleminded.[97]

Gütt and Rüdin's expanded definition of feeblemindedness provoked considerable controversy in the medical and legal literature. A few commentators defended their definition without any reservations. Thus O. Hochreuther, presiding judge of the Hereditary Health Court in Freiburg, argued that purely "moral-ethical" defects must be recognized as feeblemindedness. Likewise, Fred Dubitscher, an official in the Reichsgesundheitsamt (Reich Health Office), saw no reason why "defects in ethical value systems" should be treated differently from "qualitatively equivalent personality defects" that were primarily intellectual.[98] Other commentators acknowledged that Gütt and Rüdin had modified the traditional definition of feeblemindedness, but they endorsed the change. This position was most clearly articulated by Hans Luxenburger in a review of the Gütt-Rüdin commentary, in which he wrote:

Fundamentally new is that certain cases of asocial and antisocial psychopathies . . . can be categorized as congenital feeblemindedness, even if no real intellectual defect . . . is present. . . . From a theoretical standpoint, [this position] is not beyond criticism, because it is likely to undermine the nosologically fixed concept of feeblemindedness. . . . It will therefore be advisable to apply it only in the context of implementing the sterilization law. Here, however, it is perfectly appropriate as an interim solution . . . because it seems unacceptable to sterilize mild cases of manic depression, while allowing unstable [*haltlose*] and impulsive antisocial psychopaths to procreate, and . . . we are not yet in a position to include these psychopaths . . . in the [sterilization] law. . . . Not to take advantage of the possibility of filling this . . . gap in the law out of formal considerations would go against a healthy, rational eugenic attitude. Therefore I endorse the new interpretation as a eugenicist, even though it violates my psychiatric views.[99]

97. Ibid., 125.

98. O. Hochreuther, "Das Gesetz zur Verhütung erbkranken Nachwuchses: Anregungen zur Änderung der bestehenden Vorschriften," *JW* 64 (1935): 1382–83; Fred Dubitscher, "Asozialität und Unfruchtbarmachung: Aus dem Material des Reichsgesundheitsamtes," *MKBG* 5 (1937): 107. See also Dubitscher, "Dummheit oder Schwachsinn?" *Der Erbarzt* 1 (1935): 187–90.

99. Hans Luxenburger, review of *GRR* (2d ed., 1936), in *ARGB* 30 (1936): 422–23; for a similar admission, see Robert Müller, "Zum Schwachsinnsbegriff in der Praxis der Erbgesundheitsgerichte," *Der Erbarzt* 5 (1938): 149.

The passage just quoted is remarkable for explaining the expansion of the definition of feeblemindedness with unusual candor. Since Luxenburger was a senior researcher at the Deutsche Forschungsanstalt für Psychiatrie, where Rüdin was his boss, he undoubtedly felt some pressure to give Rüdin's book a positive review. But if Luxenburger had disagreed with Rüdin's expanded definition of feeblemindedness, he could have simply glossed over this aspect of the book.[100] While Gütt and Rüdin presented their definition of feeblemindedness as if it represented the scientific consensus, Luxenburger was too good a scientist to let this pass. He therefore acknowledged, first, that the Gütt-Rüdin commentary had modified the definition of feeblemindedness to include conditions generally classified as psychopathies; second, that this change was motivated not by scientific reasons but by a eugenic agenda, namely, to allow the sterilization of "asocials" and criminals; and finally, that Gütt and Rüdin's expanded definition of feeblemindedness amounted to filling a "gap" in the sterilization law, so that doctors were not just enforcing the law but expanding its reach in a kind of eugenic vigilantism.

Other commentators disagreed with Gütt and Rüdin's definition of feeblemindedness. Hans Gruhle, for instance, criticized the attempt to expand the notion of feeblemindedness "to everything that is mentally abnormal, and especially to asocial behavior."[101] Even Friedrich Stumpfl, who was sympathetic to Rüdin's eugenic agenda and worked under Rüdin in Munich, insisted in a 1936 article on "criminal psychopaths" that feeblemindedness referred only to mental disorders whose "core defect concerned the intellect." Since the core defect of amoral psychopaths was not an intelligence defect, he argued, persons with moral defects were not feebleminded. In a 1939 article, he explicitly rejected "the attempt to squeeze psychopaths into the [category of] feeblemindedness."[102]

The most sustained criticism of Gütt and Rüdin's definition of feeblemindedness, however, came from a jurist.[103] In a 1938 legal dissertation on the use of

100. There is a remote possibility that Luxenburger disagreed with Rüdin's position but pretended to endorse it in order to expose that Rüdin had twisted the accepted definition of feeblemindedness. But this is unlikely both because the arguments for Rüdin's expanded definition are advanced so forcefully and because Luxenburger himself had called for the sterilization of criminal psychopaths before 1933. See Luxenburger, "Psychiatrische Erbprognose"; "Zur Frage der Schwangerschaftsunterbrechung"; "Zur Frage der Zwangssterilisierung."

101. Hans Gruhle, "Forensische Psychiatrie und Kriminalpsychologie der Jahre 1938 und 1939," *AZP* 119 (1942): 332–33.

102. Friedrich Stumpfl, "Kriminelle Psychopathen: Ein kritischer Beitrag zur Frage des 'moralischen Schwachsinns,'" *Der Erbarzt* 3 (1936): 134; "Psychopathenforschung unter dem Gesichtspunkt der Erbbiologie, 1937–1939," *FNPG* 11 (1939): 415.

103. The attacks of *Reichsärzteführer* (head of the Nazi doctors' association) Gerhard Wag-

eugenics to combat crime, Hans Fickert examined the question of the extent to which the sterilization law was designed to target criminals. After taking a close look at the law and the medical literature, he concluded that Gütt and Rüdin's inclusion of emotional, ethical, and "character" defects in their definition of feeblemindedness was wrong on three counts: it deviated from the standard medical definition, which referred only to intelligence defects; it contradicted the intentions of the legislator, who had purposely omitted criminal behavior and psychopathy from the sterilization law; and finally, it contradicted other statements by Rüdin, in which he himself acknowledged the omission of criminals in the present law and called for the inclusion of asocial and criminal psychopaths through an amendment to the sterilization law.[104]

Fickert's criticism of Gütt and Rüdin's commentary on the sterilization law clearly had significant backing because both Franz Exner and Friedrich Stumpfl were explicitly thanked in the preface. What is more, Exner agreed to publish Fickert's study in his Kriminalistische Abhandlungen, the major publication series in criminology. Given the importance of the topic, it seems highly unlikely that Exner would have done this if he had disagreed with Fickert's main argument.

It was probably not an accident that the most sustained criticism of Gütt and Rüdin's expanded definition of feeblemindedness came from a jurist rather than a doctor. For Gütt's and Rüdin's high status in the German medical community surely deterred many doctors from publicly criticizing them. But there was another reason as well. As the Ministry of Justice's opposition to Gütt showed, jurists tended to be more critical of the eugenic agenda, especially as it concerned criminals. Taking a critical view of the current state of criminal-biological research, they were unwilling to implement eugenic measures against criminals. Furthermore, the jurist Fickert emphasized the need to respect the rule of law by sticking to the actual provisions of the sterilization law, while the psychiatrist Luxenburger advocated filling "gaps" in the law by adapting medical categories to a eugenic agenda.

Feeblemindedness and Crime in the Sterilization Courts

The expanded definition of feeblemindedness that Gütt and Rüdin expounded in their semiofficial commentary on the sterilization law had a profound effect on the decisions of the approximately two hundred Hereditary Health Courts

---

ner on Gütt and Rüdin's interpretation of feeblemindedness (see Weingart, Kroll, and Bayertz, *Rasse, Blut und Gene*, 472) had nothing to do with the point at issue here, that is, the extension of the diagnosis to cases of asocial or criminal behavior.

104. Fickert, *Rassenhygienische Verbrechensbekämpfung*, 41–44, 48–50.

(Erbgesundheitsgerichte) that were charged with the law's implementation. Sterilization proceedings generally conformed to the following pattern. All medical doctors had to report cases of the hereditary diseases enumerated in the sterilization law among their patients; the local public health officer (*Kreisarzt, Amtsarzt*) or, in the case of inmates, the director of the hospital, asylum, or prison would then file a motion for sterilization with the region's Hereditary Health Court. Composed of two medical doctors and a jurist as presiding judge, this court ruled on whether a particular case met the criteria for one of the hereditary diseases included in the sterilization law. If so, it ordered the person's sterilization. Decisions could be appealed to one of thirty-one Superior Hereditary Health Courts (Erbgesundheitsobergerichte), whose decisions were final in their district, since there was no national "supreme court" for hereditary health. The Hereditary Health Courts started functioning when the sterilization law took effect on 1 January 1934.[105]

From the very beginning, many Hereditary Health Courts followed Gütt and Rüdin in extending the diagnosis of feeblemindedness to include supposed "ethical defects." Even in the absence of significant intellectual defects, an "inability to integrate oneself socially" and "asocial" or criminal acts were frequently cited as proof of feeblemindedness. Some courts even referred to such cases by the term "moral feeblemindedness" (*moralischer Schwachsinn*), which had virtually disappeared from the German psychiatric literature soon after the turn of the century.[106] An unmarried day laborer in his early thirties, for instance, whose performance on the intelligence test was "not especially poor" but who had been convicted of theft in his youth and had recently killed another man during an altercation in a bar, was sterilized because the court regarded his lifelong pattern

---

105. On the functioning of Erbgesundheitsgerichte, see Bock, *Zwangssterilisation*, 182–208, esp. 184; Proctor, *Racial Hygiene*, 101–4. The figures for the number of courts are for 1935 (Proctor, 102, n. 33).

106. For such a ruling, see EOG Danzig, 2 W E 51/34, Beschluss of 16 January 1935, reported in *JW* 64 (1935): 712. The frequency of such rulings among Heredity Health Courts is attested in EOG Kiel, W Erb 79/34, Beschluss of 14 February 1935, reported in *JW* 64 (1935): 2144. See also Fickert, *Rassenhygienische Verbrechensbekämpfung*, 43–47; Bock, *Zwangssterilisation*, 319–26; Edmund Mezger, "Inwieweit werden durch Sterilisierungsmassnahmen Asoziale erfasst? Dargelegt anhand bayerischen Materials," *MKBG* 5 (1937): 88–89; Bruno Steinwallner, "2 Jahre Erbgesundheitsgesetz—1 1/2 Jahre Erbgesundheitsgerichtsbarkeit," *Psychiatrisch-Neurologische Wochenschrift* 37 (1935): 325–28; Hochreuther, "Das Gesetz zur Verhütung," 138; Robert Müller, "Zum Schwachsinnsbegriff in der Praxis der Erbgesundheitsgerichte," *Der Erbarzt* 5 (1938): 149; Fred Dubitscher, "Der moralische Schwachsinn unter Berücksichtigung des Gesetzes zur Verhütung erbkranken Nachwuchses," *ZGNP* 154 (1936): 422–57. Highly critical of this expanded notion of *Schwachsinn* is Stumpfl, "Kriminelle Psychopathen."

of "significant failures of moral judgment" as decisive proof of feebleminded-ness.[107] Another Hereditary Health Court asserted that "pathological defects in basic moral and social attitudes" were "just as heritable as intellectual feeble-mindedness" and therefore concluded that it would be "an inexplicable gap in the law if such a mental abnormality did not justify sterilization."[108]

Many Superior Hereditary Health Courts, however, soon reversed such ster-ilization decisions. When the first appeals of such cases reached them in the spring of 1935, the Superior Hereditary Health Courts in Darmstadt, Hamm, Jena, Karlsruhe, Kassel, and Kiel all overturned sterilization orders based on feeblemindedness in cases where the diagnosis was based only on asocial or criminal acts and there was no evidence of intelligence defects.[109] In one of the earliest decisions, the Superior Hereditary Health Court of Kiel ruled against the sterilization of a recidivist criminal with fourteen convictions. Lower court decisions that had based diagnoses of feeblemindedness only on asocial or crim-inal actions, the court ruled, were "in contradiction to existing medical science," which used the term "feeblemindedness" only to refer to an "intelligence de-fect." The court had no doubt that many criminals were psychopathic but pointed out that psychopaths, with the exception of chronic alcoholics, had been "intentionally left out" of the sterilization law.[110]

107. Case from Bayreuth discussed in Mezger, "Inwieweit werden durch Sterilisierungs-massnahmen Asoziale erfasst?" 88. Just as diagnoses of feeblemindedness in men were often based on criminal behavior, in women such diagnoses were often based on promiscuous sexual behavior. For such an example, see the verdict quoted at length in Fickert, *Rassenhygienische Verbrechensbekämpfung*, 44–47.

108. Lower court decision quoted in EOG Kassel, Wg 417/35, Beschluss of 28 August 1935, reported in *JW* 64 (1935): 3111–12; also quoted in *GRR* (2d ed.), 125.

109. See the following court decisions: EOG Darmstadt, EO 248/34, Beschluss of 8 April 1935, reported in *JW* 64 (1935): 1867–68; EOG Jena, Wg 135/35, Beschluss of 4 April 1935, reported in *JW* 64 (1935): 1869; EOG Jena, Wg 71/35, Beschluss of 21 March 1935, reported in *JW* 64 (1935): 1869–70; EOG Jena, Wg 68/35, Beschluss of 7 March 1935, reported in *JW* 64 (1935): 1870; EOG Kiel, Wg 134/35, Beschluss of 3 July 1935, reported in *JW* 64 (1935): 2143; EOG Kiel, WErb 79/34, Beschluss of 14 February 1935, reported in *JW* 64 (1935): 2143–44; EOG Kiel, Wg 76/35, Beschluss of 24 July 1935, reported in *JW* 64 (1935): 2743; EOG Kassel, Wg 417/35, Beschluss of 28 August 1935, reported in *JW* 64 (1935): 3111–12; EOG Hamm, Wg 1327/35, Beschluss of 8 November 1935, reported in *JW* 65 (1936): 264–65; EOG Karls-ruhe, Wg 403/35, Beschluss of 5 July 1935, reported in *JW* 65 (1936): 265. See also Fickert, *Rassenhygienische Verbrechensbekämpfung*, 47–48; Bock, *Zwangssterilisation*, 320.

110. EOG Kiel, W Erb 79/34, Beschluss of 14 February 1935, reported in *JW* 64 (1935): 2143–44. See also the decision of the EOG Hamburg in the case of "Herr S." related in Andrea Brücks and Christiane Rothmaler, " 'In dubio pro Volksgemeinschaft': Das 'Gesetz zur Ver-hütung erbkranken Nachwuchses' in Hamburg," in *Heilen und Vernichten im Mustergau Hamburg*, ed. Angelika Ebbinghaus, Heidrun Kaupen-Haas, and Karl Heinz Roth (Hamburg: Konkret, 1984), 33–34.

These decisions, however, did not put an end to the use of criminal or "anti-social" behavior as criteria for a diagnosis of feeblemindedness that justified sterilization. First, the decisions of each Superior Hereditary Health Court were valid only in its district, and not all Superior Hereditary Health Courts took such a stringent view of the law. Second, many of the higher court reversals were not as clear-cut as it might appear. Most Superior Hereditary Health Courts ruled against sterilization if the diagnosis of feeblemindedness was based *solely* on asocial or criminal behavior. If the lower court considered the case a "borderline case" between feeblemindedness and "normal stupidity," however, most Superior Hereditary Health Courts permitted the use of criminal behavior as a decisive diagnostic criterion in accordance with Gütt and Rüdin's guidelines. As a result of such higher court rulings, by 1936–37 most Hereditary Health Courts made the following distinction in treating criminal behavior. If there was no evidence whatsoever of intelligence defects, criminal behavior was insufficient to justify a diagnosis of feeblemindedness. If, however, poor performance on the intelligence test provided evidence of a "borderline case," then the door was wide open to considering criminal or other deviant behavior as decisive evidence of feeblemindedness.[111]

In many instances the distinction between normal and borderline cases depended less on the mental condition of the person under scrutiny than on the attitude of the doctor filing the sterilization motion and the court hearing the case. The court's discretion was especially great because the so-called intelligence test often included questions that uneducated persons might find difficult to answer, such as: Who discovered America? Where does coffee come from? How many Bavarian kings have there been? What is the present form of state in Germany? If the court was eager to sterilize a person with a criminal record, it was easy to interpret a few wrong answers as evidence of a borderline case that called for an evaluation of antisocial or criminal behavior as evidence of feeblemindedness.[112] That the attitude of a particular court could be crucial in determining the weight given to criminal behavior is supported by striking dif-

---

111. See, for example, EOG Kiel, WErb 64/34, Beschluss of 16 November 1934, reported in *JW* 64 (1935): 219; EOG Kiel, Wg 76/35 Beschluss of 24 July 1935, reported in *JW* 64 (1935): 2743; EOG Kiel, Wg 95/35, Beschluss of 15 May 1935, reported in *JW* 64 (1935): 2743–44; EOG Berlin, 2d Senate, Wg 1066/35, Beschluss of 13 February 1937, reported in *JW* 66 (1937): 945–46. See also Mezger, "Inwieweit werden durch Sterilisierungsmassnahmen Asoziale erfasst?" 91; Dubitscher, "Asozialität und Unfruchtbarmachung," 104, 107.

112. Initially there was a suggested list of questions; when these became too well known, doctors were asked to make up their own. On the test questions, see *GRR* (1st ed.), 76–78; Burleigh and Wippermann, *Racial State*, 138–40; Bock, *Zwangssterilisation*, 313–20.

ferences in the sterilization rates of different courts. Thus a study of Bavarian sterilization proceedings involving prisoners found that the Hereditary Health Court in Rosenheim decided in favor of sterilizing the prisoner in all such cases, whereas the court in Straubing did so in only 44 percent of cases. On average, the same study found, the Bavarian courts ruled in favor of sterilization motions involving prisoners in 80 percent of cases.[113] Another study of a large national sample determined that in cases that mentioned asocial or criminal behavior, Hereditary Health Courts ruled to sterilize in 93 percent of cases.[114]

Even if some courts, like the court in Straubing, seem to have applied stricter standards in defining "borderline cases," the crucial fact remained that once a person was classified as a borderline case, criminal behavior became a decisive criterion that would tip the scales in favor of sterilization. Even though most courts insisted on at least minimal intellectual defects for a diagnosis of feeblemindedness, Gütt and Rüdin had succeeded in making criminal behavior a decisive "symptom" of feeblemindedness in all those borderline cases that would have escaped sterilization otherwise. This practice was officially sanctioned by a decree of 6 November 1937, in which the Reich justice minister instructed the courts that "a finding of asocial or criminal behavior on the part of the person to be sterilized and his family will be of decisive importance in borderline cases."[115]

The role of criminal behavior as a criterion in sterilization proceedings probably increased over time. For when the sterilization law first took effect in 1934, the courts saw mostly serious cases of feeblemindedness that could be decided on the basis of intellectual defects alone. Once the pool of clear-cut cases was exhausted, however, the courts began to see more and more borderline cases with minor intellectual defects, in which the criterion of Lebensbewährung ("proving one's worth in life"), and therefore criminal behavior, played a crucial role.[116]

The importance of criminal behavior as a criterion in sterilization proceedings is reflected in statistical data, which demonstrate that prisoners and persons with criminal records were disproportionately targeted by the sterilization courts. A study of four thousand sterilization cases from 1934 to 1936 heard by Bavarian Hereditary Health Courts in districts that contained prisons showed that 8 percent of all cases were initiated by prison officials filing motions to have

113. Mezger, "Inwieweit werden durch Sterilisierungsmassnahmen Asoziale erfasst?" 88–91.

114. Dubitscher, "Asozialität und Unfruchtbarmachung," 100.

115. Erlass quoted in Bock, Zwangssterilisation, 326.

116. Dubitscher, "Asozialität und Unfruchtbarmachung," 104.

prisoners sterilized. If one considers men only, that percentage was even higher. Since men accounted for over 90 percent of the sterilization cases dealing with prisoners but only about 55 to 60 percent of all Bavarian sterilization cases, about 12 percent of male sterilization cases in these districts involved prisoners. By comparison, the male inmate population of the prisons, which was almost entirely male, accounted for at most 2 percent of the adult male inhabitants of the districts in question, so that male prisoners were about six times more likely to be subject to sterilization proceedings than the average male adult.[117] As we saw, the courts decided in favor of sterilization in about 80 to 90 percent of such cases.

A second, more comprehensive study of four thousand affirmative sterilization decisions (from 1934 to 1938) of Bavarian Hereditary Health Courts revealed that 15 percent of all cases involved persons with a criminal record. While sterilization cases as a whole were close to evenly split between men and women, about 90 percent of the sterilization cases with a criminal record involved men. If one looks at the figures for males only, one finds that men with criminal records accounted for no less than 25 percent of all male sterilizations.[118] Since, according to Friedrich Stumpfl's calculations, only about 5 percent of the male adult population had criminal records, this study's data suggest that men with a criminal record were about five times more likely to be ster-

---

117. Mezger, "Inwieweit werden durch Sterilisierungsmassnahmen Asoziale erfaßt?" Mezger did not break down his figures by gender. My estimate of 90 percent males among the cases involving prisoners is based on the case histories (ibid., 88–95) and the fact that all but one of the prisons were for men only (ibid., 84). My estimate of 55 to 60 percent males among all Bavarian sterilization cases is based on the figure of 53.6 percent given in Alfred Hoffmann, *Unfruchtbarmachung und Kriminalität*, Kriminalistische Abhandlungen, no. 44 (Leipzig: Wiegandt, 1940), 56. I raised Hoffmann's percentage because Mezger looked only at districts with prisons, so that the cases involving male prisoners might have raised the overall percentage of males in sterilization cases in Mezger's districts. If anything, my estimate of the disproportionate targeting of prisoners is therefore understated. The ratio of inmates to general population was estimated on the basis of inmate populations given ibid., 84, and population figures for the major towns in the Bavarian jurisdictions in question from general reference sources. The resulting inmate-to-population ratio of 1 percent is conservative because the court districts also included areas surrounding the towns. Assuming that the inclusion of out-of-town populations roughly compensates for excluding the underage population, the 1 percent figure can serve as a rough estimate of the ratio of inmates to adult population. Given that the prison population in question was 93 percent male (figures ibid.), and assuming rough parity between males and females in the adult population, it follows that the ratio of male prisoners to male adults was about 2 percent.

118. Hoffmann, *Unfruchtbarmachung und Kriminalität*, 54–98; figure of 90 percent men calculated on the basis of data on pp. 58–59. For a third statistical study of the sterilization of criminals, see Dubitscher, "Asozialität und Unfruchtbarmachung," and Dubitscher, "Der moralische Schwachsinn," 444–55.

ilized than the average adult male citizen, a figure that is remarkably close to that derived from the first study.[119]

The statistical data also confirm that the diagnosis of choice for criminals was feeblemindedness. According to the two aforementioned studies, feeblemindedness accounted for a significantly higher proportion of sterilizations of criminals: between 65 and 77 percent of criminal sterilizations, as opposed to 43 percent of all Bavarian sterilizations. Inversely, while schizophrenia made up about a third of all sterilizations, among criminals it accounted for less than 10 percent. The difference in diagnostic ratios was most dramatic in the case of severe alcoholism: whereas alcoholism accounted for less than 4 percent of sterilizations in general, it made up between 18 and 24 percent of the sterilizations of criminals. As a result, persons with serious criminal records made up a startling 56 percent of those sterilized for alcoholism in the Bavarian sample.[120]

The special targeting of criminals through a diagnosis of severe alcoholism was less controversial than the targeting of criminals through a diagnosis of feeblemindedness. Since feeblemindedness was a well-established diagnostic category referring to intellectual defects, the inclusion of characterological and social criteria necessarily provoked some criticism. Severe alcoholism, by contrast, lacked a clear-cut medical definition; nor was there any consensus on the role of heredity in alcoholism. The problematic nature of this diagnosis was reflected in the sterilization law. Whereas all other diagnoses were grouped under the heading "hereditary diseases" (*Erbkrankheiten*), severe alcoholism was mentioned in a separate paragraph that merely stated that "in addition, persons can be sterilized if they suffer from severe alcoholism." In this way the legislator avoided any claim that severe alcoholism was a hereditary disease. The official explanation accompanying the law further explained that "in the case of degenerate alcoholics, sterilization will have to be limited to the most severe forms of alcoholism because in those cases a mental and ethical deficiency will also be present so that offspring will be undesirable for several reasons."[121] Although this passage appeared to restrict sterilizations for alcoholism, it also suggested that the sterilization of alcoholics was really based on their underlying mental and ethical deficiencies, and thus opened the door to

119. Stumpfl, *Erbanlage und Verbrechen*, 18–20; Stumpfl, "Kriminalität und Vererbung," in *Handbuch der Erbbiologie des Menschen*, ed. Günther Just, vol. 5, pt. 2 (Berlin: Springer, 1939), 1264, 1266.

120. Mezger, "Inwieweit werden durch Sterilisierungsmassnahmen Asoziale erfaßt?" 87; Hoffmann, *Unfruchtbarmachung und Kriminalität*, 97.

121. Text of law and *Begründung* in GRR, 1st ed., 56, 61; Fickert, *Rassenhygienische Verbrechensbekämpfung*, 52–56.

including such deficiencies as diagnostic criteria.[122] Moreover, the reference to "several reasons" implied that the sterilization of alcoholics was justified not only for eugenic but also for social reasons, such as their inability to raise their children properly, a justification for sterilization that was first advanced in the Weimar years.[123]

The special status of severe alcoholism in the sterilization law and the official references to ethical deficiency gave Gütt and Rüdin all the justification they needed to make criminal behavior a crucial criterion for a diagnosis of severe alcoholism.[124] Even commentators who were critical of Gütt and Rüdin's expanded definition of feeblemindedness found no fault with their treatment of criminal behavior in the diagnosis of severe alcoholism.[125]

By the mid-1930s, then, the role of criminal behavior in sterilization proceedings could be summarized as follows: criminal behavior could be a decisive criterion for a diagnosis of severe alcoholism in cases of alcohol abuse or for a diagnosis of congenital feeblemindedness in "borderline cases" with slight intellectual deficiencies. If intelligence defects were completely absent, however, criminal behavior in itself did not justify a diagnosis of feeblemindedness, and the criminal in question could not be sterilized—even though he might be psychopathic. The sterilization of criminals who were neither alcoholics nor intellectually deficient thus remained a matter for future legislation.

The Treatment of Criminals under the Marriage Health Law

Although Gütt failed in his efforts to legalize the sterilization of criminals or "criminal psychopaths," he did succeed in making criminals subject to another important piece of eugenic legislation, the Law for the Protection of the Genetic Health of the German People, generally referred to as the Marriage Health Law. This law grew out of plans for a more comprehensive law against "marriages detrimental to the German people" (*volksschädliche Ehen*) that was to prohibit "healthy" Germans from marrying Jews or "genetically defective" Germans. But as it happened, this legislation was split into two separate laws: the in-

122. Hans Trunk, "Allzu großes Zögern bei der Unfruchtbarmachung wegen schweren Alkoholismus: Die Unfruchtbarmachung von Verbrechern aus Veranlagung," *Der Erbarzt* 2 (1935): 41–45.

123. This was Rüdin's interpretation in "Das deutsche Sterilisierungsgesetz: Medizinischer Kommentar," in *Erblehre und Rassenhygiene im völkischen Staat*, ed. Rüdin (Munich: Lehmann, 1934), 174.

124. *GRR*, 1st ed., 127–29.

125. Fickert, *Rassenhygienische Verbrechensbekämpfung*, 52–56.

famous Law for the Protection of German Blood and German Honor of September 1935, which banned marriages between Jewish and non-Jewish Germans, and the Marriage Health Law passed a month later, in October 1935.[126] The latter prohibited marriage if one of the partners was legally incompetent or suffering from a communicable disease, a "hereditary disease" as defined by the sterilization law, or "a mental disorder [*geistige Störung*] that render[ed] the marriage undesirable for the national community."[127] The last provision was crucial because it widened the scope of mental disorders that could be used to deny a marriage application beyond the list of hereditary diseases enumerated in the sterilization law.

By targeting "mental disorder[s] that render the marriage undesirable for the national community," the Marriage Health Law also explicitly introduced social criteria into the decision-making process. This was a clear departure from the sterilization law, which defined its "hereditary diseases" in purely medical terms. The introduction of social criteria was also reflected in the law's official "explanation" and in the semiofficial commentary coauthored by Gütt. Besides the eugenic argument that the new law would prevent the procreation of genetically defective offspring, the official "explanation" argued that a marriage must be prohibited if it "appears incapable of producing or raising healthy children."[128] This point was reiterated in Gütt's commentary, which admonished health officials to evaluate not just the "genetic quality" of a couple's potential offspring but also the parents' capacity for raising and educating such offspring.[129] Moreover, Gütt's commentary boldly justified the law as a social policy measure that was not necessarily connected with eugenic considerations: "First of all we must ask whether the personalities of the couple give us any reason to fear that their marriage would be undesirable merely as the close association of two people. Two psychopathic, hysterical, criminal or asocial

126. On the general context and the connection between the two laws, see Bock, *Zwangssterilisation*, 100–103. On Gütt's role in this legislation, see Cropp, "Fünf Jahre Abteilung 'Volksgesundheit.'" On the application of the Ehegesundheitsgesetz to criminals, see Fickert, *Verbrechensbekämpfung*, 57–66, 101–24.

127. Article 1 of the "Gesetz zum Schutz der Erbgesundheit des deutschen Volkes (Ehegesundheitsgesetz)," reproduced in Arthur Gütt, Herbert Linden, and Franz Maßfeller, *Blutschutz- und Ehegesundheitsgesetz*, 2d ed. (Munich: Lehman, 1937), 36.

128. "Begründung zu dem Gesetz zum Schutze der Erbgesundheit des deutschen Volkes," in Gütt et al., *Blutschutz- und Ehegesundheitsgesetz*, 37, 38.

129. Gütt et al., *Blutschutz- und Ehegesundheitsgesetz*, 65; see also Ernst Rüdin's reference to "Erfüllung der Eltern- und Erzieherpflichten" in "Eheverbote und Eheberatung bei Geistes- und Nervenkrankheiten" (unpublished lecture at Versammlung der Medizinaldezernenten der Länder und Regierungen, 2 April 1936), quoted in Fickert, *Verbrechensbekämpfung*, 97.

partners would have marriages that would often be undesirable for the national community, regardless of the quality of their offspring."[130]

The expansion of the Marriage Health Law's medical scope to all "mental disorders" and the introduction of blatantly social criteria made it possible to use the law to deny criminals the right to marry. The targeting of criminals was made explicit in the law's official "explanation," which stated that the law was meant to apply to persons who suffered from "mental disorders that have led to serious psychopathy, psychosis or criminal and dangerous behavior."[131] As this formulation showed, however, it was still necessary to demonstrate that a criminal suffered from a "mental disorder" in order to prevent him or her from marrying. Since the psychiatric diagnosis most widely associated with criminal behavior was that of psychopathy, the large-scale targeting of criminals would be possible only if the law's "mental disorders" included the diagnosis of psychopathy. This was by no means obvious, as even Gütt admitted that some researchers drew a sharp distinction between psychopathy and mental disorder (*Geistesstörung*).[132] Nevertheless, the law's official "explanation" as well as a circular from the Ministry of the Interior, both of which Gütt probably had a hand in, established that "serious psychopathy" did fall under the law's provisions.[133]

In practice, the provision that only mental disorders that "rendered a marriage undesirable for the national community" should result in marriage prohibitions meant that the law was used to target not all psychopaths but primarily "criminal" or "asocial" psychopaths. This left the question of what the criteria for a diagnosis of psychopathy would be. Here Gütt's commentary proposed a convenient solution: criminal behavior itself, if sufficiently serious, was to be regarded as a symptom of psychopathy. According to Gütt, a "string of constant misdemeanors or offenses" such as "constant criminal recidivism," "vagrancy, prostitution, pimping," or "pauperism from endogenous causes" was evidence of psychopathy and therefore grounds for prohibiting marriage. In some cases, even "a single offense . . . [could] demonstrate such a lack of compassion or moral sense that one must conclude that a permanent serious mental disorder in the sense of the law is present." Indeed, certain offenses should be regarded as conclusive evidence of psychopathy unless a lack of

130. Gütt et al., *Blutschutz- und Ehegesundheitsgesetz*, 65.
131. "Begründung," ibid., 39.
132. Gütt et al., *Blutschutz- und Ehegesundheitsgesetz*, 67.
133. "Begründung," ibid., 39; Point 7 of "Runderlass des Reichs- und Preussischen Ministers des Innern vom 19. Oktober 1935," quoted in Fickert, *Verbrechensbekämpfung*, 65–66.

abnormalities in the family or the "radical rehabilitation of the person in question" provided proof to the contrary.[134] Thus, for Gütt, anyone with a serious criminal record was *eo ipso* a psychopath. It would be hard to find a more blatant example of the use of moral and social criteria as "symptoms" supporting a medical diagnosis.

The targeting of criminals was also promoted by Gütt's ally Rüdin in a lecture on "marriage prohibitions" that he delivered at a meeting of health officials from all the German states in 1936. In terminology that was reminiscent of Lombroso and Kraepelin, Rüdin argued that the law was designed to target psychopaths who were "asocial or antisocial," including "all so-called morally insane or ethically defective and therefore socially inferior psychopaths . . . born criminals and enemies of society, the great army of serious, incorrigible hereditary criminals [*Anlageverbrecher*], including . . . professional criminals, habitual criminals but also habitual occasional criminals [*gewohnheitsmässige Gelegenheitsverbrecher*]."[135]

Although we do not have any good estimates of the number of persons with criminal records who were prohibited from marrying under the provisions of the Marriage Health Law, there is clear evidence that the law was used to deny such individuals the right to marry.[136] One case whose record has survived is that of Max N. and Elisabeth M. Born in 1898, Max was convicted of theft at age thirteen and placed in a home for juvenile delinquents until the age of eighteen. After briefly serving in the military at the end of the First World War, Max was again convicted for theft numerous times between 1921 and 1934, reaching a total of sixteen convictions. Released from prison in January 1936, Max had committed no further offenses when he applied for a marriage license to marry Elisabeth M. a year later, in January 1937. Because of his criminal record, the Dresden Public Health Office diagnosed Max as psychopathic and denied the couple the necessary "Certificate of Fitness to Marry" (*Ehetauglichkeitszeugnis*).[137] The couple appealed the decision to the Hereditary Health Court in Dresden, which upheld the decision in the following ruling:

> The rapid succession of offenses and the fact that . . . [Max N.'s] prison terms . . . did not prevent him from [stealing] again . . . justify the conclusion

---

134. Gütt et al., *Blutschutz- und Ehegesundheitsgesetz*, 69.

135. Rüdin, "Eheverbote und Eheberatung."

136. Fickert, *Verbrechensbekämpfung*, 63–66, 95–114, which also includes details on eight such cases from Leipzig, Dresden, and Munich.

137. Fickert's summary of "Fall 5" in *Verbrechensbekämpfung*, 108–9.

that N. is in a condition of ethical and moral decline . . . [that] is due to a lack of healthy . . . inhibitions and is rooted in his constitution and hence hereditary.

The court is therefore convinced that N. is unstable [*haltlos*] and a criminal psychopath, who is unable to conduct a marriage in the way in which it is desirable for the national community. It is to be feared that the inferior social characteristics that hold sway over him will be transmitted to his offspring or that he would, at the very least, exert negative educational influences on them that would adversely affect the national community.[138]

Debates about Expanding the Sterilization Law
to Include Criminals

The debate about the desirability of expanding the sterilization law to include criminals started even before the ink was dry on the original law. As early as 1934 Gütt and Rüdin expressed their conviction that "criminal dispositions" were hereditary in their commentary on the sterilization law. At a March 1935 meeting of the Interior Ministry's Advisory Council on Population and Racial Policy, Rüdin advocated amending the sterilization law to allow sterilization in cases of "moral feeblemindedness without intelligence defects" and called for the sterilization of "asocial and criminal psychopaths" in subsequent publications.[139] Similar demands for the extension of the sterilization law to criminals were issued by Nazi officials and prominent eugenicists, including Falk Ruttke, author of the legal sections of the sterilization law commentary; Fred Dubitscher, an official in the Reich Health Office; Karl Astel, president of the Thuringian Office for Racial Affairs; and Heinrich Kranz, director of the Institute for Hereditary and Racial Hygiene at the University of Giessen.[140]

138. Ruling of the Erbgesundheitsgericht Dresden of 12 April 1937, quoted ibid., 109.

139. *GRR*, 1st ed., 6, 215; Rüdin's presentation at Sitzung der Arbeitsgemeinschaft II des Sachverständigenbeirats für Bevölkerungs- und Rassenpolitik, 11 March 1935, quoted in Blasius, *Einfache Seelenstörung*, 169; response by Rüdin to a query from EOG Kiel, as reported in *JW* 64 (1935): 2144; Rüdin, "Das deutsche Sterilisierungsgesetz," 157; Rüdin, "Gutachten zum Thema: Organisation der Verbrechensvorbeugung in den verschiedenen Ländern," in *Römischer Kongreß für Kriminologie* (Berlin: Decker, 1939), 316–22.

140. Falk Ruttke, "Anmerkung [relating to EOG Darmstadt, EO 248/34, Beschluss of 8 April 1935]," *JW* 64 (1935): 1868; Ruttke, "Zur Unfruchtbarmachung erbkranker Verbrecher," *Ziel und Weg* 5 (1935): 310, quoted in Makowski, *Eugenik*, 210; Dubitscher, "Asozialität und Unfruchtbarmachung," 110; Karl Astel, "Die Praxis der Rassenhygiene in Deutschland," *Reichs-Gesundheitsblatt* (1938), 4. Beiheft, p. 70, quoted in Wolfgang Ayaß, *"Asoziale" im Nationalsozialismus* (Stuttgart: Klett-Cotta, 1995), 116; Heinrich Wilhelm Kranz and Siegfried Koller, *Die Gemeinschaftsunfähigen: Ein Beitrag zur wissenschaftlichen und praktischen*

Friedrich Stumpfl's position on this issue became more cautious over time. In his 1936 twin study, Stumpfl called for expanding the sterilization law to include criminals. Since he had acknowledged that it was impossible to distinguish genetic from environmental cases of recidivist criminality, he could not make sterilization dependent on specific genetic factors and simply called for the sterilization of "incorrigible recidivists" (*unbeeinflußbare Schwerkriminelle*). But since incorrigible cases could, by his own admission, result from environmental causes, he was in fact calling for the sterilization of criminals who might not be carrying criminogenic genetic traits at all. Clearly uncomfortable with this contradiction, Stumpfl began to qualify his call for new legislation in later publications. In articles written in 1938 and 1939, he still called for a "new law" for the sterilization of incorrigible recidivists but added that "such a law cannot be created immediately" because the issue of how to "delimit these cases" was still unresolved.[141]

Others unambiguously opposed the extension of the sterilization law to criminals. Probably the most influential among the opponents was Johannes Lange, whose pioneering twin study had made him a recognized expert on genetics and crime. In a 1933 article that explained the medical aspects of the sterilization law to German jurists, Lange stressed that the omission of "criminality" from the hereditary diseases enumerated in the sterilization law was "profoundly justified" because "criminality does not derive from a uniform hereditary disposition."[142] Two years later, in 1935, Lange was asked to deliver a report on the sterilization of criminals to the Eleventh International Prison Congress, which was meeting in Berlin. On this occasion, too, Lange reiterated that his twin studies did not prove the existence of a "uniform criminal disposition." Lange himself doubted that such a disposition existed and thought it more likely that certain subgroups of criminals shared certain sets of genetic traits. Even in these cases, however, it was not clear whether such traits were inherited as a whole or whether they represented a particularly unfortunate combination of inherited traits that were harmless in themselves. All these issues, Lange reported, remained unresolved because research on the heredity

---

Lösung des sogenannten "Asozialenproblems," 2 vols. (Giessen: Karl Christ, 1939, 1941). See also Alfred Schreck, "Zur Unfruchtbarmachung erbkranker Verbrecher," *Ziel und Weg* 5 (1935): 509, and Karl Hannemann, "Willensfreiheit oder Erbschicksal: Betrachtungen über die rassenpolitische Gefahr der asozialen Psychopathen," *Ziel und Weg* 9 (1939): 467–79, both quoted in Makowski, *Eugenik,* 210–11; and Ayaß, *"Asoziale" im Nationalsozialismus,* 115–18.

141. Stumpfl, *Ursprünge des Verbrechens,* 146, 174; "Über kriminalbiologische Erbforschung," *AZP* 107 (1938): 60, 61; "Kriminalität und Vererbung," 1270–71.

142. Johannes Lange, "Psychiatrische Bemerkungen zum Gesetz zur Verhütung erbkranken Nachwuchses," *ZStW* 53 (1933): 709.

of psychological traits was fraught with "extraordinary difficulties." Although Lange was convinced that the criminality of habitual criminals derived "primarily from unfavorable hereditary traits," he concluded that currently "we know so little about the genetics of criminogenic traits" that "no practical suggestions" for the use of eugenics in combating crime could be made. The necessary "scientific foundations" for sterilizations designed to "prevent the births of persons who are likely to become criminal" were simply lacking, and they were not likely to be forthcoming for "a long time to come."[143]

When the delegates to the International Prison Congress considered the question "in which cases and according to which principles" the use of sterilization was "recommended in a modern penal system," they followed Lange's advice. In a formal resolution the 1935 Congress affirmed that while sterilizations of criminals "for medical or eugenic reasons" were appropriate, "principles differing from those governing the sterilizations of other persons for medical or eugenic reasons cannot be justified for the sterilization of criminals." The congress thus endorsed the position that Lange had advocated since the Weimar years and that had prevailed in the final version of the sterilization law, namely, that criminals should be subject to a general eugenic screening for the same hereditary defects as noncriminals and duly sterilized if they suffered from such defects, but that there was no scientific justification for sterilizing criminals for supposedly genetic criminogenic traits.[144]

In the late 1930s, two legal monographs examined the question of extending the sterilization law to include criminals. In his 1938 study on the use of eugenics for combating crime the Exner student Hans Fickert conducted an exhaustive review of the relevant criminal-biological literature and concluded that "the time was not far off" when criminal-biological research would be able to attribute certain criminal behaviors to specific medical disorders, which could then be added to the sterilization law. At present, however, criminal-biological research on the role of heredity in crime had not yet produced conclusive results. Although "criminology and research on psychopaths suggest the heritability of psychopathic and criminal traits," he cautioned, "little is known

143. Johannes Lange, "In welchem Falle und nach welchen Grundsätzen empfiehlt sich im modernen Strafsystem die Anwendung der Sterilisation durch Kastration oder durch Vasectomie oder Salpingectomie?" ZStW 55 (1935): 302–6. In a 1938 article published shortly before his death, Lange mentioned a legislative "gap to be filled" with regard to the "psychopathischer Anlageverbrecher" but did not offer any specific proposals and argued that this was a very small group. Lange, "Erbgesundheitsgesetz, Ehegesundheitsgesetz, Kriminalität," Danziger Ärzteblatt 5 (June 1938): 137–38.

144. Resolutions 5 and 6 of the Eleventh International Prison Congress, Berlin, 1935, quoted in Fickert, Rassenhygienische Verbrechensbekämpfung, 17.

about the specific mode of hereditary transmission of psychopathic-criminal dispositions." Given the state of the research, Fickert concluded, it made good sense that the legislator had decided to await further research before deciding whether psychopathy should be added to the sterilization law's list of hereditary diseases. Moreover, he had recently (1938) learned from "an authoritative source" that "the passage of a sterilization law for criminals [was] not to be expected in the near future."[145] Fickert's critical stance irked eugenics enthusiasts, one of whom attacked the book as "hostile to eugenics" and found it "astonishing that such a work could appear in this [Exner's criminological] series."[146]

Two years later, in 1940, another legal monograph on "sterilization and criminality" reached the same conclusion. After a review of the "latest state of genetic research," Alfred Hoffmann found that the origins of the "criminogenic dispositions of the habitual criminal" remained unresolved and concluded that it was therefore "not justified to demand sterilization for reasons of penal policy."[147] Since both Fickert's and Hoffmann's studies appeared in the criminological publication series edited by Exner, it can be assumed that Exner supported their conclusions, especially since his own textbook of criminology, which generally examined criminal-biological issues in great detail, was conspicuously silent on the subject of sterilization. Similarly, the 1942 and 1944 editions of Edmund Mezger's criminology textbook examined to what extent current sterilizations for hereditary diseases affected criminals but did not call for new legislation to sterilize criminals as such.[148]

The debate on whether the sterilization law should be amended to allow the sterilization of criminals, recidivists, or "criminal psychopaths" thus revealed a clear pattern. The extension of the sterilization law to criminals was supported by Gütt, Rüdin, and Ruttke, all of whom were eugenic hard-liners who had participated in drafting the sterilization law but had not themselves conducted criminal-biological research. By contrast, neither Johannes Lange nor Friedrich Stumpfl, both of whom had conducted such research and therefore appreciated its complexities, shared this position. Stumpfl endorsed the extension of sterilization to criminals in principle but added that current criminal-biological knowledge did not yet allow doctors to identify the type of criminal that should be targeted. Lange squarely insisted that the scientific foundations for amend-

145. Fickert, *Rassenhygienische Verbrechensbekämpfung*, 50, 116, 120.
146. Lemme, review of Hans Fickert, *Rassenhygienische Verbrechensbekämpfung*, ARGB 33 (1939): 371–73.
147. Hoffmann, *Unfruchtbarmachung und Kriminalität*, 42–49.
148. Mezger, *Kriminalpolitik*, 2d ed. (1942), 269–73; 3d ed. (1944), 278–83.

ing the sterilization law to "prevent the births of persons likely to become criminals" were lacking. Lange's status as Germany's most distinguished criminal
biologist undoubtedly helped to win over the delegates of the International
Prison Congress and most of the jurists studying the issue. The two jurists who
wrote legal dissertations on the subject explicitly opposed the expansion of
the sterilization law to criminals at the present time, and neither Exner nor
Mezger called for the extension of the sterilization law to criminals. In the end,
the opponents prevailed. Although in the early 1940s the German police and
the Ministry of the Interior proposed to legalize the sterilization of criminals
and asocials as part of a planned Law on Community Aliens (Gemeinschaftsfremdengesetz), that law never took effect and the sterilization law was never
amended to include criminals or psychopaths.[149]

Radical Schemes and the Murder of Criminals in the "Euthanasia" Operation, 1939–1945

After the beginning of the Second World War in 1939, Nazi policy against
criminals and "asocials" became radicalized. Since criminal biology had been
unable to identify specific genetic defects underlying criminal behavior, the
sterilization law still did not include criminal behavior as a criterion for sterilization. Efforts to circumvent this "gap" by sterilizing criminals through diagnoses of feeblemindedness were severely hampered by Superior Hereditary
Health Court rulings that criminal behavior could not be considered a symptom
of feeblemindedness except in borderline cases. Frustrated by these obstacles to
a eugenic solution to the crime problem, in 1941 two eugenic hard-liners,
Heinrich Wilhelm Kranz, director of the Institute for Genetic and Racial Research in Giessen and the Hessen-Nassau branch of the Rassenpolitisches Amt
(Office of Racial Policy), and the medical statistician Siegfried Koller, proposed a
radically different approach to the issue of sterilizing criminals and asocials. In
the second volume of their work *Die Gemeinschaftsunfähigen*, discussed in the
previous chapter, Kranz and Koller claimed that twin studies had generally
proven the preeminent role of heredity in habitual criminal and asocial behavior but acknowledged that psychiatric research had failed to link such be-

149. On the Gemeinschaftsfremdengesetz, see Patrick Wagner, "Das Gesetz über die Behandlung Gemeinschaftsfremder: Die Kriminalpolizei und die 'Vernichtung des Verbrechertums,'" in *Feinderklärung und Prävention: Kriminalbiologie, Zigeunerforschung und Asozialenpolitik* (Berlin: Rotbuch, 1988), 75–100; Wagner, *Volksgemeinschaft ohne Verbrecher*, 384–93;
Werle, *Justiz-Strafrecht*, 619–80; Wolfgang Ayaß, *"Asoziale" im Nationalsozialismus* (Stuttgart: Klett-Cotta, 1995), 202–9.

havior to a specific medical diagnosis or to identify the underlying genetic factors. The concept of psychopathy, in particular, was of little use because it was very broad and applied to many persons who were neither criminal nor asocial. Kranz and Koller therefore concluded that attempts to base eugenic measures against criminals and asocials on a medical diagnosis of genetic defects were doomed to failure in the foreseeable future and proposed a radical solution: dispensing with medical diagnoses and basing the sterilization of criminals and asocials on purely "sociological criteria."[150]

Kranz and Koller proposed a new law that would authorize the sterilization of any person who was "asocial" (*gemeinschaftsunfähig*) and had two or more "asocials" among his or her close blood relatives (including grandparents, uncles, aunts, nieces, nephews, and grandchildren). This meant that persons could be sterilized if their behavior and that of two blood relatives was determined to be asocial, without any medical diagnosis of a genetic defect in the particular individual, as was currently required under the sterilization law of 1933. In Kranz and Koller's proposal persons were defined as asocial if they were "not able to satisfy the minimal demands that the national community made" on their "personal behavior" ("the duty to preserve one's honor, to work, and to perform according to one's abilities"), "social behavior" (the "duty to respect the honor, person, and property of other members of the national community"), and "*völkisch* behavior" (the "duty to preserve the honor, existence, and achievements of one's people"). Clearly, this definition was so broad that almost any nonconformist behavior could be considered evidence of an asocial personality. Asocial persons with two asocial blood relatives would not only be sterilized but also prohibited from marrying; existing marriages would be dissolved and any children would be transferred to a state home; finally, such persons could also be interned.[151]

In Kranz and Koller's eyes, basing the sterilization of asocial persons on sociological criteria (asocial behavior) rather than medical ones (genetic defects) had the additional advantage of drawing a clear line between the sterilization of the "genetically ill" according to the procedures of the sterilization law of 1933, and the sterilization of asocials, which they proposed to regulate in a separate "Law on the Denial of Rights of Honor for the Protection of the National

150. Kranz and Koller, *Die Gemeinschaftsunfähigen*, 2:29–34, 52–55, 129–30, 135–47. See also Heinrich W. Kranz, "Das Problem der 'Gemeinschaftsunfähigen' im Aufartungsprozeß unseres Volkes," *Nationalsozialistischer Volksdienst* 7 (1940): 61–66; Kranz, "Weg und Ziel bei der Lösung des Problems der Gemeinschaftsunfähigen," *Nationalsozialistischer Volksdienst* 9 (1942): 217–21.

151. Kranz and Koller, *Die Gemeinschaftsunfähigen*, 2:160–62.

Community" (Gesetz über die Aberkennung der völkischen Ehrenrechte zum Schutz der Volksgemeinschaft), whose title was meant to convey that the sterilization of asocials served not only a eugenic but also a punitive function. To emphasize this distinction, cases brought against asocials under the proposed law were to be tried by regular courts rather than the Hereditary Health Courts that heard sterilization proceedings brought under the sterilization law of 1933. Although accused asocial persons were to undergo a medical examination to determine whether they suffered from a "hereditary disease" listed in the sterilization law, the decision to sterilize them would not depend on the diagnosis of a genetic defect but on the judgment of a three-person court—composed of a professional judge, the head of the local health office (Gesundheitsamt), and the head of the Nazi Party's regional Office of Racial Policy (Rassenpolitisches Gauamt)—that they and two close blood relatives were in fact asocial according to the law's definition.[152]

Although it never became law, Kranz and Koller's proposal to jettison what they called "medical camouflage" in favor of purely "sociological criteria" for the sterilization of asocial persons is important for several reasons.[153] First, it demonstrates that even eugenic extremists recognized that psychiatric research in criminal biology had failed to identify genetic defects responsible for criminal behavior and had therefore been unable to provide the medical basis that most psychiatrists and jurists deemed necessary for introducing eugenic measures specifically targeting criminals, thus confirming the main argument of this chapter. Second, Kranz and Koller's proposal shows how some eugenic extremists were so determined to implement a eugenic solution to the crime problem, and, ultimately, a "final solution of the social question," that they were not going to let medicine's failure to identify genetic factors responsible for criminal or asocial behavior stand in their way.[154] Since eugenic measures made sense only if they targeted known genetic defects, this amounted to pursuing a eugenic policy that no longer had a rational basis. It is obvious that only persons with a complete disregard for the dignity of the individual could

152. Ibid., 145–46, 148–51, 158, 160–62.

153. The term "medizinische Tarnung" is used ibid., 137, 141. The terms "soziologische Gesichtspunkte" and "soziologische Feststellungen" are used ibid., 135, 141.

154. The phrase "final solution of the social question" was coined by Karl Heinz Roth; see Roth, " 'Asoziale' und nationale Minderheiten: Das Leben an seinen Rändern," *Protokolldienst der Evangelischen Akademie Bad Boll* 31 (1983): 120–34. For different assessments of this concept, see Wolfgang Ayaß, *"Asoziale" im Nationalsozialismus* (Stuttgart: Klett-Cotta, 1995), 217–25; Dirk Blasius, "Psychiatrie in der Zeit des Nationalsozialismus," *Sudhoffs Archiv* 75 (1991): 91; Detlev Peukert, "Die Genesis der 'Endlösung' aus dem Geist der Wissenschaft," in *Max Webers Diagnose der Moderne* (Göttingen: Vandenhoeck, 1989), 103.

allow their eugenic obsessions to run amok in this fashion. Gütt and Rüdin suffered from the same obsession, and our discussion of the "euthanasia" program will show where this could ultimately lead. Third, Kranz and Koller's proposal was unusual for its honesty in casting aside "medical camouflage," that is, for admitting that there was no medical basis for sterilizing asocial or criminal persons and acknowledging that their criteria for sterilization in these cases were "sociological." As the following pages will show, those who implemented not the sterilization but the actual murder of asocial and criminal individuals as part of the wartime euthanasia program did so very much under the cover of medical diagnoses.

Finally, Kranz and Koller's published proposal of 1941 influenced government plans for a Law on the Treatment of Community Aliens (Gesetz über die Behandlung Gemeinschaftsfremder) that formed the subject of protracted negotiations between the Reichskriminalpolizeiamt (national office of the criminal police), the Ministry of Interior, and the Ministry of Justice from 1939 to 1944.[155] Among other provisions, the 1944 draft of this law provided for the sterilization of *Gemeinschaftsfremde* (asocials) in cases where "offspring that is undesirable for the national community [*Volksgemeinschaft*] can be anticipated."[156] This vague formulation was much less restrictive than the enumeration of specific "genetic diseases" in the sterilization law of 1933 and thus made anyone a potential target for sterilization. It is worth noting, however, that even the 1944 draft of the Law on the Treatment of Community Aliens did not follow Kranz and Koller's suggestion to dispense with a medical diagnosis and base the sterilization of asocials solely on the determination that the person in question and two blood relatives had shown themselves to be asocial. Instead, the draft insisted that the sterilization of asocials be subject to the regular procedures set down in the sterilization law of 1933 and therefore required an individual medical examination, a diagnosis, and a sterilization hearing on medical grounds in a Hereditary Health Court.[157] Thus, even the Third Reich's most radical legisla-

---

155. On the *Gemeinschaftsfremdengesetz*, see Patrick Wagner, "Das Gesetz über die Behandlung Gemeinschaftsfremder: Die Kriminalpolizei und die 'Vernichtung des Verbrechertums,'" in *Feinderklärung und Prävention: Kriminalbiologie, Zigeunerforschung und Asozialenpolitik* (Berlin: Rotbuch, 1988), 75–100; Wagner, *Volksgemeinschaft ohne Verbrecher*, 384–93; Werle, *Justiz-Strafrecht*, 621–60; Ayaß, *"Asoziale" im Nationalsozialismus*, 202–9; Detlev Peukert, "Arbeitslager und Jugend-KZ: Die Behandlung Gemeinschaftsfremder im Dritten Reich," in *Die Reihen fast geschlossen: Beiträge zur Geschichte des Alltags unterm Nationalsozialismus*, ed. Peukert and Jürgen Reulecke (Wuppertal: Hammer, 1981), 413–34.

156. Paragraph 13 (1), in "Gesetz über die Behandlung Gemeinschaftsfremder" [draft of 2 February 1944], Rep. R 22 (RJM), file 944, pp. 96–97, quote p. 97, BA Potsdam.

157. Paragraph 13 (2), ibid.

tive proposal in the area of criminal justice did not drop what Kranz and Koller called "medical camouflage" in its eugenic provisions targeting asocials and criminals.

The proposed Law on the Treatment of Community Aliens, which was to provide the legal basis for expanded government powers to sterilize and intern criminals and asocials, was never enacted. But while police and the Justice Ministry were engaged in drawn-out negotiations over the law's details from 1939 to 1944, an organized killing program targeting criminals and asocials was already under way without a legal basis.

On 9 October 1939 the Department of Health in the Ministry of the Interior issued a directive (*Runderlaß*) requiring all German asylums to file official registration forms for certain categories of patients. This registration drive was the beginning of the organized killing of the mentally ill and handicapped known by the code name "Aktion T4." This "euthanasia" operation was authorized by Hitler in October 1939 in a written document dated back to 1 September, the first day of the Second World War. The patient categories subject to the registration requirement included those suffering from certain diseases, such as schizophrenia and epilepsy, those who had been interned for more than five years, and those "interned as criminal insane persons" (*als kriminelle Geisteskranke verwahrt*).[158] This phrase referred to patients who had been interned in an asylum by court order according to article 42b of the penal code. This article, which had been added to the code by the Law against Dangerous Habitual Criminals of November 1933, provided that if someone committed a crime without being legally responsible by reason of insanity or in a state of "diminished legal responsibility," the criminal court could order the person's "internment in an asylum [*Heil- oder Pflegeanstalt*] if public security require[d]

---

158. Hans-Walter Schmuhl, *Rassenhygiene, Nationalsozialismus, Euthanasie*, 2d ed. (Göttingen: Vandenhoeck, 1992), 190–214, esp. 197; Henry Friedlander, *The Origins of Nazi Genocide: From Euthanasia to the Final Solution* (Chapel Hill: University of North Carolina Press, 1995), 62–85, esp. 76; Ernst Klee, *"Euthanasie" im NS-Staat: Die "Vernichtung lebensunwerten Lebens"* (Frankfurt: Fischer, 1983), 86–95; Götz Aly, "Medicine against the Useless," in Aly, Peter Chroust, and Christian Pross, *Cleansing the Fatherland: Nazi Medicine and Racial Hygiene* (Baltimore: Johns Hopkins University Press, 1994), 52–63, esp. 60–61 (this article was first published as "Medizin gegen Unbrauchbare," in *Aussonderung und Tod: Die klinische Hinrichtung der Unbrauchbaren* [Berlin: Rotbuch, 1985], 9–74); Evans, *Rituals of Retribution*, 68–87. The registration form ("Meldebogen 1") and the accompanying "Merkblatt" of the "Runderlass" are reprinted in Klee, *Euthanasie*, 92–93, and in Ernst Klee, ed., *Dokumente zur "Euthanasie"* (Frankfurt: Fischer, 1985), 95–96; a translation of "Meldebogen 1" is printed in Burleigh and Wippermann, *Racial State*, 146–47. On the euthanasia program, see also Michael Burleigh, *Death and Deliverance: "Euthanasia" in Germany, c. 1900–1945* (Cambridge: Cambridge University Press, 1994), esp. 111–29.

it."[159] As far as registration for operation T4 was concerned, this category was generally understood to include patients interned in rehabilitation clinics for alcoholics by order of a criminal court and patients interned by the orders of police or welfare authorities without having been charged with a crime.[160]

Although we do not know exactly how many of the patients registered as "criminal insane persons" were killed by being gassed in the killing centers of operation T4, the surviving evidence suggests that a very high percentage of these patients were indeed killed.[161] According to one of the key figures of T4, there were orders to be "especially aggressive" in selecting criminal patients for the euthanasia program.[162] All of the patients classified as "criminal insane persons" in the municipal insane asylum in Berlin-Buch, for instance, were transferred to the killing centers of operation T4.[163] When one asylum doctor noticed that almost all inmates interned according to article 42b were being selected for euthanasia, he wrote his superior to explain that most of these patients suffered from only minor mental disturbances and had committed minor offenses.[164] In the Bavarian asylum Eglfing-Haar about half of those transferred to killing centers because of their criminal status had committed sexual offenses, such as sexual relations with minors and male homosexual relations, while most of the other half had committed thefts.[165]

The secrecy of operation T4 led to conflicts with the courts, which frequently retained jurisdiction over those interned as "criminal insane persons."[166] Courts inquiring about a ward of the state or conducting their periodic reviews of

159. Leopold Schäfer, Otto Wagner, and Josef Schafheutle, eds., *Gesetz gegen gefährliche Gewohnheitsverbrecher und über Maßregeln der Sicherung und Besserung* (Berlin: Vahlen, 1934), 8–9.

160. Aly, "Medicine against the Useless," 59–60; Schmuhl, *Rassenhygiene*, 199–200. T-4 administrator Herbert Linden explicitly agreed to such an expansive definition of "criminal mentally ill persons" (*kriminelle Geisteskranke*) in a letter dated 26 July 1940, quoted in Klee, *Euthanasie*, 215–16.

161. Schmuhl, *Rassenhygiene*, 198, 200; Aly, "Medicine against the Useless," 61.

162. Postwar testimony from Werner Heyde about instructions to "die Kriminellen besonders scharf zu beurteilen," quoted in Klee, *Euthanasie*, 123.

163. Norbert Emmerich, "Die Forensische Psychiatrie, 1933–1945," in *Totgeschwiegen, 1933–1945: Zur Geschichte der Wittenauer Heilstätten. Seit 1957 Karl-Bonhoeffer-Nervenklinik*, ed. Arbeitsgruppe zur Erforschung der Geschichte der Karl-Bonhoeffer-Nervenklinik, 2d ed. (Berlin: Edition Hentrich, 1989), 114, 119.

164. Letter from Dr. Weskott of the Weißenau asylum, dated 12 July 1940, quoted in Klee, *Euthanasie*, 123.

165. Report on Eglfing-Haar asylum quoted ibid., 123, and in Schmuhl, *Rassenhygiene*, 226.

166. On the judiciary's relationship to the euthanasia operation, see Gruchmann, *Justiz im Dritten Reich*, 497–534; Friedlander, *Origins of Nazi Genocide*, 116–23; Schmuhl, *Rassenhygiene*, 291–304; Klee, *Euthanasie*, 239–41, 326–33.

whether such patients should remain interned would learn that the patient in question had been transferred to another asylum and suddenly died of a "heart attack" or some other ailment.[167] When such incidents became more frequent, the courts became suspicious and rumors began to circulate. After repeated inquiries, the minister of justice, Franz Gürtner, was finally shown a copy of Hitler's secret euthanasia order in August 1940, but the judiciary as a whole remained officially uninformed.[168] In March 1941, Franz Schlegelberger, who had become acting justice minister after Gürtner's death earlier that year, decided that the situation that the euthanasia operation had created for the judiciary had become untenable and wrote a letter of complaint to Hans Lammers, the head of the Chancellor's Office (Reichskanzlei). Not only, he wrote, did courts frequently find that guardians or defendants interned in mental asylums had been transferred and died, but some medical experts were refusing to make diagnoses of "diminished responsibility" because the resulting "commitment [in an asylum] means the execution of a death sentence without trial."[169] In response to Schlegelberger's complaint, the organizers of Aktion T4 agreed to brief the judiciary on their operation. At a meeting on 23–24 April 1941 district attorneys and the presidents of state courts were thus officially informed of the euthanasia program.[170]

In April 1941 the killing operation that had so far been limited to asylums was also expanded to concentration camps under the code name "Sonderbehandlung [special treatment] 14f13." Officially, this operation targeted inmates who were unable to work. In practice, however, Jews and inmates who were diagnosed as "asocial psychopaths" or who had criminal records were also preferred targets.[171]

Aktion T4 was officially halted by Hitler in August 1941 for a number of reasons, including negative reactions among the public. In fact, however, the

167. Examples of such cases are cited in Klee, *Euthanasie*, 221, 239–41; Aly, "Medicine against the Useless," 61–62; Gruchmann, *Justiz im Dritten Reich*, 515–17.

168. Friedlander, *Origins of Nazi Genocide*, 117–21; Klee, *Euthanasie*, 241.

169. Aly, "Medicine against the Useless," 62; Gruchmann, *Justiz im Dritten Reich*, 522; Schmuhl, *Rassenhygiene*, 300; Schlegelberger's letter is reprinted as document 78 in Klee, *Dokumente*, 213–16.

170. Gruchmann, *Justiz im Dritten Reich*, 527–30; Friedlander, *Origins of Nazi Genocide*, 122; Aly, "Medicine against the Useless," 62–63; Schmuhl, *Rassenhygiene*, 303; Klee, *Euthanasie*, 331–33. Minutes and notes on the meeting of 23–24 April 1941 are reprinted as documents 79 and 80 in Klee, *Dokumente*, 216–20.

171. Schmuhl, *Rassenhygiene*, 217–18; Friedlander, *Origins of Nazi Genocide*, 142–50, esp. 144; Aly, "Medicine against the Useless," 45; Evans, *Rituals of Retribution*, 687.

euthanasia operation continued.[172] The records of the Hadamar asylum, which served as one of the killing centers, show that eighty-two "criminal insane persons" interned according to article 42b of the penal code were transferred to Hadamar from other asylums in this second phase of the euthanasia operation, between August 1942 and March 1945. Seventy-one of them (87 percent) were killed. Two-thirds of these eighty-two patients were first-time offenders; most were not convicted of serious or violent offenses. Thirty-seven percent had committed small property offenses such as theft, fraud, and the destruction of property; 20 percent had been charged under article 175 of the penal code, which criminalized male homosexual acts; several had been indicted for drug offenses, abortion, and exhibitionism. Only three had been charged with violent offenses, namely attempted homicide. Many of them were diagnosed as "feebleminded" or "psychopathic," diagnoses that were little more than medical labels for social deviance in most cases.[173]

In this second phase, after the official halt of Aktion T4 in August 1941, the Central Office of T4 also expanded its reach beyond psychiatric asylums to workhouses, old people's homes, and homes for wayward youth (*Fürsorgeheime*).[174] Thus in January 1942 a commission of high-ranking officials and medical experts, including Heinrich Wilhelm Kranz and Robert Ritter, visited the workhouse in Berlin-Rummelsburg and conducted a "model examination" (*Musterbegutachtung*) using a new registration form for "Gemeinschaftsfremde" (asocials). The commission determined that 314, or about 25 percent, of the inmates were "gemeinschaftsfremd" and should therefore be killed. In another 765 cases at least one of the examiners thought that the person ought to fall victim to the "extermination of lives not worth living." It is not known whether the 314 Rummelsburg inmates selected by the commission were indeed killed by the euthanasia operation; it is possible that they were transferred to concentration camps for "extermination through work" instead. Nor is it known to what extent similar commissions conducted such selections in other workhouses.[175]

172. Aly, "Medicine against the Useless," 46; Schmuhl, *Rassenhygiene*, 210, 220, 224; Friedlander, *Origins of Nazi Genocide*, 136, 151.

173. Rainer Scheer, "Die nach Paragraph 42 RStGB verurteilten Menschen in Hadamar," in *Psychiatrie im Faschismus: Die Anstalt Hadamar, 1933–1945*, ed. Dorothee Roer and Dieter Henkel (Bonn: Psychiatrie-Verlag, 1986), 237, 245–46, 248. I have calculated the percentages on the basis of the absolute figures reported by Scheer.

174. Schmuhl, *Rassenhygiene*, 225–26. On the Central Office (Zentraldienststelle), see ibid., 193–94, and Friedlander, *Origins of Nazi Genocide*, 69–74.

175. Aly, "Medicine against the Useless," 64–65, 68; Burleigh, *Death and Deliverance*, 250; Schmuhl, *Rassenhygiene*, 227.

In the fall of 1942 the Ministry of Justice, now headed by the fanatical Nazi Otto Thierack, adopted its own program of "extermination through work" by handing over certain categories of prisoners and "criminal insane" inmates of insane asylums to the SS to be worked to death in concentration camps.[176] On 14 September 1942 Thierack had a conversation with Joseph Goebbels, the minister of propaganda, in which Goebbels proposed "extermination through work" for Jews, Gypsies, habitual criminals held in "preventive detention" (*Sicherungsverwahrung*), and prisoners with life sentences.[177] Four days later, on 18 September 1942, Thierack's deputy, Staatssekretär Curt Rothenberger, held a meeting with Heinrich Himmler, chief of the SS and the police, in which it was agreed that the Ministry of Justice would deliver "antisocial elements from prisons" to the SS for extermination through work in concentration camps. These "antisocial elements" were to include Jews, Gypsies, all habitual criminals in "preventive detention" (*Sicherungsverwahrte*), and German prisoners with sentences over eight years.[178] Prison wardens were informed of this policy in mid-October, and by November 1942 expert commissions were visiting the prisons to make the selections. By April 1943, less than six months later, more than 12,500 *Sicherungsverwahrte* had been transferred to concentration camps, where close to 6,000 of them had already died.[179]

In July 1943 the Ministry of Justice decided to extend the policy of extermination through labor in concentration camps to the "criminal mentally ill" interned in asylums. In early August the Ministry of the Interior responded by issuing a directive informing asylum directors that persons interned according to article 42b of the penal code would be transferred to police custody.[180] In fact,

176. Klee, *Euthanasie*, 356–67; Aly, "Medicine against the Useless," 69–76.

177. Klee, *Euthanasie*, 358.

178. Ibid., 356–67, esp. 358; Aly, "Medicine against the Useless," 69–76, esp. 70; Schmuhl, *Rassenhygiene*, 227; Evans, *Rituals of Retribution*, 705. The official record of the agreement reached at the meeting of 18 September 1942, signed by Thierack, is reprinted in Karl Heinz Roth, " 'Abgabe asozialer Justizgefangener an die Polizei'—eine unbekannte Vernichtungsaktion der Justiz," in *Heilen und Vernichten im Mustergau Hamburg: Bevölkerungs- und Gesundheitspolitik im Dritten Reich* (Hamburg: Konkret Literatur Verlag, 1984), 21; and in *Im Namen des deutschen Volkes: Justiz und Nationalsozialismus* (Cologne: Verlag Wissenschaft und Politik, 1989), 268–69.

179. Klee, *Euthanasie*, 359; Wagner, "Das Gesetz über die Behandlung Gemeinschaftsfremder," 88–89. The figures are from Klee; Wagner gives the slightly higher figure of 14,700 "prisoners" transferred to concentration camps (the difference could be due to the inclusion of prisoners who were not *Sicherungsverwahrte*). Such a transfer is documented for Hamburg prisoners in Roth, " 'Abgabe asozialer Justizgefangener.' "

180. Klee, *Euthanasie*, 360; Aly, "Medicine against the Useless," 71. The ministry's directive of 8 August 1943 is reproduced in Scheer, "Die nach Paragraph 42 RStGB verurteilten Menschen," 252–53.

this directive only legitimated what was already happening. As early as October 1942 T4 doctors were visiting German asylums to evaluate inmates interned under article 42b with regard to their ability to work and making lists of such patients to be transferred to concentration camps. Surviving records for Hamburg show that at least fifty "criminal insane" patients were deported from Hamburg insane asylums to concentration camps in early 1943. By 1944 such transfers included not only those interned under article 42b but also patients who were merely diagnosed as "psychopaths" with antisocial tendencies.[181]

Conclusion

Just as the euthanasia killings in general are unthinkable without the long-term influence of the German eugenics movement, the euthanasia operation's special targeting of "criminal insane" inmates cannot be explained without the influence of criminal-biological research, which had emphasized the role of genetic factors in crime and held out the promise of a eugenic solution to the crime problem. But euthanasia is not the same as eugenics. Sterilizing people against their will reflects a fundamental lack of respect for the dignity of the individual. It is not, however, the same as killing people. (This is one reason why the euthanasia killings were kept secret, whereas the sterilization program was public.) Many German doctors took the step from endorsing compulsory sterilization to supporting or even participating in the T4 killings. But being a committed eugenicist did not necessarily entail approving of the euthanasia killings.[182] Likewise, some criminal biologists, such as H. W. Kranz and Ritter, participated in the selections of criminal insane patients for the euthanasia killings. But this does not mean that all criminal biologists endorsed the euthanasia killings of criminals. It is misleading to consider the euthanasia killings the logical or inevitable outcome of eugenics, and it is therefore equally misleading to consider the killings of criminals in the euthanasia operation or the "extermination through work" program as the logical or inevitable outcome of German criminal biology. It should be noted that drawing a distinction between eugenics and euthanasia, sterilization and killing, is not meant to advance an apologetic agenda. On the contrary, this distinction prevents defenders of the perpetrators

181. Aly, "Medicine against the Useless," 71–73; Klee, *Euthanasie*, 361–62; Schmuhl, *Rassenhygiene*, 228; Emmerich, "Die Forensische Psychiatrie," 118.

182. Paul Weindling has pointed out that "a eugenicist supporting compulsory sterilization for schizophrenics would not necessarily have supported their killing in the 'T-4 euthanasia' programme" ("Understanding Nazi Racism: Precursors and Perpetrators," in *Confronting the Nazi Past*, ed. Michael Burleigh [New York: St. Martin's, 1996], 75).

of the euthanasia program from arguing that their murderous actions reflected a common eugenic consensus of the time. They did not, and this fact only increases the moral responsibility of the perpetrators.

We do not know how many criminologists, criminal biologists, psychiatrists, or jurists besides Kranz and Ritter endorsed or would have endorsed the euthanasia killings of the criminal mentally ill and others because these killings were officially secret, so that, even if people heard about them, they could not discuss them in publications, at professional meetings, or in academic lectures. We do know that the history of sterilization policy between 1933 and 1939 presented a complex picture of opinion among criminologists, psychiatrists, and jurists. While it is conceivable that eugenic hard-liners like Gütt and Rüdin supported euthanasia killings of criminals, it does not seem likely that the people who opposed adding "criminal behavior" to the sterilization law would have endorsed the euthanasia killings of criminals. Since the euthanasia killings of criminal patients cannot therefore be considered the logical culmination of criminal biology, the sterilization debates and the development of sterilization policy that have been this chapter's main focus remain a valuable indicator of the reception of criminal-biological research.

As we look back over the Weimar debates and post-1933 sterilization practice discussed in this chapter, certain points merit special emphasis. To begin with, the debate over the sterilization of criminals among Weimar psychiatrists must be seen in the larger context of the eugenics movement and its reception in the German medical profession. This reception was overwhelmingly positive. The vast majority of German doctors endorsed the eugenic principle that persons with "genetic defects" should be prevented from procreation and supported the eugenicists' demand for the legalization of voluntary eugenic sterilization. They did so because they were convinced that many if not most mental disorders were hereditary and saw sterilization as a welcome means of eliminating disorders that they were unable to cure.

Given this support for eugenics in general, it does not at first appear surprising that most Weimar psychiatrists also advocated the voluntary sterilization of criminals. There was, however, a crucial difference between endorsing the sterilization of the mentally ill and that of criminals. While most psychiatrists believed that there was conclusive evidence for the heritability of the most important mental illnesses, especially schizophrenia and feeblemindedness,[183]

---

183. On the uncertainties, see Weingart, Kroll, and Bayertz, *Rasse, Blut und Gene*, 300–306; for the argument that there was nevertheless conclusive evidence for the heritability of certain mental illnesses, see Lange, "Referat."

almost everyone conceded that such evidence did not yet exist for the heritability of criminal behavior. As a result, most psychiatrists' position on the sterilization of criminals was paradoxical. They supported the sterilization of at least some criminals because they were convinced that heredity played the predominant role in criminal behavior. Yet they acknowledged that this conviction lacked the necessary scientific evidence because the role of heredity in criminal behavior was still poorly understood.

The fact that most German psychiatrists were convinced that criminal behavior was largely hereditary even though scientific proof was lacking reflected the strong hereditarian bias of the German psychiatric profession. At the same time, their frank acknowledgment that the necessary scientific evidence was lacking shows that most psychiatrists understood the difficulties involved in disentangling the influences of heredity and environment in criminal behavior, which demonstrates that Weimar's criminal biologists were successful in conveying these difficulties to their nonspecialist colleagues.

How, then, did Weimar psychiatrists justify the sterilization of criminals in the absence of conclusive scientific evidence? A moderate strategy, advanced by Johannes Lange, admitted that it was currently impossible to determine whether a person's criminal behavior resulted from genetic traits but proposed that criminals undergo a general eugenic screening for mental disorders whose heritability was considered well established; this was the policy that was later adopted in the implementation of the sterilization law. A more radical strategy contended that it was not necessary to prove the heritability of criminal behavior because the sterilization of criminals could be justified with the social policy argument that criminals were unfit to bring up children. This argument was later used to justify the marriage prohibitions imposed on criminals.

By the late Weimar years, the medical profession's support for eugenics had convinced most bureaucrats and politicians to support the legalization of voluntary eugenic sterilization. Despite their general support for eugenics, however, the Ministry of Justice and most political parties opposed special provisions for the sterilization of criminals. Besides legal-procedural issues, the major reason for their objection was the lack of conclusive evidence for the heritability of criminal behavior. Insisting on a higher standard of scientific evidence than the majority of psychiatrists, Weimar bureaucrats and most politicians concluded that in the absence of such evidence special provisions for the sterilization of criminals could not be justified.

The fact that the Reichstag committee's minority in favor of the sterilization of criminals included both Nazis and Social Democrats demonstrates that enthusiasm for eugenics was by no means a monopoly of the extreme right. At the same time, the Nazis' long-standing support for radical eugenic measures such as compulsory sterilization indicated that, once in power, the Nazis were likely to promote an aggressive eugenic agenda. It is therefore remarkable that even after the Nazis placed the hard-line eugenicist Gütt in charge of preparing a sterilization law, the Ministry of Justice succeeded in blocking Gütt's plans for the inclusion of criminals in the sterilization law and, when the issue surfaced again a few months later, prevented the inclusion of sterilization measures in the Law against Habitual Criminals. Although the Justice Ministry agreed to instruct prisons to screen inmates for the hereditary diseases covered by the sterilization law, the ministry continued successfully to oppose special sterilization measures for criminals throughout the Nazi period.

Even though criminals had been omitted from the sterilization law, efforts were made to stretch the law in order to sterilize criminals. Gütt and Rüdin promoted the targeting of criminals through an expanded definition of feeblemindedness and advocated amending the sterilization law to include criminals. Gütt, a medical doctor, can fairly be described as a eugenic zealot who lacked the special training in psychiatry, genetics, or criminal biology that would have allowed him to evaluate the scientific evidence supporting eugenic measures. The same was true of Kranz and Koller, and of many doctors serving on Hereditary Health Courts who went along with Gütt and Rüdin's egregious redefinition of feeblemindedness in order to sterilize criminals. The same cannot, however, be said of Rüdin, who was a distinguished psychiatrist heading the research institute where the era's most sophisticated research on human genetics and criminal biology was conducted. In his case, it appears that a dogmatic belief in the primacy of heredity and a boundless enthusiasm for eugenics enabled him to ignore the absence of scientific evidence to support his extremist eugenic program. As director of the Deutsche Forschungsanstalt für Psychiatrie, Rüdin was a scientific manager who was not directly involved in the criminal-biological research conducted by people like Lange and Stumpfl. It seems likely that his distance from the actual research made it easier for him to repeat hereditarian claims without acknowledging the complexities, uncertainties, and unresolved issues involved in the research.

As we saw, however, Gütt and Rüdin's attempt to target criminals for sterilization was challenged. In many instances, court decisions that based a diagnosis of feeblemindedness solely on criminal behavior were struck down by Superior Hereditary Health Courts. The higher court rulings argued that the medical definition of feeblemindedness referred to intellectual defects only and that the sterilization law was not intended to apply to criminals or psychopaths. These decisions by panels of judges and doctors thus checked eugenic zealotry by insisting on the rule of law and on established medical definitions. Yet even these higher court rulings permitted the use of criminal behavior as a criterion for feeblemindedness in so-called borderline cases. Since prison authorities were urged to screen prisoners for hereditary diseases, prisoners also stood a greater chance of being subject to sterilization proceedings in the first place. As a result of these screenings and the use of criminal behavior as a criterion in "borderline" cases, men with criminal records were about five times more likely to be sterilized than the average male citizen.

While the court decisions reversing the most egregious attempts to stretch the sterilization law to target criminals were based on legal and definitional considerations, the debate over whether the sterilization law should be amended to include criminals turned on the substantive issue of whether the sterilization of criminals was justified by the results of criminal-biological research. As we have seen, medical doctors who were not themselves engaged in criminal-biological research (Gütt, Rüdin) were most likely to call for the sterilization of criminals, whereas doctors who conducted criminal-biological research were more likely either to oppose the measure (Lange) or to endorse it only with reservations (Stumpfl). Furthermore, as the positions of Fickert, Hoffmann, Exner, and Mezger showed, most jurists with criminological interests opposed the inclusion of criminals in the sterilization law.

Overall, the medical profession appears to bear greater culpability regarding the sterilization of criminals than the legal profession. The Justice Ministry and most academic jurists doing criminological research opposed sterilization measures that specifically targeted criminals. Within the medical profession, three groups should be distinguished: specialists in criminal biology; eugenic policy makers without any expertise in criminal biology; and rank-and-file doctors. The criminal biologists helped to spread the hereditarian view that crime had genetic causes and that the sterilization of criminals could serve as a weapon in the fight against crime. At the same time, however, they clearly acknowledged that the role of heredity in criminal behavior was not yet fully understood and therefore did not advocate special provisions for the sterilization of criminals until further progress had been made in their research. There can be little doubt that the relative sophistication of criminal-biological research was responsible for the critical stance of the Justice Ministry and for the omission of criminals from the Nazi sterilization law. For the eugenic hard-liners like Gütt, Rüdin, Kranz, and Koller, however, the heritability of crime was an idée fixe. Neither the lack of scientific evidence nor the omission of criminals from the sterilization law prevented them from trying to implement the sterilization of criminals. Through their position of authority as authors of the semiofficial commentary on the sterilization law, Gütt and Rüdin were able to recruit many rank-and-file medical doctors as allies in this effort.

If Gütt and Rüdin succeeded in making so much headway in targeting criminals for sterilization, this was in large part because the Nazis had come to power. Although by the late Weimar years there was almost universal support for the legalization of voluntary eugenic sterilization, without the Nazi seizure of power Gütt would not have been put in charge of eugenic policy at the Interior Ministry and the sterilization law would not have introduced compulsory sterilization. The eugenic zealots Gütt and Rüdin were able to do real damage because political conditions had placed them in a position of power. At the same time, it is also important to remember that even under the Nazi regime the eugenic hard-liners suffered defeats. After all, Gütt and Rüdin's opponents succeeded in having criminals omitted from the sterilization law, limiting the consideration of criminal behavior for a diagnosis of feeblemindedness to borderline cases, and preventing the subsequent expansion of the sterilization law to include criminals. In this respect, then, our analysis demonstrates that before Nazi biological politics took its fateful turn to mass murder with the "euthanasia" operation in 1939, there was some room for debate and dissent in the area of eugenics within the Nazi racial state.

CONCLUSION

As we look back over the development of German criminology from the late nineteenth century to 1945, the most noticeable feature is the predominance of research on the biological causes of crime over research on its social causes. The criminal-biological approach prevailed in large part because most criminological research was conducted by psychiatrists. The field of criminology had originally developed from a conjunction of interests among criminal jurists and psychiatrists. The penal reformers around Franz von Liszt looked to criminological research to provide a scientific foundation for penal policy. Although the penal reformers were inclined to attribute greater importance to social than to biological causes of crime, in practice criminal-sociological investigations soon lagged behind criminal-biological research, both because German sociologists showed little interest in crime and because the penal reformers proved reluctant to undertake criminal-sociological research themselves. This situation changed only after the First World War, when a number of jurists, most notably Exner and Liepmann, did begin to conduct criminal-sociological research. But the resurgence of criminal sociology under Exner's aegis was never enough to overcome the continuing predominance of criminal biology.

Hence most criminological research during this period was conducted by German doctors, primarily psychiatrists. Why did German psychiatrists take such an interest in criminological questions? There were several reasons. First, the late nineteenth-century surge in the medical profession's interest in the etiology of crime came about because Lombroso's theory of the born criminal advanced a biological explanation of crime to which German doctors, especially prison doctors, felt compelled to respond. And when Lombroso equated his "born criminal" with the psychiatric diagnosis of "moral insanity," psychiatrists in general felt called upon to react to his theories.

Second, the reception of Lombroso's theories occurred at a time when German psychiatry was expanding its professional territory beyond the area of full-fledged mental illnesses into the borderland of minor mental "abnormalities" (now termed "personality disorders") that Koch called "geistige Minderwertigkeiten" and Kraepelin and Schneider later referred to as "psychopathic personalities." Since these conditions were associated with deviant behavior, including crime, psychiatrists' interest in colonizing this vast new borderland of "abnormalities" also fueled their interest in criminological research.

Third, psychiatrists pursued research on the causes of crime because they sought to expand the role of psychiatry in the criminal justice system. This ambition found its earliest and most radical expression in Kraepelin's *Die Abschaffung des Strafmaßes* (1880), in which he called for the abolition of fixed prison sentences in favor of indefinite, individualized treatment and the reorganization of the penal system along the lines of psychiatric clinics. Since Kraepelin's scheme sought to eliminate the distinction between punishment and medical treatment, the question of legal responsibility became moot, so that psychiatrists would no longer have to serve as expert witness in cases of the insanity plea. As a result, the traditionally adversarial relationship between criminal justice and psychiatry, in which jurists frequently resented psychiatrists for "getting criminals off," was to be transformed into a symbiotic one, in which psychiatrists played a key role in determining the proper individualized treatment for every offender. Although most psychiatrists stopped well short of Kraepelin's demands and accepted the distinction between legally responsible and irresponsible offenders (calling only for the introduction of "diminished responsibility"), they all shared the ambition of expanding the role of psychiatry in the criminal justice system. The whole idea behind criminal-biological examinations was that psychiatric evaluations ought to play a role in determining an offender's individualized penal treatment.

Finally, the psychiatric profession's eagerness to play a major role in criminal justice was closely connected to another characteristic of late nineteenth- and twentieth-century German psychiatry: its willingness to place the interests of society above the welfare of the individual patient. This attitude was clearly reflected in the pre-1914 discussions about the introduction of "diminished responsibility," in which psychiatrists seized on the "abnormality" of *Minderwertige* to justify their indefinite detention for the sake of protecting society without, however, insisting that this same "abnormality" qualify *Minderwertige* for purely medical treatment and thus exempt them from the rigors and stigma of imprisonment. The same attitude received its most explicit formulation when Aschaffenburg defended psychiatrists against the accusation that their "excessive humanitarianism" had undermined criminal justice. Psychiatrists, he insisted, routinely "deprive[d] patients of their freedom in order to protect the public" and were therefore well aware that "the interests of the patient must come second to the general welfare."[1]

Starting with the reception of Lombroso in the late nineteenth century, the biological explanations of crime offered by German psychiatrists took the form of two different paradigms. Although the turn-of-the-century pioneers of German "criminal psychology" were unanimous in rejecting Lombroso's claim that the "born criminal" represented a distinct anthropological type, the explanations of criminal behavior that they offered instead split them into two camps. The proponents of what I have called the "Kraepelin paradigm" (Kraepelin, Bleuler, and Koch) stripped Lombroso's notion of the born criminal of its anthropological characteristics and redefined the born criminal in purely psychiatric terms as someone with a "moral defect." After the First World War, this paradigm lived on in the shape of Birnbaum's and Schneider's *gemütlos* (compassionless) or "amoral" psychopaths. The most noteworthy feature of this paradigm was its conflation of moral and medical norms. Thus Kraepelin defined "moral insanity" as "the lack or weakness of those sentiments which counter the ruthless satisfaction of egotism." Remarkably, even Kurt Schneider, who criticized the conflation of medical and moral criteria in Kraepelin's definitions and made a special effort to establish objective psychological criteria for his "psychopathic personalities," committed the same error when he defined the *gemütlos* or amoral psychopathic type as lacking "compassion, shame, honor, remorse, conscience." The inclusion of moral criteria in psychiatric diagnoses greatly increased the risk of tautological reasoning in which a person's deviant or criminal behavior became a medical symptom of psychopathy simply because it violated conventional moral and social norms.

Since Schneider and Birnbaum regarded the *gemütlos* or amoral psychopathic types as a tiny minority among criminals, the scope of the Kraepelin paradigm was severely restricted from the Weimar period onward, allowing the competing paradigm to gain ascendancy. Already at the turn of the century, a second group of psychiatrists, including Aschaffenburg and Näcke, had denied the existence of a "moral defect" and taken a more complex view of the interaction of heredity and environment. They established what I have called the "Aschaffenburg paradigm," which argued that many criminals suffered from

1. Aschaffenburg, "Neue Horizonte?" *MKS* 24 (1933): 159. Although the date might lead one to wonder whether Aschaffenburg's comment was simply designed to ward off Nazi attacks, the historical record shows that this had indeed been the prevalent attitude among German psychiatrists at least since the turn of the century.

general mental abnormalities (described in terms of degeneration, *Minderwertigkeit*, or psychopathy) that made them more likely to succumb to a life of crime under adverse external circumstances—not because these abnormalities were directly criminogenic but because they handicapped their carriers in social and economic life. By the Weimar period the Aschaffenburg paradigm had become predominant. Virtually every criminal biologist of the interwar period, including those most committed to the search for genetic factors, like Lange and Stumpfl, agreed that, except for the rare cases of *gemütlos* psychopaths, the congenital or genetic factors that played a role in criminal behavior did not consist of some criminogenic "moral defect" but of various abnormal traits that were not inherently criminogenic but that could develop a criminogenic potential in certain combinations and under certain environmental circumstances.

The most important impact of the Aschaffenburg paradigm was that its complex view of the interaction of heredity and environment promoted increasing methodological and conceptual sophistication. If we compare Weimar era to pre-1914 research, there can be no doubt that the work of Birnbaum, Schneider, Gruhle, and Lange was considerably more sophisticated in its approach to the interaction of heredity and environment than the prewar theories of Kraepelin, Bleuler, Aschaffenburg, and Näcke. Remarkably, the long-term trend toward increasing methodological refinement continued in most (but not all) criminal-biological research even under the Nazi regime. Stumpfl had a much better grasp of the methodological problems of twin studies than Lange, just as Exner's 1939 survey of criminology represented a considerable advance over Aschaffenburg's standard work of 1903. This increasing sophistication immensely complicated criminal biologists' task. As their understanding of the interaction of heredity and environment became more complex, their goal of identifying criminogenic genetic factors and distinguishing between corrigibles and incorrigibles became ever more elusive.

Having established the increasing sophistication of criminal-biological research, we confront a paradox. For even though criminal biologists recognized that *both* genetic and environmental factors played a role in the etiology of crime, most (though not all) consistently privileged the search for genetic factors and argued that genetic factors were somehow of primary importance. Such an assertion would have been warranted only if it had been shown that genetic factors often led to crime without any significant environmental cofactors or that the criminogenic force of such genetic factors was not usually amenable to rehabilitative measures. In fact, however, it was widely recognized that there was no evidence for either proposition. On the contrary, Lange admitted that environmental factors played a role in the cases of *all* his criminal twins, and Stumpfl estimated that at most 20 percent of criminals could be considered incorrigible.

Why, then, did most criminal biologists nevertheless claim primacy for genetic factors? The answer, I would argue, has to do with several fundamental biases and assumptions that were characteristic of German psychiatry during the period under investigation. First, German psychiatry during this period was characterized by a strong hereditarian bias, that is, by the assumption that individual differences, including mental illness, were primarily caused by genetic factors. This hereditarianism, which was by no means unique to *German* psychiatry, derived at least in part from psychiatry's failure to make progress in the treatment of mental illnesses. Unable to cure most of their patients, psychiatrists were tempted to explain their therapeutic failures by attributing the cause of mental illness to immutable genetic factors. Furthermore, although human genetics remained in a primitive state throughout the first half of the twentieth century, hereditarianism also received a boost from the rediscovery of Mendel's laws around the turn of the century.

Second, by the mid-1920s at the latest, the vast majority of German physicians and psychiatrists were enthusiastic supporters of eugenics, at least in principle. This last qualification is important because the details of practical implementation, including the question of who exactly should be sterilized, gave rise to significant disagreements. Nevertheless, the almost universal enthusiasm for eugenics among German psychiatrists clearly helps to explain why they privileged the search for genetic factors.

Finally, although most criminal biologists acknowledged the role of social factors in crime, they were generally pessimistic about being able to change the social conditions that pushed so many people into a life of crime. Time and time again major criminal biologists, including Aschaffenburg, Näcke, and Viernstein, and even the hard-line eugenicist Rüdin, explicitly admitted that in many cases changes in the social milieu of a recidivist could, in principle, prevent that person from offending again. But such acknowledgments were always followed by the qualification that this environment could not, in practice, be changed, so that the criminal in question would have to be considered "incorrigible." In other words—and this is crucial—the prognosis of incorrigibility was not based on the conviction that the individual's criminal behavior resulted from unalterable genetic factors but on the belief that it was simply too difficult to change the social factors involved. The reasons for this pessimism about the possibility of changing the social environment and the lack of interest in trying to effect such social change were deeply rooted in the traditions of the medical profession and the political conservatism of many of its members. Psychiatrists were used to searching for the causes of mental illness in the patient rather than taking into account the patient's environment. A similar point holds for the penal reformers. For although Liszt and his fellow reformers frequently stressed the role of social factors, their reform proposals focused on the individualization of punishment, that is, on the transformation of the offender rather than social change as the most important strategy of crime prevention. From this perspective, criminal biology was welcome because it promised the knowledge about individual criminals that was crucial for an offender-oriented reform effort.

After examining the reasons why so many criminal biologists and criminologists continued to privilege biological and genetic explanations of criminal behavior over sociological ones, we must also note that the increasing sophistication of criminal-biological research did impose some checks on hereditarian beliefs and led some psychiatrists and jurists to stress the importance of environmental factors. Among the psychiatrists pursuing criminal-biological research, Hans Gruhle remained highly critical of genetic explanations of crime and emphasized the role of social factors, including social class. Moreover, jurists conducting criminological research, especially Exner and Liepmann, tended to be much more evenhanded in their treatment of biological and social factors in the etiology of crime. Most tangibly, because criminal-biological research successfully conveyed the complexity of the interaction of genetics and environment in the etiology of crime, many psychiatrists and most jurists opposed making criminality a criterion for sterilization during the Weimar and Nazi years.

In comparative perspective, the development of German criminology was by no means unique. In Italy, Lombroso's far more simplistic views on the born criminal were extremely influential throughout the first half of the twentieth century.[2] Recent research on the history of French criminology has argued that the differences between the Italian "anthropological" school and the French "sociological" school have been overstated and that even though the French, like the Germans, rejected the born criminal as an anthropological type, they shared many of the Lombrosian school's basic hereditarian assumptions.[3] Likewise, in Britain, Charles Goring's famous study *The English Convict* (1913) rejected Lombroso's born criminal but propounded a theory linking criminal

2. See Mary Gibson's forthcoming book on this subject.
3. Laurent Mucchielli, "Hérédité et milieu social: Le faux antagonisme franco-italien. La place de l'école de Lacassagne dans l'histoire de la criminologie," in *Histoire de la criminologie française*, ed. Mucchielli (Paris: L'Harmattan, 1994), 189–214.

behavior to feeblemindedness that was very similar to Aschaffenburg's views.[4] Finally, twentieth-century American criminology contained a powerful strand of what Nicole Rafter has called "eugenic criminology," which gave the United States the dubious distinction of having been one of the very first countries to sterilize criminals (starting in 1907), a practice that continued well past 1945.[5]

The relationship between criminology and Nazism was complex. On the one hand, the long-standing predominance of criminal-biological over criminal-sociological research helped to popularize the notion that it would one day be possible to provide medical solutions to the crime problem. Criminal biology thus contributed to the rise of the eugenics movement and a climate of opinion that facilitated the implementation of Nazi eugenic policy. Leading criminal biologists appealed for the Nazi regime's support by arguing that criminal-biological examinations could serve a useful function in Nazi eugenic policy, and this appeal resulted in the expansion of the Criminal-Biological Service to the national level. The research of Robert Ritter and others, the disproportionate targeting of criminals for eugenic sterilization promoted by Gütt and Rüdin, and, finally, the killing of criminal insane persons in the euthanasia operation all reflected a crude biological determinism that would have been inconceivable without decades of hereditarian criminal-biological rhetoric.

On the other hand, however, both our analysis of mainstream criminological research and our discussion of Nazi sterilization policy with regard to criminals have shown that the triumph of genetic determinism under the Nazi regime was not as complete as has often been supposed. While crude genetic determinism and racism were indeed pervasive among the Nazi elite, the leadership of the police, and significant portions of the medical profession as well as in the work of Robert Ritter and Heinrich Wilhelm Kranz, they did not supplant the more nuanced and complex discourse of most mainstream criminal biologists and criminologists.

The most tangible evidence for this argument was provided by our account of the genesis and implementation of the sterilization law, which demonstrated that the sophistication of criminal-biological research, with its emphasis on the complex interaction of genetic and environmental factors, made the sterilization of criminals controversial and contentious not only during the Weimar Republic but even under the Nazi regime. The opponents of the sterilization of criminals succeeded in having criminals excluded from the sterilization law of

4. David Garland, "British Criminology before 1935," *British Journal of Criminology* 28 (1988): 131–47; Piers Beirne, "Heredity versus Environment: A Reconsideration of Charles Goring's *The English Convict* (1913)," *British Journal of Criminology* 28 (1988): 315–39.

5. Nicole Hahn Rafter, *Creating Born Criminals* (Urbana: University of Illinois Press, 1997).

1933 and subsequently in preventing the law from being amended to include criminals. And even though Gütt and Rüdin used their influence to target criminals through an expanded definition of feeblemindedness, a significant number of Superior Hereditary Health Courts ruled against the sterilization of criminals on the basis of criminal behavior. All this suggests that the spectrum of opinion on eugenic policy was more diverse and that Nazi biological politics left more room for disagreement than historians have often assumed.

Several of the arguments advanced in this book fit in with the findings of two major strands of research on the history of science and medicine under National Socialism. After 1945 German academics, scientists, and doctors generally sought to deny or minimize the complicity of their professions with the Nazi regime through silence or apologetic accounts. When concerned scientists and historians of a younger generation finally began to investigate the history of science and medicine under the Third Reich starting in the 1980s, they therefore focused on the nazification of science, the collaboration of scientists and doctors with the Nazi regime, and their role in the organized mass murder of the euthanasia operation and the Holocaust.[6] This work has made a tremendous contribution to our understanding of the Third Reich and the role of science and the professions in it. It has definitively discredited earlier apologetic accounts and documented the central role of scientists, doctors, and other professionals in the most inhumane and murderous policies of Nazi Germany. It has shifted our attention from the irrational and antimodern aspects of Nazism to the modern, rational, and scientific features and policies of the Nazi regime.[7] And it has shown that the murder of the European Jews was part of a larger Nazi agenda of "biological politics" that targeted a wide variety of groups that were considered biologically inferior.[8] Especially in this last regard, my book agrees with and extends this strand of research by showing that criminals, too,

6. See, for example, Ernst Klee, *"Euthanasie" im NS-Staat: Die "Vernichtung lebensunwerten Lebens"* (Frankfurt: Fischer, 1983); Benno Müller-Hill, *Tödliche Wissenschaft: Die Aussonderung von Juden, Zigeunern und Geisteskranken, 1933–1945* (Reinbek: Rowohlt, 1984), translated as *Murderous Science: Elimination by Scientific Selection of Jews, Gypsies, and Others, Germany, 1933–1945* (Oxford: Oxford University Press, 1988); Robert Proctor, *Racial Hygiene: Medicine under the Nazis* (Cambridge, Mass.: Harvard University Press, 1988). Of course, there were efforts to address the history of science and medicine under Nazism before the 1980s, but they remained isolated.

7. On this point, see Anne Harrington, *Reenchanted Science: Holism in German Culture from Wilhelm II to Hitler* (Princeton: Princeton University Press, 1996), 210–11.

8. See Michael Burleigh and Wolfgang Wippermann, *The Racial State: Germany, 1933–1945* (Cambridge: Cambridge University Press, 1991).

were among the targets not only of criminal justice but of Nazi biological politics.

Other arguments in this book connect with what one might call a "second wave" of research on science under Nazism that has only begun to take shape while I have been working on this book. After the first wave of historical research documented the participation of scientists and doctors in the crimes of the Nazi regime, the most recent research has been taking both a broader and a closer look at science under the Nazis that is revealing a more complex and nuanced picture. The historian Dirk Blasius captured the agenda of this research in a brief remark on the historiography of psychiatry under the Nazi regime: "It is not difficult to document the turn away from the individual for eugenics [Rassenhygiene], but eugenics does not represent the whole of psychiatry. The real challenge for historical analysis lies in the problem of the long-term development of traditions of science that are not typical of Nazism but fell under its influence."[9]

My argument that the genetic determinism and racism characteristic of so much of the Nazi regime failed to supplant a more complex discourse on the etiology of crime in a significant portion of criminological research is in line with the findings of this second wave of scholarship. Most fundamentally, this research has called attention to the continuity of "normal" science during the Third Reich.[10] Ulfried Geuter's study of psychology in Nazi Germany, for example, has emphasized "the frightening normality of the production and use of science" under the Nazi regime. Kristie Macrakis's history of the Kaiser-Wilhelm-Society in the Third Reich has sought to "correct the prevalent view that all of science during this period was ideologically injected" and argued that "science in National Socialist Germany not only survived but often thrived." Pamela Potter's study of German musicology has suggested that "one cannot really speak of a wholesale nazification of musicology." In an analysis of eugenics and racism in the Third Reich Paul Weindling has warned against treating "every eugenicist [as] part of a homogeneous racial ideology" and argued that "race and its medical extensions were neither administratively nor ideolog-

9. Dirk Blasius, "Psychiatrie in der Zeit des Nationalsozialismus," Sudhoffs Archiv 75 (1991): 98.

10. On the historiography of this second wave (my term), see Arleen Tuchmann, "Institutions and Disciplines: Recent Work in the History of German Science," Journal of Modern History 69 (1997): 298–319; Monika Renneberg and Mark Walker, "Scientists, Engineers and National Socialism," in Science, Technology and National Socialism, ed. Renneberg and Walker (Cambridge: Cambridge University Press, 1994), 14–15.

ically monolithic." Finally, Robert Proctor's recent book on the "Nazi war on cancer" has criticized the view that "Nazi rhetoric and values . . . penetrated every crevice of German intellectual life" as a "misconception" and called attention to the "troubling phenomenon of 'quality science' under Nazism." Insisting that "Nazism was a more subtle phenomenon than we commonly imagine," Proctor's study has sought to address not only the undisputed *complicity* of science under fascism but also the *complexity* of science within fascism." In sum, these studies have argued that major areas of science continued to produce complex, sophisticated scientific research under the Nazi regime and were less pervaded by Nazi ideology than previously assumed. In this study I have sought to make exactly this argument for the field of criminology.[11]

Because any attempt to present a more nuanced picture of Nazi Germany always runs the risk of being misunderstood or misused, I wish to make it clear that by emphasizing the complexity of scientific research under Nazism, I do not intend to advance apologetic arguments that seek to minimize the complicity of many German scientists and doctors in the crimes of the Nazi regime. The more nuanced picture of scientific research under the Nazi regime is not meant to suggest that most scientists were somehow politically neutral, immune to Nazi ideology, and therefore free from responsibility for the crimes of the regime. They were not. I have shown that many prominent criminologists were eager to connect criminology to the agenda of Nazi biological politics. The more complex picture is, however, meant to show that the image of all science under National Socialism as totally nazified and, in the case of medicine, completely imbued with genetic determinism and racism is historically inaccurate and misleading. Such a view amounts to a demonization of science under the Nazi regime that can in fact have dangerous apologetic implications. For if crude genetic determinism and racism had indeed pervaded all medical and criminal-biological research during the Nazi regime, then the scientists and doctors who executed the inhumane and ultimately murderous policies of the racial state could argue that their actions simply reflected the state of scientific research at

---

11. Ulfried Geuter, *The Professionalization of Psychology in Nazi Germany* (Cambridge: Cambridge University Press, 1992), xii; Kristie Macrakis, *Surviving the Swastika: Scientific Research in Nazi Germany* (New York: Oxford University Press, 1993), 3–4, 199; Pamela Potter, *Most German of the Arts: Musicology and Society from the Weimar Republic to the End of Hitler's Reich* (New Haven: Yale University Press, 1998), 196; Paul Weindling, "Understanding Nazi Racism: Precursors and Perpetrators," in *Confronting the Nazi Past*, ed. Michael Burleigh (New York: St. Martin's, 1996), 75, 80; Robert Proctor, *The Nazi War on Cancer* (Princeton: Princeton University Press, 1999), 5–7. Geuter's book originally appeared in German in 1984. The notion of a second wave is not meant to denote a neat sequence; the two waves overlap.

the time. If it can be demonstrated, however, as I hope to have done, that the sophistication of psychiatric and criminological research gave rise to serious objections to the sterilization of criminals on the basis of criminal behavior, then the moral responsibility of men like Gütt, Rüdin, Ritter, and H. W. Kranz is much greater.

A more complex picture of science under the Third Reich also diminishes the distance that we often perceive between "Nazi science" and our own science.[12] Contemporary scientists as well as the general public often assume that science under Nazism was "bad" or "perverted" science. This view is reassuring because it suggests that our own, more "advanced" science does not have the same dangerous implications that "Nazi science" had. But if science under the Nazis was in fact more sophisticated, the distance between "Nazi science" and science in our own day is diminished, and we are forced to ask ourselves whether the role of science and medicine under the Nazi regime might point to dangers inherent in scientific research in the present. My point here is not to suggest that research on the genetic causes of crime, for instance, is intrinsically evil and dangerous and will necessarily lead to inhumane and murderous state policies. Rather, my point is that much of the scientific research conducted during the Nazi years was not as different from current scientific research as we would like to think. Like science before and after the Third Reich, scientific research in Nazi Germany was characterized by continual tension between the internal dynamics of science and the intellectual and political biases of the scientists and their society. This argument should make us uncomfortable in salutary ways. For it makes us realize that the connection between scientific research and the Nazi regime was more complicated than we might have thought, and it gives us a more critical view of science in our own time.

12. A similar point about "what would happen if certain 'us/them' distinctions were to become unstable" as a result of a more complex view of science under Nazism (in this case, its holistic side) is made in Anne Harrington, "Unmasking Suffering's Masks: Reflections on Old and New Memories of Nazi Medicine," *Daedalus* 125 (Winter 1996): 181–205.

BIBLIOGRAPHY

PRIMARY SOURCES

Archival Sources

Bayerisches Hauptstaatsarchiv, Munich
    Ministerium der Justiz (MJu)
    Ministerium des Innern (MInn)
Bundesarchiv, Abteilung Potsdam (formerly Zentrales Staatsarchiv, Potsdam)
    R 15.01 Reichsministerium des Innern
    R 18 Reichsministerium des Innern
    R 22 Reichsministerium der Justiz
    R 23.01 Rechnungshof des Deutschen Reiches
    R 30.01 Reichsministerium der Justiz
National Archives, College Park, Maryland
    Berlin Document Center Files, NS-Ortskartei (Microfilm), A-3340-MFOK

Printed Primary Sources

Periodicals
Archiv für Kriminologie
Archiv für Kriminalanthropologie und Kriminalistik
Archiv für Psychiatrie
Archiv für Rassen- und Gesellschaftsbiologie
Archiv für Strafrecht und Strafprozeß
Allgemeine Zeitschrift für Psychiatrie
Blätter für Gefängniskunde
Deutsche Juristen-Zeitung
Deutsches Recht
Deutsche Zeitschrift für die gesamte gerichtliche Medizin
Der Erbarzt
Eugenik
Fortschritte der Neurologie, Psychiatrie und ihrer Grenzgebiete

Der Gerichtssaal
Juristische Wochenschrift
Monatsblätter des Deutschen Reichsverbandes [since vol. 3: *Reichszusammenschlusses*] *für*
    Gerichtshilfe, Gefangenen- und Entlassenenfürsorge
Mitteilungen der Internationalen Kriminalistischen Vereinigung
Mitteilungen der Kriminalbiologischen Gesellschaft
Monatsschrift für Kriminalpsychologie und Strafrechtsreform
Zeitschrift für die gesamte Neurologie und Psychiatrie
Zeitschrift für die gesamte Strafrechtswissenschaft

Books and Articles

"Acht Gutachten der Bayerischen kriminalbiologischen Sammelstelle in München." *MKS* 27
    (1936): 134–52.
Adler, Alfred. "Neurose und Verbrechen." *Internationale Zeitschrift für Individualpsychologie*
    3 (1924): 1–11.
———. "Die kriminelle Persönlichkeit und ihre Heilung." *Internationale Zeitschrift für*
    Individualpsychologie 9 (1931): 321–29.
Aichhorn, August. *Verwahrloste Jugend: Die Psychoanalyse in der Fürsorgeerziehung.* Vienna:
    Internationaler Psychoanalytischer Verlag, 1931.
Alexander, Franz, and Hugo Staub. *Der Verbrecher und seine Richter.* Vienna: Internationaler
    Psychoanalytischer Verlag, 1929.
Amend, Albert. *Die Kriminalität Deutschlands, 1919–1932.* Kriminalistische Abhandlungen,
    no. 26. Leipzig: Wiegandt, 1937.
Ammann, Walter. "Die Asozialen und ihre Behandlung: Eine Aufgabe des öffentlichen
    Rechts." J.D. diss., University of Heidelberg, 1940.
Antonow, Iwan. *Die Kriminalbiologie im Dienste der Verbrechensbekämpfung und -verhütung*
    in Deutschland. Sofia: Rosowa Dolina, 1938.
Appelius, Hugo. "Die Reformbestrebungen auf dem Gebiet der Strafrechtspflege und das
    heutige Strafrecht." *ZStW* 12 (1892): 1–33.
Aschaffenburg, Gustav. *Das Verbrechen und seine Bekämpfung: Kriminalpsychologie für*
    Mediziner, Juristen und Soziologen, ein Beitrag zur Reform der Strafgesetzgebung.
    Heidelberg: Winter, 1903.
———. *Crime and Its Repression.* Boston: Little, Brown, 1913.
———. *Das Verbrechen und seine Bekämpfung.* 3d ed. Heidelberg: Winter, 1923.
———. "Zur Frage der Unfruchtbarmachung der geistig Minderwertigen." *Wissenschaftliche*
    Beilage der Leipziger Lehrerzeitung, no. 29 (1924).
———. *Psychiatrie und Strafrecht: Rede gehalten bei der Gründungsfeier der Universität Köln am*
    5. Mai 1928. Cologne: Müller, 1928.
———. "Der Einfluss Kraepelins auf die Kriminalpsychologie und Kriminalpolitik." *AZP* 87
    (1929): 87–95.
———. "Kriminalanthropologie und Kriminalbiologie." In *Handwörterbuch der Kriminologie*,
    edited by Alexander Elster and Heinrich Lingemann, 1:825–40. Berlin: de Gruyter, 1933.
———. "Neue Horizonte?" *MKS* 24 (1933): 158–62.
———. "Gleichzeitige Anordnung der Entmannung und der Sicherungsverwahrung." *MKS* 26
    (1935): 385–88.
———. "Rückblick und Ausblick." *MKS* 26 (1935): 531–35.
Aschaffenburg, Gustav, and Dr. Partenheimer, eds. *Bericht über den VII. Internationalen*
    Kongreß für Kriminalanthropologie. Heidelberg: Winter, 1912.
Aschrott, P. F. "Betrachtungen über die Bewegung der Kriminalität in Preussen während der

Jahre 1872 bis 1881." *Jahrbuch für Gesetzgebung, Verwaltung und Volkswirtschaft im Deutschen Reich* 8 (1884): 185.

Avé-Lallemant, Friedrich C. B. *Das deutsche Gaunerthum in seiner social-politischen, literarischen und linguistischen Ausbildung zu seinem heutigen Bestande*. 4 vols. Leipzig: Brockhaus, 1858–62.

Baer, Abraham. *Der Verbrecher in anthropologischer Beziehung*. Leipzig: Thieme, 1893.

Baeyer, Walter von. *Zur Genealogie psychopathischer Schwindler und Lügner*. Leipzig: Thieme, 1935.

———. "Zur Vererbung psychopathischer Eigenschaften (Familienuntersuchungen an psychopathischen Schwindlern und Lügnern)." *Der Erbarzt* 3 (1936): 137–40.

———. "Walter Ritter von Baeyer." In *Psychiatrie in Selbstdarstellungen*. Bern: Huber, 1977.

Beccaria, Cesare. *On Crimes and Punishments and Other Writings*. Cambridge: Cambridge University Press, 1995.

Berg, Hermann. *Getreidepreise und Kriminalität in Deutschland seit 1882*. Abhandlungen des Kriminalistischen Seminars. N.F., vol. 1. Berlin: Guttentag, 1902.

Beringer, K. "Zum Begriff des Psychopathen: Bemerkungen zu dem gleichnamigen Aufsatz von Prof. Mezger." *MKS* 30 (1939): 319–22.

Berlit, Bertold. "Erblichkeitsuntersuchungen bei Psychopathen." *ZGNP* 134 (1931): 382–450.

Bernhardt, Rudolf. *Studien über erbliche Belastung bei Vermögensverbrechern*. Kriminalistische Abhandlungen, no. 12. Leipzig: Wiegandt, 1930.

Berthold, Fritz. "Die Entwicklung der moral insanity und der heutige Stand der Zurechnungsfähigkeit." J.D. diss., University of Erlangen, 1937.

Birnbaum, Karl. *Die psychopathischen Verbrecher: Die Grenzzustände zwischen geistiger Gesundheit und Krankheit in ihren Beziehungen zu Verbrechen und Strafwesen*. Berlin: Langenscheidt, 1914.

———. *Kriminalpsychopathologie*. Berlin: Springer, 1921.

———. *Die psychopathischen Verbrecher: Die Grenzzustände zwischen geistiger Gesundheit und Krankheit in ihren Beziehungen zu Verbrechen und Strafwesen*. 2d rev. ed. Leipzig: Thieme, 1926.

———. *Kriminalpsychopathologie und psychobiologische Verbrecherkunde*. 2d rev. ed. Berlin: Springer, 1931.

———, ed. *Handwörterbuch der medizinischen Psychologie*. Leipzig: Thieme, 1930.

Blasbalg, Jenny. "Ausländische und deutsche Gesetze und Gesetzentwürfe über Unfruchtbarmachung." *ZStW* 52 (1932): 477–96.

Bleuler, Eugen. *Der geborene Verbrecher: Eine kritische Studie*. Munich: J. F. Lehmann, 1896.

———. "Zur Behandlung Gemeingefährlicher." *MKS* 1 (May 1904): 92–99.

Boeters, Gerhard. "Die Unfruchtbarmachung der geistig Minderwertigen." *Wissenschaftliche Beilage der Leipziger Lehrerzeitung*, no. 28 (1924).

———. "Aufruf an die deutsche Ärzteschaft." *Ärztliches Vereinsblatt für Deutschland* 51, no. 1297 (9 Jan. 1924): 3–4.

———. "Die Unfruchtbarmachung Geisteskranker, Schwachsinniger und Verbrecher aus Anlage." *Zeitschrift für Medizinalbeamte* 38 (1925): 336–41.

———. "Zur Entmannung von Sittlichkeitsverbrechern." *MKS* 25 (1934): 579–82.

———. "Zur Entmannung von Sittlichkeitsverbrechern," Part 2. *MKS* 26 (1935): 367–70.

Böhmer, Kurt. "Untersuchungen über den Körperbau des Verbrechers." *MKS* 19 (1928): 193–209.

Bohne, Gotthold. "Psychoanalyse und Strafrecht." *ZStW* 47 (1926): 439–59.

———. "Individualpsychologische Betrachtungen zu den Kapitalverbrechen der letzten Zeit." *DJZ* 33 (1928): 1502–7.

——. "Bibliographie über die Verwertbarkeit der Tiefenpsychologie (Psychoanalyse und Individualpsychologie) im Strafrecht und Strafvollzug." *ZStW* 53 (1933): 395–402.

Bondy, Curt. "Zur Frage der Erziehbarkeit." *ZStW* 48 (1927): 329–34.

——. Review of *Der Stufenstrafvollzug*. *ZStW* 51 (1930): 646.

Bonhoeffer, Karl. "Die Unfruchtbarmachung der geistig Minderwertigen." *Klinische Wochenschrift* no. 18 (1924): 798–801.

Bumke, Oswald. *Über nervöse Entartung*. Berlin: Springer, 1912.

——. *Lehrbuch der Geisteskrankheiten*. 3d ed. Munich: Bergmann, 1929.

Bürger-Prinz, Hans. "Das menschliche Triebleben und seine forensische Bedeutung." *MKS* 30 (1939): 449–60.

——. "Psychiatrie und Strafrecht." *MKS* 33 (1942): 45–52.

Cantor, Nathaniel. "Recent Tendencies in Criminological Research in Germany." *American Sociological Review* 1 (1936): 407–18.

——. "Recent Tendencies in Criminological Research in Germany." *Journal of Criminal Law and Criminology* 27 (1936–37): 782–93.

Coenen, Hans. *Strafrecht und Psychoanalyse*. Breslau: Schletter, 1929.

Creutz, Walter. "Der Einfluss der 'erblichen Belastung' und der 'Umwelt' bei Kriminellen." *AZP* 95 (1931): 73–106.

Cropp. "Fünf Jahre Abteilung 'Volksgesundheit' des Reichsministeriums des Innern unter Leitung von Ministerialdirektor Dr. Arthur Gütt." *Der öffentliche Gesundheitsdienst* 4 (1938–39): 869–97.

Dahm, Georg, and Friedrich Schaffstein. *Liberales oder autoritäres Strafrecht?* Hamburg: Hanseatische Verlagsanstalt, 1933.

Das Judentum in der Rechtswissenschaft: Ansprachen, Vorträge und Ergebnisse der Tagung der Reichsgruppe Hochschullehrer des NSRB am 3. und 4. Oktober 1936. 8 vols. Berlin: Deutscher Rechts-Verlag, 1936.

Delbrück, Felix. "Zum Schutz der Gesellschaft gegen gemeingefährliche Geisteskranke und vermindert Zurechnungsfähige." *MKS* 1 (1904): 121–23.

Der Stufenstrafvollzug und die kriminalbiologische Untersuchung der Gefangenen in den bayerischen Strafanstalten. Zusammengestellt im Auftrage des Bayerischen Staatsministeriums der Justiz. 3 vols. Munich, 1926–29.

Diagnostic and Statistical Manual of Mental Disorders. 3d ed. Washington, D.C.: American Psychiatric Association, 1987.

"Die Eugenik im Dienste der Volkswohlfahrt: Bericht über die Verhandlungen eines zusammengesetzten Ausschusses des Preußischen Landesgesundheitsrates vom 2. Juli 1932." *Veröffentlichungen aus dem Gebiete der Medizinalverwaltung* 38 (1932): 629–740.

"Die Kallikaks unserer Zeit." *Eugenik* 2 (1932): 202–8.

Dr. Joseph Galls Besuche in den merkwürdigen Gefängnissen von Preussen und Sachsen. Deutz, 1805.

Dubitscher, Fred. "Dummheit oder Schwachsinn?" *Der Erbarzt* 1 (1935): 187–90.

——. "Der moralische Schwachsinn unter Berücksichtigung des Gesetzes zur Verhütung erbkranken Nachwuchses." *ZGNP* 154 (1936): 422–57.

——. "Asozialität und Unfruchtbarmachung. Aus dem Material des Reichsgesundheitsamtes." *MKBG* 5 (1937): 99–110.

——. *Der Schwachsinn*. Handbuch der Erbkrankheiten, vol. 1. Leipzig: Thieme, 1937.

——. *Asoziale Sippen: Erb- und sozialbiologische Untersuchungen*. Leipzig: Thieme, 1942.

Dugdale, Richard. *The Jukes: A Study in Crime, Pauperism, Disease, and Heredity*. New York: Putnam, 1877.

Elster, Alexander, and Heinrich Lingemann, eds. *Handwörterbuch der Kriminologie*. 2 vols. Berlin: de Gruyter, 1933–36.

Engelhardt, Knut. *Psychoanalyse der strafenden Gesellschaft*. Frankfurt: Haag und Herchen, 1976.

"Entwurf: Gesetz über die Behandlung Gemeinschaftsfremder." In *Recht, Verwaltung und Justiz im Nationalsozialismus*, edited by Martin Hirsch, Diemut Majer, and Jürgen Meinck, 536–39. Cologne: Bund, 1984.

Entwürfe zu einem Deutschen Strafgesetzbuch. Veröffentlicht auf Anordnung des Reichs-Justizministeriums. Berlin: de Gruyter, 1920.

Exner, Franz. "Gesellschaftliche und staatliche Strafjustiz." *ZStW* 40 (1919): 1–29.

——. *Krieg und Kriminalität: Vortrag gehalten anlässlich der Universitätsgründungsfeier am 3. Juli 1926 in Leipzig*. Kriminalistische Abhandlungen, no. 1. Leipzig: Wiegandt, 1926.

——. *Krieg und Kriminalität in Österreich*. Wirtschafts- und Sozialgeschichte des Weltkrieges, Österreichische und Ungarische Serie. Vienna: Holder-Pichler-Tempsky, 1927.

——. *Studien über die Strafzumessungspraxis der deutschen Gerichte*. Leipzig: Wiegandt, 1931.

——. "Development of the Administration of Criminal Justice in Germany." *Journal of Criminal Law and Criminology* 24 (1933–34): 248–59.

——. "Kriminalistischer Bericht über eine Reise nach Amerika." *ZStW* 54 (1934): 345–93, 511–43.

——. "Aufgaben der Kriminologie im neuen Reich." *MKS* 27 (1936): 3–16.

——. "Bemerkungen zu Stumpfl: *Erbanlage und Verbrechen*. Kriminalistische Bemerkungen." *MKS* 27 (1936): 336–39.

——. "Kriminalsoziologie." In *Handwörterbuch der Kriminologie*, edited by Alexander Elster and Heinrich Lingemann, 2:10–26. Berlin: de Gruyter, 1936.

——. "Über Rückfall-Prognosen." *MKS* 27 (1936): 401–9.

——. "Die Prognose bei Rückfallsverbrechern." *MKBG* 5 (1937): 43–54.

——. "Bemerkungen zu dem vorstehenden Aufsatz von Dr. H. Trunk." *MKS* 28 (1937): 227–30.

——. "Volkscharakter und Verbrechen." *MKS* 29 (1938): 404–21.

——. "Gutachten zum Thema: Organisation der Verbrechensvorbeugung in den verschiedenen Ländern." In *Römischer Kongreß für Kriminologie*, 303–8. Berlin: Decker, 1939.

——. *Kriminalbiologie in ihren Grundzügen*. Hamburg: Hanseatische Verlagsanstalt, 1939.

——. "Die spätere Straffälligkeit jugendlicher Rechtsbrecher." *MKS* 31 (1940): 217–18.

——. *Kriminalbiologie in ihren Grundzügen*. 2d ed. Hamburg: Hanseatische Verlagsanstalt, 1944.

——. *Biologia Criminal*. Barcelona: Bosch, 1946.

——. *Kriminologie*. 3d ed. of *Kriminalbiologie*. Berlin: Springer, 1949.

——. *Criminologia*. Milan: Vallardi, 1953.

Fetscher, Rainer. "Die Organisation der erbbiologischen Erforschung der Strafgefangenen in Sachsen." *BfG* 57 (1926): 69–75.

——. "Der Stand der Frage der Sterilisierung und Schwangerschaftsunterbrechung aus eugenischen Gründen beim Menschen." *Zeitschrift für induktive Abstammungs- und Vererbungslehre* 41 (1926): 375–93.

——. *Abriß der Erbbiologie und Eugenik*. Berlin: Salle, 1927.

——. "Aufgaben und Organisation einer Kartei der Minderwertigen." *MKBG* 1 (1927): 55–62.

——. "Aus der Praxis einer Kartei." *MKBG* 2 (1928): 161–74.

——. "Kriminalbiologische Erfahrungen an Sexualverbrechern." *MKBG* 3 (1930): 172–80.

——. "Organisation familienbiologischer Karteien." *Archiv für soziale Hygiene* 5 (1930): 330.

——. "Die Sterilisierung aus eugenischen Gründen." *ZStW* 52 (1932): 404–23.

——. "Die wissenschaftliche Erfassung der Kriminellen in Sachsen." *MKS* 23 (1932): 321–35.

——. "Zur gesetzlichen Regelung der Sterilisierung." *Eugenik* 3 (1933): 110–12.

——. "Zur Theorie und Praxis der Sterilisierung." *MKBG* 4 (1933): 247–57.

——. *Abriß der Erbbiologie und Rassenhygiene.* 2d ed. Frankfurt: Salle, 1934.

Fickert, Hans. *Rassenhygienische Verbrechensbekämpfung.* Kriminalistische Abhandlungen, no. 37. Leipzig: Wiegandt, 1938.

Finger, A. "Über die 'geminderte Zurechnungsfähigkeit' und die strafrechtliche Behandlung der 'gemindert Zurechnungsfähigen.' " *Gerichtssaal* 64 (1904): 257–319.

Finke. "Biologische Aufgaben in der Kriminalpolitik." *Eugenik* 1 (1930–31): 55–58.

Fränkel. "Verbrecherschädel." *AZP* 34 (1878): 403–4.

Frégier, Honoré-Antoine. *Des classes dangereuses de la population dans les grandes villes, et des moyens de les rendre meilleurs.* 2 vols. Paris: Bailliere, 1840.

Freud, Sigmund. "Einige Charaktertypen aus der psychoanalytischen Arbeit." In *Gesammelte Werke*, 10:389–91. Frankfurt: Fischer, 1967.

Fuld, Ludwig. "Der Einfluss der Lebensmittelpreise auf die Bewegung strafbarer Handlungen." Ph.D. diss., University of Mainz, 1881.

——. "Die Entwicklung der Moralstatistik." *Deutsche Zeit- und Streit-Fragen* 13 (1884): 453.

Galton, Francis. "The History of Twins as a Criterion of the Relative Powers of Nature and Nurture." *Fraser's Magazine* (1875): 566–76.

Gaupp, Robert. "Über den heutigen Stand der Lehre vom 'geborenen Verbrecher.' " *MKS* 1 (1904): 25–42.

——. *Die Unfruchtbarmachung geistig und sittlich Kranker und Minderwertiger.* Berlin: Springer, 1925.

——. "Die Unfruchtbarmachung geistig und sittlich Minderwertiger." *ZGNP* 100 (1926): 139–81.

Gerecke, Werner. "Untersuchungen über die erbliche Belastung der Gewohnheitsverbrecher." *Der Erbarzt* 2 (1935): 107–8.

Gerecke. "Zur Frage der Rückfallsprognose." *MKS* 30 (1939): 35–38.

Gerngross, Friedrich L. *Sterilisation und Kastration als Hilfsmittel im Kampf gegen das Verbrechen.* Munich: Lehmann, 1913.

"Gesetz zur Änderung des Gesetzes zur Verhütung erbkranken Nachwuchses." *MKS* 26 (1935): 371.

Glueck, Sheldon, and Eleanor Glueck. *Five Hundred Criminal Careers.* New York: Knopf, 1930.

Goddard, Henry. *The Kallikak Family: A Study in the Heredity of Feeblemindedness.* New York: Macmillan, 1912.

Goddard, Henry, and Wilker. "Die Familie Kallikak: Eine Studie zur Vererbung des Schwachsinns." *Zeitschrift für Kinderforschung* 18 (1913–14): 132.

Gottschalk, Alfred, ed. *Materialien zur Lehre von der verminderten Zurechnungsfähigkeit.* Berlin: Guttentag, 1904.

Groß, Hans. "Aufgabe und Ziele." *AKK* 1 (1898): 1–4.

——. "Antrittsvorlesung." *AKK* 21 (1905): 169–83.

——. "Vorwort des Herausgebers zu: Bruno Meyer." *Homosexualität und Strafrecht.* *AKK* 44 (1911): 249–54.

——. "Zur Frage der Kastration und Sterilisation." *AKK* 51 (1913): 316–25.

Gruhle, Hans. *Die Ursachen der jugendlichen Verwahrlosung und Kriminalität.* Berlin: Springer, 1912.

——. "Kraepelin's Stellung zur Verbrechensbekämpfung." *AZP* 84 (1926): 205–15.

——. "Die Erforschung der Verbrechensursachen: Zum gleichnamigen Aufsatz des Grafen Gleispach." *MKS* 19 (1928): 257–68.

——. "Kriminalbiologie und Kriminalpraxis." *Kriminalistische Monatshefte* 2 (1928): 242.

——. "Wesen und Systematik des biologischen Typus." *MKBG* 2 (1928): 15–21.

——. "Geborener Verbrecher." In *Handwörterbuch der medizinischen Psychologie*, edited by Karl Birnbaum, 635–37. Leipzig: Thieme, 1930.

——. "Strafvollzug." In *Handwörterbuch der medizinischen Psychologie*, edited by Karl Birnbaum, 586–90. Leipzig: Thieme, 1930.

——. "Verbrecher." In *Handwörterbuch der medizinischen Psychologie*, edited by Karl Birnbaum, 631–35. Leipzig: Thieme, 1930.

——. "Aufgaben der Kriminalpsychologie." *ZStW* 51 (1930–31): 469–80.

——. "Schwachsinn, Verbrechen und Sterilisation." *ZStW* 52 (1932): 424–32.

——. "Vererbungsgesetze und Verbrechensbekämpfung." *MKS* 23 (1932): 559–68.

——. "Charakterologie." In *Handwörterbuch der Kriminologie*, edited by Alexander Elster and Heinrich Lingemann, 1:200–207. Berlin: de Gruyter, 1933.

——. "Kriminalpsychologie." In *Handwörterbuch der Kriminologie*, edited by Alexander Elster and Heinrich Lingemann, 1:907–14. Berlin: de Gruyter, 1933.

——. "Literaturbericht: Gerichtliche Psychiatrie und Kriminalpsychologie." *ZStW* 54 (1934): 502–9.

——. "Literaturbericht: Kriminalpsychologie." *ZStW* 55 (1935): 483–94.

——. "Psychopathie und Psychose." In *Handwörterbuch der Kriminologie*, edited by Alexander Elster and Heinrich Lingemann, 2:446–48. Berlin: de Gruyter, 1936.

——. "Vererbung." In *Handwörterbuch der Kriminologie*, edited by Alexander Elster and Heinrich Lingemann, 2:904–9. Berlin: de Gruyter, 1936.

——. "Verbrechensursachen." In *Handwörterbuch der Kriminologie*, edited by Alexander Elster and Heinrich Lingemann, 2:882–86. Berlin: de Gruyter, 1936.

——. "Kriminalitätsgeographie." *MKS* 29 (1938): 277–88.

——. "Literaturbericht: Kriminalbiologie." *ZStW* 58 (1938): 146–66.

——. "Antlitz, Gestalt, Haltung, Gebaren des Verbrechers." *MKS* 30 (1939): 215–34.

——. "Sammelreferat über Kriminalitätsgeographie." *MKS* 31 (1940): 265–69.

——. "Literaturbericht: Kriminalbiologie." *ZStW* 61 (1941): 556–69.

——. "Die Erforschung und Behandlung des Verbrechers in den Jahren 1938 bis 1940." *FNPG* 14 (1942): 123–68.

——. "Forensische Psychiatrie und Kriminalpsychologie der Jahre 1938 und 1939." *AZP* 119 (1942): 298–336.

——. "Der Täter." *MKS* 34 (1943): 65–71.

Gruhle, Hans, and Rudolf Sieverts. "Zum Geleit." *MKS* 36 (1953): 1–5.

Grunau. "Ein Jahr Gesetz zur Verhütung erbkranken Nachwuchses." *JW* 64 (1935): 3–8.

Guerry, André-Michel. *Essai sur la statistique morale de la France*. Paris: Crochard, 1833.

Gumbel, Emil Julius. *Vier Jahre politischer Mord*. Berlin: Verlag der Neuen Gesellschaft, 1922.

"Gustav Aschaffenburg zum siebzigsten Geburtstag." *MKS* 27 (1936): 294.

Gütt, Arthur, Herbert Linden, and Franz Maßfeller. *Blutschutz- und Ehegesundheitsgesetz*. 2d ed. Munich: Lehman, 1937.

Gütt, Arthur, Ernst Rüdin, and Falk Ruttke. *Gesetz zur Verhütung erbkranken Nachwuchses*. Munich: Lehmann, 1934.

——. *Gesetz zur Verhütung erbkranken Nachwuchses*. 2d ed. Munich: Lehmann, 1936.

Habel, Hans. "Die Bedeutung des Lebenswerkes von Johannes Lange für die Entwicklung der kriminalbiologischen Forschung." *MKS* 30 (1939): 1–9.

Hagemann, Max. "Rasse." In *Handwörterbuch der Kriminologie*, edited by Alexander Elster and Heinrich Lingemann, 2:454–61. Berlin: de Gruyter, 1936.

Harasser, A. Review of *Kriminalpolitik auf kriminologischer Grundlage*, 2d ed. (1942), by Edmund Mezger. *ARGB* 36 (1942): 240–42.

Hartmann, Hans. "Die deutsche erbbiologische Forschung: Zum 25jährigen Bestehen der Kaiser-Wilhelm-Gesellschaft zur Förderung der Wissenschaften." *Der Erbarzt* 3 (1936): 3–8.

Hartmann, Jakob. "Über die hereditären Verhältnisse bei Verbrechern." *MKS* 1 (1904–5): 493–520.

Healy, William. *The Individual Delinquent: A Textbook of Diagnosis and Prognosis for All Concerned in Understanding Offenders*. Boston: Little, Brown, 1915.

Heimberger, Joseph. "Sterilisierung und Strafrecht." *MKS* 15 (1924): 154–66.

Hellstern, Erwin. "Bericht über den rassen- und erbbiologischen Einführungskurs für Strafanstaltsärzte, München 27. April bis 1. Mai 1925." *MKS* 17 (1926): 63–67.

Hentig, Hans von. "Zur selektiven Funktion des Strafrechts." *ZStW* 34 (1913): 493–509.

———. *Strafrecht und Auslese. Eine Anwendung des Kausalgesetzes auf den rechtbrechenden Menschen*. Berlin: Springer, 1914.

———. "Das deutsche Sterilisierungsgesetz vom 14. Juli 1933." *MKS* 24 (1933): 538–39.

———. *Eugenik und Kriminalwissenschaft*. Berlin: Metzner, 1933.

———. "Die gesetzlichen Bestimmungen über die Entmannung gefährlicher Sittlichkeitsverbrecher vom 14. November 1933." *MKS* 25 (1934): 45–47.

Hochreuther, O. "Das Gesetz zur Verhütung erbkranken Nachwuchses: Anregungen zur Änderung der bestehenden Vorschriften." *JW* 64 (1935): 1381–84.

Hoffmann, Alfred. *Unfruchtbarmachung und Kriminalität*. Kriminalistische Abhandlungen, no. 44. Leipzig: Wiegandt, 1940.

Hoffmann, Geza von. *Die Rassenhygiene in den Vereinigten Staaten von Nordamerika*. Munich: Lehmann, 1913.

Hoffmann, Hermann. *Vererbung und Seelenleben: Einführung in die psychiatrische Konstitutions- und Vererbungslehre*. Berlin: Springer, 1922.

———. *Das Problem des Charakteraufbaues: Seine Gestaltung durch die erbbiologische Persönlichkeitsanalyse*. Berlin: Springer, 1926.

———. "Die erbbiologische Persönlichkeitsforschung und ihre Bedeutung in der Kriminalbiologie." *BfG* 58 (1927): 308–21.

Hoffmann, H. F. "Arbeitsmethode und Bedeutung der kriminalbiologischen Untersuchungsstellen für die Ermittlung des Sachverhaltes." *MKS* 23 (1932): 385–95.

Hoffmeister, Ernst. "Die Kriminalbiologie, ihre ideengeschichtliche Entwicklung und ihre grundsätzliche Bedeutung für das kommende deutsche Strafrecht." J.D. diss., University of Breslau, 1939.

Hoffner, Manfred. *Kriminalität und Schule*. Kriminalistische Abhandlungen, no. 17. Leipzig: Wiegandt, 1932.

Högel, Hugo. "Die Behandlung der Minderwertigen." *MKS* 1 (1904): 333–40.

Holub, Arthur, and Martha Holub. "Zur Frage der Charakterentwicklung bei Zwillingen." *Internationale Zeitschrift für Individualpsychologie* 12 (1933): 264.

Höpler, Erwin. "Wirtschaftslage—Bildung—Kriminalität." *Archiv für Kriminologie* 76 (1924): 81.

———. "Wirtschaftskrisen und Kriminalität." *Archiv für Kriminologie* 87 (1930).

———. "Sterilisierung und Strafrecht." *ARGB* 25 (1931): 197–216.

Hussa, R. "Die ersten Erfahrungen im kriminalbiologischen Dienst." *MKS* 34 (1943): 111–16.

Ilberg, Georg. "Über verminderte Zurechnungsfähigkeit." *AZP* 56 (1899): 474–84.

Jahrreiss. "Das Sterilisationsproblem." *MKS* 25 (1934): 255–60.

Jolly, F. "Über geminderte Zurechnungsfähigkeit." *AZP* 44 (1888): 461–78.

Jörger, Johann. "Die Familie Zero." *ARGB* 2 (1905): 494.

———. "Die Familie Markus." *ZGNP* 93 (1918): 76–116.

———. *Psychiatrische Familiengeschichte*. Berlin: Springer, 1919.

Kahl, Otto. "Die kriminalbiologische Untersuchung der Strafgefangenen in Bayern." *MKBG* 3 (1930): 18–20.

Kaiser, Günther. "Federal Republic of Germany." In *International Handbook of Contemporary Developments in Criminology*, edited by Elmer Johnson, 257–71. Westport: Greenwood, 1983.

Kankeleit, Otto. "Künstliche Unfruchtbarmachung aus rassehygienischen und sozialen Gründen." *ZGNP* 98 (1925): 220–54.

———. "Der geborene Verbrecher." *MDRG* 1 (1926): 24–32.

———. *Die Unfruchtbarmachung aus rassenhygienischen und sozialen Gründen*. Munich: Lehmann, 1929.

Kirn. "Über den gegenwärtigen Stand der Criminal-Anthropologie." *AZP* 50 (1894): 705–13.

Kitzinger, Friedrich. *Die internationale kriminalistische Vereinigung*. Munich: C. H. Beck, 1905.

Klare, Hans. *Das kriminalbiologische Gutachten im Strafprozeß*. Breslau: Schlettersche Buchhandlung, 1930.

Knecht. "Über die Verbreitung physischer Degeneration bei Verbrechern und die Beziehungen zwischen Degenerationszeichen und Neuropathien." *AZP* 40 (1884): 584–611.

Knigge, Fritz. "Vom Wesen des moralischen Defekts." *Eugenik* 3 (1933): 130–36.

Knop. "Über Moral Insanity." *AZP* 31 (1875): 697–704.

Koch, Julius. *Die psychopathischen Minderwertigkeiten*. Ravensburg: Otto Maier, 1891–93.

———. *Die Frage nach dem geborenen Verbrecher*. Ravensburg: Otto Maier, 1894.

Kohlrausch, Eduard. "Der Kampf der Kriminalistenschulen im Lichte des Falles Dippold." *MKS* 1 (1904): 16–25.

———. "Sterilisation und Strafrecht." *ZStW* 52 (1932): 383–404.

Koopmann. "Der geborene Verbrecher." *AfK* 114 (1944): 89–98.

Kopp, Walter. "Die Unfruchtbarmachung der Asozialen." *Der Erbarzt* 6 (1939): 66–69.

Koppenfels, S. von. *Die Kriminalität der Frau im Kriege*. Kriminalistische Abhandlungen, no. 2. Leipzig: Wiegandt, 1926.

Kornfeld and Raffaele Garofalo. "Zur Criminalpsychopathologie." *Gerichtssaal* 31 (1879): 348–60.

Kraepelin, Emil. *Die Abschaffung des Strafmaßes: Ein Vorschlag zur Reform der heutigen Strafrechtspflege*. Stuttgart: Enke, 1880.

———. "Lombrosos 'Uomo delinquente.'" *ZStW* 5 (1885): 669–80.

———. *Psychiatrie: Ein kurzes Lehrbuch für Studirende und Ärzte*. 2d ed. Leipzig, 1887.

———. *Psychiatrie: Ein kurzes Lehrbuch für Studirende und Ärzte*. 3d ed. Leipzig: Abel, 1889.

———. *Psychiatrie: Ein kurzes Lehrbuch für Studirende und Ärzte*. 4th ed. Leipzig: Abel, 1893.

———. *Psychiatrie: Ein Lehrbuch für Studirende und Ärzte*. 5th ed. Leipzig: Barth, 1896.

———. *Psychiatrie: Ein Lehrbuch für Studirende und Ärzte*. 6th ed. 2 vols. Leipzig: Barth, 1899.

———. *Psychiatrie: Ein Lehrbuch für Studierende und Ärzte*. 7th ed. 2 vols. Leipzig: Barth, 1904.

———. "Das Verbrechen als soziale Krankheit." *MKS* 3 (1906): 257–79.

———. *Psychiatrie: Ein Lehrbuch für Studierende und Ärzte*. 8th ed. 4 vols. Leipzig: Barth, 1909–15.

———. *Lebenserinnerungen*. Berlin: Springer, 1983.

Kranz, Heinrich (1901–79). "Die Kriminalität bei Zwillingen." *Zeitschrift für induktive Abstammungs- und Vererbungslehre* 70 (1933): 67.

———. "Das Kriminalitätsbiogramm von Zwillingen. Eine methodische Bemerkung." *Zeitschrift für morphologische Anthropologie* 34 (1934): 187.

———. "Diskordantes soziales Verhalten eineiiger Zwillinge." *MKS* 26 (1935): 511–16.

———. "Charakter und Verhalten: Untersuchungen an kriminellen und psychopathischen Zwillingen." *Der Erbarzt* 3 (1936): 98–100.

——. *Lebensschicksale krimineller Zwillinge*. Berlin: Springer, 1936.

——. "Über besondere Probleme der psychiatrischen Genetik." *Archiv für Psychologie* 116 (1964): 346.

——. "Heinrich Kranz." In *Psychiatrie in Selbstdarstellungen*. Bern: Huber, 1977.

Kranz, Heinrich Wilhelm (1897–1945), and Siegfried Koller. *Die Gemeinschaftsunfähigen: Ein Beitrag zur wissenschaftlichen und praktischen Lösung des sogenannten "Asozialenproblems."* 2 vols. Giessen: Karl Christ, 1939, 1941.

Kretschmer, Ernst. *Körperbau und Charakter*. Berlin: Springer, 1921.

——. "Biologische Persönlichkeitsdiagnose in der Strafrechtspflege." *DJZ* 31 (1926): 782–87.

——. "Gutachten zum Thema: Studium der Persönlichkeit des Verbrechers." In *Römischer Kongreß für Kriminologie*, 174–78. Berlin: Decker, 1939.

Kriener, Hubert. "Die Berücksichtigung kriminalbiologischer Forderungen im geltenden und im kommenden Recht." M.D. diss., University of Würzburg, 1936.

Krille, Hans. *Weibliche Kriminalität und Ehe*. Kriminalistische Abhandlungen, no. 15. Leipzig: Wiegandt, 1931.

"Kriminalbiologisches Institut der Sicherheitspolizei: Runderlass des RMI vom 21. Dez. 1941." *MKS* 33 (1942): 57–58.

Küper, M. "Überblick über einige in der Erbgesundheitsgerichtsbarkeit entstandene Streitfragen." *Der Erbarzt* 2 (1935): 109–11.

Kurella, Hans. *Naturgeschichte des Verbrechers: Grundzüge der criminellen Anthropologie und Criminalpsychologie*. Stuttgart: Enke, 1893.

——. *Die Grenzen der Zurechnungsfähigkeit und die Kriminalanthropologie*. Halle: Gebauer-Schwetschke, 1903.

——. "Die soziologische Forschung und Cesare Lombroso." *MKS* 3 (1906): 398–409.

——. *Cesare Lombroso als Mensch und Forscher*. Wiesbaden: Bergmann, 1910.

——. "Zu Cesare Lombrosos Gedächtnis." *MKS* 7 (1910): 1–8.

Kuttner, Ludwig. *Die Kinder der Sicherungsverwahrten*. Kriminalistische Abhandlungen, no. 31. Leipzig: Wiegandt, 1938.

Landecker, Werner. "Criminology in Germany." *Journal of Criminal Law and Criminology* 31 (1940–41): 551–75.

Lange, Johannes. "Die Frage der geistigen Entartung in ihrer Beziehung zur Irrenfürsorge." *ARGB* 20 (1928): 129–55.

——. "Psychiatrische Zwillingsprobleme." *ZGNP* 112 (1928): 283–87.

——. "Über die Anlage zum Verbrechen." In *Der Stufenstrafvollzug*, 2:141–67. Munich, 1928.

——. "Leistungen der Zwillingspathologie für die Psychiatrie." *AZP* 90 (1929): 122–42.

——. *Verbrechen als Schicksal: Studien an kriminellen Zwillingen*. Leipzig: Thieme, 1929.

——. *Crime and Destiny*. New York: Boni, 1930.

——. *Crime as Destiny: A Study of Criminal Twins*. London: Allen and Unwin, 1931.

——. "Verbrechen und Vererbung." *Eugenik* 1 (1931): 165–73.

——. "Referat." Part of "Die Eugenik im Dienste der Volkswohlfahrt: Bericht über die Verhandlungen eines zusammengesetzten Ausschusses des Preußischen Landesgesundheitsrates vom 2. Juli 1932." *Veröffentlichungen aus dem Gebiete der Medizinalverwaltung* 38 (1932): 655–70.

——. "Kriminalität und Eugenik." *Medizinische Welt* 7, no. 22 (3 June 1933): 761–65.

——. "Psychiatrische Bemerkungen zum Gesetz zur Verhütung erbkranken Nachwuchses." *ZStW* 53 (1933): 699–711.

——. "Bemerkungen zu der Abhandlung von Boeters: Zur Entmannung von Sittlichkeitsverbrechern." *MKS* 25 (1934): 582–87.

——. *Psychopathie und Erbpflege*. Berlin: Metzner, 1934.

———. "In welchem Falle und nach welchen Grundsätzen empfiehlt sich im modernen Strafsystem die Anwendung der Sterilisation durch Kastration oder durch Vasectomie oder Salpingectomie?" *ZStW* 55 (1935): 291–306.

———. "Bemerkungen zu Stumpfl: *Erbanlage und Verbrechen*. Psychiatrische Bemerkungen." *MKS* 27 (1936): 329–36.

———. "Erbgesundheitsgesetz, Ehegesundheitsgesetz, Kriminalität." *Danziger Ärzteblatt* 5, no. 6 (June 1938): 134–38.

Lange, Johannes, and Franz Exner. "Die beiden Grundbegriffe der Kriminologie: Anlage und Umwelt." *MKS* 27 (1936): 353–74.

Leers, Johann von. "Die Kriminalität des Judentums." In *Das Judentum in der Rechtswissenschaft*, vol. 3, *Judentum und Verbrechen*, 5–60. Berlin: Deutscher Rechts-Verlag, 1936.

———. *Judentum und Gaunertum*. Berlin, n.d.

Legras, A. M. *Psychose en Criminalität bij Tweelingen*. Utrecht: Kemink, 1932.

———. "Psychose und Kriminalität bei Zwillingen." *ZGNP* 144 (1933).

Lehmann, Guenter. "German Democratic Republic." In *International Handbook of Contemporary Developments in Criminology*, edited by Elmer Johnson, 235–56. Westport: Greenwood, 1983.

Lehmann, Möller, Grunau. "Ein Jahr Gesetz zur Verhütung erbkranken Nachwuchses." *JW* 64 (1935): 1376–81.

Lemme. "Fünf Jahre Abteilung Volksgesundheit im Reichsministerium des Innern." *ARGB* 33 (1939): 89–90.

———. Review of *Rassenhygienische Verbrechensbekämpfung*, by Hans Fickert. *ARGB* 33 (1939): 371–73.

Lenz, Adolf. "Kriminalbiologischer Unterricht mit Demonstrationen an Sträflingen." *MKS* 16 (1925): 30–37.

———. *Grundriss der Kriminalbiologie*. Vienna: Springer, 1927.

———. "Probleme der Kriminalbiologie." *MKBG* 1 (1927): 11–18.

———. "Der kriminalbiologische Untersuchungsbogen des Grazer Institutes und der Wiener Polizeidirektion." *MKBG* 2 (1928): 125–44.

———. "Begrüssungsansprache." *MKBG* 4 (1933): 16–19.

Lenz, Fritz. Review of *Verbrechen als Schicksal*, by Johannes Lange. *ARGB* 21 (1929): 335–36.

———. "Zur Frage eines Sterilisierungsgesetzes." *Eugenik* 3 (1933): 73–76.

Leppmann, F. "Die Eigenart des heutigen gewerbsmässigen Verbrechertums." *MIKV* 9 (1901): 149–71.

Lersch, Emil. "Die strafrechtliche Verwertung der kriminalbiologischen Gutachten." *MKBG* 3 (1930): 41–54.

Liepmann, Moritz. "Die Problematik des 'progressiven Strafvollzugs.'" *MKS* Beiheft 1, *Beiträge zur Kriminalpsychologie und Strafrechtsreform* (1926): 56–68.

———. *Krieg und Kriminalität in Deutschland*. Wirtschafts- und Sozialgeschichte des Weltkrieges, Deutsche Serie. Stuttgart: Deutsche Verlagsanstalt, 1930.

Lilienthal, Karl von. "Eugenik und Strafrecht." *ZStW* 39 (1918): 255–76.

Liszt, Franz von. "Eine internationale kriminalistische Vereinigung." *ZStW* 9 (1889): 363–72.

———. "Die strafrechtliche Zurechnungsfähigkeit: Eine Replik." *ZStW* 18 (1898): 229–66.

———. "Schutz der Gesellschaft gegen gemeingefährliche Geisteskranke und vermindert Zurechnungsfähige." *MKS* 1 (1904): 8–15.

———. "Entwurf eines Gesetzes betreffend die Verwahrung gemeingefährlicher Geisteskranker und vermindert Zurechnungsfähiger." *MIKV* 11 (1904): 637–58.

———. *Lehrbuch des deutschen Strafrechts*. 14th ed. Berlin: Guttentag, 1905.

——. *Strafrechtliche Aufsätze und Vorträge.* 2 vols. Berlin: Guttentag, 1905.

Liszt, Franz von, Karl Birkmeyer, and Emil Kraepelin. *Vergeltungsstrafe, Rechtsstrafe, Schutzstrafe.* Munich, 1906.

Lombroso, Cesare. "Über den Ursprung, das Wesen und die Bestrebungen der neuen anthropologisch-kriminalistischen Schule in Italien." *ZStW* 1 (1881): 108–29.

——. *Der Verbrecher (homo delinquens) in anthropologischer, ärztlicher und juristischer Beziehung.* Translated by M. Fränkel. 2 vols. Hamburg: Richter, 1887–90.

——. "Virchow und die Kriminalanthropologie." *Die Zukunft* 16 (29 August 1896): 391–96.

——. *Die Ursachen und die Bekämpfung des Verbrechens.* Translated by Hans Kurella. Berlin: Bermuhler, 1902.

Lombroso-Ferrero, Gina. *Criminal Man according to the Classification of Cesare Lombroso.* 1911. Reprint, Montclair: Patterson Smith, 1972.

Loos, Otto. "Die kriminalbiologische Forschung, ihre Durchführung und die praktische Verwendung ihrer Ergebnisse." *Die innere Mission* 31 (1936): 290–306.

Luxenburger, Hans. "Die sogenannte verminderte Zurechnungsfähigkeit: Bemerkungen zu Wilmanns Buche." *MKS* 19 (1928): 304–13.

——. "Anlage und Umwelt beim Verbrecher." *AZP* 92 (1930): 411–38.

——. "Psychiatrisch-neurologische Zwillingspathologie." *ZGNP* 56 (1930): 145.

——. "Psychiatrische Erbprognose und Eugenik." *Eugenik* 1 (1931): 117–24.

——. "Zur Frage der Schwangerschaftsunterbrechung und Sterilisierung aus psychiatrisch-eugenischer Indikation." *ZStW* 52 (1932): 432–39.

——. "Zur Frage der Zwangssterilisierung." *Eugenik* 3 (1933): 76–79.

——. "Spezielle empirische Erbprognose in der Psychiatrie." In *Erblehre und Rassenhygiene im völkischen Staat,* edited by Ernst Rüdin, 143–49. Munich: Lehmann, 1934.

——. Review of *Gesetz zur Verhütung erbkranken Nachwuchses,* 2d ed., by Arthur Gütt, Ernst Rüdin, and Falk Ruttke. *ARGB* 30 (1936): 421–25.

Maier, Hans W. *Die nordamerikanischen Gesetze gegen die Vererbung von Verbrechen und Geistesstörung und deren Anwendung.* Juristisch-psychiatrische Grenzfragen, vol. 8, nos. 1–3. Halle: Marhold, 1911.

——. "Zum gegenwärtigen Stand der Frage der Kastration und Sterilisation." *ZGNP* 98 (1925): 200–219.

Mayer, Hellmuth. *Das Strafrecht des deutschen Volkes.* Stuttgart: Enke, 1936.

——. "Kriminalpolitik als Geisteswissenschaft." *ZStW* 57 (1937): 1–27.

——. "Gutachten zum Thema: Studium der Persönlichkeit des Verbrechers." In *Römischer Kongreß für Kriminologie,* 188–92. Berlin: Decker, 1939.

Mayr, Georg von. *Statistik der gerichtlichen Polizei im Königreiche Bayern und in einigen anderen Ländern.* Vol. 16 of *Beiträge zur Statistik des Königreichs Bayern.* Munich: Statistisches Bureau, 1867.

——. "Wesen und Ziele der Kriminalstatistik." *Jahrbücher für Kriminalpolitik* 1 (1895): 257–74.

——. "Die Nutzbarmachung der Kriminalstatistik." *MKS* 1 (1904–5).

——. "Forschungsgebiet und Forschungsziel der Kriminalstatistik." *ZStW* 32 (1911).

——. "Kriminalstatistik und Kriminalätiologie." *MKS* 8 (1911–12): 333.

——. "Nochmals Kriminalstatistik und Kriminalätiologie." *MKS* 9 (1912–13): 129.

——. *Statistik und Gesellschaftslehre.* Vol. 3, *Moralstatistik mit Einschluß der Kriminalstatistik.* Tübingen: Mohr, 1917.

Meggendorfer, Friedrich. "Klinische und genealogische Untersuchungen über 'moral insanity.' " *ZGNP* 66 (1921): 208–31.

——. Review of *Verbrechen als Schicksal,* by Johannes Lange. *Deutsche Zeitschrift für Nervenheilkunde* 108 (1929): 311–12.

"Menschen vor dem Richter." Special issue of *Internationale Zeitschrift für Individualpsychologie* 9, no. 5 (1931): 321–407.

Mergen, Armand. *Methodik kriminalbiologischer Untersuchungen.* Stuttgart: Enke, 1953.

——. *Die Kriminologie.* Berlin: Vahlen, 1967.

——. *Der geborene Verbrecher.* Hamburg: Kriminalistik-Verlag, 1968.

——. *Das Teufelschromosom: Zum Täter programmiert.* Essen: Bettendorf, 1995.

Merker, J. F. K. *Die Hauptquellen der Verbrechen gegen die Eigenthums-Sicherheit in Berlin mit Hindeutung auf die Möglichkeit der Verminderung derselben.* Berlin, 1839.

Meywerk, Wilhelm. "Beitrag zur Bestimmung der sozialen Prognose an Rückfallsverbrechern." *MKS* 29 (1938): 422–44.

——. "Zur Frage der kriminalbiologischen Prognosestellung." *MKS* 30 (1939): 287–89.

Mezger, Edmund. *Moderne Strafrechtsprobleme.* Marburg: Elwert, 1927.

——. "Anlage und Umwelt als Verbrechensursache." *MKS* 19 (1928): 141–47.

——. "Konstitutionelle und dynamische Verbrechensauffassung." *MKS* 19 (1928): 385–400.

——. "Verminderte Zurechnungsfähigkeit und Gewohnheitsverbrecher." *Gerichtssaal* 96 (1928): 69–90.

——. "Psychoanalyse und Individualpsychologie in der Strafrechtspflege." *Gerichtssaal* 102 (1932): 1–29.

——. "Die Arbeitsmethoden und die Bedeutung der kriminalbiologischen Untersuchungsstellen." *Gerichtssaal* 103 (1933): 127–90.

——. *Kriminalpolitik auf kriminologischer Grundlage.* Stuttgart: Enke, 1934.

——. "Inwieweit werden durch Sterilisierungsmassnahmen Asoziale erfaßt? Dargelegt anhand bayerischen Materials." *MKBG* 5 (1937): 81–98.

——. "Erwiderung." *MKS* 30 (1939): 322–24.

——. "Gutachten zum Thema: Studium der Persönlichkeit des Verbrechers." In *Römischer Kongreß für Kriminologie*, 192–202. Berlin: Decker, 1939.

——. "Die künftigen Aufgaben kriminologischer Arbeit." In *Römischer Kongreß für Kriminologie*, 83–91. Berlin: Decker, 1939.

——. "Zum Begriff des Psychopathen." *MKS* 30 (1939): 190–92.

——. *Kriminalpolitik auf kriminologischer Grundlage.* 2d ed. Stuttgart: Enke, 1942.

——. "Zwanzig Jahre *Körperbau und Charakter.*" *MKS* 33 (1942): 187–91.

——. *Kriminalpolitik und ihre kriminologischen Grundlagen.* 3d ed. Stuttgart: Enke, 1944.

Michel, Rudolf. "Körperbau, Charakter und Verbrechen." *Wiener medizinische Wochenschrift* 75 (1925): 45–50.

Mikorey, Max. "Das Judentum in der Kriminalpsychologie." In *Das Judentum in der Rechtswissenschaft*, vol. 3, *Judentum und Verbrechen*, 61–82. Berlin: Deutscher Rechts-Verlag, 1936.

Mittermaier, W. "Zur Sterilisationsfrage." *MKS* 25 (1934): 346–50.

Möckel, W. "Sterilisation und Kastration." *Sozialhygienische Mitteilungen* 9 (1925): 97–102.

Mönkemöller. "Psychopathie und Gesetzgebung." *AfK* 77 (1925): 31–50, 114–25, 210–22, 281–87.

Moll, Albert. "Sterilisierung und Verbrechen." *Kriminalistische Monatshefte* 3 (1929): 121–26.

Moser, Tilmann. "Psychoanalyse und Strafrecht." In Moser, *Repressive Kriminalpsychiatrie*, 226–36. Frankfurt: Suhrkamp, 1971.

Muckermann, Hermann. "Eugenik und Strafrecht." *Eugenik* 2 (1932): 104–9.

Müller, Robert. "Zum Schwachsinnsbegriff in der Praxis der Erbgesundheitsgerichte." *Der Erbarzt* 5 (1938): 149–51.

Näcke, Paul. *Verbrechen und Wahnsinn beim Weibe. Mit Ausblicken auf die Criminal-Anthropologie überhaupt.* Vienna: Braumüller, 1894.

——. "Degeneration, Degenerationszeichen und Atavismus." *AKK* 1 (1899): 200–221.

———. "Die Kastration bei gewissen Klassen von Degenerirten als ein wirksamer socialer Schutz." *AKK* 3 (1899): 58–84.

———. "Drei kriminalanthropologische Themen." *AKK* 6 (1901): 261–72.

———. "Die Hauptergebnisse der kriminalanthropologischen Forschung im Jahre 1901." *AKK* 9 (1902): 141–56.

———. "Forensisch-psychiatrisch-psychologische Randglossen zum Prozesse Dippold, insbesondere über den Sadismus." *AKK* 13 (1903): 350–72.

———. "Über den Wert der sogenannten Degenerationszeichen." *MKS* 1 (1904): 99–111.

———. "Die Überbleibsel der Lombrososchen kriminalanthropologischen Theorien." *AKK* 50 (1912): 326–39.

Nagler, Johannes. "Anlage, Umwelt und Persönlichkeit des Verbrechers." *Gerichtssaal* 102 (1932): 409–85.

Nationalsozialistische Leitsätze für ein neues deutsches Strafrecht, herausgegeben vom Reichsrechtsamt der NSDAP. Part 1. N.p., 1935.

Neureiter, Ferdinand von. "Zu den biologischen Problemen in Strafvollzug." *Beiträge zur gerichtlichen Medizin* 6 (1924).

———. "Die Ausgestaltung des Kriminalbiologischen Dienstes in Lettland." *Beiträge zur gerichtlichen Medizin* 7 (1927).

———. "Der kriminalbiologische Dienst in Belgien und Lettland." *MKBG* 1 (1927): 19–25.

———. "Die Organisation des kriminalbiologischen Dienstes in Deutschland." *MKBG* 5 (1937): 21–28.

———. "Der kriminalbiologische Dienst in Deutschland: Text und Erläuterung der AV. des Reichsjustizministers vom 30. November 1937." *MKS* 29 (1938): 65–81.

———. *Kriminalbiologie*. Berlin: Heymanns, 1940.

Oberholzer, Emil. *Kastration und Sterilisation von Geisteskranken in der Schweiz*. Juristisch-psychiatrische Grenzfragen, vol. 8, nos. 1–3. Halle: Marhold, 1911.

Oberthür, Gerd-Rainer. *Kriminologie in der Strafrechtspraxis: Kriminologischer Dienst und Zentralinstitut für Kriminologie*. Stuttgart: Enke, 1976.

Ochs, Gerd. "Die Lehre Lombrosos: Darstellung, Genealogie und Kritik der positiven Strafrechtslehre." J.D. diss., University of Frankfurt, 1957.

Oettingen, Alexander von. *Die Moralstatistik*. Erlangen: Deichert, 1868.

———. *Die Moralstatistik*. 2d ed. Erlangen: Deichert, 1874.

———. *Die Moralstatistik*. 3d ed. Erlangen: Deichert, 1882.

Ostermann, A. "Zum Sterilisierungsgesetz." *Eugenik* 3 (1933): 137–40.

Pelman, Carl. "Strafrecht und verminderte Zurechnungsfähigkeit." *Politisch-Anthropologische Revue* 2 (1903–4): 63–72.

———. "Bemerkungen zu dem Prozesse des Prinzen Prosper Arenberg." *MKS* 1 (1904): 60–63.

Pelman, Carl, and Karl Finkelnburg. *Die verminderte Zurechnungsfähigkeit*. Bonn: Röhrscheid and Ebbecke, 1903.

Petrzilka, Werner. *Persönlichkeitsforschung und Differenzierung im Strafvollzug*. Hamburg: de Gruyter, 1930.

Ploetz, Alfred. *Die Tüchtigkeit unserer Rasse und der Schutz der Schwachen*. Berlin: Gustav Fischer, 1895.

———. "Der Sachverständigenbeirat für Bevölkerungs- und Rassenpolitik." *ARGB* 27 (1933): 419.

———. "Lebensbild Arthur Gütts." *ARGB* 30 (1936): 279–83.

Ploetz, Alfred, and Ernst Rüdin. "Ministerialdirektor Dr. Arthur Gütt 5 Jahre Leiter der Abteilung für Volksgesundheit im Reichs- und Preussischen Ministerium des Innern." *ARGB* 33 (1939): 88.

Poll, H. "Über Zwillingsforschung als Hilfsmittel menschlicher Erbkunde." *Zeitschrift für Ethnologie* 46 (1914).

Popenoe. "Eugenische Sterilisierung in Kalifornien." *ZStW* 53 (1933): 721.

Prichard, James. *A Treatise on Insanity and Other Disorders Affecting the Mind.* London: Sherwood, Gilbert, and Piper, 1835.

———. *On the Different Forms of Insanity in Relation to Jurisprudence.* London: Bailliere, 1842.

Psychiatrie in Selbstdarstellungen. Bern: Huber, 1977.

Quetelet, Adolphe. *Recherches sur le penchant au crime aux differens ages.* 2d ed. Brussels: Hayez, 1833.

———. *Sur l'homme et sur les développements des ses facultés, ou Essai de physique sociale.* Paris: Bachelier, 1835.

Rabl, Rupert. *Strafzumessungspraxis und Kriminalitätsbewegung.* Kriminalistische Abhandlungen, no. 25. Leipzig: Wiegandt, 1936.

Rath, Carl. *Über die Vererbung von Dispositionen zum Verbrechen: Eine statistische und psychologische Untersuchung.* Stuttgart: Spemann, 1914.

Reik, Theodor. *Gedächtniszwang und Strafbedürfnis.* Vienna: Internationaler Psychoanalytischer Verlag, 1925.

Reiss, Eduard. "Über erbliche Belastung bei Schwerverbrechern." *Klinische Wochenschrift* 1 (1922): 2184–87.

Renger, Ewald. *Kriminalität, Preis und Lohn.* Kriminalistische Abhandlungen, no. 19. Leipzig: Wiegandt, 1933.

Reuter. "Sterilisierung der Verbrecher." *Medizinische Welt* (1929): 60.

Reuter, Fritz. "Sterilisation und Kastration in ihrer strafrechtlichen Bedeutung." J.D. diss., University of Breslau, 1932.

Reuter, Fritz, and Wätzold. *Aufartung durch Ausmerzung: Sterilisation und Kastration im Kampf gegen Erbkrankheiten und Verbrechen.* Berlin: Hobbing, 1936.

Riedl, Martin. "Ein Beitrag zur Frage der Fortpflanzung von Verbrechern." *ARGB* 25 (1931): 257–67.

———. "Über Beziehungen von geistig-körperlicher Konstitution zur Kriminalität und anderen Defekten." *MKS* 23 (1932): 473.

———. "Studie über Verbrecherstämmlinge, Spätkriminelle und Frühkriminelle." *AfK* 93 (1933): 7–13, 125–35, 238–57.

Riffel. "Die kriminalbiologische Untersuchung von Strafgefangenen und Fürsorgezöglingen in Baden." *BfG* 61 (1930): 262.

Rinderknecht, Gertrud. "Über kriminelle Heboide." *ZGNP* 57 (1920): 35–70.

Ritter, Robert. *Ein Menschenschlag.* Leipzig: Thieme, 1937.

———. "Primitivität und Kriminalität." *MKS* 31 (1940): 197–210.

———. "Die Aufgaben der Kriminalbiologie." *Kriminalistik* 15 (1941): 38–41.

———. "Das kriminalbiologische Institut der Sipo." *Kriminalistik* 16 (1942): 117.

———. "Erbärztliche Verbrechensverhütung." *Deutsche Medizinische Wochenschrift* (22 May 1942): 535–39.

Rochlitz, Chr. *Das Wesen und Treiben der Gauner, Diebe und Betrüger Deutschlands.* Leipzig: Schmidt, 1846.

Rodewald. "Die Unfruchtbarmachung geistig Minderwertiger im Lichte der Medizin und des Rechts." *MKS* 22 (1931): 705–20.

Roesner, Ernst. "Der Einfluß von Wirtschaftslage, Alkohol und Jahreszeit auf die Kriminalität." In *Bericht der Zentralstelle für das Gefangenenfürsorgewesen der Provinz Brandenburg.* Berlin, 1931.

———. "Die Ursachen der Kriminalität und ihre statistische Erforschung." *Allgemeines Statistisches Archiv* 23 (1933): 19–35.

——. "Kriminalstatistik." In *Handwörterbuch der Kriminologie*, edited by Alexander Elster and Heinrich Lingemann, 2:27–54. Berlin: de Gruyter, 1936.

——. "Wirtschaftslage und Straffälligkeit." In *Handwörterbuch der Kriminologie*, edited by Alexander Elster and Heinrich Lingemann, 2:1079–1116. Berlin: de Gruyter, 1936.

Rohden, Friedrich von. "Körperbauuntersuchungen an geisteskranken und gesunden Verbrechern." *Archiv für Psychiatrie* 77 (1926): 151–63.

——. "Kriminalbiologische Untersuchungen an gesunden und geisteskranken Verbrechern." *DZGGM* 10 (1927): 620–33.

——. "Lombrosos Bedeutung für die moderne Kriminalbiologie." *AZP* 92 (1930): 140–54.

——. "Vom geborenen Verbrecher." *MDRG* 6 (1931): 54–57.

——. *Einführung in die kriminalbiologische Methodenlehre*. Berlin: Urban, 1933.

——. "Gibt es unverbesserliche Verbrecher?" *MKS* 24 (1933): 74–92.

Rohland, Woldemar von. "Der Prozess Dippold: Eine juristische Betrachtung." *DJZ* 8 (1903): 486–88.

Römischer Kongreß für Kriminologie: Kameradschaftsarbeit von Teilnehmern und Mitarbeitern am Ersten Internationalen Kongreß für Kriminologie in Rom, Oktober 1938. Berlin: Decker, 1939.

Rosanoff, Aaron, Leva Handy, and Isabel Rosanoff. "Criminality and Delinquency in Twins." *Journal of Criminal Law and Criminology* 24 (1933–34): 923–34.

Rosenberg, Alfred. *Der Mythus des 20. Jahrhunderts*. Munich: Hoheneichen, 1930.

Rosenfeld, Ernst. "Die strafrechtliche Verwertung der kriminalbiologischen Gutachten." *MKBG* 3 (1930): 55–65.

——. "Fünf Forderungen an die rechtliche Regelung der Sterilisation." *MKBG* 4 (1933): 259–66.

Rüdin, Ernst. "Über Vererbung geistiger Störungen." *ZGNP* 81 (1923).

——. "Psychiatrische Indikation zur Sterilisierung." *Das kommende Geschlecht* 5 (1929): 1–19.

——. "Wege und Ziele der biologischen Erforschung der Rechtsbrecher mit besonderer Berücksichtigung der Erbbiologie." *MKBG* 3 (1930): 164–71.

——. "Schwangerschaftsunterbrechung und Unfruchtbarmachung, insbesondere bei sozialer und eugenischer Indikation." *MIKV* N.F. 6 (1932): 49–62.

——. "Das Reichsgesetz zur Verhütung erbkranken Nachwuchses." *AfK* 93 (1933): 1–4.

——. "Die Bedeutung Arthur Gütt's für die Erb- und Rassenforschung und deren praktische Anwendung." *Der öffentliche Gesundheitsdienst* 4 (1938–39): 897–99.

——. "Gutachten zum Thema: Organisation der Verbrechensvorbeugung in den verschiedenen Ländern." In *Römischer Kongreß für Kriminologie*, 316–22. Berlin: Decker, 1939.

——, ed. *Erblehre und Rassenhygiene im völkischen Staat*. Munich: Lehmann, 1934.

——. *Rassenhygiene im völkischen Staat: Tatsachen und Richtlinien*. Munich: Lehmann, 1934.

Rusche, Georg, and Otto Kirchheimer. *Punishment and Social Structure*. New York: Columbia University Press, 1939.

Ruttke, Falk. "Rassenhygiene und Recht." In *Rassenhygiene im völkischen Staat: Tatsachen und Richtlinien*, edited by Ernst Rüdin, 91–103. Munich: Lehmann, 1934.

——. "Erb- und Rassenpflege in Gesetzgebung und Rechtsprechung des 3. Reiches." *JW* 64 (1935): 1369–76.

——. "Kommentar zu EOG Darmstadt, 8 April 1935." *JW* 64 (1935): 1868.

Sander, W., and Alfred Richter. *Die Beziehungen zwischen Geistesstörung und Verbrechen: Nach Beobachtungen in der Irrenanstalt Dalldorf*. Berlin: Fischer, 1886.

Sauer, Wilhelm. *Kriminalsoziologie*. Berlin: Verlag für Staatswissenschaften und Geschichte, 1933.

——. "Anlage und Umwelt als Verbrechensursachen." *Zeitschrift der Akademie für deutsches Recht* 2 (1935): 250.

Schäfer, Leopold, Otto Wagner, and Josef Schafheutle, eds. *Gesetz gegen gefährliche Gewohnheitsverbrecher und über Maßregeln der Sicherung und Besserung*. Berlin: Vahlen, 1934.

Schallmayer, Wilhelm. *Über die drohende physische Entartung der Culturvölker*. 2d ed. Berlin: Heuser, 1895.

Scheel, H. von, and A. Hesse. "Kriminalstatistik." In *Handwörterbuch der Staatswissenschaften*, edited by Ludwig Elster et al., 6:1–54. Jena: Fischer, 1925.

Schmid, Albert. *Anlage und Umwelt bei 500 Erstverbrechern*. Kriminalistische Abhandlungen, no. 24. Leipzig: Wiegandt, 1936.

——. "Zur Geschichte der Kriminologie in Deutschland seit den Anregungen der Lehre Lombrosos vom geborenen Verbrecher." J.D. diss., University of Munich, 1951.

Schmidt, Eugen. "Verbrechen und Strafe." In *Handbuch der Individualpsychologie*, edited by Erwin Wexberg, 2:150–79. Munich: Bergmann, 1926.

——. *Verbrechen als Ausdrucksform sozialer Entmutigung: Eine einführende Betrachtung über das Werden und die Behandlung der kriminellen Persönlichkeit auf Grund der Erkenntnisse der modernen Psychologie*. Munich: Schweitzer, 1931.

Schneider, Kurt. "Körperbau und Charakter." *MKS* 12 (1921): 370–75.

——. *Die psychopathischen Persönlichkeiten*. 1923. 2d ed. Leipzig: Deuticke, 1928.

——. *Die psychopathischen Persönlichkeiten*. 3d ed. Leipzig: Deuticke, 1934.

——. "Über Psychopathen und ihre kriminalbiologische Bedeutung." *MKS* 29 (1938): 353–67.

——. *Psychopathic Personalities*. London: Cassell, 1958.

Schnell, Karl. *Anlage und Umwelt bei 500 Rückfallsverbrechern*. Kriminalistische Abhandlungen, no. 22. Leipzig: Wiegandt, 1935.

Schöch, Heinz. "Die gesellschaftliche Organisation der deutschsprachigen Kriminologie." In *Gedächtnisschrift für Hilde Kaufmann*, edited by Hans-Joachim Hirsch, Günther Kaiser, and Helmut Marquard, 355–72. Berlin: de Gruyter, 1986.

Schoetensack, August. "Strafe und sichernde Maßnahme." In *Denkschrift des Zentralausschusses der Strafrechtsabteilung der Akademie für deutsches Recht über die Grundzüge eines Allgemeinen Deutschen Strafrechts*, 90–99. Berlin: Decker, 1934.

Schreck, A. "Gedanken eines Strafgefangenen zur Sterilisierung." *Eugenik* 2 (1932): 209–12.

Schröder, Paul. "Psychopathen und abnorme Charaktere." *Münchner medizinische Wochenschrift* no. 26 (1933): 1007.

——. "Der Psychopath vor dem Strafrichter." *MKS* 25 (1934): 106–14.

——. "Kriminalbiologische Untersuchung des Gemütslebens." *MKS* 29 (1938): 367–81.

Schütt, E. "Die erbbiologische Bestandsaufnahme." *Der öffentliche Gesundheitsdienst*, ser. B, 2 (1936): 241.

——. "Erläuterungen zur erbbiologischen Bestandsaufnahme." *Der öffentliche Gesundheitsdienst*, ser. A, 2 (1936): 255.

Schwab, Georg. "Über die Beziehungen der körperlichen Konstitution zum Verbrechertyp." *MKS* 32 (1941): 213–36.

Schwind, Hans-Dieter. "Die 'Neue Kriminologische Gesellschaft' (NKG) und ihre Vorgeschichte: Ein kurzer Überblick, 1927–1988." In *Kriminalität: Persönlichkeit, Lebensgeschichte und Verhalten. Festschrift für Hans Göppinger*, edited by Hans-Jürgen Kerner and Günther Kaiser, 633–54. Berlin: Springer, 1990.

Seibert, Otto. "Die Unfruchtbarmachung des Verbrechers." *Der Erbarzt* 6 (1939): 51–52.

Sichart, E. "Über individuelle Faktoren des Verbrechens." *ZStW* 10 (1890): 37–50.

Siegert, Karl. *Grundzüge des Strafrechts im neuen Staate*. Tübingen: Mohr, 1934.

Siemens, Hermann. *Zwillingspathologie*. Berlin: Springer, 1924.

Sieverts, Rudolf. "Gedanken über Methoden, Ergebnisse und kriminalpolitische Folgen der kriminal-biologischen Untersuchungen im bayrischen Strafvollzug." *MKS* 23 (1932): 588–601.

——. "Gedanken über den kriminalbiologischen Dienst im bayrischen Strafvollzug: Ein Nachwort." *MKS* 24 (1933): 107–16.

——. "Kriminologische Forschung als Landschafts-Teilaufgabe der deutschen Hochschulen." *MKS* 26 (1935): 1–10.

Sommer, Robert. "Die Criminalpsychologie." *AZP* 51 (1895): 782–803.

Sommer, W. "Beiträge zur Kenntnis des kriminellen Irren." *AZP* 40 (1884): 88–178.

Staemmler, Martin. "Die Sterilisierung Minderwertiger vom Standpunkt des Nationalsozialismus." *Eugenik* 3 (1933): 91–110.

Starke, Wilhelm. *Verbrechen und Verbrecher in Preussen, 1854–1878: Eine kulturgeschichtliche Studie*. Berlin: Enslin, 1884.

Steinwallner, Bruno. "2 Jahre Erbgesundheitsgesetz—1 1/2 Jahre Erbgesundheitsgerichtsbarkeit." *Psychiatrisch-Neurologische Wochenschrift* 37 (1935): 325–28.

Stemmler, L. "Die Unfruchtbarmachung Geisteskranker, Schwachsinniger und Verbrecher aus Anlage." *AZP* 80 (1924): 437–68.

——. "Der Stand der Frage der Sterilisierung Minderwertiger." *Archiv für soziale Hygiene und Demographie* N.F. 1 (1925–26): 209–18.

Sternberg, Theodor. *Die Selektionsidee in Strafrecht und Ethik*. Berlin: Puttkammer, 1911.

Stolz. "Gedanken über moralisches Irresein (moral insanity)." *AZP* 33 (1877): 732–44.

Storch. Review of Schneider, *Die psychopathischen Persönlichkeiten*. *MKS* 14 (1923): 304–9.

Stumpfl, Friedrich. "Erbanlage und Verbrechen." *ZGNP* 145 (1933): 283–326.

——. "Die kriminelle Familie." *Volk und Rasse* 8 (1933).

——. "Die kriminellen Verwandten." *AfK* 93 (1933): 80–86.

——. "Grundlagen und Aufgaben der Kriminalbiologie." In *Erblehre und Rassenhygiene im völkischen Staat*, edited by Ernst Rüdin, 317–32. Munich: Lehmann, 1934.

——. *Erbanlage und Verbrechen: Charakterologische und psychiatrische Sippenuntersuchungen*. Berlin: Springer, 1935.

——. "Kriminalität und Rasse." *Deutsches Recht* 5 (1935): 31–34.

——. "Kriminalbiologische Forschung und der Vollzug von Strafen und sichernden Massnahmen." *Gerichtssaal* 108 (1936): 338–61.

——. "Kriminelle Psychopathen: Ein kritischer Beitrag zur Frage des 'moralischen Schwachsinns.'" *Der Erbarzt* 3 (1936): 134–37.

——. "Untersuchungen an kriminellen und psychopathischen Zwillingen." *Der öffentliche Gesundheitsdienst* 2 (1936).

——. *Ursprünge des Verbrechens: Dargestellt am Lebenslauf von Zwillingen*. Leipzig: Georg Thieme, 1936.

——. "Die Vererbung des Charakters" In *Die Persönlichkeit im Lichte der Erblehre*, edited by Johannes Schottky. Leipzig: Teubner, 1936.

——. "Erbanlage und Verbrechen: Eine Erwiderung auf die Bemerkungen von Prof. Lange und Prof. Exner, sowie Prof. H. Mayer." *MKS* 28 (1937): 92–98.

——. "Psychopathenforschung und Kriminalbiologie: Erbbiologische Ergebnisse, 1933–1937." *FNPG* 9 (1937): 167–76.

——. "Über Erbforschung an Rechtsbrechern." *MKBG* 5 (1937): 111–15.

——. "Vortrag auf der Jahresversammlung der Vereinigung für gerichtliche Psychologie und Psychiatrie am 17.4.1937." *Deutsches Recht* 7 (1937): 336.

——. "Geistige Störungen als Ursache der Entwurzelung von Wanderern." In *Der nichtseßhafte Mensch*, edited by Alarich Seidler. Munich: Beck, 1938.

——. "Über kriminalbiologische Erbforschung." *AZP* 107 (1938): 38–63.

——. "Verbrechen und Vererbung." *MKS* 29 (1938): 1–21.

——. "Gutachten zum Thema: Studium der Persönlichkeit des Verbrechers." In *Römischer Kongreß für Kriminologie*, 217–27. Berlin: Decker, 1939.

——. "Kriminalität und Vererbung." In *Handbuch der Erbbiologie des Menschen*, edited by Günther Just, vol. 5, pt. 2, 1223–74. Berlin: Springer, 1939.

——. "Probleme der Erbcharakterforschung." *AZP* 113 (1939): 25–31.

——. "Psychopathenforschung unter dem Gesichtspunkt der Erbbiologie, 1937–1939." *FNPG* 11 (1939): 409–16.

——. *Motiv und Schuld: Eine psychiatrische Studie über den Handlungsaufbau bei kriminellem Verhalten*. Vienna: Deuticke, 1961.

——. "Asozialität." In *Handwörterbuch der Kriminologie*, edited by Rudolf Sieverts, 1:62–75. 2d ed. Berlin: de Gruyter, 1966.

——. "Kriminalbiologie." In *Handwörterbuch der Kriminologie*, edited by Rudolf Sieverts, 1:496–519. 2d ed. Berlin: de Gruyter, 1966.

——. *Kriminalität, Pathorhythmie, Wahn: Psychosomatisch-dynamische Strukturgesetzlichkeiten menschlicher Handlungen in Konfliktsituationen*. Berlin: Springer, 1975.

Stursberg, H. *Die Zunahme der Vergehen und Verbrechen und ihre Ursachen*. 5th ed. Düsseldorf: Rheinisch-Westfälische Gefängnisgesellschaft, 1879.

Tönnies, Ferdinand. "Das Verbrechen als soziale Erscheinung." *Archiv für soziale Gesetzgebung und Statistik* 8 (1895): 329–44.

——. *Uneheliche und verwaiste Verbrecher: Studien über das Verbrechertum in Schleswig-Holstein*, Kriminalistische Abhandlungen, no. 14. Leipzig: Wiegandt, 1930.

Trunk, Hans. "Allzu großes Zögern bei der Unfruchtbarmachung wegen schweren Alkoholismus." *Der Erbarzt* 2 (1935): 41–45.

——. "Soziale Prognosen an Strafgefangenen." *MKS* 28 (1937): 209–27.

Verhandlungen des Reichstags, 3. Wahlperiode (1924–27). Berlin: Reichs-Druckerei.

Verhandlungen des Reichstags, 4. Wahlperiode (1928). Berlin: Reichs-Druckerei.

Verhandlungen des Reichstags, 5. Wahlperiode (1930). Berlin: Reichs-Druckerei.

Verhandlungen des 26. Deutschen Juristentages. 3 vols. Berlin: Guttentag, 1902–3.

Verhandlungen des 27. Deutschen Juristentages. 4 vols. Berlin: Guttentag, 1904.

Verhandlungen des 28. Deutschen Juristentages. 3 vols. Berlin: Guttentag, 1906–7.

Vierkandt, Alfred, ed. *Handwörterbuch der Soziologie*. Stuttgart: Enke, 1931.

Viernstein, Theodor. "Ärztliche Untersuchungen an Kaisheimer Gefangenen." *Münchener medizinische Wochenschrift* 58 (1911): 2322–25.

——. "Einführung eines Stufensystems in den bayerischen Strafanstalten." *Zeitschrift für Medizinalbeamte* 35 (1922).

——. "Biologische Probleme im Strafvollzuge." *DZGGM* 3 (1924): 436–53.

——. "Entwicklung und Aufbau eines kriminalbiologischen Dienstes im Bayerischen Strafvollzug." In *Der Stufenstrafvollzug*, 1:68–85. Munich, 1926.

——. "Der Kriminalbiologische Dienst in bayerischen Strafanstalten." *MKS* 17 (1926): 1–21.

——. "Kriminalbiologische Grundlagen für die Reform des Strafvollzuges in Bayern." *DJZ* (1926): 1142–46.

——. "Die kriminalbiologischen Untersuchungen in den deutschen Strafanstalten." *BfG* 58 (1927): 322–38.

——. "Über Typen des verbesserlichen und unverbesserlichen Verbrechers." *MKBG* 1 (1927): 26–54.

——. "Typen des besserungsfähigen und unverbesserlichen Verbrechers (Selbstbericht)." In *Der Stufenstrafvollzug*, 2:168–81. Munich, 1928.

——. "Kriminalbiologie." In *Der Stufenstrafvollzug*, 3:7–50. Munich, 1929.

——. "Die Kriminalbiologische Untersuchung der Gefangenen in Bayern." *MKBG* 3 (1930): 30–38.

——. "Die psychologisch-soziologische Erfassung der Fürsorgezöglinge." Unpublished manuscript, 1930. Bayerisches Staatsarchiv.

——. "Biologische Aufgaben in der Kriminalpolitik." *Eugenik* 1 (1930–31): 213–17.

——. "Die kriminalbiologische Forschung in Bayern." *MDRG* 6 (1931): 118–32.

——. "Stufenstrafvollzug, Entlassenenfürsorge, Sicherungsverwahrung." *MDRG* 7 (1932): 132–46, 166–76.

——. "Über Kriminalbiologie." *AZP* 98 (1932): 277–99.

——. "Die Bekämpfung der Kriminalität vom bevölkerungspolitischen, erbbiologischen und rassenhygienischen Standpunkt." *Zeitschrift für Medizinalbeamte* 46 (1933): 532–48.

——. "Neuordnung des Stufenstrafvollzuges." *AfK* 93 (1933): 31–39.

——. "Erbwertliche Erforschung und Beurteilung abgrenzbarer Bevölkerungsschichten." In *Erblehre und Rassenhygiene im völkischen Staat*, edited by Ernst Rüdin, 333–47. Munich: Lehmann, 1934.

——. "Stellung und Aufgaben der Kriminalbiologie im Hinblick auf die nationalsozialistische Gesetzgebung." *DZGGM* 26 (1936): 3–16.

——. "Schlußansprache." *MKBG* 5 (1937): 117–21.

——. "Die soziale Prognose bei der Entlassenenfürsorge." *MKBG* 5 (1937): 55–64.

Viernstein, Theodor, and Ed. Schütt. *Die Bekämpfung der Kriminalität vom bevölkerungspolitischen, erbbiologischen und rassenhygienischen Standpunkt*. Leipzig: Fischer, 1933.

Virchow, Rudolf. "Über Criminalanthropologie." *Correspondenz-Blatt der Deutschen Gesellschaft für Anthropologie, Ethnologie und Urgeschichte* 27 (1896): 157–62.

Vorentwurf zu einem deutschen Strafgesetzbuch. Bearbeitet von der hierzu bestellten Sachverständigenkommission. Veröffentlicht auf Anordnung des Reichs-Justizamts. 2 vols. Berlin: Guttentag, 1909.

Wachenfeld. "Zur Frage der Strafwürdigkeit des homosexualen Verkehrs." *ASS* 49 (1902): 37–66.

Wahlberg, Wilhelm. *Das Princip der Individualisirung in der Strafrechtspflege*. Vienna: Carl Gerold's Sohn, 1869.

Warstadt, Arno. "Vergleichende kriminalbiologische Studien an Gefangenen." *ZGNP* 120 (1929): 178–235.

Wasserman, Rudolf. *Beruf, Konfession und Verbrechen: Eine Studie über die Kriminalität der Juden in Vergangenheit und Gegenwart*. Munich: Reinhardt, 1907.

——. "Wandlungen der Ansichten über Wesen und Zweck der Kriminalstatistik." *Gerichtssaal* 75 (1910): 369 and 76 (1911): 136.

——. "Die Entwicklung der Kriminalstatistik von Quetelet bis G. von Mayr." *Annalen des Deutschen Reiches für Gesetzgebung, Verwaltung und Volkswirtschaft* (1911): 81.

——. *Die Entwicklungsphasen der kriminalstatistischen Forschung*. Kriminalistische Abhandlungen, no. 5. Leipzig: Wiegandt, 1927.

——. "Ist die Sterilisierung von Männern durch Kastration als Mittel zur Verhinderung von Sittlichkeitsverbrechen angebracht und zuverlässig?" *AfK* 86 (1930): 199–207.

Weber, F. A. "Die Unfruchtbarmachung Geisteskranker, Schwachsinniger und Verbrecher aus Anlage." *Zeitschrift für ärztliche Fortbildung* 22, no. 5 (1 March 1925): 152–55.

Weber, Hellmuth von. "Der Psychopath vor dem Strafrichter." *ZStW* 53 (1933): 656–75.

——. *Kriminalsoziologische Einzelforschungen*. Jena: Biedermann, 1939.

Weber, L. W. "Kastration und Sterilisation geistig Minderwertiger." *ZGNP* 91 (1924): 93–113.

Weingart, Albert. "Die verminderte Zurechnungsfähigkeit." *ZStW* 19 (1899): 133–48.

Welsch, Xaverius. *Entwicklung und heutiger Stand der kriminologischen Persönlichkeitsforschung und Prognose des sozialen Verhaltens von Rechtsbrechern in Deutschland.* Hamburg: Kriminalistik Verlag, 1962.

Wennmohs, F. A. *Über Gauner und über das zweckmässigste, vielmehr einzige Mittel zur Vertilgung dieses Übels.* Güstrow: Ebert, 1823.

Weygandt, W. "Die Entwicklung der gerichtlichen Psychologie und Psychiatrie." *MKS* 8 (1911): 209–20.

Wiethold, Ferdinand. "Psychoanalyse." In *Handwörterbuch der Kriminologie*, edited by Alexander Elster and Heinrich Lingemann, 2:441–46. Berlin: de Gruyter, 1936.

Wilmanns, Karl. "Zustände verminderter Zurechnungsfähigkeit einst und jetzt." *ZStW* 44 (1923): 89–97.

———. *Die sogenannte verminderte Zurechnungsfähigkeit.* Berlin: Springer, 1927.

Wilson, James Q., and Richard Herrnstein. *Crime and Human Nature.* New York: Simon and Schuster, 1985.

Wittels, Fritz. *Die Welt ohne Zuchthaus.* Stuttgart: Hippokrates, 1928.

Woytinski. "Kriminalität und Lebensmittelpreise." *ZStW* 49 (1928): 647–75.

Würtenberger, Thomas. "Die Kriminalbiologische Gesellschaft in Vergangenheit und Gegenwart." *Kriminologische Gegenwartsfragen* 8 (1968): 1–9.

Wulffen, Erich. *Kriminalpsychologie: Psychologie des Täters.* Berlin: Langenscheidt, 1926.

Zimmermann, Karl Wilhelm. *Die Diebe in Berlin.* Berlin: Reichhardt, 1847.

SECONDARY SOURCES

Ackerknecht, Erwin. *Kurze Geschichte der Psychiatrie.* 3d ed. Stuttgart: Enke, 1985.

Adams, Mark, ed. *The Wellborn Science: Eugenics in Germany, France, Brazil and Russia.* New York: Oxford University Press, 1990.

Allen, Garland, and Andrew Futterman. "The Biological Basis of Crime: An Historical and Methodological Study." Unpublished paper for "Genetics and Crime" conference, University of Maryland, 1995.

Aly, Götz. "Medicine against the Useless." In *Cleansing the Fatherland: Nazi Medicine and Racial Hygiene*, by Götz Aly, Peter Chroust, and Christian Pross, 22–98. Baltimore: Johns Hopkins University Press, 1994.

Aly, Götz, Peter Chroust, and Christian Pross. *Cleansing the Fatherland: Nazi Medicine and Racial Hygiene.* Baltimore: Johns Hopkins University Press, 1994.

Aly, Götz, and Karl Heinz Roth. *Die restlose Erfassung: Volkszählen, Identifizieren, Aussondern im Nationalsozialismus.* Berlin: Rotbuch, 1984.

———. "Siegfried Koller." In *Die restlose Erfassung*, by Götz and Roth, 96–115. Berlin: Rotbuch, 1984.

Anderson, Dennis L. *The Academy for German Law, 1933–1945.* New York: Garland, 1987.

Angermund, Ralph. *Deutsche Richterschaft, 1919–1945.* Frankfurt: Fischer, 1991.

Arbeitsgruppe zur Erforschung der Geschichte der Karl-Bonhoeffer-Nervenklinik. *Totgeschwiegen, 1933–1945: Zur Geschichte der Wittenauer Heilstätten. Seit 1957 Karl-Bonhoeffer-Nervenklinik.* 2d ed. Berlin: Edition Hentrich, 1989.

Ayaß, Wolfgang. *"Asoziale" im Nationalsozialismus.* Stuttgart: Klett-Cotta, 1995.

Bajohr, Frank, Werner Johe, and Uwe Lohalm, eds. *Zivilisation und Barbarei: Die widersprüchlichen Potentiale der Moderne.* Hamburg: Christians, 1991.

Baldwin, P. M. "Liberalism, Nationalism and Degeneration: The Case of Max Nordau." *Central European History* 13 (1980): 99–120.

Becker, Peter. "Vom 'Haltlosen' zur 'Bestie': Das polizeiliche Bild des Verbrechers im 19. Jahrhundert." In *"Sicherheit" und "Wohlfahrt": Polizei, Gesellschaft und Herrschaft im 19. und 20. Jahrhundert,* edited by Alf Lüdtke, 97–131. Frankfurt: Suhrkamp, 1992.

——. "Kriminelle Identitäten im 19. Jahrhundert: Neue Entwicklungen in der historischen Kriminalitätsforschung." *Historische Anthropologie* 2 (1994): 142–57.

——. "Randgruppen im Blickfeld der Polizei: Ein Versuch über die Perspektiven des 'praktischen Blicks.' " *Archiv für Sozialgeschichte* 32 (1994): 283–304.

——. "Une sémiotique de l'escroquerie: Le discours policier sur l'escroc au XIXe siècle." *Déviance et Societé* 18 (1994): 155–70.

——. "Der Verbrecher als 'monstruoser Typus': Zur kriminologischen Semiotik der Jahrhundertwende." In *Der falsche Körper: Beiträge zu einer Geschichte der Monstrositäten,* edited by Michael Hagner, 147–73. Göttingen: Wallstein, 1995.

——. "Physiognomie des Bösen: Cesare Lombrosos Bemühungen um eine präventive Entzifferung des Kriminellen." In *Der exzentrische Blick: Gespräche über Physiognomik,* edited by Claudia Schmölders, 163–86. Berlin: Akademie Verlag, 1996.

——. " 'Gefallene Engel' und 'verhinderte Menschen': Über Erzählmuster, Prostituierte und die Kriminalistik des vorigen Jahrhunderts." In *Die Konstruktion der Wirklichkeit durch Kriminalität und Strafe,* edited by Detlev Frehsee et al., 329–49. Baden-Baden: Nomos, 1997.

——. "The Triumphant Advance of Degeneration: Medical Sciences and Criminal Law in Nineteenth-Century Germany." In *Medicine and the Law: Proceedings of the 19th International Symposium on the Comparative History of Medicine—East and West,* edited by Yasuo Otsuka and Shizu Sakai, 83–128. Tokyo: Ishiyaku EuroAmerica, 1998.

Beirne, Piers. "Heredity versus Environment: A Reconsideration of Charles Goring's *The English Convict* (1913)." *British Journal of Criminology* 28 (1988): 315–39.

——. *Inventing Criminology: Essays on the Rise of "Homo Criminalis."* Albany: State University of New York Press, 1993.

——, ed. *The Origins and Growth of Criminology: Essays on Intellectual History, 1760–1945.* Aldershot: Dartmouth, 1994.

Bellmann, Elisabeth. *Die Internationale Kriminalistische Vereinigung.* Frankfurt: Peter Lang, 1994.

Berg, Manfred, and Geoffrey Cocks, eds. *Medicine and Modernity: Public Health and Medical Care in Nineteenth- and Twentieth-Century Germany.* Cambridge: Cambridge University Press, 1997.

Berger, Thomas. *Die konstante Repression: Zur Geschichte des Strafvollzugs in Preussen nach 1850.* Frankfurt: Verlag Roter Stern, 1974.

Berrios, German. "Personality Disorders: A Conceptual History." In *Personality Disorder Reviewed,* edited by Peter Tyrer and George Stein, 17–41. London: Gaskell, 1993.

Berrios, German, and Roy Porter, eds. *A History of Clinical Psychiatry.* New York: New York University Press, 1995.

Biagioli, Mario. "Science, Modernity and the 'Final Solution.' " In *Probing the Limits of Representation: Nazism and the "Final Solution,"* edited by Saul Friedlander, 185–205. Cambridge, Mass.: Harvard University Press, 1992.

Blackbourn, David, and Geoff Eley. *The Peculiarities of German History.* Oxford: Oxford University Press, 1984.

Blanckert, Claude. "Des sauvages en pays civilisé: L'anthropologie des criminels (1850–1900)." In *Histoire de la criminologie française,* edited by Laurent Mucchielli, 55–88. Paris: L'Harmattan, 1994.

Blasius, Dirk. *Bürgerliche Gesellschaft und Kriminalität: Zur Sozialgeschichte Preussens im Vormärz.* Göttingen: Vandenhoeck, 1976.

——. *Kriminalität und Alltag: Zur Konfliktgeschichte des Alltagslebens im 19. Jahrhundert.* Göttingen: Vandenhoeck, 1978.

——. *Umgang mit Unheilbarem: Studien zur Sozialgeschichte der Psychiatrie.* Bonn: Psychiatrie-Verlag, 1986.

——. "Ambivalenzen des Fortschritts: Psychiatrie und psychisch Kranke in der Geschichte der Moderne." In *Zivilisation und Barbarei: Die widersprüchlichen Potentiale der Moderne*, edited by Frank Bajohr, Werner Johe, and Uwe Lohalm, 253–68. Hamburg: Christians, 1991.

——. "Die 'Maskerade des Bösen.' Psychiatrische Forschung in der NS-Zeit." In *Medizin und Gesundheitspolitik in der NS-Zeit*, edited by Norbert Frei, 265–85. Munich: Oldenbourg, 1991.

——. "Psychiatrie in der Zeit des Nationalsozialismus." *Sudhoffs Archiv* 75 (1991): 90–105.

——. *"Einfache Seelenstörung": Geschichte der deutschen Psychiatrie, 1800–1945.* Frankfurt: Fischer, 1994.

Bock, Gisela. "Racism and Sexism in Nazi Germany: Motherhood, Compulsory Sterilization and the State." *Signs* 8 (1983): 400–421.

——. *Zwangssterilisation im Nationalsozialismus.* Opladen: Westdeutscher Verlag, 1986.

——. "Sterilization and 'Medical' Massacres in National Socialist Germany: Ethics, Politics and the Law." In *Medicine and Modernity: Public Health and Medical Care in Nineteenth- and Twentieth-Century Germany*, edited by Manfred Berg and Geoffrey Cocks, 149–72. Cambridge: Cambridge University Press, 1997.

Brucker-Boroujerdi, Ute, and Wolfgang Wippermann. "Die 'Rassenhygienische und Erbbiologische Forschungsstelle' im Reichsgesundheitsamt." *Bundesgesundheitsblatt* 32 (1989), Sonderheft (March 1989): 13–19.

Burchell, Graham, Colin Gordon, and Peter Miller, eds. *The Foucault Effect: Studies in Governmentality.* Chicago: University of Chicago Press, 1991.

Burleigh, Michael. " 'Euthanasia' in the Third Reich: Some Recent Literature." *Social History of Medicine* 4 (1991): 317–28.

——. "Between Enthusiasm, Compliance and Protest: The Churches, Eugenics and the Nazi 'Euthanasia' Programme." *Contemporary European History* 3 (1994): 253–63.

——. *Death and Deliverance: "Euthanasia" in Germany, c. 1900–1945.* Cambridge: Cambridge University Press, 1994.

——. *Ethics and Extermination: Reflections on Nazi Genocide.* Cambridge: Cambridge University Press, 1997.

——, ed. *Confronting the Nazi Past.* New York: St. Martin's, 1996.

Burleigh, Michael, and Wolfgang Wippermann. *The Racial State: Germany, 1933–1945.* Cambridge: Cambridge University Press, 1991.

Busse, Falk. "Gustav Aschaffenburg (1866–1944): Leben und Werk." M.D. diss., University of Leipzig, 1991.

Bynum, W. F., Roy Porter, and Michael Shepherd, eds. *The Anatomy of Madness: Essays in the History of Psychiatry.* London: Tavistock, 1985.

Centrum Schwule Geschichte, ed. *"Das sind Volksfeinde!" Die Verfolgung von Homosexuellen an Rhein und Ruhr, 1933–1945.* Cologne: Emons, 1998.

Chevalier, Louis. *Classes laborieuses et classes dangereuses à Paris pendant la première moitié du XIXe siècle.* Paris: Plon, 1958.

Chickering, Roger, ed. *Imperial Germany: A Historiographical Companion.* Westport: Greenwood, 1996.

Christiansen, Karl. "A Review of Studies of Criminality among Twins." In *Biosocial Bases of Criminal Behavior*, edited by Sarnoff Mednick and Karl Christiansen, 45–88. New York: Gardner Press, 1977.

Clark, Michael, and Catherine Crawford, eds. *Legal Medicine in History*. Cambridge: Cambridge University Press, 1994.

Cocks, Geoffrey. "German Psychiatry, Psychotherapy, and Psychoanalysis during the Nazi Period: Historiographical Reflections." In *Discovering the History of Psychiatry*, edited by Mark Micale and Roy Porter, 282–96. New York: Oxford University Press, 1994.

——. *Psychotherapy in the Third Reich: The Göring Institute*. 2d ed. New Brunswick: Transaction, 1997.

Coffin, Jean-Christophe. "La 'folie morale': Figure pathologique et entité miracle des hypothèses psychiatriques au XIXème siècle." In *Histoire de la criminologie française*, edited by Laurent Mucchielli, 89–106. Paris: L'Harmattan, 1994.

Coid, Jeremy. "Current Concepts and Classifications in Psychopathic Disorder." In *Personality Disorder Reviewed*, edited by Peter Tyrer and George Stein, 113–64. London: Gaskell, 1993.

Cornel, Heinz. *Geschichte des Jugendstrafvollzugs*. Weinheim: Beltz, 1984.

Dahrendorf, Ralf. *Society and Democracy in Germany*. New York: Norton, 1967.

Darmon, Pierre. *Médecins et assassins à la Belle Epoque: La médicalisation du crime*. Paris: Seuil, 1989.

Deichmann, Ute. *Biologists under Hitler*. Cambridge, Mass.: Harvard University Press, 1996.

Dell, Suzanne, and Graham Robertson. *Sentenced to Hospital: Offenders in Broadmoor*. Oxford: Oxford University Press, 1988.

Dickinson, Edward Ross. *The Politics of German Child Welfare from the Empire to the Federal Republic*. Cambridge, Mass.: Harvard University Press, 1996.

Dölling, Dieter. "Kriminologie im 'Dritten Reich.' " In *Recht und Justiz im "Dritten Reich,"* edited by Ralf Dreier and Wolfgang Sellert, 194–225. Frankfurt: Suhrkamp, 1989.

Dowbiggin, Ian. "Degeneration and Hereditarianism in French Mental Medicine." In *The Anatomy of Madness: Essays in the History of Psychiatry*, edited by W. F. Bynum, Roy Porter, and Michael Shepherd, 188–232. London: Tavistock, 1985.

——. *Inheriting Madness: Professionalization and Psychiatric Knowledge in Nineteenth-Century France*. Berkeley: University of California Press, 1991.

Downes, David. "The Sociology of Crime and Social Control in Britain, 1960–1987." *British Journal of Criminology* 28 (1988): 175–87.

Dreier, Ralf, and Wolfgang Sellert, eds. *Recht und Justiz im "Dritten Reich."* Frankfurt: Suhrkamp, 1989.

Dürkop, Marlis. "Zur Funktion der Kriminologie im Nationalsozialismus." In *Strafjustiz und Polizei im Dritten Reich*, edited by Udo Reifner and Bernd Sonnen, 97–120. Frankfurt: Campus, 1984.

Eley, Geoff. "German History and the Contradictions of Modernity." In *Society, Culture and the State in Germany, 1870–1930*, edited by Geoff Eley, 67–103. Ann Arbor: University of Michigan Press, 1996.

——, ed. *Society, Culture and the State in Germany, 1870–1930*. Ann Arbor: University of Michigan Press, 1996.

Emmerich, Norbert. "Die Forensische Psychiatrie, 1933–1945." In *Totgeschwiegen, 1933–1945: Zur Geschichte der Wittenauer Heilstätten. Seit 1957 Karl-Bonhoeffer-Nervenklinik*, edited by Arbeitsgruppe zur Erforschung der Geschichte der Karl-Bonhoeffer-Nervenklinik, 105–23. 2d ed. Berlin: Edition Hentrich, 1989.

Emsley, Clive. *Crime and Society in England, 1750–1900*. 2d ed. London: Longman, 1996.

——. "Albion's Felonious Attractions: Reflections upon the History of Crime in England." In *Crime History and Histories of Crime: Studies in the Historiography of Crime and Criminal Justice in Modern History*, edited by Clive Emsley and Louis Knafla, 67–86. Westport: Greenwood, 1996.

Emsley, Clive, and Louis Knafla, eds. *Crime History and Histories of Crime: Studies in the Historiography of Crime and Criminal Justice in Modern History*. Westport: Greenwood, 1996.

Engstrom, Eric. "Emil Kraepelin: Psychiatry and Public Affairs in Wilhelmine Germany." *History of Psychiatry* 2 (1991): 111–32.

——. "Kraepelin: Social Section." In *A History of Clinical Psychiatry*, edited by German Berrios and Roy Porter, 292–301. New York: New York University Press, 1995.

——. "Kulturelle Dimensionen von Psychiatrie und Sozialpsychologie: Emil Kraepelin und Willy Hellpach." In *Kultur und Kulturwissenschaften um 1900 II: Idealismus und Positivismus*, edited by Gangolf Hübinger, Rüdiger vom Bruch, and Friedrich Wilhelm Graf, 164–89. Stuttgart: Franz Steiner, 1997.

——. "The Birth of Clinical Psychiatry: Power, Knowledge, and Professionalization in Germany, 1867–1914." Ph.D. diss., University of North Carolina, 1997.

Evans, Richard. *Rituals of Retribution: Capital Punishment in Germany, 1600–1987*. Oxford: Oxford University Press, 1996.

——. "In Search of German Social Darwinism: The History and Historiography of a Concept." In *Medicine and Modernity: Public Health and Medical Care in Nineteenth- and Twentieth-Century Germany*, edited by Manfred Berg and Geoffrey Cocks, 55–79. Cambridge: Cambridge University Press, 1997.

——. *Tales from the German Underworld: Crime and Punishment in the Nineteenth Century*. New Haven: Yale University Press, 1998.

——, ed. *The German Underworld: Deviants and Outcasts in German History*. London: Routledge, 1988.

Feinderklärung und Prävention: Kriminalbiologie, Zigeunerforschung und Asozialenpolitik. Beiträge zur NS Gesundheits- und Sozialpolitik. Berlin: Rotbuch, 1988.

Finder, Gabriel. "Education, Not Punishment: Juvenile Justice in Germany, 1890–1930." Ph.D. diss., University of Chicago, 1997.

Finzsch, Norbert, and Robert Jütte, eds. *Institutions of Confinement: Hospitals, Asylums and Prisons in Western Europe and North America, 1500–1950*. Cambridge: Cambridge University Press, 1996.

Fischer, Isidor. *Biographisches Lexikon der hervorragenden Ärzte der letzten fünfzig Jahre*. Berlin: Urban und Schwarzenberg, 1932.

Foucault, Michel. *Surveiller et punir: Naissance de la prison*. Paris: Gallimard, 1975.

——. *Discipline and Punish: The Birth of the Prison*. New York: Pantheon, 1978.

——. "About the Concept of the 'Dangerous Individual' in Nineteenth-Century Legal Psychiatry." *International Journal of Law and Psychiatry* 1 (1978): 1–18.

Frei, Norbert. "Wie modern war der Nationalsozialismus?" *Geschichte und Gesellschaft* 19 (1993): 367–87.

——, ed. *Medizin und Gesundheitspolitik in der NS-Zeit*. Munich: Oldenbourg, 1991.

Friedlander, Henry. *The Origins of Nazi Genocide: From Euthanasia to the Final Solution*. Chapel Hill: University of North Carolina Press, 1995.

Frommel, Monika. "Internationale Reformbewegung zwischen 1880 und 1920." In *Erzählte Kriminalität: Zur Typologie und Funktion von narrativen Darstellungen in Strafrechtspflege, Publizistik und Literatur*, edited by Jörg Schönert, 467–95. Tübingen: Niemeyer, 1991.

Gadebusch Bondio, Mariacarla. *Die Rezeption der kriminalanthropologischen Theorien von Cesare Lombroso in Deutschland von 1880–1914*. Husum: Matthiesen, 1995.

Garland, David. *Punishment and Welfare: A History of Penal Strategies*. Aldershot: Gower, 1985.

——. "Politics and Policy in Criminological Discourse: A Study of Tendentious Reasoning and Rhetoric." *International Journal of the Sociology of Law* 13 (1985): 1–33.

——. "The Criminal and His Science." *British Journal of Criminology* 25 (1985): 109–37.
——. "Foucault's *Discipline and Punish*: An Exposition and Critique." *American Bar Foundation Research Journal* (1986): 847–80.
——. "British Criminology before 1935." *British Journal of Criminology* 28 (1988): 131–47.
——. *Punishment and Modern Society: A Study in Social Theory*. Chicago: University of Chicago Press, 1990.
——. "Criminological Knowledge and Its Relation to Power." *British Journal of Criminology* 32 (1992): 403–22.
Gasman, Daniel. *The Scientific Origins of National Socialism: Social Darwinism in Ernst Haeckel and the German Monist League*. London: Macdonald, 1971.
Gellately, Robert. *The Gestapo and German Society: Enforcing Racial Policy, 1933–1945*. Oxford: Clarendon Press, 1990.
Geschichte der Rechtswissenschaftlichen Fakultät der Universität Graz. Vol. 3, *Strafrecht—Strafprozessrecht—Kriminologie*. Graz: Akademische Druck- und Verlagsanstalt, 1987.
Die Geschichte des Paragraphen 175: Strafrecht gegen Homosexuelle. Berlin: Verlag Rosa Winkel, 1990.
Gibson, Mary. "The 'Female Offender' and the Italian School of Criminal Anthropology." *Journal of European Studies* 12 (1982): 155–65.
Giles, Geoffrey. " 'The Most Unkindest Cut of All': Castration, Homosexuality and Nazi Justice." *Journal of Contemporary History* 27 (1992): 41–61.
Gilman, Sander, and J. Edward Chamberlin, eds. *Degeneration: The Dark Side of Progress*. New York: Columbia University Press, 1985.
Glass, James. *"Life Unworthy of Life": Racial Phobia and Mass Murder in Hitler's Germany*. New York: Basic Books, 1997.
Göppinger, Horst. *Juristen jüdischer Abstammung im "Dritten Reich."* 2d ed. Munich: Beck, 1990.
Goldstein, Jan. *Console and Classify: The French Psychiatric Profession in the Nineteenth Century*. Cambridge: Cambridge University Press, 1987.
Gould, Stephen Jay. *The Mismeasure of Man*. New York: Norton, 1981.
Graff, Helmut. *Die deutsche Kriminalstatistik: Geschichte und Gegenwart*. Stuttgart: Enke, 1975.
Grassberger, Roland. "Hans Groß." In *Pioneers of Criminology*, edited by Hermann Mannheim, 305–17. 2d ed. Montclair: Patterson Smith, 1972.
Green, Thomas A. "Freedom and Criminal Responsibility in the Age of Pound: An Essay on Criminal Justice." *Michigan Law Review* 93 (1995): 1915–2053.
Gruchmann, Lothar. *Justiz im Dritten Reich, 1933–1940: Anpassung und Unterwerfung in der Ära Gürtner*. Munich: Oldenbourg, 1988.
Güse, Hans-Georg, and Norbert Schmacke. *Psychiatrie zwischen bürgerlicher Revolution und Faschismus*. 2 vols. Kronberg: Athenäum, 1976.
Hacking, Ian. "Degeneracy, Criminal Behavior and Looping." Unpublished paper for Genetics and Crime Conference, 1995.
Hagner, Michael. *Homo cerebralis: Der Wandel vom Seelenorgan zum Gehirn*. Berlin: Berlin Verlag, 1997.
Hamer, Dean, and Peter Copeland. *Living with Our Genes: Why They Matter More Than You Think*. New York: Doubleday, 1998.
Hannover, Heinrich, and Elisabeth Hannover-Druck. *Politische Justiz, 1918–1933*. Frankfurt: Fischer, 1966.
Harrington, Anne. *Reenchanted Science: Holism in German Culture from Wilhelm II to Hitler*. Princeton: Princeton University Press, 1996.

——. "Unmasking Suffering's Masks: Reflections on Old and New Memories of Nazi Medicine." *Daedalus* 125 (1996): 181–205.

Harris, Ruth. *Murders and Madness: Medicine, Law, and Society in the Fin de Siècle*. Oxford: Oxford University Press, 1989.

Harvey, Elizabeth. *Youth and the Welfare State in Weimar Germany*. Oxford: Clarendon Press, 1993.

Harwood, Jonathan. *Styles of Scientific Thought: The German Genetics Community, 1900–1933*. Chicago: University of Chicago Press, 1993.

Hasenclever, Christa. *Jugendhilfe und Jugendgesetzgebung seit 1900*. Göttingen: Vandenhoeck, 1978.

Hay, Douglas, Peter Linebaugh, John Rule, E. P. Thompson, and Cal Winslow, eds. *Albion's Fatal Tree: Crime and Society in Eighteenth-Century England*. New York, Pantheon, 1975.

Hentig, Hans von. "Gustav Aschaffenburg" (1954). In *Pioneers in Criminology*, edited by Hermann Mannheim, 421–28. 2d ed. Montclair: Patterson Smith, 1972.

Hering, Karl-Heinz. *Der Weg der Kriminologie zur selbständigen Wissenschaft*. Hamburg: Kriminalistik Verlag, 1966.

Herman, Arthur. *The Idea of Decline in Western History*. New York: Free Press, 1996.

Heuß, Herbert. "Wissenschaft und Völkermord: Zur Arbeit der 'Rassenhygienischen Forschungsstelle' beim Reichsgesundheitsamt." *Bundesgesundheitsblatt* 32 (1989), Sonderheft (March 1989): 20–24.

Hohmann, Joachim S. "Fanatischer Nazi und Zigeunerforscher: H. W. Kranz." In *Robert Ritter und die Erben der Kriminalbiologie: "Zigeunerforschung" im Nationalsozialismus und in Westdeutschland im Zeichen des Rassismus*, 297–302. Frankfurt: Peter Lang, 1991.

——. *Robert Ritter und die Erben der Kriminalbiologie: "Zigeunerforschung" im Nationalsozialismus und in Westdeutschland im Zeichen des Rassismus*. Frankfurt: Peter Lang, 1991.

Hoff, Paul. *Emil Kraepelin und die Psychiatrie als klinische Wissenschaft*. Berlin: Springer, 1994.

Hüser-Goldberg, Ruth. "Das kriminalpolitische Programm von Moritz Liepmann (1869–1928)." J.D. diss., University of Hamburg, 1974.

Ignatieff, Michael. *A Just Measure of Pain: The Penitentiary in the Industrial Revolution, 1750–1850*. New York: Pantheon, 1978.

——. "State, Civil Society and Total Institutions: A Critique of Recent Social Histories of Punishment." In *Social Control and the State*, edited by Stanley Cohen and Andrew Scull, 75–105. Oxford: Robertson, 1983.

Im Namen des deutschen Volkes: Justiz und Nationalsozialismus. Cologne: Verlag Wissenschaft und Politik, 1989.

International Biographical Dictionary of Central European Emigrés, 1933–1945. 3 vols. Munich: K. G. Saur, 1980–83.

Irro, F., and P. Hagemann. "Karl Birnbaum: Versuch einer Würdigung der Lebensarbeit eines bedeutenden Psychiaters und zugleich ein verspäteter Nachruf." *Psychiatrie, Neurologie und medizinische Psychologie* 25 (1973): 117–23.

Jeffery, Clarence. "The Historical Development of Criminology." In *Pioneers in Criminology*, edited by Hermann Mannheim, 458–88. 2d ed. Montclair: Patterson Smith, 1972. First published in *Journal of Criminal Law, Criminology and Police Science* 50 (1959).

Jellonnek, Burkhard. *Homosexuelle unter dem Hakenkreuz*. Paderborn: Schöningh, 1990.

Jenkins, Philip. "Varieties of Enlightenment Criminology." In *The Origins and Growth of Criminology*, edited by Piers Beirne, 79–97. Aldershot: Dartmouth, 1994.

Jessen, Ralph. *Polizei im Industrierevier: Modernisierung und Herrschaftspraxis im westfälischen Ruhrgebiet, 1848–1914*. Göttingen: Vandenhoeck, 1991.

John, Michael. "Constitution, Administration and the Law." In *Imperial Germany: A Historiographical Companion*, edited by Roger Chickering, 185–213. Westport: Greenwood, 1996.

Johnson, Eric. "The Roots of Crime in Imperial Germany." *Central European History* 15 (1982): 351–76.

———. *Urbanization and Crime: Germany, 1871–1914*. New York: Cambridge University Press, 1995.

Jones, David. *History of Criminology: A Philosophical Perspective*. Westport: Greenwood, 1986.

Justizministerium des Landes Nordrhein-Westfalen, ed. *Kriminalbiologie*. Juristische Zeitgeschichte NRW, vol. 6. Düsseldorf, 1997.

Kaiser, Jochen-Christoph, Kurt Nowak, and Michael Schwartz, eds. *Eugenik, Sterilisation, "Euthanasie": Politische Biologie in Deutschland, 1895–1945*. Berlin: Buchverlag Union, 1992.

Kanner, L. "In Memoriam: Gustav Aschaffenburg." *American Journal of Psychiatry* 101 (1944): 427–28.

Käsler, Dirk. *Die frühe deutsche Soziologie 1909 bis 1934 und ihre Entstehungsmilieus*. Opladen: Westdeutscher Verlag, 1984.

Kater, Michael. *Doctors under Hitler*. Chapel Hill: University of North Carolina Press, 1989.

———. "Die Krise der Ärzte und der Medizin im Dritten Reich." In *Der Wert des Menschen: Medizin in Deutschland, 1918–1945*, edited by Christian Pross and Götz Aly, 357–73. Berlin: Edition Hentrich, 1989.

———. "Die unbewältigte Medizingeschichte: Beiträge zur NS-Zeit aus Marburg, Tübingen und Göttingen." *Historische Zeitschrift* (1993): 401–16.

Kaufmann, Doris. "Eugenik—Rassenhygiene—Humangenetik." In *Die Erfindung des Menschen: Schöpfungsträume und Körperbilder, 1500–2000*, edited by Richard van Dülmen, 347–65. Vienna: Böhlau, 1998.

———. "Psychiatrie und Strafjustiz im 19. Jahrhundert: Die gerichtsmedizinischen Gutachten der medizinischen Fakultät der Universität Tübingen, 1770–1860." *Medizin, Gesellschaft und Geschichte. Jahrbuch des Instituts für Geschichte der Medizin der Robert Bosch Stiftung* 10 (1991): 23–39.

———. "Boundary Disputes: Criminal Justice and Psychiatry in Germany, 1760–1850." *Journal of Historical Sociology* 6 (1993): 276–87.

———. *Aufklärung, bürgerliche Selbsterfahrung und die "Erfindung" der Psychiatrie in Deutschland, 1770–1850*. Göttingen: Vandenhoeck, 1995.

———. "Science as Cultural Practice: Psychiatry in the First World War and Weimar Germany." *Journal of Contemporary History* 34 (1999): 125–44.

Kebbedies, Frank. "Kriminalbiologie und Jugendkriminalrecht—Verwissenschaftlichung und Moralisierung während der NS-Zeit." In *Kriminalbiologie*, edited by Justizministerium des Landes Nordrhein-Westfalen, 151–67. Düsseldorf, 1997.

Kerckwoorde, Jacques Van. "Statistique morale et statistique criminelle au XIXème siècle." In *Histoire de la criminologie française*, edited by Laurent Mucchielli, 253–68. Paris: L'Harmattan, 1994.

Kersting, Franz-Werner, Karl Teppe, and Bernd Walter. "Gesellschaft—Psychiatrie—Nationalsozialismus. Historisches Interesse und gesellschaftliches Bewußtsein." In *Nach Hadamar: Zum Verhältnis von Psychiatrie und Gesellschaft im 20. Jahrhundert*, edited by Franz-Werner Kersting, Karl Teppe, and Bernd Walter, 9–61. Paderborn: Schöningh, 1993.

———, eds. *Nach Hadamar: Zum Verhältnis von Psychiatrie und Gesellschaft im 20. Jahrhundert*. Paderborn: Schöningh, 1993.

Kisker, K. P. "Kurt Schneider." *Der Nervenarzt* 39 (1968): 97–98.

Klee, Ernst. *"Euthanasie" im NS-Staat: Die "Vernichtung lebensunwerten Lebens."* Frankfurt: Fischer, 1983.

——, ed. *Dokumente zur "Euthanasie."* Frankfurt: Fischer, 1985.

Kolle, Kurt. "Emil Kraepelin." In *Große Nervenärzte*, edited by Kurt Kolle, 1:175–86. Stuttgart: Thieme, 1956.

——. "Hans W. Gruhle." In *Große Nervenärzte*, edited by Kurt Kolle, 3:69–76. Stuttgart: Thieme, 1963.

——, ed. *Große Nervenärzte.* 3 vols. Stuttgart: Thieme, 1956–63.

——. *Große Nervenärzte.* Vol. 1, 2d ed. Stuttgart: Enke, 1970.

Kranz, H. "In memoriam Kurt Schneider." *Archiv für Psychiatrie* 211 (1968): 1–6.

Kreuter, Alma. *Deutschsprachige Neurologen und Psychiater: Ein biographisch-bibliographisches Lexikon von den Vorläufern bis zur Mitte des 20. Jahrhunderts.* Munich: Saur, 1996.

Kreutzahler, Birgit. *Das Bild des Verbrechers in den Romanen der Weimarer Republik.* Frankfurt: Peter Lang, 1987.

Kühl, Stefan. *The Nazi Connection: Eugenics, American Racism and German National Socialism.* New York: Oxford University Press, 1994.

——. *Die Internationale der Rassisten: Aufstieg und Niedergang der internationalen Bewegung für Eugenik und Rassenhygiene im 20. Jahrhundert.* Frankfurt: Campus, 1997.

Kuhn, Robert. *Die Vertrauenskrise der Justiz (1926–1928): Der Kampf um die Republikanisierung der Rechtspflege in der Weimarer Republik.* Cologne: Bundesanzeiger, 1983.

Lanteri-Laura, Georges. "Phrénologie et criminologie au début du XIXème siècle: Les idées de F. J. Gall." In *Histoire de la criminologie française*, edited by Laurent Mucchielli, 21–28. Paris: L'Harmattan, 1994.

Larson, Edward. *Sex, Race, and Science: Eugenics in the Deep South.* Baltimore: Johns Hopkins University Press, 1995.

Ledford, Kenneth. *From General Estate to Special Interest: German Lawyers, 1878–1933.* Cambridge: Cambridge University Press, 1996.

Lees, Andrew. "State and Society." In *Imperial Germany: A Historiographical Companion*, edited by Roger Chickering, 215–43. Westport: Greenwood, 1996.

Leps, Marie-Christine. *Apprehending the Criminal: The Production of Deviance in Nineteenth-Century Discourse.* Durham: Duke University Press, 1992.

Lerner, Paul. "Rationalizing the Therapeutic Arsenal: German Neuropsychiatry in World War I." In *Medicine and Modernity: Public Health and Medical Care in Nineteenth- and Twentieth-Century Germany*, edited by Manfred Berg and Geoffrey Cocks, 121–48. Cambridge: Cambridge University Press, 1997.

——. "Hysterical Cures: Hypnosis, Gender, and Performance in World War I and Weimar Germany." *History Workshop Journal* 45 (1998): 79.

Lévy, René. "Crime, the Judicial System and Punishment in Modern France." In *Crime History and Histories of Crime: Studies in the Historiography of Crime and Criminal Justice in Modern History*, edited by Clive Emsley and Louis Knafla, 87–108. Westport: Greenwood, 1996.

Lewis, A. "Psychopathic Disorder: A Most Elusive Category." *Psychological Medicine* 4 (1974): 133–40.

Liedtke, Hartwig. "Karl Birnbaum: Leben und Werk." M.D. diss., University of Cologne, 1982.

Lifton, Robert Jay. *The Nazi Doctors.* New York: Basic Books, 1986.

Lindesmith, Alfred, and Yale Levin. "English Ecology and Criminology of the Past Century." *Journal of Criminal Law and Criminology* 27 (1937): 801–16.

——. "The Lombrosian Myth in Criminology." *American Journal of Sociology* 42 (1937): 653–71.

Linton, Derek. *Who Has the Youth Has the Future: The Campaign to Save Young Workers in Imperial Germany*. Cambridge: Cambridge University Press, 1991.

Lüdtke, Alf, ed. *"Sicherheit" und "Wohlfahrt": Polizei, Gesellschaft und Herrschaft im 19. und 20. Jahrhundert*. Frankfurt: Suhrkamp, 1992.

Lüdtke, Alf, and Herbert Reinke. "Crime, Police and the 'Good Order': Germany." In *Crime History and Histories of Crime: Studies in the Historiography of Crime and Criminal Justice in Modern History*, edited by Clive Emsley and Louis Knafla, 109–37. Westport: Greenwood, 1996.

Lüken, Erhard-Josef. "Der Nationalsozialismus und das materielle Strafrecht." Ph.D. diss., University of Göttingen, 1988.

Macrakis, Kristie. *Surviving the Swastika: Scientific Research in Nazi Germany*. New York: Oxford University Press, 1993.

Majer, Diemut. *Grundlagen des nationalsozialistischen Rechtssystems: Führerprinzip, Sonderrecht, Einheitspartei*. Stuttgart: Kohlhammer, 1987.

Makowski, Christine. *Eugenik, Sterilisationspolitik, "Euthanasie" und Bevölkerungspolitik in der nationalsozialistischen Parteipresse*. Husum: Matthiesen, 1996.

Mann, Gunter. "Medizinisch-biologische Ideen und Modelle der Gesellschaftslehre des 19. Jahrhunderts." *Medizinhistorisches Journal* 4 (1969): 1–23.

——. "Biologie und der 'Neue Mensch': Denkstufen und Pläne zur Menschenzucht im Zweiten Kaiserreich." In *Medizin, Naturwissenschaft, Technik und das Zweite Kaiserreich*, edited by Gunter Mann and Rolf Winau, 172–88. Göttingen: Vandenhoeck, 1977.

——. "Dekadenz, Degeneration, Untergangsangst im Lichte der Biologie des 19. Jahrhunderts." *Medizinhistorisches Journal* 20 (1985): 6–35.

Mannheim, Hermann, ed. *Pioneers in Criminology*. 2d ed. Montclair: Patterson Smith, 1972.

Maretski, Thomas. "The Documentation of Nazi Medicine by German Medical Sociologists: A Review Article." *Social Sciences and Medicine* 29 (1989): 1319–32.

Martin, J. P. "The Development of Criminology in Britain, 1948–60." *British Journal of Criminology* 28 (1988): 165–74.

Martin, Randy, Robert Mutchnick, and W. Timothy Austin, eds. *Criminological Thought: Pioneers Past and Present*. New York: Macmillan, 1990.

Marxen, Klaus. *Der Kampf gegen das liberale Strafrecht*. Berlin: Duncker & Humblot, 1975.

Massin, Benoit. "From Virchow to Fischer: Physical Anthropology and 'Modern Race Theories' in Wilhelmine Germany." In *Volksgeist as Method and Ethic: Essays on Boasian Ethnography and the German Anthropological Tradition*, edited by George Stocking, 79–154. Madison: University of Wisconsin Press, 1996.

Matza, David. *Delinquency and Drift*. New York: Wiley, 1964.

Mayr, Ernst. *The Growth of Biological Thought: Diversity, Evolution, and Inheritance*. Cambridge, Mass.: Harvard University Press, 1982.

Mechler, Achim. *Studien zur Geschichte der Kriminalsoziologie*. Göttingen: Otto Schwartz, 1970.

Medizin im Nationalsozialismus. Munich: Oldenbourg, 1988.

Mergel, Thomas. "Geht es weiterhin voran? Die Modernisierungstheorie auf dem Weg zu einer Theorie der Moderne." In *Geschichte zwischen Kultur und Gesellschaft: Beiträge zur Theoriedebatte*, edited by Thomas Mergel and Thomas Welskopp, 203–32. Munich: Beck, 1997.

Meyer-Lindenberg, Johannes. "The Holocaust and German Psychiatry." *British Journal of Psychiatry* 159 (1991): 7–12.

Micale, Mark, and Roy Porter, eds. *Discovering the History of Psychiatry*. Oxford: Oxford University Press, 1994.

Morris, Norval, and David Rothman, eds. *Oxford History of the Prison.* Oxford: Oxford University Press, 1995.

Morris, Terence. "British Criminology, 1935–1948." *British Journal of Criminology* 28 (1988): 150–64.

Mucchielli, Laurent. "Hérédité et milieu social: Le faux antagonisme franco-italien. La place de l'école de Lacassagne dans l'histoire de la criminologie." In *Histoire de la criminologie française,* edited by Laurent Mucchielli, 189–214. Paris: L'Harmattan, 1994.

———. "Introduction générale: Naissance de la criminologie." In *Histoire de la criminologie française,* edited by Laurent Mucchielli, 7–15. Paris: L'Harmattan, 1994.

———, ed. *Histoire de la criminologie française.* Paris: L'Harmattan, 1994.

Müller, Christian. *Das Gewohnheitsverbrechergesetz vom 14. November 1933.* Baden-Baden: Nomos, 1997.

Müller, Ingo. *Furchtbare Juristen: Die unbewältigte Vergangenheit unserer Justiz.* Munich: Kindler, 1987.

———. *Hitler's Justice: The Courts of the Third Reich.* Cambridge, Mass.: Harvard University Press, 1991.

Müller, Joachim. *Sterilisation und Gesetzgebung bis 1933.* Husum: Matthiesen, 1985.

Müller-Hill, Benno. *Tödliche Wissenschaft: Die Aussonderung von Juden, Zigeunern und Geisteskranken, 1933–1945.* Reinbek: Rowohlt, 1984.

———. *Murderous Science: Elimination by Scientific Selection of Jews, Gypsies, and Others, Germany, 1933–1945.* Oxford: Oxford University Press, 1988.

———. "Selektion. Die Wissenschaft von der biologischen Auslese des Menschen durch Menschen." In *Medizin und Gesundheitspolitik in der NS-Zeit,* edited by Norbert Frei, 137–55. Munich: Oldenbourg, 1991.

Newman, Graeme, and Pietro Marongiu. "Penological Reform and the Myth of Beccaria." In *The Origins and Growth of Criminology: Essays on Intellectual History, 1760–1945,* edited by Piers Beirne, 3–24. Aldershot: Dartmouth, 1994.

Noakes, Jeremy. "Nazism and Eugenics: The Background to the Nazi Sterilization Law of 14 July 1933." In *Ideas into Politics,* edited by R. J. Bullen, H. Pogge von Strandmann, and A. B. Polonsky, 75–94. London: Croom Helm, 1984.

NS-Recht in historischer Perspektive. Munich: Oldenbourg, 1981.

Nye, Robert. "Heredity or Milieu: The Foundations of Modern European Criminological Theory." *Isis* 67 (1976): 335–55.

———. *Crime, Madness, and Politics in Modern France.* Princeton: Princeton University Press, 1984.

———. "The Rise and Fall of the Eugenics Empire: Recent Perspectives on the Impact of Biomedical Thought in Modern Society." *Historical Journal* 36 (1993): 687–700.

Olesko, Kathryn. "Introduction to Special Issue: Science in Germany." *Osiris* 5 (1989): 7–14.

Ostendorf, Heribert, ed. *Von der Rache zur Zweckstrafe: Hundert Jahre Marburger Programm von Franz von Liszt.* Frankfurt: Alfred Metzner, 1982.

Pasquino, Pasquale. "Criminology: The Birth of a Special Knowledge." In *The Foucault Effect: Studies in Governmentality,* edited by Graham Burchell, Colin Gordon, and Peter Miller, 235–50. Chicago: University of Chicago Press, 1991.

Paul, Diane. *Controlling Human Heredity, 1865 to the Present.* Atlantic Highlands: Humanities Press, 1995.

Pauleikhoff, Bernard. *Das Menschenbild im Wandel der Zeit: Ideengeschichte der Psychiatrie und der klinischen Psychologie.* 4 vols. Hürtgenwald: Pressler, 1983–87.

———. "Karl Birnbaum." In *Das Menschenbild im Wandel der Zeit,* 3:270–88. Hürtgenwald: Pressler, 1987.

——. "Hans Walter Gruhle." In *Das Menschenbild im Wandel der Zeit*, 4:51–72. Hürtgenwald: Pressler, 1987.

Peukert, Detlev. "Arbeitslager und Jugend-KZ: Die Behandlung Gemeinschaftsfremder im Dritten Reich." In *Die Reihen fast geschlossen: Beiträge zur Geschichte des Alltags unterm Nationalsozialismus*, edited by Detlev Peukert and Jürgen Reulecke, 413–34. Wuppertal: Hammer, 1981.

——. *Volksgenossen und Gemeinschaftsfremde*. Cologne: Bund-Verlag, 1982.

——. *Grenzen der Sozialdisziplinierung: Aufstieg und Krise der deutschen Jugendfürsorge von 1878 bis 1932*. Cologne: Bund-Verlag, 1986.

——. *Inside Nazi Germany*. New Haven: Yale University Press, 1987.

——. *Die Weimarer Republik*. Frankfurt: Suhrkamp, 1987.

——. "Die Genesis der 'Endlösung' aus dem Geist der Wissenschaft." In *Max Webers Diagnose der Moderne*, 102–21. Göttingen: Vandenhoeck, 1989.

——. *The Weimar Republic*. New York: Hill and Wang, 1992.

——. "The Genesis of the 'Final Solution' from the Spirit of Science." In *Nazism and German Society*, edited by David Crew, 274–99. London: Routledge, 1994.

Pichot, P. "Psychopathic Behaviour: A Historical Overview." In *Psychopathic Behaviour: Approaches to Research*, edited by Robert D. Hare and Daisy Schalling, 55–70. Chichester: Wiley, 1978.

Pick, Daniel. *Faces of Degeneration*. Cambridge: Cambridge University Press, 1989.

Pilgram, Arno. "Theorie der Kriminalitätsentwicklung—ein retardierter Spross der Kriminologie. Kritik der Kriminalitätsentwicklungstheorie am Beispiel der 'Monatsschrift für Kriminologie und Strafrechtsreform,' dem 'Zentralorgan' deutschsprachiger Kriminologie." In *Kriminalität in Österreich*. Vienna: Verlag für Gesellschaftskritik, 1980.

Pine, Lisa. "Hashude: The Imprisonment of Asocial Families in the Third Reich." *German History* 13 (1995): 182–97.

Polsky, Andrew. *The Rise of the Therapeutic State*. Princeton: Princeton University Press, 1991.

Potter, Pamela. *Most German of the Arts: Musicology and Society from the Weimar Republic to the End of Hitler's Reich*. New Haven: Yale University Press, 1998.

Prins, Herschel. *Offenders, Deviants or Patients?* 2d ed. London: Routledge, 1995.

Prinz, Michael, and Rainer Zitelmann, eds. *Nationalsozialismus und Modernisierung*. 2d ed. Darmstadt: Wissenschaftliche Buchgesellschaft, 1994.

Proctor, Robert. *Racial Hygiene: Medicine under the Nazis*. Cambridge, Mass.: Harvard University Press, 1988.

——. *The Nazi War on Cancer*. Princeton: Princeton University Press, 1999.

Pross, Christian, and Götz Aly, eds. *Der Wert des Menschen: Medizin in Deutschland, 1918–1945*. Berlin: Edition Hentrich, 1989.

Radzinowicz, Leon. *In Search of Criminology*. Cambridge, Mass.: Harvard University Press, 1962.

——. *Ideology and Crime*. New York: Columbia University Press, 1966.

——. *The Roots of the International Association of Criminal Law and Their Significance: A Tribute and Reassessment on Its Centenary*. Max-Planck-Institut für ausländisches und internationales Strafrecht, 1991.

Radzinowicz, Leon, and Roger Hood. *History of the English Criminal Law and Its Administration from 1750*. Vol. 5, *The Emergence of Penal Policy*. London: Stevens, 1986.

Rafter, Nicole Hahn. *Creating Born Criminals*. Urbana: University of Illinois Press, 1997.

Rautenberg, Erardo. *Verminderte Schuldfähigkeit: Ein besonderer, fakultativer Strafmilderungsgrund?* Heidelberg: Kriminalistik Verlag, 1984.

Rehbein, Klaus. "Zur Funktion von Strafrecht und Kriminologie im nationalsozialistischen Rechtssystem: Eine Wissenschaft begründet die Barbarei." *MKS* 70 (1987): 193–210.

Reilly, Philip. *The Surgical Solution: A History of Involuntary Sterilization in the United States.* Baltimore: Johns Hopkins University Press, 1991.

Reiner, Robert. "British Criminology and the State." *British Journal of Criminology* 28 (1988): 268–88.

Reinke, Herbert, ed. ". . . nur für die Sicherheit da . . . ?" *Zur Geschichte der Polizei im 19. und 20. Jahrhundert.* Frankfurt: Campus, 1993.

Renneberg, Monika, and Mark Walker, eds. *Science, Technology and National Socialism.* Cambridge: Cambridge University Press, 1994.

Renneville, Marc. "Entre nature et culture: Le regard médical sur le crime dans la première moitié du XIXème siècle." In *Histoire de la criminologie française,* edited by Laurent Mucchielli, 29–53. Paris: L'Harmattan, 1994.

——. "La réception de Lombroso en France (1880–1900)." In *Histoire de la criminologie française,* edited by Laurent Mucchielli, 107–35. Paris: L'Harmattan, 1994.

——. *La médecine du crime: Essai sur l'emergence d'un regard médical sur la criminalité en France.* Villeneuve d'Ascq: Presses Universitaires du Septentrion, 1997.

Rennie, Ysabel. *The Search for Criminal Man: A Conceptual History of the Dangerous Offender.* Lexington: D. C. Heath, 1978.

Robert, Philippe. "The Sociology of Crime and Deviance in France." *British Journal of Criminology* 31 (1991): 27–38.

Rock, Paul. "Introduction: The Emergence of Criminological Theory." In *History of Criminology,* edited by Paul Rock, xi–xxix. Aldershot: Dartmouth, 1994.

——, ed. *History of Criminology.* Aldershot: Dartmouth, 1994.

——. *A History of British Criminology.* Oxford: Clarendon Press, 1988. First published as a special issue of *British Journal of Criminology* 28.

Roer, Dorothee, and Dieter Henkel, eds. *Psychiatrie im Faschismus: Die Anstalt Hadamar, 1933–1945.* Bonn: Psychiatrie-Verlag, 1986.

Roseman, Mark. "National Socialism and Modernization." In *Fascist Italy and Nazi Germany,* edited by Richard Bessel, 197–229. Cambridge: Cambridge University Press, 1996.

Roth, Karl Heinz. "Erbbiologische Bestandsaufnahme—Ein Aspekt ausmerzender Erfassung vor der Entfesselung des 2. Weltkrieges." In *Erfassung zur Vernichtung: Von der Sozialhygiene zum Gesetz über Sterbehilfe,* edited by Karl-Heinz Roth, 57–100. Berlin: Verlagsgesellschaft Gesundheit, 1984.

——. "Schein-Alternativen im Gesundheitswesen: Alfred Grotjahn (1869–1931)— Integrationsfigur etablierter Sozialmedizin und nationalsozialistischer 'Rassenhygiene.' " In *Erfassung zur Vernichtung: Von der Sozialhygiene zum Gesetz über Sterbehilfe,* edited by Karl Heinz Roth, 31–56. Berlin: Verlagsgesellschaft Gesundheit, 1984.

——, ed. *Erfassung zur Vernichtung: Von der Sozialhygiene zum Gesetz über Sterbehilfe.* Berlin: Verlagsgesellschaft Gesundheit, 1984.

Rothmaler, Christiane. " 'Prognose: Zweifelhaft': Die kriminalbiologische Untersuchungs- und Sammelstelle der Hamburgischen Gefangenenanstalten, 1926–1945." In *Kriminalbiologie,* edited by Justizministerium des Landes Nordrhein-Westfalen, 107–50. Düsseldorf, 1997.

Rusche, Georg, and Otto Kirchheimer. *Punishment and Social Structure.* New York: Columbia University Press, 1939.

Sass, H., S. Herpertz, and W. Ernst. "Personality Disorders." In *A History of Clinical Psychiatry,* edited by German Berrios and Roy Porter, 633–55. New York: New York University Press, 1995.

Scheer, Rainer. "Die nach Paragraph 42b RStGB verurteilten Menschen in Hadamar." In *Psychiatrie im Faschismus: Die Anstalt Hadamar, 1933–1945,* edited by Dorothee Roer and Dieter Henkel, 237–55. Bonn: Psychiatrie-Verlag, 1986.

Scherer, Klaus. *"Asozial" im Dritten Reich: Die vergessenen Verfolgten*. Münster: Votum, 1990.

Schildt, Axel. "NS-Regime, Modernisierung, Moderne: Anmerkungen zur Hochkonjunktur einer andauernden Diskussion." *Tel Aviver Jahrbuch für deutsche Geschichte* 23 (1994): 3–22.

Schmidt, Eberhard. *Einführung in die Geschichte der deutschen Strafrechtspflege*. 1947. 3d ed. Göttingen: Vandenhoeck, 1964.

Schmiedebach, Heinz-Peter. "Zum Verständniswandel der 'psychopathischen' Störungen am Anfang der naturwissenschaftlichen Psychiatrie in Deutschland." *Der Nervenarzt* 56 (1985): 140–45.

——. "The Mentally Ill Patient Caught between the State's Demands and the Professional Interests of Psychiatrists." In *Medicine and Modernity: Public Health and Medical Care in Nineteenth- and Twentieth-Century Germany*, edited by Manfred Berg and Geoffrey Cocks, 99–119. Cambridge: Cambridge University Press, 1997.

Schmuhl, Hans-Walter. "Die Selbstverständlichkeit des Tötens: Psychiater im Nationalsozialismus." *Geschichte und Gesellschaft* 16 (1990): 411–39.

——. "Sterilisation, 'Euthanasie,' 'Endlösung.' Erbgesundheitspolitik unter den Bedingungen charismatischer Herrschaft." *Medizin und Gesundheitspolitik in der NS-Zeit*, edited by Norbert Frei, 295–308. Munich: Oldenbourg, 1991.

——. *Rassenhygiene, Nationalsozialismus, Euthanasie*. 2d ed. Göttingen: Vandenhoeck, 1992.

——. "Kontinuität oder Diskontinuität? Zum epochalen Charakter der Psychiatrie im Nationalsozialismus." In *Nach Hadamar: Zum Verhältnis von Psychiatrie und Gesellschaft im 20. Jahrhundert*, edited by Franz-Werner Kersting, Karl Teppe, and Bernd Walter, 112–36. Paderborn: Schöningh, 1993.

——. "Rassismus unter den Bedingungen charismatischer Herrschaft." In *Deutschland, 1933–1945*, edited by Karl-Dietrich Bracher, Manfred Funke, and Hans-Adolf Jacobsen, 182–97. 2d ed. Düsseldorf: Droste, 1993.

——. "Reformpsychiatrie und Massenmord." In *Nationalsozialismus und Modernisierung*, edited by Michael Prinz and Rainer Zitelmann, 239–66. 2d ed. Darmstadt: Wissenschaftliche Buchgesellschaft, 1994.

Schneider, Hans-Joachim. *Kriminologie*. Berlin: de Gruyter, 1987.

Schneider, Wolfgang, ed. *"Vernichtungspolitik": Eine Debatte über den Zusammenhang von Sozialpolitik und Genozid im nationalsozialistischen Deutschland*. Hamburg: Junius, 1991.

Schönert, Jörg, ed. *Literatur und Kriminalität: Die gesellschaftliche Erfahrung von Verbrechen und Strafverfolgung als Gegenstand des Erzählens. Deutschland, England und Frankreich, 1850–1880*. Tübingen: Niemeyer, 1983.

——. *Erzählte Kriminalität: Zur Typologie und Funktion von narrativen Darstellungen in Strafrechtspflege, Publizistik und Literatur zwischen 1770 und 1920*. Tübingen: Niemeyer, 1991.

Schoppmann, Claudia. *Nationalsozialistische Sexualpolitik und weibliche Homosexualität*. 2d ed. Pfaffenweiler: Centaurus, 1997.

Schulte, Regina. *Das Dorf im Verhör: Brandstifter, Kindsmörderinnen und Wilderer vor den Schranken des bürgerlichen Gerichts*. Hamburg: Rowohlt, 1989.

——. *The Village in Court: Arson, Infanticide, and Poaching in the Court Records of Upper Bavaria, 1848–1910*. Cambridge: Cambridge University Press, 1994.

Schütz, Reinhard. "Kriminologie im Dritten Reich: Erscheinungsformen des Faschismus in der Wissenschaft vom Verbrechen." J.D. diss., University of Mainz, 1972.

Schwartz, Michael. *Sozialistische Eugenik: Eugenische Sozialtechnologien in Debatten und Politik der deutschen Sozialdemokratie, 1890–1933*. Bonn: Dietz, 1995.

——. "Kriminalbiologie und Strafrechtsreform: Die 'erbkranken Gewohnheitsverbrecher' im Visier der Weimarer Sozialdemokratie." In *Kriminalbiologie*, edited by Justizministerium des Landes Nordrhein-Westfalen, 13–68. Düsseldorf, 1997.

Seiffert, Dorothea. "Gustav Aschaffenburg als Kriminologe." J.D diss., University of
    Freiburg, 1981.
Sharpe, J. A. "The History of Crime in England." *British Journal of Criminology* 28 (1988):
    254–67.
Shorter, Edward. *A History of Psychiatry*. New York: Wiley, 1997.
Siemen, Hans-Ludwig. *Menschen blieben auf der Strecke: Psychiatrie zwischen Reform und
    Nationalsozialismus*. Gütersloh: van Hoddis, 1987.
——. "Reform und Radikalisierung. Veränderungen der Psychiatrie in der
    Weltwirtschaftskrise." In *Medizin und Gesundheitspolitik in der NS-Zeit*, edited by Norbert
    Frei, 191–200. Munich: Oldenbourg, 1991.
——. "Die Reformpsychiatrie der Weimarer Republik: Subjektive Ansprüche und die Macht
    des Faktischen." In *Nach Hadamar: Zum Verhältnis von Psychiatrie und Gesellschaft im 20.
    Jahrhundert*, edited by Franz-Werner Kersting, Karl Teppe, and Bernd Walter, 98–108.
    Paderborn: Schöningh, 1993.
Sieverts, Rudolf, ed. *Handwörterbuch der Kriminologie*. 2d ed. 5 vols. Berlin: de Gruyter,
    1966–75.
Simon, Jürgen. "Kriminalbiologie—theoretische Konzepte und praktische Durchführung
    eines Ansatzes zur Erfassung von Kriminalität." In *Kriminalbiologie*, edited by
    Justizministerium des Landes Nordrhein-Westfalen, 69–105. Düsseldorf, 1997.
Skultans, Vieda, ed. *Madness and Morals: Ideas on Insanity in the Nineteenth Century*.
    London: Routledge, 1975.
Smith, David. *Minds Made Feeble: The Myth and Legacy of the Kallikaks*. Rockville: Aspen
    Systems, 1985.
Smith, Roger. *Trial by Medicine: Insanity and Responsibility in Victorian Trials*. Edinburgh:
    Edinburgh University Press, 1981.
Sparing, Frank. ". . . wegen Vergehen nach Paragraph 175 verhaftet": Die Verfolgung der
    Düsseldorfer Homosexuellen während des Nationalsozialismus*. Düsseldorf: Grupello, 1997.
——. "Zwangskastrationen im Nationalsozialismus: Das Beispiel der kriminalbiologischen
    Sammelstelle Köln." In *Kriminalbiologie*, edited by Justizministerium des Landes
    Nordrhein-Westfalen, 169–212. Düsseldorf, 1997.
Spencer, Elaine Glovka. *Police and the Social Order in German Cities: The Düsseldorf District,
    1848–1914*. DeKalb: Northern Illinois University Press, 1992.
Strasser, Peter. *Verbrechermenschen: Zur kriminalwissenschaftlichen Erzeugung des Bösen*.
    Frankfurt: Campus Verlag, 1984.
Streng, Franz. "Der Beitrag der Kriminologie zu Entstehung und Rechtfertigung staatlichen
    Unrechts im Dritten Reich." *MKS* 76 (1993): 141–68.
——. "Von der 'Kriminalbiologie' zur 'Biokriminologie'? Eine Verlaufsanalyse
    bundesdeutscher Kriminologie-Entwicklung." In *Kriminalbiologie*, edited by
    Justizministerium des Landes Nordrhein-Westfalen, 213–44. Düsseldorf, 1997.
Stümke, Hans-Georg, and Rudi Finkler. *Rosa Winkel, Rosa Listen: Homosexuelle und
    "gesundes Volksempfinden" von Auschwitz bis heute*. Reinbek: Rowohlt, 1981.
"Symposium on Genetics and Crime." In *Politics and the Life Sciences* 15 (1996).
Tatar, Maria. *Lustmord: Sexual Murder in Weimar Germany*. Princeton: Princeton University
    Press, 1995.
Thom, Achim. "Die Entwicklung der Psychiatrie und die Schicksale psychisch Kranker sowie
    geistig Behinderter unter den Bedingungen der faschistischen Diktatur." In *Medizin
    unterm Hakenkreuz*, edited by Achim Thom and Genadij Caregorodcev, 127–65. East
    Berlin: Verlag Volk und Gesundheit, 1989.
——. "Die rassenhygienischen Leitideen der faschistischen Gesundheitspolitik—die
    Zwangssterilisierungen als Beginn ihrer antihumanen Verwirklichung." In *Medizin*

unterm Hakenkreuz, edited by Achim Thom and Genadij Caregorodcev, 65–90. East Berlin: Verlag Volk und Gesundheit, 1989.

Thom, Achim, and Genadij Caregorodcev, eds. *Medizin unterm Hakenkreuz.* East Berlin: Verlag Volk und Gesundheit, 1989.

Thompson, E. P. *Whigs and Hunters: The Origin of the Black Act.* New York: Pantheon, 1975.

Trent, James. *Inventing the Feeble Mind: A History of Mental Retardation in the United States.* Berkeley: University of California Press, 1994.

Tuchmann, Arleen. "Institutions and Disciplines: Recent Work in the History of German Science." *Journal of Modern History* 69 (1997): 298–319.

Voss, Michael. *Jugend ohne Rechte: Entwicklung des Jugendstrafrechts.* Frankfurt: Campus, 1986.

Wagner, Patrick. "Das Gesetz über die Behandlung Gemeinschaftsfremder: Die Kriminalpolizei und die 'Vernichtung des Verbrechertums.' " In *Feinderklärung und Prävention: Kriminalbiologie, Zigeunerforschung und Asozialenpolitik,* 75–100. Berlin: Rotbuch, 1988.

———. *Volksgemeinschaft ohne Verbrecher: Konzeptionen und Praxis der Kriminalpolizei in der Zeit der Weimarer Republik und des Nationalsozialismus.* Hamburg: Christians, 1996.

Weber, Matthias. "Ein Forschungsinstitut für Psychiatrie: Die Entwicklung der Deutschen Forschungsanstalt für Psychiatrie in München zwischen 1917 und 1945." *Sudhoffs Archiv* 75 (1991): 74–89.

———. *Ernst Rüdin: Eine kritische Biographie.* Berlin: Springer, 1993.

Weckowicz, Thaddeus, and Helen Liebel Weckowicz. *A History of Great Ideas in Abnormal Psychology.* Amsterdam: North-Holland, 1990.

Wehler, Hans-Ulrich. *Das deutsche Kaiserreich, 1871–1918.* Göttingen: Vandenhoeck, 1973.

———. *The German Empire.* Leamington Spa: Berg, 1985.

———. "A Guide to Future Research on the Kaiserreich?" *Central European History* 29 (1996): 541–72.

Weindling, Paul. "Eugenics and the Welfare State during the Weimar Republic." In *The State and Social Change in Germany, 1880–1980,* edited by W. R. Lee and Eve Rosenhaft, 131–60. New York: Berg, 1990.

———. *Health, Race and German Politics between National Unification and Nazism, 1870–1945.* Cambridge: Cambridge University Press, 1989.

———. "The 'Sonderweg' of German Eugenics: Nationalism and Scientific Internationalism." *British Journal for the History of Science* 22 (1989): 321–33.

———. "The Survival of Eugenics in Twentieth-Century Germany." *American Journal of Human Genetics* 52 (1993): 643–49.

———. "Understanding Nazi Racism: Precursors and Perpetrators." In *Confronting the Nazi Past,* edited by Michael Burleigh, 66–83. New York: St. Martin's, 1996.

Weingart, Peter. "German Eugenics between Science and Politics." *Osiris* 5 (1989): 260–82.

———. "Politik und Vererbung." In *Wissenschaft auf Irrwegen: Biologismus, Rassenhygiene, Eugenik,* edited by Peter Propping and Heinz Schott, 23–43. Bonn: Bouvier, 1992.

———. "Eugenics—Medical or Social Science?" *Science in Context* 8 (1995): 197–207.

Weingart, Peter, Jürgen Kroll, and Kurt Bayertz. *Rasse, Blut und Gene: Geschichte der Eugenik und Rassenhygiene in Deutschland.* Frankfurt: Suhrkamp, 1988.

Weiss, Sheila Faith. *Race Hygiene and National Efficiency: The Eugenics of Wilhelm Schallmayer.* Berkeley: University of California Press, 1987.

———. "Die Rassenhygienische Bewegung in Deutschland, 1904–1933." In *Der Wert des Menschen: Medizin in Deutschland, 1918–1945,* edited by Christian Pross and Götz Aly, 153–73. Berlin: Edition Hentrich, 1989.

———. "The Race Hygiene Movement in Germany, 1904–1945." In *The Wellborn Science:*

Eugenics in Germany, France, Brazil and Russia, edited by Mark Adams, 8–68. New York: Oxford University Press, 1990.

Weitbrecht, H. J. "Kurt Schneider 80 Jahre—80 Jahre Psychopathologie." *FNPG* 35 (1967): 497–515.

Werle, Gerhard. *Justiz-Strafrecht und polizeiliche Verbrechensbekämpfung im Dritten Reich.* Berlin. de Gruyter, 1989.

Werlinder, Henry. *Psychopathy: A History of the Concepts.* Uppsala: University, 1978.

West, D. J. "Psychological Contributions to Criminology." *British Journal of Criminology* 28 (1988): 207–22.

Wetzell, Richard. "Criminal Law Reform in Imperial Germany." Ph.D. diss., Stanford University, 1991.

———. "The Medicalization of Criminal Law Reform in Imperial Germany." In *Institutions of Confinement: Hospitals, Asylums and Prisons in Western Europe and North America, 1500–1950,* edited by Norbert Finzsch and Robert Jütte, 275–84. Cambridge: Cambridge University Press, 1996.

Wiener, Martin. *Reconstructing the Criminal: Culture, Law, and Policy in England, 1830–1914.* Cambridge: Cambridge University Press, 1990.

Wolff, Jörg. *Jugendliche vor Gericht im Dritten Reich.* Munich: Beck, 1992.

Wolfgang, Marvin E. "Cesare Lombroso." In *Pioneers in Criminology,* edited by Hermann Mannheim, 232–91. 2d ed. Montclair: Patterson Smith, 1972.

Wright, Gordon. *Between the Guillotine and Liberty: Two Centuries of the Crime Problem in France.* New York: Oxford University Press, 1983.

Wright, Lawrence. *Twins and What They Tell Us about Who We Are.* New York: Wiley, 1997.

Wright, William. *Born That Way: Genes, Behavior, Personality.* New York: Knopf, 1998.

Young, David. "Cesare Beccaria: Utilitarian or Retributivist?" In *The Origins and Growth of Criminology: Essays on Intellectual History, 1760–1945,* edited by Piers Beirne, 25–34. Aldershot: Dartmouth, 1994.

Zehr, Howard. *Crime and Development in Modern Society: Patterns of Criminality in Nineteenth-Century Germany and France.* London: Croom Helm, 1976.

Zimmermann, Michael. *Verfolgt, vertrieben, vernichtet: Die nationalsozialistische Vernichtungspolitik gegen Sinti und Roma.* Essen: Klartext, 1989.

———. *Rassenutopie und Genozid: Die nationalsozialistische "Lösung der Zigeunerfrage."* Hamburg: Christians, 1996.